W9-DBW-555

The Soviet Union and the Challenge of the Future

The Soviet Union and the Challenge of the Future

Volume 1: Stasis and Change

edited by Alexander Shtromas and
Morton A. Kaplan

A PWPA Book

PARAGON HOUSE PUBLISHERS

New York

First edition

Published in the United States by

Paragon House Publishers
90 Fifth Avenue
New York, New York 10011

Copyright © 1988 by Paragon House Publishers

A Professors World Peace Academy book

Library of Congress Cataloging-in-Publication Data

The Soviet Union and the challenge of the future.

"A PWPA book."
Includes index.
Contents: v. 1. The Soviet system.
1. Soviet Union—Social conditions—1945–   —
Congresses. 2. Soviet Union—Politics and govern-
ment—1945–   —Congresses. I. Shtromas,
Alexander, 1931–   II. Kaplan, Morton A.
HN523.5.S69   1987   306'.0947   87-6904
ISBN 0-943852-29-3 (v. 1)

Contents

v

PART II

CRISIS OF THE SOVIET SYSTEM

PART III

PROSPECTS FOR TRANSITION

APPENDIX

Introduction

The Soviet System: Stasis and Change is volume 1 of *The Soviet Union and the Challenge of the Future*. Volumes 2, *Economy and Society*, 3, *Ideology, Culture, and Nationality*, and 4, *Russia and the World*, will soon follow. These books are the product of the second international conference of the Professors World Peace Academy in Geneva, Switzerland. Despite the claim of one picketing group that the conference was part of a Soviet-KGB plot and the claim of a Geneva newspaper that the conference was dominated by a reactionary anti-Soviet Jewish conspiracy, the editors, who take full responsibility for the intellectual structure of the conference and of the invitation list, are confident that it was the largest and intellectually most systematic conference ever held on the Soviet Union. The conference examined practically all aspects of Soviet reality—politics, economics, and various aspects of the social system, Soviet science, art, humanities, and ideas—and it did so within a time continuum that included the U.S.S.R.'s past, present and projected future. As with all symposia, contributions to these books are not of uniform quality. But the editors believe that they are presenting here as comprehensive and as scholarly distinguished a symposium on the subject as has ever been held, that the books make an important and innovative contribution to the knowledge about and understanding of the U.S.S.R. and also that these volumes contain exciting teaching materials.

Although the task of organizing the conference—Shtromas as organizing chairman and Kaplan as president of the organization—and of editing the books was carried out congenially, the editors are not in complete agreement with each other or with the papers included in these volumes. Furthermore, it was their deliberate policy to invite contributions from scholars holding different, and sometimes opposite, views on the subjects under discussion, so that the widest possible spectrum of opinion would be represented and discussed both at the conference and in the books. However, the editors did not include any papers that lacked intellectual value. In fact, one paper in a later volume was rewritten three times until most of what the editors regarded as merely polemical and distortive anti-Soviet bias had been eliminated.

The sharpest controversy at the conference concerned what Alexander Shtromas called "the Soviet crisis," a crisis that he argued could shake and eventually would lead to the change of the regime. Many disagreed, some extremely strongly, with his thesis, which he has proposed for several years now. But he had his supporters. And even some who had been strongly opposed to his views, after they heard his presentation, conceded them to be plausible and deserving of serious consideration. Virtually none, however, doubted that the Soviet Union was in a crisis resulting from the management of its economy—a crisis that in the future would affect the role the Soviet Union plays in the world and that might affect accordingly its foreign policy—even if they thought the Soviet political system itself would survive.

In contrast to the subsequent volumes, all of which concentrate on particular aspects of the Soviet system, the present volume is devoted to the discussion of the Soviet system as a whole. It starts with a debate on the Soviet system's nature, continues with the analysis of its present critical state, and then considers the prospects for transition to and, consequently, the possible character of an alternative non-Soviet and post-Soviet system. The volume is, accordingly, divided into four main parts that, in the editors' opinion, are organically interrelated and that, as a consequence, overcome the usual shortcomings of conference proceedings. We believe that the book comprehensively and systematically covers its subject.

Part I, "The Nature of the Soviet System," opens with Michael Voslensky's discussion of the relationship between the concept of the *nomenklatura*, that is, the ruling bureaucracy, and the totalitarian state—the thesis that Voslensky made famous. Voslensky effectively argues that all totalitarian states are of one and the same type and that "left" and "right" have little meaning when dealing with them, and that in any event these systems start with leftist slogans and afterwards move to the right. Richard Löwenthal counters that Voslensky has left out of his account all the historical and other concrete factors that determined the specific contents of totalitarian regimes. In any event, he says, Mussolini began by imposing control over the unions, hardly a leftist beginning. One can thus only ask, he states, in what respects totalitarian states are similar or different.

Methodologically, the editors are forced to agree with Löwenthal that one can ask only in what respect regimes are the same or different. Specific histories do determine specific contents. And yet Löwenthal himself fails to obey his own caveat when he argues that Mussolini's move against the unions was rightist. After all, the Socialists, who controlled many of the unions, were his competitors on the left. In Germany, Italy, and Russia the ideology was antibourgeois and the concept of socialism prominent. It was in other respects that the regimes differed. Fascism and Nazism were initially nationalistic, a development that came only later to Communism. But then we are not sure that "left" and "right" are clear concepts. And in the more fundamental ideological aspects—leaving out nationalism and racism—there were striking similarities as there were also in their methods, as Voslensky points out in his rejoinder.

Löwenthal argues that Voslensky was wrong in considering ideology to be unimportant and power the only goal of totalitarian states. Ideology was important to Stalin and also to Khrushchev. Only in the post-Khrushchev era did the maintenance of power rather than ideology become the goal. And this coincided, as Löwenthal argues in his own chapter, following that of Voslensky's and discussing the problems of stabilization of the extant regimes in both the U.S.S.R. and China, with collective rule at the apex of the Soviet system (something that also was true until 1924 and perhaps to 1934 depending upon how one assesses the evidence).

Up to this point in the argument the editors agree with Löwenthal. Moreover, his argument that the rulers of the Soviet Union might be able to solve the problem of reform sufficiently to maintain control is the majority view and plausible, even if doubtful. However, his failure to recognize that the present Soviet leaders remain Leninists, even if not pure Marxists, is the lacuna in his argument. They may have ruined the economy—and they all recognize the need for some changes—but the Leninist system produced a state that is equal, if not superior, to the United States militarily. This alone keeps the Soviet Union intact against fissiparous tendencies and permits control of the satellites. Furthermore, whether the ruling *nomenklatura* would survive the collapse of Leninism is doubtful. Therefore, reform under Gorbachev is likely to involve only a mere tinkering with the centralized system. It is this that makes successful transformation in a nonrevolutionary fashion to an authoritarian state doubtful. For reasons too extensive for discussion in an introduction, the prospects for internal reform leading to systemic changes in China, even if doubtful, are greater. Suffice it to state here that calls for political pluralism have been made from high places in the

Chinese party and that differences in society, culture, and party organization make the process of transformation in China less "unthinkable," if still less than likely, than in the Soviet Union. It may have been Löwenthal's neglect of Leninism that led him to tell Kaplan that it is "nonsense" to deny that the Sandinistas are pluralistic.

There follows a short definitional comment by Kaplan, who does not regard the Fascist and Nazi systems as totalitarian. Whether the current Soviet system is totalitarian depends upon the degree of subsystem dominance and directivity required for use of the term. But the system remains Leninist and, thus, fundamentally different from authoritarian systems such as those of Franco or Pinochet.

Shtromas' comment includes the ideological component—an attempt to transform society—into the concept of totalitarianism. For Kaplan, this component is epiphenomenal. (This is a methodological, not a substantive disagreement between the editors.) Although the actuating element in Soviet society for transformation was ideological, in Kaplan's view the transformation is required if one wants to impose a Leninist-type, that is, as Shtromas prefers to call it, a totalitarian regime. In Aristotelian terms, this would be a distinction between the initiating and the final cause. But different initiating causes are possible, and élites that desire totalitarian rule will adopt the ideology to legitimate the result. Once imposed—that is, once there is a "fit" between society and regime—there is no need for further transformation, though there may be a need for organized activities to inhibit the growth of organizations that could mediate between individuals or groups and the state and, by thus enhancing group autonomy generally, put the imposed "fit" at risk.

The former is the reason, as Shtromas argues in his commentary, why the Soviet rulers continue to insist upon an ideology in which they do not believe, for they wish to retain what Shtromas calls a totalitarian and Kaplan would call a Leninist regime. Shtromas ends with an analysis of the Chinese situation. Here there are differences of emphasis between the editors, with Kaplan being less skeptical than Shtromas about the possibility for the present reforms to become irreversible.

This wide-ranging theoretical discussion of the Soviet system's substance —a discussion, the editors would like to stress again, which was conducted among scholars holding very different views on that issue indeed—is followed by two chapters, one of which is seeking to clarify the appeal that the Soviet-type ideology and system exert, and the other is examining the relationship between the Soviet ideology and system and the concept of human rights.

In the former chapter, "Communism as a Cultural Phenomenon," Leszek Kolakowski shows how Soviet-type Communism managed to absorb all the important and popular social issues and, by making them its own, forged them into tools to be used for its particular purposes of getting, maintaining, and expanding exclusive political power. According to Kolakowski, it was the partial success of Communism in attaining these particular goals that has undermined its initial appeal and precipitated the bankruptcy of its ideas, first of all in the countries where it has been established in power, but also to a large extent worldwide.

The chapter, "Human Rights and the Soviet Future" by Eugene Kamenka, concludes the first part of this volume. Marx, Kamenka notes, had no concept of essential conflict. In a Communist society, a division of labor would arise naturally without coercion or rule. Thus, Marx was never able to understand that there would be a public political life under a Communist regime. Law was necessary, in his opinion, only in bourgeois states, a view that early Soviet authors still accepted but that was rejected in developed Soviet society, particularly under Stalin. Law is now seen in the Soviet Union as the means by which the state steers society. There is no theory of justice or of rights in Soviet law, and law tends, with some exceptions, to be subsumed under public law, a position also adopted by some Western Marxists. Even where Soviet law now does recognize certain rights, it does not recognize them as a corresponding duty of the state but rather as a grant by the state. They are conditional and depend upon individuals fulfilling their corresponding duties to the state. Kamenka notes that the Soviet Union needs a system of rights to cope with the complexities of modern society, but in the limits of the present political régime is unable to provide it in unconditional form.

Part II, "Crisis in the Soviet System," opens with a rich chapter by Richard V. Burks on "The Coming Crisis in the Soviet Union." Burks cites the economic crisis (a zero growth rate or worse), disaffection, strikes, and alcoholism as causes and symptoms of oncoming régime crisis. To make the system work at all, the régime must tolerate extensive corruption. Even so the population no longer sees hope of substantial improvement as it once did under Khrushchev. Solidarity in Poland was a distinct threat to the Soviet Union because of possible contagion. Even a successful invasion of Poland against armed resistance might have brought the régime to crisis, and similar outbreaks in Eastern Europe cannot be precluded. Acceptance of market methods might serve to create nationality conflict. In sum, Burks believes that a "landslide" crisis resulting in the change of the régime has a better than even chance of materializing within the life of this generation.

Peter Wiles in his commentary on Burks notes that the British economic deterioration may rival the Russian, but that it does not shake the legitimacy of the public order because the people freely choose their governors. Furthermore, he says, the Soviet ideology sets not merely comparative but absolute standards that the system has no hope of approaching. This further undermines its legitimacy. He believes that any efforts to establish a market economy within the current régime structure will fail for largely the same reasons Kosygin's abortive efforts failed. And he doubts that it would lead to rapid growth in the Soviet Union in any event. Brezhnev's proposed solutions would not work either, he thinks. Détente would produce technological and financial borrowing, but the first is difficult to assimilate and the second creates debt problems. A third approach would be to permit a widened second or nonofficial economy. He elaborates on this in his chapter for volume 2. But its moral and economic costs would be stupendous, for it would constitute recognition of the bankruptcy of socialism.

Nonetheless, Wiles does not see system breakdown in the near future because Gorbachev really is a new broom, because only the élite understands the nature of the crisis, and it is not going to revolt because all Burks' examples of breakdown were foreign and thus contained a large element of nationalist revolt, and above all because of the foreign policy gains of the Soviet Union. It is this need of the Soviet Union for continued foreign policy gains to service its legitimacy that Kaplan will cite in volume 4, and not some doctrine of world control, that makes the Soviet Union dangerous to the peace of the world unless the free countries remain united and strong.

In his chapter, "The Function and Fate of Law in the Transition to a Post-Soviet Era," Ferdinand Feldbrugge complements Burks's and Wiles's mainly social and economic analyses of the coming crisis in the Soviet Union by looking at that same problem from a political and legal perspective. He cites the reasons why the Soviet leadership cannot make the concessions required to improve the economy. Both vagueness and excessive detail in Soviet law respond to the need of the political leadership to maintain political control of the systems of production and distribution. Paradoxically, however, the means required for control also impede the acquisition of information. And hence power, but not effective power in terms of rational results, is maintained by the régime. Feldbrugge also cites the second economy which, according to him, plays an ever-increasing role in Soviet life. Although Soviet officialdom occasionally attacks the second economy, it is largely ignored, for the chief requirement of officials is that they speak not truth but the current party line. This leads to a withdrawal by citizens to the realm of private lives.

The nationality problem is serious, Feldbrugge says. The official constitutional line—true multinationalism—has little relationship to the actual state of affairs. The Russians are predominant in fact. (There has been somewhat enhanced representation of nationalities in the Central Committee and the

Politburo since Feldbrugge wrote his paper, but this has not fundamentally changed the dominance of the Russians in the system yet.) Feldbrugge thinks the Soviet Union has reached the limit of its expansion because of the support required by client states and the fact that the Russians will not be satisfied short of control. The editors doubt this. They think that the Sandinistas or the Dergue in Ethiopia have their own reasons for desiring a Leninist state, that this makes them natural allies of the Soviet Union, and that there is an historical basis for anti-Americanism in Latin America that feeds on the *macho* attitudes of Leninist élites.

The Soviet Union, Feldbrugge notes, exacerbates the faults of the rationalist world view. Soviet law supports this rationalistic world view by providing a blueprint and also by trying to influence behavior. The chief purpose of Soviet law is to maintain order. But this runs into dangers. The blueprint may be too difficult to interpret or it may begin to acquire an independence of its own. Although all-embracing political control would seem to prevent the emergence of an independent system of law in the Soviet Union, the extreme conservatism of the political system, its inherent resistance to all change, enhances a situation under which the legal order may achieve a certain *de facto* independence.

Feldbrugge then examines a number of scenarios that would have conflicting consequences in terms of possible crisis. But the only viable one may be economic deregulation. This would involve at least a partial private sector with corresponding amendments introduced into the law. That, in turn, would call for the introduction of some real civil rights. Pluralism would begin to develop and the Party would be unveiled publicly as merely the ruling élite, which would require it to justify its assumption of this role.

Part III, "Prospects for Transition," opens with Shtromas' key and controversial chapter about the ways in which the Soviet system may end. In a longish exposé, too complex and detailed to present in this introduction, Shtromas argues that the Soviet system will fall when the existing political system will split, producing a "second pivot," which was the usual method whereby régimes changed in the past. This is illustrated by the fall of the *ancien régime* in France and several other historical precedents. But Shtromas, quoting Lenin, says that a nationwide crisis also is necessary.

The Soviet élite usually is identified with the *nomenklatura*, but the intellectual class is much wider. Most of the experts and professional administrators are not part of the *nomenklatura*. In every Soviet office there is friction between these groups, i.e. between those who rule and those who try to carry through a professional function. But the two million-strong *nomenklatura* is itself too large for it to be unified and monolithic. And the inequalities within it are staggering. There are conflicts of interest even within the two thousand at the top of the *nomenklatura*. Although these conflicts of interest do not yet produce interest groups or aggregations as these are known in the West, informal groups do exist, develop and consolidate, nurtured by that anti-collectivistic institution, the family. The largest and most powerful informal group, the technocrats, as opposed to the partocrats, know that their interests would be not only safe but most likely strongly enhanced by a change of régime. (Most recently the Shah's SAVAK, or secret police, except for a few top officials, is being used by Khomeini's régime in Iran.)

According to Shtromas, the credited legitimacy of the régime already has been used up. All that is required is a nationwide crisis. But will this take place as a transformation at the top in which the technocrats gradually take over from the partocrats or by a revolution from the top? Although Gorbachev has long been identified as a technocratic reformer, he did not take over with the mission of transforming, rather than reforming, the system. His selection, Shtromas says, was in this respect premature. Hence, eventually, the revolution from above is the more likely scenario.

But there are other alternatives, which involve confrontation between contending groups in the Soviet system. The Prague Spring is one model. The 1956 Revolution in Hungary is another. The Polish (Solidarity) model is yet another possibility that should not be dismissed. The military also may play a decisive role in changing the régime. Their inherent Russian nationalism, Shtromas says, is in organic conflict with the values and goals of the régime. Although they would not support democracy, an authoritarian regime that they would be likely to install would be compatible with pluralism. As these alternatives opened up, the Party in its attempt to stay in power would have to call upon outside allies, a course that would also change the régime. (To avoid a compromise with the Christian Democrats that would have sidetracked Allende's socialist revolution from above, Allende called upon the assistance of Pinochet, with consequences that he did not foresee.)

This part concludes with commentaries by Burks and Alexander Matejko who critically assess Shtromas's propositions and discuss various aspects of the problem of transition.

Part IV, "The Alternative," is subdivided into two subparts—"The Visions" and "The Proposals." The former consists of two chapters—the first by Terry McNeill about the Western debate on the Soviet future and the second by Vladislav Krasnov on the émigré and *samizdat* debate.

McNeill agrees that there are five alternatives, as seen in the West, from the collapse of the régime to its continued stability. The extreme thesis of stable totalitarianism, McNeill feels, has few supporters. The view that the current Soviet system is merely a necessary stage in assuring Russia's development also has lost much support as has the image of future convergence between East and West. A further thesis is that of the eventual crumbling of the Soviet régime. This view was criticized by Jerry F. Hough for failing to recognize the ability of the Soviet system to transform itself. But others thought that Hough was talking about pluralism with respect to a system in which real pluralism was impossible. The social and political stagnation accompanied by an economic crisis in the Soviet Union seems to rule out the stability thesis. Others see difficulties arising also from nationality problems. The régime-destabilizing role of Russian nationalism is stressed by other writers.

McNeill concludes that conceptual models such as the totalitarian one have little to say. Development and convergence models were too deterministic. Reform from above is possible but not likely to be of a significant extent. There are no signs indicating an imminent collapse of the Soviet system either. The most likely alternative is that the régime will find some way to "muddle through." But in the end, he says, all empires die.

The internal debate, which Krasnov analyzes, does not include many conceptualizers although there is an occasional convergence theorist. The range is from Amalrik, who thought the system was ready to collapse, to those who believed that the task of change is most formidable—from nationalists to liberal anti-nationalists, from those who support Solzhenitsyn to those who detest him, from democratic socialists to anti-socialists, from Christians to secularists, from those who fight the system to those who, like Zinoviev, hate it but believe in its permanence. These various groups also have programs, but their differences are as rich and as complicated as the doctrinal positions that the author already had had difficulty summarizing and describing in his chapter. The reader will find this a rich harvest.

Subpart B, "The Proposals," starts with the chapter by Anatoly Fedoseyev. Fedoseyev is an engineer, and social scientists will quickly recognize that his proposals for a democratic structure of government with a market economy are too detailed to provide a workable framework. They are more notable for the fear they express of governments out of control and for the search for legal means to prevent excessive or unrepresentative governmental activities. Their detail is interesting less for the hardly existing possibility that they could be implemented than for the attitudes that underlie them which have developed in response to the system now operative in the Soviet Union. But they also manifest an attitude that is more widespread in the Soviet Union than we recognize: fear of the violence and disorder that characterize Western societies. It is in this sense that Fedoseyev's proposals for the control of disorder without excessive governmental power also are of interest.

Alice Erh-Soon Tay begins her chapter, "Law and the Soviet State," with the recognition that some degree of socialist mentality now influences even Western law—that *Gemeinschaft*-based concepts are now important also in Western legal systems. Thus, the influence of *laissez-faire* and liberalism are on the decline. The editors believe that this was indeed the case through the seventies but that a strong reversal is occurring in the eighties. They do agree with Tay, however, that the attraction of socialism as a solution to national problems is vanishing and that some of the major problems of the present era have to do with the nature of industrial society, regardless of whether the economic system is capitalistic or socialistic.

The focus of Tay's attention, however, is the rule of law as a major achievement of civilized society and of its weak status in socialist systems. While the significance of the rule of law is declining in the West, she says, rudimentary aspects of it are developing in the Soviet system. The bureaucracies that operate in the modern world, she says, are comprehended completely neither in *Gemeinschaft* or *Gesellschaft* terms. Administrative law is now assuming increasing importance. This occurs both in government and business, where *Gemeinschaft* attitudes influence some aspects of bureaucratic procedures and *Gesellschaft* others. Whether the term "law" can be used to denote both aspects of bureaucratic procedures is an important question.

Tay argues that experience in the Soviet Union dims the hope once felt that *Gesellschaft* features of administrative law would increase there, thus diminishing important aspects of domination-submission relationships. China has now moved closer to an appreciation of *Gesellschaft* aspects of law than has the Soviet Union, she says. If the collapse of the Soviet system took place there would likely be a return to *Gesellschaft* aspects of law. If as a result of this collapse the republics became independent, this return would be more pronounced in the Ukraine and the Baltic republics than in Russia or the Central Asian republics. The formal structure of Soviet law is *Gesellschaft*, and only its setting within Party control emphasizes *Gemeinschaft* features. But, she argues, the means needed to produce these results must consist of subtle political and legal measures rather than of the morally motivated and sweeping constitutional changes proposed by Fedoseyev.

Following is George Brunner's chapter on what needs to be changed in Soviet constitutional law if there is to be a genuine governing constitution. Brunner points out that the Soviet constitution is proclaimed to be merely a means to an end—the building of Communism—and, therefore, that it does not have any independent force. He shows how Soviet practice proves this to have been the case. Articles 2 and 6 dealing with the supremacy of the people and the Party respectively are in conflict, and the latter provision, which is the dominant one, must be changed if the constitution is to have any independent force. The other dangerous principle in the constitution is that of socialist legality which establishes a contradiction between the rule of law and the dominant political implementation of Party purposes. That also needs to be changed, Brunner says. He then discusses the additional four most important aspects of constitutional change that he sees as prerequisites for establishing an alternative political system. These should be directed at sorting out or bringing to an end the nationality issue, economic stagnation, political rigidity, and the monocratic power structure.

Brunner believes that the nationality issue requires genuine decentralization of authority. Economic stagnation can be overcome only by changing those sections of the constitution that establish a socialist economy. He is also opposed to having a range of stipulated social and economic rights in a post-Soviet constitution because it is difficult to define them properly and because they depend on economic performance. The reservations on civil and political rights in the present Soviet constitution must either be eliminated or amended in a satisfactory fashion. The Soviet constitution is not particularly lacking in provisions for democratic rights, which have little basis in Russian culture, but they are not implemented in practice. That needs to be changed, Brunner says.

The final chapter in this section is by Olimpiad S. Ioffe, "Prospects for the Reception of Soviet Law After the Collapse of the Soviet System." Ioffe argues that the chief defect in Soviet law lies in the political monopoly of power over the legal (as opposed to the underground) economy. Because of the problems that derive from this, the Soviet system is engaged in a constant alternation between centralization and decentralization, a process, he says, that is not inexhaustible. But this problem, he argues in contradiction to Harold Berman, cannot be solved within the Soviet system.

If the Soviet system changes, as he thinks it will, much of Soviet law cannot be received because, unlike Roman law, it is based on socialism rather than the implementation of general rules. Nonetheless, he believes, many aspects of Soviet law can and should be received in a post-Soviet state if they are stripped of the elements of practice that make them tyrannical. Moreover, Soviet jurisprudence has evolved principles that because of their abstractness could be fruitfully applied anywhere. Even some of the demagogic preambles to Soviet laws have proved useful in the hands of Soviet jurists in correcting some of the problems in Soviet society. And he prefers the Soviet legal standard (though it is ignored by judicial practice), according to which the defendant in a libel suit must prove the truth of his allegations, to the Western model in which the complainant must prove falsity. Although the editors think that it is sometimes more difficult than desirable to prove libel, they would like at the same time to stress that the Soviet alternative would have a chilling effect on free discussion of public issues. Ioffe wants justice for the individual, and so do we, but we are also concerned about keeping the political system honest, which also will have salutary consequences for individuals. And the Western standard is preferable for these reasons.

The volume concludes with an appendix in which Robert F. Byrnes provides perhaps the best discussion of American research and instruction on the Soviet Union in the literature.

Inevitably the above brief summary does not do full justice to the ingenious and innovative contributions of which this volume consists. To be properly appreciated they deserve to be carefully read by every person interested in Soviet and world affairs. The benefits will be great. For never before have discussions of the critical problems that the Soviet Union faces, its stability and viability, and the possible alternatives to the Soviet political status quo been brought together in such a comprehensive, systematic, and imaginative manner as they are in this volume.

Alexander Shtromas
Morton A. Kaplan

PART

I

THE NATURE OF THE SOVIET SYSTEM

1

The Soviet System

Historical and Theoretical Evaluation

MICHAEL VOSLENSKY

In the summer of 1946, that is 40 years ago, I came to Nuremberg as a Soviet interpreter at the trial of the major German war criminals. After two decades of unchallenged exposure to Soviet propaganda, I was for the first time brought face to face with the realities of the defeated National Socialist Reich. They differed from the pictures painted in our imaginations by *Pravda*. Of course, the day-to-day brutal cruelty of the national socialist regime proved to be in fact even more abhorrent than what was pictured by Soviet propaganda. But the most striking discovery was the undeniable similarities between the structure and the functioning of the political machine in Hitler's Reich and in Stalin's U.S.S.R. The bewildering similarities appeared even in details; so, for instance, Hitler and Stalin were each hailed during the war by their respective propaganda services as "the greatest warlord of all times" (*der grösste Feldherr aller Zeiten, velichaishiy polkovodets vsekh vremyon*)—with the addition in Stalin's case of "and peoples" (*i narodov*). Some details were less amusing for us. In 1946 it was no joy to read about how Stalin, when introducing the almighty Beria to Ribbentrop, made the jovial remark, "This man is our Himmler."

3

Five years later, Hannah Arendt published her book, *The Origins of Totalitarianism*.[1] This work was very instrumental in establishing the fact that both allegedly opposite régimes belonged to the same totalitarian type.

Later this scholastic conclusion was proclaimed "cold war propaganda." Without producing any evidence, revisionist historians of the post-cold war period declared that the similarities between fascism and Soviet socialism were superficial and accidental. They did not reflect the nature of both systems, which were clearly the opposites of one another, since fascism was a product of the decaying and reactionary monopolistic capitalism, whereas the Soviet system, albeit not without some bureaucratic deviations, was, on the whole, socialist and thus progressive.[2] In the 1970s it was nearly impossible to speak in the West about totalitarianism without being immediately labelled "cold warrior."[3] After the sad experience of détente the use of the term *totalitarianism* does not provoke any more open attacks, but neo-détentists cannot dissimulate their uneasiness at hearing it.[4]

It is time to put an end to this period of uncertainty about the notion of totalitarianism and, insofar as the roots of the evident similarities between "real" and "national" socialism are concerned, to arrive at clear conclusions.

Can the Similarity Be Accidental?

This is the first point to be cleared. Accidental similarities do exist. Sometimes we meet people with a certain resemblance to other people we know but who are certainly not their relatives. Such vague resemblance differs distinctly, however, from what the French call *un air de famille*. Even doubles never reach the similarity of twins.

History shows that similarities in the structure and functioning of different societies arise either as the result of analogous development or as a result of one society's having copied the ways and achievements of another. Since both fascism and national socialism were adamant in stressing their enmity toward the Bolshevik régime, there is indeed no evidence of the former having copied the latter. If this is so, the apparent similarities had to develop as expressions of the organically similar nature of these régimes.

Maybe these similarities were only those of form, not of substance. From the Marxist point of view, however, such an admission would be completely false. In dialectical materialism any form is nothing but the form of a substance. Thus the similarities between "national" and "real" socialism are neither accidental nor purely formal. They show inescapably that these régimes are organically close to each other. Indeed, they belong to one and the same type of régime that has been dubbed *totalitarianism*.

Totalitarianism vs. Pluralism

The prevailing opinion considers democracy to be the opposite of totalitarianism. This is wrong; the opposite of democracy (the rule *of* the people) is autocracy, dictatorship, or oligarchy (the rule *over* the people). Totalitarianism has a different meaning; it is the total control by an undemocratic power over all spheres of life in society. Hence, the opposite of totalitarianism is *pluralism*. This is an important point. Not every nondemocratic régime is totalitarian, but every totalitarian régime is antidemocratic. Absence of democracy is not the dividing line between totalitarian and other socio-political structures, but rather the monopoly of all, not just political, power.

A society is pluralistic not because there are several political parties in it (there are, for example, several parties in East Germany) and not even because the mass media reflect different points of view. A pluralistic society is pluralistic in its very structure. This society has no class possessing the monopoly of rule over all spheres of life. Modern pluralistic societies do have an élite, but this élite is also pluralistic. It consists of a *political* class that has political power, a *bourgeois* class that has economic power, and the *intelligentsia* that is shaping the culture and ideology. A totalitarian society is different; it has only one ruling class—the political bureaucracy that exercises full monopoly over decision-making in politics, economy, society, and ideology. The same group of people at the top of society decide what should be produced by industry and agriculture, which novel is good, and what kind of painting is bad. These people are not specialists; they are neither engineers nor agronomists nor artists. They are Party *apparatchiks* with a total monopoly of power in the country. Totalitarianism vs. pluralism—this is the formula of the historical conflict of our century.

Totalitarianism and Authoritarianism

The rejection of totalitarianism as a concept comprising fascism, "national" and "real" socialisms, and other similar régimes caused much harm to the objective analysis of the historical conflict indicated above. Not less harmful were the results of two other terminological manipulations.

The first consisted of the tacit acceptance of the Comintern's notion of fascism, according to which not only Italian fascism but all totalitarian régimes, with the notable exception of the communist ones, were fascist. This permitted the substitution of the notion of fascism for that of totalitarianism, while excluding communism from the latter.

The second manipulation was a continuation of the first. Every dictatorship, with the exception of that of the *nomenklatura*, was labelled fascist. This, too, was invented by the Comintern and successfully led away from classifying nondemocratic régimes according to their real structures and ways of functioning.[5]

These two semantic manipulations should be explicitly rejected. The nonmonopolistic, i.e. military and other personal dictatorships, which do not bring to the position of rulership a new class of political bureaucracy that monopolizes power over all walks of life, are not totalitarian; they are *authoritarian*.

This means that the dictator or the dictatorial junta impose themselves upon society as supreme, nondemocratic and repressive political authorities, but do not attempt to change the society, to create a new class, and by doing so, to perpetuate the kind of rule that has thus been imposed. An authoritarian régime considers itself to be provisional, limited only to its task of solving a certain real or imaginary crisis that has befallen the country. Being determined to use drastic and sometimes most cruel means for the solution of that crisis, it does not, however, pretend to open a new era in history. The authoritarian dictators admit that their seizure of power is no more than a temporary takeover; they do not pretend that it is a social revolution. Authoritarian régimes base their power on military force and seek support from the traditional social groups that may be sympathetic to the dictators' aims. Neither hereditary nor self-reproducing, the authoritarian régimes, particularly the military ones, are in most cases shortlived. Usually they are right-wing and tend to be nationalistic, traditionalist, and religious. While undemocratic, they still tolerate a moderate opposition and do not fully eradicate civil rights and liberties, although they are suspicious of them. The authoritarian régimes are unstable, and the transition from them to democracy is rather easy, because they tolerate the remnants and bear the germs of pluralism. Thus authoritarianism is clearly different from totalitarianism.

Totalitarianism: Neither Right nor Left

Rather often we read about totalitarianisms of the left and of the right, "real" socialism allegedly belonging to the left, and fascism and "national" socialism to the right.[6] This distinction has become a commonplace and thus an axiom. But as a matter of fact no evidence has been produced that could properly substantiate such a classification. Indeed, what could the evidence be? The social origin of the leadership? Hitler was a worker in Vienna, a jobless artist, and a private in the army. Lenin and Krupskaya were members of the gentry. Trotsky came from a wealthy bourgeois family. Who then belongs to the right, and who to the left?

Maybe the evidence lies in the proclaimed class associations of the totalitarian parties. Hitler's party was called the National Socialist German Workers' Party; Lenin's, the Russian Social Democratic Workers' Party. The alleged aim of both was the creation of socialism—in Hitler's case, of "German national socialism," in Stalin's, of "socialism in one country," the U.S.S.R. Both parties were equally anticapitalist; Lenin's party was struggling against the bourgeoisie, Hitler's against the plutocracy. In national socialist publications, Hitler was hailed as "the greatest socialist of all times."[7] Italian fascism was not different either. Mussolini had been a left-wing socialist, and it was in that spirit that he organized his fascist party.[8]

Maybe the conclusion about who was on the right and who on the left could be drawn on the basis of the sources financing these parties. Hitler's party had among its financial backers big German capitalists, Lenin's party, big Russian capitalists (e.g. Savva Morozov) and the general staff of the German armed forces.

As we see from the above, there really is no evidence to substantiate the claim that Hitler's party belonged to the right, whereas Lenin's was on the left. As a rule, all totalitarian movements and parties start on the radical left. After they come to power, however, they establish régimes that by all usual standards should be attributed to the extreme right. They are police régimes of "law and order," extremely hierarchical in their structure, with a highly privileged élite placed at the top that is hermetically sheltered from the rest of the population. Totalitarianism is also a type of theocracy, for it is based on an obligatory ideology that substitutes for religion—the leader is worshiped like a god or at least as his prophet. This is what the so-called personality cult is all about. The explanation of this left-right confusion is rather simple. The right, the center, and the left are categories of a *pluralistic* structure. *Monopolistic* totalitarianism does not belong to that structure and that is why it is neither left nor right. It has to be interpreted in different categories.

Totalitarian forces are obsessed by power and power alone, and they seek to seize it by all available means. Since it is easier for them to get support for their endeavor to overthrow the existing government by playing the part of the radical left, they willingly play this part. After having seized power, however, the totalitarians behave as the most reactionary right. They continue to pay lip service to leftist slogans only to simulate continuity and to win support for their expansion in foreign countries. As Hitler duped his leftist sympathizers abroad, so are the Soviet politbureaucrats duping the left in the West and in the Third World.

The Main Features of Totalitarianism

We have delimited totalitarianism. Let us now consider its main features.

1. The most important feature is the birth of a new ruling class—the political bureaucracy, the *nomenklatura*—that holds a monopoly on decision-making on all issues relevant to its interests.
2. The most important assistant of this class is the party "of a new type"—a totalitarian party organized as a military unit and led by the party apparatus, the core of the *nomenklatura*. The party pretends to be a workers' party, later a people's party engaged in the construction of a new society.
3. The stabilizers of the régime that insure the totality of the *nomenklatura*'s power are the political police and the military-industrial complex. Accordingly, the régime is characterized by state terror and militarism.
4. This régime consolidates its power and enhances its total control over the population by imposing upon society, and ruthlessly enforcing, an obligatory ideology that is messianic and has in principle the task of replacing traditional religion, although, for tactical reasons, the church is still tolerated.
5. The singleness and totality of the official ideology is reinforced by total ideological censorship applied, without exception, to all the media and all artistic and scientific works, with a view to barring any idea that is not in full conformity with the totalitarian ideology from entering the domain of public consumption.
6. Ideological censorship is amplified by overall secrecy and by the draconian punishments meted out to those who violate the secrecy rules.
7. The totalitarian ideology is spread and enforced by a huge propaganda machine which is the most powerful instrument the party apparatus uses in conducting both its internal and foreign policies.
8. The propaganda conducted by this machine is unavoidably based on xenophobia, nationalistic chauvinism, and state anti-Semitism.

Should one go deeper into the details, one could mention many other characteristic features of totalitarianism. But even this list, certainly not exhaustive, is sufficient for identifying a totalitarian society and distinguishing it from any other type of socio-political organization.

Some Objections

Some objections have been formulated regarding close links between "national" and "real" socialism.

1. "National" socialism did not abolish capitalism in its own country, the satellites and the occupied countries; "real" socialism did.

This is correct. But in fact the national-socialist rulers fully controlled the German national economy.[9] Without such a control, the four-year plan would have been impossible. Those repeating the Comintern's formula that "the Nazis were puppets of the German capitalists" cannot explain why, if this was so, the national-socialist rulers imposed a plan upon the capitalists and not the capitalists upon the national-socialist rulers.

Soon after the October revolution, Lenin began advocating the build-up of a state capitalistic system in Soviet Russia, along the lines of the German war economy. Three years later, in March 1921, he initiated the New Economic Policy (NEP). Under its provisions, Lenin permitted a certain development of capitalistic elements in society that were strictly controlled by the Soviet state retaining in its hands the "commanding heights of the economy." This formula was akin to the economic practice of the Nazis. After Lenin's death, Bukharin insisted on pursuing NEP But Stalin's *nomenklatura* wished to concentrate all economic power in their own hands. Ten years after the October revolution the NEP was dropped. Ten years after the Nazi seizure of power, the army of Field-Marshall Paulus capitulated in Stalingrad. At that point, a change of the Reich's economic policy was out of the question. It is possible that, under different circumstances, the Nazi leaders would have also given up the market economy during those ten years, because it was certainly hampering the totality of their power. But another development was possible, too—the continuation of NEP, a policy adopted by Hungary two decades ago and by China in our days.

2. National socialism and fascism were the enemies of the U.S.S.R.

This is not quite correct. The relations between the Mussolini government and Moscow were for many years quite satisfactory. As for Germany, Stalin kept confidential channels to Hitler open through Kandelaki and others.[10] In 1939, the U.S.S.R. and the German Reich became allies against Poland and delimited their respective spheres of interest in Eastern Europe. At the end of 1939, Stalin agreed to join the Axis powers as the fourth major partner. In the end this plan failed, but only because Hitler was not prepared to pay the price Stalin requested for it—ceding to Moscow Eastern Europe as well as parts of Turkey, Persia, and Iraq. Only because of this did the war between Germany and the U.S.S.R. begin. It is, therefore, a travesty to dub it, as the Soviets do, an antifascist war. Moreover, even during the war, secret contacts between Soviet and German representatives took place; the conditions of a separate peace treaty were under discussion.[11]

It is also necessary to stress that there has not been much harmony among the countries of "real" socialism themselves. The break between the U.S.S.R. and Yugoslavia, Albania and China, the alienation from the U.S.S.R. of North Korea and Romania, and the attempted alienation from the U.S.S.R. of Hungary in 1956 and of Czechoslovakia in 1968, both of which ended in Soviet military intervention, have all shown that sharp conflicts are also possible within the camp of "real" socialism. The military clashes on the Soviet-Chinese border, the wars between the Communist régimes, first waged by Vietnam against Pol Pot's Campuchea, and then by China against Vietnam, as well as Soviet intentions to start a nuclear war against China, demonstrate clearly that there is no substantial difference in the nature of the relations between the totalitarian régimes.

3. The sharp contradiction between the Soviet and the Nazi ideologies.

This is no argument at all. There was a clear difference between the national socialist and the Italian fascist ideology. Every totalitarian régime has an ideology of its own.[12] There are good reasons for this being so. A totalitarian ideology is a reflection, projected in a propagandistic form, of those real objectives of the ruling political bureaucracy that cannot be attained without mass support. Since these objectives differ from country to country, the contents of totalitarian ideologies have to differ, too. Total-itarian ideologies are important in the analysis of the totalitarian political planning, but they are irrelevant to the study of the totalitarian phe-nomenon. In this respect, only the *role* that ideology plays in totalitarian societies is important.

Some Conclusions

We have accepted the term totalitarianism. It would also be possible for us to accept the word fascism, with which millions of people are much more familiar—of course on the condition of extending this word to *all* totalitarian régimes without exception. It is, however, not the term, but the substance which is here most important. And the social and political substance of "real" and "national" socialisms as well as of fascism is the same. Real socialism is not only similar to, it is identical with, fascism and national socialism. Those who have lived in the Soviet Union know it; they know that they have lived under a totalitarian, fascist régime.

Notwithstanding the barrage of official propaganda, many people in the U.S.S.R. clearly understand this reality. Under Khrushchev a well-known

Soviet film director, Mikhail Romm, produced a documentary film, *Ordinary Fascism*, using excerpts from national socialist films. Although the movie showed another land and another epoch, the similarity was so clear that even in the Soviet press an orthodox Soviet writer angrily remarked that some movies "seem to deal with fascism, but one gets the impression that they are about us." Romm was summoned to the Party's Central Committee where Suslov directly asked him, "Mikhail Ilyich, why do you dislike us so much?" Yes, at the top of the *nomenklatura* its members are, at least subconsciously, aware of the identity between the "real" and "national" socialisms, between the totalitarian socialism and fascism. Against their own will the Soviet leaders had to state this awareness quite plainly when they stigmatized Tito's Yugoslavia and Pol Pot's Campuchea as fascist régimes, although they were the same régimes that only a short time before the Soviets had hailed as perfectly socialist.

* * * * *

At the end of her book, Hannah Arendt wrote pessimistically, "The crisis of our time and its central experience have brought forth an entirely new form of government which as a potentiality and an ever-present danger is only too likely to stay with us from now on, just as other forms of government which came about at different historical moments and rested on different fundamental experiences have stayed with mankind regardless of temporary defeats—monarchies and republics, tyrannies, dictatorships and despotism."[13] We can afford to go further in our conclusions.

I started my paper with a reminiscence of Nuremberg where I had the privilege to assist at the final act of the "national" socialist tragedy. I do not expect to assist at the final act of the tragedy of "real" socialism. Maybe not many of my contemporaries will. But I have no doubt at all that this final act will come. The historical experience regarding the fate of national socialism and fascism has shown that totalitarian structures disappear, and what follows is neither chaos, nor a new totalitarianism; it is democracy and pluralism. The spontaneous assumption of freedom is irresistible. After Nuremberg I worked at the Allied Control Council for Germany, and saw for myself how difficult it was to stop the process of spontaneous assumption of freedom in the Soviet zone of occupation. Now I live in Munich and am an Austrian citizen. I see how strong the roots of democracy and pluralism are in both these countries where "national" socialism and its Führer were born and grew up.

Totalitarianism is monolithic and therefore looks strong, but its roots are shallow. If shaken in the ground, totalitarianism gets radically uprooted, ceding place to a normal, pluralistic society and a parliamentary democracy, spontaneously formed by all the major forces of society after they are liberated from totalitarian oppression. Therefore, I am convinced that also in Russia, instead of ordinary fascism, pluralism and democracy will come one day to flourish.

NOTES

 1. Hannah Arendt, *The Origins of Totalitarianism* (New York and London: Harcourt Brace Jovanovich, 1973).
 2. Wolfgang Wippermann, *Faschismustheorien. Zum Stand der gegenwärtigen Diskussion* (Darmstadt: Wissenschaftliche Buchgemeinschaft, 1972), 3-4, 7-9. See also: V. Gransow, *Konzeptionelle Wandlungen der Kommunismusforschung. Vom Totalitarismus zur Immanenz* (Frankfurt/M.-New York: Campus Verlag, 1980).
 3. See as a specimen: R. Kühnl, "Zur politischen Funktion der Totalitarismustheorien in der BRD," in Greiffenhagen u.a., *Totalitarismus* (München: List Verlag, 1972).
 4. A good specimen is Richard Saage, *Faschismustheorien. Eine Einführung* (München: Beck, 1981).
 5. Georg Stadtmüller, *Sozialismen -Nationalsozialismus -Faschismus* (München: Hanns-Seidel-Stiftung e.V., Akademie für Politik und Zeitgeschichte, 1981), 133-134.
 6. See W. Wippermann, *Faschismustheorien*, 6.
 7. Karl Albrecht, *Der verratene Sozialismus* (Berlin-Leipzig: Nibelungen-Verlag, 1941), 5.
 8. See Daniel Guérin, *Fascisme et grand capital. Italie -Allemagne* (Paris: Gallimard, 1945); Giorgio Bocca, *Mussolini socialfascista* (Milano: Garzanti, 1983), 9-10.
 9. So did the Italian fascists. Mussolini told Emil Ludwig in an interview, "We are, like in Russia, in favour of a collectivist essence of individual life. We have put private capitalism under our control, the Russians have suppressed it." Quoted from G. Bocca, *Mussolini socialfascista*, 20.
10. Sven Allard, *Stalin und Hitler. Die sowjetrussische Aussenpolitik 1930-1941* (Bern-München: Francke Verlag, 1974), 31-44, 52-59, 94-102.
11. Peter Kleist, *Zwischen Hitler und Stalin 1939-1945* (Bonn: Athenäum Verlag, 1950), 230-284.
12. The common denominator of all totalitarian ideologies is, according to Lubomir Sochor, the following: they strongly claim to be revolutionary but are very conservative in their contents. See L. Sochor, *Contribution to an Analysis of the Conservative Features of the Ideology of "Real Socialism"* (Cologne: Research Project Crises in Soviet-Type Systems, Study No. 4, 1984). Cfr.: Konrad Löw, *Marxismus und Nationalsozialismus. Unterschiede und Gemeinsamkeiten* (Sonderdruck) (München: Olzog Verlag, 1980).
13. H. Arendt, *Origins of Totalitarianism*, 478.

2

Beyond the "Institutionalized Revolution" in Russia and China

RICHARD LÖWENTHAL

Introduction

One way of trying to forecast the prospects for the transformation of a political system, or of a group of such systems, is to analyze the forces that have determined the creation and evolution of those systems so far. In fact, while historical experience shows that unforeseen factors always intervene to limit the value of our forecasts of major developments, an understanding of the forces that have so far determined the course of events in the field in question appears to me as the only basis for looking at its future, at least with a minimum of security. In the case of the Communist party dictatorships that have arisen not as secondary products of the impact of greater powers from abroad, but from indigenous, original forces, we are entitled to the statement that the uniqueness of those "homegrown" communist dictatorships have been due to the fact that for a long time the pursuit by their rulers of utopian aims has forced them to follow up the original revolution that established their power by recurrent revolutions from above, thus trying to institutionalize revolution; and further, that the major turning point in their history so far occurred when, due to the increasing incompatibility of the practice of recurrent revolutions from above with the growing economic needs for modernization, institutionalized revolution had to be abandoned, and utopianism with it.

It has long been my view that the uniqueness which originally distinguished authentic, "homegrown" Communist party dictatorships from the countless other dictatorships of history was precisely that serious and persistent commitment not only to keeping power, but also to using power for ever new attempts to achieve utopian goals, leading to recurrent revolutions from above, and that only this unique and distinct character justified the description of this type of dictatorship as "totalitarian." I have concluded that, by the same token, Communist party dictatorships that have abandoned the search for utopia and the practice of recurrent "revolutions from above"—as the Soviet Union did towards the end of the Khrushchev era and Communist China did within a few years of Mao Zedong's death—no longer fit the epithet of totalitarianism, however certainly they have remained dictatorial systems.[1] I believe that an understanding of the dynamic process that has produced this crucial turning point in the two major communist powers will also enable us to make some tentative guesses on the prospects of their further transformation.

To understand the roots of Communist totalitarianism, it is essential that we recognize that the Communists first took power in the name of a utopian goal of perfect equality having its origin in the radical wing of the Western enlightenment of the 18th century, and more particularly of the French Revolution. Rousseau and others had developed visions of an ideal society based on a unanimous "general will" before that revolution. Robespierre and his supporters had tried to achieve it by force, even though their goals still fell short of *social* equality, and, after their fall, the more radically egalitarian Gracchus Baboeuf, who never achieved power, had conceived the idea that a lasting success for utopia could only be assured by the revolutionary rule of a strictly centralized single party. In 19th century France, Baboeuf's ideas were taken over by Blanqui, but his uprisings failed again and again, and his contemporary Karl Marx drew the conclusion that the goals of revolutionary socialism could only cease to be utopian and become practicable in a highly productive industrial society where they would not require a party dictatorship. But when the industrial workers of the West became both more numerous and more organized, as Marx had expected, and their struggle for political and economic rights became less revolutionary as it became more successful, the echoes of the original utopian vision gradually faded away throughout Western and Central Europe.

The course of history was sharply different in Russia, where political and social progress had remained much slower despite some acceleration of industrial progress since the turn of the century. Among the Russian

Marxists, Lenin interpreted the doctrine of the master as a kind of conditional utopianism, in the sense that the original utopian vision must be the goal after the revolutionary seizure of power, but could be achieved only on the basis of a highly developed economy, which he knew was still far away. But he also believed, in the tradition of Baboeuf and Blanqui, that revolutionary power could only be conquered by a strictly centralized "party of a new type." He proceeded to build it before the unsuccessful revolution of 1905 and rebuilt it afterwards, and he saw the outbreak of the first World War from the start as a chance for successful revolutions both in Russia and in other belligerent countries. His conquest of power in the October Revolution of 1917 was still not aimed at the immediate building of a socialist, let alone communist utopia in Russia. Having won in alliance with a movement of radical peasants eager to take their lands from the landlords, and with the peasant soldiers determined to get home to have their share of them, he concentrated on getting out of the war and encouraging revolution in other European countries that would have an economic basis for building socialism at home, and making possible a similar development in Russia by their help. When, by the end of the Russian civil war, no successful revolutions of the expected kind had taken place anywhere in industrially advanced Europe, Lenin accepted the harsh lesson that the conditions for utopia were not ripe in his country. In early 1921 he ended "wartime communism" and introduced the "New Economic Policy," thereby protecting the vital needs of the peasant majority so as to restore their production and end famine, and permitting considerable scope for private trade between town and country. But he also stabilized the dictatorial single-party rule that had developed in the course of the civil war, finally destroying the remnants of other leftwing parties that had fought on the Communists' side, and forbidding the formation of organized factions within his own party on the ground that they might give access to the influence of the "class enemy."

Lenin's final policy, then, was still a form of what we have called "conditional utopianism", *not* an attempt at achieving a utopian system here and now, but an insistence on consolidating total one-party rule in the hope that changes in other countries would make possible the fulfillment of utopian expectations at a later time. In particular, his paper on cooperation with the peasants, written on his deathbed,[2] insisted that the concessions made to them in the New Economic Policy could and should be maintained for a long time. But the doubt about the lasting effectiveness of that policy, expressed by some of the leading party specialists within a few years, was confirmed at the turn of 1927-1928 when increasing difficulties of obtaining grain from the peasantry were reported. The crisis was not the result of "sabotage" by the "kulaks," as the leftwingers in the party charged, but

neither could it be overcome by mere good will and concessions. Its roots
were the insufficient supplies of industrial products to the peasants, which
could not be cured without major changes of policy. But this was the
moment when one communist leader decided in fact to change the policy
radically—to achieve *his* vision of utopia by brute force. That leader was
Stalin.

Stalin's new policy led not only to a massive effort to speed the growth of
state industry, but also to the forced collectivization of the peasantry within
a few years, including a period of hunger and the transfer of millions of
peasants to camps of imprisonment where most of them eventually died.
Stalin himself later called the entire proceedings "a second revolution—but
this time a revolution from above."

The Running Down of the
"Institutionalized Revolution" in Russia

What we have called the system of "Institutionalized Revolution," then,
began with Stalin. It was not foreseen, let alone intended, by Lenin—yet it
was a consequence of his kind of long-term utopianism and its failure. It was
a consequence also of his belief that the advanced countries would sooner or
later produce revolutions based on ideas similar to his own, whereas, in fact,
communist revolutions were never actually to succeed in any advanced
industrial countries. It was a consequence further of his insistence on creating
and retaining single-party power in a country where, as he knew, the ideas of
that party were far from being shared by the majority of the people, so that
its control in any crisis could be secured only by force. And it was a
consequence, finally, of the kind of people that were bound to come to the
top in a party that, whatever its original beliefs, eventually found the
preservation of its power by every available means to be its most crucial
task.

As Stalin's characteristic economic policy took shape from 1928 onward, it
turned out to produce very different mixtures of utopian and developmental
features in the industrial and the agricultural fields. In industry, despite all
the harm done by excessive plans, neglect of expert advice, and poor
training of both technicians and workers, the developmental results on the
whole outranged the damages caused by utopian illusions. In agriculture,
despite all the efforts at mechanization and all the input of enthusiastic
volunteers filled with utopian hopes, the loss of peasant responsibility, of
livestock, and of total output caused by Stalin's "second revolution" had still
not been overcome by the time of his death in 1953. Broadly, the develop-

mental side of the ideological paradox proved predominant in Stalin's industrial economy, while the utopian side retained its power to ruin Soviet agriculture throughout Stalin's lifetime.

In changing the policy of the ruling party of the Soviet Union and the means of carrying it out, however, Stalin also changed one vital element of the utopian ideas from which it sprang; he totally dropped the belief in equality that had been the central value of traditional leftwing utopianism. As his power increased, there developed both an anti-egalitarian wage system in industry and a system of arbitrary privileges within the party. There were, of course, good reasons for thinking that the forced training of technically educated workers and the forced increase of industrial output in general could not be achieved by equality of wages, and the communist trade union leaders understood this, but Stalin insisted on the highest possible differentials. Similarly, there may have been good reasons why party functionaries charged with tasks of special difficulty for a long time should be rewarded not only with praise, but also with material gifts, particularly in conditions of general scarcity, but Stalin made such gifts so excessive that they had to become largely secret. His later rearrangement of access to higher education had a similar character.

Stalin had succeeded in overcoming the peasants' desperate resistance against his "revolution from above" by using the full powers of the party's General Secretary, not yet of a despot *above* the party. The bulk of the party activists, including many who had been critical at the beginning, came to believe that the party would not be able to survive the crisis without his authority. One famous proof that he was not yet a despot is the fact that his attempt to have one Ryutin, the author of a secretly-circulated pamphlet which blamed him for the crisis and demanded his replacement, handed to the courts for calling for Stalin's murder was rejected by the Politburo as late as 1932. Another proof is that at the 17th Party Congress of 1934, when the crisis was over, his title of General Secretary was reduced to First Secretary, and in the final election for the Central Committee, 292 secret votes were passed against him, as was disclosed many years later to a post-Stalin Central Committee (though not to the public) from documents.[3] It was probably that event, combined with the rising popularity of his long-time supporter Kirov, that caused Stalin to plan henceforth for the position of a despotic ruler *above* the party—a position he achieved by the great blood-purge following the assassination of Kirov.

There is no need in this context to retell that frightful story. What matters for our purpose is that from that time to Stalin's death in March 1953, the Soviet Union had a dictator who no longer depended on the officially ruling party, but used the party as merely one of the instruments of his power, on a par with the army and the government and somewhat below the secret police. It was during this time that Stalin made his pact with Hitler and fought his war against Hitler when attacked by him, that he became a wartime ally of the Western powers and their post-war enemy. It is not unnatural that many students of the period think that Stalin by that time, if not long before, believed in nothing but his power—that there was no remnant of ideological commitment left in him. But this is not true.

Stalin did not use the great purge just for his personal power, but for a systematic renewal and rejuvenation in the party and all branches of government—his second "revolution from above." Later, too, having had to make various concessions to the peasants and to religious believers during the war, he soon withdrew them. In 1950, he began, with the help of Nikita Khrushchev, a campaign to reduce the number of collective farms by merging them into greater units (by the time of the 19th Party Congress of 1952 little more than one third were left) which assured more effective control over them by the party apparatus. Most important, in his last (1952) pamphlet, "Economic Problems of Socialism in the USSR," Stalin developed an utterly utopian vision for an economic system in which all trade between the state-owned industrial units and the formally independent collective farms would be run without exchange of money—by a form of centrally organized barter.

It may be only due to Stalin's death soon afterwards that the people of the Soviet Union have been spared this ultimate form of a "revolution from above." Yet even the death of Stalin, while opening the door to Khrushchev's "destalinization" and to the liberation of most, and the rehabilitation of many, though by no means all, of Stalin's surviving victims, did not yet bring the final end of utopian experiments for the Soviet Union. The very man who was decisive for restoring the primacy of the Communist party, and who took the initiative for destalinization and at least partial rehabilitation of the victims, did so precisely because he believed in his own version of the utopian ideology—a version rather more humane, even more egalitarian, but not always more realistic than that of Stalin. Khrushchev's reforms included a reduction of the excessive wage differentials for the workers, and an abolition of the collective farms' dependence on state-run machine stations. But they also included repeated doubtful reorganizations of economic planning, from the partial regionalization of the middle fifties to the last attempt at a radical division of party organs into those administering urban and rural areas. Worst of all, they included the 1959 attempt to get the members of the collective farms to sell their private cattle "voluntarily" to the collective, and to move from their homes and their adjacent private land to new central "agro-towns" with more remote and smaller private plots. These were, in fact, old pet ideas of Khrushchev which had once failed in Stalin's time; now they were much propagated before the negative effects had to be recognized by the well-meaning initiator.

When the new party program—the same that was revised by Gorbachev's staff after 25 years—came out in 1961, it showed a curious contrast between Khrushchev's old attachment to utopian aims and his new caution concerning attempts to achieve them by command. The glorious promises of overtaking American food output by 1970 and reaching the "higher stage of communism" by 1980 were compelling reasons for Khrushchev's successors to avoid using the program. But the general text of the document had already made it clear that further advances to the "higher stage of communism" would not be the result of further enforced transformations of the social structure, but the automatic products of the steady improvement of productivity and of the standard of living of the masses. This must be regarded as the definite end for Russia of the age of institutionalized revolutions from above.

In fact, among the leaders responsible for Soviet policy, Khrushchev was the last true believer in the utopian goals of Marxism-Leninism—in his case, including the egalitarian element to some extent. The end of his leadership also marked the end of their relevance—the utopian goals, while still repeated, quickly lost their inner-party credibility. Among Khrushchev's successors, the hope for a better future, and the efforts for it, naturally have remained, but the belief in such utopian formulas as the "higher stage of Communism" soon became a joke among them, with possible individual exceptions among the last survivors of a bygone generation.

Achievements and Utopian Near-Chaos Produced by the Institutionalized Revolution in Mao's China

When the Chinese Communists finally took control of the whole of mainland China after their prolonged and bitter struggle for power, they had two apparent advantages: a ready-made model for building a socialist economy as presented by the Soviet Union, and a revolutionary leader of uncontested authority in his party with the will and ability to cooperate with Stalin without necessarily imitating him in every field. Mao Zedong not only survived his victory much longer than Lenin, but for more than a decade had no need to replace Leninist party leadership by Stalinist personal despotism. Given the fact that Stalin's despotism ended with his death less than four years after Mao's rise to full national power, Mao could soon afford to modify, in the light of Chinese experience, even those models that he had at first been ready to accept.

The first attempt at such a modification concerned Mao's first "revolution from above"—as in Russia, the forced collectivization of the peasantry. Mao originally had hoped to avoid the enormous damage done to Soviet agriculture and the massive terror against the peasantry which had characterized the Stalinist original by stretching the operation over three five-year plans. Like Stalin, however, he was driven to concentrate the campaign in two to three years by a sudden, unforeseen shortage of rural deliveries to the state. Afterwards, also not unlike Stalin in 1934, Mao in 1956 followed up the completed operation by announcing, at the First Session of the 8th Party Congress, a period of national reconciliation by simultaneous concessions of the regime to peasants, workers, and intellectuals.

Beginning in 1957, however, the evolution of Chinese communism went a way of its own—not primarily because the intellectuals used the right of criticism offered to them in the "Hundred Flowers' campaign" more vigorously than Mao and his party had expected, but because the disproportion between the rate of growth of the enormous Chinese population and the limited capital available for industry created urgent economic problems quite different from the Soviet model. The issue was made acute when long overdue wage increases for the industrial workers, conceded by the 1956 Party Congress, produced a rush from the overpopulated countryside into the cities, while the hope of getting more Soviet capital for the development of Chinese industry went unfulfilled. Under those circumstances Mao Zedong decided, with the initial approval of the party leadership, to impose two new forms of a "revolution from above" without a parallel in Soviet history: the "Great Leap Forward" in the organization of industry, encouraging a race of regional party officials for higher production targets over the heads of both the planning of the central ministries and the competence of the local managers, and the "People's Communes" in the countryside, bringing the collective farms of entire districts under a single command in order to employ all their members—not only in agricultural work and both local and large-scale irrigation, but also in improvised on-the-spot industrial work, including improvised steel furnaces! The common denominator of both aspects of this second "revolution from above" was Mao Zedong's reacting to increased economic difficulties by an increased reliance on the power of utopian faith.

The story of the crisis of Mao's uncontested authority is identical with that of the process leading from this, his second "revolution from above," to his third—the "Great Proletarian Cultural Revolution" of 1966. The former was launched in stages in 1958, beginning with the Second Session of the 8th Party Congress early in that year, which proclaimed the "Great Leap Forward" and prepared the first experiments with the "Peoples' Communes," and leading to the Central Committee meeting at the end of the year which officially proclaimed the Communes while seeking to limit the wildest utopian hopes and excesses that had developed in the meantime around them. The years of 1959-1962 brought a reduction of Mao's influence on the conduct of economic affairs due to growing critique of his utopian tendencies in the party leadership and government administration, as well as an increase in his influence on the training of the young generation and armed forces, and on the developing debate with the Soviet leaders on Marxist-Leninist theory in general and Communist world policy in particular. By the time of the CPC's official break with the Soviet Communist Party in the summer of 1963, Mao's series of answers to the Soviet "Open Letter" became the recognized official canon of Chinese Communist ideology, including his doctrine that counterrevolution had succeeded in the Soviet Union and could still occur in China in the course of the next "five to ten generations or one or several centuries." His campaigns for "socialist education" and "learning from the army" had begun to organize a radical Maoist following independent from the regular party institutions. At the same time, Mao's increasingly rigid doctrine that socialist achievement in the economy depended exclusively on the right spirit of all people involved in the process of production, independent of any offer of material incentives—a doctrine never accepted by any of the Soviet leaders in any stage of Soviet history—created an unbridgeable gulf between him and the serious practitioners of economic policy and administration.

The sanction of the "Great Proletarian Cultural Revolution" by the Party's Central Committee meeting of August 1966, called in an *ad hoc* composition with military assistance, marks the beginning of the third of China's, and Mao's, great revolutions from above, as well as the overthrow of the rule of the Party he had led to its revolutionary victory in favor of his attempt at personal despotism. The change had become inevitable because the gulf between his increasingly extreme utopianism (produced in large part by his horror at the post-Stalinist evolution in the Soviet Union) and the view of much of the Chinese party bureaucracy had to Mao become incapable of compromise. But while the aged Mao succeeded in paralyzing the party organization for a number of years, he did not succeed in creating an alternative order; nor did he succeed in acquiring the independence of a true despot. In the early years of the Cultural Revolution, Mao became increasingly dependent on the army, which had first helped to transport the mass movement of the young Red Guards to its Beijing demonstrations, and then had helped to send them back to the countryside when they were fighting each other and ransacking the documents of the Ministry of Foreign Affairs. It was the army representatives who played a key role in the forming of new revolutionary committees from whose work a reorganized party was to be eventually created; and when the first congress of this "resurrected" party was held, it was the army leader Lin Biao who was not only elected as Mao's deputy, but designed by statute as his eventual successor. After Lin Biao died in an unexplained air accident, allegedly due to his treacherous machinations, the generals are not known to have protested, but their role was considerably reduced; yet Mao himself was now heard of less and less, and no uncontested leading figure was recognizable any longer. Before the death of Mao in 1976, ten years after his assumption of the role of a would-be despot, an undecided factional struggle seemed to swing between ultra-Maoist utopians and more practical-minded administrators, with a remnant of order maintained by the outstanding administrator Chou Enlai and a few collaborators assembled by him, among whom Deng Xiaoping was one; but Chou died before Mao, and Deng was sent into provincial exile for a second time by the extremist clique. In the last phase of Mao's would-be despotic rule, Communist China had no recognizable government at all.

Even more strikingly than in the Soviet Union, the period of institutionalized revolution had ended in China with a disorganization of the régime's institutional structure and a profound discredit of the idea of further revolutions. The only major decision carried out by Hua Guofeng, a former provincial party leader and security chief, allegedly appointed successor by the dying Mao, with the help of Mao's personal guards and the Beijing garrison, and to the apparent relief of most of the party organization, was the arrest of the leading radical utopians, including Mao's wife Jiang Ching, for having attempted to seize power by force. But Hua apparently had no political concept of his own, except the absurd pretense that all Mao's ideas had been correct and must be carried out—though he had enough common sense not to attempt to follow this prescription in practice. As the party cadres who had been trained before the Cultural Revolution and survived it recovered their self-confidence, they not only called back Deng from his second exile to become their effective, though never their nominal leader, in late 1977, but also decided a year later to give priority to the modernization policy advocated by the late Chou Enlai in Mao's last years. By 1981 they not only elected a new leadership oriented towards this non-utopian and non-revolutionary goal, but adopted a remarkable document concerning Mao's historical role since the party's conquest of power. It combined praise for his original revolutionary victory and his creation of a powerful and independent Chinese state, criticism of his policies of the "Great Leap Forward" and the "Peoples' Communes" as at least partly ill-conceived, and outright condemnation of the "Cultural Revolution" as wholly destructive in its effects. At the same time it spared the dead leader the charge of personal responsibility for the organized crimes of that period by ascribing them to his arrested and sentenced radical supporters, now known as the "Gang of Four." The post-revolutionary and post-totalitarian era of Communist China, which may be said to have begun with the death of Mao and the arrest of his extremist advisers, was thus definitely established with the 1981 reorganization of the party leadership and its document on party history.

Post-Revolutionary Russia:
The Struggle Between Stagnation and Reform

The decision of the Politburo and Central Committee of the Soviet Communist Party to remove Khrushchev from his position as party leader by an overwhelming vote—an event unprecedented in the history of independent, ruling communist parties—was consciously intended not only as a change of the person, but of the role of the party leader. Indeed, that role had been ill defined in the Khrushchev era. The man who had dared to expose the inner-party terror of Stalin and his regime of personal despotism, thus consciously restoring the physical security of the members of the party élite, had not been able, and indeed not willing, to establish a binding procedural rule for the decisions of the "collective leadership" which, after the shock of "destalinization," was clearly needed. Given to frequent new inspirations of uneven value, he had not offered to the country the stability that both the people and most of the party bureaucrats strongly desired, and had increasingly tended to announce publicly his political proposals before they had been discussed, let alone approved, by the Politburo. What probably did most to turn the leading party strata against him, however, was one of his great potential merits; he who had restored the physical security of the members of the *nomenklatura* remained to the end unwilling to give them job security regardless of their performance, and was rather inclined to cause repeated upheavals within the apparatus—thus eventually turning the *nomenklatura* against him.

The new leadership of Brezhnev and Kosygin impressed both subordinates and general public at first by its air of calm, moderation and stability. The only field where it was in a hurry was the dismantling of some of Khrushchev's organizational devices—the recent partition of the party organizations between industrial and rural sections, and the older replacement of a number of economic branch ministries by regional institutions. The new men did not attempt to undo destalinization, but they began to softpedal it—making both the literary treatment of the purges and the still far from complete rehabilitation of their victims increasingly difficult. The attempt to improve industrial productivity by reducing the imposition of detailed central commands to the managers, expected since the Liberman discussion, was undertaken experimentally on a limited scale by Kosygin. A more massive effort to overcome the persistent backwardness of Soviet agriculture was made by increased expenditure for chemical fertilizers and improved equipment for a number of years; even more important efforts to improve productivity by introducing the "link" system in the collective farms were attempted to in various regions and centrally favored for a time, but eventually were crushed almost everywhere by the regional bureaucracy. But the strongest impression of unity and progress was probably created by the new kind of "cabinet discipline"—the fact that disagreements witin the leadership were not allowed to become visible, that it tended to speak with a single voice. This apparent unanimity, which in Stalin's time could only have been achieved by fear of punishment, had become much easier in a post-revolutionary period, where no member of the *nomenklatura* could believe any longer that the fate of the cause depended on his particular recipe.

In fact, one of the major innovations of the new leadership was the silent abandonment of Khrushchev's utopian faith; it was not announced with fanfare, but understood from the start by the entire leadership. To the outsiders, it was recognizable by the prompt dropping of the timetable for the fulfillment of future achievements contained in Khrushchev's party program, and by the general decline in the use of that document—a phenomenon which caused some hopeful Western observers to expect not only a post-utopian and post-revolutionary, and in that sense post-totalitarian, but a post-ideological Soviet Union that would at last become a "satisfied power." But the new leadership was no less aware than its predecessors that the monopoly of power for their single party could not be maintained without an ideological justification, and if any of them had doubted that need, they were soon reminded of it not only by a growing wave of dissident *samizdat* literature at home but by the Czechoslavakian heresy seeking a new road towards a "socialism with a human face." It was in April 1968 that Brezhnev, in a speech to Moscow party activists, announced a non-utopian justification of the single-party regime; it was needed to defend the achievements of the "socialist system" against the unending attempts of its capitalist enemies to create conflicts among its social strata and nationalities. The argument contained the core of a new version of official communist ideology, based no longer on utopian goals and expectations, but on the need for eternal vigilance against the capitalist world as the price of the "socialist achievements" already gained and still to be improved under communist rule. Soon afterwards, the so-called Brezhnev Doctrine was to justify the invasion of Czechoslovakia by its Warsaw Pact allies under Soviet leadership with the need to practice the same vigilance in protecting the unity of the communist-governed nations against the intrigues of the capitalist world.

This shift of the center of communist ideology from the promise of utopia to the need for unity and strength in defense of past and future achievements against the capitalist enemy had, of course, its background in the trauma of Khrushchev's spectacular defeat in the Cuban missile crisis, and in the consequent decision of the new leadership to try and change the East-West balance by a massive increase in armaments, notably in intercontinental missiles and in long-range naval and air transport. Its success was facilitated in part by the weaknesses of its rivals—by the involvement of the United States in the Vietnam war, and of China in the throes of the "Cultural Revolution." For a number of years it was also helped by the Soviet Union wisely avoiding the use of its new weapons in zones of vital interest to its political main opponent, the U.S., and thus ensuring that the latter's attention to the Soviet massive military build-up was not duly aroused. Even the supply of Soviet weapons to North Vietnam, hampered as it was at times by Chinese sabotage, did not alter President Johnson's belief that Russia was a satisfied power while China was preparing a major offensive in Southeast Asia that had begun in Vietnam, and the same president saw no cause for concern in the Soviet-led intervention of the Warsaw Pact against the "Prague Spring," since it took place within the part of Europe long conceded to Soviet hegemony.

The undisturbed change in the relation of forces between the superpowers, achieved without excessive provocation on the Soviet side and without noticeable awareness on the American side, only reached an end when a new American administration realized that the Soviets had reached an approximate parity of nuclear strength, and offered negotiations aimed at stabilizing the balance. The resulting first SALT agreement of 1971 and its sequels were, from a Soviet point of view, the greatest peaceful success in the history of their foreign policy; and it was accompanied during the same years by equally successful negotiations of the Soviets and their European allies with the Federal Republic of Germany, resulting in the *de facto* recognition of the East-West borders, created in Europe after World War II, after a quarter of a century. By speaking of those negotiations as successful for the Soviets, I do not mean that they were in their nature defeats for the West; given the preceding development, both the American and West German negotiators had good reasons to welcome their results as factors of stability and alternatives to a dangerous and futile arms race. Yet parallel with those negotiations, unplanned internal changes occurred in the Soviet Union which were soon to result in unforeseen changes in East-West relations.

The internal changes in the Soviet Union were pointing to the victory of stagnation over reform under an aging leadership. Kosygin's experiment with greater autonomy for the industrial managers had soon been abandoned under the pressure of the bureaucracy, and so had the leadership's support for experiments with agricultural "links." Even more important than the obvious increase in the average age of the members of the Politburo was the growing age and corresponding traditionalism of the bulk of the *nomen-klatura*—a bureaucracy the members of which had become effectively unremovable under the post-Khrushchev regime. The hope that the end of enforced revolutions from above, and of the utopian dreams inspiring them, might open the way to unplanned, "spontaneous" initiatives from below, as in the normal evolution of Western history (and in the Marxian interpretation of history based on it) had once again not been fulfilled in Russia—as little as in tsarist times. A great historian of tsarist Russia, Kliuchevsky, had pointed out long ago that in the pre-revolutionary empire the most effective impulses for economic and social change had hardly ever come from the pressure of the common people, whose institutional means of influence were too limited, but again and again from above and outside—to wit from the real or imagined foreign dangers perceived by the tsars, and from their corresponding efforts to increase their country's military strength and develop the economic and educational institutions needed for that purpose.

In the conditions of modern Communist Russia, a temporary victory of the forces of stagnation represented by an overaged *nomenklatura* can hardly produce total stagnation for any length of time, because there are always the claims of the armed forces notoriously difficult to reject. It can only produce partial stagnation in the civilian sector combined with increased influence of military dynamism. This is what seems to have happened in the second half of the seventies, when a temporary weakening of the influence of American presidential leadership, due to the effects of the aftermath of Vietnam and Watergate on public opinion and through it on Congress, made it equally difficult for successive administrations to obtain approval for the results of new negotiations with the Soviet Union as for resisting its actions in the Third World.

True, the fact that the détente agreements did not and could not end the conflict between the superpowers, but could at best offer means for controlling its forms, must have been clearly understood by all concerned after the experience of the Yom Kippur war of 1973 and its aftermath, which showed that the Soviets had advance knowledge of the Arab attack but, while refraining from supporting it, also had refrained from warning the Americans; that on the eve of a decisive Israeli victory over Egypt, the Soviets had threatened with military intervention, and that the United States, while neutralizing the threat, had succeeded in limiting the Israeli counter-offensive sufficiently to save Egypt's integrity and honor, and had used it to win Egypt over to their own camp; and that Washington afterwards had rejected any proposal for a broad international conference on the Middle East including the Soviet Union.

But a deliberate decision of the Soviets to react to the growing inadequacy of U.S. economic cooperation and to the temporary U.S. near-paralysis in taking foreign policy initiatives by, on the one hand, expanding their interventions in the Third World and, on the other hand, by their installing modern intermediate range missiles aimed at Western Europe, seems to have occurred only in 1975. The aging Brezhnev, who had achieved his country's unique success in being recognized as an equal partner of the other superpower, undertook in his final years to undermine the basis of that success, not by formally cancelling the SALT agreements, but by seeking new positions of power in various parts of the Third World and attempting to put pressure on the European allies of the United States with a reckless boldness utterly unlike his previous caution, and different from the wilder international enterprises of Khrushchev only on the basis of a military strength that had certainly grown impressively in more than a decade, but was still likely to prove inadequate in a serious test.

Due to the alarm caused in the Western alliance as this reckless turn of Soviet policy came to be generally understood, the famous "double-track" decision of NATO, calling on the Soviets to reverse their new establishment of nuclear weapons directed at Western Europe or face the stationing of corresponding American weapons in Western Europe directed at the Soviet Union, seemed inevitable. In the new atmosphere, the negotiations proposed by NATO started only with great delay and little prospect of success, as the leaders of both superpowers were now in a mood clearly opposed to détente. But while both sides appeared to this observer to march with flying colors into parallel and opposing blind alleys, the economic effectivity and political credibility of the Soviet system suffered worse. During the last years of Brezhnev and the subsequent leadership of two other men of similar age and feeble health, however different in quality and outlook, the belief in an inevitable and accelerating decline spread widely both inside and outside the Soviet empire, and the combination of economic stagnation, political ineffectiveness, and militarism sketched above came to be widely regarded as the necessary character of a great Communist power in the stage I have here characterized as post-utopian and post-revolutionary.

Yet both the differences between the post-revolutionary evolution of the Soviet Union and that of Communist China, discussed in the following section, and the ups and downs in the evolution of the Soviet Union itself should have warned us against taking "the fall of the Soviet Empire" for granted. It is true that the factors of stagnation had become particularly strong in the Soviet Union for more than a decade, with strikingly harmful effects in the economic field and in the selection of political leaders. It is also true that the main factor of stagnation had long been the higher and middle bureaucracy—the *nomenklatura*—and that its role in Russia had become incomparably stronger than in Stalin's time, owing to its strong links both with the building of industry and the control of peasants, its post-Stalin gain of physical security and its post-Khrushchev gain of job security, and not the least because of the element of solidarity which, despite endless personal rivalries, arose from its peculiar kind of class consciousness. But even in Russia, there is a fundamental difference between longevity and eternity, and an overdue generation crisis may greatly change the trend if used by skilled leaders, and especially if the natural harmony between the Soviet's military machine and their civilian bureaucratic apparatus, which has been the conventional wisdom of the Brezhnev era, is no longer taken for granted.

It is here that the potentially crucial role of the first party leader of a new generation may become decisive. When Gorbachev was new in his office, there was much speculation in the West that the new general secretary, being not only more vital and innovative but also more cultured, might be interested in better relations with the West. Even assuming the likelihood of this hypothesis, it does not follow that Gorbachev would feel free to make major steps in that direction in the near future—certainly not at the expense of Soviet military strength. But it has been beyond doubt, both before his rise to the highest party office and even more since then, that Gorbachev is passionately concerned with fighting economic stagnation. Yet anybody who wishes to fight the established, largely overaged bureaucracy—or more precisely, to rejuvenate it—cannot possibly afford to fight the military leadership, which is at least as cohesive and more publicly respected, at the same time.

I conclude that the present, long-established, backward-looking bureaucracy is strong, but not by nature invincible. Its breakup and rejuvenation are by no means certain, but conceivable, and may be seriously attempted in the course of the generation change that is now in progress. A simultaneous correction of the overstressing of military strength practiced in the last decade is *not* likely because, from an internal Soviet point of view, the revamping of the economic bureaucracy is more urgent. It could only come more slowly—and whether it comes may depend on changes on the Western side as well.

Post-Revolutionary China: Some Causes for the Breakthrough of Reform

Since the official rejection of the ultra-utopian policies of the late Mao Zedong and his limited number of convinced supporters, the effort at modernizing China has assumed the character of a true breakthrough of the forces of reform. While the period during which we have been able to observe this remarkable phenomenon is as yet limited, the contrast to the increasing stagnation of the post-revolutionary Soviet Union in recent years, at least where economic and social policies are concerned, has been so striking that it requires an attempt at explanation.

The major factors of a different development start with the different popular memory of the worst actions of Stalin and the worst actions of Mao. Though Stalin's "Great Purge" affected millions of families and was bitterly debated in the years of "destalinization," there was always the counterweight of the argument that Stalin had led Russia to victory in the Great War and had raised her to the rank of a world power; and in the mind of most of the younger generation, the glorious memory of Stalin seems to be more alive than the shocking one. The horrors of Mao's "Cultural Revolution," which occurred in the final phase of his rule, and of the near chaos which continued down to his death, are still in comparatively recent memory. For the younger generation they seem to have overshadowed his real revolutionary achievements and his important merit in establishing China's complete independence from Soviet tutelage.

A second major difference concerns the relative stability of the party bureaucracy in both countries. Stalin destroyed a generation of major party functionaries, but he replaced them at once by the next generation. He kept the individuals in fear but treated the institution as indispensable. When, after his death, the personal security of the bureaucrats was assured as well, their role became stronger than ever before—strong enough to gain also an unprecedented job security in the Brezhnev era and a corresponding influence. Mao, in the early phase of his "Cultural Revolution," had come close to treating the bureaucracy of party and state as his main enemies, excepting only the army. His appeal to the Red Guards to "bombard the headquarters" was directed precisely against the bureaucracy and led to the effective paralysis of the party institutions, and when the party was reorganized anew, from the top downwards, many of the former bureaucrats eventually reappeared, but in a situation of extreme insecurity.

Finally, when the utopian elements of the traditional communist doctrine were at last abandoned in Russia after the fall of Khrushchev, this was done without resistance and without fanfare, simply by concentrating the doctrine on the real achievements, their steady pursuit and their defense against the capitalist enemy. The new Chinese leader had at first really to fight against the utopian tradition, to tell the truth about how insufficient the real achievements had remained in the economic field, and to stress that good Marxists had to learn to find truth from the facts.

All this has meant that the new Chinese leadership around Deng Xiaoping had to start work with a considerably disorganized party apparatus in which the surviving upstarts from the young "Red Guard" generation, if they were not still secretly trying to pursue the rejected policy of the "Gang of Four," were as insecure as the oldtimers rehabilitated in Mao's final years after their persecution during the early Cultural Revolution. If there was little competence for carrying out the new task of serious modernization at a realistic pace, there was also little self-confidence left in this repeatedly and thoroughly shaken bureaucracy. Most likely it was that insecurity of a shaken and mixed bureaucratic personnel that enabled Deng to carry out his new economic ideas as soon as they had become sufficiently clear in his own head.

This could not happen without trial and error; for Deng, though clearly both an unusually able and decisive man in his old age, had little personal experience in the problems of economic and social modernization that he recognized as decisive for China's future. (He did not at once correct the exaggerated plans for the pace of industrial expansion which had still been sanctioned by Hua Guofeng, and he started with exaggerated hopes for the amount of credit and technological support China could quickly get from the West, and above all from the United States, for its industrial development. He also misjudged, on the occasion of a border-conflict with Soviet-supported Vietnam, the strength of the Chinese armed forces, with their longstanding war inexperience and their clinging to glorious but outdated guerrilla practices, in case of a serious conflict with the Vietnamese, given their almost uninterrupted history of fighting.) But faithful to his belief in learning truth from facts, Deng learned quickly and acted accordingly; he moderated the initial pace of the industrial program to more realistic proportions, and he stopped the adventure at the Vietnam border in time to limit the damage.

Above all, Deng developed, after the initial period of trial and error, three major reform programs: a program for dramatically improving Chinese agricultural production by decisively encouraging the peasants' own interests; a program for giving both greater scope for industrial factory management and greater freedom for private trade in consumer goods; and a program for the massive rejuvenation of leading personnel in party, administration, and army. The agricultural reforms (for which first steps had been taken before by reducing the "people's communes" to a purely administrative function and restoring to the peasant families some limited scope for private production within the collective farms) have recently been developed so far that private production has apparently become the main part of Chinese agriculture, resulting in enormous, if regionally uneven, improvement of both the peasants' income and the food supply of the city population. The major reforms in industry were only started when the success in agriculture was already assured, and seem to have given the factory managements the degree of independence within the framework of general directives which Soviet reformers have proposed for their much more developed industries again and again—so far without major success. The greater managerial freedom in China includes the right to sell consumer goods to private traders, again with the corresponding advantage for the living standard of large numbers of consumers, but without an attempt to overcome the considerable regional unevenness of those standards, at least for the time being. At the same time, the official press is at pains to explain that those highly popular changes are not part of a return to capitalism, but take place in a framework of public ownership of industry and public planning of the general directions of its growth, which are viewed, now as before, as the essentials of a socialist economy.

Finally, the deliberate rejuvenation of leading personnel in party, administration, and army has begun in the last few years, and it has begun where it was most needed—at the top. Deng, who is 80 years old himself, seeks to avoid people above the forties and fifties in most key roles; he is clearly not only concerned with the working capacity of those responsible, but also with their final liberation from memories of a distant past that he knows have little relevance for the problems of the present. Obviously, his economic and political reforms could not have succeeded as much as they have if they had met the resistance of a solid phalanx of the senior officials, but for reasons indicated above, no such phalanx was noticeable among the bureaucracy of party and state in post-Mao China, and he is now evidently concerned that no anti-reform phalanx should develop in a post-Deng China either. The one group of major importance where traditional elements for such a phalanx were still recognizable was the military establishment, and this is the organization where Deng has been careful to make his earlier changes most cautiously and for which he has announced the principles of a general "generation change" only in the course of 1985. Here even more than in other fields, he has been generally careful to arrange the retirement of the seniors with all honors and praise for their past merits. But he has also taken care to make clear the qualification required for their successors and those of their ranking subordinates—not only regarding their loyalty to the Party or their socialist patriotism, but also their thorough, wide-ranging education on the level of contemporary experience, problems, and technologies. (Looking at the picture of many American universities today, I should not be surprised if quite a few of those coming men of Communist China would turn out to have obtained part of their education in the United States; but looking at the care taken by present Chinese foreign policy to preserve its freedom of movement in world affairs and keep the door open to an eventual normalization of relations with Moscow, I should not be surprised either if at a not so distant time, quite a few of them might also obtain a part of their education in the Soviet Union again. For the long-term interest of successfully modernizing Communist China in a world divided between two superpowers will clearly require its ability to balance between them.)

Conclusion: A Final Word on Prospects

For all the obvious differences between the conditions of origin, the evolution, and the present problems of Communist party rule in the Soviet Union and China, it seems clear to me that their prolonged periods of what I have called "institutionalized revolution" had common basic characteristics that sharply distinguished them from other dictatorships and tyrannies in history. Because the original seizure of power was based on a commitment of both parties to goals that were utopian in the strict sense of being incapable of fulfillment on this earth, both felt forced to follow up the original revolutionary seizure of power in due course by repeated revolutions from above, but were also forced eventually to abandon the attempt in the interest of economic modernization and political survival. I believe that it was this utopian-inspired dynamic of the institutionalized revolution that was the distinguishing characteristic of Communist totalitarianism, and that gave this totalitarianism the quality not of a final blind alley of history, as some of its early critics had feared, but of a truly historic phenomenon with a beginning and an end.

The present, post-utopian and post-revolutionary Communist regimes, the two outstanding examples of which I have tried here to sketch, are therefore also post-totalitarian in my sense of the term. They both are, however, still party dictatorships who cling to their power—not in order to achieve utopia, in which they no longer believe, but in order to advance the economic modernity and political greatness of the nations they govern. In ruling nations without a political tradition of democracy or a strong cultural tradition of human rights, their leaders and functionaries see no reason why their single-party rule should not continue indefinitely, provided they succeed in making reasonable progress in the pursuit of those non-utopian economic and political goals.

It is at this point, however, that the necessary parallelism of the two leading communist powers comes to an end. Prerevolutionary Russia, while backward in comparison with the Western nations, was much farther advanced on the road to modernity than prerevolutionary China. When the

Soviet Union entered the post-revolutionary phase in the sixties while Mao's China entered the paroxysm of the "Cultural Revolution," the distance in favor of the older communist power still increased. But after the middle seventies, the Soviet Union entered, as we have seen, a period of increasing bureaucratic stagnation, while soon afterwards the post-revolutionary China that emerged from the death of Mao Zedong entered a period of accelerating reform.

Now I am not suggesting that this recent separation of trends, not to speak of an at least temporary reversal of roles between the two major communist powers, indicates any new law of development. On the contrary, it indicates that the evolution of the post-revolutionary communist party regimes no longer necessarily follows a common law. In the absence of a still effective common tradition and of recognizable major forces of popular pressure, the decisive factors of evolution in both countries at any given moment appear to be the relative strength of dynamic leadership versus bureaucratic stagnation, not to mention possible factors of outside international aid or pressure.

At some junctures, the course of history may be influenced by major events for some time to come, as after great wars or revolutions. At others, it may be shaped by the rise of great movements or by leaders of unusual vision and energy. But it is never predetermined, and at the present time and for the two great powers with which I have been dealing here, its future seems to me less foreseeable than ever.

NOTES

1. For my first statement of this view, see R. Löwenthal, "Development vs. Utopia in Communist Policy," in Chalmers Johnson, ed., *Change in Communist Systems* (Stanford, Ca.: Stanford University Press, 1970). For recent developments, see R. Löwenthal, "Totalitarianism and After in Communist Party Regimes," in *Totalitarian Democracy and After* (Jerusalem: Israel Academy of Science and Humanities, 1984), and R. Löwenthal, "Beyond Totalitarianism," in Irving Howe, ed., *1984 Revisited: Totalitarianism in our Century* (New York: Harper & Row, 1983).
2. I am referring to Lenin's famous article "On Cooperation," which Bukharin was to describe in his last public argument against Stalin's turn towards collectivization as "Lenin's political testament."
3. The disclosure was made by V. M. Verkhovykh, the surviving deputy chairman of the Elections Commission of the 17th Congress, to an investigating commission of the Party's Central Committee in 1957, and is confirmed by the fact

that the stenographic record of the 17th Congress lists 1225 participants, while the official summary cites only 935 voting delegates. The difference of 289 votes corresponds to the 292 votes against Stalin minus the 3 that were admitted in the record. The facts were first published broadly in Roy Medvedev, *Let History Judge* (New York: Alfred Knopf, 1971), 155-6, and later in full detail in Anton Antonov-Ovseyenko, *Portret Tirana* (New York: Khronika Press, 1980), 113-118.

3

A Theoretical Evaluation Without Historical Contents

A Commentary on Section 1

RICHARD LÖWENTHAL

Professor Michael Voslensky has called his paper "A Historical and Theoretical Evaluation of the Soviet System." But while the paper is extremely clear in a kind of evaluation that may be described as theoretical, defining the Soviet system as a type of totalitarianism on a par with Italian fascism and German national-socialism, it has virtually no historical content at all. There is no hint on how the ruling parties of those totalitarian systems arose and came to power, except by their, or their leader's, will to total power. Voslensky clearly takes it for granted that the founders of those systems care for power and nothing else, and that their different ideologies were important only as different means to an end that he describes as "identical." As a result, he also has virtually nothing to say about the prospect of transformation in the Soviet Union—except his confidence that somehow, sometime it will come to an end and be replaced by some kind of democratic system, as successfully as the fascist totalitarianism of Italy and the national-socialism of Germany were eventually replaced by democratic systems, wholly in the Italian and at least partly in the German case.

I.

In addition to the absence of reflection on the origin of Soviet communism and the possible road to its future disappearance, there is an equally total refusal to discuss the forms of transformation that have already taken place in the almost 70 years since Lenin took power—against an absence of the historical element. In what follows, I propose to discuss briefly the consequences to Voslensky's understanding of the Soviet Union of what I regard as the two major weaknesses of his approach, namely his assumption of the "identity" of all forms of totalitarianism, and his neglect of the importance of the phases of change in the history of the Soviet Union.

Having been confronted in my life and work from an early time with the new forms of communist and fascist dictatorships, I have long accepted the concept of totalitarianism as meaningful in the double sense: of describing by it a new type of dictatorship aiming at an ideological-model-based total transformation of society, and of applying this concept to movements and systems driven by opposite ideological goals of the communist and the fascist-national-socialist variety. To that extent Voslensky and I would appear to have a common basis for our argument. But I have never accepted Carl Friedrich's formula that communism and Nazism could be described as "basically alike," because I felt their ideological and political differences were sufficient to make the decision whether they were more alike or more different dependent on the concrete issue under discussion—say, more alike in some of their methods of rule, more different on some issues of economic and foreign policy. Even less can I accept Voslensky's formula of their "identity," which could only be put forward by an observer who believes that political systems can be characterized *completely* by their methods of rule (or even only a few of them), regardless of their ideological aims which are shoved aside as mere verbal eyewash. Voslensky does indeed go as far as to suggest that all totalitarian systems necessarily start with an apparent left-wing attitude, and, once in power, develop an apparent rightwing policy, because they must begin to conquer power from below and go on to strengthen and defend it from above. But nobody who has seen or studied the road to power followed by Mussolini and Hitler could seriously maintain that they followed a left policy, when the former broke up the trade unions and peasant organizations by brute force and with the funds of the rich, and the latter treated the German labor movement as his main enemy (next to the Jews), nor could anybody familiar with the policy of Lenin in power maintain seriously that, for all its twists and turns, it had become a rightwing policy during NEP. The underlying error, and it is a fundamental error, is the assumption that the founders of totalitarian movements and régimes did not believe in their ideologies, but only believed in power; I can understand how a student of the latter-day *nomenklatura* could have arrived at this view by his experience, but that is a misleading key to an understanding of the origins of the totalitarian phenomenon.

The underlying fact neglected by Voslensky is that before there were totalitarian régimes, there were totalitarian movements inspired by ideologies of a utopian type, and that the utopian contents of the communist ideologies on one side and the fascist and national-socialist ideologies on the other were diametrically opposed: the communists looked for a utopia of perfect equality, the fascists and national-socialists for one of perfect hierarchy. Of course, the evolution of Stalin's Soviet Union moved toward a radical neglect of the egalitarian dream, and Stalin's successors also made only very moderate concessions to it, while Mao Zedong's China moved in its later phase toward an attempt at its almost literal fulfillment and only turned toward a compromise with the possibilities of the real world after Mao's death.

But the different ideological starting points of the two types of totalitarian systems had lasting effects on the organization and role of their ruling parties. The fascist and national-socialist systems were officially based on the *Führerprinzip*, the leadership principle of one-man rule, and Dr. Voslensky's assumption that they could have moved to a collective system if only they had survived for a longer period shows a lack of understanding of their nature. By contrast, the Soviet and Chinese systems, while of course never democratic, started with a concept of so-called party democracy, which did mean, under Lenin and for a long time under Mao, a considerable freedom of discussion within the Politburo and even within the Central Committee. Even under Stalin remnants of this democratic element continued throughout the horrors of his forced collectivization and as late as 1932, prevented him by majority decision from ordering the death sentence against an inner-party critic. The complete one-man rule, which Voslensky treats as the original system, was only achieved by Stalin's blood purge of 1937 and coincided with a period in which the party was merely one of several tools of the rule of the despot. A corresponding change occurred in China only with Mao's "Great Proletarian Cultural Revolution" in 1966. Both forms of despotism ended with the death of the despots, when party rule, with a measure of inner-party discussion, was restored in both Russia in 1953 and China in 1976-1977.

II.

This brings us already to the importance of the successive transformations in the Soviet system, which Voslensky's paper neglects but which I regard as crucial for any analysis directed to the future evolution of that system, so that they form the main subject of my own paper. It would obviously be redundant if I repeated them here in detail. A few main points must suffice.

When Lenin took power in Russia in the course of its defeat in World War One, he believed that his utopian aims could only be fulfilled with the help of revolutionary victories in more advanced European countries. When no such victories had been forthcoming by the end of the Russian civil war, he decided that his party dictatorship should be maintained with a cautious, non-utopian economic policy in expectation of a later fulfillment of the revolutionary hopes abroad. It was Stalin who, faced with the contradictions of a non-utopian economy under communist rule, decided to create a non-egalitarian utopia under communist rule, and increasingly under his personal despotic rule, by repeated "revolutions from above" demanding millions of victims but also producing at that cost a great industrial power that was able to fight and survive Hitler's war. But even in his post-war years, he did not abandon either his personal despotism or his plans for further utopian revolutions from above.

No other despot has followed Stalin. His successors have restored the principle of party rule and, towards the end of the Khrushchev era, abandoned not only the belief in further revolutions from above, but the utopian goal itself in favor of more realistic goals of economic improvement and increased military power, while maintaining the principle of the fundamental division of the world into a capitalist and a socialist part. As the utopian frenzy passed and the tasks of the régime became more normal, the chief object of recurrent major decisions turned out to be the choice between unchanging stability, beloved by the *nomenklatura* but amounting to stagnation in its economic consequences, or effective reforms needed both for improving living conditions and for keeping pace with the non-communist world, but hated by the self-satisfied bureaucracy. At present, following the generation change both symbolized and promoted by Gorbachev, we seem to be at the turn from a phase of stagnation to a phase of reform, but the amount of success of the latter is still uncertain.

On the basis of this analysis, I see no compelling reason why the Soviet system should collapse sometime in the foreseeable future. It is true, of course, that no system of government produced by the human spirit can be expected to last forever in this imperfect world. But Voslensky's pointing to the eventual successful democratization of the formerly totalitarian Italy, Austria, and West Germany ignores two crucial differences—that their to-talitarian régimes only collapsed as a result of a lost war, and that all of them had lived through important periods of some kind of democratic rule, even if of a rather imperfect kind, before their totalitarian régimes were created. By contrast, tsarist Russia could never be described as even an imperfect form of democracy, and neither its history nor that of the period between the February and October revolutions of 1917 are likely to have left a longing for the traditions of the past among the Russian people. Moreover, the vast majority do not believe that Western institutions would be a better way to solve their problems. They might well be—Voslensky thinks so, and this is one point on which I, as a Westerner, am naturally inclined to agree with him. But the experience of the century now drawing to its close should have shown us that the majority of mankind, having developed from vastly different starting points, has little understanding of the institutions of the West and less longing for their blessings. The Russians, while no longer very popular as an alternative in the Third World, are on the whole likely to remain part of this non-Western majority.

4

Rejoinder to Löwenthal's Commentary

MICHAEL VOSLENSKY

The experience of *nomenklatura* rule shows to its subjects the unimportance of the formal contents of the official ideology and the overwhelming importance of the real ways of governing and shaping the society, all Professor Löwenthal delicately calls "the methods." When I went to school in 1929, the word *patriot* was an offence; *Russia* and *motherland* were reactionary, white-guardist terms. When I graduated from the same school in 1939, all of us were "patriots" loving our "motherland Russia." Nevertheless, quite correctly, we considered it to be the same ideology of Marxism-Leninism, independent of its contents. It was the obligatory, unquestioned, official ideology enforced by the despotic ruling class upon the society. Not the claim, but only the aim of this ideology was important and this has always been the same—to assure the rule of this class, the *nomenklatura*, and to extend this kind of rule to other countries.

Even more important were the "methods" of this rule. I hope that Professor Löwenthal agrees that these "methods" were identical in Stalin's Soviet Union and in Hitler's German Reich. That is why I write about the *identity* of "real" socialism and "national" socialism. Frankly speaking, I think that every democratic socialist should consider them so.

But we are told that the communist rulers are left, and the national-socialist rulers right. Then I may ask, "What is left and what is right?" For me, left means freedom and social justice with a clear trend toward equality, as well as many other things, absolutely incompatible with a despotic police state and the institutionalized privileges of the ruling class. Concentration camps, torture, show trials, an almighty secret police, a theocratic rule of a Fuhrer (in Italian, *duce*; in Russian *vozhd*—so Stalin was called; in Romanian, *conducator*—Antonescu and Ceaucescu being so called), and a *de facto* rule of party functionaries—can all this be left? I know there are people in some social-democratic parties who would answer in the affirmative. But I very earnestly hope that Professor Löwenthal does not share their opinion, that he shares the opinion of Kurt Schumacher: "*Weltkommunismus ist Weltreaktion.*" (World communism is the world's reaction.)

And *this* is what I wished to show in my paper—nothing but *this*.

5

The Necessary Conditions for Characterizing a State as Totalitarian

A Commentary on Section 1

MORTON A. KAPLAN

Michael Voslensky, in discussing the similarities between Nazi Germany and the Soviet Union, raises anew the issue of the conditions according to which a state should be characterized as totalitarian. In attempting to address this question, I shall not stress definitions as such but shall attempt to elucidate the analytic features that I believe should be included in this inquiry: for, in my opinion at least, the differences between the Soviet Union, Nazi Germany and Fascist Italy, for instance, are as important as the similarities.

The first pair of concepts I wish to use is that of system and subsystem. Technically a system is any set of variables and functions. However, I shall restrict the meaning of system to those aspects of the real world that are meaningfully related in terms of a research objective. In this particular context, I shall use the term system to refer to an entire society. A subsystem, as I shall use the term here, will refer to any at least partly independent part of a society, for instance, church, economy, police, army, and so forth. The environment of a society is composed of all those aspects of the world that affect the society but that are not internal to it, for example, the weather, resources, culture, the personality and memory of individuals, and informal social processes.

Two sets of paired concepts will now be used in my analysis—system and subsystem dominance on the one hand, and greater or lesser directivity on the other. These concepts are employed in scalar fashion, not dichotomously.

A system dominant system is one in which the equilibrium of the system presents itself to the actors within the system as a parametric given. For instance, in a perfect market, price operates as a simple environmental constraint for any individual buyer or seller even though it is the product of all the transactions within the market. In a modestly subsystem dominant system, the behavior of the individual actors has a noticeable impact on the equilibrium of the system. For instance, in an oligopolistic market, any deviation from the equilibrium price by one of the actors will change the price unless the other actors engage in countervailing behavior. In a fully subsystem dominant system, the dominant subsystem determines the equilibrium of the system subject only to extra-systemic or environmental constraints. If there is a true monopoly, the monopolist determines price subject only to demand elasticity. Stalin's farm collectivization policy, for example, could be imposed upon the peasants, subject only to their killing of their cattle.

A system is directive to the extent that decisions flow unimpeded from top to bottom; the number of roles diminishes as one moves to the top of the system, and the number of roleholders in any particular role is smaller as one moves to the top of the system. So, the directivity of the Soviet system diminished as the Politburo changed from one in which the General Secretary was the *Vozhd*, in effect, in a different and higher role, to one in which he was merely the first among equals. Thus, in principle, the system could be every bit as subsystem dominant as in Stalin's time while being less directive. It is important to note, however, that even at the height of Stalin's power, the Soviet system was not as directive as contemporary textbooks asserted. Had it been, it would not have been necessary for Stalin to prepare his purges as carefully as he did or to institute them serially, procedures that inhibited potential victims from coalescing against him.

If we choose to define a totalitarian system as one in which the top role controls all the subsystems of the society, subject only to environmental constraints, then it would be acceptable to call the present Soviet system totalitarian, although obviously the Politburo is less active in changing the system than it was in Stalin's time. This, in principle, could be the result of reduced directivity, in which conflicts within the ruling role impede change. It could also be the result of environmental constraints in the form of the desire of the high *nomenklatura* for class security, or of the enhanced expectations of the population, which would increase the cost of shifts in policy so much that they become counterproductive. Environmental constraints might have produced the same diminished activity in Stalin's time, however, if, for instance, he had become apathetic or depressive.

On the other hand, a system may be both less subsystem dominant and less directive than the Soviet system under Stalin, or even than in the present circumstances of the Soviet system, and still exhibit rapid social change directed from the top. This could occur because the roles in effective control, or the goals of those who hold the roles, are so threatened by external forces that they have no option but to remain united while they crush these forces. Some might argue that this was the case in the U.S.S.R. under Lenin or even during Stalin's early period. France under Robespierre would seem also to qualify.

Whether one defines totalitarianism in terms of extreme subsystem dominance or in terms of some combination of subsystem dominance and directivity—there seems little point in arguing over definitions as long as we remain clear about our assertions—it would seem that there has been only one system that can be called totalitarian—the Soviet system, at least under Stalin. If we include great directivity in the definition, then the present Soviet system would not fit. However, neither the Nazi or fascist systems, let alone such authoritarian systems as Franco's, could be called totalitarian. The Nazis never abolished at least partly independent sources of economic, political, or armed power. They reduced and managed them but never had the kind of subsystem control that characterizes even the present Soviet system. Moreover, Hitler never deliberately compartmentalized the secret police in a divide-and-rule strategy, as did Stalin. Nor did he ever deliberately emasculate the party, although he did purge Ernst Roehm to maintain army support. Moreover, although Hitler was the unchallenged leader, he exercised that role only fitfully. Mussolini had to cope with a king, an established aristocracy, the army, economic strength, and the sharing of directive authority with the fascist Grand Council.

Voslensky is probably correct in believing that the communist and Nazi regimes shared common tendencies, at least while Stalin was alive. We do know that both Hitler and Mussolini at times expressed profound admiration of the thorough character of Stalin's revolution. But that this was seriously meant is doubtful in Mussolini's case. Franco never had such goals. The circumstances that attended the accession of Stalin, Hitler, and Mussolini to power also may account for some differences. The régimes were far from identical.

As we examine the Soviet system for signs of possible change, we must look at system dominance, directivity, and environmental factors. Will some technocratic features of the system become so important that they become independent sources of power? What about the army during succession conflicts? What about environmental factors like enhanced expectations or demographic change? Is it possible that the response to those may bring about two pivots within the régime, perhaps between those who think that accommodation of the nationalities is the way to maintain the system and those who want to protect the privileged positions of the Russians, in which case the two pivots could originate within the Russian nationality?

On Totalitarianism and the Prospects for Institutionalized Revolution in the U.S.S.R. and China

A Commentary on Sections 1 and 2

ALEXANDER SHTROMAS

I

Professor Michael Voslensky defines totalitarianism as "total control by an undemocratic power over all spheres of life in society" and calls its opposite pluralism.[1] One could accept this definition but not without certain qualifications. For as long as control, however total it may be, is exercised by human beings over human beings, it can never become perfect either in scope or in effectiveness. There will always remain some flaws and loopholes which people will use, acting individually and in groups, to their own advantage and in surreptitious defiance of the exigencies of the controlling power. Even the very agents of that power on all its levels, while ostensibly acting on that power's behalf, will be in fact pursuing, in the first place, their particular individual or group interests in preference to any other such interests. To be sure, sometimes these individual and group interests may more or less fully coincide with those of the power in whose name they are pursued (sometimes certain individuals and groups may even persuade the power to take up their interests as its own), but more often they will not. This is to say that no totalitarian system can ever reach the ideal of an absolute "ant-hill type" uniformity and that it thus will always remain to a certain extent pluralistic, or, which is one and the same thing, that no totalitarian power is, or ever has been, truly totalitarian.

Totalitarianism is, however, a reality. In real life, as Voslensky rightly suggests, it has been embodied at least in the Soviet, Nazi and Fascist systems. What these systems have in common is indeed a certain mode of social organization under which all outwardly extant and functioning groups or institutional bodies—be they political, economic, cultural, social or any other—are incorporated as mere structural elements into a fully monolithic and all-encompassing political system headed either by a sole leader or by an oligarchic clique acting as a single institution of leadership. The basic task of any kind of such totalitarian headship is to ensure the preservation and reproduction of the monolithic and all-encompassing nature of the system over which it presides. The actual performance of the bodies of which that system consists, as well as the real behavior of groups and individuals operating within those bodies, is for the totalitarian headship a task of secondary significance, as long of course as the quality of performance of these particular bodies or the character of actual behavior of people do not represent a real threat to the totalitarian monolith itself, i.e. as long as political control over the whole of the system remains intact.[2] This implies the necessity of distinguishing, within the overall concept of totalitarian power, between two of its basic aspects—political control and actual rule. Totalitarian systems, in order to survive, have to be fully effective in exercising political control, while they may remain rather inept in actual rule.

Analysing social relations inside Soviet industry during 1928-1941, Moshe Lewin succinctly observed that even in Stalin's time the Soviet political centre found industrial enterprises "difficult to rule—but easy to control."[3] The difficulties of ruling Soviet society have since been greatly exacerbated while the effectiveness of exercising political control over it has remained on the whole almost as effective as it has ever been. In Michael Urban's words, the contemporary Soviet Union represents a "spectacle of omnipotent impotence in the total power state."[4] Although this may be a somewhat exaggerated characteristic, there is no doubt that the basic substance of totalitarian power in contemporary U.S.S.R. is described in it quite accurately. "Intrastructural dissent,"[5] which is a negative reflection of the Soviet system's capacity to rule, has by now become ubiquitous indeed and is not significantly receding under the attack launched against it by Gorbachev's Politburo.

The totalitarian system's capacity to rule is, however, not entirely unrelated to its ability to exercise political control. The reduction of the capacity to rule proportionately advances "intrastructural dissent" which, in its turn, gradually forms an alternative society in the U.S.S.R. While operating within the limits of the official system and thus not having as yet overcome the overall framework of totalitarian political control exercised by that system, this alternative society itself is by no means subject to the official system's control. Hence, the growth and consolidation of the alternative society, being the direct result of the reduction of the totalitarian power's capacity to rule, inevitably limits also that power's ability to exercise political control. This process has the potential of undermining in due course the totalitarian power's ability to exercise total political control altogether. The realization of this potential that would have to be expressed in the alternative society's overcoming of the limits of the official system would mark the end of both Soviet totalitarianism and "intrastructural dissent."

Voslensky's definition of totalitarianism, however, even if modified and elaborated upon in the above way, is incomplete. It subsumes not only the modern totalitarian systems under Voslensky's own scrutiny, but also the traditional despotic societies which were the subject of Karl Wittfogel's *Oriental Despotism* and which do not belong to the totalitarian category, despite Wittfogel's conviction that they do. In order to define totalitarianism fully and adequately, it is necessary to identify certain specific traits which would thoroughly distinguish it from mere despotism. In this respect, Professor Richard Löwenthal's concept of totalitarianism seems to be very helpful indeed. According to Löwenthal, totalitarianism is "a new type of dictatorship aiming at an ideological-model-based total transformation of society."[6] Differently from all other dictatorships (e.g. despots), the totalitarian ones have seriously and persistently been committed "not only to keeping power, but also to using power for ever new attempts to achieve utopian goals, leading to recurrent revolutions from above."[7] Indeed, whereas mere despotism is a conservative and routine orientated system, totalitarianism is a revolutionary and supreme-goal-achievement oriented one. While both these systems may be equally ideocratic, with only their ideologies being polarly different in substance (the despotic ideology will glorify the eternal yesterday whereas a totalitarian, the perfect tomorrow), only the totalitarian system is also teleocratic.

Voslensky's and Löwenthal's definitions of totalitarianism stress different aspects of this system and are therefore mutually complementary. One without the other would remain incomplete. It is true, however, that while being all revolutionary and future-orientated, some totalitarian systems have not managed to reach the level of mature despotism. As Professor Morton Kaplan rightly remarked, according to the above criterium, "there has been only one system that can be called totalitarian—the Soviet system."[8] The fact of the matter is that systems that are merely despotic are naturally so formed at the outset, whereas those that are totalitarian, after having been brought into existence by revolutionary action, inherit an old non-despotic society that it is the totalitarian system's task to transform into one that would possess all the traits of mature despotism. It took the Soviets about twenty years to get to the level of "despotic totality," and without Stalin it would have taken them most probably much longer to get there. Neither Mussolini nor Hitler had at their disposal the amount of time necessary for achieving their ultimate goals.

Again, Löwenthal's reference to totalitarian movements[9] which precede the totalitarian régimes and which create them by superimposing themselves upon society as supreme political authority, helps us to identify a totalitarian system even before it has acquired its really full despotic scale. In those terms one may define as totalitarian a system in which a totalitarian movement managed to establish itself as the supreme political authority of the land, and to consolidate this position to the extent of full subordination to itself of the state machinery, thus acquiring the capability of using this machinery unrestrictedly for the successful advancement of its rule over the rest of society. This implies the necessity of distinguishing between the maturing and mature, or developing and developed, totalitarianisms. In these terms the Nazi and Fascist systems were maturing or developing totalitarianisms, whereas the Soviet system, from the mid-1930s until the present day, is a mature or developed totalitarianism.

II

My recognition of the present-day Soviet society as totalitarian puts me at odds with Löwenthal who maintains that since the end of Khrushchev's era it is not totalitarian anymore.[10]

According to Löwenthal, in the first half of the 1960s the U.S.S.R. entered into the post-utopian, post-revolutionary and, consequently, post-totalitarian stage of its development. Among the Soviet rulers "Khrushchev was the last believer in the utopian goals of Marxism-Leninism. . . .The end of his leadership also marked the end of their relevance."[11] For Russia the age of institutionalized revolutions from above had thus come to a definitive close.[12] In Löwenthal's view, the post-Khrushchevian Soviet rulers continue to cling to their dictatorial power not "in order to achieve utopia, in which they no longer believe, but in order to advance the economic modernity and political greatness of the nations they govern."[13]

Assessing this state of affairs against the background of his definition of totalitarianism, Löwenthal logically concludes that the U.S.S.R. has not simply outgrown its former totalitarianism (that it had already done by the

mid-1960s), but also is now fully transformed into an ordinary non-totalitarian dictatorship.

While fully agreeing with Löwenthal's definition of totalitarianism and
sharing many (but by far not all) of his above arguments, I nevertheless find
his conclusion concerning the non-totalitarian nature of the present Soviet
régime wrong, not only by my standards but also his own. First of all, it
seems to me that neither the present Soviet rulers disbelief in Marxism-
Leninism or in any communist ideals at all—a fact strongly stressed by
Löwenthal and undoubtedly true—nor the analysis of actual policies the
Soviet régime pursues, points to Soviet abandonment of utopian goals, let
alone to their exclusive concentration on pragmatic tasks related to the
execution of the functions of a national government.

One cannot simply dismiss the official claim about the whole Soviet
domestic policy being centered around the utopian task of building a communist society in the U.S.S.R. or explain it away as a mere codephrase for
furthering the country's economic and social development. This will not do
for the simple reason that communist construction in the U.S.S.R. continues
to be conducted in the same old ideological manner as before, that is, by
putting conceptual considerations above economic dictates. Nor is communist
construction neutral with regard to achieving economic and social results. By
giving priority to central planning and state economic management, communist construction tends to stagnate society and impedes rather than
induces the country's economic, technological, and cultural progress.

Löwenthal would no doubt try to account for that by referring to the
absence in Russia of "a political tradition of democracy or a strong cultural
tradition of human rights,"[14] which enables the Soviet rulers to seek economic progress without altering their dictatorial system of rule. But this
particular system of rule encompassing control over all walks of life is as
unprecedented in Russia as elsewhere. However much Russia lacked the
democratic and human rights traditions, she had a highly developed tradition of small private enterprise and autonomous economic activity which the
Soviet régime, instead of putting to rational use, continues vigorously to
suppress—yet another instance of the pragmatic national interest being sacrificed by the Soviet régime to its ideologically-conceived utopian goal.

Even more obviously ideological is Soviet foreign policy. Its antagonistic
attitude toward the "capitalist West" has no foundation in Russia's national
interests whatsoever. There are no clashes between authentic Russian national interests and those of the U.S.A. or any other Western country over
any substantive issue or in any territorial area. The actual East-West conflicts
are all artificially construed by the Soviets on purely ideological grounds and
to the detriment of authentic Russian national interests. For it is not

confrontation but cooperation with the West that would benefit Russia most. Even Russia's imperial interests, let alone the political, economic and military ones, would be best served by ending the confrontation between the two superpowers and substituting for it genuine cooperation. This is not to be, however, for the Soviet rulers, again, will never allow pragmatic national interests to prevail over the ideologically-conceived communist utopian ones. Hence, the East-West confrontation continues unabated, also the relentless Soviet foreign expansion, which, far from strengthening the power of the Soviet state and contributing to its assets, is an ever-increasing factor of political destabilization and a huge drain on Russia's national resources.

It follows from the brief analysis given above that the present Soviet régime is not as post-utopian as Löwenthal would have it, and also that its policies are determined largely by motives superseding those that derive from the tasks of simply advancing economic modernity and political greatness of the area under the Soviet régime's control.

What then are the true interests motivating Soviet policy-making if both genuinely ideological and purely pragmatic national commitments have to be excluded? Dealing with this problem elsewhere, I have arrived at the conclusion that these are the self-serving interests of the Soviet rulers themselves.[15] The Soviet Party state established itself as an ideocratic and teleocratic entity whose utopian commitments and goals were not simply alien but contrary to the self-perceived interests and genuinely held views of the overwhelming majority of the people that it had undertaken to rule. As such it was bound to be a clique-state whose only purpose was to enhance and promote at all costs the interests and goals of the small ideologically zealous ruling clique against those of the people at large. Hence, Löwenthal's recurrent "institutionalized revolutions" from above.

The present Soviet rulers may not care about ideals, but they care most strongly about the preservation of their power. And the power that they have inherited, and are bound to cling to, is representative of no one, except the "infallible ideology of Marxism-Leninism" of which they are the ex-officio "high priests." Since it is only that ideology, and nothing else beside, that invests the present Soviet rulers with the exclusive and inalienable right to absolute power, they have to stick to it whether they believe in it or not. For these purely pragmatic reasons the present Soviet rulers must remain unswervingly committed to Marxism-Leninism and to the pursuit, domestically and worldwide, of the utopian goals of communism inherent in it. This is to say that the more cynically pragmatic the Soviet rulers become, the more ideologically intransigent communists they are bound to be.

To sum it up, the present Soviet rulers are not essentially different from their predecessors. They are in charge of a communist-ideocratic and teleocratic clique-state and have to act accordingly. From this perspective it is indeed "of secondary importance whether, as in the beginning, this ruling clique consists of idealistic believers in a higher and better order of things, which they are determined to bring about against all odds by a revolutionary (e.g. terrorist) action, or of cynical opportunists who do not believe in any ideals at all, but who, in order to survive, do everything they can to perpetuate the single ideology and teleology of the power they have inherited. The clique nature of this state remains the same at all times and so remain also its basic policies and activities."[16]

This, I believe, fully explains why I insist on defining the present Soviet system as totalitarian. To me it is largely irrelevant whether communist revolutionary utopian goals are pursued out of conviction or sheer opportunism. What matters is the fact that they continue to be pursued today as much as they were yesterday. And if this is so, the Soviet Union remains totalitarian according to Löwenthal's own standards.

Löwenthal may, however, disagree. He would most probably point out that the main feature of totalitarianism—the recurrent "institutionalized revolutions" from above—have gone from the Soviet scene forever. The Soviet society, he would most probably say, has acquired today a constant and stable socio-political shape, and this is the real background against which all talk about further pursuits of any utopian revolutionary goals amounts to nothing more than sheer phraseology that may have only one practical purpose, that of embellishing the boring conservative routine into which the Soviet society has in fact grown. I could not agree more. Indeed, in the Soviet Union today there is no room left for any more of the recurrent "institutionalized revolutions" from above which were so typical of Stalin's time and, though to a lesser extent, also of Khrushchev's. Khrushchevian-type erratic upheavals could not be repeated because of the danger to the system's stability this would inevitably involve, and all the conceivable measures aimed at further enhancement of the totality of the Soviet Party state's control over all walks of Soviet life have already been taken, with nothing else left to accomplish.

In the U.S.S.R. today the only "institutionalized revolution" from above that may still be envisaged is the one that would be aimed at restoring the civil society as an entity autonomous from the state and subordinated only to the rule of law. This would be, however, already an anti-totalitarian revolution. In the series of "institutionalized revolutions" from above this one would surely be the last since it would be launched by a totalitarian power with the view of self-destruction.

The Soviet system—one in which totalitarianism, through all the recurrent "institutionalized revolutions," has acquired a fully developed despotic dimension (thus exhausting the potential for and putting a limit on further such revolutions)—is, however, in itself a remarkable revolutionary-type phenomenon. Never before has a nationwide social-political structure been created by the conscious revolutionary effort of a committed minority following a certain ideological blueprint and forcing, when needed by the means of indiscriminate mass terror, the unwilling majority to adapt to its constraints. This unprecedented revolutionary achievement is, however, cast into the shade by the permanent revolutionary action the Soviet Party state has conducted for more than half a century in order to keep the Soviet society in its artificially created shape. When looking at the Soviet Union from that perspective, it is not so much the conservative routine that is emerging, but rather a ceaseless "institutionalized revolution" aimed at preventing the artificially created Soviet totality from falling to pieces.

On the other hand, Soviet international politics can also be seen as the Soviet Party state's permanent engagement into what one could call an "institutionalized revolution" on a global scale. One may be skeptical about the extent of the Soviet commitment to world revolution, but one cannot deny that many a recent victorious communist revolution in Asia and Africa never would have materialized were it not for the Soviet Party state's active "institutionalized" involvement in their making.

Hence, I believe that even by what is in Löwenthal's terms the decisive criterion, the Soviet Union remains today a fully fledged, mature and developed totalitarian system. I hope that Löwenthal agrees.

III

In Löwenthal's view* the post-totalitarian era began in China with the death of Mao and the arrest of the so-called "Gang of Four," being "definitely established with the 1981 reorganization of the party leadership and its document on party history."[17] However not every student of contemporary China would agree with this view.

---

* This last part of my comment will be devoted to Löwenthal's treatment of China. Not being a sinologist myself, I asked my sinologist friend, Miriam London, to present her own comment on Löwenthal's paper with the view of publishing it in this volume under a separate title. Although she turned down this request, Miriam London nevertheless most kindly supplied me with many written remarks on Löwenthal's text, permitting me to use them in my comment. She also provided me with other specialists' literature on the problems of China that Löwenthal undertook to discuss. For all this I am extremely grateful to her. Although much of what is written below is based on Miriam London's facts, views and sources (always acknowledged), the full responsibility for the following text is, naturally, entirely mine.

As Miriam London pointed out in a letter to me, that school of thought in Western sinology to which she herself belongs "sees something quite different, complicated and unstable. Basically," she continues, "we see the economic reform as a sort of Chinese NEP, originally undertaken as measures of expedience and crisis-management."* This seems to me to be exactly the situation which at a certain point in time the Chinese communist authorities might be tempted to solve by yet another "institutionalized revolution" from above. Hence, Löwenthal's conclusion that "the period of institutionalized revolution had ended in China with a disorganization of the régime's institutional structure and a profound discredit of the idea of further revolutions" (i.e. with the Great Cultural Revolution) may be somewhat premature.[18]

Let us, however, begin where Löwenthal does—namely with the Maoist collectivization of Chinese agriculture.

According to Miriam London:

> Collectivization began almost immediately, albeit in stages, after the land reform of 1950-53, during which at least 5 million—one recent report alludes to 9 million—"landlords" (landowners) and "rich" peasants were cruelly executed. A new "kulak" element, formed of the more enterprising "middle" peasants, had barely a chance to assert itself.
>
> The entire families and descendants of the landowners and better-off peasants were, along with any survivors, permanently stigmatized as members of "black classes." However poor they now were, peasants belonging to these newly defined hereditary classes were essentially outcasts, denied even the meager rights of other peasants, systematically persecuted, and made the perennial targets of brutal "struggle" during the incessant political campaigns (*yundong*) of the following two decades.[19]
>
> Whatever caused Mao Zedong later to launch the "Three Red Flags" campaign, of which the Great Leap Forward and the establishment of communes were part, the result was the worst disaster of the century, and particularly for rural China, where 80 percent of the population lives. The official P.R.C. press has most recently admitted to 20 million people dead of hunger in the years 1959-1962—twice the figure first acknowledged in an earlier publication.[20] The more probable conservative figure is 25 million to 30 million dead.[21] In Jürgen Domes's estimation, the Great Leap set the country *back* "five years in industry and at least twelve years in agriculture."[22]
>
> Mao Zedong not only failed to solve the old economic, political, and cultural problems which impeded China's modernization in the past, but he created new and more insoluble problems. For example, in agriculture, his policies not only reduced the peasantry to grinding poverty, but, because of

* September 25, 1985

amateur interference in the agricultural process, they resulted in a huge loss, through soil erosion and salinization, of already scarce arable land. The failure of his utopian venture of 1958 did not prevent Mao from trying partial experiments with the commune system again during the cultural revolutionary decade of 1966-76. The resultant crisis in agriculture, the foundation of the Chinese economy, left the Dengist coalition no choice but to undertake reform. China could not afford any other solution. A recent editorial in a Peking newspaper, *Nongmin Ribao*, inadvertently explains why:

> "At present, 80 percent of the Chinese people's means of sub-sistence . . . comes from agricultural products directly or indirectly. Would it do for such a great country like ours to rely on imported grain to solve its food problems? No. With a population of 1 billion, we shall need 500 million tons of grain annually to get along but there are only 200 million tons of commodity grain on the world market. The Soviet Union and Japan purchase about 80 million tons of grain annually. If 20 percent of our population were to rely on imported grain for food, we would need 100 million tons of grain. This is unmanageable. We do not have that much foreign exchange and, even if we managed to buy the grain, it would be impossible to transport it."[23]

In industry, Mao initially achieved much more, within the limits of the Soviet model. But scarcely had industry recovered from the setbacks of the Great Leap when the worse disruption of the Cultural Revolution took over. In many parts of the country factories closed down altogether, while opposing worker-factions battled each other. (When foreign reporters were first allowed into previously closed areas in 1977, they discovered several major factories still closed.) Thus, in addition to the usual ills of a socialist state-run industry—operation at a loss, overstaffing, inefficiency, sloth—the final decade of Maoism introduced the divisiveness of factionalism, which survives in submerged form to this day.

Stagnation in industry, population growth, and Mao's virtual dismantling after 1968 of the educational system all exacerbated another problem—unemployment. When Deng assumed power he was faced with two genera-tions of "unemployables." The Red Guard generation of students had merely been handed diplomas for schooling never completed, and the next generation entered schools with newly revised curricula which deliberately discouraged academic learning. But even had these students acquired the requisite knowledge and skills for modern technology (they did not), they would have found scarcely any opportunity to apply them. Mao "solved" the problem by dumping millions of young people on the countryside. Many, however, slipped back illegally into the cities, where some found odd jobs in the "black" economy and others turned to crime.

As though this were not enough, the new leadership also faced the psychological consequences of the preceding Cultural Revolution, especially among the young. These consequences were, in brief, a widespread disillusionment, not only in Maoism, but in the communist *system*, and a loss of faith in the Party and its ability to lead. A saying echoed among young people all over China and even found its way into the official press: "[(We, I)] have seen through everything." What this meant was that they could no longer be taken in by Party propaganda or the Communist myth. In fact, many young people came to view the Cultural Revolution in retrospect paradoxically as "a good thing" because it irrevocably demolished false illusions. (I have heard such a view repeated lately by mainland students in the U.S.)

The members of the coalition that formed around Deng Xiaoping were well aware of all this and more—a veritable Pandora's box of revelations had opened in the late seventies. Extraordinary measures were necessary not only to restore the economy but to counter the "crisis of confidence" in the Party and its ideology. Deng Xiaoping had already become the symbol of revisionism, which in the popular mind signified a turn to a more tolerable, normal way of life. Moreover, he had clear seniority and controlled an old-power network with strong military ties. He was the only living leader who could possibly salvage the country and the Party. (In the late seventies many educated Chinese expressed the view that if Deng were suddenly to die at this time, the situation in China could rapidly disintegrate into regional factional warfare—in effect, warlordism.)

All these factors combined to secure Deng the leverage he needed to initiate NEP, Chinese-style.*

In Soviet communist perception, NEP, it should be remembered, was not a policy of continuous, stable development but only a temporary retreat from the steadfast pursuit of socialist goals—a retreat necessitated by critical circumstances and aimed at preserving in these circumstances the monopoly of power in the hands of the Communist Party. After NEP had played its role by having cured the country's most disastrous social and economic ills, an outright communist attack on NEP followed, resulting in the total destruction of the social system shaped by NEP and the re-introduction of full-fledged socialism or, what in Soviet communist perception is one and the same thing, total state control over all walks of life in society. The Communist Party had no choice but to launch such an attack, for if it failed to do so and allowed capitalist elements and market forces to develop unabated, the Party's power over the state and society sooner or later would be inevitably and irreversibly undermined.

* This large extract is from Miriam London, "Remarks" (see note 19).

The Soviet Communists were perfectly aware of this and from the very outset of their embarkation on NEP started preparations for reversing and abolishing it. In the Soviet Union during the 1920s, economic liberalization related to NEP was, with that view in mind, accompanied by simultaneous measures drastically suppressing all remnants of opposition to Communist rule and eradicating the slightest potential for the re-emergence of such opposition within both the society at large and the Communist Party itself.[24] At the same time, Soviet rulers started to prepare their future attack on NEP by building up the machinery of the Party and the state with the view towards increasing its repressive power to unprecedented proportions. One of the most telling examples of this preliminary build-up for a future attack was the 1922 reorganization of the security police (the Cheka) into the GPU with special military detachments put at its disposal.[25] Only after the completion of all these preparations, in the end of the 1920s, did the Soviet rulers feel secure about being able to win a decisive battle against the thus disarmed society, and only then did they dare launch their "institutionalized revolution" from above that abolished NEP and established the Stalinist variety of socialism.

The present situation in China in this respect (i.e., of securing Communist power in an NEP-type situation and asserting it when necessary against the revived "capitalist elements") is not entirely different. Wild Western hopes about Marxism being made obsolete in China, based on one leading article in the Party's central organ, *Renmin Ribao* (The People's Daily), did not materialize. On the contrary, the Marxist ideological grip on the country has been significantly tightened of late. Even the resolution of October 20, 1984, that officially launched the latest and most radical reforms, reiterated with strong words the Four Basic Principles, particularly the one concerning the leadership by the Party.[26] As the prominent Sinologist L. Ladany has observed, "the party schools in Peking and elsewhere still teach the old Stalinist Marxism. Also several manuals on Marxism have been published recently by official publishing houses. They, too, teach the old theory, a rigid form of Stalinist Marxism." Ladany also noted that "a disturbing nostalgia for things Russian is noticeable in China today. It was recently announced that 20,000 Russian book titles . . . are being imported into China this year. Some books written recently in China present the Soviet economic system in bright colours—and this is new."[27]

In a recent article Miriam London pointed out that

Peking is also calling for more subtle and effective political indoctrination programs in the schools in order to instill patriotism—which is flatly equated with loyalty to the Communist Party—and to demonstrate the superiority of so-called scientific Marxism over capitalism and discredit

Western "bourgeois notions" of freedom and democracy. In a notorious speech in February 1985, [then] Party General Secretary Hu Yaobang, regarded as one of the most "advanced" reformists, explicitly stated that the role of the press in China was to serve as the "Party's mouthpiece." And a *Renmin Ribao* article last September warned the populace to beware of foreign spies, even among travelers, visiting relatives, trade representatives, and participants in scientific, technological and cultural exchanges.[28]

All this was further corroborated by the September 1985 National Conference of the Communist Party which made it clear that the Party would *not* countenance any attempts at introducing "bourgeois liberalism" in the name of Marxism and would seek to strengthen the Party's ideological and propagandistic work.

The ideological limits have been set accordingly and were vigorously reiterated by the 1987 campaign against 'bourgeois liberalism' launched in response to the students' demonstrations of December 1986. There was not much new in this campaign. A decisive crackdown on open dissent took place in China in 1979 and culminated in the campaign against 'spiritual pollution' of 1983. What in China is called 'the changes of weather' have brought about a period of expanding relaxation in 1984-86, but even then, political repression of 'counterrevolutionary elements' was not abandoned. No one knows how many or how few political arrests had been made during that period, since such data are not available; but the New China News Agency reported, for example, that in 1984-85 armed police squads patrolling large and medium-sized cities arrested about 170 'counterrevolutionaries.'[29]

Neither has 'relaxation' been extended to political prisoners, all of whom continued to serve their sentences through these years. International pleas for the release of China's most famous dissident, Wei Jingsheng, serving a fifteen-year sentence for advocating a 'fifth modernization—democracy' were ignored by Chinese authorities. When a participant in a conference of about sixty overseas scholars, sponsored by the United Front Department in June 1985 in Peking, asked Deng to free Wei, the latter snapped back angrily that as soon as Wei got out, he would only start creating chaos.[30] But the real precursor of the 1986 events and the resulting unleashing of the campaign against 'bourgeois liberalism' in 1987 was the paranoid reaction of the central leaders to the anti-Japanese student movement that suddenly took off in Peking in September 1985 and spread to universities across the country. It was suppressed, although its slogans and demands, from the official point of view, were not as controversial as those under which the students mounted their protests in 1986.

The overriding message of the central leaders was unmistakable: no student movement must be initiated outside the Party, which alone has the right to lead. The rationale—betraying shrill notes of defensiveness and anxiety this time around—was that only unity under the Communist Party can assure China's bright future and prevent chaos.[31]

Also, as it was the case in the U.S.S.R. during the NEP, the central authorities were rapidly beefing up the security police during the period of "relaxation."

Enrollment in three major higher institutions for the police is reported by a well-informed Hong Kong journal to have increased more than 210 percent in 1985 over the previous year, and new professional security schools have recently been established.[32]

All that and other similar data did not at all indicate, as Löwenthal suggested, that China has passed the stage of "institutionalized revolution" and firmly entered into a post-revolutionary and thus post-totalitarian stage of its development. On the contrary, it rather pointed to the fact that, unless Communist rule in China is for some reason going to disintegrate, China would soon face the possibility of yet another "institutionalized revolution," bringing down the present reforms and establishing a "Soviet-type system of enlightened Stalinist control."[33]

Already the Dengist reforms experience serious problems and lack of control. It is true, as Miriam London suggested before the student demonstrations of 1986, that

The new economic policies brought fast, dramatic improvement in agricultural production and living standards, especially in good farming areas near large cities, with resultant benefit to urban dwellers. But improvement was extremely uneven and, along with the more complicated reform efforts in industry, gave rise to new situations and unexpected difficulties, which in turn led to periodic retrenchments or "pauses for breath." (The leaders admitted being taken by surprise by some of these developments and the extent of difficulty. Ideologists with a central-blueprint mentality never realize that the unexpected is to be expected.) However, there is evidence. . . that the reform faction does not see any road back, at least for the foreseeable future. Despite the seemingly intractable problems and complications that have arisen, often amounting to economic chaos, the reformists argue that there is no alternative to going ahead, even if this means "feeling one's way across the river by stepping stones." At the same time, they have had to defend this position repeatedly before the ideologically orthodox members of the top coalition, whose instinctive reaction to chaotic conditions is always to pull back and tighten controls. Such action, the reformists maintain, would mean a vicious circle dooming all hope of modernizing China by the middle of the twenty-first century. A recent article in the *Renmin Ribao* presents this argument in a nutshell: "If you tighten control whenever confusion occurs, this leads to rigidity, which leads to loosening of control, which leads to confusion, which leads to tightening control again.[34]

A fundamental cause of this "confusion" is that the loosening of central control takes place in the absence of any internal regulatory mechanism or accurate information feedback, which are essential to the operation of a freer economy. Articles in the press call for more economic laws and regulations, but also disclose that the qualified personnel needed to formulate and implement such laws are lacking.

The trouble is that the Party cadres want to remain the law—and generally manage to do so. China has many little kingdoms within the larger kingdom. The central authorities periodically berate the middle-level cadres for merely going through the motions of reform, but, in fact, doing much as they please.[35] The wild policy swings and insecurity that have marked Chinese Communist rule have, indeed, affected these cadres but not as Löwenthal imagines. Many are digging in their heels, waiting for a new tide, after Deng's death, to sweep the reforms away. Uncertainty about central policy has also increased these cadres' dependence on local networks of "relationships," especially on tried and trusted friends of the same faction during the Cultural Revolution.[36] Since such networks operate for the exclusive benefit of the clique, they have wreaked havoc with many reform measures in practice, contributing to economic chaos and corruption.

It should also be held in mind that the great majority of the 40 million Party cadres have an extremely low educational level and lack the competence to deal with the complex changes involved in "modernization." They perceive an ultimate threat to their power in the new emphasis on learning and expertise, against which many of them also retain an old Maoist prejudice.

The dissension within the top circles of power in Peking provides the middle-level cadres with good reason for continued uncertainty. The revisionists, centrists, and more orthodox Stalinists who basically constitute the top coalition have thus far managed to practice "compromise politics." As official statements sufficiently reveal, the present leaders understand that, after three and a half decades of extremely fickle policy, consensus and a public image of stability and unity have become a "life-and-death" matter for the Party. Nevertheless, dissension at the top is an open secret and has caused continual, perceptible wavering of the policy line to the present. The more orthodox Stalinists at the power center blame the reforms, including the "open door" policy, for the rampant economic corruption and "spiritual pollution"—that is, the spread of "decadent bourgeois" and "capitalist" ideas, which they regard as alarmingly out of control. The entire leadership appeared greatly disturbed by elite university student demonstrations in the autumn of 1985 [let alone those of winter 1986], which blew the cover on popular resentment about perceived consequences of the reforms, notably rising prices, growing income disparity, and the self-enrichment of many Party cadres and some of the leaders' "princeling heirs," through privileged business connections. Party Central's measures to deal with this worrisome popular mood have included defensive articles in the press "explaining" the "transitional" problems of the reforms, sometimes quite sensibly; exhortations to the Party cadres to "obey the law" (meaning little more in practice than to "be good"); and the executions of several criminal playboy-sons of influential fathers, in order to cleanse the Party image by demonstrating that everyone is "equal before the law." The last two measures hardly reassure the many Chinese who know well the fruitlessness of hortatory politics and economics and the arbitrary justice of Party crackdowns.

The reporter-analyst Mary Lee recently noted: "Even sanguine observers say that until the back of (China's) economic and social problems is broken, Deng's "organizational guarantee" (of policy continuity through picked younger successors) will only last as long as he does."[37] It is in the nature of these problems to intensify, especially if the régime continues, at the same time, to pursue the inherently conflicting course of consolidating Soviet-type political and ideological controls. Quite a solid "phalanx" of more orthodox Stalinist cadres, backed by entrenched middle-level cadres with Maoist leanings, waits in the wings for the right moment to gain ascendance.*

I would like to conclude with the following thoughts that were formulated by one of the leading Western authorities on China, Jürgen Domes. "If the policies of a 'socialist market economy' should be continued until the end of this century, the forces they are bound to unleash in the urban society will sooner or later demand first a revision and then possibly even an abolition of the Four Basic Principles,[38] which, for all practical purposes, would mean the abolition of the totalistic single-party system." Since, in that case, the Chinese Communist Party would commit political suicide, and that can hardly be expected, "the possibility of a return to a Soviet-type system of centralized planning and a reduction of private initiatives has not significantly decreased during 1984 . . . all economic reforms and theoretical revisionism notwithstanding.[39]

"It is exactly in this projection that China's most severe developmental problem can be found. For following is the historical experience the world has witnessed since the Russian October revolution of 1917 and the system that it created. Between socialism on the one hand and modernity and social progress on the other there exists—to put it into Marxist-Leninist terms—an antagonistic contradiction. They are incompatible."[40]

* This is another large extract from Miriam London's "Remarks" (see note 19).

Contrary to what Löwenthal suggests, the situation in China is far from settled. Communist China is at the crossroads. The reforms introduced by Deng represent a lethal challenge to the embattled communist totalitarian system of rule. This system can be saved only by its launching of yet another "institutionalized revolution" from above. Nobody can say with assurance that this is what will inevitably happen. But it very well may happen, which Löwenthal either fails to realize or refuses to admit. If, however, it does not, then the still-totalitarian (not yet post-totalitarian, as Löwenthal would have it) communist régime in China will eventually crumble. Only at this stage will one be able to speak about China's transition from totalitarianism to post-totalitarianism.

NOTES

1. M. Voslensky, "The Soviet System: An Historical and Theoretical Evaluation," in the present volume, Chapter 1.
2. This particular feature of totalitarian systems is elaborated in more detail, but under a different angle, in F. Feher, A. Heller, and G. Markus, *Dictatorship Over Needs* (Oxford: Basil Blackwell, 1983), 110-116; and A. Arato, "Critical Sociology and Authoritarian State Socialism," in J.B. Thompson and D. Held, eds., *Habermas: A Critical Debate* (Cambridge, Mass.: The M.I.T. Press, 1982), 200-206.
3. M. Lewin, *The Making of the Soviet System* (London: Methuen, 1985), 257.
4. M.E. Urban, "Conceptualizing Political Power in the U.S.S.R.: Patterns of Binding and Bonding," in *Studies in Comparative Communism*, Vol. XVIII, No. 4 (Winter 1985): 209.
5. For my more extensive treatment of Soviet "intrastructural dissent" and its ubiquity, see: A. Shtromas, *Political Change and Social Development: The Case of the Soviet Union*, (Frankfurt a/M.: Verlag Peter Lang, 1981), 67-82. See also Part III, Section 1 of this volume.
6. R. Löwenthal, "A Theoretical Evaluation Without Historical Contents—A Commentary on Section 1," Part I, Section 3 of this volume, hereafter referred to as R. Löwenthal, "Comments."
7. R. Löwenthal, "Beyond the 'Institutionalized Revolution' in Russia and China," Part I, Section 2 of this volume, hereafter referred to as R. Löwenthal, "Paper."
8. M. A. Kaplan, "The Necessary Conditions for Characterizing a State as Totalitarian—A Commentary on Section 1," Part I, Section 5 of this volume.
9. R. Löwenthal, "Comments."
10. R. Löwenthal, "Paper."
11. Ibid.
12. Ibid.
13. Ibid.
14. Ibid.
15. See "To Fight Communism: Why and How?" in *International Journal on World Peace*, Vol. 1, No. 1 (Autumn 1984): 20–44.

16. Ibid., 37.
17. R. Löwenthal, "Paper."
18. Ibid.
19. Miriam London elaborates: "In a 1972 interview, a peasant refugee told us: 'I don't know whether you understand this, but on the China mainland human beings are not all the same anymore. We (who belong to the black classes) are like earthworms on chicken farms. We can die at any time.'" (Remarks on Löwenthal's paper attached to a letter to Shtromas [March 25, 1986], hereafter referred to as "Remarks.") For a detailed analysis by the Londons of refugee accounts on hunger in China, see: M. London & I.D. London, "The Other China," in *Worldview*, Vol. 19 (No. 5): 4-11, and (No. 6): 43-48.
20. *Jingji Guanli* (Economic Management), No. 3 (March 1981): 3.
21. Roderick MacFarquhar has calculated a range of 16.5 to 29.4 million deaths (see his *The Origins of the Cultural Revolution*, Vol. 2, *The Great Leap Forward, 1958-1960* [London & Kuala Lumpur: Oxford University Press, 1983], 335). According to John S. Aird's analysis done for the U.S. Bureau of Census, "the net population loss during the famine years of 1959-61 reached perhaps as much as 25 million people" (as quoted from V. Smil, "China's Food," in *Food Policy* [May 1981]: 76). As Jürgen Domes noted, even the minimal figure of 20 million is more than the number of people who died from famine in India in the thirty years from 1950 to 1980 (see his *The Government and Politics of the PRC: A Time of Transition* [Boulder & London: Westview Press, 1985], 38).
22. Domes, ibid.
23. *Nongmin Ribao*, September 28, 1985, as published by Foreign Broadcast Information Service, October 15, 1985. Miriam London remarks: "When China exports grain, this does not mean, therefore, that all hinterland areas have sufficient food, but only that export from rich coastal areas is more feasible and earns foreign exchange." ("Remarks," as in note 19.)
24. Simultaneously with the introduction of NEP, drastic measures were taken by central authorities in Soviet Russia to suppress and liquidate entirely the remnants of other socialist parties, to reduce dramatically the influence and undermine the organizational strength of the Russian Orthodox Church and other churches, and to destroy all other public bodies that were in any measure autonomous from the Bolshevik Party. At the same time the 10th Congress of the Party that in 1921 introduced NEP adopted the notorious resolution, "On the Unity of the Party," which prohibited within it any factional activity and, in fact, all discord with the Party leadership's views. For accurate reviews of these measures with the notable exception of those taken against the churches, see E.H. Carr, *The Bolshevik Revolution, 1917-1923*, Vol. 1 (London & Basingstoke: Macmillan, 1950), chapters 8 and 9; C. Bettelheim, *Class Struggles in the U.S.S.R. First Period: 1917-1923* (Hassocks: Harvester Press, 1976). For a brief account of the early (1921) assault on the Russian Orthodox Church, see W.C. Fletcher, *A Study in Survival: The Church in Russia 1927-1943* (London: S.P.C.K., 1965), chapter 1; for a more detailed one, see D. Pospielovsky, *The Russian Church Under the Soviet Régime,* Vol. 1, (Crestwood, N.Y.: St. Vladimir's Seminary Press, 1984), 93-112.

25. For details on the GPU and its comparison with the Cheka, see E. H. Carr, *Bolshevik Revolution*, 179-183; C. Bettelheim, *Class Struggles*, 287-288.

26. Besides the leading role of the party, these are: socialism, proletarian dictatorship, Marxism-Leninism, and Mao Zedong thought.

27. *The Wall Street Journal*, September 30, 1985, 21.

28. M. London, "China Mirages," in *Freedom at Issue*, No. 89 (March-April 1986): 18.

29. Ibid., 17

30. Ibid.

31. Ibid., 18.

32. Ibid.

33. The expression is J. Domes's; see *The Government and Politics of the PRC*, 238, 253, et al.

34. *Renmin Ribao*, October 17, 1985.

35. The saying in China is: "The top has policies and the bottom has countermeasures." The fact that such a saying is making the rounds and has been mentioned several times in the press (for example, in *Renmin Ribao* of January 17, 1986) indicates that this phenomenon is indeed widespread and cannot be ignored.

36. For more details of this particular form of factionalism in the Party, see M. London and Ta-ling Lee, "China's Party Cadres Hedge their Bets," in *The Asian Wall Street Journal*, July 16, 1985.

37. *Far Eastern Economic Review*, March 20, 1986.

38. For them, see note 26.

39. J. Domes, *The Government and Politics of the PRC*, 257-258.

40. Ibid., 253.

7

On Different Types of Modern Dictatorships

A Rejoinder

RICHARD LÖWENTHAL

Alexander Shtromas has done me the honour of presenting substantial critical comments on my views concerning the recent developments in both the U.S.S.R. and China. In the part of his comment dealing with the evolution of the Soviet Union, he disagrees with my views of its history since the end of the Khrushchev era; his disagreement is partly based on a use of terms that happen to be different from mine, but also on a rather serious difference in the estimate of the relation of achievements and failures in Soviet history. In either case, I hope that a brief reply may be fruitful for the reader. By contrast, in the part dealing with the evolution of Communist China, he relies mainly on the views of a school of Sinologists dealing with the *prospects* of that country's recent, post-Maoist development—views that deserve the respect owed to serious experts, but are rendered questionable, as I hope to show in my reply, by a mistaken analogy to a very early period of Soviet history.

I.

In the beginning of his second section, Shtromas sums up my view of the evolution of the Soviet system since the final years of the Khrushchev era as its transformation into "an ordinary non-totalitarian dictatorship." This is

fair enough, provided the reader understands that an "ordinary non-totalitarian dictatorship" is not a nice, pleasant régime by either his standards or
mine. In non-totalitarian dictatorships, whether of the Chilean type or of the
latter-day Soviet Union, people are still arrested for their opinions. In the
Soviet case, some of these people are sent to psychiatric institutions. In the
Chilean case, torture is used against them, and in both cases, these people
are deprived of their jobs. Non-totalitarian dictatorships, however, do not
practice repression—as did the Soviets in their totalitarian period—against
entire *categories* of people regarded as hostile to their systems on "theoretical" grounds, without caring whether the individuals concerned have actually
shown such hostility. In recent years, Pinochet has probably killed proportionately more of his subjects than recent Soviet leaders—yet he is not, in
my terms, a totalitarian, though very much a dictator.

I see the distinguishing mark of a true totalitarian dictatorship in the fact
that, in the effort to achieve a strictly utopian aim, it is forced again and
again to submit its people to new revolutions from above—which no other
dictatorship has ever done. Shtromas correctly points out that, owing to the
present economic level of the Soviet system, continuing revolutions from
above are no longer possible. That is precisely why I do not regard it any
longer as totalitarian, but he argues that the system's policy has remained
just as utopian without revolutions from above, as shown by its economic
policy. Clearly, we disagree about the meaning of the word *utopian*. To me,
utopian describes a goal which by its nature is not achievable, such as an
economy without scarcity or a "classless society." But while the Soviet
leaders may sometimes still refer to such utopian dreams—which most of
them have long treated as jokes—their economic policy, while different from
ours and often irrational in its methods, is not utopian. It has not only
produced failures, but has succeeded in creating one of the two major powers
of the world, including its greatest and highly modern army—but by no
means only its army.

While I strictly deny the alleged utopian character of the present Soviet
system, I agree with Shtromas on its ideological character; this constitutes
the advantage of this ex-totalitarian dictatorship over a non-totalitarian
dictatorship without such a past, like Chile. But at the core of its ideology
are no longer the dreams of a distant future, but the partly real, partly
imagined achievements—in production, in living standards slowly improving
in the long run, in the power represented in the world. All this, both the real
and the imagined part, is ideologically ascribed to the party and its system,
and ideologically described as always threatened by the capitalist enemy. Of
course, this ideological picture of the Soviet Union and the world is very far
from the truth. But it would not be as effective as it is within the system if it

did not also contain part of the truth. I wish Shtromas and his friends would take into account that large numbers of Soviet citizens believe that the foreign and economic policies of Stalin and his successors have made their country both more powerful and more productive—even if at a terrible price in human suffering—and that a very substantial part are proud of it.

In the same context, I do not agree with the view that the motives of Soviet policy are nothing but "the self-serving interests of the Soviet rulers themselves." All rulers who wish to keep their position have to try to produce some success in order to impress the largest possible part of the people. What the Soviet rulers are trying to promise the people is a combination of the impressive national greatness of a "superpower" with gradually increasing productivity, and hopefully leading to a more or less steady, if slow, improvement of conditions of life, without further major upheavals, unless the wicked enemies force them from outside. This is the vision, not of a hell of unending, institutionalized revolutions, but of a would-be stable, would-be benevolent-looking dictatorship. We do not have to believe in the success of that vision, but we ought to recognize that the political system that it requires is utterly different from the former unique dream of the totalitarian dictatorship and the efforts of fulfilling it by ever new, institutionalized revolutions.

II.

In dealing with Chinese Communism, Shtromas has rightly concentrated on my treatment of post-Mao China, which I call post-revolutionary China.

Our argument on China, then, starts after the final period of Mao's "Great Proletarian Cultural Revolution," the totally destructive character of which I publicly analyzed as early as 1967 and after the period of extreme uncertainty preceding his death.[1] It begins with the search for a post-Maoist régime to reach our central issue with the era of Deng Xiaoping, which I regard as a clear case of a post-revolutionary era. Indeed, I have not for a moment believed that China would become either capitalist or democratic under the present régime; I even would have grave difficulty imagining that this nation, with its history and its more than a thousand million people, could become a democracy under any régime. But I do not believe either that Deng's efforts at reform can be understood, and its prospects judged, by the totally artificial comparison between it and Lenin's "New Economic Policy" of 1921. It is a radically different attempt to deal with a very different situation.

Lenin's NEP was conceived little more than three years after he had taken power. He had won a dreadful civil war, but paid for it, not only with terrible losses of life, but also with a disastrous disorganization of the economy that ended in famine. He had not believed that this absurd disorganization was communism; on the contrary, he still believed that backward Russia by herself did not have the preconditions for communism and that communism would only become possible if communists conquered power in more advanced countries. He knew by then that this might take years, but he did not foresee that it might take decades. During those years, NEP was intended as a means to establish a stable, uncontested rule of his Communist Party in an as yet non-communist Russia, while allowing the minority of industrial workers to restore, and to gradually improve, the state-owned factories, and the majority of peasants to produce and sell their goods while slowly learning to cooperate in voluntary organizations and improve their output. Thus, living conditions would get better slowly, while the party ruled and waited for the arrival of more advanced allies. There is documentary proof that Lenin still believed in this evolution on his deathbed; he did *not* think in terms of another "revolution from above."[2]

Some of Lenin's followers, particularly ideological leftists and experienced economists, doubted that this would work for a prolonged period of time. As the wait for revolutionary allies lengthened, the operation of the NEP economy became more difficult, with hungry workers unwilling to produce enough industrial goods for the peasants, and poorly supplied peasants unwilling to give a large part of their output to the cities. It was the experience of this unforeseen economic crisis, not a long preconceived plan, which caused Stalin in late 1927 to start to prepare for measures that culminated in the "Second revolution, but this time from above"—the forced collectivization. It was certainly not the only way to deal with the crisis, but it was Stalin's way, and it created Stalin's system.

Deng's reforms in China have come in a completely different situation. What they have in common with Lenin's NEP is that they attempt to "normalize" the life of a communist-ruled country after a period of terrible economic disorganization. But they are not conceived for waiting for help from abroad. China today is not remotely as isolated as Lenin's Russia was, and its present leaders do not look for a breathing space, but for a new long-term road for their régime. They want this new road to remain communist in the sense of a new definition—no big capitalist firms, but more flexibility at the lower levels, no return to brutal exploitation of the peasants, but gradual improvement even for those of them who have not yet profited from the reforms, better education as more trained teachers become available, more contact with the outside world, whether capitalist (first, because they have more to offer) or communist (second and with caution, because of past experience with Russia, but gradually nevertheless as a balance to capitalist influence). And they will insist on propagating the new ideas as part of the old ideology, even if most people do not believe in it, because an old coat is better than nothing.

This, I say, is what the Chinese communist leaders, or the main tendency among them, intend to do. It is not, in my view, an unreasonable attempt in the Chinese situation. But, of course, its success in the longer run is anything but assured, not because the organizers do not really want it, but because its execution in this vast land with its countless factors of disorganization is immensely difficult. Its chance—and I do not offer percentages of its probability—is that it may still be somewhat less difficult than anything else, and that the Chinese, who have shown so much talent in all parts of the world, may learn from their past suffering, as their rulers have learned from their past absurdities, to find tolerable ways of living together.

NOTES

1. See my article "Mao's Revolution: The Chinese Handwriting on the Wall," in *Encounter* (London) 28, no. 4 (April 1967).
2. The evidence for this is in the 5th, post-Stalinist edition of Lenin's *Sochineniya* (Moscow, Marx-Lenin Institute, 1958-65), and is quoted in this context in Moshe Lewin, *Lenin's Last Struggle* (New York: Random House, 1968), notably in chapter 8, 111-113.

8

Communism as a Cultural Phenomenon

LESZEK KOLAKOWSKI

There is a Polish anecdote about a little girl who was assigned a school essay entitled, "Why We Love the Soviet Union." Unsure of the answer, she asked her mother, "Mummy, tell me, why do I love the Soviet Union?" "What a thing to say," her mother cried. "They're criminals, no one loves them, everybody hates them!" She then asked her father. "Don't be so silly," her father cried angrily, "they're our oppressors, invaders, the whole world hates them!" The little girl was at a loss. She asked a few more adults the same question, but they all answered in a similar vein. Finally she wrote: "I love the Soviet Union because nobody loves it."

I would like to proceed rather like that little girl. I would like, namely, to consider a question which has seldom, if we disregard communist propaganda (although even its authors do not take the matter seriously), received serious treatment—the issue of communism as a source of cultural inspiration in our century. Admittedly, anthropologists try to avoid using the word *culture* in a value-laden sense, using it instead to refer to all the means of communication peculiar to a given community, such as its customs, laws, and educational institutions, its mechanisms of power and religious beliefs, its art, its family bonds, sexual norms, and so forth. All these things can, of course, be described without making any assumptions as to the superiority or inferiority of some cultures with respect to others. In this sense communist culture encompasses both the poems of Mayakovski and the mouldy cliches churned out by every scribe in a provincial propaganda office; the same principle sets classical Chinese works of art alongside the pictures produced by Maoist artists, which have still a long way to go in order to attain the level of the comic strips in American newspapers.

The sense in which I use the word *culture*, however, is much more restricted. It is, moreover, one which does entail a value judgement. Included, then, in this sense, are, firstly, original, and not merely imitative, works of literature, art and the humanities; secondly, I have in mind works which can be assumed genuinely to have entered into the essential make-up of that culture whose scope is the traditional range of the Christian religion, and whose roots are to be found in Greece and Rome, Judaism and Christianity. To a great extent Russia, too, belongs within this scope, even though in its politics it can be said to be closer to its Tatar traditions.

My question, then, is the following: how are we to understand the fact that international communism has, both in power and as an aspirant to power, shown itself during certain historical periods to be culturally fruitful? I mean by this that it has been capable both of inspiring original work of a kind that should be considered a part of the European civilization, by no means relegated to its dustbin, and at the same time of attracting a significant part of the culture-forming élite, including some of its most distinguished members. The question is worthy of consideration not only because the destructive and anticultural force of communism is well-known to us all, but also because there is reason to claim that this force was built into the system from the very beginning. This is an aspect of the communist system of rule that has been often described, and there is no need to dwell on it. But it should be recalled that communism, unlike other tyrannies, ancient and modern, engaged in the destruction of culture not only, indeed not even primarily, by negative means such as censorship, prohibitions, and the repression of the disobedient. Simple tyrannies are less destructive insofar as their aims are restricted to preventing centers of political opposition from forming, and to eradicating all those elements in cultural life which might pose a threat to the system of political power. The government itself, however, wanting mainly to be undisturbed and undivided, does not insist on spreading its influence over all spheres of life, and can therefore tolerate cultural expression as long as it remains politically indifferent. Communism, on the other hand, from the outset intended its rule to be all-encompassing, and aimed, not merely to liquidate threats, but also actively to control all forms of collective life, including ideology, language, literature, art, education, the family, and even dress. It is, no doubt, extremely difficult for a system of all-encompassing rules to attain a state of total perfection. Nevertheless, we remember the days when the pressure to attain this ideal weighed heavily upon us—days when ideological norms defined what we should think about relativity theory as well as what forms of music were correct or prohibited, and what trouser width was in accordance with the requirements of socialist life.

The most impressive results of this striving towards all-encompassing regulation were obtained in the People's Republic of China. Those of the Soviet Union in the last years of the Stalinist era were also very considerable, albeit not quite as outstanding; the pressures of reality demanded a partial sacrifice of the ideal. For instance, the regulation of the content of natural sciences was abandoned. Other regulations proved too troublesome to execute, for example, those concerning dress. In most of the European Soviet protectorates, particularly in Poland, such regulations never attained the Soviet level; the principle itself, however, has never been abandoned, and the extent to which it can be put into practice depends simply on the strength of the ruling apparatus when pitted against the natural tendencies of social life. From the point of view of cultural oppression, Poland for many years was, and to this day remains, closer to a traditional tyranny than to a totalitarian régime. The apparatus of government is geared there mainly towards negative means such as censorship and the oppression of dissidents or politically uncertain elements, but its attempts to impose value regulations on cultural works, when there are any, are incompetent and ineffective. It hardly needs pointing out that this is not the result of any benevolent intentions of this apparatus, but rather only of its weakness.

My interest, however, does not lie here. On the contrary, I want to look at communism as a force that was culturally active. It would seem hard to deny that it was such a force. Talented writers and men of ideas such as Vladimir Mayakovski, Sergei Yesenin, Isaac Babel, Pilniak, the young Fadeyev, Erenburg identified with the Bolshevik coup; distinguished film-makers such as Eisenstein and Pudovkin; avant-garde artists such as Malevich, Deyneka, Rodchenko, even, for a short time, Chagall; and some of the intelligentsia and writers in the humanities. The later fates of this considerable category of creative artists and writers were, as we know, varied; some died by their own hand, some by the hand of an executioner, while others sold out to the tyranny or else ended their life in bitterness and inactivity. In the twenties communism proved to be a considerable force attracting Western artists and intellectuals; among the literary and artistic avant-garde, men such as Aragon and Eluard, Picasso and Leger, as well as a great number of other genuinely outstanding people in France, Italy and Germany were Communist Party members throughout their lives. Even in countries such as Great Britain and the United States, where communism never attained political significance, the list of intellectuals, artists and writers who were, for varying periods of time, if not party members, then Stalinist or Trotskyist sympathizers, is quite impressive; likewise the intelligentsia in Mexico and Brazil. In independent Poland, the political influence of communism was, albeit noticeable in the union movement, on the whole negligible; the fact that its centre of influence lay in a country which was considered to be an old enemy was also a natural barrier. And yet, despite this, it did manage to attract a certain number of genuinely original people, such as Broniewski, Jasienski, Wandurski, Wat, Zegaldowicz, Kruczkowski, and intellectuals such as Stefan Czarnowski in the last stages of his life, Nowakowski, and Natalia Gasiorowska. In the first post-war decade the Communist government found considerable support among artists and writers, some of them undeniably distinguished. This was also the case in Hungary and Czechoslovakia.

But there is little point in multiplying examples and names; the list could obviously be very long. It is incontestable that in certain historical conditions communism was not only a strong center of gravitational force attracting a culturally active milieux, but also, as it turned out, a source of inspiration for works that have since become a part of the artistic and intellectual life in our century. It was present not only as a separate form of civilization which ravaged, and continues to erode, the historical continuity of Europe, extinguishing spiritual expression wherever its power could reach, but also as a source of the energy which kindled such expression.

The least credible means of explaining this, and the most naïve, is to spout generalities to the effect that "people are easily deceived, bribed and frightened—that is the secret of communism's success." Dismissing the history of communism with formulations of this kind is as easy as it is ineffective, indeed counter-productive, since it makes it impossible to understand important parts of history. Such formulations also have the merit of being applicable to everything that incites our outrage or displeasure, but their very all-explanatory power reveals their emptiness. The history of communist culture is not so easily explained away; it was made up of social processes, which in turn should be examined as such, and not merely as results of the unsavoury motives of individuals. Indeed, if the question could so easily be disposed of in this way, it would be inconceivable why communism in power, while it continues to wield all its instruments of deceit, bribery and fear, should have lost so entirely, and quite a long time ago, its ability not only to kindle artistic and intellectual creativity, but also to attract the sympathy of people who are culturally active; and that it should have lost this ability also in Europe and North America, countries beyond the reach of its power.

How was it that Stalinism could, when in power, enlist considerable support among the intellectual élite while the régimes currently in power, which are after all less cruel and bloodthirsty, are unable to do so? And why have various other despotic and revolutionary régimes failed to display a similar capacity? Fascism and Nazism in culture were, after all, mainly destructive, leaving only ruins in their wake; but although they occasionally managed to awaken the sympathy of various people from the Western cultural élites (Heidegger, Ezra Pound, Céline, and Knut Hamsun being the most illustrious examples), they nevertheless proved, when compared to Stalinism, exceedingly weak in this respect.

One important field in which communism proved to be almost entirely fruitless is philosophy. Official Soviet philosophy has left behind nothing worth mentioning; its history could be studied profitably only to show the inevitable degradation of thought when it is reduced to a helpless instrument of the party. Lukacs and Bloch, two genuinely interesting thinkers who continue to attract a certain amount of attention, are counter-examples only to a certain extent. Lukacs is worth reading as an extraordinary example of an intellectual of great talent who throughout his life, and despite various conflicts and episodes, offered up his mind into the service of a tyranny; but his work no longer provides any intellectual stimulation and is considered, also in Hungary, to be dead. As for Bloch, only those elements of his thought that have little to do with either communism or Marxism could possibly be of any interest. In Poland and Czechoslovakia, also, the philosophical writings that grew out of the communist spirit are now a rubbish dump—although, of course, for archeologists, even rubbish dumps hold some interest.

* * *

Communism has a history dating back many centuries. But even in its earliest forms, in the utopian literature of the Renaissance and the Enlightenment, it already revealed its incurable contradiction. For these utopias, sometimes inspired by religion, appealing to sharing of goods by the apostles and condemning private property as a sin, were at the same time egalitarian and despotic; they preached both absolute equality and the need for the rule of an enlightened élite which would protect that equality. Communism as a political movement, no longer merely as a literary genre, grew out of the Jacobinic left, where the conflict between equality on the one hand, treated as an absolute and supreme value, and freedom on the other, was even more prominent. The ideal society was to be at once strictly egalitarian and despotically governed—in short, a square circle. The nineteenth century, the age of Marx, an age that witnessed the growth and development of the modern socialist movement, was by no means fertile soil for communism. Certainly, particular theoretical strands of it were continued, but as a political movement it hardly existed. The First International was not the organ of communism; Marx himself, despite his theoretical authority, was practically of no account as a political activist; and the socialist parties of the Second International, albeit sometimes in conflict and split into various factions, assumed, in their overwhelming majority (Marxist included), the legitimacy of democratic institutions and the belief in cultural freedoms.

Social criticism in the nineteenth century was highly developed and sometimes acerbic, but it had nothing to do with communism. Modern communism in the proper sense arose at the turn of the century as Lenin's faction; until World War I its influence on the socialist movement outside Russia was negligible; indeed for a long time it remained unrecognized as something ideologically and politically new rather than as part of the various and sundry tactical or doctrinal differences within one movement. It was not until 1910 that it slowly began to emerge and become visible. It did not conceal the fact that it was a harbinger of despotism; its totalitarian potential was there from its inception. If in time it succeeded in bringing Russia's revolutionary wave under its yoke and establishing its rule on its crest, the conditions of this success admittedly lay in a string of extraordinary accidents of history, but it was not only these accidents that brought it to the top. It was also the ability it had quickly to absorb all the important social issues and make them its own, forging them into tools for its own use. This ability was later to become, in its developed form, the basis of the future successes of Sovietism.

In other words, communism has, from the very beginning, both in its strategy and its ideology, been a parasite; it has successfully lived off all those relevant and important social issues which were also worthy causes true to the intentions of a large part of an intelligentsia nourished on ideals of Enlightenment humanitarianism. Before World War I, communism did more than protect the interests of workers; it also unmasked national oppression, took upon its shoulders the aspirations of poor peasants, protested against censorship, in a word allied itself, in a way that was not doctrinaire, with all possible sources of resistance to tsarist autocracy, aiming to channel them all in one direction. The communists had almost no hand in the February revolution and the overthrow of the tsar; and the October Revolution took place under two slogans that had nothing communist about them—peace and land for the peasants. The dominant ideology of the masses during the revolutionary process was not communism but anarchism, expressed in the slogan, "All power to the Soviets." This slogan was at one point taken over by the Bolsheviks and later (when the Soviets could no longer be used against the Provisional Government) abandoned; they then took it up again and again, only in order to exploit the anarchist utopia with the purpose of destroying all remaining state institutions and imposing their own rule on a disorganized and demoralized society. Lenin clearly admitted that the reason the Bolsheviks won was that the agrarian program they implemented was not their own but that of the Socialist Revolutionary Party. Another slogan, in addition to peace and land, which was instrumental in the disintegration of the old state, was the slogan of a nation's right to self-determination. The subsequent fate of this program we know—the slogan of land for the peasants was to be put into practice by expropriating the peasants and chaining them to the land on the principle of feudal servitude; the slogan of peace, by building the most highly militarized empire on earth, unsated in its lust for conquests and aggression; the slogan of national self-determination, by systematically quashing all the aspirations and traditions of the nations swallowed up by the empire; the other slogan of workers' control over factories, by depriving the working class not only of having a say in the factories' management, but also of trade union rights and any other means of resisting exploitation and oppression.

Nevertheless, many intellectuals saw Bolshevism not merely as a collection of slogans meant to satisfy immediate, albeit primary, social claims, but rather as a global utopian ideology, as the beginning of a new world and a new time in which all human problems would be solved once and for all, and all misfortunes remedied. Particularly sensitive, of course, were the issue of peace and war and the issue of internationalism connected with it. International communism as we know it today is a product of World War I. The Poles have a natural tendency to view this war through the prism of what was most important for them, namely the rebuilding of an independent Polish state after years of bondage. This result, however, had not figured in the intentions of any of the powers that had started the war. The war itself was a savage slaughter of millions of people, and the longer it lasted, the more clearly it revealed itself to be just what the socialist left claimed it was—an imperialist war, a struggle in which nations massacred each other in the interests of the ruling classes.

It is difficult indeed to overestimate the role which anti-war passions played in the Bolshevik sympathies of European intellectuals during the early twenties. Bolshevism was the sole clear beneficiary of the embarrassing failure of the Second International of 1914 when it turned out that international workers' solidarity, the ideological backbone of the socialist movement, was but a useless, empty phrase which vanished like a ripple on the water as soon as it was put to the test. The USDP, the anti-war faction of German social-democracy established in 1917, was a hatchery of communism for this very reason, and for European writers like Arnold Zweig, Bertold Brecht, Henri Barbusse, Romain Rolland, Anatole France and Jaroslav Hašek, to name a famous few, who espoused communism at the time or sympathized with it, the horror of war served as the main stimulus. Communism was the promise of a world without war; in other words, it was successfully parasitic on the human desire for peace, which has become one of our century's most strongly felt human sentiments. Before the war communism in Russia was a small sect, and in the years between the first and second Russian revolutions the influence of communism and Marxism on the Russian intelligentsia was considerably weakened, so that many of the most outstanding members of the intellectual élite launched a fierce attack on the historical and philosophical dogmas which, until only recently, they themselves had espoused. Thus it was not without good cause that Gorky said at a writers' conference in 1934, by which time his devotion to Stalinism was total, that the years 1907-1917, a great era in the history of Russian poetry, represented the most shameless and disgraceful decade in the history of the Russian intelligentsia.

There were, of course, also other motives. There was that fascination with barbarism often found in intellectuals, in other words with the absolute beginning of a new era, the break with the past, the freedom from the burden of time past. Both in Russia and in the West, this ethos of cultural rootlessness, the release (illusory, need I add) from the heritage of tradition, the cult of a youth unencumbered by the weight of history, and the desire to shock and offend the bourgeois public all provided strong motives for supporting Bolshevism as the bringer of a radical newness, the hammer that, in accordance with the call of the International "du passé faisons table rase," would crush a burdensome past. For Alexander Blok, for Mayakovski, for futurists and French surrealists, this motive played an important role. Its presence in the magnetic force of communism at the time can perhaps be explained by historical circumstances. World War I was indeed the close of the nineteenth century, it was indeed the beginning of a new era in all spheres of human life, and this was something the Bolsheviks realized earlier and better than anyone else. Thus, for a time, they were able to become a part of European culture as the incarnation of the new age, and this helped lend to the communist civilization a certain, albeit brief, authenticity.

The first half of the thirties brought with it new social upheavals—the great economic crisis, the triumph of national socialism in Germany—and later the civil war in Spain and the great storm in China. On all these things communism successfully continued to feed. It was all very urgent and very real; the great depression and its effects—poverty, despair, millions of unemployed—were communism's great opportunity. For communism came now as the promise of a society free from uncertainty and unemployment, and as the fiercest foe of the fascist cancer which, feeding off the same disasters, seemed to be consuming Europe. In the same years when millions of people were dying in the Ukraine, from starvation, artificially organized by the government, and from torture, cold, exhaustion and bullets in Stalinist prisons, camps and in various stages of displacement, a considerable portion of the Western intelligentsia saw the Soviet state as a bastion of peace, the watchfire of revolutionary humanism, and the harbinger of a new world in which people are equal, trusting in the future and free from the uncertainty of what tomorrow will bring. People like André Malraux, Walter Benjamin, Theodor Plivier, Jean-Richard Bloch, Theodore Dreiser, John Dos Passos, and Upton Sinclair all sympathized or identified with communism; Leon Feuchtwanger and Romain Rolland greeted the macabre farce of the Moscow trials as a triumph of justice. And here, too, lamenting human blindness and naïveté is of no avail when we try to understand why this was so. Here, too, there are social and cultural processes which have to be explained as such. The Popular Front of the mid-thirties was, of course, the product of Sovie manipulation, but it was not only that; if it had any effect, it was because its slogans reflected the real hopes, fears, and experiences of Europe. Fascism was not merely something communism thought up in order to frighten; it was a terribly real, mortal threat to nations and civilizations, and although it fed on the same social diseases as communism, the people drawn to it were of an entirely different mold, while its cultural vitality was almost nought. The often timid and unstable policies of the Western democracies in the face of this threat were deftly exploited by communism, and anti-fascism could be, and in fact was, a culturally inspiring force. The social disasters caused by inflation and the depression were quite real. The two-year Soviet-German friendship did cause some people to waver, certainly, but the further course of the war soon erased that unsightly stain. Between 1941 and 1945 the Soviet giant reassumed, with some effect, the role of the main protector of the world against Nazi barbarism, and turned its military successes into strong support for the new ideological invasion in Europe.

That is similar to the Central and East European cultural élites. Those members who clearly pronounced themselves in favour of a communist régime were for the most part from a socialist or left-liberal background, not a communist one. In Poland, for example, their support was to a large extent defined by negative reactions to pre-war Poland, particularly the Poland of recent years, after the death of Marshall Pilsudski. The Poles have an understandable tendency to idealize that period, since, for all its sins, Poland was independent then, and its various faults and afflictions shrink to the size of minor discomforts when compared with the new "progressive" system. Censorship was minimal in comparison with the systematic destruction of the progressive muzzle with which the national culture has been struggling for so many years; instances of police lawlessness fade into insignificance in the face of a Polish People's Republic in which lawlessness has been elevated to a system. Nevertheless, that part of the intelligentsia which in 1945 or 1946, after the horrors of the war and occupation, identified, more or less ardently, with the new system, saw things in a different light. Those who remembered the Bereza camp, the Brzesc trial, the disgusting wave of virulent anti-Semitism, and the intrusive, all-pervasive clericalism, saw in communism a continuation of the enlightenment, a turning against that old Polish, clerical, chauvinistic trend in the national tradition. That trend was one against which the more enlightened and cosmopolitan sections of the educated nobility had waged a struggle since at least the 17th century, long before the formation of the intelligentsia in the modern sense. Similarly, the agrarian reforms which had been announced from the start reflected many of the traditional demands of the non-communist left. So did the expansion of general education that communism in fact promoted.

To say all this is by no means to justify anything, least of all the participation of this section of the intelligentsia in the mass communist lie; nonetheless, communism is, to repeat a banal observation, a historical phenomenon of great significance, and cannot be understood simply by condemning or sneering at the gullibility or corruptibility of its advocates. If it managed successfully to feed off genuine social concerns, largely those to which both European liberalism and socialism were sympathetic, this does not mean that it solved them, nor even that it attempted to do so. On the contrary, it brought to ruin all the social, cultural, national, and international concerns that it claimed to champion. One ostensible example is the issue the Soviet Union constantly and proudly presents as its particular achievement—unemployment. This is ostensibly an exception only in the sense that unemployment was banished in the Soviet Union through the system of forced work; it is indeed true that there has never been any unemployment among slaves. Nazism also successfully defeated unemployment. Nevertheless unemployment remains a bane for democratic societies. When it occurs on a large scale it invariably becomes a life-giving source for communist promises, and the hope, not always illusory, that many people will be prepared to forsake their freedom in exchange for the security of enslavement.

Communism was a gigantic facade that in reality concealed a pure striving for power, absolute power, as an end in itself. The rest was a tool, a strategy, enforced self-limitation. But the facade was far from being mere decoration;

it was not only communism's condition of life, its respiratory system, but also an ineradicable remnant of the tradition of nineteenth century socialism and the Enlightenment, of which communism was indeed the degenerate progeny. Progeny, even when degenerate, nevertheless retains a variety of discernible genetic traits, and these were also discernible in communism. The Enlightenment gave birth to rationalism, contempt for tradition, and hatred of the entire mythological layer in culture. The brutal persecution of religion was not the only form in which these trends blossomed in communism; they also found expression in the principle, put into practice rather than voiced outright, whereby human individuals are entirely exchangeable, the life of those individuals counting only insofar as they are tools of the higher cause, namely the state, since there is no rational basis for attributing any kind of special, non-instrumental status to the human personality. Thus rationalism was transformed into the idea of slavery. On the other hand, the romantic and early socialist tenets in communism—the search for the lost community and solidarity of people, the protest against the social disintegration caused by the progress of industrialisation and urbanization—were expressed in caricature, as the principle of a forced solidarity, in other words as the attempt to create a facade of unity, the unity of despotism.

Nonetheless, both the phraseology of solidarity and the rationalist and Promethean kind were markedly visible in communist language from the outset, attesting to its connections, however perverted, with the tradition of romanticism and the Enlightenment, and also lending to its ideology that particular pathos which, being undoubtedly authentic in the minds of its believers, seemed to endow communism with some kind of participation in the truth. During the period of communism's ideological blossoming this was of course its strength but also exposed it to considerable danger. For this facade, to the extent that it was taken seriously within the movement, inevitably tended toward independence and questioning of its own sub-servient role; taking the facade seriously also meant confronting it with the reality of the state or the political movement, and thanks to this communism could, indeed had to, produce a constant stream of its own internal critics, heretics and apostates, who appealed to original sources, ever present in the phraseology, in order to unmask the poverty of reality. This was something that was barely discernible in other totalitarian movements, where the gap between the facade and the reality was small (the ideology was generally quite blunt in voicing its real intentions) and the strength of the ideological tradition feeble. Hitler could be the counterpart of Stalin, but there was no Nazi Marx, Engels, or even Lenin behind him. The genealogy which he created for himself was artificial.

Thus communism, to use the idiom it applied to the bourgeoisie, was constantly forced to send its own grave diggers out into the world. In the intellectual and moral criticism which finally brought about the collapse of communist ideology, a particular, and particularly effective, role was played by former communists or left-wing socialists, people who not only knew but had internalized the political and psychological mechanisms of communism—an experience difficult to replace. Arthur Koestler, Ignazio Silone, Boris Souvarine, Bertram Wolfe—they had all been communists; Orwell was a left-wing socialist. The part played by former communists, Milovan Djilas foremost among them, in the ideological disintegration of the communist countries of Europe during the fifties and sixties was considerable if, indeed, not too decisive.

There is an important distinction to be made here. When we talk about the attracting force of the communist idea and about its cultural fertility, we may have in mind one of two things—either the work of artists, writers and intellectuals who identified or sympathized with communism, or works whose discernibly ideological nature clearly reveals the source of their inspiration. There have been many distinguished artists and writers connected with communism whose works either did not contain unequivocal testimony of their political sympathies or did so only incidentally and indirectly. Some, for example, although dealing with matters championed by the claims of communism and to that extent in agreement with it, did not reveal this identification in their actual content, since the subjects they dealt with were such that they did not require one to be a communist or a sympathizer in order to be able to defend them. Aragon was beyond doubt a great poet whose works have a permanent place in French literature, but his poetical works can be distinguished from his mendacious Stalinist journalism and propaganda novels. The poetry of Pablo Neruda is, in part, of a clearly discernible communist nature, but the canvases of Siqueiros, a painter of great stature, contain nothing that could possibly lead one to see him as a complete Stalinist. Dreiser was a communist sympathizer and joined the party towards the end of his life, yet his novels are in the rich American tradition of social criticism, not in the tradition of communist propaganda. In Broniewski's pre-war poetry one can easily distinguish the lyrical from the political, and indeed this latter also contains, in my view, some works that are worthy of note; unlike his post-war poem on Stalin, they bear witness, in some sense, to the fact that communism at one stage was able to absorb a certain amount of the energy that was present in the history of genuine social conflicts, and not merely in the history of Soviet imperialism. Similar observations could be made about many of the artists and writers whose names I have mentioned.

Apart from works by people who allied themselves politically with communism, however, there were—and I stress the past tense—literary, artistic, and intellectual works which were specifically communist in their actual content and which became established in the history of culture. It is safe to say that the longer communism remained in power, the fewer such works there were. Works that were genuinely inspired by communist ideas all but vanished in the Soviet Union in the thirties; not only, or perhaps not mainly, because of the purges and massacres, but above all because of the growth and consolidation of totalitarian forms of rule that left no place for personal expression, replacing it instead with the national agit-mush, and thus effectively drying up any remnants of authenticity in the communist ideology. Admittedly some writing of good quality did come out of World War II, but by then the ideas inspiring such works were patriotic rather than communist; they describe the horrors of the war from the point of view of people who, at knifepoint, fought for their lives and for the life of their nation, not for the triumph of the revolution. In Poland and in other Soviet protectorates, post-war works of communist inspiration were no longer able to contribute much that was worth remembering; socialist realism in art and literature was a still birth. Those writers, too, who made their début after the war and seriously accepted the communist faith made their real entry into national writing only when they had abandoned that faith. Granted, such an assessment is rough-hewn and general. It does not take into account transitional stages, possible exceptions, or ideologically mixed works, but it is not possible for me to discuss individual works or biographies here. If there are instances of communist works of this period whose merits leave room for reasonable argument, it is also certain that after a few years what is worthwhile in the culture of countries taken over by communism was created either despite communist ideology or alongside it, bypassing it as it were. It should be said, however, that when an ideology pretends to omnipotence and all-encompassing rule, to create alongside it is already to create against and despite it. Works that simply ignore the ideology, the doctrine and the government are admittedly tolerated, to some extent even in the Soviet Union, but this is the result of the ideology's debilitating state of senility, not homage deliberately paid to liberal values. Criticism of communism from within has practically ceased to exist; it has no social use. Communism has ceased to produce its own critics who appeal to its doctrinal premises, and every critical comment is immediately an attack on its principles, not on their alleged deformations. In Western Europe, in communist countries, and in North America there is no longer anyone of any cultural standing whose works are inspired by the communist faith; the drying-up is almost total, and certainly irreversible. In Latin American countries, with their enormous social problems, their poverty, their backwardness, and their blatant inequalities, the ideas of communism have perhaps retained something of their former power. But the actual ideology that continues at least to remain alive in the Soviet Union is not communism but the idea of imperialism. In other words, communism as a particular form of culture in this sense—as an energy capable of producing works that find a permanent place in culture—has ceased to exist in the civilized world. It remains, of course, a military and political power that can frighten and invade, and also mobilize those forces in the Third World that want to take power as cousins of the great empire. But it cannot spread its influence through the culture-forming élites.

To say this much is not yet to explain why communism became, and succeeded in maintaining itself, as an extraordinary powerful source of ideas with which so many people identified, including a considerable section of the leading milieux of cultural life. That is a separate matter, and I do not intend to consider it here. I will only repeat that appealing to fear and stupidity in an attempt to explain this process is a coarse and much over-simplified way of going about it. It is of no more help than an attempt to explain the rise and successes of early Islam by the claim that Arabs were stupid, and consequently, that instead of believing in Christ, they believed in the false prophet Mohammed. Indeed, I doubt that communism's rise and spread throughout the world can even be explained causally in the sense in which floods or droughts can be explained. Looking back, all historical events, including sudden outbreaks of great religious movements, seem to be connected to particular circumstances. It is always possible to discover causes *ex post*. Just how tenuous, however, such explanations are can be seen when we consider that, if they really exposed the sufficient conditions for these historical changes, then surely we would also be able, with the same degree of certainty, to predict such changes; but we cannot. Communism was born as a quasi-religious movement—that is, as the ideological expression of the need for ultimate salvation. This need, one may assume, is a permanent and ineradicable feature of all civilizations, but its presence alone does not suffice to explain why, at certain times and in certain places, it finds expression in the form of acute historical convulsions that overcome large parts of populations and lead to violent and unexpected changes that overturn the established order. Communism is an instance of such a convulsion, born from a desperate need for the ultimate salvation, a new age. An outgrowth of the Enlightenment tradition at a time when the traditional faiths had to a large degree been abandoned by the educated élites, it took on the inconsistent form of a secular religion. The psychological mechanisms of its expansion were similar to those to which the traditional faiths owed their effectiveness in their time of vigour; similar, also, were the workings of the missionary energy of its militant atheism. Its doctrines, however, were a caricature of religion, for communism demanded at the same time blind faith and the recognition that it was the rational interpretation of the world; and

since it could not have both at once, its thrashings between these two
contradictory demands brought about, within the range of its influence, the
fall both of religion and of rational knowledge. The bankruptcy of its ideas
is also the defeat of that very Enlightenment of which it was the ultimate
and most consistent, and thereby self-destructive, expression.

All this, I stress once again, fails to explain its genesis. At most it enables
us to understand the authenticity that originally characterized its message,
and hence its short-lived and now past effectiveness as a catalyst of cultural
life. But why history should have chosen those times and those places to
bring forth this self-destructive potential of the Enlightenment we do not
know. All powerful and significant social movements are really products of
many random circumstances stuck together; they include not only the economic, political and psychological moods and conditions of a given time, but
also the characters and creative initiative of the individuals actively involved,
as well as, finally, the weight of the residue of tradition. There is no one who
can boast of having a method of reducing this multiplicity of coincidences to
a measurable and uniform scale that could serve as a basis for providing an
explanation of historical events. There is little doubt, however, that this
convulsion is nearing its end, and that the loss of the ability to mobilize
culturally active forces is an extremely significant measure of its decline.
Communism is more and more visibly becoming a matter of pure force, but
it would be false to claim that it was never anything but that. As to the
specific forms this decline will take and the length of time it will span, we are
forced to rely on the divinations of soothsayers.

Translated from Polish by AGNIESZKA KOLAKOWSKA

9

Human Rights and the Soviet Future

EUGENE KAMENKA

I

At first sight, the Soviet Union strikes the outside observer as an intensely political and politicized society. "Official" ideology, political in form and content, pervades and controls all "licensed" public utterance. That which is not licensed is quickly driven underground by censorship, exclusion from educational institutions, expulsion from professional organizations, dismissal from work, and police measures and administrative harassment. It is treated as an anti-social, anti-Soviet, illegal act.

The politicization of Soviet society, the ubiquity of censorship, dogma and control—in short, the fundamentally totalitarian character of Soviet society —find their initial justification in the ideology of Marxism-Leninism itself and beyond that in some of the central doctrines and attitudes of Karl Marx.

Karl Marx, as I have written elsewhere, was the greatest thinker in the history of socialism.[1] For one hundred years, he gave socialism much of its intellectual respectability and its theoretical self-confidence. From diverse sources and materials, from phrases in radical pamphlets and slogans at socialist meetings, from German philosophy, French politics, and English economics, he created a socialist system of thought, a total socialist critique of modern society. He refined and systematized the language of socialism; he explained and expounded the place of socialism in history; he reconciled, or seemed to reconcile, its conflicting hopes and theoretical contradictions. His work—itself a process of self-clarification—set the seal upon the transition from the romantic revolutionism of the 1840s to the working-class movement of the 1860s through the 1880s. It fused into a single body of connected doctrine moral criticism and economic analysis, revolutionary activism and social science, the longing for community and the acceptance of economic rationality and industrial progress. It clothed the interests and demands of a still largely nascent and despised working class in the dignity of a categorical imperative pronounced by history itself. It laid some of the important foundations for a critical account of the birth and development of modern society. For Marx correctly recognized the world-historical importance of the French Revolution and the Industrial Revolution. He saw that, in Europe at least, they were part of one development. He realized that they had inaugurated a new era in history, an era in which civil society—the world of industry and trade—had moved to the center of the stage and was being driven by violent internal compulsions to ever more rapid change and expansion. Marx recognized more clearly than others the birth of modern society with the tensions and conflicts involved in its internal dynamic. Since the Napoleonic wars set the seal of destruction upon the old order and the old régime in Europe, we have been living through a continuing crisis, one which has spread outward from Europe until it engulfs the world. Marx was the first, and in many respects greatest, student of that crisis. His predictions have proved at least partly false, and his presentation of the issues may now seem far too simple, but he saw where many of the issues lay, not only of his time but of ours. The study of modern society still cannot bypass the work of Karl Marx.

Marxism as social theory is one thing and Marxism as ideology another, though the two are related in a variety of interesting ways. It has often been claimed that the great success of Marxism came when armed Bolsheviks burst into the streets of Petrograd in October/November 1917 and established the first Marxist government in the world. That government has since grown from strength to strength. Communist states now govern much more than one third the population of the world. Yet only some—and they are a marked minority—socialists in advanced industrial societies have seen this as a realization of Marx's predictions and a vindication of his hopes. The Communist revolutions took place at first sight in defiance of Marx's theory of history and not in accordance with it. The practical actions and theoretical proclamations of the governments that were brought into being have seemed to many a far cry from Marx's vision of a free, cooperative, and ultimately stateless workers' community, in which class division, alienation, and all forms of coercion would be totally overcome. Neither do those governments confront us as genuine workers' governments, putting the interest of the proletariat first, cherishing proletarian organization and proletarian freedom, for instance, confident and independent trade unions. They are, as Rosa Luxemburg and others predicted they would be, dictatorships over the proletariat, not of the proletariat.

For much of his life Karl Marx had little time for the Russians. The tsarist autocracy was, for him, the cornerstone of European reaction; in 1848 he called for war against it. Later he was to see in the British Foreign Secretary, Lord Palmerstone, a Russian spy. Russia's government was the cornerstone of reaction in Europe, but her people, too, were for Marx products and carriers of Asiatic barbarism, shaped by the 250 years of Tartar overlordship and, according to Marx in the 1850s, by the "Mongolizing and Tartarizing nature of the terrain." Russians were a spiritless, servile people, accustomed to the knout.

Paradoxically, it was in Russia that Marx gained the most attention and respect among serious intellectuals in his own lifetime. They welcomed his call for revolution, but they welcomed even more his implicit assurance that the capitalist, individualistic, competitive West was not the ultimate model for mankind, but would itself be replaced by a higher and communitarian society. By the 1870s, Marx was changing his view, learning Russian and taking an intense interest in Russia as the country where his doctrines had "great currency." In 1879, the English liberal M.P., Sir Mountstuart Elphinstone Grant-Duff, reported back to the Empress Frederick of Prussia (eldest daughter of Queen Victoria) on a visit he had paid to Marx at his home. Marx spoke of her and of the Crown Prince with "due respect and propriety" and his opinions, if slightly cynical, were largely correct when concerned with the past and the present. On the future Marx was vague and unsatisfactory. "He looks, not unreasonably, for a great and not distant crash in Russia, thinks it will begin by reforms from above which the old bad edifice will not be able to bear and which will lead to its tumbling down altogether. As to what would take its place he had evidently no clear idea, except that for a long time Russia would be unable to exercise any influence in Europe."[2]

Marx died too soon to consider where his theories had led or what was new and what was old in the politics, system of government, and national lifestyle of the Soviet citizen. There has been a flood of literature since, some of it placing Soviet reality in the context of Russian history rather than of Marxism. Marx would have found such books much more interesting, exciting, and congenial than the current typical Western Marxist concerns like Marxism and the multi-nationals, Marxism and feminism, Marxism and gay liberation, Marxism and the counter-culture. He would want to know about Russia rather than ignore it as an embarrassment for Marxism. For history, Marx knew and said, was not made by the people but by great historic nations and by great socio-economic classes that were carriers, organizers and overlords of new productive forces and modes of production. Such classes were made and shaped by their role in history, i.e. by their role in production. That very general view of Marx's—that power and not just ideas or ideals shapes the course of history, and that revolutions have a logic independent of the will of those who make them—is not palatable to many people today, but it has been thoroughly borne out by the history of the Communist states that his writing helped to create. The details of his theory of the coming socialist revolution, and of revolution generally, on the other hand, are not.

The rise and spread of communism, of communist revolution and communist take-overs in .the twentieth century bear out, without question, Marx's insistence that bourgeois society or industrial capitalism had an internal expansionary dynamic that would undermine and unsettle traditional, non-industrial nations throughout the world, that would drag all nations into action in, and reaction to, the history of Europe. In spite of its subsequent concern with, and manipulative use of, the theme of national liberation, communism can be seen as a principal agent in underdeveloped countries of the practice and ideology of (limited) modernization, of industrialization, and of the development of state economic and political power. Its most effective cutting edge, like that of Marxism, was directed not against capitalism, but against pre-capitalist modes and formations, against feudal dependence and exploitation especially. Marx, however, saw the socialist revolution as far more than that. It would be a great historic advance upon capitalism and industrialization and not simply an alternative route to the latter. It would occur in or depend upon the support of the most advanced industrial societies. It would be the work of the proletariat, the most advanced, industrialized and consciously rational and collectivized part of the population. It would result in the abolition of private property and the disappearance of classes and, consequently, in the withering away of state and law. It would see, therefore, the inauguration of a new unalienated cooperative society of human self-determination and freedom. The proletariat would bring this about because it was the truly universal class that had no particular standpoint or interest but represented the whole of humanity. The proletariat, indeed, became for Marx the philosopher-king, combining rational knowledge and rational action, knowing and doing in one. For Hegel, the great actors in history—Alexander, Napoleon, etc.—had served the cunning of reason, not appreciating themselves the significance and inevitable results of their own action. Hegel's philosopher, on the other hand, did understand the significance of history, but, like the owl of Minerva, was wise only after the event. The proletariat would both understand and act rationally and with increasing self-consciousness, as the revolution took shape.[3]

In the end, both the rise and the development of communist states point to the untenability of Marx's essentialist theory of history as progression through successive, logically inevitable "social formations" and of his picture of the working class and the coming socialist revolution. The working class, both before and for a century since Marx's death, has shown no signs of fitness for the role of philosopher-king. It has shared in all the prejudices and confusions of the age and added many of its own. It has not been the bearer of rationality in industry but, on the contrary, a frequent enemy of industrial progress and rationalization. Proletarians (i.e. workers) have supported their countries in war, and, as industrial civilization progressed, they have turned more and more to what Lenin called "economism," the pursuit of sectional material interests and of short-term goals. They neither made this century's communist revolutions nor did they come to control them. Affluence under capitalism, not deprivation, has widened their vision in recent years. The communist revolutions that can genuinely be called revolutions and not military take-overs or coups—those in Yugoslavia and China, for instance—have not been the result of an uprising by a conscious and disciplined proletariat, but the result of a collapse of the old régime either in war or because of its financial incompetence, aggravated by the sufferings of the peasantry and the landless and, most importantly, precipitated by the alienation of growing numbers of a special, non-Marxist class, the intelligentsia. They have been rebellions or revolutions against the old order, against pre-capitalist attitudes, traditions, and methods of government. They have been most strikingly successful not in societies where industrialization is very advanced and the proletariat is a significant section of the population, but in peasant societies that could also plausibly be called highly authoritarian or even, in Marx's sense, Asiatic despotisms—societies in which the state has long been stronger than the rest of society and the controller and initiator of all social and economic progress. The basis of communism is not Marx's vision of a spontaneous uprising by the working class that would represent the majority of the nation. It is Lenin's tactically brilliant elaboration of techniques for capturing state power through a disciplined and conspiratorial party that represents "consciousness" instead of spontaneity; it is his blueprint for a system of one-party rule that would subordinate all significant social activity to the control of a one-party state. That is not what Marx intended; it is what many aspects of his theory and especially his conception of the proletariat's "historical role" made possible.[4]

The outstanding thing about organized Marxists, as distinct from other socialists, has been their keen appreciation of the importance of power. The doctrine of the inevitability of revolution, the doctrine that state and law represented the will of the ruling class, the doctrine that the bourgeoisie would fight bitterly and relentlessly to retain its privileges and the doctrine that the economic arrangements of society were the key to everything else implied precisely what Lenin believed—that social progress was a matter of war, that the so-called dictatorship of the proletariat must be relentless and pervasive, and that a disciplined conscious party that understood and used power could change the character of society and control the destiny of mankind, provided it understood the direction of economic organization and development and the role that the state could play in both this and the moral, social and political transformation of mankind.

In communist and most Western views, then, Soviet culture is a profoundly politicized and consciously totalitarian culture. The Communists, admittedly, object to the word *totalitarian* in so far as it is used to imply that there is a specific societal type transcending the orthodox Marxist classification or in so far as it is used to suggest important parallels between communist government on the one hand and fascist or Nazi government on the other. But they, too, will concede that Marxism-Leninism as the "guiding ideology" of Soviet people, and the Communist Party as the supreme expression of historical destiny and the true social interest, do and should permeate and control all aspects of life in the Soviet socialist society. The distinction between private and public, the emphasis on individual values abstracted from social life, and the alleged autonomy of separate social or cultural spheres, they will argue, are categories based on the vicious separation of man from man that are characteristic of bourgeois production and bourgeois life. Human rights, taken by themselves, are empty abstractions that do not pervade society logically or historically, and cannot be treated as standing either above or outside class and political struggles.

The two fundamental features of Marxism that made it an effective ideological weapon in the struggle against autocracies—its monism and its progressivism, rightly criticized by Professor W. W. Bartley III as ascribing to reason a certainty that it cannot attain—also combined to make Marxism a suitable ideological basis for totalitarian control. Marx's insistence on the absence of social discontinuities, his emphasis on the social character of man and of all human activities, struck squarely and not entirely ineffectively at the nineteenth century liberal's elevation of the private conscience and the private sphere of life. The Marxist classification of societies in terms of essential characteristics, and the Marxist view that historical developments flowed in a single stream, implied the view that any given society was a finite whole, ruled by pervasive principles, subject to domination by a single class. That is why, in the face of all the evidence of complexity, Marxists still persist in talking about *the* ruling class and *the* system. Much as the Marxist doctrine of the class struggle may have done to inspire and strengthen the development of truly pluralistic views of society, this development took place entirely outside the Marxist fold. For the Marxist, the doctrine of the class struggle carried an essential anti-pluralistic message—like Hegel's dialectic, class conflict was but a phase in the development of the One. The final goal of history lay in the coming to power of a single class that was no longer a class, but the whole of Man, in the creation of a society that was free, but no longer rent by competing interests and "plurality of thinking." Even before the achievement of this goal, the doctrine of a pervasive class struggle denied the autonomy or independence of any political field or demand, just as the admittedly complex strain of economic reductionism in Marxism denied the autonomy or independence of any social or cultural field. Nothing could claim the right to be considered apart from the "social base" that gave it birth and the social interest it served.

Faced by autocracy and involved in revolutionary struggle, men and women tend to follow those who can point to a single, concrete, and yet seemingly all-embracing aim. Because Marxist theory had been elaborated in the context of the advancing industrial economies of the West, and because Marx was more than a mere ideologue of revolution, it was not at all clear by Marxist standards that Russia had reached, in 1881, in 1905, or in 1917, the stage that made it ripe for a proletarian revolution. In fact, it was clear it had not, and the decision to go ahead amounted to a radical rejection of Marxist "historical materialism," of the Marxist belief that history could not be made by will, and that the state only served and reflected economic realities independent of it. But once such doubts were suppressed or swept aside by the Bolshevik victory and Lenin's elaboration of the claims of "consciousness" as opposed to those of "spontaneity," Marxist essentialism—as expressed in the theory of revolutions and the doctrine of the dictatorship of the proletariat—was able to provide such an aim. From the transfer of power, everything would follow; the dictatorship of the proletariat was the necessary and the sufficient ground for socialism, for communism, for the complete liberation of man. Combined with Marxist teleology, with the belief in history's progress toward an ultimate end, Marxist monism was also able to reduce what others had thought of as the realm of values. The Revolution, the "historic role and tasks of the Party," and the coming of Communism became the ultimate moral end in terms of which all was to be judged. Nor were such judgments mere individual judgments, they were the judgments of history itself. No wonder that the revolutionary Angelica Balabanoff could write, after reading Plekhanov's *The Development of the Monistic View of History* (the primer of a whole generation of Russian Marxists): "I found it exactly what I needed at the time, a philosophy of method that gave continuity and logic to the processes of history and endowed my own ethical aspirations, as well as the revolutionary movement itself, with the force and dignity of an historical imperative."[5] To rule in the name of history is to rule completely. To the imperatives of history there can be no opposition. The continuing importance and appeal of Arthur Koestler's *Darkness at Noon* lies in its appreciation of the role of this belief in the shaping of the Marxist mentality. But we know now, from the *Confessions of an Old Bolshevik* and other revelations about Bukharin's motives for "confession," that Koestler overrated, even then, the extent to which old Bolsheviks still believed.

II

The logical structure and ambitions of Marx's theory made it easily convertible into the ideological foundation of totalitarian rule. But the empirical content on which it based much of its appeal was a content tied to specific social circumstances and events. Marxism was an ideology and a critique of the period of transition *into* fully-fledged industrial society; in the *Communist Manifesto*, one might almost say, Marx and Engels mistook the birth-pangs of a new social order for its death-pangs. Its claim to be a universal science reflects a period of cultural and technological development in which science was beginning to replace religion and morality as the guide and hope of mankind, but in which the intellectual division of labour and the accumulation of knowledge had not yet reached the point where the conception of a universal science absorbing and explaining all specialisms would become wildly implausible. Its emphasis on economic organization and economic interests as the foundation and content of power was born of a period of almost violent economic and social change, in which tradition, custom, and habits of ruling and of obedience seemed to have been swept away in a flood of economic innovation and reorganization.

Karl Marx, as Alfred G. Meyer has argued for instance, wove three fundamental strands into a single, majestic system—a radical critique of bourgeois industrial civilization as dehumanizing man, an optimistic theory of progress pointing to the ultimate overcoming of all such dehumanization and alienation, and a sober and respectably scientific investigation of society.[6] The unity of this system, the suppression of contradiction between the three strands, depended upon Marx's conception of the historical role of the proletariat as the bearer of further progress, as the group that would unite theory and practice to overcome the exploitation and dehumanization of man. When events in the advanced industrial societies began to show that Marx's conception of the proletariat and its inevitable destiny was false, as events indeed began to show from 1848 onward, the disintegration of classical Marxism began.

The point may be approached in yet another way, as it has been approached by Adam B. Ulam.[7] The birth and rapid development of industrial society in an initially agrarian social setting impose enormous strain and social dislocation upon those who are torn out of their agrarian environment and the placid idiocy of rural life to become the new urban, industrial proletariat. Ulam suggests that the peasant's reaction to the new social role forced upon him is at first fundamentally anarchist in content; he combines strong hostility to the machine and industrial society with a longing for an idealized version of the village commune. But this only creates an unbearable tension in his daily life; slowly he must learn to stop dreaming that someone will smash the machines and accept the new industrialization on which his whole power of earning has come to depend. It is at this stage that Marxism evolves as an ideology for the new working class. On the one hand, it promises the worker the same as the anarchists promise: a true community of mankind, in which the *Gemeinschaft* of agrarian life will be re-established in freer and more splendid form. On the other hand, it teaches the worker to accept industrialization as the very means by which this truly human freedom will be brought about. It sings paeans to the bourgeoisie's role in extending man's productive capacities. It deflects the worker's hostility away from the machine toward the owner of the machine and the government that protects the owner; it shows the worker the power he can have within the industrial system itself. Marxism, thus, "receives its historical significance from its ability to combine anarchism—the most violent protest against industrialism —with an intense cult of technology and a conviction of the historical necessity and blessings of industrialism;"[8] it becomes (as it became in Germany) the inspirer and educator of many workers in their transition to a fully industrial life. But when the industrial society and the industrial ethos have become firmly established (as they did in Germany around 1900, and in England earlier), Marxism loses its relevance. The workers turn to laborism and the demand for better housing and higher wages, the middle classes look for status and security. The disintegration of Marxism referred to by Meyer sets in apace precisely because the proletariat ceases to perform the function vital for Marxist hopes. Thus in Germany, from 1900 or so onward, the Marxism of the German Social-Democratic Party served mainly to frighten the middle classes; it had less significant effect on social policies or even on the practical demands of the working class and of the SPD itself. In Russia towards the end of the nineteenth century, on the other hand, Marxism was relevant as it is relevant in agrarian societies turning toward industrialization today. Russia was being rapidly precipitated into the industrial age while her society was of the type to maximize anarchist reactions. It was on a wave of anarchist reaction that the Bolsheviks came to power in 1917, when Lenin deliberately deepened the anarchist content of Marxism to make a direct appeal to the peasant with his slogan of "Land, Peace and Bread"; once in power, he used Marxism to intensify the cult of technology, to make socialism depend upon electrification. Just as Marxism could make bearable for the worker the smoke and misery of the growing industrial settlements of the West, so it could palliate for the Russian the crash programmes of the Stalinist dictatorship, just as it palliated the crash programmes of the Chinese dictatorship in the period now called "the rule of the Gang of Four." (The revival of Marxism in Western European societies in recent years is not based on the industrial worker, but on new crises of post-industrial society and of the cult of technology in general; it is based on the Marxism of 1844-48 rather than the Marxism of the 1870s.)

To what extent the Bolshevik and Communist Chinese rise to secure power can be ascribed to the appeal and legitimizing function of their ideology and to what extent it was a result of cynical opportunism and single-minded use of terror (not to speak of invasion and the incompetence of those who opposed Communism) is a matter of dispute, and it will no doubt remain so. There is no dispute among serious students of communist societies that Marxism as a legitimating ideology disintegrates as those societies pass beyond the mobilizational stages of rapid revolutionary change and forced industrialization into a modern industrial and post-industrial ethos and as the government relaxes political control of all areas of social life. Complexity, the need for state and legal organization, the emergence of classes, strata, and interest groups become all too evident. Marxism begins to be judged by its present achievements and not its future claims, and it is found wanting—implicitly by the leadership, explicitly by the population. In area after area, Marxist categories are quietly dropped, reinterpreted, combined with non-Marxist positions.

The growth and stabilization of Soviet power, then, has been accompanied by a drastic decline in Soviet prestige, internally and externally—a decline exacerbated by the enormous gap between Soviet and Marxist ideological pretensions and the realities of "actually existing socialism" in the communist world. Of course, the Soviet Union still has its clients, driven by hatreds at home rather than admiration for the Soviets abroad, by their need for support or even more disreputably by the sympathy that one dictator readily feels for another. Nevertheless, the disintegration of Marxism as a social theory, as an ideology, and above all as a moral beacon for mankind, has been consummated by the widespread recognition that it helped to produce and justify, as the socialist humanist Steven Lukes puts it, "the Bolshevik terror during and after the Civil War. . .Stalin's terror, the purges and trials, the mass deportations and the vast network of labor camps . . . the social catastrophe of Mao's Cultural Revolution . . . the 'murderous utopia' of Pol Pot's Cambodia . . . [and] the grim, surveillance-minded, demoralized world of contemporary 'actually existing socialism', above all in the U.S.S.R. and Eastern Europe, where civil society and public life have been destroyed, and both marxist and moral vocabulary have become wholly devalued, the worthless currency of an empty rhetoric."[9] The sensitive outside observer of the Soviet Union is now struck, above all, by the pervasiveness of cynicism among Soviet people, by the sharp distinction they draw between "us" and "them" (the leadership or the *nomenklatura* or the Communist Party and the people, ideologists and "honest" people, intellectuals and workers, etc.). This is not to say that there are no ideological components in Soviet society that do command fairly widespread support, e.g. patriotism (even in the midst of self-deprecation on the technological, productive and economic side), populism, and dislike of foreigners and nations that are well-off. But they have broken loose from Marxism, if they ever were part of it, though they have also given the Soviet Union a Third World clientele, which shares with them prejudices and emotive slogans more easily once Marxism is no longer a more tough-minded complex ideology getting in the way of both sides in their increasingly unprincipled alliances.

III

What began, then, as the world's most political society, with the most pervasive politicizing ideology, has ended, in an important sense, as a society that has no true politics at all. Of course, if, as many of its students believe, politics is simply about who gets what, when, and how—about the allocation, or the authoritative allocation, of goods in a social system—then the Soviet Union is still supremely political. From this view, politics, government, and administration are closely linked, perform the same tasks, and all societies, including the U.S.S.R., are political societies. In so far as the allocation of goods is made much more directly and pervasively by means of governmental authority in the Soviet Union, the U.S.S.R. is indeed a supremely political society. Many have seen it and still see it as such.

An older, and in my view better, tradition deriving from Aristotle's *Politics* sees the political more narrowly. It draws a sharp distinction, as Aristotle does, between true politics or political government on the one hand and other (administrative, authoritarian) arrangements and forms of government or administration on the other. For Aristotle, political rule was that which is exercised among citizens who are free and equal in birth. It is to be sharply distinguished from family relationships, economic hierarchies, monarchical or tyrannical government, and even the rule of the *demos* or the people. Politics, in short, was for him the science of freedom, the public activity of free men, and in some societies women, who come to agreement through discussion, compromise, conciliation and bargaining, through reconciling diverse interests and defining particular common interests. Politics presupposed interests prior to politics. The existence of politics in this sense marked off the Greek world, or more accurately parts of the Greek world, from the empires surrounding it. That free world was fundamentally different from the universal dependence and subordination of all except the emperor in what Herodotus and subsequent theorists from Montesquieu to Hegel and Marx in his concept of the "Asiatic mode of production" have seen as satrapy or Oriental despotism. There, politics and constitutions were replaced by administration, public discussion between free citizens by the concept of service, of fulfilling one's duties. Of course, even in such societies, there may be forms of palace politics, but they are indulged in restricted circles and in a semi-clandestine fashion; they are not elevated into a public principle of social life.

That, I believe, also applies to the Soviet Union as opposed to the democratic world. The difference derives both from Russia's state-centered history since the Tartar yoke and from Marxism and Marxism-Leninism. For both classical Marxism and Soviet-inspired Marxism-Leninism, as I have striven to show, have no concept of politics, in the sense of a science of freedom, as part of the socialist society. Lenin, in the period between 1917 and 1924, paid some lip service to it. He may have actually believed that, as material and educational standards rose, a workers' democracy based on discussion between free and equal citizens would become possible, though he had no qualms in suppressing the Kronstadt Soviet. Trotsky and the Left Opposition at least half strove against Stalin, but not against Lenin, for party democracy as opposed to democratic centralism by violating the ban on fractions and seeking genuine party discussion at all levels. But crucial aspects of classical Marxist doctrine, and of their own interpretation of Marxism, were against them and continue to be against their successors. The concept of mobilization, by which the state and the party act on society, continues to replace the concept of politics in all non-dissident, non-revisionist communist thinking. The attempt to re-establish politics, indeed, has been the central issue between dissidents and suppressed revisionists on the one hand and their suppressors on the other. The image-building of a new generation of Soviet leaders, their interest in communication, is no substitute unless they go on to elevate politics over administration—and thus threaten both their dominance and the cohesion of the empire they control.

"The conflict of rights and duties," Marx wrote in *The German Ideology*, "is a contradiction that belongs only to bourgeois society."[10] Similarly, the conflict of interests was for him a contradiction that belonged only to the prehistory of mankind, to the societies of alienation, exploitation, and class division. In his early writings, his belief that rational democracy, rational law or rather rational freedom and true universality were possible, rested on a confused contrast between particularity and universality as qualitative, not quantitative, distinctions. Particularity, specificity and consequent conflict, divisiveness and disharmony were, for the young Marx, products of external determination, or heteronomy, of alienation. The truly self-determined was also the truly universal and the truly free, internally coherent, and rational, incapable of coming into conflict with that which was simply itself once more. In his doctoral thesis, Marx resolved the contradictions between the Epicurean atom as free and the attraction and repulsion between atoms with breathtaking sophistry; in being repelled or attracted by another atom, the atom is simply repelled or attracted by itself, since one atom is indistinguishable from another. It thus remains self-determined and therefore free.[11] In the end, Marx took the same view about people once they were truly rational and self-determined; conflict of interests between them became a logical impossibility.

Only a few years later, Marx resolved with the same sophistry the contradiction between the political state or community as a legislative power and as a representative power:

> The legislative power is representative here in the same sense as every function is representative, in the sense, for instance, that the cobbler, in so far as he fulfills a social need, is my representative, in the sense that every specific social activity, as a species of activity, represents only the species, i.e., a character of my own being, in the sense that every man represents the other. He is a representative in this case not through something else, which he symbolizes, but through that which he *is* and *does*.[12]

This, as I argued many years ago in my *The Ethical Foundations of Marxism*, is Marx's vision of the moral and historical end of man—the rational state which is the state of a human essence that is qualitatively and essentially universal. As such, it is self-distinguishing, but it absolutely precludes separation or conflict. We find in it a division of functions, but one that arises naturally and spontaneously, and that is not, allegedly, a fixed division of labour. Since each function is a manifestation of activity of the human essense, since each truly represents man's universal being, all functions are naturally harmonious components of a united social life. There is no call for an external power to apportion or to harmonize their various roles; there is no need for a coercive political state outside or above the society that rationally arranges itself, and there is no call for guarantees against such a state, tyrannical majorities, or abuse of power. The conflict of rights and duties, of private and public wills, of individual and society, disappears from the arena of history.

The conception of rational law and of a rational state with which Marx was still working in 1842 and the early part of 1843 quickly disappeared from his work to be replaced by a concept of a truly free and cooperative society in which people participate in free and cooperative activities. For Marx, they thus became truly universal, seeing in all their human fellows merely representatives of themselves, performing general human functions, having general human interests. In such a society, a society based on the free labour of the creative artist, there is no systematic conflict of interests and no politics; the choices that have to be made are technical choices of how best to use resources for agreed common ends. In so far as Marx continued to believe that the overcoming of alienation and the beginning of the true history of mankind would be attained with communism, he continued to reject the conception that politics was necessary for freedom, that a society based on voluntary associations of workers could not resolve all discussion into technical consideration of means. Whatever communist administrators may believe and act on privately, they still pretend publicly that all social and economic decisions are rational, technical decisions, scientific in character.

Marx's lack of a theory of politics is linked with but also accounts for the widely recognized principal weaknesses of Marxist social theory—the tendency towards class and economic reductionism, towards seeing all significant social conflict as reflecting or derived from one central and resolvable conflict—that between economic classes or between productive forces and relations of production. Revolutions are messy and bloody attempts at social reorganization that have well-known, widely recognized, and long-lasting negative features and effects. Honest men and women would not readily embark on pervasive revolution and social reconstruction unless other forms of protest and reform were impossible, if they did not believe that total social reconstruction was feasible, that there was a single factor or action from which all else would follow, making possible the millennium. Marxism, for a period, offered some that hope. It argued that private property and the division of labour were the necessary and sufficient base of all alienation, exploitation, and social conflict. Abolish them and conflict and divergence of interests would disappear. Politics would become unnecessary; government would cease to be coercive; rights would be unnecessary and people univerally respected; law would be replaced by self-administration. The inability of classical Marxism to come to grips with the concept of public political life, with political freedom and political democracy, with politics as the science of freedom, is one factor that accounts for its constantly decreasing legitimacy and relevance in established Marxist-Leninist states, but its refusal to acknowledge the problem is, like stupidity, also a source of strength. The concessions that have to be made and are being made in official Marxist-Leninist theory amount to a limited and controlled lip service and basically incoherent acceptance into Marxist theory of limited phrases from conventional democratic theory, bereft of political substance or bite. The state, we are told, is, under the conditions of socialism, no longer a class state but the state of all the people; even in class societies state and law serve some general, non-class functions—those of promoting and safeguarding interests common to the whole society or necessary to any society at all. The political functions of citizens are now divided, in contemporary Soviet theory, into representative, expert or professional, and direct functions, not all to be performed by all the people and treated virtually as separate inputs into a system of social administration, though they are also to be subordinated to the state-defined and above all Party-defined interests of socialist society.[13]

The problem may also be illustrated by considering Marxist-Leninist attitudes to law. The leading Soviet legal thinker of the period 1924-34, E.B. Pashukanis, was a good and perceptive Marxist, utterly true to Marx's thought, in developing the view that law was a bourgeois phenomenon to be contrasted with socialist administration. Law, he argued, as understood in the Western legal tradition and in the phrase "the rule of law" was a system of adjudication or of bargaining between equal and equivalent right-and-duty-bearing individuals; it involved presumptions against status, hierarchy, and the elevation of the public over the private or of the state over the individual. It was a system of horizontal relations between people and interests that were formally treated as equal. Administration and socialism, for Pashukanis on the other hand, rejected this equality and multiplicity of abstract interests and individuals; they elevated the socio-technical norm, social policy, and technical requirements, and rejected, in principle, so-called individual rights. They created a vertical system of subordination and sub-subordination that distinguishes administration from law.[14]

Pashukanis' interpretation of law is not that adopted in Marxist-Leninist theory today. His "legal nihilism" is flatly rejected, though both Soviet and Chinese theorists have come to see the point in Pashukanis's distinction as a distinction within legal systems between horizontal right-and-duty-oriented law and vertical subordinating administration-oriented regulation. The Chinese, for instance, believe that their economic law will be partly of the one type and partly of the other. All communist societies have taken over to some extent formal categories and structures, institutions and procedures of the Roman-based Western civil law system, though they subordinate all these to politics and policy and confine true civil relations to the unplanned economic sphere—at the time of the New Economic Policy in Russia and in China now as part of modernization—and to unpolitical aspects of civil life. But, since the 1960s, they have increasingly elevated the role of law in society and the importance of socialist legality by bureaucratizing the concept and the content of law. Law is now increasingly defined as "steering society," as representing the command of the state and the general social interest. The most striking feature of Marxist-Leninist theory of law is the glaring absence within it of a theory of justice as opposed to a theory of legal correctness, of legality, and the absence of a theory of rights. The trend, parallelled but not carried to the same extremes by Western Marxists, is to elevate public law over private law where those terms are used in the sense noted and developed by Gustav Radbruch, in his earlier period, when he contrasted the vertical elevation of policy and social interest in public law with the determination of rights and the elevation of a multiplicity of competing particular interests and individuals in private law. All societies and legal systems face a problem of reconciliation and accommodation, of compromise, between these trends or approaches. But Marxist-Leninist theory, like classical Marxism, does not admit that the problem exists. That is why it still has no theory or conception of politics as the science of freedom, and why it is inhospitable to a theory of rights even at the theoretical level, let alone at the practical. Liberal democrats see rights, as Carl Wellman does, as a "cluster of ethical liberties, claims, powers and immunities that together constitute a system of ethical autonomy possessed by an individual. . .vis-à-vis the state."[15]Social democrats accept this but add certain group rights—those of trade unions, minorities, etc. But collectivist socialists, above all Marxist-Leninists, when they leave behind utopia, see rights as essentially a matter for society, the state, to regulate—as deriving from society, not preceding it, as exercisable only with its approval. The growing strength of this view in the West is often underrated.

IV

Critics of the Soviet Union, external and internal, are rightly conscious of the extent to which the Soviet government and Party apparatus, in trampling on democracy, on civil and political liberties, also trample on rights. There is a rich and detailed literature about the extent to which the Soviet government limits rights at the theoretical level and disregards them, in utter defiance of its own international obligations under the U.S. Conventions and the Helsinki Accord at the practical level.[16]

Primarily, the significant human rights pressure on Soviet leaders, nevertheless, comes internally from Westernized intellectuals and Westernized nationalities in the Baltic states and the Ukraine, and externally from the satellites and international opinion. Russia itself, as countless historians and social theorists have noted, missed out on those European developments that gave rise to Western individualism, pluralism, and the concept of the rule of law, as well as to the doctrine of human rights. For centuries, the Russian state has been more powerful than all the rest of society put together and all classes and institutions, for some three hundred years, have been defined by and dependent on the state. Marxist theory, Leninist practice, and Russian realities and traditions have thus all combined to rob the demand for human rights and the observance of them of any strong institutional or internal ideological bases. Dissatisfaction with the government—and there is much dissatisfaction—focuses, especially among Russians, on such traditional complaints as the distinction between "us" and "them," shortages and mismanagement, corruption and hypocrisy, failure to respect or encourage honesty and decency—but not on the violation of rights. Thus the very language that Andrei Sakharov, for instance, has to use to promote the concept and cause of human rights does not appeal to Russian cultural and linguistic tradition; it reads like a translation from a *Time* or *Newsweek* editorial. The language of Solzhenitsyn, which does constantly appeal to Russian themes, makes no use of the concept of human rights, but concentrates instead on Russian conceptions of moral justice, righteousness, honesty and decency.[17]

Paradoxically, those who place hope on the development of a demand for actual, observed human rights in the Soviet Union fall back on the changes introduced by Marxist-Leninist ideology and Bolshevik administration, both of which, though for limited purposes and in limited ways, emphasize concepts of civil, political, economic, social, and cultural rights and, also to a limited extent, acknowledge these in Soviet legislation.

Professor Tay and I, like many others, have traced in detail elsewhere the human rights provisions in the various Soviet constitutions from the Declaration of the Rights of the Toiling and Exploited Peoples in 1918 to chapters 6 and 7 of the 1977 Soviet State Constitution (Articles 33-69) dealing with the "basic rights, freedoms and duties of citizens."[18] There has been a clearly discernible movement away from seeing class-rights in the context of class-struggle, and the now superseded dictatorship of the proletariat, towards seeing them as inhering in individual citizens; there has also been an excision of the discriminatory concepts of class-origin and class-affiliation from the constitutions and the law. Since 1936 there has been a formal acceptance of certain traditional civil and political rights—including, allegedly, equality before the law, equality of men and women, right of participation in management and administration of the state, voting and election, freedom of speech, press, assembly, meetings, street processions and demonstrations, right to asylum for foreigners, rights to associate in public organizations, right to profess any religion and to conduct religious worship, inviolability of the person and the home, right of privacy of correspondence and of telephone and telegraphic communication, and the right to complain against state action of officials. There has also been a growing emphasis on and extension of various economic and social rights—the right to work in appropriate occupations in so far as social requirements and opportunities permit, the right to housing, education, cultural benefits, to leisure and rest, paid holidays, extensions of social service and sport, health protection, maintenance in old age, sickness or disability. A certain growing convergence between the definition of rights, at the formal level, in the West and in Soviet society both reflects and makes possible the definition of such rights by international agreements and by the United Nations and its instrumentalities.

Nevertheless, as almost all foreign writers have also noted, there is a fundamental difference between the official Soviet conception of rights and the traditional Western conception, which goes not only to the matter of their observance, but to their very formulation. The Soviet state bluntly rejects any conception that individual human rights precede, logically, historically or morally, any form of political association or that they inhere in human beings as such. Rights have been presented in Soviet constitutions as conferred on individuals by society, acting through the state and the party. They are defined by the state; they may not be exercised except in conformity with the interests of society and the socialist aims of the state; they involve corresponding but logically unrelated duties to society and the state. They are not absolute rights but conditional rights; they are rights not against the state but rights designed to strengthen the bonds between the individual and the state. At the theoretical level, these openly expressed qualifications—more openly expressed in the 1977 constitution than in

Stalin's 1936 constitution, which no one expected to be observed—provide the formal justification for the abrogation of rights in any particular case where the state regards them as amounting to criticism or rejection of the socialist system. At the practical level, such justification is rarely required. Soviet constitutions and laws do not provide for the citizen directly to challenge the powers of the state or any infringements of his or her rights by the state. Such infringements, in theory, have to be pursued by the Procuracy. What is more, Soviet courts, as well as the Chinese, who follow the Soviet example, take the view that the constitution is not itself a law citable in court, but a 'basic law' that is in fact only *a basis for law.* Its provisions do not come into effect unless and until enacted in specific legislation. In the field of human rights, or at least of review of administrative actions, it is being called for—but has not yet come.

Recent developments in the Soviet Union—its growing economic complexity, educational sophistication, and social differentiation, as well as its greater reliance on legal-administrative forms of control—have involved an increasing elevation of legal-rational patterns of legitimacy that stand in some tension with the traditional pattern of Marxist-Leninist and Stalinist ideology. The declining role of direct commands, and the increase of exchanges between various institutions and groups, do involve greater autonomy, and "rights-claims" vis-à-vis the state apparatus. Some think that Soviet society, in becoming a modern industrial and post-industrial society, cannot escape Weberian legal rationality and, in the process, increasing rights-talk and rights-claims.

In principle, there is truth in this; in practice, the development of rights ideology in the Soviet Union is subject to very severe limitations, and not only to those of control from above. One has only to compare the social position and social role of the Workers' Defense Committee (KOR), the Human Rights Committee (ROPC:O) and Solidarity in Poland with the marginal nature of the Initiative Group for the Defense of Human Rights in the U.S.S.R., the Human Rights Committee of the U.S.S.R., the Moscow Branch of Amnesty International, etc., in the Soviet Union. For virtually all the satellites, and some of the non-Russian Soviet Republics, Marxist-Leninist ideology, the Soviet pattern adopted by their rulers, and the anti-human rights provisions of their constitutions can easily be presented and are mostly seen as foreign impositions, violating local traditions. In the R.S.F.S.R., and for Russians in the rest of the Soviet Union, they are less patently so. The bad things about Soviet rule, no doubt, are often ascribed by Russians to foreigners or Jews (especially Jews). But the Soviet state does elevate the Russian core of the Soviet empire above others internally, and Soviet power above foreigners abroad. I suspect it still commands an overwhelming loyalty and legitimacy from the vast mass of Russians, when confronted by foreign, including satellite, criticism or hostility. The state is widely criticized and distrusted in economic matters, but it is not, I believe, confronted by a developed and widespread ideology of human rights clung to by Russians in principle as a weapon against Soviet authoritarianism.

Nevertheless, as many contributors to these volumes emphasize, there are great tensions and dissatisfactions in the Soviet Union. There are economic dissatisfactions that are widespread among Soviet people, and signs that the Soviet system cannot improve its performance without serious loss of authority. There are urgent regional, ethnic, national, and religious dissatisfactions, that affect a smaller range of people but are felt much more sharply. The latter will perhaps latch most readily on to human rights claims and demands and welcome their becoming matters of international concern. The ideology of human rights, in short, gives support to those who, primarily for other reasons, are sharply critical of the Soviet system and may become more critical. But a principled demand for human rights is not, I believe, a major component of the mass Soviet scene.

V

The international campaign for human rights, promoted by the United Nations and its agencies, and for a period adopted as a major U.S. foreign policy plank by President Carter, unquestionably does give great encouragement to many of the justified critics and protesters in the Soviet Union. The Soviet government, however, has been far from inept in taking advantage of the readiness with which questions of human rights can be obfuscated, politicized and made the subject of shameless selectivity as a result of the political divisions of the world, the comparatively narrow range of democratic regimes and convictions in the world, and major stresses and strains within Western democracies themselves.

The thrust of the United Nations *Declaration on Human Rights* and the subsequent conventions, confirmed to some degree by the Helsinki Accord, distinguishes the conceptions of international law taking shape under the United Nations from those that had been promulgated by the League of Nations. The notion that rights under international law can be vested in groups of individuals or in individuals as such, and not only in states, is gaining ground, even though United Nations provisions can only extend this conception through the agreement of parties to be bound. The Soviet Union totally rejects this view of international law, at least in respect of individuals or groups within its own territory. This is true not only in relation to the traditional political and civil liberties, but in relation to economic, social and cultural rights and to the new collective rights, including the rights of peoples, that are now being promoted in the United Nations by sections of the Third World, with at least some selective support from the Soviet Union. The increased role of the Third World in the United Nations during the 1970s—one might say indeed its dominance—has certainly helped the Soviet Union in achieving a major shift of emphasis and direction in United Nations conceptions of human rights. The Covenant on Civil and Political Rights and Covenant on Economic, Social and Cultural Rights were proclaimed and opened for signature at the same time, in 1966. In the last decade, however, there has been increasing propaganda, especially within UNESCO, that economic, social and cultural rights are at least fully as important as civil and political rights and in fact provide their necessary foundation. Now, a new group of collective rights, the so-called third generation of "rights of solidarity," is being promoted as also having equivalent status and as involving significant tinkering with the rights of individuals and with civil and political rights. Something like agreement on the rights of (some) peoples and the rights of self-determination (for some) has been reached in the United Nations only by interpreting self-determination not to mean democratic self-government, but merely the rejection of formal colonial rule and Western economic imperialism or neocolonialism. In the rhetoric of the U.N. General Assembly, all this has become identified with racism and western European domination; economic, military, and political hegemony on the part of socialist African or Asian states is passed over in silence. An eminent international lawyer, Antonio Cassesse, has summarized the totally different conceptions of self-determination and the rights of people represented in the United Nations. He writes:

> Socialist countries understand self-determination essentially as the liberation of non-self-governing peoples from colonial domination. They have broadened the concept—under pressure from African and Arab countries—to include liberation from racist domination (South Africa and Southern Rhodesia) and from foreign occupation (Arab territories occupied by Israel). Moreover, with the support of Afro-Asian countries (which are worried lest the collapse of colonialism should involve the breaking up of colonial territories), the socialist countries deny that self-determination can legitimate secessions. Thus, to socialist countries, self-determination means only "external" self-determination and only for peoples subject to colonial or racist rule or to foreign occupation. The achievement of independent status by peoples living in non-racist sovereign States entails the implementation of self-determination. This applies in particular to socialist States: "only in socialist States and through the sovereignty achieved by them can self-

determination be completely realized." Ultimately, for sovereign and independent States self-determination becomes tantamount to the right of nonintervention. This point is very important and deserves to be particularly
stressed. According to socialist countries, self-determination, considered as
the right to nonintervention, means the right that foreign States shall not
interfere in the life of the community *against the will of the government*. It
does not include the right that a foreign State shall not interfere in the life
of the community *against the interests of the population* but at the request
or at any rate with the tacit approval of the government.

Western countries have, on many occasions, attacked this outlook for
being too restrictive and one-sided. They maintain that the right of peoples
oppressed by totalitarian regimes must be recognized and that in any case
self-determination must include respect for fundamental freedoms and the
basic rights of individuals. The close link between self-determination and
individual human rights is one of the main features of the Western doctrine.
As was stated in 1972 by the U.S. delegate to the Third Committee of the
General Assembly, "Freedom of choice is indispensable to the exercise of
the right of self-determination." For this freedom of choice to be meaningful, there must be corresponding freedom of thought, conscience, expression, movement and association. Self-determination entails legitimate, lively
dissent and testing at the ballot box with frequent regularity.[19]

A second distinguishing trait of the Western view, according to Cassesse,
is its emphasis on the universality of self-determination. For Western states
the principle of self-determination must be regarded as applying to all
peoples, not just to certain specific categories of peoples, those suffering
from racism or imperialism, where any non-European, non-Western state is
automatically and wrongly taken to be incapable of either. The question of
indigenous peoples, for example, is certainly treated more sympathetically by
prosperous Western states than by Afro-Asian, Islamic, or Marxist-Leninist
blocs, though no country is fully at ease with the problems involved in
recognizing them as nations within a nation, peoples within a people.

The literature on human rights is voluminous and presents us with no sign
of general agreement on their nature, their definition or their source, or on
the basic moral principle or justification on which they rest. The lists of
human rights contained in the U.N. *Declaration on Human Rights* and the
Covenants on Civil and Political, and Social, Economic, and Cultural Rights
are widely recognized, by philosophers at least, as being conceptually
disparate and muddled, containing rhetoric and crucially important inner
conflicts. The rights elevated in the Declaration are the most coherent—but
their coherence derives from their close connection with European liberalism
and democratic traditions, and they are in fact being safeguarded to a
reasonable degree only in countries that have that tradition. Even so, they

cannot be and are not presented as uniformly absolute; various escape clauses recognize that they have to be considered in a concrete social context. The social climate and demands furthered by many of their Western radical supporters are often destructive of many of these rights and shamelessly selective and biased in elevating some of them and not others. We do not hear much today of the primacy that the U.N. *Declaration* ascribes to the family, or of the U.N.-endorsed right of parents to choose the kind of education (which includes moral education) they would like their children to have. The right of property guaranteed in the *Declaration*—and in respect of personal property such guarantee is part of the constitutions of most communist countries—was simply dropped from the *Covenant on Civil and Political Rights*; it has not been heard of again. Of direct interest and concern to the philosopher is the failure of the U.N. documents to distinguish between absolute rights ascribed to human beings as a direct consequence of their being simply human (e.g. not to be tortured), rights ascribed to them in virtue of their entering into specific relationships (e.g. as employees entitled to certain labour conditions, etc.), and rights dependent on their capacities or those of the society (e.g. pensions and education). The documents fail to distinguish between rights that are immunities, imposing clear duties of noninterference on all others, and not normally dependent on general social conditions and variations, and rights that are claims to benefits, which are both dependent on social conditions and variations and which, unlike immunities, do not impose duties on a clearly defined addressee. Nor have the proponents of the U.N. *Covenants*, as opposed to their critics, been willing to consider seriously the sharp and fundamental clash between civil and political rights, that limit the power of the state, and social, economic, and cultural rights that positively demand ever-increasing state organization of society. The only constitutions that successfully but brutally resolve these serious conflicts in the theory of rights are the communist constitutions which provide, on the model of the constitution and legal codes of the U.S.S.R., that all rights granted by the constitution or in the codes shall be exercised only in conformity with the social, economic, and political system of the country and the purposes of building socialism. The United Nations, indeed, and the organizations concerned to promote it, might have been expected to be an arena for discussion, an intellectual battleground, between the very different approaches to human rights, and conceptions of their role in social and political life, that mark off democratic societies from non-democratic ones. There is no serious engagement between these views in the U.N. or its propaganda organs, because democratic representatives there have simply shirked real battle, honestly admitting their shortcomings and exercising restraint in drawing attention to the dishonesty and cynicism of the vast majority of signatories to the *Declaration* and *Covenants* and the shameless selectivity they exercise in criticizing other countries.

Despite Marx, governments and even social formations fall not as the result of iron necessity, of internal contradictions that burst through the integument, but from a host of contingent and often unforeseeable factors—financial crisis, war, incompetence at the top, rising expectations, and actual improvements confronted by a sharp and sudden reversal. There is, as the Soviet government is well aware, less danger in trying to sit on bayonets for an extended period than in removing them and then wanting to put them back. Autocracy, historically, has proved no stronger than the weakest and most stupid autocrat; collective leadership, backed by a systematic, experienced and pervasive party apparatus clear about its goals and how to achieve them in the selection of leading personnel, is much stronger. The Party in the Soviet Union may not deliver the economic goods to the people, but it has not lost its political grip over the society, its capacity to run many lines at once or, above all, the glory of having turned the militarily declining Russia of 1850-1917 into a great superpower, capable of confronting the only other superpower. Its achievements rest not on having the better or the more convincing ideology, or on satisfying the needs and demands of its population to a greater extent than other governments. Its achievements rest on the willingness to do whatever is necessary to carry out the goals of the leadership—no matter how great the brutality, the cynicism, the indifference to justice, liberty, equality, or material welfare required.

The concept of human rights, certainly, provides one basis for justified criticism of the Soviet Union. Personally, I believe that concepts of justice, of freedom, and, above all, of care and compassion for one's own population provide an even stronger basis. Not only rights, but justice, morality, intellectual honesty, and ordinary decency are totally discounted in Soviet official ideology and by Soviet official life.

At the same time, this ruthless goal-oriented form of rule by command is increasingly recognized not to produce at all efficiently or impressively for the majority of the population those material satisfactions for which many people, though not all, will surrender much of their liberty and self-respect. In a fiercely competitive world, these inefficiencies may threaten increasingly the independence of action and the international pretensions and internal self-satisfaction of the régime. Above all, as the Soviet régime well appreciates, it is seriously threatened by allowing expectations, material and spiritual, to rise too quickly, or by permitting Soviet citizens to believe that their lives can and should be constantly compared with the lives of people in more affluent and freer countries. This problem, too, the Party continues to handle with relative skill—effectively bribing those who can compare on condition of their loyalty to the régime and its policy of suppression, censorship, and lies.

In the long term, in the very long term, isolation, censorship, playing on ignorance and chauvinism are made more difficult by the increasing need for technological sophistication, rising standards of living in many parts of the world, and increased communications throughout all of it. In these matters, too, the Soviet leadership has proved itself to be superficially adaptable without being willing to dismantle or even prejudice any of the essential bases of its control. If and when a collapse of the Soviet system occurs, its immediate cause will have been a contingent and I believe unpredictable fact—a small thing, in retrospect, to bring down such a mighty régime if it had not been morally, rather than physically, rotten to the core.

NOTES

1. Eugene Kamenka, ed., *The Portable Karl Marx* (New York and Harmondsworth: Viking Penguin, 1983), xi. See that volume generally for selections illustrating the assertions about Marx in this paper.
2. For more details see *The Portable Karl Marx*, 67.
3. The concept of the proletariat in Karl Marx, on which my former Ph.D. student, Dr. David Lovell, has completed a book, is a subject surprisingly, or perhaps not surprisingly, neglected by Marxists. Lovell's work shows quite clearly how Marx sees the proletariat conceptually, as a logical category that reconciles the contradiction between Communism as the movement of the deprived working class and nineteenth century socialism as the proclamation of the general social interest, by being itself a "universal" class. Philosophically, at first, then politically and finally economically as "labour," the proletariat is a vital component in Marx's system, its nature determined by the logical requirements of the system and not by the empirical development of the working class as an existing social group.
4. A recent addition to the prolific literature on this point is David Lovell, *From Marx to Lenin: An Evaluation of Marx's Responsibility for Soviet Authoritarianism* (Cambridge: Cambridge University Press, 1984).
5. Angelica Balabanoff, *My Life as a Rebel* (London: Hamish Hamilton, 1938), 13.
6. In his *Marxism: The Unity of Theory and Practice. A Critical Essay* (Cambridge, Mass: Harvard University Press, 1954 and subsequent reprints), *passim.*
7. In his *The Unfinished Revolution* (New York: Random House, 1960), *passim.*
8. Adam B. Ulam, *The New Face of Soviet Totalitarianism* (Cambridge, Mass.: Harvard University Press, 1963), 21.
9. Steven Lukes, *Marxism and Morality* (Oxford: Oxford University Press, 1985), xii.

10. Marx and Engels, *Gesamtausgabe*, (Moscow, Frankfurt a.M.: Marx-Engels Institute, 1927) f. Abt. I, Band 5, s.192.

11. See Marx's doctoral dissertation "The Difference between the Democritan and the Epicurean Philosophy of Nature" and the discussion in E. Kamenka, *The Ethical Foundations of Marxism*, 2nd ed. (London: Routledge & Kegan Paul, 1972), 17-47, esp. 20-23.

12. Karl Marx in his 1843 (Manuscript) critique of Hegel's *Philosophy of Right, Marx-Engels Gesamtausgabe* (1927f), Abt. I, Band I-i, s.542, discussed in my *Ethical Foundations of Marxism*, 32-47.

13. For (German) translations of representative Soviet texts and an excellent discussion, see Friedrich-Christian Schroeder, *Wandlungen der sowjetischen Staatstheorie* (Munich: C.H. Beck, 1979. See also Yu. A. Tikhomirov, "Razdelenie vlastei ili razdelenie truda," *Sovetskoe gosudarstvo i pravo* no. 1 (1967): 14, transl. in *Soviet Law and Government* 5, no. 4 (Spring 1967): 11-19, and "Vlast,' demokratiya, professionalizm" ("State Power, Democracy, Professionalism"), *Sovetskoe gosudarstvo i pravo* no. 1 (1968): 24.

14. See E.B. Pashukanis, *Obshchaia teoriya prava i Marksizm* (Moscow: Sotsialisticheskaia Akademia, 1924). There are now several English translations. For references and discussion, see E. Kamenka and A.E.S. Tay, "Public Law—Private Law," in S.I. Benn and G.F. Gaus, eds., *Public and Private in Social Life* (London: Croom Helm, 1983), 67-92.

15. Carl Wellman, "A New Conception of Human Rights," in E. Kamenka and A.E.S. Tay, eds., *Human Rights* (London: E. Arnold, 1978), 48-58.

16. See, for instance, Georg Brunner, "Recent Developments in the Soviet Concept of Human Rights," in F.J.M. Feldbrugge and W.B. Simons, eds., *Perspectives on Soviet Law for the 1930s* (The Hague: Martinus Nijhoff Publishers, 1982), 37-52; Richard N. Dean, "Beyond Helsinki: The Soviet View of Human Rights in International Law," in *Virginia Journal of International Law* 20, no. 1 (Fall 1979): 55-95; John T. Evrard, "Human Rights in the Soviet Union: The Policy of Dissimulation," *De Paul Law Review* 29 (1980): 819-68; F.J.M. Feldbrugge, "The Soviet Human Rights Doctrine in the Crossfire Between Dissidents at Home and Critics Abroad," *Vanderbilt Journal of Transnational Law* 13, no. 2-3 (Spring-Summer 1980): 451-66; Eugene Fryer, "Soviet Human Rights: Law and Politics in Perspective," *Law and Contemporary Problems* 43, no. 2 (Spring 1979): 296-307; David Kowalewski, "Human Rights Protest in the U.S.S.R.: Statistical Trends for 1965-78," *Universal Human Rights* 2, no. 1 (Jan.-Mar. 1980): 5-29; Christopher Osakwe, "Soviet Human Rights Law under the USSR Constitution of 1977: Theories, Realities and Trends" in *Tulane Law Review* 56 (1981): 249-93; Peter B. Reddaway, "Theory and Practice of Human Rights in the Soviet Union," D.P. Kommers and G.D. Loescher, *Human Rights and American Foreign Policy* (Notre Dame, Ind.: University of Notre Dame Press, 1979), 115-29; Daniel C. Turack, "Freedom of Transnational Movement: The Helsinki Accord and Beyond," *Vanderbilt Journal of Transnational Law* II, no. 4 (Fall 1978): 585-608; and the voluminous

and harrowing internal and emigré dissident literature. Each of the International Covenants—economic, social and cultural, as well as civil and political, and all the associated rights—are constantly and directly violated by Soviet authorities.

17. It should be noted, however, that a consciously liberal elevation of law and legal rights as foundations for democracy and progress was gaining strength in pre-revolutionary Russia from the 1860s onward. Its main carriers, the Kadets, were the strongest party in Russian cities. For a vindication of views unjustly ignored and vilified in revolutionary literature and Soviet accounts of Russian legal history, see A. Walicki, *The Legal Philosophies of Russian Liberalism*, (Oxford: Clarendon Press, 1986).

18. E. Kamenka and A.E.S. Tay, "Human Rights in the Soviet Union," *World Review* 19, no. 2 (June 1980): 47-60.

19. Antonio Cassesse, "Political Self-Determination—Old Concepts and New Developments," in A. Cassesse ed., *U.N. Law—Fundamental Rights: Two Topics in International Law*, (Rockville, MD: Sijtoff & Noordhoff, 1979), 154-5.

PART

II

CRISIS OF THE SOVIET SYSTEM

1

The Coming Crisis in the Soviet Union

R. V. BURKS

The thesis of this essay is that the chances of system breakdown in the Soviet Union within the next five to ten years are probably better than even.[1] By system breakdown I mean a Soviet version of the crises which took place in Hungary in 1956, in Czechoslovakia in 1968, in Yugoslavia in 1971, and in Poland in 1980. I do not, however, necessarily mean to assert that the existing Soviet regime might not in the end recover some form of control; but even in that case its mastery of the population would at the least have been severely put to the test.

The Failure of Central Planning

The secular slowdown in the rate of growth of the Soviet gross national product (GNP) which reached new and unforeseen lows beginning in about 1978, is likely, in my view, to provide the underlying cause of the event that I am attempting to envision. The rate of increase in the Soviet GNP has fallen from an annual average of seven percent in the 1950s, to five percent in the 1960s, and to three percent in the 1970s. Since 1978 it has hovered around two percent, and the Central Intelligence Agency has forecast that it will remain at that level throughout the present decade. Private scholars, however, have argued that there has been no increase per capita in net material product in recent years, and have even asked whether the Soviet economy has not stopped growing altogether.[2] Indeed the question may well be asked whether the decline will not continue until the rate of growth is clearly negative and headed on down.

For the primary cause of the decline in the rate of growth appears to be the nature of the Centrally Planned Economy (CPE), whose crucial weakness—at least in its Soviet version—has been its inherently low rate of technological innovation. Throughout its history the Soviet Union has had to import virtually every new technology from its point of origin, the industrial West and, despite vast expenditures, has, after an early spurt, gradually fallen further and further behind.[3] The low Soviet innovation rate results in a growth primarily dependent upon increased inputs of the factors of production, of labor, and of capital, and only secondarily upon increases in the productivity of these factors. In this respect the CPE is the exact opposite of the market economy.[4]

Soviet dependence upon inputs has become more important as the pace of technological change in the West has continued to accelerate. The Soviet economy has so far been unable to absorb the technology of the latest (or third) industrial revolution through which the West has begun to put itself, that concentrated in the information processing and service industries. At the present day Moscow has made little progress in absorbing into its productive system such new breakthroughs as computers, microprocessors, fiber optics, xerography, lasers, and robots.[5] And this at a time when increments to inputs are becoming smaller and smaller.

Let us look at the Soviet economic problem in some detail, beginning our analysis with the decline in the availability of labor. In 1928, when forced-draft industrialization began, 82 percent of the Soviet population lived in villages; today the figure is 36 percent. As is generally recognized, urban dwellers have difficulty reproducing themselves, a problem which in the U.S.S.R. has been exacerbated by a perennial housing shortage. Even today one-fifth of all apartments are shared by two families. Moreover, Soviet contraceptives are difficult to find and, when available, not very reliable. Thus, Soviet woman rely primarily on abortion. In 1980 the number of abortions was admitted officially to be greater than the number of live births and in fact was probably much greater. Furthermore, the decline in the crude birth rate has been accompanied by a sharp increase in infant mortality, at one end of the life span, and by a rise in the proportion of pensioners, at the other.[6] Consequently the net annual addition to the labor force which was two million or more as late as the 1970s, will only average about 550,000 per year in the present decade. Meanwhile the Kremlin is already importing satellite labor: lumberjacks from Bulgaria, coal miners from North Korea, common labor from Vietnam assigned to stations in Siberia. It is said that Hanoi has agreed to pay off its war debt of $3 billion to Moscow with "guest" workers of this ilk.[7]

The impact on the rate of growth of GNP of this decline in increments to labor is magnified by the fact that although two-thirds of the Soviet gross industrial product is turned out in the Russian and Ukrainian Republics, their populations are not reproducing themselves. The current increase in the Soviet population overall is concentrated instead in the Muslim republics of the Caucasus and Central Asia. Workers of Mohammedan faith, however, even if they are unemployed, are reluctant to accept assignment outside their homelands.[8] Thus, in the present decade it appears no longer possible to raise the gross national product by massive additions to the labor force, and the annual rate of growth is likely to remain flat unless the volume of new investment can be raised enough to compensate, or unless the productivity of capital and labor can be elevated, or both.

But as the annual rate of growth of GNP has declined, the absolute quantity of the total product that could be siphoned off for investment has fallen proportionately. Already in the years 1961-1975 that share ran between 26 and 28 percent of the total, a proportion which is close to the upper limit that an economy can invest without limiting either consumption or defense. Thus Brezhnev and his colleagues were forced, as early as 1975, to face the Hobson's choice of cutting either defense, consumption or investment. They chose investment, so that its share fell to 23 percent of GNP, by far the lowest in all of socialist Europe. Meantime, however, measured in terms of productive capacity created, the amount of additional capital required to produce a given unit of output had climbed steeply.[9] That left increased factor productivity as the one remaining hope of the Soviet leadership. And indeed we find that between 1965 and 1977 the Brezhnev leadership quadrupled Soviet importation of Western technology for that very reason, accepting a not inconsequential increase in the country's hard currency debt as it did so. Nonetheless, from the early seventies combined factor productivity suffered an annual decline of 0.8 percent.[10]

Thus the Soviet leadership seems to be trapped. It appears that for the foreseeable future there will be no substantial additions to the labor force, no significant increase in investment, and a slowly declining factor productivity. But before we undertake to examine the possible political consequences of this unexpected *cul-de-sac*, we must look at other aspects of the Soviet economic problem, those of infrastructure, energy, and health of the population.

Much of the rather astonishing Soviet achievement in rapid industrialization has been made possible by the deliberate neglect of infrastructure, of which agriculture is a prime example. Approximately one-fourth of the total crop is lost regularly, either because storage facilities are lacking or the network of rural roads is inadequate, not to speak of insufficient supplies of synthetic fertilizer—only now being corrected—and a farm population that is both overage and preponderantly female.[11]

Railroads are another problem. For want of highway and pipeline construction they are constantly overworked. Today much of the country's rolling stock, especially locomotives, is no longer reparable and must be replaced, while many marshaling yards have to be relaid. Perhaps the biggest problem of all, however, is a mounting shortage of energy, and indeed of raw materials generally. For some years it has been evident that extraction costs of these substances from traditional sources in the Ukraine and European Russia were becoming prohibitive. In 1982, for example, the investment cost per additional barrel of oil was about ten times what it had been in 1974. Today it seems clear that the energy and raw material base of the Soviet economy must be transferred from Europe to an inhospitable and distant Siberia, or to the even farther removed Soviet Far East. Delay appears to be out of the question as shown by the fact that two-thirds of Soviet hard-currency earnings, vital to the continued importation of advanced technology as well as of foodstuffs, are obtained through the sale of oil and gas.[12] And yet without massive foreign help it seems reasonable to believe that Soviet resources may not be equal to this monumental task.

The government in Moscow now finds itself faced with a situation in which the bulk of its industry is to be found in European Russia and the Ukraine, most of its cheap energy and raw materials in Siberia and the Far East where there is little in the way of infrastructure, and future increments to its labor force so far immovably located in Soviet Central Asia—the three elements being connected primarily by a railway network which needs to be rebuilt.

To the additional constraints on future growth imposed by the matters mentioned above must be added an additional factor, namely a deterioration in the health of the population. Among industrial states the Soviet Union has today the unique distinction of experiencing, after years of normally declining mortality rates, a sudden and significant increase in these rates, so much so that relevant demographic data, such as death rates by age and sex, are no longer made public.[13] By 1964 the crude death rate in the U.S.S.R. had fallen as low as 6.9 per thousand. Thereafter, however, it began to rise again and by 1980 had reached 10.3, an increase of 50 percent. This reversal is partly to be explained by the aging of the population, but virtually all age groups are affected. The increase in infant mortality, the rate of which is now probably three times that in the U.S., and the rise in the death rate among males 20-44 years of age, have been little less than startling. Male life expectancy has been shortened by an estimated four years, from age 66 to age 62, while female expectancy has remained at 73.5 years, causing the disproportion between the sexes to reach a new high and contributing to the growing number of one-parent families.[14]

The rise in infant mortality rates is due to a number of factors. That the average female undergoes three or four abortions in her lifetime (as compared with the .75 of her American counterpart) contributes, as does the spread of alcoholism and the growing number of fatherless families. Eighty-eight percent of working age people are gainfully employed in the Soviet Union, and the participation of females in the labor force is perhaps the highest in the world. This situation places a great burden on factory creches, which are inadequate both in the number and the training of their personnel. In contrast to conditions prevailing in the U.S., furthermore, such diseases as influenza, rickets, diphtheria and typhoid fever remain serious threats in the Soviet Union. The creches are frequently victimized by influenza.[15]

The prime cause of early death among males is, of course, alcoholism. Traditionally endemic in the U.S.S.R., the disease now has become pandemic. In 1978, there were 51,000 deaths in the Soviet Union from alcohol poisoning alone, more than 100 times the number in the U.S. Alcoholism is now spreading among women—especially those who are divorced, widowed, or single—at an annual rate of increase of five percent. For the first time there are child alcoholics. The addiction is the primary cause of requests for divorce and is also a factor in the increasing incidence of mental retardation among children. In the seventies such retardation ran to three percent of live births, as compared with the United Kingdom, where it was 0.75 percent. Alcohol is also a problem in maintaining worker discipline in the factories. The disease is concentrated in the Slavic and Baltic republics. Almost as much of the family budget is spent for alcoholic beverages as is spent for food by an American family. As under the tsars, the sale of these beverages is a monopoly of the state and today the revenue from it is equal to the officially admitted expenditure for defense.[16]

Along with the increase in alcoholism we are witnessing a failure of Soviet socialized medicine, its primary cause again being the shortfall in resources. The great majority of physicians and surgeons are women, while nurses are hard to find, even though the absolute number of Soviet medical personnel is double the American. The workweek of the typical Soviet doctor is 28 hours and her pay is less than that of the average manual worker. Clinics are crowded and open only part of the day, while medical equipment is for the most part obsolescent, and outside of Moscow there is a shortage of ordinary medicaments, such as aspirin. Often it is possible to get satisfactory service only by means of bribery. The proportion of the Soviet budget alloted to health care has fallen from 6.6 percent in 1965 to 5.2 percent in 1978. The reader will note that it was during these same years that Soviet mortality rates began to climb.[17]

The picture I have painted is a bleak one and the reader who has followed the argument thus far is entitled to ask how an economy endowed with so many inherent weaknesses could, in the historically brief space of 57 years, make of backward, rural, isolated Russia a nuclear-armed superpower. The explanation is to be found in the fact that the weaknesses of the Soviet C.P.E. have been the obverse of its strengths. As we have seen, a command economy, for example, enabled the Russians to neglect infrastructure for years and employ the capital thus saved to build steel mills. It made possible the location of these mills (and of armament plants) in western Siberia, beyond the reach of the Nazi German military, in blithe disregard of the fact that both the steel and the tanks would have cost a great deal less had they been produced in the Donbas in the Ukraine. A command economy could also distribute its steel at a price well below the cost of production thus facilitating the use of the product throughout the economy.

To raise the capital with which to build such expensive plants and distribute such costly steel, the Soviet government forced the peasant mass of the population into collective farms which it then utilized as mechanisms for forcing the *kolkhozniki* to produce the grain at prices fixed so as to keep their living standards at the level of subsistence. By introducing machinery on the huge fields created by collectivization from innumerable tiny private strips, the command economy could also and at the same time release the bulk of the peasantry for work in burgeoning cities. Meanwhile the grain produced and paid for in this cruel way could be sold on the world market and the hard currency proceeds employed to pay for imports of advanced Western machinery and equipment to be used in the manufacture of steel and tanks. In short, the Russian version of the CPE is an extreme form of the kind of economy a Western industrial state might develop for the purpose of waging a prolonged and decisive war. In Soviet Russia, preparation for war, or the waging of it, has been the overwhelming concern of the rulers of the country for the last 57 years. It would not be far from the truth to assert that in an international situation of nuclear stalemate, waging "cold war" is a necessary correlate of a command economy of the Soviet type.

But clearly there were some things the CPE could not do. It could not achieve a high level of efficiency, for example. Central planners fix prices for their own purposes, not to measure relative scarcities, with the result that they end up not knowing what anything costs. As a consequence, costs tend to be underestimated and output overestimated, labor productivity gains are exaggerated, and the volume of investment is overstated while personal incomes tend to rise faster than production, creating a constant—if suppressed—inflation. A high rate of technological innovation remains beyond reach, since managers are concerned to meet exaggerated physical production targets, while the introduction of new technology and new industries must await the decision of the planners at the top. Thus economic growth becomes ever more dependent upon annual increments to factor inputs while the demographic changes wrought by the industrialization process itself reduce their availability.

Clearly the high costs of central planning are at last becoming evident. As the annual GNP rate of increase has gradually fallen since the sixties because of the various constraints outlined above, and since repeated efforts to improve the productivity of the CPE by means of within-system reform have failed, why should we now believe that the rate of growth will not continue to fall, eventually becoming negative, and confronting the Soviet leaders with an insuperable requirement for system change? Is not the continuing decline in the rate of growth of the Soviet GNP inherent in the nature of the CPE?[18] Many Western economists have now come to believe that only the introduction of a socialist market, i.e. one combining state ownership of the means of production with primary reliance on market forces for the allocation of labor and capital, can give the U.S.S.R. a reasonably efficient economy. Apparently many Soviet economists are in agreement. A recent memorandum written by economists at the Soviet Academy of Sciences in Novosibirsk for the use of the central planning authorities (and subsequently leaked to the West) asserts that "The system of centralized administrative direction of the economy has reached the outer limits of its productive power."[19]

To put the matter in historical perspective, however, I would assert that the Soviet régime has brought cold, backward and isolated Russia to the standing of a nuclear superpower in an historically brief period of time. But this remarkable success has been achieved not only by the leadership's adoption of shortcuts in the industrialization process, but also by the employment of one-party dictatorship, the use of political terror and the lowering of an iron curtain in order that the industrial shortcuts might be put in place. Now, after six decades of rapid growth, the bill for both the industrial shortcuts and the extreme political techniques is coming due and the wherewithal to pay it is lacking. In brief, the Soviet economy has run out of significant additional annual increments to factor inputs, and the political system is showing signs of failure.

It is time to turn our attention to some of these signs.

The Erosion of the Régime's Control

From Stalin's death in 1953 to the last years of Brezhnev's leadership, the population of the Soviet Union experienced for the first time a significant and continuing improvement in living standard, i.e. an average increase in real income of 3.4 percent per annum.[20] This rate resulted in a near tripling of Soviet living standards, an amelioration probably unique in Russian history. It no doubt prepared the average Soviet citizen to believe Khrushchev when, in 1959, he told a Party congress that by 1975 the U.S.S.R. would have surpassed the U.S. in *per capita* production of such items as meat, milk and butter, thus guaranteeing the Soviet people the highest living standard in the world![21]

But as we have seen the living standard of the Soviet people has begun to be adversely affected. Indeed, except for consumer durables, it has, since 1975 or shortly thereafter, become stagnant at a level about one-third of the American. This change for the worse was announced to the general public with fanfare, by the failure of four harvests in a row, those of 1979, 1980, 1981 and 1982. At the same time the sugar content of Soviet beets and grapes fell, as did the amount of oil in Soviet oil seeds, and of starch in Soviet potatoes. In fact, between 1976 and 1981 imports provided all the increased availability of comestibles. By 1981 food was rationed in at least 20 major cities, while today many essential foods are available in the provinces only at the higher prices of collective farm markets. In cities there is increasing dependence upon distribution at the place of work, a practice which favors selected groups of laborers.[22]

The question that arises at this point is how the Soviet citizenry is likely to react to the onset of a long period of stagnant or declining living standards, especially after it has experienced a period of significant improvement in those standards for the first time since the onset of collectivization in 1928. The answer to this question we may know already. As early as 1962, Khrushchev undertook to order a 30 percent increase in the price of meat. But, instead of the grumbling compliance he had no doubt expected, he was faced with an open revolt in Novocherkassk, a port with Cossack traditions on the lower Don. Order had to be restored by units of the regular army, which at first apparently refused to fire. Novocherkassk set off a series of riots and disorders in such widely scattered places as Moscow, Leningrad, Baku, Kamenets-Podolski in the Ukraine, Termir-Tau in Kazakhstan, Chirchik in Uzbekistan and Kaunas in Lithuania.[23] These disorders took place many years before strikes and riots in Poland brought down two first secretaries, fathered an opposition party disguised as a labor union, and did other devilment besides.

In the days of Stalin food shortages would not have represented a danger to public order. Why should they have done so in 1962-1963? One answer is the régime's abandonment, back in 1953, of reliance on the systematic use of political terror. As Khrushchev made clear when the Kremlin first began to import sizeable quantities of food from the West, under Stalin the population of shortage areas would have been left to starve. But during the nine years that had elapsed since the death of the great dictator, the régime had attempted to replace systematic reliance on terror with the appeal of material incentives. Thus, the cost of defiance was by no means as high for the individual participant as it had been under Stalin.

Willingness to risk the wrath of a police state over a 30 percent increase in an artificially low price for meat suggests that other factors were at work, in addition to the suspension of systematic terror. Undoubtedly one of them was the beginning of a basic change in popular expectations. The truth seems to be that in the 1960s the Soviet masses were for the first time beginning to get a picture of living conditions in Europe. As a result of the introduction of universal secondary education, virtually the entire adult population was becoming literate. But to this salient fact must be added another—the growing availability of radio and television to the average citizen. By 1980, there would be 85 radios and 85 television sets per 100 Soviet families.[24] While foreign broadcasts in Soviet languages are, in general, jammed electronically, both the broadcasters and the listeners can make use of counter-jamming techniques. A significant percentage of radio programs reaches diligent ears, particularly in rural areas. Though slanted, Soviet television newscasts do broaden the popular perspective, particularly when the reporting is from the European satellites.

In addition to the suspension of systematic terror and the impact of an ongoing revolution in communications, there was also the ebullient Khrushchev's opening to the West. Under him came the first important inflow of tourists from the outside world. Their clothing, their cars, their segregated hotels, and the luxury offerings of the dollar and native crafts shops opened especially for them had also had their influence, especially since by far the largest number of travellers came from the satellite states. To the tourist trade must be added the presence on the shop floor of machinery of Western provenance. In Tolyatti, for example, the Russian version of the Fiat was manufactured with Italian machinery and equipment. Little wonder that the foreign product now appeared to be regarded by the average denizen as inevitably superior to its domestically produced counterpart.

That the average Soviet adult is aware that living conditions are much better in the West is certain, but exactly what he knows is uncertain. Is he aware that his per capita consumption is substantially less than that of the dweller in the satellite? That his consumption is two-thirds of the Italian but a mere one-third of the American?[25] Or does he believe that all Westerners live like capitalists? The sociologist refers to an International Demonstration Effect (IDE) which he defines as the unrealistic and even irrational expectations produced in a developing and formerly isolated population by its sudden awareness that life is very much better elsewhere.

While the results of Soviet public opinion polls, if any, on this point are not available, there is some evidence of this kind available from Poland. After an unprecedented annual increase in Polish real income per capita during the period from 1971 to 1978, a sample of Polish manual workers was asked the question: Generally speaking, did you and your family's living conditions improve during the last eight years? Two-fifths answered saying that there had been no change in those conditions or that a deterioration had set in, while almost two-thirds described their family budgets as highly strained.[26]

In view of the evidence, then, it seems to me that it would be unwise to discount the political significance of the food issue in the U.S.S.R. and what has become its chief symbol, meat. Apparently what the Soviet masses have been saying is that "real Socialism" must, as a minimum requirement of their allegiance, provide them with an acceptable diet. By acceptable they seem to mean no less than what the satellites peoples are accustomed to eating, but they may also mean a great deal more. Shortly before his death, Brezhnev warned the Central Committee that food was not only the key economic issue facing the leadership, but the key political problem as well!

Some two years after the Union-wide rash of disorders which began at Novocherkassk and to which we have already referred, the Kremlin undertook to raise agricultural procurement prices in the hope of improving output. At the same time it was decided not to raise the prices charged the public for staple foods which meant that the government would pay the difference out of the all-Union budget. With the passage of time the amount of this subsidy has grown until, if it were now abolished, the official prices of staples would rise by 40 percent. Of course real prices have in fact gone up, publicly at the collective farm markets and surreptitiously in the state stores, where the clerks engage in such subterfuges as short weighting, false grading or bribe extraction. Yet the Kremlin remains unwilling to reduce or abolish a subsidy which has had only a minor effect on agricultural productivity and by 1980 was costing roughly as much as half of the contribution of agriculture to the national income.[27]

As early as Khrushchev's time the Kremlin began a serious effort to increase the public availability of meat, in the per capita production of which the U.S.S.R. ranks very low among European states, partly because the country lies too far north to be able to produce much in the way of maize, a principal animal fodder. Even in 1978, Soviet consumption of meat was only 49 kilograms per person per year, as compared with a Polish consumption figure of 86 kilograms. To maintain even this low rate of consumption Moscow has found it necessary to import huge quantities of fodder grains and large amounts of meat for human consumption as well. The grain contracts into which Moscow has presently entered with Washington, Ottawa, Buenos Aires, and Paris commit it to a policy of subsidizing meat production with hard currency purchases for the foreseeable future.[28] On average, one quarter of Soviet hard currency earnings are spent in this way, even though such purchases reduce substantially the amounts available for the importation of advanced technology or for steadying shaky satellite economies.

The subsidization of food prices and the importation of fodder grain turned out not to be enough, however, at least in the view of the men in the Kremlin. Therefore the effort to sweeten the pot of material incentives went further, involving the expansion of the so-called second economy, to perhaps as much as 15 percent of GNP, no doubt in the expectation that the mass of the population would thereby improve its living conditions sufficiently to make the existing state of affairs acceptable.

Of the second economy there was already a lawful version: the private plots of the *kolkhozniki*, the *sovkhozniki*, and the urban dwellers which, altogether, represent only three percent of Soviet arable land but produce roughly thirty percent of the dairy products, the meat and the vegetables which are available to the general citizenry.[29] If it be asked why the Soviet leaders do not permit the doubling of the area of private plots in order to help solve its food problems, a good, tentative answer is that such an action might further endanger both the physical and the institutional integrity of the collective farm, the inefficiency of which must be endured in order, among other things, not to raise the question of "why all those people had to die" during the forcible collectivization of agriculture in the 1930s.

But the private plots and the collective farm markets had existed all along. The expansion of the second economy beyond their activities has been made possible largely by régime toleration of unlawful enterprise. This takes a number of forms. One is the theft of materials from the place of work and their sale on the black market. Such theft made it possible for members of the élite to secure parts for their privately operated automobiles since centrally planned factories are notorious for their failure to provide an adequate supply of spare parts. The sale of materials and tools taken from the place of work also makes possible the repair of consumer durables and the construction of private dachas.

Another form taken by the illicit second economy was camouflaged production of scarce consumers' goods. This is done either in parallel, along with legitimate products in a government factory, or as a separate enterprise, a clandestine version of the putting-out-system, with piece-work carried out in private apartments. Ladies' lingerie is a typical product of these systems. Whatever the output, it is marketed black. Obviously, either type of production requires the complicity of highly placed authorities and both are capable of creating secret millionaires. The entire economy of Kirghizia is reported to have been turned into a semiprivate enterprise as early as the 1950s.[30] Today corruption has become well-nigh universal. In addition to the forms noted above, workers soldier on the job, unqualified students use bribery to secure entrance to medical faculties, physicians find hospital beds only for those able to offer them a private gratuity, while in some minority republics even ministerial offices are said to be bought and sold.

Apparently the authorities tolerate such behavior because it permits the gears of the CPE to turn more freely. The availability of spare parts and the theft of tools and materials from the place of work make it easier for families to keep their consumer durables in operation, for example, and this lightens the burden of what has come to seem to the average Soviet a rather spartan lifestyle. Toleration of corruption also gives the authorities an added element of control. Almost every Ivan could be brought before the authorities for corrupt practices, but the police only intervene when the true dereliction is serious, e.g. the son of a corrupt Jewish surgeon applies for emigration papers, thus raising with his non-Jewish neighbors the question of why a Jewish youth should be vouchsafed the privilege of leaving the country.[31] To be sure, a wide-ranging toleration of crooked practices by the authorities undermines respect for the law, runs counter to official Communist doctrine, and helps explain the low productivity of the Soviet factory. But the Soviet citizen has never known the rule of law. The reigning doctrine, it would appear, he has not taken seriously for years. And while the faltering discipline of the labor force might be somewhat improved by systematic resort to the police power, in any case it is not the primary cause of the steady decline in the rate of growth of Soviet GNP.

But even with subsidized food prices, fodder imports, and the toleration of a nearly universal corruption, many Soviet citizens find the world in which they live intolerable and seek relief in one form of withdrawal or another. The pandemic nature of present-day Soviet alcoholism has already been alluded to. The government's financial interest in the sale of alcoholic beverages, a state monopoly—although there is also a readily available *samogon* or moonshine—is often mentioned. But from the view in the

Kremlin it may seem better to have unhappy people regularly drunk inside the factory than soberly engaged in political demonstrations on the street.

Another form of withdrawal is to be found in the clandestine spread of Protestant sectarianism, especially of the officially unrecognized sects, the evangelical Baptists, the Pentecostalists, and the Seventh Day Adventists. As in the United States, evangelical movements attract the poorer and less literate elements of the population. At the same time, this form of sectarianism constitutes an outright—if implicit—rejection of the régime, the individual human conscience replacing the Communist Party as the highest earthly authority.[32]

Churches, as distinguished from sects, also tend to become deviationist under totalitarian rule. In the western Ukraine, traditionally the seedbed of Ukrainian nationalism, there appears to exist an underground Uniate Church, its hidden hierarchy in clandestine contact with Rome. There has also been a return of Russians to Orthodoxy, to whose clergy even some members of the Party hierarchy now repair for the sacraments of baptism and marriage. In my view the Orthodox renewal is a manifestation of a Russian backlash, a rejection of the notion that what is being created under socialism is a new Soviet man.

All of which—the concern of Moscow for the price and availability of food, the expansion of the second economy by means of corruption, and the withdrawal of large elements from active participation in Soviet life—brings us back to what appears to have become the key political issue as far as the masses of the Soviet population are concerned: the present-day quality of Soviet life, especially as that is evidenced in the shortage and unappetizing character of the country's food.

The first of the four failed harvests came in 1979. In May, 1980, two months before the emergence of Solidarity in Poland, food shortages produced a two-day wildcat strike of 70,000 workers at the Lada (Fiat) automobile plant in Tolyatti. This incident was followed by strikes at the auto and truck plant in Gorki and reportedly at the Kama River truck plant at Brezhnev, and by strikes at tractor plants in Cheboksary on the Volga and in Estonia as well.[33] In Tolyatti and Gorki the strikers went back to work only after fresh supplies of food were rushed in from surrounding territories. Units of the regular army were also deployed but did not otherwise intervene, although severe punishment was administered to the strike leaders. For some months food supplies remained above normal. It is evident that those involved in the strike were, like the shipworkers at Gdansk later that summer, among the most highly skilled and best-paid members of the urban proletariat. Like the shipworkers, they felt they deserved better treatment by a government that ruled in their name. But their action in open defiance of

an authority that was, at the same time, a police state with a long record of
the systematic use of violence against domestic opposition, must also have
reflected feelings of bitterness and even despair.

Perhaps, therefore, we should give greater credence to that current Western reportage from the U.S.S.R. which finds widespread and deep discontent
among the masses. Popular pessimism with respect to the future is said to be
profound, and parents fear for the fate of their children. Large numbers of
common people have reportedly come to feel that Marxism-Leninism is not
a proper basis of the social order. In practice, they say, central planning
does not work. It cannot even provide the workingman with a decent
standard of living. It appears that the man on the street now tends to see the
Soviet Union as possessing a more or less hereditary ruling class that
remains indifferent to the suffering of the proletariat and enjoys an abundant
life only by means of the ruthless exploitation of the country's extraordinary
natural resources, a wealth that in justice is the property of all. One evidence
of this change in outlook is the increasing importance of the "pecking order"
in Soviet society.[34]

In short, the food issue may also be a surrogate for other grievances, as in
the case of Poland. The most immediate is the increase in the time which
ordinary citizens must spend standing in queues. With the failure of the
economy to grow and of living standards to improve, consumer goods are
scarcer and the inflationary overhang of purchasing power more depressing.
A major reason for the decline in labor discipline is the growing length of
the lines, both before and after working hours. Workers characteristically
take a shortcut by leaving their places of employment, e.g. in the middle of
the morning. Otherwise, the time spent in the line amounts to a lengthening
of the working day and therefore in effect to a cut in take-home pay.
Furthermore in the queue the standees have time to commiserate with each
other on their mutual plight, a situation which is likely to radicalize the
views of the participants and to make them see their circumstances as worse
than, in objective fact, they are.[35]

Another source of grievance that could surface in the form of concern
over food is the perceptible decline in social mobility which has characterized recent years; the hardening of class lines has been sufficiently pronounced as to raise in the mind of the average citizen the question whether
Soviet Russia is not in fact becoming a society of estates, or hereditary
classes. Such a transformation is perhaps inadvertently admitted by official
adoption of the formula according to which contradictions do exist in
Soviet society but they are of a "non-antagonistic" character. While the job
security of the Soviet citizen is proverbial, it is presently difficult to find
work that matches one's training. A survey made in Ufa, the capital of the
Bashkir Autonomous Republic, shows that 72.5 percent of the children of

the intelligentsia become members of that class, while only 31.4 percent of workers' progeny do. Another study suggests that while 76 percent of agricultural workers hoped to enter university, only 10 percent actually did so, as compared with the 93 percent of urban intellectuals who proposed to enroll, of whom 61 percent achieved that goal.[36]

But perhaps the most serious sublimated grievance of all is the ramshackle state of the Socialist health-care system, particularly as it affects children, and the evident decline in the health of the general public, as described earlier in this essay.

Food shortages may possibly be surrogate to still a fourth issue, that of ethnic conflict. Elements thereof seem to have been present in the public disorders of 1980, as well as those of 1962-1963. In some places the language in which orders were to be given to the work force was questioned. Nine of the eleven incidents of 1962-1963 took place in minority republics. The food issue, and the deeper grievances which it may represent, may even affect the legitimacy of the Soviet régime, in the sense that the real, if inarticulate, grievance of the masses of the population runs to the effect that the human costs of Soviet rule are very high and in the long run are acceptable only if the gap in living standards between East and West is narrowed perceptibly. Legitimate is the régime that catches up with the West. And on that score the present régime is currently an egregious failure. Khrushchev's 1959 promise is further than ever from realization.

At the same time, however, it must be kept in mind that there is one other major source of régime legitimacy, and one of which the Kremlin makes every effort to remind the Soviet public, i.e. the unbelievable triumph of the Red Army over the *Wehrmacht* in World War II, especially when that is combined with the present military standing of the U.S.S.R. as one of two superpowers on earth, a fact which in itself constitutes a certain guarantee of the physical security of the Soviet peoples. In my view, it is the need of this second legitimizing factor that explains why Moscow will in the end find unacceptable any general relaxation of international tension such as would follow, for example, a reduction in the NATO and Warsaw Pact forces in central Europe by perhaps one-third.

It is, I think, important in this connection to attempt to understand the nature of the disorders that afflicted the Soviet polity in 1962-1963 and again in 1980 and also, if more devastatingly, afflict the satellites because the régimes imposed by Moscow on them are of the Soviet type. To begin with, these outbreaks of demonstrations, strikes, and riots on a country-wide scale are spontaneous events. They are, generally speaking, not organized and, given the extensive character of régime controls, probably could not be. Of all the instances we have, those in the German Democratic Republic in 1953 and in Poland in 1970, 1976 and 1980, as well as those in the Soviet Union in 1962-1963 and 1980, only the most recent Polish outbreak was organized and that only in the sense that a group of dissident intellectuals, most of them former Party members, realized that, after the disorders of 1970 and 1976, another upheaval was likely. Forming a clandestine committee, the KOR, they proceeded to publish and circulate to factories through Poland a weekly *samizdat* newspaper whose editorials carried the ideas which later gave rise to the political program embodied in Solidarity.

Since the strikes, the demonstrations, and the riots are spontaneous, there is no way of predicting their occurrence. The mass of the population in the larger cities must become emotionally so depressed and feel such a sense of hopeless entrapment that some trivial event will set it off without warning but which, like a fuse laid round the country, triggers comparable explosions in a series of other cities, threatening to engulf the country.

Despite its possession of a huge and efficient repressive apparatus, the government has real difficulty in dealing with these outbreaks. Most of the people involved are workers, so the disorders at once raise the question of whether the official picture of a workers' state inhabited by happy families has much validity, the question being repeated in headlines around the world, much to the embarrassment of the régime, whose legitimacy has been questioned before the court of world opinion. Because of the extreme centralization of a Socialist government, local authorities are unable or unwilling to react to so momentous a happening. In any case, their forces feel themselves faced with a tidal wave. But in the central political command confusion is compounded by a lack of information. To deal with the crisis either the demands voiced by the strikers and rioters must be acceded to, or units of the regular army must be deployed, whether as a presence in the streets, implicitly backing the activities of the riot troops of the security police, as in Poland in 1980; as by themselves a threatening presence (Tolyatti in 1980); or as firing on the mob (after refusing to fire?) as at Novocherkassk in 1962. This set of facts reveals the Achilles heel of the decadent totalitarian regime: its rule is ultimately dependent upon an army made up of persons recruited from the mass of the population, which is itself alive with disaffection.

In August 1980, a third effort of the government in Warsaw to raise retail prices of foodstuffs produced a third upheaval, this time leading to the formation of a new, nationwide union of urban workers, Solidarity. In effect, however, Solidarity was not a labor union but an opposition political party, demanding to share, with the Polish Communist Party, which would represent the Soviet interest, in the governance of the country. Moscow refused absolutely to countenance such a rearrangement, since if it were granted to the Poles it could not be denied the East Germans or the Czechs, and, by extension, perhaps not even to the peoples of the Soviet Union itself.

Within its own territory the Kremlin took a number of precautionary measures directed against the potential appeal of Solidarity within Soviet Russia. The Soviet-Polish frontier was closed and troops mobilized along it, although the primary purpose of this maneuver was to threaten Poland with occupation. Electronic jamming of the broadcasts of the "Voice of America" and the BBC was resumed. A propaganda campaign in the Ukrainian media emphasized Polish claims to Galicia. The directors of the KGB in the western minority republics made rare appearances in Party journals explaining to the comrades the need for increased vigilance against the bourgeois poison emanating from Poland. Preoccupation with Solidarity thus appears to have been widespread within the Soviet new class.

It seems to me that the Polish crisis must be viewed as a serious threat to the stability of the Soviet polity. Five years after its inauguration the issues raised by the crisis remain unresolved and, even though the country is effectively under martial law, the population still seethes. The régime is driven to the murder of priests and then to the trial and condemnation of the security personnel who committed murder under orders. The most numerous of the European satellite populations, the most strategically located and perhaps the wealthiest in natural resources, the Poles have gradually refused to wear the totalitarian Soviet straitjacket. By way of a series of crises, more particularly that of 1956, they have wrung from their masters concessions which already mark a certain progress toward a pluralist polity.

In order to understand the extent of the threat to Soviet stability which the Polish situation provides, it will be helpful to deal briefly with the political gains which the Poles have so far been able to book. In the crisis of 1956, the Poles obtained three concessions. They persuaded Khrushchev to recall the Soviet "advisers" who had theretofore actually governed the country. Thereafter the Polish Party attempted to rule on its own, with considerably less than outstanding success. (Khrushchev was also forced to withdraw his "advisers" from the other satellites, a retreat which he camouflaged by the proclamation of a new era in the imperial relationship, what he called the epoch of the Socialist Commonwealth. What he meant was that each satellite would now be administered by its own Communist Party, but within the framework of overall Soviet policy.) Moreover, a new Polish first secretary, understanding that no one could administer Poland without a minimal cooperation from the Catholic hierarchy, in 1956 released the Polish primate from prison and permitted him to resume his position at the head of the Polish Church. Thereafter Poland had two governments, one *de jure*, the Communist, the other *de facto*, the Catholic. And in major matters the first found it necessary to secure the cooperation of the second.

Thirdly, in 1956 Poland acquired a free press, even if one by way of shortwave radio. During the crisis of that year mobs destroyed the ground-wave jammers in all the country's principal cities and the régime never quite mustered the courage to put them back up. Since Warsaw had to pay for the skywave jamming, which for technical reasons had to be based on the territory of neighboring Socialist states, and since that form of jamming was both expensive and not especially effective without the support of the groundwave stations, interference with Western broadcasts was brought to an end. This meant that the transmissions of "Radio Free Europe" in Munich, whose airtime constituted something like 80 percent of all Western broadcasts in the Polish language, and which included a newscast in each of its 20 hours, was contacted by insiders from both Polish governments and from the disaffected intelligentsia in the hope of having their respective points of view put on the air.

The new political arrangement sputtered along in fits and starts for a number of years until the incompetence and mismanagement of a weak régime brought visible expression to what all along was probably a hidden crisis. Large-scale outbreaks of disorder, concentrated along the Baltic coast, where the public was more generally aware of Western living standards, took place, as we have seen, in 1970, 1976, and 1980. In each instance the immediate cause was an attempt of the authorities to raise the price of food, after having, for a quarter of a century, pointed to fixed food prices as proof that under socialism inflation did not exist.

Between 1970 and 1980 the government—which was faced with an in-creasingly burdensome financial problem because of the rate at which its annual subsidy of food prices was growing, and which believed that if there were a marked improvement in the national diet increased prices would be acceptable to the public—borrowed heavily in the West in order to pay for greater imports of comestibles. While Polish living standards improved at a steady and significant rate, Warsaw also borrowed in order to create an export industry which would permit repayment of the now burgeoning hard-currency debt. Between the intractability of the CPE and the incom-petence of the Communist authorities, the product of the new export industry proved to be unsaleable in the West. A second attempt to raise food prices (1976) produced a new round of disorders and a new government retreat. But Poland was now on the verge of bankruptcy. In desperation the government tried a third time to raise food prices and got Solidarity for its pains.

As I have already suggested, Solidarity represented a good deal more than an attempt to punish an incompetent (and foreign-dominated) government for having made a foolish promise. Solidarity was in fact an attempt to transform Poland into a genuine socialist commonwealth, a country which accepted the right of the Soviet Union to protect its vital interests in the Polish state by way of the Communist Party while, at the same time, permitting the population an equal voice in its affairs through what was formally a labor union.

Since, as has been argued, Moscow could in no way tolerate such an arrangement without itself risking the danger of Soviet destabilization, and since the Polish Communist Party had miserably failed in its duties, the government of the unruly population was turned over to the Polish army. This action was not only a public admission of political failure and even, perhaps, a harbinger of the future, but it was also a substitute for the military occupation of the country by the Soviet forces which for many months had surrounded it.

Evidently the Kremlin was most reluctant to order the occupation of Poland. No doubt it believed the Polish claim that the country would resist, arms in hand. While this resistance could be overcome in no more than a couple of weeks, the effect on the world Communist movement might be disastrous. A Western people who had experienced the benefits of socialism for 40 years was now willing to accept heavy casualties in a hopeless effort to rid itself of the system. How would that play in Namibia? In any case it seemed certain that such an outcome would cause the Italian Communist Party to declare its independence of Moscow. Furthermore, once occupied, Poland would be Moscow's immediate responsibility. The population would have to be fed, subsidization of its faltering economy increased, and order maintained, and all this by a country facing serious economic difficulties itself.

Nonetheless, the rule of the Polish military has so far proved no more than an interim solution to the Polish problem. To govern effectively the dictatorship needs the willing cooperation of the population. This it has been unable to obtain because of the repressive measures it must take in order to preserve public order. Without the willing cooperation of the Polish people, the military dictatorship cannot introduce the marketizing reform of the economy which almost all educated Poles now agree is the *sina qua non* of any long-term economic recovery. It does seem to be the case that the Polish people are now more determined than ever not to put up indefinitely with a rule which is despotic as well as foreign and incompetent. The world, and the Kremlin, can only wait for the slumbering Polish crisis to break out into the open in some new form. I argue, in other words, that Poland is now a kind of time bomb that still may set off an explosion in its giant neighbor.

The View From the Kremlin

An Unfavorable Correlation of Forces

From the foregoing analysis it would appear that the ruling elements in the Soviet polity are faced with serious and even unprecedented problems. There is first of all the question of what should be done to revive the rate of growth of the GNP to three or four percent per annum. At the same time there is the related problem of how to cope with the erosion of regime control of the mass of a population which has suffered much and which has now, for the first time, become reasonably well aware of the living conditions prevailing in Western countries.

At the level of the new class, however, these two basic problems may appear in a somewhat different light, refracted, as it were, in the twin mirrors of Communist ideology and the prerequisites of totalitarian power. In the perception of the new class the two problems just listed may appear rather as a set of four: 1) a correlation of forces in the world at large which is currently unfavorable to the CPSU; 2) the nature and extent of the risks to political control of any reform of the economy sufficient to make its operation primarily reliant on market forces; 3) how to overcome a current malfunctioning of the dictatorship of the proletariat so as to end the present period of comfortable but perilous drift; and 4) finally, whether, while attempting to cope with these first three problems it will be possible to maintain and strengthen the internal cohesion and the military discipline of the ruling élite.

* * *

In the brief course of Soviet history the ruling élite has been bound together by its belief that fate has given it a supernal mission, one which justifies beyond any reasonable doubt the enormous sacrifices that it has had to impose upon the masses, i.e. sacrifices that will ultimately bring happiness to all mankind. This rationalization, it seems to me, is one key to the integrity of the régime.

Unfortunately the supernal mission has had to be redefined, not once but a number of times. At first (1917-1924) the leadership taught that its harsh and extreme policies were justified by the imminence of a world revolution which would bring an end to capitalism's exploitation of man by man and to the endless wars which were its inevitable by-product. But after a first struggle over the post of secretary general and the installation of a new leadership, the supernal mission became in 1928-1941 the "building of socialism in one country" in order to preserve the revolution from the capitalist enemies which had temporarily encircled it. This sacred duty was followed by those of saving European civilization from fascism (1941-1945), a degenerate form of capitalism. Subsequently the mission was the reconstruction of a devastated "socialist motherland" (1946-1953). After a second succession struggle, the overriding vocation of the new class became (1957-1964) the construction of a welfare state at home, and the exploitation of a favorable correlation of forces abroad so as to force the capitalist states to surrender one strategic position after another in preparation for the day when socialism would triumph throughout the world. We note, however, that the mission of 1957-1964 failed of realization on both counts.[37]

Indeed, Brezhnev and his successors, it seems to me, have been left hanging by events, without any overriding Elysian objective other than a very slow progress through "real socialism" toward a socialism that is only a final preparation for the realization of Communism. When, following the failure of their Cuban adventure in 1962, the Soviet leaders decided that they would have to acquire a nuclear military capability at least equal to that of the most powerful capitalist state, the Soviet edition of the welfare society, if ever it had been realistic, became unrealizable. Yet even the Soviet nuclear accomplishment, I would submit, is today in question. The annual increase in allocations to defense—which the CIA thought had held in real terms at three to four percent between 1976 and 1981—now turns out to have been reduced to two percent. The great sensitivity of the Soviet leaders to President Reagan's recent "star wars" proposal points in the same direction, as does the removal of Soviet Chief of Staff Marshal Nikolay Ogarkov for having complained publicly that, in the event of a conventional war in Europe, Soviet forces would have to do battle without the advantage of high technology command and control systems which, the Marshal asserted, NATO already possesses.[38]

Meantime, various states which are members of the socialist community and are faced with a reduction in Muscovite economic subsidies have begun to diverge more openly from Soviet policies. Many of them borrowed heavily from the West during the seventies—as did the U.S.S.R. itself—in order to raise living standards, in addition to promoting industrial growth. But by the eighties most of the satellite governments had lost their creditworthiness in Western eyes because of poor economic performance. They have since had to don the mantle of austerity, a garment unexpectedly converted into a hair shirt by a reduction in the anticipated deliveries of Soviet oil and gas, on which their industries are roughly 80 percent dependent, and upon an increase in the price of oil. In these circumstances, and naturally much to the annoyance of the Kremlin, some have attempted to negotiate a new relationship with the West in the hope of offsetting the reduction in the subsidy from the East.

Perhaps the most striking example of this disintegrative trend was the lawful emigration early in 1984 of 26,000 persons from the German Democratic Republic, in exchange for a substantial increase in the subsidy which the Federal German Republic has all along provided Communist Germany. There was a sudden cut-off to the exodus, however, and subsequently a campaign in the satellite press attempting to dissuade the East German First Party secretary from paying an official visit to Bonn, whence, by the way, his Bulgarian colleague had already also announced his intention of going.[39] For another example, Poland has been attempting to ease its way into membership in the International Monetary Fund, accepting thereby a degree of Western supervision of its economy in order to facilitate the granting of new loans. Both Cuba and Nicaragua have made a pretense of opening negotiations with the U.S.A., while North Korea, after years of ignoring her neighbor to the south, suddenly has taken steps to prepare the way for the opening of trade negotiations with her. Most important of all, perhaps, has been the announcement from Budapest that the market reform of the Hungarian economy, which had been begun in 1968 and which had been cut back during the period 1972-1978, partly in consequence of Soviet pressure, would now be accelerated to a point at which it will probably become very difficult to reverse. Most of these changes have represented small steps toward the greater integration of the various socialist countries with the world market and, to that extent, constitute a diminution of Soviet influence. This trend appears likely to continue. The 1984 meeting of the Comecon, the international organ for the coordination of the socialist economies, was the first since 1971, and achieved little or nothing. Romania has long been guilty of national deviation, while China, Yugoslavia and Albania have for many years asserted their complete independence of Moscow.[40]

Obviously, if the Soviet Union could maintain its imperial subsidies at the old and slowly rising levels, it would today be faced with less enfeeblement of the imperial nexus. To be sure there are bright spots in the picture, the establishment of a Communist base in Central America, the prospect of an explosion in the Philippines, the occupation of Kampuchea by North Vietnam. But are these indicative of the real balance of forces?

Actually, to the dilution of the imperial nexus there is being added still another factor, namely a deterioration in the Soviet standing as a superpower, a trend in some part also related to the inherently greater long-run efficiency of the market economy. At the time of Stalin's death, the world appeared to fit the Marxist book, divided, as it was, between two nuclear powers in bitter conflict at various points around the globe, one socialist, the other capitalist, each with its troop of lesser allies and client states echeloned in military alliance around it.

Today, however, the world is more nearly multipolar, with the future of the socialist superpower seemingly beclouded. To be sure, the German power has been destroyed; Hitler's Third Reich partitioned as three survivor states; the *Volksdeutschen* for the most part driven out of Eastern Europe. Yet in the place of the Reich there has arisen a new potential enemy, one which can be variously described as a Common Market, a European Community or a NATO alliance, three entities embracing virtually all the states of Western Europe and reinforced by the presence of an American garrison intended to serve as a trip-wire in the event of a sudden Soviet attack.

Since its formation, this triple new Europe has experienced a long, if occasionally interrupted, period of economic growth, despite the dissolution of her overseas empires. The loss of these empires alone has deprived Soviet ideologues of one of their most convincing arguments, i.e. Lenin's theory according to which countries experiencing the higher stages of capitalism required colonies as the prerequisite of their domestic stability, thus making war among the imperialist powers inevitable in the long run. For his part, Khrushchev attempted to set Lenin's doctrine right again by wooing the third world with arms and economic handouts, hoping thus to turn the former colonies against the West. But in this his success was only partial.[41]

Furthermore, at the other end of the Eurasian land mass a crushed and defeated Japan, also shorn of her overseas empire, has undergone since World War II a rapid recovery, becoming indeed a leading member of the club of advanced industrial nations. By 1971 the market economy of Japan produced a volume of exports twice that of the U.S.S.R., although the island kingdom has virtually no mineral resources, produces only two-thirds of the Soviet GNP and possesses only 44 percent of Russia's population.[42]

Then there is the case of mainland China, where the Communist triumph in 1949 appeared to add one fourth of the earth's population to the Soviet camp. Today Beijing is not only defiantly independent of Moscow but also has de facto marketized its agrarian communes by the introduction of so-called material incentives. In consequence over the last seven years China's agricultural output has actually doubled, and the country has been transformed from a food-importing to a food-exporting state. Currently attempting to marketize its industrial production, the Chinese leadership has declared publicly that Marx was a nineteenth century thinker whose teachings do not constitute an adequate basis for the modernization of a backward country.[43]

Finally, there is the example of market America herself, a country which, instead of staggering from one economic crisis to the next, each being more severe that its predecessor, has grown prodigiously since 1945—with interruptions to be sure—and is now the world center of a third industrial revolution, one powered by the digital computer, and is proposing to extend the military competition with the U.S.S.R. into outer space. The Soviet Union, on the other hand, still relies on second-generation mainframe computers, having made her own computers IBM compatible in order to offset the difficulties the CPE manifests in the production of spare parts and the provision of services. The introduction of robots into Soviet industry, as we have said, has only just begun.

In short, Marxism-Leninism appears less and less to be an accurate description of the secular forces that govern the world, and the Soviet régime is not only less able to dominate its clones but is also in danger of running out of credible enemies.[44] There must be elements within the Soviet new class who have begun to wonder whether the CPE is, after all, a satisfactory basis for the maintenance of the country's status as a superpower. All of which is another way of saying that probably the régime itself now faces a legitimacy problem where it is most dangerous, among its own cadres. There must be a growing, if indeterminate, number who no longer believe in the system, except in the sense of a personal source of livelihood *pro tem*.

The Risks of Marketization

In the event of the introduction of a market reform, the immediate problem which the new class would have to face would be the unemployment within its own ranks. For the massive bureaucratic establishment which is the new class has as one of its principal functions that of substituting for the market, e.g. fixing thousands of prices, allocating virtually the totality of capital and labor, clearing up bottlenecks, and the like. Those who are not eligible for retirement or who could not survive in a competitive environment—and I think we must assume that the numbers of both would be legion—would have to stomach a return to the ranks of the proletariat. Such considerations no doubt go far to explain the intransigent opposition of the bureaucrats to virtually any economic reform, but more particularly to one which is moving toward a market.

A second danger that would come with market reform applies only to totalitarian states formally organized as federations, such as Yugoslavia or the U.S.S.R., i.e. the threat of the gradual transformation of such a federation into a set of semi-autarkic economies with all that that might imply for the exacerbation of the national problem. One of the great advantages of the CPE is that it automatically places all but the most unimportant economic decisions in the federal capital, in our case Moscow, thus precluding different decisions from being taken in Kiev, Vilnius or Dushanbe.

All this is another way of saying that the national problem is a major obstacle to the marketization of a centrally planned economy. The prime illustration of this fact is to be found in Communist Yugoslavia. For a proper appreciation of the danger a brief review of the Yugoslav experience will be of help.

In 1952 the Yugoslav leadership undertook, as part of its effort to reach a *modus vivendi* with its population in the circumstances of excommunication by the Cominform, to transfer a significant share of investment decision-making from the central planners to the lowly commune, the basic unit of local government within each federal republic. As it turned out, however, it was not the communes who ended up making the newly decentralized investment decisions but instead the distinct and separate Party apparatuses in each of the republics. And by 1959 Marshal Tito and his closest associates found themselves facing a situation in which each republican Party was pursuing an investment policy which could only be justified, if at all, in the event of an ultimate break-up of the Yugoslav Federation! For each republic, even Montenegro, was building its own steel mill, each was attempting to build or extend its own port facilities, many planned for an automotive industry of their own, and so on. This was not exactly what the central leadership had had in mind. The best solution to the new problem turned out to be the marketization of the federal economy as a whole, so that the play of market forces would cause the less efficient of these operations to close down, leaving only the efficient to survive.

Market forces took hold only by fits and starts, however. The poorer and more agrarian southeastern republics contested bitterly the reduction in the federal subsidy of their new factories which the reform brought with it. They refused to close unprofitable enterprises on the ground that the economic consequences of such action would be politically destabilizing. Since Belgrade agreed, the southerners managed to obtain federal help for specific enterprises so as to postpone the evil day indefinitely. The more prosperous northern republics for their part countered by successfully pressing for constitutional reform which relieved the federal government and the federal Party of much of their authority. The dominant faction in the Croatian Party, moreover, took advantage of its increasingly greater autonomy secretly to encourage an ancient Croatian literary society, with a press of its own and branches in every important Croatian town, to assume the role of a camouflaged opposition political Party and openly to advocate the acquisition by all republics of constitutional rights which would make Croatian secession from the Federation only a cautious after-thought. In Croatia the popular response to the new 'party' was enormously, even hysterically, favorable. To bring the Croatians to their senses Tito was forced to purge (December 1971) the Croatian Party leadership, as well as the liberals in the other leaderships. He told his intimates that the country was on the verge of civil war and that he was prepared to occupy the deviant Republic with forces of the Yugoslav People's army, whose officers' corps was, as everyone knew, made up primarily of Serbs and Montenegrins.[45] (One of the Croatian demands—to which Tito had not acceded—would have assigned all Croatian recruits to units stationed in Croatia and placed all troops in that Republic under the command of a Croatian general officer. The commander in Croatia had always been a Serb.)

I venture to think that the Soviet leaders were neither surprised nor chagrined by the Yugoslav misadventure. They have to deal with a national problem of their own. The long delay in the adoption (1977) of the Brezhnev revision of Stalin's 1936 constitution is apparently to be explained by persistent if unavailing efforts of the Soviet minority republics to put real meaning into the federal language of that document. Another index of national dissidence is the intensification of anti-Semitism among Slavs.[46] Partly in consequence, some 400,000 Jews, out of a total of perhaps two million, have asked to emigrate, with all the immediate costs to the individual and his family that such an application brings with it. Nor is the language situation in the Soviet Union undergoing improvement. While the percentage of citizens who can communicate in Russian is growing, the proportion of minority nationals who use their native tongue on a daily basis is also rising. One third of the population of the U.S.S.R.—and this one-third includes the Muslims—still attends schools that teach Russian as a foreign language. The Kremlin now attempts to introduce instruction in Russian in minority areas at the preschool level.[47]

The enlivenment of minority nationalism has also triggered a Russian backlash. From 1965 until the accession of Mikhail Gorbachev to the position of secretary general in 1985, minority representation at the top, i.e. at the level of the secretariat and the Politburo, was limited to candidate members of the latter body, where their role was largely formal since they remained residents of their national republics and did not normally take part in its deliberations. The backlash has also become visible in the foundation of a genuinely voluntary but exclusively Great Russian "Society for the Preservation of Historical Landmarks" which, in addition to the purpose indicated by its name, seeks to protect the environment against the ravages of thoughtless industrialization. The Society played a major role in the cleaning up of Lake Baikal. To me this organization has the earmarks of a covert national party; in any case, I doubt if an analogue presently exists elsewhere under socialism.

Thus in the event of a Soviet attempt to introduce market reform, Moscow would probably face a problem similar to that which Belgrade has already experienced. Indeed, the native Party leaders in Soviet Central Asia attempt regularly to persuade Moscow that the area should be allowed to develop a heavy industry of its own, a plea which the Muscovite politicians as regularly ignore. But there are other indications that the Muslim population of the U.S.S.R., whether that in Central Asia or the much smaller body of the faithful in the Caucasus, do not willingly accept their Soviet citizenship or, at the least, remain unwilling to accommodate to the practical requirements of residence in the Soviet state.

There is not only the fact that as a rule Muslims refuse to accept employment outside Muslim-inhabited areas, an attitude which embarrasses the Soviet government considerably, since the annual increment to its labor force is presently found in Soviet Central Asia and the Caucasus. But it is also true that Muslims in Central Asia refuse to accept employment in the cities in their own area, since they believe that leaving the community into which they were born is almost an act of treason. Thus it is the cities of Central Asia that contain the one-fourth of the total population of the area which is non-Muslim, i.e. Slavic. The Central Asian urban proletariat is by and large made up of Slavic speakers. Finally, intermarriage between the Slavic settlers and local Muslims is a rare event. In fact, a Muslim who joins the Party and accepts a responsible position in, say, government is regarded by the natives as having turned Russian and abandoned his people.

The Russians return the compliment. Interrogation of recent emigrants from the U.S.S.R. indicates that draftees from the Muslim populations are not as a rule assigned to combat units but instead to railway and construction battalions, where they receive minimal military training. These units have taken over much of the physical labor formerly allotted to some of the more notorious but now dissolved corrective labor camps. One specialist thinks that the high differential between Muslim and Christian birthrates in the U.S.S.R. makes it certain that the Kremlin will have either greatly to increase the strength of the noncombat military or to lengthen the term of service for combat troops. More recent evidence suggests, however, that Soviet authorities are now giving a larger share of noncombat roles within combat divisions to non-Slavs.[48] It has occurred to me that the Muslim experience in the labor battalions could turn out to be a major event in the emergence of a Soviet Muslim, as distinguished from an Uzbek or a Tadzhik, national consciousness.

When the Soviets first invaded Afghanistan, in December, 1979, they pulled together some four divisions from Muslim reservists in Central Asia, believing that, since these soldiers were native speakers of Tadzhik and Uzbek, languages spoken widely in northern Afghanistan, they could serve as interpreters and intermediaries with the local population and smooth the way for Soviet intervention. But the Muslim reservists sold their weapons in order to buy Korans, which are difficult to obtain in the U.S.S.R. The reservists also evinced a notable reluctance to use force against the Afghani, whom they regarded as fellow Muslims.

There also is other evidence of an emergent Muslim national consciousness among the peoples of the Caucasus and Central Asia. These areas are the only Mohammedan regions in the world where Shiites and Sunnites worship cheek by jowl in the same mosques (in this case mainly private homes). The existence of a cultural pride is suggested by the celebration amid pomp and circumstance of the millenium of the birth of the Uzbek scholar Al-Khwarizmi (780-850), who has among his credits the transmission to the West what are today called Arabic numerals. Moreover, a favorite religious shrine of Soviet Muslims is the tomb of one Bahautdin Naqshband, the founder of a dervish order which preaches resistance to foreign oppression and was instrumental in organizing armed opposition to the Russian take-overs of the Caucasus and Turkestan in the early nineteenth century.[49] To one acquainted with the national liberation movements in the nineteenth century Balkans all this has a familiar ring.

The attempt of the Soviet government to establish a Communist régime in Afghanistan also seems to me to raise questions about the situation now prevailing—under the typical socialist facade of unanimity, progress, and joy—in the Muslim-inhabited areas of the Soviet state. Certainly no one could have believed that Afghanistan was ripe for socialism. The social order there is tribal. The economy is agricultural, producing a per capita national income of $250. Male life expectancy at birth is 39.9 years while the literacy rate is 12 percent.[50] In 1979 it would have been difficult to visualize Afghan society as even having entered the stage of progressive bourgeois nationalism, usually ascribed by Mowcow to third world countries whose governments are Soviet dependencies.

Could Moscow have wished to assure itself of control of the energy supplies of the country? Afghan reserves of methane gas have already been tapped by a pipeline terminating on Soviet territory. Or was there thought of a Soviet Afghanistan as providing access to a warm water port? The overland route to the Arabian sea is without hard-surfaced roads or railways and goods must not only cross the mountains of Afghanistan, but they must also brave the open desert of the Pakhistani province of Baluchistan. A shorter route, with better roads, leads over the mountains and arid valleys of Iran to the Persian Gulf, the occupation of whose shores would put Moscow in command of the oil reserves of the Middle East. While such an act would no doubt precipitate an international crisis of the first order—the Japanese economy imports some 90 percent of its oil through the Straits of Hormuz —it appears to be the case that 24 Soviet divisions are stationed permanently in the southern Caucasus.

Another possible explanation for the invasion of Afghanistan might be a strongly felt need for the Politburo to restore a sense of momentum to the world Communist movement, as well as to Soviet cadres whose morale may have been affected by the unfavorable correlation of forces, as seen from Moscow and referred to earlier in this essay. On the list of Soviet third-world dependencies the number of deviant, ailing or escaped clients is more impressive than the number of successful and obedient ones. But if this explanation has any validity, it implies that the accuracy and pertinence of the information supplied by the KGB agents in Afghanistan left a great deal to be desired. It does appear that Soviet authorities have been astonished and angered by the stubborn character of Afghan resistance.

As early as 1973 Moscow had established in Kabul a native military dictatorship to its own liking, but that dictatorship had gradually escaped the clutches of the local Afghan Communists and their Soviet advisers. Presumably the Kremlin believed that a strictly Communist régime would be more responsive to its wishes than a "progressive bourgeois" one. But this begs the question as to why the Soviet government wanted control of Afghanistan in the first place.

Let me offer an additional hypothesis: an important Soviet motive for the installation of a Communist government in Afghanistan was the fear that that country would otherwise end up as an Islamic republic and that this would tend to make worse an already difficult situation in the Muslim Caucasus and Soviet Central Asia. The evidence is circumstantial but I find its cumulative effect impressive.

Why, for example, should Soviet Muslims be exempt from the appeals of Islamic republicanism? Egyptian Muslims are not, nor are Saudi Arabians, nor (to be sure) Iranians. The standard counter argument runs to the effect that Central Asians must reasonably be grateful for the greater literacy, the improved living standards, the urbanization and modernization that Soviet rule has brought with it. These claims have a solid factual foundation. Living standards in the Muslim-inhabited regions of the U.S.S.R. are sub-stantially higher than those prevailing in Afghanistan and Iran, countries just to the south. Irrigation has made Soviet Central Asia the prime supplier of raw cotton to the countries of the socialist community. There are now also in these areas textile and food processing industries, as well as oil extraction and a nuclear missile testing facility.

Yet in its origin Islamic republicanism was primarily the reaction of an illiterate Iranian peasantry to the impact of a forced-draft modernization sponsored by the shah. This reaction played into the hands of a Muslim clergy, the *mullahs*, who had come to be largely ignored by educated Iranians, but who now managed to seize control of the government and attempt to return the country to the way of life of the ninth century caliphate, insofar as that was compatible with the continued flow of oil revenues. The leaders of Islamic republicanism soon conceived of themselves as the founders of a world movement within the confines of Islam. The long and bloody war between Iran and Iraq is one manifestation of this outlook.

The question that must be asked is whether the rural populations of the Caucasus and Soviet Central Asia have reacted more favorably to forced-draft modernization Soviet style than the Iranian peasantry did to the modernization of the shah. And a related question: why should it be assumed that indigenous Communist movements would strike deeper roots in the Caucasus and Soviet Central Asia than they had in any of the independent Islamic countries where, except for Indonesia, they have so far remained tiny and despised political sects?

Between Iran, on the one hand, and Egypt on the other, there exists no physical contiguity nor any linguistic corridor. Iran and Afghanistan, however, share a long common border while half of the population of Afghanistan speaks Pashtu, a member of the Iranian language group, and all educated Afghani, whether Pashtu speakers or not, are fluent in Dari Persian, the form of Iranian spoken in Teheran. Furthermore the Tadzhiks, who comprise 25 percent of the population of Afghanistan, speak a form of Iranian identical with that spoken by the population of Soviet Tadzhikistan, which lies just across the Soviet frontier from them and in numbers is roughly equal in strength. It would appear that the existence of this linguistic corridor considerably increases the chances of Islamic republican doctrine making its way in Soviet Central Asia.

It is also worth noting that a Soviet-sponsored Communist régime was first installed in Afghanistan in April 1978, only three months after the *ayatollah* Khomeini had seized control of the government in Teheran. This first Communist government survived in Kabul only some 23 months, however, the brevity of its career being largely the result of a frontal attack which it launched upon the power and influence of the rural Afghan *mullahs*. The assault precipitated a popular rising with which the new régime could not cope. This first régime, however, was shortly replaced by a second, which was imposed by a sizable influx of Soviet troops, in December 1979. The insurgency continued, however, and competent observers have estimated that some two-thirds of the Afghan *mujaheddin*, or crusaders, as these guerrillas are known, are of Islamic republican persuasion. So far the Islamic republicans are the only guerrillas who have been able to organize resistance forces with personnel from more than one tribe. It is thus not impossible that should Moscow ever admit defeat and withdraw its forces, it would be confronted by an Islamic republic in Afghanistan. In any case, it does not take much imagination to understand that this bitter and barbaric military struggle may turn out to be the first stage in the development of an Afghan national consciousness, one based not on ethnic factors but on a religiously configured, anti-Soviet sentiment.

Like the Polish crisis, the Afghan guerrilla war seems likely to continue for a long time. The Afghani appear to be determined. Probably a third of their population—some five million people—has taken refuge in northern Pakistan, which is Pashtu speaking, and in Iran. These asylums also serve as sanctuaries, where the guerrillas rest and re-equip. Small arms from the West make their way to those operating out of Pakistan, including more recently the "stingers" they so badly needed to cope with the enemy's helicopter gunships.

The Soviet leaders are embarrassed by this situation. To deal decisively with the *mujaheddin* they would need approximately to double the number of their forces in Afghanistan, to some 300,000, but they fear this would attract worldwide attention and bring down upon them widespread moral opprobrium which, apparently, at this time they are anxious to avoid. So on the one hand they quietly negotiate in Geneva, attempting to arrange for a withdrawal on favorable terms. They fear that the abandonment of the régime in Kabul, and its subsequent inevitable collapse, would impair the stability of others of their dependencies. On the other hand, they exclude the foreign press from the country and attempt to depopulate strategic areas so that the guerrillas will not be able to find food or shelter in them.

Meantime, returning Soviet casualties have apparently made an impression inside the U.S.S.R. A new form of corruption now protects young recruits, whose parents can afford to pay, from being assigned to Afghanistan. The Soviet population seems to be learning that the war is a "dirty" one, and they are angry that the Afghani refuse to be reasonable and give up a war they can't win. For a long time the Soviet public has been aware of the falsity of the government's claims in domestic affairs; this they can see for themselves. But until now they had been inclined to take the official declarations on foreign policy at face value. For the first time they appear to be harboring doubts in this area also. It has been argued that defeat in Afghanistan could cause sufficient disillusionment to set off a general crisis in the U.S.S.R. itself.[51] If this is indeed the case, Afghanistan has become a slow-burning fuse on the south, as is Poland, on the west.

It occurs to me, by way of concluding this discourse on the risks of marketization, that together the Polish and Afghan cases suggest that the Soviet polity, for all its astonishing accomplishments, may in the long term be incapable of acculturating and absorbing distinctively foreign cultures. The phenomenon, which I have elsewhere called "political landslide," has so far been limited to countries with a Catholic heritage: Hungary in 1956, Czechoslovakia in 1968, Croatia in 1971, Poland in 1981. The Afghan war, especially if it proves to be connected with the spread of Islamic republicanism, suggests that Communism and the Muslim faith also suffer from a basic incompatibility. In any case, the evidence indicates that the Muslim populations of the Soviet Union would not be the last to utilize decentralization of the Soviet economy to pursue economic policies of their own.

We have already seen that in Yugoslavia the effort to shift from central planning to reliance on market forces resulted in Belgrade's temporary loss of political control in Croatia, a situation which was corrected only by the threat of military occupation of the deviant republic. But earlier, in 1968, what began as the marketization of the Czechoslovak economy, had led to a similar result. Under the leadership of a new secretary general, Alexander Dubcek, the ruling elements, in virtual unanimity, undertook to dismantle the machinery of totalitarian control. Censorship was abolished and government television was permitted to produce a documentary concerning the mysterious death, in 1948, of Jan Masaryk, Czechoslovak foreign minister and son of the founder of the Republic. Interest groups were allowed to form, such as a national association of collective farms, to press for concessions to their constituents before government officials in Prague. New political parties were permitted, and old ones were allowed to expand their memberships and the press runs of their newspapers, although the official sources made no reference to the possibility of free elections. The universities recovered their autonomy and their standards. It appeared as though the country was on the way to becoming a one-party social democracy, that it was developing what its spokesmen referred to as a socialism "with a human face" in which the rights of the individual human being would be accorded some respect, when forces of the Warsaw Pact (mainly Soviet) entered the country and put an end to the experiment.[52]

Today it is clear that the rapid evolution of the Czechoslovak polity from January 1968 until the Soviet occupation in August was causally related to a market reform which had gotten under way a few years earlier. The nexus between marketization and the loss of control of a totalitarian polity, however, is not immediately apparent. But it may be understood if we begin with the proposition that marketization automatically involves the restoration of a significant measure of consumer sovereignty, i.e. by its purchases the consuming public, and not the government, largely determines what goods and services shall be produced. In the Soviet case, the restoration of consumer sovereignty would limit considerably the proportion of the GNP that could be earmarked for the use of the military-industrial complex. Marketization thus would constitute a threat to the enormous present Soviet military establishment, albeit one which that establishment may have to accept in the light of the alternative, i.e. an unacceptable decline in the rate of growth of GNP. To put the matter in other terms, one purpose of the CPE is to enable the political authorities to dictate to the public what goods and services it shall be able to spend its money for, even if this involves a deliberate lowering of popular living standards. Thus, in the first place, consumer sovereignty places limits on political power. It is probably incompatible with a totalitarian, though not necessarily with an authoritarian, polity.

If Soviet Russia should marketize, to take the argument one step further, it would have to accept a high degree of integration with the world market, specializing in the export of those products and services in which it enjoyed a natural advantage and in the import of those in which it did not. If in this situation it should turn out that employment opportunities abroad were often more rewarding than those at home, emigration would have to be permitted in the interests of efficiency and the greatest return on capital. Yet freedom to emigrate would give everyone a political as well as an economic alternative and thus make it very difficult for the government deliberately to lower living standards very far. The potency of the police power would be greatly reduced.

Finally, in a market economy labor would have to be free to bargain with capital in respect of its wages and conditions of work. To make these negotiations meaningful it would have to possess the right to strike. But unless there were a free press, in which the claims of labor could be put before the court of public opinion, and a government that was enough beholden to labor to take a serious view of its problems, the right to strike would be a feeble weapon. Consumer sovereignty does not by its nature require a democratic form of government, but it is certainly not incompatible with it.

In the case of Czechoslovakia, which alone of the present-day socialist states possessed in the interwar period something of a democratic government and tradition, the leaders of the reform movement seem to have understood from the beginning the relationship between market reform and political pluralism and deliberately have pushed the latter simultaneously with marketization. Such an acceleration, however, would be unlikely in the case of the U.S.S.R.

A Malfunctioning Dictatorship

All these problems—the failure of central planning, the erosion of régime control, the unfavorable correlation of forces, as well as the risks of marketization—have to be dealt with by a government that, in my view, is no longer working as it was designed to do. The dictatorship of the proletariat has begun to malfunction. The most visible evidence of this malfunction is the indecisive character the current succession struggle has assumed. Between 1975 and 1985, the Union was governed by three walking corpses, Brezhnev, Andropov and Chernenko. This shadow dictatorship appears in part to have resulted from the reluctance of the old guard, those who came up through Stalin's massive purges, to admit to the seats of power a younger generation that did not have blood on its hands. Was it feared that this new generation might fail to understand how easily control of the huge, powerful but unwieldy system could be lost?[53]

The succession, in 1985, to the post of general secretary of 54-year-old Mikhail Gorbachev represents the beginning of the long-awaited generational changeover, but it remains to be seen how long the new man will have to rule by consensus, as his immediate predecessors did, or how soon (if at all) he can secure firm control of all the levers of power.

But there is also the consideration that, as with any self-selecting body—and more especially in one in which supreme power is ill-defined and brooks no constitutional limits—the tendency has been to select a secretary general who will not represent a threat to the political careers of those who made the choice. The result has been a steady decline in the personal qualities of that all-important official, as is easily seen if we recall the progression from Lenin to Stalin to Khrushchev to Brezhnev, Andropov and Chernenko.

Since the leadership was faced with increasingly divisive issues, it not unsurprisingly manifested a growing tendency to temporize. Brezhnev was the first to embody this trend. He was chosen to succeed a leader who had come to understand that the Soviet polity was itself malfunctioning and who had therefore attempted to repair it through measures of reform. One need not agree with Khrushchev's specific diagnosis of the problem to understand that he had indeed come to envision the need for some modification of the system. But in attempting reform, Khrushchev inevitably threatened the perquisites of various hierarchies and was at last overthrown for his trouble.

His successor Brezhnev not unnaturally took the position that there was nothing wrong with the Soviet polity that a little fine-tuning would not take care of. The result of this attitude was that for the first time the Union had a secretary-general who governed, not by fiat, but by negotiating out compromise arrangements among his contentious senior colleagues. In some instances, as in the decision to occupy Czechoslovakia in 1968, the secretary-general apparently ended up holding the casting vote. But the overall consequence of the new distribution of power at the top was that divisive issues no longer produced bloody purges and sharp changes of line. Instead they resulted in a creeping form of political paralysis.

Further analysis of the new malady will suggest that it was at bottom rooted in the emergence of a new veto power, one exercised de facto through discrete noncompliance by any of the major bureaucratic establishments: the party apparatus, the military, the security police, and the state bureaucracy. The capability of noncompliance was in turn derived from a kind of self-denying ordinance which the leadership had adopted shortly after the death of Stalin in 1953, when they all foreswore the systematic use of political terror. They apparently took this action primarily because they had learned from bitter experience that when terror is used regularly to control and direct the mass of the population—as distinct from its occasional employment to mark off the boundaries of tolerated behavior —quarrels within the élite end up being decided in the offices of the security police who eventually assume control of the polity as a whole. Hardly a family in the *nomenklatura* had not suffered grievous personal loss as a result. Some leaders may have also understood that the systematic use of terror was not in the long run compatible with the successful functioning of a modern industrial society. At the same time, however, the deprivation of the secretary-general of his personal control over the secret police made it impossible for him to insist on full compliance with his instructions. Thus, much to the astonishment of almost everyone, it had even become possible for an élite conspiracy to exercise the new veto power by overthrowing a reforming first secretary and replacing him with one who was content to rule by consensus.[54]

This growing indecisiveness on the part of the leadership was perhaps also related to a long-term tendency for the less talented and the more unprincipled to come to sit in the seats of power. This proclivity was first seen in the mass liquidation of the old Bolsheviks in the late 1930s, when these brilliant and polyglot revolutionaries—most of them with professional credentials—were replaced by illiterate peasants and workers who had never been abroad and who were content to rise in power at the cost of the physical annihilation of their superiors. Not surprisingly, conformity and seniority appear today to be the twin keys to promotion, generally speaking, especially since in the meantime Brezhnev had granted tenure to all bureaucratic personnel, thus blocking the possibility of transfer to less important or more distant positions, the one last lever of bureaucratic sanction available to the secretary-general.[55]

In sum, the transformation of the secretary-general into a walking corpse is symptomatic of a graver illness, one which might be diagnosed as the bureaucratic degeneration of a totalitarian régime. To operate successfully, a polity of this nature must be charged with an overriding objective, such as the need to manage a world revolution, build socialism in one country, or repulse the invasion of an overpowering hereditary enemy. Even the cold war defense of the homeland against capitalist encirclement does not appear to be enough to stabilize the system over many years, or to provide it with decisive leadership, without which it tends to drift.

Divisions Within the New Class

What Milovan Djilas refers to as the new class can perhaps be best understood as an intelligentsia in power, an intelligentsia being the class of people in a developing country who serve as the transmission belt for introducing into their homeland the knowledge and techniques of developed countries.[56]

In the Soviet Russia of today admission to this class is by way of graduation from domestic universities, but all members of the new class have some claim to professional standing. In a modernizing totalitarian polity, however, where the gap between facade and reality is often cavernous, the members of this class face a special problem, that of the two truths, the truth that they must always and everywhere publicly proclaim, and the truth they can utter only in the company of intimates, if at all. For under Communism success in a professional career has so far been dependent not so much on professional accomplishment as it is on political loyalty and backstairs intrigue. The typical member of the new class is thus faced with a constant trade-off between career advancement and professional standards.

It seems reasonable to believe that in coping with the problem of two truths the new class can be divided into three subgroupings. The first is made up of those for whom two truths are not a problem. Such people are interested in power and its perquisites and will do whatever is necessary to retain and enjoy them. I would venture to assert that this group is, on the whole, made up of the less talented and the less educated. Especially the senior members of this group are for the most part of humble (primarily) peasant origin, have as a rule only grammar school education, and have come up as beneficiaries of Stalin's great purges. This kind of background would go far to explain strict adherence to established institutions and policies as well as ignorance of and suspicion toward the world outside the U.S.S.R.[57] All these people, young and old, I would call politicians, and it is they who now make the basic political decisions.

As for the unfavorable correlation of forces discussed in the third section of this essay, the politicians would no doubt insist that it represented a third temporary stabilization of international capitalism, after those which began in 1924 and in 1949, and that in the meantime it behooved good revolutionaries to hold onto the gains that had already been made. There should be no retreat in Afghanistan, no reduction in the clandestine sponsorship of international terrorism, and no arms limitation agreement unless the bourgeois powers were prepared to concede unilateral advantage. The politicians emphasize the dangers of capitalist encirclement and the innate hostility of the bourgeois world, propositions which, in their hands, amount to self-fulfilling prophecies.

As for economic reform, I believe the politicians would advocate "further perfection" of the mechanism of central planning, combined with more consistent use of the police power in the maintenance of labor discipline—this in the face of accumulated evidence showing that established bureaucratic interests have in the past always defeated even minor reform efforts. To cope with the possibility of widespread rioting, perhaps the number and equipment of the security divisions assigned to the ministry of the interior should be beefed up, in the view of the politicians.

The second grouping within the new class, as I see it, is composed of those whose instincts and interests are primarily professional. Mostly of the younger generation, they have survived a rigorous training and tend to believe that they should be given full responsibility for the practice of their callings. They feel that all positions should be filled by the best qualified and that if this were the case many if not most of the problems faced by the régime could be dealt with successfully.[58] The two truths are inherently troublesome for anyone of truly professional orientation. The members of this subgrouping I shall refer to as technocrats.

No doubt the technocratic view of the international prospects of the Soviet Union is that as a state with a run-down centrally planned economy it is fighting a losing battle. The so-called unfavorable correlation of forces is no more than a Marxist-Leninist misunderstanding of the more or less progressive way in which the world persists in moving. In my view the technocrats will, on the whole, tend to support market reform, believing that under it their professional skills would have greater value, that they would be better able to adjust to the cold winds of competition, even though masses of them would at first experience dismissal as the reform proceeded. The memorandum advocating market reform prepared for the use of the leadership by the Academy of Sciences at Novosibirsk has already been referred to.

No doubt the technocrats hope that in the end they will replace the politicians as the ruling element within the new class. This may help explain the reluctance of the Brezhnev faction to admit representatives of the younger generation to the highest office. Some observers of the Soviet scene are now asserting that Gorbachev himself is the first of the technocratic element to reach the position of supreme power, and it does seem that in addressing audiences of university students in speeches (which do not appear in the press) he is more or less openly appealing to them as the future leaders of Soviet Russia. In the speeches that are published the new Soviet leader leans more heavily on factual data and reasoned analysis than did his predecessors. He insists that the way the economy is run must undergo a thorough change and must be brought up to Western levels of efficiency. At the same time, however, he avoids discussion of the specific changes he has in mind.[59]

The third sub-category of the new class I would refer to as the *literati*. While the first grouping holds the reins of power and is to be found primarily in the Party apparatus and the *nomenklatura*, and while the second is responsible for the implementation of policy and is concentrated in the various bureaucratic establishments, including the military, the *literati* tend to be located in the writers' unions, in the academies, within the artistic community, and on university faculties. While there are conservative and reactionary elements here also, the *literati* are inclined to be the most troubled by the problem of the two truths. This is partly because this group is the special heir of the East European tradition according to which an intelligentsia is obligated to serve as "the voice of the people," especially when the people suffer from oppression. It is also partly because Soviet citizens of Jewish background are more strongly represented among the *literati* than elsewhere in the new class, but mainly because of the nature of their daily tasks. "Socialist Realism," in form a school of literature but in fact a device that makes each author his own censor, was introduced in order to keep the Communist *literati* under Party control and deny them the opportunity to morally undermine the new régime as they had the old.

Because the new class is an intelligentsia in power, I believe that intellectual dissidence constitutes the greatest threat to the stability of the Soviet régime, greater I would argue, than any other. For intellectual dissidence tends to formulate and dwell upon the second truth, and, in consequence, it has a tendency to raise the moral issue and thus to precipitate the factional division that is a principal prerequisite of régime destabilization. In the satellites dissidence has even led to mass desertion from the teachings of Marx and Lenin. Intellectual dissidence is largely peculiar to the new class, and especially to the *literati*; it does not much affect either the workers or the *kolkhozniki* whose opposition is more likely to take such forms as Protestant sectarianism or wildcat strikes.

There is a public form of intellectual dissent: the rare cases of those writers who make use of their official positions to narrow somehow the gap between the two truths. Perhaps the outstanding example is the editorship of the literary journal *Novyi Mir* by Konstantin Simonov and Alexandr Tvardovsky during the years 1954-1970.[60] It was *Novyi Mir* that published (in 1962 and to be sure with the personal permission of N. S. Khrushchev) "One Day in the Life of Ivan Denisovich," paving the way for the literary greatness of Alexander Solzhenitsyn. There is also the case of nuclear physicist Andrei Sakharov, father of the Soviet hydrogen bomb, who undertook to circulate private memoranda within the new class over his own name and to grant interviews to the Western press. Even in the best of times the régime simply cannot tolerate for very long people of such prestige questioning its policies. Because of the extent of the influence of these people, as well as because of their devotion to the second truth, they are sooner or later ordered to cease and desist, or face the consequences. Those who refuse to comply become in their suffering international martyrs, much to the annoyance of the Kremlin. But such cases suggest what the outcome might be if censorship were to be abolished, or even to be relaxed.[61]

The extent of the threat to new class cohesion represented by works devoted to the second truth first became publicly evident in 1956, when the Hungarian *literati* realized that General Secretary Matyas Rakosi had persuaded them to engage their literary talents in defense of the progressive character of his régime, while at the same time he practiced in secret the worst forms of tyranny against the Hungarian opposition. To make public amends the *literati* took advantage of Khrushchev's newly introduced policy of destalinization to organize a series of discussion clubs, the Petoefi Circles, for the purpose of promoting discussion within the new class of the nature of the Hungarian Socialist régime. These discussions helped precipitate the insurrection of late October and early November 1956, during which Western correspondents complained that they could find no one in the streets of Budapest who would admit to having ever been a member of the Communist Party.

An even more spectacular example of the mass defection of a new class is to be found in the history of socialist Czechoslovakia, where the ruling élite suddenly (in the spring of 1968) opted for a socialism "with a human face." This transformation took place, however, only after the failure of the local version of the CPE threatened to undermine Czechoslovakia's relatively high living standard. To counter this threat a market reform had been resorted to, based on the Yugoslav model. Meantime, however, the literature of dissidence had surfaced in the official Slovak media, an oddity to be explained by the fact that Slovakia possessed a separate Party apparatus but one which had been denied the full autonomy which Prague had promised. Once the second truth appeared in the Slovak media it literally flooded the Czech press, radio, and television.[62]

While Czechoslovakia in 1968 is the clearest case of a *trahison des clercs* triggered by a sudden flood of second truth publication, the crisis of 1971 in Yugoslavia, to which I have referred elsewhere, also illustrates the point. For the separatist movement in Croatia of that year was preceded by a campaign in the publication of the *Matica Hrvatska*, a Croatian literary society of nationalist orientation, as well as by Party-tolerated public rallies in which patriotic speeches aroused mass audiences to a fever-pitch of excitement.[63]

The crises in Hungary, Czechoslovakia, and Croatia were produced and accompanied by a suspension of official censorship. But if censorship is not tampered with, the threat of the second truth takes the form of an underground press the product of which is known collectively as *samizdat*. The essence of this threat is not that *samizdat* reveals to the new class so much that it hadn't already known, or even that some of this news returns to Russia by way of Western broadcasts. The primary threat lies rather in the danger of the moral condemnation of the régime, in the implication that the socialist community itself is, in the words of an American president, an "evil empire," and in bringing the evidence relevant to this judgment to the level of everyday awareness.

The underground press also makes it possible for the opposition to formulate a concrete program of its own. After the Polish disorders of 1970 and 1976 the volume of *samizdat* reached flood proportions. While continuing to maintain its censorship of all official publications, Warsaw seemed unable to cope with the output of the private typewriter, the mimeograph machine or the secret press. There was even a so-called flying university, i.e. lectures given in one private apartment after another, the professor explaining what he really thought, as distinguished from what he was required to say in his official lecture hall. Among the flood of clandestine publications was a newspaper which was somehow distributed to factories throughout the country. Edited by a committee of intellectuals, known by the acronym KOR, some of whom were former members of the Polish Party, its editorial content would later reappear as the program of Solidarity. Some members of KOR served the leadership of the new union as an informal brain trust.

It should be pointed out that, currently, even under martial law, the output of Polish *samizdat* continues virtually unabated. While the universities are being brought once again under state control, the church buildings of the more courageous priests are now serving as centers of public discussion, as formerly the flying university did. Churches, furthermore, are able to provide stages for the presentation of plays and auditoria for the screening of films with political content. I would imagine that, translated into various Soviet languages, much of this current clandestine intellectual and artistic product is now read—at dictation speed—over the facilities of Radio Liberty in Munich.

Some members of the new class are more affected by the problem of professional integrity than others, but perhaps the majority are vulnerable in some circumstances, e.g. should it appear that the existing polity is in real trouble, or that the national interest is no longer served by it, or that the régime can be viewed as a moral monstrosity, or, most perilous of all, some combination of these.

Given the vulnerability of its European satellites to the threat of intellectual dissidence, the Kremlin must be fully alert to the danger it represents at home in its clandestine form. For the time being at least, the great flow of these unauthorized publications—including a *Chronicle of Current Events* in whose production elements of the KGB must have had a hand—which characterized the late sixties and early seventies in Soviet Russia has been dammed up. Not only do Soviet authorities punish the authors and distributors of *samizdat* with expulsion, exile, imprisonment, or confinement to psychiatric hospitals, but they also register the imprints of typewriters. They limit the number and availability of photocopy machines, placing them under twenty-four-hour KGB guard, virtually forbid the possession of personal computers, jam foreign radio transmissions in any of the Soviet languages, and suspend direct dial telephone service to Western Europe and the United States. It is also true that telephone books are not available to the general public.[64]

But the cost of reducing the flow of *samizdat* to its present trickle may turn out to be very high. For such restrictions have the effect of blocking the Soviet Union from participating in the so-called "informatics" revolution, which is now central to the continuing industrialization of the West and in which the U.S.S.R. must somehow participate if it is to remain competitive, even in the military field, with its capitalist enemies. Without a much freer flow of information than is currently politically acceptable and without the massive computerization of the economy, how can the Soviet manufactured product ever become competitive in the world market?

The Danger of Political Landslide

It is time to return to the estimate that I made at the beginning of this paper. The crises to which I refer in the very first paragraph are, in my judgment, of a special kind. They are political landslides.

By political landslide I mean a sudden and unexpected loss of political control by a totalitarian régime. The key symptoms may differ. Free elections are called or censorship is formally abolished. A secession movement is organized or an opposition party masquerading as a free labor union suddenly emerges. These symptoms are characteristic because totalitarian control by its very nature attempts to suppress the essential pluralism of traditionally or newly pluralist or even partly pluralist societies such as autocracies by using violence, or the threat of violence, to obliterate the distinction between state and society. In a political landslide, total control has ended by producing total dissent.[65] So far, however, all examples of political landslide come from European countries with a Catholic tradition. To date there have been none in European countries of Orthodox religious tradition.

A final question at issue is whether the Soviet Union, a superpower located culturally as well as physically somewhere between the Catholic and the third worlds, is in serious danger of undergoing an analogous system breakdown. The answer to the question is that all social orders will experience breakdown if the stress to which they are subjected becomes severe enough, i.e. if the vital interests of the dominant Great Russians are placed in jeopardy.

The basic fact is that the present Soviet economic system, despite its enormous accomplishments in the past, now appears to have exhausted its ability to grow. Indeed, the Soviet leaders may even be confronted with an irreversibly negative rate of economic growth. When a market economy enters a period of low or negative growth, i.e. enters a depression, such as the one which began in 1929, it at once begins to accumulate reserves of labor (the unemployed) and of capital (an unusually high rate of capital accumulation). Once the market has gone through a period of basic readjustment of economic relationships—liquidation of both reparations and war debts as in the 1929 depression—it can put the accumulated reserves of capital and labor to work to produce a new period of growth, or prosperity.

But in the U.S.S.R. with a per capita rate of growth that is probably zero, there is full employment and individual savings accounts are at or near an all-time high.[66] Both labor and capital are in short supply. In addition, the economic tasks that face the government are mountainous: not only must the raw material and energy base be transferred from European Russia to Siberia and the Far East, but agricultural productivity must be raised, public health succored, the railways partially rebuilt, and the informatics revolution imported.

Now on the one hand, it must be clear to leading members of the new class that the CPE is no longer productive enough to maintain the rough military parity with the capitalist West, which they must regard as a vital Russian interest. This parity has been won at a heavy cost and has become one of the main claims of the régime to legitimacy. On the other hand, the only promising solution to the problem of declining productivity appears to be the marketization of the economy (if there is no unemployment is there not much underemployment?) and precisely this seems to carry with it the threat, if not the promise of destabilization.

The current stagnation of living standards, the decline of social mobility and the worsening of the public health, together with a new awareness on the part of the general public that living standards are much higher in the West, have made the availability of food supplies and the character of the popular diet prime political issues. So far as the evidence goes, the mass of the population appears to be dispirited and inclined to profit from a spreading corruption, while concentrating on its material needs and withdrawing from public concerns.

The new class has to fear that food shortages can at any time set off demonstrations, wildcat strikes and riots ranging over wide areas of the U.S.S.R. In such an event, probably only the intervention of the army would suffice to restore order. But it must not be entirely clear to the Communist leaders whether they could confidently rely upon the rank and file to do their duty or whether, indeed, the high command might not profit from the occasion to install a régime that promised greater success in dealing with the problems facing the country.

Censorship and emigration policies tend to conceal from the outside world the erosion of régime control that has already taken place. Categories of officials, such as the *advokatura*, now lobby the *nomenklatura* which today adjudicates conflicts of interests between an office in the central committee apparatus and its opposite number in an important ministry. The growth of the second economy by way of corruption amounts to a partial if clandestine reversion to the New Economic Policy of 1921-1928, i.e. to a degree of marketization. The trend is reinforced by the proliferation of professionals, engineers, economists, physicists, whose efficient employment by itself requires a lessening of central control. The continuing revolution in communication pushes in the same direction; until the Kremlin can tolerate small, autonomous computer programming units it will have to continue to import virtually all its software from the United States. Other forms of pluralization than the economic are also evident, although stoutly resisted by Moscow, such as the enhancement of e.g. Bashkir nationalism or the spread of Protestant sectarianism. And just below the ostensibly placid surface of Soviet society can be sensed the beating pulse of *samizdat*, itself an incipient and already variegated public opinion.[67]

In my view this new, Brezhnevian equilibrium of corruption, consumerism, and conformity, interest groups and all, is not as stable as its terror-ridden Stalinist predecessor, despite its being the silent product of forty-two years of covert negotiation and compromise. An incipient if disguised pluralism scarcely provides a firm support for a Communist hierarchy. The measures necessary to prevent a new outpouring of *samizdat* serve almost as a guarantee that the computerization of the economy will be impeded, if not stultified. National consciousness grows rapidly under the impact of the world revolution in communication, totalitarian controls to the contrary notwithstanding. It seems clear that the Communist *imperium* has been able to reconcile to its rule neither the satellite European populations to its west nor the Muslim peoples to the south, even if, for the sake of argument, we

grant the reconciliation of the non-Muslim Soviet minorities. Just as shortages of food within the U.S.S.R. may serve to trigger internal disorders
widespread and serious enough to set off the systemic crisis which is the
subject of this paper, so either the ongoing tide of Polish dissidence or the
long-continuing trickle of Soviet casualties from Afghanistan could serve in
the same way.

Communist Moscow's dilemma may be formulated as follows: it probably
cannot bring to an end the present perilous economic stagnation without
marketizing the Soviet economy, yet it cannot tolerate stagnation indefinitely.
But if it does undertake marketization, and is able to overcome the stubborn
resistance of major elements of the new class thereto, it risks the loss of
central control and must in any case accept an automatic shift in priorities
from the military-industrial complex to popular consumption. It begins to
look as though the *tour de force* we call Stalinist forced-draft industrialization has only temporarily created a superpower.

In my view, to repeat the principal theme of this essay, the chances of a
political landslide in the Soviet Union within the next five to ten years are
better than even. Let us hope that the Soviet new class and the Great
Russian people can accept a reduction to mere great power status without
involving themselves, and the rest of the world, in a nuclear crisis.

NOTES

1. In the beginning I envisioned the possibility of a system breakdown as being
   better than even within five years. See my "Die nahende Krise in der Sowjetunion," *Osteuropa* XXXIII (1983): 449-462, 555-568, 705-723. After the selection
   of Mikhail Gorbachev as secretary general I lengthened the period by five years
   on the ground that he would probably make a serious effort at economic reform
   and thus lengthen the time in which my percentages (say 60-40) were at work.
   Marshall I. Goldman, *U.S.S.R. in Crisis. The Failure of an Economic System*
   (New York: W.W. Norton, 1983), xiv, takes a position similar to my own. He
   argues that the Soviet economy is already in crisis in the sense that it can only
   recover the power of growth if it is marketized and such a change may be
   impossible politically.

   For contrary views see Robert F. Byrnes, ed., *After Brezhnev. Sources of
   Soviet Conduct in the 1980s.* (Bloomington, IN: Indiana University Press, 1983),
   xviii, and Timothy J. Colton, *The Dilemma of Reform in the Soviet Union*
   (New York: Council on Foreign Relations, 1984). My review of Byrnes is to be
   found at pp. 380-381 of *Osteuropa* (Stuttgart), XXIV (1984), and of Colton pp.
   177-181 of *The Washington Quarterly* (Winter 1985).

2. Henry Rowan, "Central Intelligence Agency Briefing on the Soviet Economy,"
   Before the Subcommittee on International Trade, Finance and Security Eco-

nomics, 1 December 1982, mimeograph, 5-6. *Allocation of Resources in the Soviet Union and China—1983. Hearings Before the Subcommittee on International Trade, Finance, and Security Economics of the Joint Economic Committee Congress of the United States. Ninety-Eighth Congress, First Session. Part 9: Executive Sessions, June 28 and September 20, 1983* (U.S. Government Printing Office, 1984): 2, hereinafter cited as *Resources 1983*; to my knowledge the first to assert, if provisionally, that there had probably been no per capita growth since 1978 was Michael Ellman, "Did Soviet Economic Growth End in 1978," in Jan Drewnowski, ed., *Crisis in the East European Economy. The Spread of Polish Disease* (New York: St. Martin's Press, 1982), 131-142. Alexander Nove puts the case in "Has Soviet Growth Ceased?" *Manchester Statistical Society* (November 1983).

3. Cf. Anthony Sutton, *Western Technology and Soviet Economic Development,* 3 vols. (Stanford, Calif.: The Hoover Institute, Stanford University, 1968-1973).

4. Two other factors are also in part responsible for the secular decline in the rate of growth of Soviet G.N.P. One is the fact that the increasing complexity of the economy gradually magnified the informational and decision-making requirements of the central planners so that the number of bottlenecks and shortages which they could not foresee has grown disproportionately, the other a general failure of worker morale, particularly after 1978, when stagnation of living standards set in. To the best of my knowledge, reasons for the downward secular trend were not looked into until the rate of growth of GNP reached two percent per annum. Economists specialized in the analysis of the Soviet Union generally appeared to assume that the rate would one day level off at a comfortable four or five percent per annum.

5. Marshall I. Goldman, "Gorbachev and Economic Reform," *Foreign Affairs* (New York), Fall 1985: 56-73.

6. "Statement of Murray Feshbach," *The Political Economy of the Soviet Union. Joint Hearings Before the Subcommittee on Economic Goals and Intergovernmental Policy of the Joint Economic Committee Congress of the United States and the Subcommittee on Europe and the Middle East of the Committee on Foreign Affairs, House of Representatives, Ninety-Eighth Congress. First Session. July 26 and September 29, 1983* (Washington D.C.: U.S. Government Printing Office, 1984): 95, 119, 121, 102-103.

7. Ibid., p. 90; Cullen Murphy, "Watching the Russians," *Atlantic Monthly,* February 1983: 33-52.

8. "Statement of Murray Feshbach," *The Political Economy of the Soviet Union,* 90, 94-95.

9. Franklyn D. Holzman, *The Soviet Economy, Past Present and Future. Foreign Policy Association Headline Series,* No. 260 (September/October 1982): 49-50; "Statement of Herbert Levine," *The Political Economy of the Soviet Union: 57; Deutsches Institut fuer Wirtschaftsforschung (DIW), "Die UdSSR an der Schwelle des elften Fuenfjahrplanes," Wochenbericht* 19/81: 219-226, hereinafter cited as "An der Schwelle"; Rowan, 48-49. The rate of growth of government spending on scientific research, whether basic or applied, has fallen from 11

percent per annum in 1971-1975 to some four percent by the eighties, no doubt affecting adversely the already negative rate of growth of combined factor productivity. Michael Binyon, "Soviet Science," *The Chronicle of Higher Education*, 20 January 1982: 19.

10. Morris Bornstein, "Soviet Economic Growth and Foreign Policy," in Seweryn Bialer, ed., *The Domestic Context of Soviet Foreign Policy* (Boulder, Colorado: 1981), 232-234; Statement of Robert W. Campbell, *The Political Economy of the Soviet Union*: 10.

11. Bornstein; 236-237; "An der Schwelle," 222.

12. Bornstein; 238-239, 237, 240; "An der Schwelle," 221; John P. Hardt, "Soviet Non-fuel Minerals Policy: Global Context," *The Journal of Resource Management and Technology* XII (1983): 57-62; Peter Wiles, "The Worsening of Soviet Economic Performance," in Drewnowski, ed., 143-146.

13. Murray Feshbach, *The Soviet Union: Population Trends and Dilemmas. A Publication of the Population Reference Bureau, Inc.* XXXVII, no. 3 (August 1982): 6.

14. Ibid., 30-33; "Statement of Murray Feshbach," *The Political Economy of the Soviet Union*, 127.

15. Ibid., 120-121, 125; Feshbach, *The Soviet Union*, 34; Murphy, "*Watching the Russians.*"

16. Ibid., 35; "Statement of Murray Feshbach." *The Political Economy of the Soviet Union*, 141-142; Murphy, "Watching the Russians;" Wiles, "The Worsening of Soviet Economic Performance," in Drewnowski, p. 152.

17. "Statement of Murray Feshbach," *The Political Economy of the Soviet Union*, 134-137; Murphy, "Watching the Russians"; for a revisionist view of the Soviet demographic problem see Sergei Maksudov, "The Challenge From the Side of Demography," in the present series, Volume II.

18. Nove, "Has Soviet Growth Ceased?"; Alec Nove, "Soviet Economic Performance: A Comment on Wiles and Ellman," in Drewnowski, 164-171.

19. "Veraenderungen im sowjetischen Wirtschaftssytem? Diskussionen und Experimente," DIW, *Wochenbericht* 38/83 (22 September 1983): 473-477; Thomas H. Naylor, "A 'Menu' of Options by Soviet Economists," *New York Times*, 16 October 1982, p. 27, cols. 1-5.

20. Gertrude E. Schroeder, "Soviet Living Standards: Achievements and Prospects," in John P. Hardt, ed., *Soviet Economy in the 1980s: Problems and Prospects. Part 2. Selected papers submitted to the Joint Economic Committee Congress of the United States, 31 December, 1982* (Washington, D.C.: U.S. Government Printing Office, 1983): 367–87 states that "since 1950, real per capita consumption in the U.S.S.R. has risen at an annual average rate of 3.4 percent." For the C.I.A. estimates for the various five-year plan periods cf. Holzman, p. 21.

21. N.S. Khrushchev, *Target Figures for the Economic Development of the Soviet Union 1959-1965: Report to the Special 21st Congress of the Communist Party of the Soviet Union, 27 January 1959 and Reply to Discussion* (London: Soviet Booklet No. 47, 1959), 48-49.

22. Feshbach, *The Soviet Union*, 9; Schroeder, "Soviet Living Standards," *Soviet Economy in the 1980s*, 367-368, 370, 372, 383; "An der Schwelle"; Bureau of Intelligence Research, Department of State, "The Soviet Economy in the 1980s: the Political Setting," mimeograph 14, September 1982, 2. According to press reports the 1984 Soviet grain crop was 65m tons short of its 240m target. Cf. "Soviets Call Grain Crisis Acute," *Detroit Free Press*, 23 October 1984, p. 7A, cols 1-3.

23. Blair A. Ruble, "Soviet Trade Unions and Relations After 'Solidarity'," *Soviet Economy in the 1980s*, 349-366; Alexander Shtromas, *Political Change and Social Development: the Case of the Soviet Union* (Frankfurt a/ Main-Bern: Verlag Peter Lang, 1981), 66; *Allocation of Resources in the Soviet Union and China 1981. Hearings before the Subcommittee on International Trade, Finance and Security Economics of the Joint Economic Committee of Congress of the United States. Ninety-Seventh Congress, First Session. Part 7: Executive Sessions July 8 and October 15, 1981* (Washington D.C.: U.S. Government Printing Office, 1982): 111, 174; *Allocation of Resources in the Soviet Union and China 1980. Hearings Before the Subcommittee on Priorities and Economy in Government of the Joint Economic Committee Congress of the United States. Ninety-Sixth Congress. Second Session. Part 6: Executive Sessions June 30 and September 25, 1980* (Washington, D.C.: U.S. Government Printing Office, 1981): 114, hereinafter cited as *Resources 1980*; Goldman, *U.S.S.R.* in Crisis, 110.

24. "Household Stocks of Consumer Durables, 1980," *U.S.S.R.: Facts and Figures Annual* VII (1983): 61, as cited and updated in a mimeographed handout distributed by Ben Eklof, Indiana University, in a lecture at the University of Michigan, Ann Arbor, 12 February 1985.

25. Schroeder, "Soviet Living Standards," *Soviet Economy in the 1980s*, 367.

26. George Kolankewicz, "Poland, 1980: The Working Class Under 'Anomic Socialism,'" in Jan F. Triska and Charles Gati, eds., *Blue-Collar Workers in Eastern Europe* (London: George Allen and Unwin, 1981), 136-156. Between 1973 and 1976 household expenditures on non-foodstuffs rose at a rate of 17 percent per annum for manual worker households, Ibid., 142-143, Paul A. Smith, Jr., "Will Soviet Workers take to the Streets in the Eighties?" *U.S. News and World Report*, 11 August 1980: 46-47.

27. Vladimir G. Treml, "Subsidies in Soviet Agriculture: Record and Prospects," *Soviet Economy in the 1980s*, 171-185; M. Elizabeth Denton, "Soviet Consumer Policy: Trends and Prospects," in John P. Hardt, ed., *Soviet Economy in a Time of Change. A Compendium of Papers Submitted to the Joint Economic Committee Congress of the United States. Volume 1: October 10, 1979* (Washington, D.C.: U.S. Government Printing Office, 1979): 759-789.

28. Ibid., 761-763; *Resources 1980*, 116; Goldman, "Gorbachev and Economic Reform," 64-66; "Ost-West Handel Weiter unter Schwierigen Bedingungen," *DIW Wochenbericht 46/82*, 18 November 1982, 567 and note 10 as well as that chart on p. 569.

29. Bornstein, 236-237; "An der Schwelle," 222. The percentage of the total fruit

crop produced on the private plot is 40. For potatoes it is 60. Cf. also
Holzman: 135.

30. A. Shtromas, *Political Change and Social Development*, 71-73.

31. A detailed account of the pervasiveness of corruption in Soviet society is to be
found in Konstantin M. Simis, *U.S.S.R. The Corrupt Society. The Secret
World of Soviet Capitalism*, trans. Jacqueline Edwards and Mitchell Schneider
(New York: Simon and Schuster, 1982).

32. I owe this insight to Professor Earl A. Pope, Department of Religion, Lafayette
College.

33. *Resources 1980*, 145; Goldman, *The U.S.S.R. in Crisis*, 110-111.

34. A lecture by Professor Ben Ecklof at the University of Michigan, Ann Arbor,
12 February 1985; George Feifer, "Russian Disorders. The Sick Man of
Europe," *Harper's*, February, 1981: 45 ff., 52; Thomas Powers, "An Interview
with Kenneth Lipper on the Nature of the Soviet Leadership. Why the Russians
Need to Make a Deal," *Rolling Stone*, 21 January 1982: 11-14; Robert Tucker,
"Swollen State, Spent Society. Stalin's Legacy to Brezhnev's Russia," *Foreign
Affairs*, Winter 1981-1982: 414-435, also speaks of a crisis of faith in the
Soviet Union. For a more recent sample cf. Robert G. Kaiser, "Accelerating
Pace of Decay Faces U.S.S.R.," *Manchester Guardian Weekly*, 7 and 14
October 1984.

35. Wiles, "The Worsening of Soviet Economic Performance," 147, 150. For the
relationship of political radicalism to working arrangements which give rise to
prolonged conversation in adverse economic circumstances cf. R.V. Burks,
The Dynamics of Communism in Eastern Europe (Princeton, N.J.: Princeton
University Press, 1961), 55-56.

36. "Veraenderungen," 474, n. 7; N.A. Aitov, ed., *Nekotorye problemy sotsial'nykh
peremeshchenii v SSSR* (Ufa: 1978), 36, where N was 2000 adults all over 25
years of age, reproduced in a handout distributed by Professor Ben Eklof in
conjunction with his lecture at the University of Michigan, Ann Arbor, 12
February 1985; R.W. Davies, ed., *The Soviet Union* (London: 1978), 82.

37. Robert G. Wesson, *The Russian Dilemma. A Political and Geographical View*
(New Brunswick, N.J.: Rutgers University Press, 1974), 78-115 *passim*. The
following pages owe much to the insight of this work.

38. "Statement of Herbert Levine," 60; "Statement of Gertrude Schroeder." *The
Political Economy of the Soviet Union*, 64; *Resources 1983*, 44; "Sorry, I'll
Count That Again." *Economist* (London), 10 November 1984: 54; James
McCartney, "Soviet Military Might Invades Defense Debate," *Detroit Free
Press*, 10 February 1985, p. 6B, cols 3-6; "Soviet General Staff: Red Star
Wars," *Economist*, 15 September 1984: 46-47.

39. Jane P. Shoemaker, "Brief Exodus Puzzling. E. Germany Breaches Wall,"
Detroit Free Press, 18 June 1984, p. 7C, cols 3-4; "Bulgarian Cancels German
Visit," *idem.*, 10 September 1984, p. 4A, cols. 1-3.

40. For an analysis of the present status of the Hungarian New Economic Model
cf. Rudolph L. Toekes, "Hungarian Reform Imperatives," *Problems of Communism* (Washington, D.C.), September-October 1984: 1-23. Actually, Moscow

could ease its hard currency difficulties considerably were it to cease providing dollar subsidies to certain of its satellites. In 1981 these subsidies amounted all told to $6.3 billion, of which Cuba, Poland and Vietnam together took $4.8 billion. But of course withdrawal of this largesse might destabilize the régimes in question, a political price the Kremlin cannot afford to pay. "Now Russia Asks for Time to Pay," *Economist*, 6 February 1982: 79-80. The figures are based on material provided by the U.S. National Foreign Assessment Center and the Joint Economic Committee of Congress.

41. Wesson, 182-185.
42. Ibid., 186.
43. "Peasants Rising," *Economist*, 2 February 1985: 11-12; Ann Scott, "China Says Marxism is Obsolete," *Detroit Free Press*, 8 December 1984, p. 1A, col. 1, p. 7A, cols. 1-3.
44. Wesson, 182-185.
45. Dennison Rusinow, *The Yugoslav Experiment 1948-1974* (Berkeley, Calif.: University of California Press, 1977), 245-312. For a more somber view cf. R.V. Burks: *The National Problem and the Future of Yugoslavia* (Santa Monica, Calif.: Rand Corporation P-4761, 1971), *passim*.
46. For an update see Grigori Freeman, "A Soviet Teacher's 'J'accuse,'" *New York Times Magazine*, 25 November 1979, 121, 123-127.
47. Murphy, "Watching the Russians."
48. Robert Martin, "Ethnic Minorities in the Soviet Military. Non-Combat Units as an Ethnic Sponge," paper presented to the 1982 annual meeting of the American Association for the Advancement of Slavic Studies, Washington, D.C., 42 pages. Cf. also S. Enders Wimbush and Alex Alexiev, *The Ethnic Factor in the Soviet Armed Forces* (Santa Monica, Calif.: Rand Publication R-2787/1, March 1982); Susan L. Curran and Dimitry Ponomareff, *Managing the Ethnic Factor in the Russian and Soviet Armed Forces: An Historical Overview* (Santa Monica, Calif.: Rand Publication R-2640/1, July 1982); and Alexander Alexiev and S. Enders Wimbush, *The Ethnic Factor in the Soviet Armed Forces: Historical Experience, Current Practices, and Implications for the Future,* an Executive Summary (Santa Monica, Calif.: Rand Publication R-2930/1, August 1983).
49. Alexandre Bennigsen, "Mullahs, Mujahidin and Soviet Muslims," *Problems of Communism* (Washington, D.C.), November-December 1984, 28-44; as well as a lecture given by him at the University of Michigan, Ann Arbor, 23 November 1981.
50. A scholarly and knowledgeable account of the Soviet penetration of Afghanistan is Anthony Arnold, *Afghanistan: The Soviet Invasion in Perspective* (Stanford, Calif.: Hoover Institution Press, 1981), xviii.
51. Anthony Arnold, "The Situation in Afghanistan: How Much of a Challenge is it for the Soviet Imperial State?" in the present series, Volume III. For a shortened version, see *The World & I*, Volume 1, no. 1, 1986: 351-367.
52. R. V. Burks, "The Decline of Communism in Czechoslovakia," *Studies in Comparative Communism: An Interdisciplinary Journal.* II (1969): 21-49.

53. Seweryn Bialer, "The Harsh Decade: Soviet Policies in the 1980s," *Foreign Affairs*, Summer 1981: 999-1020.

54. For an earlier version of this analysis see R.V. Burks, "The Arcane Art of Kremlinology," *Encounter* (London), March 1983: 20-30. For a contrary view see the letter of Ernst Lowe in *Encounter*, April 1985: 79.

55. Wesson, 152-155, 158.

56. While we differ on some essentials, my thinking on the subject matter of this entire section has been considerably influenced by conversations with Vladimir Shlyapentokh of Michigan State University on 20 June and 4 July 1985.

57. Recently, sixteen Greek military police who had served as torturers under the dictatorship of the lieutenant colonels (1967-1974) together with some of their associates, were interviewed. Court records involving the sixteen were also gone over. The evidence collected in this fashion reveals that the sixteen had in common humble birth, a poor opinion of their own merits, an unusual respect for authority, e.g. a strong need to stand in well with their parents, exceptional physical stamina and endurance, and a strong dislike of Communism and Communists. People of this sort tended to be selected by the police authorities for special training as torturers. During training these recruits were subjected to heavy anti-Communist indoctrination. They were taught that they constituted the most élite service in the nation. They were subjected to severe physical hazing, including floggings, illogical and degrading commands and the requirement that they spy on one another. Toward the end of their training they were required to attend practice torture sessions so as to desensitize them gradually to their own participation. Even so, only about 1.5 percent of the total number of recruits in a given year survived the course of training and became torturers. The evidence further indicates that the sixteen graduates under study had not been battered children nor were they sadists. They viewed their work as routine and, after the fall of the dictatorship, settled back into normal life. The research would seem to indicate that the course of training was a more important element in the development of the torturer than the personality type although both were essential. Richard E. Snow, "Torturers," U.S. Office of Naval Research (London), *European Science Notes* XXXIX (1985): 406-408. I have to thank A.W. Burks of the University of Michigan for bringing this article to my attention. It appears to me that this study, put together by a Ms. Haritos-Fatouros, may have some relevance to our understanding of particularly the elderly element among the politicians. Most of them are of humble origin and have little in the way of formal education. (Gorbachev is the first general secretary to have attended university.) All have been subjected to intensive indoctrination and treated as members of an élite, key to the very survival of the régime. All have been expected to spy on each other. Almost all came up through the great purges, frequently, if not usually, playing a role in the disappearance of the men whom they replaced. All are at least aware of the conditions prevailing in corrective labor camps. If the Haritos-Fatouros research is relevant, the changeover to the Gorbachev generation now at last underway may indeed bring about significant changes in Soviet policy.

58. Shtromas, 75-77.
59. Conversations with Ernst Kux of the *Keue Zuercher Zeitung*, Geneva, Switzerland, 14 and 15 August 1985; Dusko Doder, "Looking Ahead. Gorbachev Boosts Nation's Morale But Bureaucratic Change Unlikely," *Ann Arbor News*, 17 September 1985, C1-C2.
60. Shtromas, 75.
61. Ibid., 62-67.
62. R. V. Burks, "The Decline of Communism in Czechoslovakia."
63. Information derived from seminars I offered at Wayne State University in 1972-1975. Cf. also Rusinow, 287-307.
64. The Soviet government has apparently also promulgated a law making it a crime for Soviet citizens to pass information obtained from their employment on to foreigners without first procuring official permission. This action is evidently intended to make the broadcasts of Western radios less interesting. Furthermore, Soviet authorities now refuse to accept prepayment of customs duties on packages mailed from abroad. This is meant to curtail shipment of books and clothing to dissidents and would-be immigrants. Cf. F. Stephen Larrabee, "Higher, Thicker Kremlin Walls," *Detroit Free Press*, 29 May 1984, p. 25, cols. 3-4.
65. Shtromas, 67-71.
66. Igor Birman, "The State of Soviet Economic Affairs," *Russia* (Silver Spring, Md.), no. 11 (1985): 56-67.
67. Wesson, 165-166; Shtromas, 67-71. Michael Voslensky, *Nomenklatura. The Soviet Ruling Class. An Insider's Report.* trans. Eric Mosbacher (Garden City, N.Y.: Doubleday, 1984) is an original contribution to our understanding of Soviet politics.

2

The Economic Crisis in the U.S.S.R.

A Commentary on Section I

PETER J. D. WILES

The word crisis is greatly overused, and this conference may well be about to offend in this way. It deserves prominence, if only in the end to be played down. Yet undoubtedly this word must be applied to the over-centralized non-market system. True, by ordinary statistical indicators Britain is in a worse state than the U.S.S.R., but it is much easier for a totalitarian régime to get into a crisis than for a democratic one. Let us pause here, then, on the very notion of crisis. Why is the British economic failure less important to Britain than the statistically less severe Soviet failure is to the U.S.S.R.? Why is the latter, but not the former, a real crisis?

There are many reasons:

1. Every British government is legitimate. None seized power by force since 1688; all have been voted in without monarchical interference since 1832 at the latest. The electoral system is unfair, the people do not know exactly what they are voting for, etc.; but they rightly put the ultimate blame on themselves for the government they have chosen, and the

disasters (including economic ones) that this particular government has caused.[1]
2. Historically legitimacy has taken other forms than that bestowed by parliamentary democracy. The other main form is divine appointment. Thus the kings of France were divinely appointed, and Napoléon is said to have remarked how unfair this was. When he came back from Moscow defeated, his subjects held him to have violated their contract with him, whereas if he had been Louis the "nth" they would have rallied behind him in sympathy and love.
3. The CPSU is a Napoléon, not a Bourbon. It seized power forcibly, without the people's permission, claiming not divine but Hegelian, or historical, appointment. This claim is validated only by itself. So it is on neither count legitimate. It imposes, much like Napoléon, a mere contract instead. This is largely implicit, and says, basically, "shut up and we'll give you security and sausage." So this contract stipulates, *inter alia*, top-class economic performance, much as Napoléon's stipulated perpetual military victory. The CPSU wrote the whole contract itself, of course, so it cannot complain about any clause. But if it cannot fulfill one of its own self-designed, forcibly imposed clauses, it has no legitimacy whatever.
4. Therefore quite minor failures in absolute terms, like growth of consumption at merely 1% per head per annum (my upper estimate for 1978-85), trigger for U.S.S.R. a regime crisis, while in Britain the more serious fact that unemployment won't come down, as the government promised, simply causes it to lose by elections. The system remains entirely legitimate.

Moreover the CPSU's contract stipulates not merely absolute but also relative success.[2] U.S.S.R. must "catch up and surpass" the West, but it isn't doing that either any more. This goal is also self-imposed. Failure here too adds to her crisis of legitimacy. U.S.S.R. is certainly not catching up and surpassing Japan, and South Korea has pre-empted her future export markets.

Many ways out of the Soviet crisis suggest themselves. First we can reform the system by introducing market elements, as Kosygin tried to do in 1965. Kosygin's reform was undoubtedly very radical, almost Hungarian, but Brezhnev did not allow it to happen. This way out has been sufficiently discussed, and we shall not deal with it here. Suffice it to note four points:

1. There seem to be insuperable ideological objections to an inter-enterprise market in socialist industry, transport, and construction (note the careful

choice of words). Brezhnev ousted Kosygin on this issue from all but the shadow of power in 1971. Other markets, especially in agriculture and housing, there may be, but never this one. The strictly socialist sector is somehow sacred. Even Gorbachev, the "young radical," seems to share this opinion.[3]

2. Other ideologically serious countries, like the G.D.R. and Bulgaria, let alone more independent countries like Albania and North Korea, take the same view.

3. But first Hungary and now Poland and China have broken ranks. Of these the first two have not shown brilliant results, and many capitalist countries equally do not show them. China has, but it is plausible to argue that the Cultural Revolution was like a civil war, and the present success is "postwar recovery," normally a period of rapid growth. One way and another, the market has *not* shown itself overwhelmingly superior as an instrument of growth.[4]

4. For the U.S.S.R., "export-led growth in the bracing atmosphere of the world market" would simply mean more gas, gold, timber, and oil. It would not subject her manufacturers to this treatment, much though they undoubtedly need it. In economic jargon, the U.S.S.R. has had the "Dutch disease" for centuries.

There are two other ways out of the crisis, both stumbled upon by Leonid Brezhnev. One is to import technology. This had been recommended by Kosygin and so rejected by Brezhnev until he took sole charge in 1971. Then he canceled the reforms and declared détente instead—in order to enable him to borrow money and import technology on a scale that Kosygin had not envisaged. Thus technology and, in Poland's case, even financial capital are imported in order to avoid reform. On this also much could be said, but it is not our subject. In any case, capital importation leads to debt crises, and foreign technology proves unexpectedly difficult and expensive to assimilate.

A third way out of the crisis suggests itself: let the second economy or 2E, as I shall call it hereafter, flourish. This is a genuine if partial solution in economic terms, but its moral and ideological costs are stupendous. Above all, it threatens the CPSU's legitimacy!

If the large 2E does not exactly betoken a crisis, it is tempting, nay it is a duty, to examine whether Richard Burks's other constituents of an economic and general crisis are really persuasive. The comprehensiveness and accuracy of his excellent description of various "negative phenomena" are beyond cavil. Indeed let us add to it: the real growth of consumption and investment is not even as high as the CIA's low figures because the CIA is very bad on prices, and regularly overstates price stability.[5]

The doubt is whether all this adds up to system breakdown within five years. Let us state dogmatically a more pessimistic (i.e. pro-Soviet!) view:

1. Economic growth never actually ceased. It will probably pick up a little now, as harvest luck improves, and the new broom gets sweeping.
2. Gorbachev really is a new broom. He really is interested in moderate reforms. Between moderate and radical reform—Burks's sole prescription—there is no great difference of promise (see above).
3. Perceived economic crisis, on the Klopper-Dirksen rules (above) means what the élite perceives. *They* are not going to revolt! What the people perceive is not 1% growth versus 2% growth, but *sudden* large movements in their own circumstances, as when Khrushchev raised meat prices and caused the big riots in Novocherkassk (1962).
4. Burks's foreign examples of breakdown all had a very big component of nationalism. In the U.S.S.R. 70% of the population (nearly all Russians, for the most Belorussians and most Ukrainians) have united their ethnic loyalty with Soviet patriotism. On this, compare Maksudov's impressive contribution in volume III on the spread of the Russian language.
5. Above all, and here alone I disagree with Burks on a factual point, is what the Kremlin cannot but call foreign policy success: the slow spread of Soviet-type Marxism-Leninism within the Third World. Since the initial burst of successes in the late seventies,[6] we must add, effectually: Nicaragua, which the White House will clearly never regain; continued good possibilities in Guyana, Congo, Benin, Seychelles, Madagascar; and the slow approach to military victory in Afghanistan and Cambodia. The Kremlin is very British; it likes to see the map painted red. Nor is it wrong; real estate victories are very genuine ones, and if they go on long enough they mean, by definition, total victory. There is, then, no crisis of foreign policy failure, rather the contrary, "history" is slowly moving in the direction Lenin predicted.

This point is a crucial one, nay the crucial one. If we hold on, the "objective process" of history in the Third World will float us off. Meanwhile, then, let us merely

   . . . . Keep hold of Nurse
For fear of finding Something Worse.

NOTES

1. Disasters merely suffered—say due to OPEC—are of course irrelevant.
2. This is the doctrine of the two criteria of Soviet economic crisis. I owe it to

Messrs. Dirksen and Klopper of Amsterdam University.

3. Revising this in April 1987, I stand by it as a statement of Gorbachev's state of mind in May 1985.

4. On the capitalist side one often hears South Korea mentioned. While South Korea certainly participates enthusiastically in the world market as an exporter, and is a prime example of export-led growth, she is grossly protectionist and avoids market decisions in her domestic economy. Japan, the older champion of the market economy, is a still less convincing example. Monopoly, protectionism, and state intervention are at least as evident as in South Korea, *and the defense burden is uniquely low*. If we take this point seriously, Japan is a much less convincing protagonist than South Korea.

5. Cf. the sources quoted in Burks, in Chapter 11, (notes 2, 13, and 14).

6. Cf. P. J. D. Wiles, ed., *The New Communist Third World* (London: Croom Helm, 1983).

3

The Function and Fate of Law in the Transition to the Post-Soviet Era

FERDINAND J. M. FELDBRUGGE

The Present Crisis and the Role of Law Therein

The Soviet system is moribund, but linked to an efficient life-support machine. Law is part of this machine, but also, less visibly, a contributing factor to the various crises which beset the Soviet system. Both elements of this statement deserve further elaboration. The most convenient approach would be to begin with the most obvious insufficiencies, shortages, stresses in the Soviet system, to try to identify the underlying problems which cause them, and to point out in particular how they are related to law. The visible problems can easily be defined in terms of shortages—of economic performance, of internal and external political control, of ethnic cohesion, of societal purpose, of information—but these are themselves manifestations of more basic stresses which have to be laid bare in order to understand why the shortages have occurred and why they threaten the survival of the existing Soviet system. Such an analysis, it is to be expected, will show that the various insufficiencies observable with the naked eye are in fact intimately connected and cannot therefore be correctly understood in isolation from each other.

Economic Stagnation

The symptoms of the economic difficulties are clear enough: low growth, poor quality, and chronic shortages, particularly of consumer goods. In several areas the gaps that separate Soviet economic performance and the performances of the most advanced free market economies seem to have widened, instead of narrowed, as Soviet political leaders and the official ideology claimed they would. It would be a simplification to attribute Soviet economic stagnation to a single factor; however, both Soviet comments and external analyses indicate that organizational as well as motivational factors are among the principal causes of the present predicament.

In terms of organization, the problem is well known and much discussed. The Soviet economy suffers from excessive centralization; decisions are taken at levels that are too high, on the basis of defective information, resulting in inefficient procedures, organizational rigidity, and ultimately low yields. It has to be remembered, of course, that the problem of setting up and running a Soviet-type economy is a much more arduous task than the management of a free market economy. The experience of the Soviet Union and its associated states shows that a comprehensive, centrally planned and controlled economy which pretends to embrace virtually the entire national economy of a country, requires a very elaborate support system of legal and administrative measures. Soviet criminal law serves primarily to prevent the collapse of the state-run economy; its chapters on economic crimes and crimes against socialist property are the most frequently applied. Soviet administrative and financial law are almost exclusively concerned with the excessively complicated juggernaut of the official production and trading system, and with the problem of how to keep it from grinding to a halt.

Lurking beneath these organizational difficulties is what could be called in Marxist terms consciousness lagging behind the economic basis. The socialist economy has failed to produce the anticipated change in man's attitudes; the Soviet citizen is still motivated by self-interest; he will only work for a commensurate reward or in fear of punishment. This is implicitly recognized in the new Soviet Constitution which continues to proclaim: "In accordance with the principle of socialism: 'From each according to his abilities, to each according to his work,' the state supervises performance and consumption" (Art.14, para.2, first sentence).[1] The same principle lies at the basis of the ambivalent attitude towards work. Work is romanticized as the supreme and heroic self-realization of man and simultaneously employed as one of the ultimate instruments to discipline the recalcitrant individual. From the times of Lenin, labor camps have both physically and metaphorically ringed the centers of Soviet power. Soviet constitutional theory regards the right to work as the nucleus and origin of all other fundamental rights of citizens but at the same time proclaims labor not only the basic right but also the basic duty of the citizen.[2]All this goes to show that the Soviet régime recognizes realistically the unreformed mentality of its own citizens. Its constant appeals to lofty ideals, to the selfless commitment of the individual in the interests of society, ring ever more hollowly, while at the same time the performance of essential social activities are ensured by effective systems of individual incentives and disincentives.

Why then, one might ask, has the Soviet government failed to involve the full power of the self-interest motive for the improvement of the country's economy? The answer to this question lies in the peculiar political framework of the Soviet Union which pretends to embrace all other sectors of social life, including the economy. By the same token the organization of the economy is made subject to overriding considerations of a non-economic, political nature. The admission that a centrally controlled economy will not produce acceptable results unless its participants derive some degree of individual advantage from increased performance was made many years ago, already in the times of Lenin. The leadership would certainly prefer to have to deal with a completely docile and obedient population, which would execute orders like robots. On the surface the Soviet people are indeed exceptionally disciplined in a double sense; strict discipline is imposed and enforced, and the population normally behaves in a very disciplined manner —to an outside observer Soviet society may create the impression of an old-fashioned and strict boarding school. But the ideal of communist man requires more than punctual execution of orders; it asks for heroic sacrifice, total commitment. While these are not forthcoming, any extra effort by the citizen will have to be bought by the régime through concessions: material goods, status, freedom. This process is basically a zero-sum game—anything granted to the individual is given away by the régime. The latter, rationally enough, strives to pay the lowest price for the most advantageous (from its point of view) package of individual incentives.

In democracies, economic performance and the material well-being of citizens are among the most central concerns of the governments of the day, because the continuation of an administration is dependent on the outcome of the next elections and thereby on the citizens' judgment of the official economic policies. In the Soviet Union the connection between economic performance and the position of the government is quite different. Soviet economic policy is much more clearly subordinate to other and more general policy demands. As a result, Soviet economic policy is specifically subject to two decisive considerations. One is that improved performance is desired for the sake of strengthening the external power position of the régime, and the other that a minimally acceptable level of economic perform-ance begins at a point, below which serious unrest among the population, such as would threaten the stability of the régime, would occur. In this context it is worth pointing to the large-scale famines that the Soviet and other communist régimes have countenanced with equanimity, so long as they did not feel that the suffering of the population posed any real threat to their position.[3]

In other words then, the Soviet government must be considered entirely capable of bringing about spectacular economic improvements, but is un-likely to do so within the immediate future if the economic rationality of such reforms is not based on their political expediency. With regard to the latter, the Soviet leadership is certainly aware of the fact that genuine economic reforms (as distinct from the incessant organizational tinkering that has gone on, often with great fanfare, since the death of Stalin) will most likely result in serious loss of central power. The political value of the increased wealth under central control will be outweighed by the conse-quences of shifting control over certain sectors of the economy away from the center. Such a step would affect the nature of the Soviet system and is unlikely to be taken under present circumstances. In the long run, however, it will be inevitable, a point to which we shall return at the end of this paper.

Political Rigidity

In some respects the political machinery of the Soviet system, constructed by Lenin, perfected by Stalin, and lovingly maintained by their successors, must be regarded as phenomenally successful. Not only has it proved to possess greater tenacity than the longest living right-wing dictatorships of modern times, but it has in fact been going from strength to strength. This machinery has allowed a small band of people to build for themselves a position of absolute domestic power which has become completely un-assailable, and to transform a peripheral European state into a superpower. Why then is it still possible to talk of a political crisis in the Soviet Union, and what are the symptoms and causes of this crisis?

A recent indication that all is not well with the Soviet political system is the insecurity that surrounds the succession of the top leader, the general secretary of the Communist Party. The fairly frequent changes that have taken place during the last few years have indeed not affected the basic characteristics of the system, but, on the other hand, it would be hard to argue that the personality of the top leader is of little relevance. Soviet leaders of the second echelon have a deceptive knack of looking colorless and faceless; once they have been promoted to the front rank this impression is faulted, witness the performances of Khrushchev, Brezhnev, Andropov, Chernenko, and Gorbachev.

In an excessively centralized system the death or removal of the top leader is a deeply traumatic event. The replacement of any other prominent politician or official can be arranged through reference to the top leader, but when the latter disappears off the stage the system itself is thrown into disarray. The top leader functions within an ambivalent relationship with the Politburo. He owes his position initially to commanding a majority of supporters in the Politburo. As time passes, the leader is usually able to put more distance between himself and his colleagues on the Politburo. He becomes less dependent on them and new networks of power relationships emerge, defined by their connection with the leader himself. The longer the leader remains in power, the more the original pattern of his relationship with the Politburo will change. At the moment of his demise, however, a sudden and catastrophic transformation occurs. The political landscape is hit by an earthquake. Persons who held high office under the old leader suddenly find themselves friendless, and others who were in semi-disgrace are momentarily catapulted into a position of great influence: genuine participation in the election of the new leader. Then the cycle starts again.

The serious instability inherent in the recurrent leadership successions is not the only intractable political difficulty that besets the Soviet government. In a more general manner, the régime appears to be unable to tackle effectively certain other prominent issues. In the preceding section we have pointed out how overriding political considerations prevent the adoption of the most obviously desirable economic reforms. Then the Soviet Union is faced with a complex and pressing national problem, inherited from tsarist Russia. This problem has only become worse during the Soviet era. Alcoholism has assumed the proportions of a national disaster in the U.S.S.R.; it has deep effects on economic performance, on mortality rates and general levels of health, and on most types of crime. One could continue in this vein. The only public institutions that seem to function properly are the main instruments of physical force available to the régime: the KGB and the Armed Forces. The situation recalls the closing decades of Imperial Russia when the army and the police held together the disaffected sections of a disintegrating body politic.

The most comprehensive explanation for this extraordinary collection of unsolved problems lies in the self-induced paralysis of power of the Soviet régime. The Marxist-Leninist frame of mind favors extreme ideological and political intolerance; every form of social organization outside the Party, or rather outside the control of the Party leadership, is utterly suspect and regarded as dangerous and potentially hostile. For long periods, even within the Party itself, there was a constant search for enemies going on. In this climate, the elimination of all independent forms of social life—independent that is of the Party center—became the all-absorbing obsession of this

center. Basically, this elimination was realized under Stalin, but the maintenance of this status quo required ceaseless effort and constant vigilance. As
a result the Soviet leadership became more and more inclined to view
matters in the exclusive perspective of their potential to increase or decrease
central power, and, by the same token, more and more unable to influence
the outcome of autonomous processes. In the end, total power engendered
total impotence.

In a curious manner, this situation is reflected in Soviet law. One of the
pervasive official attitudes running through most sectors of Soviet law is the
fear that the legal structures created by the state will inadvertently result in
positions which would allow citizens or institutions a viable legal defense
against the state. To prevent such things happening, the Soviet legislator
employs a two-pronged device. Firstly, there is the use of vague and open-
ended terminology that has to be given exact meaning in an interpretive
process controlled by the authorities. This allows extension of the demands
of the state and the corresponding extension of the duties of the state and
the corresponding curtailment of the rights and entitlements of citizens and
institutions. Secondly, the legal position of citizens and institutions may also
be defined in a very precise and detailed manner, where it concerns the
enunciation of their respective duties. The use of vague terminology is most
noticeable in the elaboration of the politically most sensitive civil rights.
Their exercise is conditional upon their being "in the interest of socialism"
(or some similar formula), and additionally the Constitution states in more
general terms that civil rights may not be exercised against the interests of
the state or of society, and that their exercise is inextricably connected with
the observance of civil duties, which embrace, among others, the duty to
safeguard the interests of the Soviet state and to promote the growth of its
power and authority.[4]

Legal regulation that is excessively elaborate and detailed is very current
in Soviet administrative law, in the regulation of the colossal organizational
complex formed by the Soviet state economy. The complexity of this branch
of law is regularly bemoaned in Soviet legal literature; the point is frequently
made that numerous officials are unaware of certain legal rules which
specifically concern their own activities.[5]

Both vagueness and excessive detail in legal regulation have the same
background: the wish of the régime to retain maximum power and discretion. Vagueness allows the authorities to interfere at will; detailed regulation
aims at reducing discretionary powers of lower administrative levels to nil.
The paradoxical result of all this, however, is that law fails in its primary
task—to regulate behavior. Vague rules do not regulate anything, but rather
only disguise arbitrariness. The regulatory potential of excessively detailed

rules diminishes sharply as it becomes practically impossible to observe or even know them. In this way the erosion of legal control only mirrors the more general impotence of the supreme rulers of the U.S.S.R.

Informational Distortions

The growing inability to exercise power effectively may also be connected with the defective knowledge of the external world with which Soviet leaders have to operate. First of all, the internal political dialogue among members of the Soviet leadership circles is predominantly couched in the terminology of Marxism-Leninism. This means that even if one assumes that most Soviet leaders are realists, opportunists, even cynics, rather than ardent believers in communism, they will still be inclined to interpret reality largely through concepts derived from the state's official ideology. It can be doubted whether the latter offers the most useful conceptual framework for understanding the present problems of Soviet society. The most obvious application of Marxist-Leninist stereotypes in this respect is at the same time the most inappropriate one for psychological reasons. What I have in mind is a view of the Soviet system as being dominated by a ruling class, which owns (in a non-legal, economic sense) the principal means of production, exploits the subordinate of state ideology, institutions, law, etc., in such a way as to safeguard its privileged position. Such a view may be incomplete and one-sided (as I believe any Marxist view is), but it contains a large element of truth. It is hardly going to be popular, however, with Soviet leaders, since it would destroy any legitimacy that the status quo may possess. Rather, they will continue to identify the maintenance of present privilege as the building of communism, their domestic critics as enemies of socialism and agents of imperialism, etc. In particular, the conceptual toolkit of Marxism-Leninism is singularly ill-suited to interpret contemporary developments in the Western world. For decades Soviet media have painted a picture of ceaseless and ever deepening crisis. Undoubtedly, this picture can be very substantially retouched with the aid of numerous items of unofficial information; many Soviet citizens, certainly including the leading political strata, are aware of the greater wealth of Western societies and their citizens, and of the vigor of their economies. Nevertheless, it has to be feared that dogmatic thought patterns, derived from official ideological fixations, have a seriously distorting effect on the perception of domestic and foreign political and social developments by the Soviet ruling élite.

Thus ideology affects the interpretation and digestion of information. Another problem concerns the sources of information themselves. This is most obvious in the area of public opinion. In most Western societies, public opinion is of an almost debilitating confusion, on account of its extraordinary richness. A very extensive freedom of varied means of communication, an economic climate which allows wide access to these means, political polycentrism, and a vast array of parties, factions, pressure groups and other forms of association, make it possible that almost any viewpoint can be heard. Although this situation possesses its own informational weaknesses, the Soviet scene is affected by difficulties of an opposite nature. Independent public opinion is reduced to nil; in representative bodies, such as the soviets, nothing is discussed, nobody disagrees; the media present a picture of monolithic uniformity; a small stage-managed area of discussion is made available to the public, but the topics and scope of the discussion are tightly controlled. Among the most blatant disadvantages of this system of communications control are the reduced level of information available to Soviet leaders with regard to the ideas and opinions of the population, and the loss of constructive suggestions which do not reach the leadership on account of the lack of suitable channels.

A further serious information problem exists in the Soviet economy. The latter should ideally embrace the virtually complete complex of productive activities in the entire country, on the basis of socialist (i.e., directly or indirectly state) ownership of the means of production and comprehensive economic planning by the state. Such a system, to function satisfactorily, requires that those at the summit be well informed. The central planners can only exercise effective control over the economy if they possess adequate knowledge of what is going on at lower levels and if their directives encounter a high degree of observance at these lower levels. An analysis of available materials leads one to doubt whether these conditions are generally met. It appears that throughout the hierarchical system of Soviet economic relationships subordinate levels frequently have a vested interest in disguising the actual state of affairs from their superiors. The latter are then expected to make decisions which the subordinates believe to be to their own advantage. As these distortions may work their way through the entire hierarchy of economic relationships, the ultimate result may be a grossly unreliable picture. It should be added, however, that some corrections may be introduced in the process and that the leadership has other independent sources of information at its disposal. Nonetheless, it may be assumed that the central planners are seriously hampered by a lack of adequate information concerning at least certain sections of the economy.

But even if central planners were perfectly aware of what was going on in all areas of the economy, genuine control from the center would still require the undistorted transmission of central directives to addresses at lower levels, and the correct execution of such directives by the latter. In this respect, it is also doubtful whether the actual performance of the Soviet economic system gets anywhere close to the proclaimed ideal. This ideal represents the Soviet version of the rationalist illusion of control which deceives the leaders of many modern societies. The rise of the social sciences, coupled with the great advances of technology, has created the belief that social processes are understood and have become controllable. Policy makers are then tempted by the desire to draw up a grand design for the future of society, into which all intermediate objectives and sector policies are required to fit.

For the Soviet régime, such a self-perception is particularly seductive, because it already possesses a grand design in the shape of the communist view of the world, and it has, feeling itself legitimized by this ideology, already ascribed itself all powers necessary to translate its views into reality.

The Soviet Second Economy

The Soviet second economy is not only of great practical importance in the daily lives of Soviet citizens and for the overall performance of the Soviet economy, it also throws new light on the basic structure of the Soviet system and the motivational forces which activate it. For this reason it has to be mentioned, however briefly, in a survey of the main problems of modern Soviet society.

For the purposes of this paper, the Soviet second economy (or unofficial, unobserved, shadow, parallel economy, or similar designations) can be defined as that part of the Soviet economy which remains largely outside the central planning and control mechanism.[6] The legal foundation of the socialist economy is Art.10, para.1 of the U.S.S.R. Constitution which provides that "The foundation of the economic system of the U.S.S.R. is socialist ownership of the means of production . . . ." This rule should be read in conjunction with Art.16 which provides that the economic system of the U.S.S.R. constitutes a single whole and is managed on the basis of state plans. In other words, socialist ownership of the means of production and central planning together make up the official socialist economy or first economy of the U.S.S.R. It is to be noted that the existence of economic activities outside the socialist complex is already recognized in the Constitution itself: the private plots of citizens in Art.13 and "individual labor activity" of citizens in Art.17. This means that the second economy, in the sense attributed to it here, also embraces legal activities.

There can be no doubt that the illegal sector of the second economy predominates in quantitative terms. More importantly, in the context of this essay, the illegal second economy lays bare certain inconsistencies in the official self-perception of the Soviet régime and offers an insight into the genuine forces that hold the Soviet system together. The main questions calling for an answer in this respect are: why did a second economy emerge in the Soviet Union, and, how does the régime react to it?

In one of the foregoing sections it has been argued that the official Soviet economy is a highly artificial structure that has to be supported by an elaborate network of legal and administrative measures; elsewhere it has been pointed out that a centrally controlled economy suffers from inbuilt and virtually insurmountable obstacles to its internal flow of information, which turn the pretense of effective central control in all but the most exceptional circumstances into an illusion. Under these circumstances it would probably be more sensible to inquire why a second economy has not emerged in the Soviet Union, if this would have been the case. In other words, it is only to be expected that pockets and then areas of economic activity outside central control will come into being, and that it will prove to be impracticable for the state to proscribe any such activity or to enforce all of its prohibitions of such activity. One example may suffice. The final link in the chain of economic processes is the sale of a finished product to its ultimate user. Maintenance of central control over the economy requires therefore that also this final step is kept within the ambit of the official economy. The legal translation of this requirement is in Art.154 of the RSFSR Criminal Code, the prohibition of "speculation": the buying and selling with the aim of making a profit. It needs little imagination to understand that in an economy beset by scarcity of numerous kinds of consumer goods, private buying and selling, i.e., "speculation," will occur as naturally as grass after rain, and that the official ban against it will be unenforceable under normal conditions.

Although the official stance of the Soviet régime vis-à-vis the illegal sector of the second economy is inevitably negative or even hostile, factual official treatment of the second economy displays a far wider spectrum of nuance, from virulent rejection to open encouragement. This can be explained by the fact that second economy activities, including illegal ones, may be of greatly different value, positive as well as negative, for the régime.[7] At one end of the spectrum one finds, for instance, the activities of private money changers ("currency speculators" as they are termed by the Criminal Code), which are of no benefit to the rulers, but only to the participants in the transaction, and which involve indirect financial loss to the state. Currency speculation attracts heavy penalties, up to and including capital punishment. At the other end, construction work for state enterprises by private building gangs (*shabashniki*), although unlawful, is of great usefulness in coping with one of the traditional bottlenecks in the economy. For this reason, it seems that very little is put in the way of these unsocialist "heroes of labor."

The picture of official treatment is even more complicated. Not only are second economy activities classed according to their value—positive or negative—for the régime, but within each group one also has to look at who is the beneficiary. Foreign currency dealings may change their character, depending on whether they have been conducted by a street operator or by a member of the élite returning from an official trip abroad.

The important principle behind this is that the acquisition of benefits derived from second economy activities is a constituent part, and a rather major one at that, of the status of élite members. It is especially through the publications of numerous emigrés, former members of the Soviet élite, that we have become aware of the essential function of the second economy as a primary source of remuneration for *nomenklatura* members.[8] This leads to the conclusion—which may appear startling to the unprepared observer—that the second economy, far from being some sort of foreign body in the Soviet politico-economic system, is in fact one of its principal structural elements. The members of the élite have their loyalty rewarded in part by being allowed to participate in the advantages and privileges bestowed by the second economy; consequently, the élite has a strong vested interest in maintaining a vigorous second economy.

One should not be led astray by the occasional exposure of members of the élite for engaging in forbidden economic activities. Participation by the élite in the second economy is governed by a network of informal rules, wholly comparable to the informal rule systems which govern corruption in other parts of the world. Violation of these rules may result in drastic sanctions, but these are not aimed at uprooting the second economy, but at maintaining its orderly functioning.

Moral Crisis

The Soviet world view was forced upon an unwilling population by a comparatively small group of zealots after the October Revolution, but there is no point in denying that they were fired by a genuine and most ardent élan. Most of them perished in the GULAG. The moral implications of this course of events are still a source of confusion and controversy. I myself am inclined to believe that Stalinism was indeed engendered by Leninism. Lenin's maniacal hatred of opponents, his moral nihilism, were the most natural prelude to the diabolical régime over which Stalin presided. But whether one agrees with this or not, Stalinism happened and the present rulers of the Soviet Union are the legitimate successors of it. (The term "legitimate" is indeed bizarre in this respect.) Stalin justified his actions by reference to Marxist-Leninist doctrines, which he interpreted in his own peculiar way. His successors first condemned him, somewhat, but did not reject the doctrines and values by which he had ruled. Gradually, Stalin himself was also partially rehabilitated. All these operations could only take place by engaging in dishonesty and mendacity of such proportions as have

never before been observed in human history. Emigrants from the U.S.S.R.
generally agree that the most unbearable aspect of Soviet rule is not political
oppression, lack of democracy, poverty and material deprivations, but the
all-pervasive lie from which there is no escape. Can it be a coincidence that
the leading newspaper is called *Pravda*? The culture of lying among Soviet
officialdom is universal and at the same time most complex. Official Soviet
statements are often true because they contain a double lie. The truth
usually ends up under such a layer of untruths that it becomes an almost
futile exercise to unearth it, because by that time new heaps of lies have
accumulated all around it.[9]

The principal concern of a Soviet official is to know which line has to be
followed at a given moment; it is not simply a matter of truth being
regarded as untruth, but of the effortless alternation between mutually
exclusive viewpoints. Any reasonably intelligent participant of public life in
the U.S.S.R. must realize that the price to be paid for a position of public
importance, with the accompanying status and advantages, includes at least
incessant sacrifices on the altar of the god of lies. Under such circumstances
one cannot expect a high level of morality in public life. In this sphere the
integrating factors are not common ideals and individual moral convictions
supporting these ideals, but rational calculations of common interest.

Lip service to official ideals is still paid, because, threadbare as they are,
they still offer the most convenient justification for the political status quo.
Increasingly, however, one notices that where there is a genuine need to
encourage popular support for some public task, the authorities do not use
the waveband of their official ideology of Marxism-Leninism, but strike the
more emotive chord of patriotism. This was already done in World War II.
As has often been remarked, patriotism is the last fallback position when
other societal ideals have paled; in its lowest form it is only collective
egotism.

The barrenness, in a moral sense, of the public scene in the U.S.S.R. has
caused a certain atomization of Soviet society. People withdraw, if they
have no specific reason to get involved in public activities, into their private
spheres. This is where, in a small network of personal relationships, life is
effectively lived. This is where, presumably, another and more genuine
morality operates.

The National Question

Among the various stresses to which the Soviet system is subject, the
national issue occupies a peculiar position. First of all, compared to the
factors which have been discussed until now, it stands apart by its independence. If the Soviet Union were populated by nothing but ethnic Russians,

the present malfunctioning of the economy, the political defects of the Soviet systems, and the other elements that constitute a single complex of malaise would not be altered very much. Conversely, if the Soviet Union were to be replaced by a politically, economically, morally healthy organism, than the national question would still be there, requiring, if not a solution, then at least certain adaptations.

Secondly, the national question in the Soviet Union appears in an unusual shape. The most commonly encountered formula, both in European states and in Third World countries, is the cohabitation within a single state of one numerically dominant ethnic group and one or more ethnic minorities; in such situations it is usually accepted that the major nationality is strongly identified with the state itself and occupies the center of the stage. Then there are the true multinational states where no single ethnic entity commands a majority (e.g., Switzerland, Yugoslavia). Both types of states have their own specific political problems; in the first type the main question is to find a mutually acceptable package of concessions to be offered to the minority nations; in the second type the principal difficulty is to find a workable balance of power between the various competing national groups. The peculiarity of the national set-up in the U.S.S.R. is that it finds itself about halfway between the two models referred to here. The Russian nation is roughly as numerous as the host of other Soviet nations put together. The tension inherent in this situation is further aggravated by a historical and a demographic factor. The Soviet state came into being as the successor to the Russian empire and as the heir to the Russian national tradition. The present demographic trend is most clearly in favor of the increase of the non-Slavic population of Central Asia and the parallel relative decrease of the Russians.

The official constitutional solution of the national question, adopted in the U.S.S.R., is the formula of true multinationalism: recognition of the equal national rights of the constituent nations. But even in the Constitution itself this solution has not been applied consistently. Only fifteen nations, essentially selected on the basis of political expediency, are the recipients of full national recognition. Other national groups, occasionally more numerous than some of these fifteen leading nations, have to be satisfied with a lower constitutional status.

When one takes a closer look at the more detailed elaboration of the formula of multinational equality among the fifteen leading nations of the U.S.S.R., it becomes clear that this equality is not implemented in a number of specific legal arrangements, and even less so in administrative practice. One of the favorite devices utilized in this respect is the failure to include the Russian union republic, the R.S.F.S.R., in arrangements applying to all

other union republics. The best known example is the absence of a separate
Communist Party organization in the R.S.F.S.R., along with the existence
of such organizations in the fourteen other republics; but this example is
joined by a multitude of others (the ministries of internal affairs, for instance,
or the KGB organization). The background to this is quite simply that the
R.S.F.S.R. is to some extent the *alter ego* of the federal state, the U.S.S.R.;
it is the metropolitan unit, with the other fourteen republics not only
geographically, but also politically peripheral; not for nothing do the leaders
of the smaller southern republics regularly and solemnly refer to the
R.S.F.S.R. as "our elder brother."[10]

The predominance of Russia and the Russians is even more pronounced
in the reality of political life, away from official legal or administrative
constructions. The federal structure of the U.S.S.R. is best compared with a
facade; it really exists, it is not a mirage, but behind it is nothing. Or rather
behind it is the centralized and unitary power of the Communist Party of
the Soviet Union. The Party is absolutely dominated by Russians; and the
non-Russians who occupy positions of importance in the Party usually
outdo the Russians themselves in their allegiance to Great Russian nationalism, as Lenin already observed.[11]

All this creates a complicated map of national aspirations. Great Russian
nationalism is in an uneasy alliance with the régime, which attempts to
harness the genuine force of Russian nationalism to the interests of Soviet
patriotism. The particular nationalisms of the numerous minority nations
are affected by their attitudes towards the Soviet system, as the most potent
external force, and towards Russia, as the most intrusive external national
element on the domestic national scene. National feelings are strongest
where they are fed by both anti-Soviet and anti-Russian sentiment (e.g., in
Lithuania).

In the context of an inventory of fundamental problems afflicting the
Soviet régime, one final observation regarding the nationality issue is worth
making. It concerns a certain parallel between nationalism and religion. In
either case the Soviet régime is faced with a force which cannot be con-
veniently accommodated within the officially professed value system, and
which therefore tends to be regarded as hostile. (As stated in the previous
paragraph, the situation is somewhat different with regard to Russian nationalism; it is possible to justify the privileged position of the Russians by
reference to their unique merits in establishing the first socialist state in the
world—and that all by themselves—and to their continued leading role
among the nations of the socialist world. Moreover, the by now obvious
failure of the official ideology to offer a credible set of socio-political ideals
and to provide a genuine motivational force has inevitably led to the rise of

nationalism as an *ersatz* ideology, and of course only Russian nationalism can fill this role under the present circumstances.)

International Failure

From the moment Moscow stepped onto the stage of history as an insignificant principality in the Russian middle ages, the territory controlled by its rulers has grown almost uninterruptedly. This seemingly inexorable process entered a new stage after World War II. New territories brought under Moscow's control were then no longer legally incorporated in the metropolitan state, but were reduced to the position of client states, retaining a modicum of legal, but almost no political independence.

The ideology provides a general conceptual framework for supporting an expansionist foreign policy, by holding out the ultimately inevitable future of world communism and by exhorting purposive activity to bring this future about. Ideology apart, at the level of *realpolitik*, it has often been remarked that Russian attitudes towards the West are strongly tinged by fear, particularly of invading armies. In this respect it is usual to refer to the Mongols, Poles, Swedes, French, and Germans. Russia, one might argue, is not so much a huge, as a vast country; its empty plains seem to invite incursions.

While admitting that ordinary Russians might still be inclined to harbor such feelings of fear, I believe that it is naive to think that the leaders in and around the Politburo and the General Staff still operate with such unrealistic stereotypes. They must know that there is absolutely no genuine possibility of a Western army invading the U.S.S.R. unprovokedly within the fore-seeable future. How then is the expansionist tendency in Soviet foreign policy to be explained, if not by a mistaken obsession to surround the U.S.S.R. with an ever larger glacis?

The answer to this question is to be found in the mold of political thought engendered by the domestic situation. The Soviet leaders have created conditions which make it unbearable for them to tolerate any internal institutions which represent independent power, whether politically, economically, or socially. Anything new which arises spontaneously, outside the Party's central control is immediately suspect. What is not under control is "objectively" an enemy, something that must be subjugated or eliminated. When this attitude is transferred to foreign policy, truly neurotic behavior must result. The Soviet Union, in its own view, does not have friends, but, on the one hand, clients, subordinate powers, vassals, and on the other hand, enemies. It is little wonder that the U.S.S.R. has made little progress in expanding its reach after World War II. A number of third world states have temporarily drifted into the Soviet orbit, but only Cuba seems to have remained a steady member of the club. An unsteady régime, in a situation of political volatility, may be tempted to cuddle up to the U.S.S.R., in an effort to maintain itself. But eventually it will transpire that nothing short of installing a Soviet-type system will satisfy the new friend and that ultimately the Soviet Union will be unwilling or unable to uphold its allies on other continents indefinitely.

It would seem, therefore, that the centuries-old expansion of Russia has reached its limits, at least for the foreseeable future, because overseas expansion has turned out to be a risky and unprofitable business and extension of the contiguous land mass around the U.S.S.R. is interdicted by the presence of unyielding neighbors. This is a basically new configuration and one with which Soviet foreign policy will eventually have to come to grips. Of course, the Soviet government may continue for a long time to use its standard procedures of looking for weak spots among the states which surround it and of encouraging rifts among them. In the end, however, Russia will have to accept its place among the nations of the world, which implies the recognition of international pluralism and genuine peaceful coexistence, rather than the Soviet interpretation of it as a way station on the road to communist (read, Soviet) domination of the world.

Anthropological Dimensions of the Crisis of the Soviet System

We have argued in the preceding paragraphs that, apart from the question of nationalism, the various crisis factors in the Soviet Union are closely connected. This can be most readily demonstrated by focusing on the function of power. The pursuit of power, its accumulation, and the elimination of alternative, independent centers of power, define to a very great extent the landscape of public life in the U.S.S.R. They account for the enormous political, economic, and military strength of the system, but also for its low level of economic performance, its political paralysis, its poor perception of reality, its lack of international success. Power is unquestionably what holds the Soviet system together, but its disruptive potential has gradually become increasingly visible. Soviet leaders, beginning with Lenin, have been fascinated by power and obsessed with its acquisition and maintenance; now one wonders if these inclinations have not become fatal and self-destructive.

Looking for an explanation, one would probably have to go back to the philosophical roots of enlightenment and rationalism. Marxism itself and the Soviet version of it are manifestations of more general views on man and society which became prominent during the last two centuries. The rise of science gave European man the belief that he mastered the natural world; then the social sciences provided an understanding of society and man's place in it. The weakening of a religiously determined world view favored the idea that a rational organization of society could be designed. Once such a design were available, the insights produced by social science would allow its realization. The principal tool required would be power.

Soviet Marxism, by eliminating all nuances and counterbalances, has become the most extreme expression of this rationalist world view. It pretends to possess perfect knowledge of social processes and of the ultimate course of world history; it posits a totally materialist world view and rejects any heteronomous morality. Everything is subordinated to the realization of the communist future; it requires and legitimizes the appropriation of unlimited power.

The weaknesses of the rationalist world view, enlarged by their Soviet Marxist exaggerations, become manifest in the present troubles of the Soviet Union. Our understanding of society and man's place in it is fragmentary, and is distorted rather than aided by a Marxist approach. The tools for reshaping society are anything but efficient. Governments have in fact little idea of what they are effecting through their policies, but the Soviet rulers live in the even worse illusion that they know where they are going. The malleability of the individual and the plasticity of society are far from endless. Not only do they resist the efforts of the leaders to be cajoled into the desired shapes, they even respond with strange tricks.

The Soviet leaders originally held that the reform of the basis, the socialization of the means of production, would in the end produce a new type of society populated by a new kind of inhabitant, the new Soviet man. This person would be mentally attuned to socialism, free of any individualistic strivings, totally committed to the advancement of the common good. But what we see almost seventy years after the Revolution is a legal, administrative, political, economic, and social system where every moving part is propelled by self-interest, whether fear of punishment or desire of profit. The new Soviet man seems to be nobody else but old Adam. Looking closer, however, certain contours of a yet unknown person are discernible. He or she has developed a capacity for smoothly adapting to the demands of the government, voicing his support where required, and generally going through the expected motions. On the other hand, this allegiance is shallow. The deepest interests of the individual concern the sphere of his private life, a small and manageable number of intimate relationships with family members, close friends, and colleagues at work. Social commitments on a wider scale are pointless, because everything is predetermined here and there is no scope for a truly individual contribution. The real new Soviet man has therefore become a very private person who presents a bland and almost faceless exterior towards society. "Who wants to spit in the wind?" as Vladimir Bukovskii put it.[12]

The Present Crisis and the Role of Law

Is there sufficient reason to talk of a crisis in the Soviet system, and, if so, how does law relate to such a crisis? I believe that it makes sense to speak of a crisis when stresses or tensions or dysfunctions appear in a non-static complex, or in other words in a process, that threaten to disrupt its normal course or its continued existence. This definition admittedly contains ample ambiguities, but it may at least offer a starting point.

From the previous argument it is obvious that I see the Soviet system primarily as one which is most fundamentally determined by its relationship to power, and its acquisition, expansion, and maintenance. The ideological component in particular, which many regard as the most essential constructive element of the system, is in my eyes rather to be considered as one of several factors which affect the basic question of power relationships.

As a machine for amassing power the Soviet system has proved itself unprecedentedly successful. But, as I have attempted to explain, this arrangement carries the seeds of its own destruction. Put in the most general terms, the present Soviet régime seems to have lost the ability to tackle, let alone solve, almost any important social issue. Its excessive fear of abandoning power induces it to weigh every policy option in this light. Consequently, no constructive policies are embarked upon and neither are any independent initiatives allowed. The protection and safeguarding of the status quo, at least in domestic affairs, gradually becomes the exclusive preoccupation of the government. In the meantime, certain issues remain unsolved, while in other instances solutions are produced by spontaneous processes (the emergence of the second economy, of the real new Soviet man, undesired and unplanned). The régime seems to be as powerful as ever, but in reality its control over certain basic social factors is slipping out of its hands. In a manner which is perhaps not even clearly realized by the leadership, its power is becoming irrelevant in a number of sectors; other forces have taken over. In this sense, the Soviet system can be said to be in a crisis. This does not mean that the system as we know it is in danger of imminent collapse.

The Soviet system, obsessed with the preservation of its power, has always attached great importance to protective mechanisms, supporting constructions. In this respect, one may distinguish between purely conceptual systems and systems manifesting themselves in visible organizations. Among the former, Marxist-Leninist ideology is the most prominent; another conceptual factor that reinforces, to some extent, the Soviet system is Russian nationalism. Without the support provided by a number of visible organizations, the Soviet system would not survive for long. In this respect the principal guarantors of the system are the Party, the KGB and the Police, the Army, and the governmental and legal system. They all play different roles; here we want to consider in particular the role of law.

Soviet law supports the Soviet system mainly in two ways. Soviet law provides a significant part of the system's organizational blueprint, and it influences behavior in a direction desired by the rulers. The first task is standard and unspecific, but still quite essential. Soviet law defines the administrative-territorial structure of the land, the various levels of public power and their relative competences, the formal organization of the economy and the functioning of its constituent parts, etc. This task is not fundamentally different from similar ones existing in states with other socio-economic systems, but for two exceptions. One is that in the U.S.S.R. the area covered by the legal organization of the state is considerably larger, particularly because it embraces a far greater sector of economic activities. The other exception is connected with the nature of the relations between law and politics in the U.S.S.R.: the decisive factor in public affairs is the Party top, rather than the state, and for this reason organizational schedules laid down by the state (in other words, the legal structure of the society), may be openly or tacitly superseded by instructions emanating from the Party.

In a more active and ongoing way Soviet law supports the system by influencing behavior. One important area which has already been mentioned concerns the protection of the state-controlled economy by criminal law. This economy would collapse without the continuous enforcement of strict prohibitions against numerous types of economic activities which detract from the centrally controlled economy. The dynamic character of this aspect of law is demonstrated by the incessant changes, necessitated by newly emerging types of behavior.[13] In this kind of law we are not dealing with a static organizational blueprint, but with a sector of social life where the government is in constant interaction with some of its citizens, where it attempts to achieve certain results, and where state and citizens are locked in an endless dialogue of reactive behavior. Next to economic criminal law, other such areas are to be found in housing, family, and labor law.

In sum, the two modes in which Soviet law supports the Soviet régime are those of creating and maintaining order. This assumes that order is an element which is included in the régime's general objective, the acquisition and preservation of power. This assumption suggests under which circumstances law may become an anti-systemic, disruptive, dysfunctional factor in the perspective of the Soviet rulers: when law-induced order detracts from the general objective of the system. Two broadly defined situations should be considered in this respect.

The order-creating function of law may be affected by hypertrophy. In such cases the command of the legislator, embodied in a law which describes a specific organizational structure or process, is not heard sufficiently clearly.

This may be because the message is too complicated, or because the audience is not disposed to listen. This situation regularly occurs in the Soviet economy, but also in other areas of public administration. The regulative system imposed by the authorities fails to be fully implemented, for whatever reason. The most common manifestation is overregulation, a phenomenon which is connected with what has been discussed above under the heading of informational distortions. Central agencies, on the basis of incorrect information on what is going on at lower levels, issue directives which for various reasons are not obeyed lower down the line. This will result in distorted reporting on performance and thereby in even less information available to the central authorities. A realization that something is amiss may evoke corrective legislation, but then there is always the risk that the situation will get even worse. There are areas of Soviet legislation, especially in economic-administrative law, where there seems to be a continuous stream of look-alike legislative directives, disappearing into a black hole of stubborn non-implementation.

On a quite different note, the order maintained by law has an inherent tendency to become an independent order, independent especially of the vital interests of the régime. In liberal democracies this problem does not arise in principle, because the independence of the legal order itself is defined as one of the basic interests of the political system. In a Soviet-type system, however, law is both officially regarded and actually utilized as nothing more than an instrument of politics. Under such conditions it is to be avoided that the legal order acquire an existence which is in some way independent of the order desired by the rulers. The problem may be solved by legal or extra-legal means. The latter route is followed when political or administrative measures are allowed to override legal arrangements. The total subservience of law can also be guaranteed by legal means when the precedence of political interests is included within the law itself. This procedure is common in the area of civil rights and also in criminal law. The constitutional elaboration of civil rights makes it abundantly clear that such rights can never be used against the interests of the Soviet régime. In criminal law one may point to the existence of vaguely defined crimes, such as anti-Soviet propaganda or hooliganism, which allow the repression of undesired behavior without much further specification.

Still, if this were the entire picture, the conclusion would simply be that the independence of the legal order cannot emerge as an anti-systemic factor, because this independence itself has been effectively prevented. The present climate, however, is one of fundamental political conservatism, in which no important objectives are contemplated as deserving of realization, not even economic ones, because objectively necessary economic reforms are not engaged in, and simply improved economic performance cannot very well be regarded as a genuine political objective. In such a climate the preservation of the status quo acquires paramount importance and consequently maintenance of the established legal order moves to the forefront. Under such circumstances, the legal order may achieve a certain de facto independence, not because it has freed itself of its political shackles, but because the political interests themselves have somehow faded.

Future Course of the Present Crisis

At the beginning of the foregoing section it has been argued that the Soviet system is subject to tensions that threaten its continued existence and functioning, and that in this sense one may refer to a crisis of the Soviet system. Looking at the present state of the Soviet Union from a somewhat different angle one might also say that the Soviet régime has lost, to a considerable degree, the capacity for purposive, peaceful change. Again, this by no means signifies that the Soviet system is faced with imminent collapse. Its further fate will depend on the way the various disruptive and conjunctive factors will interrelate.

The various stress factors described above differ not only in an inherent disruptive potential, but also in internal mobility. The economic, political and informational constraints which affect the functioning of the Soviet régime may be quite serious, but they are also relatively stable. The leadership is more or less aware of the shortcomings in this respect and accepts them as inevitable for the time being. While no external factors interfere, poor economic performance, defective political control, and distorted knowledge of what goes on in society can be expected to remain at tolerable levels. They will not by themselves lead to the downfall of the Soviet system.

Other stress factors are less stable. The most obvious example is the international situation, in particular developments in the vassal states. The Soviet régime is only partially in control in Poland, Hungary, and Eastern Germany (to name the most critical instances), and developments in these countries may present crucial challenges. Similar factors are the national question in the U.S.S.R., the second economy, and, less tangibly but most intriguingly, the moral crisis. All these factors are capable of independent growth, and if this takes place the Soviet government must decide whether it is going to take any action.

The disruptive factors are counterbalanced by a complex of guarantors, of régime supports. These are grouped around the most central conjunctive element, the Party élite. This élite controls the entire society through the

Party organization, legitimizes its position through reference to Marxist-Leninist ideology, safeguards its internal cohesiveness through a system of political and material privileges (including participation in the second economy), is supported by the ultimate physical force of Army and KGB. Real reform will occur only when a change of the external factors evokes a régime reaction which brings about a lowering of the degree of integration of the system. The process can best be described in a step-by-step manner. It goes without saying that the following scenario is only meant to describe a possible course of events, in order to demonstrate the ideas outlined above, and does not claim to be the most likely development.

1. The Soviet leader decides that the situation does not call for significantly new policies; the Brezhnev-Chernenko pattern is followed. One must wait for a new leader, or for a revision of the decision, prompted by new autonomous developments of stress factors.
2. The leader decides that new policies are called for. He has reached his position by being an exceptionally able manipulator of political power. One of the most basic considerations for the leadership is the awareness that much of its own power is lost within the Party-state apparatus. This loss is partly due to bureaucratic entropy (naturally occurring processes in large organizations and information networks), partly to a deliberate compromise, manifested by the fall of Khrushchev and the ascent of Brezhnev. The loyalty and cooperation of medium and lower levels of the Party machine have been bought by granting them reasonably comfortable positions. For all these reasons I believe that the most likely first step to be taken by the leader will be an attempt to reclaim some of the power lost within the apparatus.
3. For his new policies the leader will require allies. The most obvious ones are the Army and the KGB. The Army will have to be rewarded with a maintenance of high military spending, which requires improved economic performance. The Army will probably favor a strong posture towards the West and inflexibility in military matters vis-à-vis the vassal states. Increased stress on Soviet patriotism, rather than on ideological purity, is also indicated. The KGB might receive Politburo representation again (as they already have, since this was written).
4. In more concrete terms the new policies would entail the reinforcement of genuine central control over the economy and the concurrent decrease of local power and initiative. The second economy would also suffer in two ways: extra-systemic second economy activities would be repressed as rivals of the official network; institutionalized second economy activities connected with the operation of the lower levels of the official economy would also be under pressure.

5. The tendency of such reforms would be to push the lower levels of the Party-state machine, or at least certain sections of it, out into the area of anti-systemic forces. They would find their most natural allies in there in the forces of nationalism and in societal sectors connected with the second economy.

6. Judging from past experience, increased economic centralism will not result in improved performance and will get bogged down in grass-roots unwillingness. The accompanying tensions in the Party may lead to the downfall of the leader (à la Krushchev) and the election of a new one, or to a radical change of course by the old leader.

7. The new leader designs a new policy and seeks new allies. A prominent option would now be a certain amount of economic deregulation. Such a policy would allow the growth of a legitimate second economy. By the same token it would provide an opportunity for the manifestation of national differences, at first at an economic level. Local Party and state functionaries would support such developments. The Army would not object, provided its resources remained unimpaired. The main opponent would be the KGB.

8. The emergence of a legitimate private sector in the economy will be accompanied by the incipient articulation of the interests of particular groups, whether economic or national. As the state network (the "elected" soviets) lacks the proper channels, the Party will initially be the most suitable vehicle for the expression of such interests. If a split were to occur between the local Party-state bosses and private economic interests, the entire development might abort. An arrangement along Yugoslav lines—a decentralized, localized, but socialist economy—is therefore more likely than downright privatization (such as in Hungary). The latter road may be acceptable (as it was in Hungary) for relatively small-scale, ancillary economic units.

It should be repeated that the scenario outlined above is designed mainly to convey an impression of a possible course of events, taking into consideration the various crisis factors which have been discussed in an earlier part of this essay. A very probable event which has not been included is a loop-back, which might occur at almost any stage; for a variety of reasons it may turn out that one phase is followed by an earlier phase, which has already been traversed in the past. Recent Soviet history offers several examples of such situations. Under Brezhnev there was a return to a number of Stalinist practices; the short Chernenko era revived in many respects the reign of Brezhnev. It is entirely to be expected that future Soviet leaders will occasionally deem it wise to return to tried policies of the past. The entire development process will accordingly be much slower and more complicated than the one that had been outlined here. But regardless of such complications, two factors stand out as the most serious obstacles to fundamental change: economic centralization, particularly in the rigid form of central planning and state ownership of the entire productive process, and strict adherence to Marxist-Leninist ideology. The former will lead to increasingly material backwardness of the U.S.S.R., which is politically, socially and morally an ultimately untenable position. The latter prevents the adoption of a rational view of society and the world and thereby blocks the acceptance and implementation of genuine reform proposals.

Consequences for Soviet Law

In one of the previous sections we have analyzed how law is simultaneously a conserving and a disruptive factor in relationship to the Soviet system. It bolsters the position of the régime by creating and maintaining order, while at the same time it may, through overregulation, lead to the failure of effective control, or it may tend to hamper the government in the untrammeled pursuit of its interests. What now, in the light of the possible future developments outlined in the foregoing section, is the contribution which Soviet law might make to these developments, and how would Soviet law itself change in this process?

Any attempt by the leadership to recapture lost ground in the control of the productive process will inevitably entail a considerable involvement of law. Through a complex of new rules the government will try to create an organizational framework of exercising effective central control over the economy. More elaborate prohibitions to combat the increasing pluriformity of the second economy will be needed, backed up by more detailed instructions to police, procuracy, courts and other law enforcement agencies. Although some results may be expected from the latter sets of measures, the implementation of the entire policy will also carry the seeds of its own frustration, because it leads to estrangement of lower levels of the bureaucratic pyramid, to local sabotage of law enforcement, and consequently to the ultimate irrelevancy of the reforms.

Eventually the only policy option that is not sterile will turn out to be economic deregulation, which in political terms is nothing else but the conscious abandonment of a certain amount of power. By itself economic deregulation requires only modest adaptations in Soviet law. These concern mainly the rules on economic decision-making and profit distribution, as contained in the specialized laws on state enterprises and their associations.[14] It is, however, to be expected that economic deregulation will almost automatically entail the emergence of a growing private sector in the economy. Such a sector, to be legal, needs first of all the repeal of certain rules of criminal law, in particular the present prohibitions against speculation, private enterprise, commercial representation, etc. Furthermore, present Soviet law lacks the legal institutions necessary for the proper development of private economic activities. It will therefore be inevitable that suitable forms of corporations, companies, partnership, and so forth are created.

Economic reforms may gradually prepare the ground for the defenestration of the present ideology. Once the essential steps towards economic deregulation and the abandonment of Marxism-Leninism have been taken, it will be possible to proceed to alterations of the constitutional system. The first change, and in many ways the most urgent, is the autonomization of civil rights. By this I understand primarily the severance of the most important political freedoms from the interests of the state. It would be of tremendous ideological and practical importance if the Soviet state were to recognize that the exercise of the freedoms of speech, of the press, of association is to be absolute, within certain wide confines, and not tied to the promotion of the interests of the state.

The recognition of genuine civil rights would also serve as a suitable starting-point for a process of increased political pluralism. Such a process would present very serious problems, of a moral as well as an organization nature. The Russian tradition is extremely weak in this respect and the Soviet politico-legal framework offers almost no institutional basis. The most readily available differential criterion in this respect is not political orientation, but nationality. As argued above, local Party agencies, which have at least a certain experience in genuine political decision-making and which will probably be an element of great importance in a future reform of the Soviet system, appear to be a better vehicle for emergent political pluralism than local soviets or competing political parties.

The Party, at this stage, will have shed its ideological mask and appear more truthfully as what it actually has been for a long time already, an élite, a ruling class which occupies a leading position in Soviet society. This will undoubtedly weaken the Party's position, because its legitimation will now have to be derived exclusively from performance, and not anymore from its ideological anointment. On the other hand, experience shows that such ruling classes, encumbered by little ideological baggage, propelled mainly by their own privileged positions, are often able to function reasonably well, provided access to them is relatively open and profits accruing from the arrangement are not too unevenly distributed over the various classes.

The further fate of law in the U.S.S.R. would depend very much on the political future of the U.S.S.R. itself. Would it survive as a multinational unitary state, or as a federation, or would it break up into a number of independent states? What would the successor states ultimately adopt as their political régimes: one-party autocracies, military dictatorships, socialist or liberal democracies? We shall not enter into speculations on these questions.

NOTES

1. It is intriguing that the words "of socialism" were included in the corresponding provision (Art.12, par.2) of the previous Soviet Constitution of 1936, omitted in the draft Constitution of 1977 and restored in the final text. This might indicate that the draftsmen of the 1977 Constitution initially decided to be realistic and to admit tacitly the lasting character of the 'socialist' self-interest motive. Subsequently, it was probably found to be too embarrassing.

2. 1977 Constitution, Arts. 40 and 60. On the double function of law as reward and punishment see M. Heller, *Le monde concentrationnaire et la littérature soviétique* (Lausanne: Terre des Hommes, 1974), 11-53.

3. ". . . dans un système socialiste la pénurie aléatoire des produits de consommation est aussi *naturelle* que l'abondance dans nos régions." A. Kriegel in *Pouvoirs* 6 (1978): 126.

4. 1977 Constitution, Arts. 39, 50, 51, and 59.

5. Even Brezhnev himself complained in 1974 that in the various branches of the economy "there are thousands of different prescriptions and instructions . . . Many of these instructions are obsolete, contain unjustified restrictions or overly detailed regulation." L. I. Brezhnev, *Leninskim kursom*, T.6 (Moscow: Gospolitizdat, 1976), 73.

6. On the definition of the Soviet second economy see G. Grossman, "The Second Economy of the U.S.S.R." *Problems of Communism* 26 No.5 (1977): 25-40; P. Wiles, *Die Parallelwirtschaft; eine Einschätzung des systemwidrigen Verhältens im Bereich der Wirtschaft unter besonderer Berücksichtigung der UdSSR*, (Köln: Bundesinstitut für ostwissenschaftliche und internationale Studien, 1981), 8-10; A. Katsenelinboigen, "Coloured Markets in the Soviet Union," *Soviet Studies* 29 (1977): 62-85.

7. Cf. A. Shtromas, *Political Change and Social Development: The Case of the Soviet Union* (Frankfurt am Main/Bern: Verlag Peter Lang, 1981), 73-74; F. Feldbrugge, "Government and Shadow Economy in the Soviet Union," *Soviet Studies* 36 (1984): 528-543.

8. E.g., M. Voslensky, *Nomenklatura* (English edition, 1985) and earlier German and French editions.

9. Cf. A. Solzhenitsyn, *Zhit' ne po lzhi: Sbornik materialov, August 1973-Fevral' 1974* (Paris: YMCA Press, 1975), esp. 194–198; for this text in English translation see L. Labedz, ed., *Solzhenitsyn: A Documentary Record*, 2nd edition (Hammondsworth: Penguin, 1974), especially the essay "Live not by Lies."

10. Cf. F. Feldbrugge, "The Elder Brother in Russia. Seniority in Russian Politico-Legal Discourse." *Sowjetsystem und Ostrecht. Festschrift für Boris Meissner zum 70. Geburtstag* (Berlin: Duncker & Humblot, 1985), 211-225.

11. Lenin, *Sochineniia* 45: 358: ". . . it is well-known that russified foreigners always overdo it where it concerns genuinely Russian attitudes."

12. In *To Build a Castle.*

13. Very extensive amendments in the chapter on economic crimes were introduced on 3 December 1982 in the Criminal Code of the R.S.F.S.R.; *Vedomosti Verkhovnogo Soveta RSFSR*, 1982, No. 49, item 1821.

14. Particularly the Statute on the Socialist State Production Enterprise of 4 October 1965 and the Statute on the Production Association of 27 March 1974.

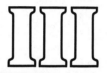

PROSPECTS FOR TRANSITION

1

How the End of the Soviet System May Come About

Historical Precedents and Possible Scenarios

ALEXANDER SHTROMAS

Introductory Remarks on Revolution and Political Change

When Lenin formulated his "fundamental law of revolution"—the law according to which "for a revolution to take place it is not enough for the exploited and oppressed masses to realize the impossibility of living in the old way, . . . it is essential that the exploiters should not be able to live and rule in the old way"[1]—he, in fact, only reaffirmed an old and much more fundamental truth, first stated by Plato, that "changes in any constitution originate, without exception, within the ruling class itself, and only when this class becomes the seat of disunion";[2] "while so long as they" (i.e. the ruling class) "are of one mind . . . the city cannot be changed."[3]

Indeed, all revolutions that have changed an established and consolidated political order (or a city, a constitution, a commonwealth) into a new one, were the result of disunion and ensuing confrontation between the élites. Spontaneous popular uprisings and revolts have never been able, on their own, to produce a revolutionary change, for the simple reason that they do not, and cannot, carry with them a political alternative to the existing system of rule. Even if an uprising or revolt were to shatter the existing

201

political institutions to the extent of causing a power vacuum, as, for example, the revolt of Petrograd workers in February 1917 did, a united élite would have rapidly filled it by restoring the shattered institutions and putting them back into the position of political control. If, however, the élite were split, its change-oriented part could take full advantage of the power vacuum produced by a popular revolt for filling it by institutions under its own control, and to the exclusion of those of the shattered sovereign state power. This is what actually happened in Petrograd in February-March 1917, when the liberal "Progressive Bloc" took advantage of the power vacuum in the capital city, produced by a spontaneous workers' revolt, and through the State Duma in which it had an absolute majority, abolished the monarchy, formed the Provisional Government and thus assumed political power in Russia.

Along the same lines have developed also all other "great revolutions" known to history.[4] Among them the Russian revolution of February-March 1917 was, perhaps, unique in the sense that in its process a popular revolt had played a certain role, however secondary and subordinated, whereas in any other such revolutions it did not. There were, for sure, no popular revolts to play any part during either the English Revolution of 1642 or the Great French Revolution of 1789. Such "negative" facts concerning the role of the "people's action" in making a revolution allowed Jean Baechler to arrive at the quite categorically stated conclusion that "the seizure of power by the people, whether the proletariat or the bourgeoisie, is a pure myth, unsupported by a single fact,"[5] and thus historically to confirm Vilfredo Paretto's theoretical contention that "the essence of all revolutions is a change of the ruling élite," or even more simply, "a change of élites."[6]

This does not mean that in a revolution the attitudes of the grassroot population do not matter at all. They do matter indeed, and a great deal so. As all theorists of revolution have quite unanimously acknowledged, a profound all-round dysfunction between the civil society and the polity or, as Chalmers Johnson has put it, "a disequilibrated and dyssynchronized social system" is a prerequisite for a revolutionary change.[7] Such a dysfunction implies that in the population at large the desire for political change has become more powerful than whatever has been left of the allegiance to the political status quo. It is the population's indifference to the fate of the old régime, sometimes amounting to direct hostility toward it, that provides the necessary conditions for making the change-oriented élite's bid for "reconstitution of the state" realistic; nobody then prevents it from combatting the conservative ruling élite and the polity it commands. In other words, for the revolution to be successful, the "reciprocity of expectations between rulers and ruled"[8] must first be broken down, to the extent of the old régime's total loss of legitimacy in the eyes of the overwhelming majority of the people.

In that sense the change-oriented élite acts in a revolution as the legitimate representative of the population, as the champion of the population's aspirations for a better future and thus enjoys the population's implicit and, when stimulated, also explicit support. This support, however passive, is especially crucial in the aftermath of the revolution. Even if rendered in the form of failing to rally around the forces of restoration, it is usually sufficient to consolidate the victory of the revolution over the old régime.

There is no doubt whatsoever that the French Revolution of 1789, made by the representatives of the Third Estate in the Estates General, did enjoy such kind of support from the overwhelming majority of Frenchmen. Only one rather backward group of peasants in western France, the so-called Chouans, actively opposed the revolution and joined forces with the royalists enabling them to wage in the Vendée a local civil war which for a few years represented a major threat to the new, not yet properly consolidated post-revolutionary order; but, since there appeared no larger social group to follow them in rallying round the royalist cause, their resistance was doomed to fail. In Russia, there were no signs of loyalty to the old tsarist régime even on the scale of the Chouans. The February Revolution of 1917 that did away with the tsar was greeted with unqualified joy and enthusiastically accepted by all larger sections of Russia's population without exception. It is in this sense that a revolution is a truly popular event. Although its champion is the change-oriented part of the élite, that élite acts as if in the name and on behalf of the people, and the people recognize it as such.

The kind of revolution for which Lenin formulated his "fundamental law" and for which to materialize the élite championing it has to enjoy sufficient popular support, can be directed only against an oppressive autocratic régime that either bars the way for introducing change or imposes changes that the people cannot accept and deeply resent. It was because of that property of every revolution that Marx qualified what he termed to be a bourgeois revolution by the word democratic. For Marx, every revolution deserving that name had to be democratic, even if it was only a bourgeois-democratic revolution. When predicting the inevitability of the proletarian socialist revolution, Marx always stressed that it will have to take place because bourgeois democracy effectively excludes the workers from participation in it and, as far as they are concerned, is no more than an oppressive dictatorship.[9] For Marx, the socialist revolution by raising the proletariat, "the nine-tenths of the population," "to the position of ruling class" becomes tantamount to nothing more than "winning the battle of democracy."[10] The faithful followers of Marx who, unlike Marx, had witnessed the active and fruitful involvement of the proletariat into "bourgeois

democracy," split their ranks because one part of them (e.g. Eduard Bern-
stein) proclaimed that the idea of the proletarian revolution had, in such
new circumstances, become obsolete, whereas the other part (e.g. Lenin)
intransigently stuck to it in spite of all change. But even the latter ones (e.g.
Lenin himself), when trying to justify the inevitability of the proletarian
socialist revolution, had to associate the moment for it to come about with
such times when the ruling bourgeoisie would have no choice but to abolish
democracy altogether and start ruling by employing openly dictatorial and
terroristic means.

It was, in fact, Alexis de Tocqueville who first established that only in
conditions of autocratic or authoritarian minority rule (which he, in breach
with the classical Aristotelian tradition, called aristocracy) is revolution an
adequate, and in some cases even inevitable, vehicle of political change.[11]
According to him, revolutionary change in a democracy is totally out of
place and completely unnecessary; democracy, being the most dynamic
system, at the same time "renders society more stationary than it has ever
been."[12]

This is not to say, and de Tocqueville himself never said so, that democracy cannot be overthrown by subversive, conspiratorial, and/or violent
means. Contemporary history is a witness to only too many successful
conspiracies and plots against democracy which, after having been destroyed,
was replaced by ruthless, and, in most cases, sectarian, dictatorship. This is
especially true in the case of infant post-revolutionary democracies, such as
the one born in Russia in March 1917 and overthrown by the Bolshevik
coup d'état in October of that same year, or the one established in Germany
in November 1918 and destroyed from within by the Nazis in 1933-35, or the
one brought about in 1931 by the republican régime in Spain and devoured
by the flames of the civil war that ensued five years later. All of them
followed the regular, historically set pattern for post-revolutionary developments whereby one of the few totalitarian movements operating on the
margins of the society's political spectrum hijacks the revolution and, riding
high on its tide, establishes itself as the total dictatorial state. All revolutions
went through such spells of "millenarian dictatorships,"[13] and in this sense
the "millenarianisms" of Peisistratus in Athens of the sixth century B.C. and
of the Jacobins in eighteenth-century France are phenomena of the same
order as the Bolshevik and Nazi "millenarianisms" of the twentieth century.

Not only such infant democracies but every unstable democracy—a democracy that is established either in a country still besieged by acute social
antagonisms or even in one which, in spite of being socially quite cohesive, is
actively subverted by foreign-sponsored political groups—is prone to col-
lapsing and yielding power to one kind of dictatorship or another. It is the

first instance, that of acute social antagonisms, that makes democratic institutions so fragile in Latin America, Turkey or Pakistan; and the second, that of foreign-sponsored subversion, that has driven most countries of Central and Eastern Europe between the two world wars from democracy to dictatorship. I leave here aside those obvious instances when democracies have been destroyed and oppressive dictatorships imposed in their stead by direct foreign intervention as was the case of most countries of Central and Eastern Europe in the aftermath of World War II.

Nevertheless, the political acts leading to a democracy being overthrown have never assumed the character or dimension of a revolution. They were always perpetrated as coups d'état, although not always necessarily did they take also the form of a coup de force. (Hitler, for example, in 1935, entrenched himself in power by a coup d'état that was not at all a coup de force.)

It was again Lenin who stressed that "revolution is impossible without a nationwide crisis."[14] For only a crisis of such dimensions exposes the rottenness of the old régime, its total inability to cope with the problems society faces, its full functional inadequacy as far as the discharging of the state's normal duties is concerned—in other words, the profound all-round dysfunction referred to above. And it is also only such a crisis that provides the change-oriented part of the élite with the right opportunity to step in with its counter-proposals and counter-policies, pressing the ruling élite either to accept and carry them out or, alternatively, to abdicate and be replaced by the counter-élite.

If the ruling élite, or at least some of its powerful elements that would be able to prevail, accepted the counter-proposals and counter-policies, co-opted their movers into the ruling élite and introduced together with them the systematic changes sought, the revolution would be carried out from above, in an orderly though quite drastic manner. This process, which Chalmers Johnson calls conservative change, is nevertheless revolutionary for it not only results in the "reconstitution of the state," but also, sooner or later, involves a complete change of the ruling élite. But what if the revolution were to be carried out in a situation where the ruling élite would prove to be non-caring or "intransigent"[15] and thus unwilling to go for change even when faced by a raging national crisis? In such a situation are there any ways of removing the existing ruling élite and putting the counter-élite in its place? History shows that there are many such ways. Below I will try to show how some of them could be applicable to the Soviet Union. But before I do that, I would like to draw the attention to a certain general rule common to all revolutionary transitions. This is the rule of the "second pivot," and it was first formulated by a Soviet samizdat writer, F. Znakov.

The "Second Pivot"

According to Znakov, for a revolution to take place the division between the élites has to be expressed in an institutional form. No other form will suffice. This means that the counter-élite has to assume control of a certain public or state body either already in existence as an integral part of the official system or called into existence by that system for the special purpose of crisis management and resolution. In some cases, one could add, such an institution may be formed without official sanction but has later to be officially recognized and thus incorporated into the official system as in the case of "Solidarity" in the Poland of 1980.

Alternatively, an existing public or state body where members of both parts of the élite were doing business and discussing outstanding issues together, may at a certain point be split into two, with one of the parts coming under the control of the counter-élite and thus becoming its spearhead, not any more for mere demands and pressures, but for bringing about practical political change directly, independently, and with disregard for the proper order of subordination and procedure. Such a split would already divide the existing "one-pivotal" political system into two separate pivots of power and social integration engaging in a confrontation for the assumption of full power.

Revolution, Znakov maintains, is on only when such a split of "one into two" occurs and an open confrontation between the thus formed two pivots of power and social integration ensues. Again, alternatively, a public or state body fully integrated into the official political system, if it came under the full control of the counter-élite, may, at a certain point in time, be split off from the integral systemic pattern and used as the "second pivot," too. Znakov calls the split of "one" (political system) "into two" the "critical mass" that unleashes the chain reaction called revolution. He summed it up by saying that "the emergence of the second pivot" *(vtoroy sterzhen')* . . . "of power and social integration . . . is the general law of a revolutionary process." Elaborating on it, he wrote: "The experience of history indicates that the most essential requisite of any revolution, and the main fact portending its outbreak, is the formation on the legal surface of society of an institution, independent of the existent system of power and capable of setting itself off against it . . . After such a *second pivot* of society's organization comes into being, the course and the fate of the revolution depends on the correlation of forces representing the old system of power and that second pivot, as well as on what shape their confrontation is taking."[16]

Indeed, if we look at the revolutionary developments in seventeenth century England, eighteenth century France, and Russia of February (March) 1917, they will all confirm F. Znakov's "second pivot" theory, as would also other less famous revolutions if they really were revolutions and not mere putsches, coups d'état, or spontaneous uprisings and insurrections. The characteristic feature of all these revolutionary developments is the split of the existing autocratic political system into "two pivots" with each of them trying to establish itself as the "sole pivot," which in the case of the "first pivot" means restoration of the old order, and, in the case of the "second pivot," the creation around it of a new political system into which the "first pivot," if it is not entirely abolished, could be assimilated as a body of secondary importance.

In seventeenth century England, the Long Parliament emerged as the "second pivot" challenging the authority of the king, Charles I, who, by declaring war on Parliament in 1642, finally split the political system of the country into two warring "pivots." In eighteenth century France, the role of the "second pivot" was assumed by the representatives of the Third Estate in the Estates General, when they, on June 17, 1789, with the support of some representatives of other estates, proclaimed themselves the National Assembly of France and on June 23, 1789, refused to obey the orders of the king, Louis XVI, to dissolve this newly and spontaneously created body—the "second pivot" of the Great French Revolution of 1789. I always wondered why the French celebrate the 14th of July, the historically meaningless event of the storm of the Bastille, which took place even after the National Assembly was proclaimed the National *Constituent* Assembly of France (9th of July), rather than the 17th of June, which really marked the beginning of the French Revolution.

In Russia of 1917, the "second pivot" was instituted by the Provisional Committee of the State Duma, which was formed on February 27 (March 12), 1917, by the deputies of that semi-parliamentarian body who thus decided to disobey the tsar's decree of February 25 (March 10), 1917, about the State Duma's dissolution (mainly members of the ''Progressive Bloc'' led by the centrist Kadet—Constitutional Democratic—Party with the representatives of the left and some right-wing parties joining in).

F. Znakov's "second pivot" theory unites all the elements of revolutionary political change described above. It emphasizes that revolution is a result of a confrontation of élites, shows that its success is dependent on at least passive mass support for political change and, accordingly, on the degree to which the "old régime" has lost its legitimacy; but, most importantly, it shows the general way in which dictatorial political systems, be they autocratic, or oligarchic, enter into a "nation-wide crisis" and, subsequently, meet their end. The way is that of these systems being blown up from within and split into two, each organized around a separate pivot; it is in the ensuing battle between these two pivots for the restoration of a "one-pivotal" political system that the fate of the revolution is decided.

Before trying to apply all these theoretical considerations and models to prospective developments in the U.S.S.R. one should, however, say a few words about the state of the Soviet élite and the conflicting forces within it.

The Soviet Ruling Élite and the Counter-Élite

The Soviet ruling élite is usually identified with *nomenklatura*, the group of people holding the most important positions in all walks of Soviet life; or, to be more precise, those positions which it is the exclusive prerogative of the Party apparatus—the only truly sovereign body of authority in the land—to make appointments to. The social-political role of the *nomenklatura*, as well as its very existence, was convincingly established in 1969 by the works of Bohdan Harasymiv[17] and Jerry F. Hough.[18] Gradually, the term *nomenklatura* has become common currency, and today it is widely used, not only in Soviet studies, but also by the media and in all other forms of communication concerning the U.S.S.R. Mikhail Voslensky, himself a former member of Soviet *nomenklatura*, defined it as "the ruling class of the Soviet Union," and that definition stuck, since it was his book that contributed most to the popularization of this peculiarly Soviet institution in the West.[19] It is, indeed, a good working definition which can be accepted even by those who have their queries with the concept of class.

The Soviet élite is, however, much wider than *nomenklatura*. In every factory or plant, collective or state farm, scientific or educational institution—in brief in every Soviet office of whatever kind—only the very top officials are *nomklats* whereas their numerous expert-subordinates—engineers, economists, agronomists, lawyers, scientists, scholars, etc.—are not. Neither are the even more numerous members of the administrative and clerical personnel.

In every Soviet office there exists strong tension between the so-called "power" and "business-oriented" factions of its personnel, that often spills over into acute conflict. In essence it is a conflict between Party apparatus management and professional expertise, the former being usually represented by *nomklat-apparatchiks* and their sycophants occupying most of the leading posts in the office, and the latter by specialists occupying in that same office positions of secondary and tertiary rank.

The interests of the Party apparatus and those of the professional strata are inimical by definition. The Party apparatus is primarily interested in maintaining and consolidating ever further its total control over all socially relevant activities. For that sake, and that sake only, it needs to run the centralized system of detailed planning and all-round regimentation of all such activities, however irrational, counterproductive and even damaging in terms of utility such a system may be. The professional strata are, on the contrary, chiefly interested in achieving, by whatever they do, maximum utility which coincides entirely with the professional person's natural striving for full realization of his potential. The professionals therefore instinctively oppose the restrictive practices of centralized planning and all-round regimentation, automatically trying to respond to them by defiance. In order to be able to counter that defiance and enforce the system it runs, the Party apparatus has to maintain a huge network of plenipotentiary representatives, the *nomklats*, ubiquitously ramified throughout the country and reaching every workplace that exists. This is how the antagonism between the power and the expert élites shapes itself in the workplace, the primary "socialist *kollektiv*," which is supposed to be the elementary cell of Soviet society. This antagonism, to a lesser or greater degree, permeates all hierarchical levels of that society for, in the final end, all of them consist of workplaces, offices and institutions.

Could this antagonism be simply defined as that between the consolidated power élite, the *nomenklatura*, and all other non-*nomklatist* élites? I do not think it can. The *nomenklatura* is too big and too complex a body to be able to exist and function as a monolithic whole. It comprises not less than 2 million officials, and in fact maybe more than twice that number,[20] engaged in various occupations and discharging on all levels of social hierarchy very different responsibilities. Its membership ranges from, say, chairmen of collective farms, directors of small factories or workshops, and headmasters of schools, on the one hand, to the very top officials, including the "portraits" themselves, on the other.[21]

The inequalities within the *nomenklatura* are staggering indeed. Scores of different clusters of minutely defined privileges divide it into a host of mutually impenetrable casts with each such lower cast being put in a position of total subordination, moreover of full submission, to the higher ones. Perhaps only a few upper casts enjoy a relationship of a certain interdependence which puts them into an entirely different category strictly dividing these upper casts as the top echelon of *nomenklatura* from the rest of it.

There are perhaps about 2000 officials that belong to this top echelon of *nomenklatura*. Beside the "portraits," one should include into it the heads of the CC's departments and their deputies; members of the all-Union Council of Ministers; the heads of main "public organizations," such as the trade unions, unions of creative artists, the Communist Youth League, etc.; chiefs of all-Union media; some top civil servants (e.g. diplomats) and military commanders; and, last but not least, the chief Party and government bosses in the republics and provinces. It was during Brezhnev's times that all these people became practically unremovable from office, were thus endowed with real influence on policy decision and top appointment-making and, as a result, consolidated themselves into a ruling oligarchy, encompassing also the "portraits" whose status was thus reduced to that of "the firsts among the equals." These oligarchs are no more mere members of *nomenklatura* as they used to be under Stalin and, partly, also under Khrushchev; by having become such well-entrenched "solid assets" of that body, they became also its real and sovereign masters. Mere members of *nomenklatura* are the rest, those whom one could call its "liquid assets" and who, as much as the rest of the population (and, because of a direct relationship, perhaps even more), are entirely at the mercy of these masters.

But even the masters do not form a fully coherent social stratum. Those of them who depend on, and represent, territorial and branch interests are in constant strife with one another and both of them—with the ones who are in charge of the central authority of the state and whose business it is to assure social and political integration throughout the country. In those strifes all parties tend to form and lead coalitions that consist not only of members of the lower echelons of *nomenklatura* but also of non-*nomklatist* élites. The "territorial" and "branch" *nomklats* are far from being united within themselves either. There is fierce competition between different territorial and branch interests which all are involved in "zero-sum games." Indeed, the differences of interests between the civilian and military branches, the suppliers and the receivers of supplies, the producers and the traders, the practitioners and the academics, to name but a few, are so formidable that the interests of the ones can be defended and promoted only at the expense of the interests of the others.

Faced with the ample evidence of such strifes and cleavages within the Soviet élite, a number of Western students of the U.S.S.R. concluded that the purportedly united Soviet ruling stratum in fact consists of numerous competing "interest groups."[22] It would be wrong, however, to identify these groups exclusively with offices and institutions and, accordingly, to interpret the state of the Soviet system as that of "institutional pluralism."[23] The competition between offices and institutions is unable on its own to pluralize the Soviet system, let alone to undermine its basic unity, because, as I have argued elsewhere, the Soviet system consists "not only of particular 'group bureaucracies' 'freely' competing with each other but also possesses a supreme, unifying 'super-bureaucracy'—the Party *apparat*—for whose favours all other groups are compelled to compete."[24] The whole substance of the *nomenklatura* system is that of making all offices of the country ultimately and utterly dependent on the Party apparatus and thus of virtually transforming them into its mere extensions. Hence, "Soviet offices, as such, seldom act as distinctive groups whose interests compete with those of the Party apparatus. They only compete among themselves *before* the Party apparatus, using the latter's values and priorities as arguments to win their particular case."[25]

This is to say that, as long as the system of *nomenklatura* remains functional and keeps the Party apparatus in effective control of all walks of Soviet life, there will be no way for the office and/or institution-based groups completely to separate themselves from the Party "super-bureaucracy." If one accepts that self-consciousness is one of the "sociological requisites of a group"[26] and that in the Soviet political context such self-consciousness means that groups "must conceive of themselves as a group distinct from the Party *apparatchiki*,"[27] then, logically, one has to admit that purely office or institution-based competing practices are, under the present circumstances, in themselves insufficient to provide for the formation by respective "competitors" of proper, full-fledged "interest groups."

Authentic interest groups in the Soviet Union are formed and already exist not so much within offices or any other formally definable structures (such as different layers and sections of *nomenklatura*), but mainly as informal social entities that fall into line not so much on institutional as on functional, i.e. within-, inter- and extra-institutional, grounds. For example, those who are actively involved today in competition on behalf of their particular office interests may be seen as such an informal group whether already actual or merely as yet potential. For there is very little doubt that if not for the systemic compulsion, the great majority of these competitors would opt for competition not before the Party apparatus, whose decisions are bound to be arbitrary and erratic, but on a free market where one's own efforts and performance matter most. By seeing in the Party apparatus an obstacle for their own development and by being thus ready to discard it altogether, these people already conceive of themselves as a group not simply "distinct from the Party *apparatchiki*" but entirely opposed to them. This is the kind of self-consciousness that should unite all competing-between-themselves office-based groups into a single interest group seeking by a common effort to acquire the best conditions of fighting out the differences of interests among themselves.

That at least the specialist élites are already united into such an interest group was proved in a meticulous manner and with the support of a wealth of factual and statistical data by Milton C. Lodge. From his thorough research he drew the empirically substantiated conclusion that "all the specialist élites record a marked increase in self-awareness"[28] and that "throughout the later period" (he talks here about the second half of the 1960s). . .

[the] "Party-specialist. . .conflict is in the 'active-interest-group' range."[29] One should not hesitate to extend the same conclusion to the creative intelligentsia; a large part of the managerial stratum (which, as just shown, although they belong formally to the *nomenklatura*, increasingly share the values and goals of the specialists, thus gradually acquiring a double identity); and also to certain elements within the professional administrative and clerical personnel of the state, the notorious Russian *chinovniki*, who always considered themselves as the backbone of the nation, the vital element securing social order within it, and, as such, traditionally opposed erratic rulers whose policies threatened to undermine social cohesion and were prone to sow the seeds of unrest.[30]

These informal interest groups take on different and flexible shapes, such as, for example, what in H. Gordon Skilling's terms are "opinion groups"[31]— groups that extend over all narrowly-defined organizational or institutional boundaries—or, indeed, a great variety of other similarly structured groups that, according to Jan T. Gross, are constantly being created by the "continuous extension of organized social life outside the framework of official social institutions, as networks of social relations cease to overlap with organizational structures approved and supervised by the régime."[32] One could point here to the ubiquitous informal groups of *samizdat* and *tamizdat* readers and circulators that have developed into a huge network covering the whole country and comprising scores of thousands upon scores of thousands of people, among whom the active dissidents form only the tip of the iceberg; or to the massive "colored market" activities involving, in one way or another, practically every Soviet citizen[33]—not least those belonging to the *nomenklatura*, even to its top echelon.[34] But above all, one should point to the anti-collectivist, and thus anti-socialist, institution of the family that is, in fact, the ultimate springboard from which all other informal activities and networks are generated. As the genuine cell of society, it increasingly outbalances the socialist working *kollektiv* as its artificial cell and, by extending into multiple and overlapping networks of "friendly families," builds up within the U.S.S.R. a "counter-society" that gradually transforms the official society of working *kollektivs* into an empty shell.

In an earlier work I have described the Soviet Union as a society of total dissent disguised as one of almost total compliance with the régime.[35] In another work, I have analyzed at greater length the informal interest group activities, the ones briefly mentioned above as well as some others, within the conceptual framework of "intrastructural dissent."[36] This analysis allowed me to come to the conclusion that Soviet society as a whole—not only the élites but also the masses—is striving for political change and has become sufficiently ripe for accomplishing it. It is the pattern of intrastructural dissent that transcends all the formal social boundaries—those between the élites and non-élites, between the *nomklatist* and non-*nomklatist* élites, between the members and non-members of the Party—and that makes the *nomenklatura* itself a "seat of disunion," as Plato would have it.

Broadly speaking, the basic disunion stretching across all formally defined boundaries of Soviet society is that between two distinct categories of people. To the first of these two categories belong those whose position in society entirely depends on the peculiarities of the Soviet system and the institution of *nomenklatura* that goes with it. These people would simply lack the skills or ability to remain functional on a comparable level in any non-Soviet social and political system. Since most of these people are members of the Soviet ruling élite, the change to a non-Soviet system would mean for them the loss of élite status and for some also criminal liability for acts they committed in order to get themselves into the élite and remain within its ranks. All these people are bound therefore to be staunch defenders of the political status quo and resist by all means in their power any attempts to change it.

To the second category belong all those people whose positions cannot be adversely affected by a systemic change and who, on the whole, rightly or wrongly, feel that under a different, less rigid political system, their chances for both upward mobility and self-realization would substantially improve. That applies to the ordinary people—workers and collective farmers—as much as to all specialist élites, including those of their members who are in the *nomenklatura*. Certainly, different groups within that large category concentrate in their aspirations for change on different priorities. For some such a priority is the legalization of private enterprise, for others the right to be organized into genuine trade unions, yet for others intellectual and creative freedom. For the specialist élites, working in the economic sector, such a priority would be the reconstitution of the country's system of planning and management into one which would put them in sole effective charge of all organized productive processes and managerial activities—a priority that would entail the abolition of all presently existing feudal-type fetters on such processes and activities, including the *nomenklatura*, and the whole system of absolute rule by the Party apparatus inseparable from it.

These social or functional priorities could be accompanied across the board by certain ideological ones, such as, for example, religious and national freedoms.

There is nothing in those differences of priorities and aspirations which would make them incompatible with one another, let alone mutually exclusive. All of them can be easily accommodated for simultaneously and alongside of one another. That is why all the different groups of which this second category consists may be treated as a single, though only loosely amalgamated, "interest group" whose unity is based upon its common desire to advance political change and to see it through.

The people of the first category are still prevalent among the masters of *nomenklatura*, its so-called "frozen assets." By continuing to dominate the top echelon of the *nomenklatura* these people effectively maintain themselves in full control of the country, forcing all others to play their tune and behave in accordance with their whims. The few people of the second category who made it to that top echelon were accepted by its dominant group only on the condition that they function on its behalf and in its interests, behaving so as if they were wholeheartedly and completely sharing all its values and goals.

Among the mere members of *nomenklatura*, its so-called "liquid assets," the proportion of these two categories of people is already about 50-50; moving further down the social ladder the proportion of people of the second category is rapidly increasing until, on its lowest scale, they become as prevalent as the people of the first category were on the top. These proportions are, however, not at all steady. At time passes by, the proportion of people of the second category is quite rapidly increasing on all scales of Soviet society, including the top one. With the natural change of generations that is what is bound to happen, whether the masters of *nomenklatura* like it or not.

The people of the first category, whom one could, for the sake of brevity, call the *partocrats* and who form the Soviet ruling élite, belong to a certain generation and social type.[37] They have an almost identical background and their biographies hardly differ. They come from humble origins, are ill-educated (most, however, have university-level degrees without having ever accomplished primary education), and usually started in life as simple laborers. Generationwise, they were born before or soon after World War I, which means that they rose in their party-apparatus-sponsored careers at some point in time between the end of the 1920s and the mid-1940s, which is to say that they were the notorious promotees of Stalin, people who rose from rags to riches amidst terror and purges of which they managed to become the main beneficiaries. One has to possess special qualities of character to be able to survive, let alone to prosper and advance in careers, under such circumstances. Above all these people had to be great survivors and masters of "security technique." They also had to excel in the Party-apparatus intrigues and be sufficiently unscrupulous to denounce and send to their deaths the very people under whose auspices they started work as Party *apparatchiks*. To be able to combine inconspicuous cautiousness with murderous pursuits is a special skill of which these people, no doubt, were the grand masters. For only the species with such outstanding skills qualified for survival according to the Stalinist iron laws of natural selection of Party cadres; all other species had to go.

People whose only skills are in the realm of Party-*apparat* intrigue, who by actively engaging in the application of those skills disposed of many innocent lives, have no choice but to cling to the Soviet system of rule by all means in their power. Without believing in the Marxist-Leninist (or, by the same token, in any other) ideology they are bound to stick to it most firmly as it is that ideology that endows them with unchecked absolute power and provides the only basis for its legitimation. Therefore the more unideological and pragmatically self-interested these partocrats are, the more ideologically intransigent communists they are bound to be.

The people of the second category, whom for the same sake of brevity one should call the *technocrats,* are those who possess universally applicable skills and whose livelihood depends on the successful application of those skills.[38] Boris M. Meissner succinctly characterized them as a group whose power "is rooted in the authority and prestige inherent in the *functions* it performs" which distinctively separates the members of this group from, and opposes them to, the partocrats whose power "rests in the *positions* they hold."[39] The technocrats do not belong to any specific generation or class. They can be of any age and come from any social background.

It is, however, true that after Stalin most of the young people selected for political careers accomplished specialist education that was preceded by a normal period of study in both primary and secondary schools. This is why, within the *nomenklatura* the younger generation is predominantly technocratic (but not entirely, since the tendency to promote to the leading posts non-professional people or professionally inadequate people is still strong), whereas the older one consists almost exclusively of partocrats. On lower scales of the social ladder the generation gap between the partocrats and the technocrats drastically diminishes. While the partocrats everywhere belong almost exclusively to the older generation, the technocrats on the lower scales of the social ladder represent a normally balanced generational structure. This is to say that the conflict in the Soviet Union is not between different generations—although in the highest echelons of *nomenklatura* it appears mainly in that form—but between intergenerational interest groups which only in the case of the partocrats acquires a generational dimension.

As opposed to the partocrats, the technocrats do not have any vested interest in maintaining the Soviet system of rule. They know their talents and skills will make them properly functional under any political circumstances. This does not mean, however, that they are politically indifferent. Rightly or wrongly, they are convinced that as far as they, and the country and people at large, are concerned, any systemic change can be only for the better, and therefore they are ready to promote, and contribute to, such a change. Of course, the overwhelming majority of the technocrats are not prepared to wreck their professional careers and try as much as they can to comply with all the partocratic political demands, posing as totally loyal Soviet citizens and even as ardent supporters of the Communist Party and the Soviet government. However, insofar as a technocrat really cares about the optimal performance of his function, and the social issues implicit in it, he is bound to involve himself in intrastructural dissident activities in one way or another and does it with increasing intensity.

Milovan Djilas, who in his book *The New Class* (1957) made one of the first attempts to analyze the new partocratic "upper class" of socialist societies, has later also identified the existence in those societies of a "new new class" or, in other words, of the technocratic "middle class." In his *Unperfect Society: Beyond the New Class*, he wrote: "In the whole of the East European Communist world . . . ground has already been covered for the creation of a new social stratum—a special middle class . . . The sum and substance of this new stratum of society are specialists of all kinds . . . The very fact that the growing strength of this class cannot now be restrained . . . means that this is the class of the future. . .I feel that I am in a sense its spokesman because I can at least envisage the inevitability of its progress."[40]

The German political scientist, H.F. Achminov, stated simply that "the technical intelligentsia are the gravediggers of Communism."[41] And F. Znakov declared that in an industrial society, into which the Soviet Union has developed in the course of the last decades, the partocratic stratum (he calls it "supermonopolistic") became superfluous, with no constructive function to perform or role to play.[42] Its continuing leading role in society has therefore no social or moral justification; by persisting with it, the partocrats only pervert the natural hierarchy of such a society and, constantly using coercion to keep society in this artificial shape, stifle all its creative forces. According to F. Znakov, the present-day Soviet technocratic "middle class," in the natural social hierarchy of an industrial society, has to become the "upper class," and it is its destiny to establish itself in this position by removing the "superfluous" partocrats and thus destroying the whole perversive and stagnant system of the totalitarian partocratic rule.[43] F. Znakov also argues that "the middle class gradually becomes conscious of its real potential and fundamental interests and rapidly develops from a 'class in itself' into a 'class for itself',"[44] thus becoming sufficiently mature to act in accordance with its objective mission.

It is obvious, however, that the intrastructural dissident ventures of the technocrats cannot produce any significant changes as long as the partocrats stay in power. These ventures, under the present circumstances, will always be only partial successes and overall failures. But such ventures do produce a real awareness of the directions that the technocrats as a social group would like to see the country take and a consciousness of the impossibility of initiating and carrying out such change under partocratic rule.

Even now the technocrats are not a powerless group. In the age of the scientific-technological revolution their share of influence and power in society is rapidly increasing, though the partocrats remain supreme. As Frederick J. Fleron, Jr. has shown in his analysis of the composition of the Party's Central Committee, the proportion of specialists in that supreme body of power grew from 25.6% in 1952 to 44% in 1961,[45] a trend that continued unabated into the early 1970s, and, although it has been on the decline since, resuming again only in 1985 with Gorbachev's accession, the technocratic proportion of around 40% has remained pretty steady throughout all these years.[46]

Similarly the role of professionals in Soviet society as a whole is rapidly increasing, making them one of the most important interest groups (as a whole "multistructured" social stratum but not as institutionally identifiable bodies) in the country. Here are some statistical data clearly illustrating this point: the average annual increase of "scientific workers" amounts in the Soviet Union to 12.3 percent, that of industrial workers only to 3.5 percent; the number of "scientific workers" doubled between 1956 and 1960 and doubled again between 1960 and 1966.[47] Between 1970 and 1979 the number of people who completed higher education rose from 8,261,541[48] to 14,826,000,[49] i.e. increased about 80%. This, I think, speaks for itself. Also, as some Soviet scholars are publicly stating, experts are taking a much more important part than before in the process of political decision-making.[50]

This near-to-power position inevitably tempts the technocrats to utilize it fully, especially when till now they have been so persistently unable to determine policy, even on issues concerning their immediate professional interests. How and in what way could the technocrats realize this "temptation"—remove the partocrats and get themselves to political power? To this question I shall address the rest of my paper.

At this point it should be sufficient to state that, as it was established above, all the necessary conditions for such a revolutionary change are already present in the U.S.S.R.: the Soviet régime has spent whatever "credited" legitimacy it originally had, and continues to exist thanks only to the inertia of oppression and fear that this oppression induces; the Soviet élite is utterly divided with its technocratic part determined to oust the ruling partocrats and constitute itself as the sole ruling élite; in this confrontation, the disaffected and politically apathetic masses would support the party of change rather than defend the political status quo. All this being so, what remains now is to look forward to the breakout of a nationwide crisis that could start moving the Soviet counter-élite into action with its institutionalization and the "second-pivot" effect to follow and, consequently, to bring about political change.

But maybe such dramatic developments will not be necessary? Maybe political change in the Soviet Union will take place in the form of a peaceful technocratic succession to the partocrats which will have to come about anyway in the course of the natural change of generations? Or, maybe, political change will be initiated by the top rulership itself joining ranks with the technocrats and staging an "anti-partocratic" revolution from above? These questions are becoming particularly relevant at the time when the now only fifty-six-year-old Mikhail Gorbachev occupies the highest office in the land, and when over 40% of the top Party and government personnel have been already replaced, mainly by members of his generation, with this process likely to continue unabated.

Technocratic Succession or Revolution from Above?*

All available evidence points to the fact that Gorbachev is not a typical partocrat. When Stalin died Gorbachev was twenty-two, a student at the Law Faculty of the University of Moscow. Before entering the university he had had the advantage of a full-time primary and secondary education from which he graduated with a "silver medal," the second-highest award, allowing for two good marks among twenty-plus excellent marks. After summa cum laudae graduation from Moscow University (another rare distinction), Gorbachev was sent to his native Stavropol to assume a post in the Komsomol (Communist Youth League) Committee of an agricultural

---

*This section, as the whole paper, was written in the first half of 1985 and revised before submission for publication, in June 1986. Inevitably, by now (this is being written at the end of April 1987), the account and assessment of recent Soviet policy developments given in it are already to some extent out of date. Indeed, in June 1986 the policy of *glasnost'* (openness), which is now so central, was only beginning to evolve, and there was very little talk then of *demokratizatsiya* (democratization), a policy now under heated discussion, according to which not only the deputies to the Soviets, but also factory managers and some party and government officials would be periodically submitted to reelection by secret ballot in multi-candidate slates. Nevertheless, I decided to leave the main bulk of this section of my paper intact. For one, my general evaluation of both Gorbachev and the 'new' Party line which he represents and tries to implement has not changed; secondly, it seems to me that there is some historical value in presenting to the reader a relatively early attempt at making sense of the 'Gorbachev phenomenon.'

However, in order to prove that this early attempt is still valid, the new policies of *glasnost'* and *demokratizatsiya* must be accounted for and put into the overall framework of Soviet policy development since Gorbachev's accession. This I will try to do, however briefly, in a postscript to this section of the paper.

district (*sel'skiy rayon*) in the Stavropol province. This assignment prompted him to become a part-time student of Stavropol's Agricultural Institute from which he successfully graduated too. There is no doubt whatsoever that he undertook that "additional study" on his own initiative and that it was his own sense of propriety in doing a job that motivated him to get yet another systematic specialist education. This urge for acquiring specialist knowledge in the field within which he had to discharge only the duties of political leadership makes Gorbachev unique among Party and Komsomol *apparatchiks*, most of whom are remarkably indifferent to academic study of any kind. They usually study only when ordered to do so by their superiors, and in most cases are assigned by them to special Party and/or Komsomol schools, rather than to ordinary institutions of professional training. Gorbachev, on the contrary, has never been a student of a Party or Komsomol school, opting instead for straightforward professional training.

Gorbachev was neither a promotee of Stalin (he started to work as a low-grade *apparatchik* in 1955, two years after Stalin's death) nor at any time a Stalinist in his convictions. In the University of Moscow, where he was a Komsomol activist, he tried to use his influence to defend those fellow-students who fell victims to the unending political persecution campaigns characteristic of Stalin's rule. Coming from a rural background, he was realistic about, and therefore acutely critical of, the Stalinist collective farm system and did not try too much to hide it. Sometimes he quite openly mocked the falsehood of Stalinist propaganda, especially when presented in the form of art, such as, for example, the notorious film, *The Cossacks of Kuban*. Under the circumstances of raging Stalinism such behavior was outstandingly bold and honest by any standards.[51]

That Gorbachev is fully aware of the defects and dysfunctions of the Soviet system and that he personally stands for far-reaching systemic reforms is a fact, too, best proven in a number of works by Archie Brown.[52]

But do all those personal properties of Gorbachev really matter insofar as policy decision-making is concerned? To answer this question one has to remember that Gorbachev was selected to the General Secretaryship of the CPSU's CC by the same Politburo (except for Ustinov who died in the meantime) that a year before had chosen Chernenko for that post. To be sure, Gorbachev's selection for this post was not unanimous.[53] A strong contender to assume it was Viktor Grishin, another septuagenarian, and the most natural candidate of the partocrats for Chernenko's succession. It was established with sufficient certainty that Chernenko himself had sent a message from his deathbed to the Politburo, nominating Grishin as his successor, and that Grigory Romanov—at that time, beside Gorbachev, the only other full Politburo member and CPSU CC's Secretary—formally proposed Grishin for that post.[54]

If, in spite of it all, the partocrats' choice went for a younger man, it was because they were fed up with the instability and uncertainty that the annual funerals of their "Number Ones" entailed, as well, no doubt, as with Western and domestic reaction to the succession of septuagenarian rulers in the Kremlin which, they deemed, was strongly undermining the credibility of the régime, and extremely damaging to its prestige, both at home and abroad.[55] If that younger man happened to be Gorbachev rather than the much more partocratic Romanov, it was because Romanov, having recently come from Leningrad, had not yet established a power base of his own in Moscow and, as a heavy drunkard, corrupt person, and a lout, did not command the necessary respect and trust of his colleagues.[56] In that situation Gorbachev, with his already established favorable image in the West, was perhaps the only viable choice, for whom, despite certain misgivings, Chernenko's Politburo finally had to opt. There should be, however, no doubt whatsoever that the ruling partocrats on that Politburo would never have appointed Gorbachev to lead them if they had been even in the slightest doubt about his ability and willingness to do their bidding, precisely following the brief with which they issued him. Gorbachev was hired as Number One, not to be his own man, but to serve the collective interests of the partocrats as arranger of and spokesman for the conservative oligarchic consensus.

Gorbachev's mandate could be briefly described as the Soviet system's invigoration without innovation involving systemic change. His task is to seek maximum improvement of the system's failing performance by "within-system" means or, in other words, the preservation in the best possible way of the Soviet political status quo. This mandate does not allow Gorbachev even to start contemplating reforms that could in any way at all affect that status quo, but it gives him certain freedom to take the necessary measures aimed at repairing and reconstructing the present Soviet system's most inefficient, superfluous, or obviously failing parts.

The content of Gorbachev's mandate was concisely formulated by the Politburo in its first publicly reported session after Chernenko's funeral. The following quotations from that official report, in my view, adequately summarize that mandate:[57]

Domestic policy

1. "Definitively to turn the economy onto the road of intensification."
2. "To tighten the work, state and party discipline."
3. "To fight the phenomenon of dressed-up boasting (*paradnost'*) and

irresponsibility, everything that contradicts the norms of socialist life."
4. "To continue with the programme of further developing and raising the effectiveness of irrigational agriculture." (This programme was announced by Chernenko personally and has never been explicitly approved or even voiced by Gorbachev though he was in charge of Soviet agriculture.)

Relations with socialist countries
5. "To move economic cooperation between socialist countries along the path of further development of their socialist integration."
6. "To give priority to socialist countries in foreign affairs."

International politics
7. "To treat the non-aligned countries of Asia, Africa, and Latin America as the U.S.S.R.'s partners and friends in the struggle for peace and for the establishment of equal relations among nations."
8. "To develop relations with the capitalist countries in the spirit of peaceful co-existence and cooperation which, as the experience of détente in the 1970s has proven, may be possible when mutual readiness for it is present."
9. "To treat as the main task the prevention of the arms race in space and its stopping on earth with the view, in the final end, of liquidating nuclear arms altogether and everywhere."
10. "To take notice of the closeness of positions of the U.S.S.R. and France on the return to the policies of détente, strengthening of the European security, maintaining the balance of power on a minimal level, prohibiting the arms race in space [and] of the mutual striving of the U.S.S.R. and France for further expansion of mutually beneficial (bilateral) cooperation."
11. "To develop contacts with the U.S.A., e.g. between the legislative institutions, in the interest of better mutual understanding and the establishment of mutually beneficial cooperation in the interest of strengthening peace."[58]

The ruling partocrats set these strict limits for Gorbachev to operate within, and he had fully to accept them, together with his acceptance of the General Secretaryship. In his acceptance speech and, two days later in the speech delivered at Chernenko's funeral, Gorbachev especially went out of his way to stress that the "strategic line elaborated at the 26th Congress of the Party" (in 1981, i.e. still in Brezhnev's times) "was and will remain immutable" and to pledge himself "steadfastly to follow the Leninist course of our Party."[59] In a number of policy speeches delivered since, he has always been careful to praise the achievements of the past first, and, only after having done so, to start criticizing backwardness, sluggishness, indiscipline, and other negative phenomena that "hinder our further progress."[60]

In Gorbachev's presentation of the Party's policies, there is, however, a remarkable discrepancy between style and substance. The style is vigorous, enthusiastic, creating the impression that from this time on everything will be very different from what it used to be; the substance, however, amounts to nothing else but a more vigorous restatement of past policies. The only difference, as Gorbachev himself is constantly implying, is that in the past these policies remained largely on paper, whereas he will see to their being decisively implemented in practice.

What are these policies? In the Dnepropetrovsk speech Gorbachev succinctly summed them up by saying that "the main road" (to solve the problems that the U.S.S.R. faces) "is the acceleration of the scientific-technological progress."[61] This, however, he emphasized, is a long-term task. Meanwhile, one has to concentrate on improving performance by better use of the already existing resources. According to him, these resources are immense. For example, on the day when a special team of the U.S.S.R.'s Central Office of Statistics watched the work of Odessa's milling machines factory, that factory's productivity rose by 19%. Hence, he concluded, productivity may be very substantially increased by merely having more order, more responsibility, and more work discipline. Another way of improving performance here and now consists in reducing the tremendous waste of energy and raw materials and in implementing a strict régime of all-round economizing of all resources. Yet another measure that, according to him, should also be taken immediately relates to the restructuring of capital investment. From now on the main bulk of such investment should go not into the building of new productive capacities but into the technical reconstruction and re-equipment of the existing ones. When delivering this speech, he, significantly, also included into the same category of proper usage of the existing resources the eternal Soviet problem of raising the quality of goods produced. For, as he said, quality could be substantially improved simply by "strict observation of technological discipline and each worker's performance of his duties with a sense of high responsibility";[62] of course, he continued, one should at the same time also think about how "to increase the influence of economic incentives on the improvement of the quality of production," but did not offer any explicit ideas on this at all.[63]

When elaborating on the same subject in his report at the 27th Congress of the Party, Gorbachev was unable to come up with anything better than the following suggestion: "To exclude the production of defective wares, of low-quality goods, radical measures are necessary. One has to apply, with this task in mind, all the power of material and administrative measures, to use our laws. There is apparently also a necessity to promulgate a special law on the quality of production."[64] Rounding up his discussion there on the better usage of existing resources, Gorbachev, predictably, pointed out that "The decisive condition for the achievement of the goal set is the industriousness and talent of the Soviet people. And in this respect it is difficult to overestimate the role of socialist emulation."[65] Have we not heard it all before from Brezhnev? For the whole period of his incumbency he insistently tried to hammer home all those ideas, however, to no avail.

The typical Gorbachev technique of presenting old wine as if it were now in new bottles could be demonstrated by the following phrase from his report to the April (1985) Plenary Session of the CPSU's CC: "What is needed is *revolutionary change* (emphasis added)—a transition to fundamentally new technological systems, to the latest generations of technology, providing for the very highest efficiency."[66] If, after almost two decades of constant urgings by Brezhnev and his associates to intensify the process of the "scientific-technical revolution" in the country, this is "revolutionary change," what then is routine?

As I have already mentioned, Gorbachev established his reputation as a reformer a long time before he became General Secretary. When still the First Secretary of Stavropol's Provincial Party Committee (*kraykom*), he made himself prominent as an advocate of the so-called *zvenyevaya sistema* (family-based productive link system). He had publicly urged a wider application of that system, akin to the one now introduced with such success in China, even in 1976, that is, after the Party in 1973 had condemned the Khudenko experiment with such links as an attempt at restoring capitalism, refuting at the same time the whole idea of replacing the "sacred" brigade by such independent links. Although the links were not formally prohibited, they were allowed to function only as subdivisions of brigades and thus were deprived of their very substance—of the right directly to enter into a "collective contract" with the farm independently of the brigade. It was under these circumstances that Gorbachev argued forcefully for the legitimization of the "collective contract" and thus, in fact, for the restoration of the links as autonomous economic units.[67] That his ideas on this key issue remained unaltered is seen from the fact that he repeated them as late as 1983, when already CPSU CC's Secretary for agriculture and full member of the Politburo.[68]

Rumors have been widely circulating in Moscow about Gorbachev's "progressive" and "reformist" attitudes on all other issues, too. It was said that he was strongly in favor of extending the whole package of the Hungarian economic reform to the Soviet Union, that he was constantly trying to promote the idea of stricter observation of the norms of "socialist legality," thus in fact advocating the gradual transformation of the U.S.S.R. into a kind of "socialist *Rechtstaat*."[69] Archie Brown's arguments about these rumors being not entirely unfounded are, in my view, convincing enough.[70]

However, all these progressive ideas were and are conspicuously absent in the policy pronouncements that Gorbachev made in his capacity of General Secretary of the CPSU's CC, demonstrating only too clearly the real limits of his mandate, notwithstanding the fact that he got sufficient room for maneuver and independent action for, as was said, the system's invigoration without innovation.

As General Secretary, Gorbachev spoke on agricultural policies for the first time at the 27th Congress of the Party. Typically, his first point was about the better use of available resources. According to Gorbachev, by simply reducing the losses of agricultural products usually incurred during their harvesting, transportation, storage and processing, one could "increase the resources for consumption by up to 20 percent, and for some products— even by 30 percent."[71] But how is one going to achieve this result? Gorbachev only says that the CC and the Government have defined drastic measures for reducing these losses, without specifying what these measures are. One could reasonably surmise these measures to be mostly disciplinarian in nature.

Among other specific measures to be taken by the Party with the view of increasing the agricultural output Gorbachev mentioned the following two:

1. the integration of agriculture with related branches of industry by the means of creating, in the center and in all the administrative-territorial divisions of the country, unified organs of management for the whole agrarian-industrial complex (A.I.C.; a giant superministry, the *Gosagroprom*, was created in November 1985 for this purpose) which is nothing more than yet another attempt at solving economic problems by taking administrative measures.
2. the introduction for collective and state farms of definite annual plans of deliveries to the state "which will not be changed. At the same time they will be entitled to use whatever they have produced above the plan—and for potatoes, fruit, vegetables, a significant part of the planned production itself—as they please." The same principle, defined by Gorbachev as "the creative application to contemporary circumstances of Lenin's (1921) idea on *prodnalog* (the tax in kind), will be applied to the republics and provinces, which could keep all the "above-plan" supplies of agricultural products for satisfying the needs in food provision of their own localities.

There was nothing in Gorbachev's report that would stress the idea of introducing the autonomous links which he so much cherished before becoming General Secretary. He mentioned the "collective contract" only once and in the very ambiguous context of introducing it equally on the level of the brigade, link and the family.[72]

The Joint Decree of the CPSU's CC and the U.S.S.R.'s Council of Ministers "On Further Improvements of the Economic Mechanism of Management in the Agrarian-Industrial Complex of the Country," issued after the 27th Congress of the Party,[73] has significantly watered down even these rather modest plans for economic independence of agricultural enterprises. The emphasis in this decree is not any more on leaving to these enterprises whatever they have produced above the plan for their free disposition, but on stimulating them to sell all their products to the state. The republican and provincial administrative organs, on the other hand, were unconditionally entitled by that decree to retain for their local needs whatever agricultural products they managed to get from the farms as above-the-plan supplies to the state. As a result, the administrative pressure on the collective and state farms to deliver all they can to the state will now inevitably double. The decree foresees that and obligingly provides the local party and soviet organs with a host of devices for controlling and interfering in the farms' economic activities and everyday life. Even the farms' use of meat and milk for their internal needs has now become subject to strict administrative regulation and control.[74] The collective contract is encouraged by the decree exclusively for the brigades as the means of reducing the farms' (and thus the state's) overall responsibility for remunerating the workers, in a way reminiscent of the Stalinist *trudoden'* (workday) system, under which there was no guarantee that the farm worker would receive a single kopeck for his toil. Family and individual contracts are allowed in state farms and recommended in collective farms only for vegetable-growing and livestock breeding, and only on the same conditions as those foreseen for collective contracts with brigades, i.e. with very little real autonomy of choice or activity left.[75]

As a corollary to this decree, another more recent one stipulates the strengthening of state control over the markets in towns where collective farms, individual farmers, and other food producers sell the foodstuffs they produce directly to the consumer.[76] The latter decree is aimed at eliminating the incentive for the food producers to sell their products directly to the consumer in preference to the official state and cooperative organizations which are supposed from now on themselves to dominate these town markets. To that effect the U.S.S.R.'s Council of Ministers has decided to introduce into these markets set price limits (under the code name of "observation of the rules of trade") as well as official registers of the town markets' sellers of agricultural products.[77]

The issue of town markets is only one of a whole range dealt with in the above decrees on elimination of unearned income with a view towards

comprehensively curbing the possibilities for people to earn an income
independently from the state. In addition to new measures aimed at combatting more effectively embezzlement, corruption, speculation, and other traditional criminal activities, it introduces regulations that put under the state's
strict supervision and regimentation private economic activities hitherto
almost entirely outside the sphere of the state's interference and control (e.g.
private renting of accommodation, rendering of services in construction and
other fields, small-scale production of some consumer goods and their free
sale). The decrees prohibiting 'unearned income' were later supplemented by
the law 'On Individual Working Activities' which has allowed individuals to
engage, with the state's explicit permission and under the state's direct
control and supervision, in certain (very limited and with the specific exclusion of trading) economic activities outside the state system. With that
law coming into force on May 1, 1987, the boundary between 'earned' and
'unearned' income will be set in definite terms—the money earned by individuals for their work outside the state system will be treated as 'earned
income,' and thus as legitimate, only if the work has been done with the
permission and under the control of the state; the money received for the
same work, done by an individual outside the state system without an
explicit authorization by the state, will be qualified as 'unearned income' for
which the individual who received it will be held legally liable. Far from
promulgating 'a new edition of NEP,' the law 'On Individual Working
Activities,' if taken in tandem with the series of decrees aimed at combatting
'unearned income,' appears as yet another device for subjecting the private
lives of individual Soviet citizens to greatly invigorated control of the state.[78]
Together with other Soviet policy decisions promulgated in the aftermath of
the Party's 27th Congress, the ones on "unearned income" and "individual
working activities," perhaps more saliently than the others, reflect the presently overriding tendency of Soviet policy to try to solve the critical problems
the U.S.S.R. faces by applying administrative and disciplinary measures
and, consequently, by further centralization of management and enhancement of the state's control over all economic and social activities performed
outside the state system.

    This tendency seems to break with the usual socialist cycle, or the cyclic
development of the socialist system, so brilliantly described by Professor
Olympiad Ioffe. According to him, the Soviet system, as "unlimited political
power based on economic monopoly," in order to avoid economic collapse, is
bound periodically to introduce decentralizing reforms which after having
accomplished their "healing tasks" are repealed. Hence, the Soviet system
develops "in the form of periodic shifts from strong centralization to limited
decentralization that then reverts back to strong centralization." These
periodic shifts or cycles in Soviet history saw the transitions from "war

communism" to NEP, from NEP to Stalin's absolute centralization, from Stalin's absolute centralization to Khrushchev's and Kosygin's decentralizing reforms, and from them to Brezhnev's recentralization. At present, in Ioffe's view, the Soviets "have reached the stage when the cycle is on the point of reverting to decentralization." Therefore, he says, "I must confess that I cannot predict whether Gorbachev. . .will be a Soviet Stolypin or a Soviet Pobedonostsev; the only thing which to me is beyond doubt is that at the given stage of Soviet economic development, Gorbachev, in order to retain unlimited political power, needs to relax centralization."[79]

This, however, seems not to be the case. The ruling Soviet partocrats have apparently decided that in the present circumstances it is too dangerous for them to move even an inch toward decentralization, for by doing so they are afraid of provoking in the enterprises an enthusiastic "counterwave" response which could easily lead to their irreversible and irretrievable loss of control over those enterprises and thus of political power altogether. Hence, palliatives to decentralizing reforms had to be sought in order to remedy the failing economic performance, and the partocrats found these palliatives in such a further enhancement of their centralized political power that would hopefully make it able forcefully to impose the measures that in their view could, without decentralization, assure the needed higher economic efficiency, e.g. introduction of modern technology, concentration on intensive economic development, but, first and foremost, implementation of truly effective administrative control over the people's economic and social behavior. The key word coined at the 27th Party Congress for describing these policies, and now ubiquitously used, is *uskorenie* (acceleration), not reform (the word still mentioned by Gorbachev in his Report to the Congress, though only once) or decentralization.[80] Another key word coined concurrently to describe the means by which this acceleration should be achieved is *perestroyka* (restructuring) by which not so much the structure or functioning of the system but people's attitude to their performance at work is meant. These policies are indeed opposite to those that one could have expected the reform-minded Gorbachev to pursue.

All this is to say that there is a strongly pronounced discrepancy between Gorbachev, the persona, and Gorbachev, the functionary. Such a discrepancy between the persona and the function is easily recognizable in any Soviet official, but it becomes more difficult to see when the persona in question is that of the General Secretary himself. The point is that today this is true about the General Secretary as much as about any other Soviet official. It is the failure to see this point clearly enough that at present causes, in my view, so much confusion in Soviet policy analysis.

Until Brezhnev's death it was indeed extremely difficult to dissociate Soviet rule from the personality of the ruler who, from the late 1920s, was undoubtedly always the man who occupied the position of the CPSU's CC General Secretary. Even Andropov, who should have known best, mis-evaluated the strength of the post that he took over from Brezhnev after the latter had passed away. He assumed that this post was as strong as ever and that only the man who held it, Brezhnev, was a weak and unambitious person, neither able nor willing to put it to proper use. He was absolutely sure therefore that his accession to that post would make a cardinal dif-ference, but very soon he had to realize how wrong he was. None of the campaigns and policy changes that he had so vigorously tried to initiate during the first few months of his ascendancy ever took off in any real terms. No new initiatives had been launched since March 1983, and by June of that same year those which were already in process either came to a virtual halt, including the famous anti-corruption campaign,[81] or were so revised that they practically reverted to Brezhnev's policies of procrastination and inactivity.

Andropov, I am sure, died a bitter and disappointed man. I think that he was profoundly frustrated and distressed by his discovery of the fact that the post of General Secretary no longer carried any real personal power, and that this discovery precipitated his physical decline and early death. I also believe that the easy selection of Chernenko as Andropov's successor was due mainly to the resignation of the Andropovites on the Politburo to the political reality under which no General Secretary could make a real differ-ence as far as introducing change was concerned. They obviously took the view that if Andropov, with his most powerful KGB and Party apparatus background, was unable to start things moving, no one else would be able even to try to begin to; and, if this was the case, the best thing to do (and the most innocuous, too) was to select Chernenko as the living embodiment of the late Leonid Brezhnev, to carry on with the Brezhnevite policies of defensive immobility and mechanistic opportunism. Gorbachev's selection, as his mandate shows, is not too different from that of Chernenko, although it indicates that at present both the Andropovites and the Chernenkoites agree on the urgent need of forcefully invigorating the system though by the old "within-system" means.

Indeed, during the eighteen years of Brezhnev's General Secretaryship, the real role and the real power of that post changed quite dramatically. After the palace coup that on October 14, 1964 disposed of Khrushchev, Brezhnev and the Brezhnevites managed to alter the Soviet system of rule by effectively beheading it—the position of the sole and all-powerful leader was trans-formed by their collective effort into that of a mere spokesman for a broad oligarchic consensus of the ruling partocrats. In other words, *autocratic totalitarianism*, characteristic of the Soviet system under Stalin and, to a lesser degree, under Khrushchev, was transformed, under Brezhnev, into an *oligarchic totalitarianism.*[82]

As long as that system persists, any General Secretary, whatever his personal qualities and ambitions, will be bound to function as if he were another Brezhnev. Andropov was forcefully reduced to the role of Brezhnev Mark II, Chernenko voluntarily played a weakened Brezhnev Mark III, and Gorbachev was hired to do the job of an invigorated Brezhnev Mark IV. There is very little doubt that, at least for the time being, Gorbachev will have to stick to that Brezhnev Mark IV position, whether he personally likes it or not; for if he does not, he risks the loss of office, thus becoming Khrushchev Mark II.

I believe that Gorbachev would have been much more fortunate had he not gotten the top job now. If, for example, Grishin had succeeded Chernenko, and in several years Grishin had been succeeded by another typical septuagenarian partocrat—generally speaking, if the series of successions of one traditional septuagenarian partocrat by another had lasted for about another decade, and if Gorbachev, by outlasting them all, had only then inherited the top job—he may have found himself in the position of being able to be true to himself and of pursuing policies of his own making; for, during that decade or so he, as Number Two, could have filled with qualified technocrats (or, in other words, meritocrats) all the leading posts that the dying-out or retiring partocrats would have vacated, and then succeed to the top post as the established and recognized champion of technocracy and the leader of the "technocratic troops" all firmly entrenched in key posts and ready for action.

The new technocratic élite, with Gorbachev at its helm, would certainly not hesitate to introduce the long overdue radical systemic reforms that, being incompatible with totalitarian communist rule, would inevitably lead to its dismantlement. There would be nothing in it for them to lose and everything to gain. The same would apply to Gorbachev himself even to a much greater degree, for he would then be able to enter into history as the man under whose leadership the Russian state was, at last, reconstituted from a backward and artificial Soviet communist political entity into one that is genuinely popular, national, and advancing. And what can be a greater bonus for a political leader than that?

There is no need to guess what kind of reforms entailing such a reconstitution of the Russian state a freed technocratic élite would introduce. A program of such reforms has already been elaborated by a typical representative of the Soviet technocratic élite, Anatoly P. Fedoseyev,[83] whose views, it seems to me, are most congenial to the ideas and plans besetting the whole Soviet technocratic stratum. I am sure that if and when Gorbachev, or any other similar leader, together with all the technocrats, were in the position seriously to embark on the road of reforms, they would be bound to move on that road along the lines suggested in the "Fedoseyev plan," even if they had never heard about it before.

The realization of this scenario of change, based on a smooth "generation-type" technocratic succession to partocracy, has been strongly upset by the "premature" elevation of Gorbachev to the top office in the Party. But even in the case of Gorbachev remaining a contender for the top post for a longer period of time, this scenario could still not materialize because of a possible "premature" outbreak of a nationwide crisis, precipitating change and bringing it about in a much more abrupt manner. However, despite all these upsetting factors or possibilities, one should not readily discard this scenario, dismissing it altogether. For Gorbachev may still fall out with the partocrats before their full eclipse, forcing them to oust him as they earlier ousted Khrushchev. In this case they would have to restore the series of gerontocratic successions and thus pave the way for a Gorbachev Mark II to rise and prepare for a definitive technocratic succession that would materialize after a certain period of time.

If this were the case, and nothing in the meantime did interfere with the development of such a smooth "generation-type" technocratic succession, political change in the Soviet Union would assume a form very similar, or even analogous, to that which took place in Spain after Franco's death in 1975. It is interesting to note that after Franco's death, previously inconspicuous and fully obedient to the dictator middle-rank Party *apparatchiks*, such as the first democratically elected Prime Minister and former chief of propaganda in the ruling Falangist Party, Adolfo G. Suarez, and his colleagues (not to mention the king, Juan-Carlos I, who was specially trained by Franco for the succession), by the radicalism of their drive for change greatly surpassed the liberal wing of the Francoist establishment (e.g. Manuel Fraga Iribarne, Count José de Areilza, et al.), which was seen as the most formidable force working for change within the system when it was in full operation. I could only add that I personally know quite a number of high (though not at the very top and thus obscure) Soviet officials (e.g. in the Central Party apparatus) who could be seen as Suarez's potential counterparts in the Soviet Union; I would not at all be surprised if by the radicalism of their drive for change these semi-obscure officials would greatly surpass many well-known Soviet dissidents.

This is to say that under certain circumstances briefly described above, the *Spanish model of change* may be applicable to the Soviet Union. However, if in Spain this model brought about a democratic succession, in the Soviet Union it would hardly bring about the same result. Russia has been stifled under a totalitarian régime for too long to be able to produce a democracy immediately in the aftermath of transition; what was in her power in 1917 is no longer within her reach. The succession in Russia no doubt will most likely be, at least in the beginning, an authoritarian one. Hence, the Spanish model of change may apply to the U.S.S.R. only insofar as the mode of change is concerned; as for its results, it may not.

But let us come back to Gorbachev and to the chances of his breaking through the limits of his mandate, starting to do his own bidding and thus launching a technocratic revolution from above.

Most observers would argue that by now (April 1987) Gorbachev is powerful enough to go ahead with any reforms of his own choosing and, consequently, if he still sticks to his original mandate, he must be doing so out of his own free will. The old-timer partocrats, the argument goes, should no longer be a stumbling block for Gorbachev, since during his ascendancy about 40% of them were removed from office and replaced by members of Gorbachev's own younger generation.

Let us start with the latter argument about the partocrats having practically lost power. This argument is wrong, not only because of the fact that about 60% of them have retained their posts, but also because many of the newcomers are not that much younger than, and different in character from, those whom they have replaced. All the new appointees to the ministerial posts and the first secretaryships of the provincial party committees—and these are the crucially important positions—were either the deputies of the men they have replaced, or, in the case of outsiders to the particular office, members of the *nomenklatura* on the level normally qualifying for such promotions. There were no new appointees to high offices either from outside the *nomenklatura* or such that would have meteorically risen from the lower to the highest levels within the *nomenklatura*. In other words, the old *nomenklatura* system has remained totally unaltered, which ensures the unabated continuation of partocratic supremacy.

Secondly, not all among those who have gone have gone really. Some former high officials—among them the retired Chairman of the Council of Ministers, Nikolai Tikhonov; the former First Deputy Chairman of the Presidium of the Supreme Soviet, Vasily Kuznetsov; and the veteran ex-Secretary of the CPSU's CC, Boris Ponomarev—have retained their seats in the Central Committee of the Party selected by the 27th Congress and with them positions of significant influence over the Politburo's decision-making, an event as yet unprecedented in the Party's history.

Thirdly, among the new recruits to "Gorbachev's Politburo" only three—Nikolai Ryzhkov, Nikolai Talyzin and Boris El'tsin—have a proper technocratic background, and one more—Eduard Shevardnadze—is, as are those

above, also in his fifties, whereas most of the others—Lev Zaikov, Yegor
Ligachev, Viktor Chebrikov, Sergei Sokolov, and Yury Solovyov—are in
their sixties and seventies. All this is to say that the partocratic grip on
political power in the U.S.S.R. has remained on the whole intact.

Equally wrong therefore is the assumption that by now Gorbachev has
managed to consolidate his personal power to the extent of being able to
introduce the reforms he would wish to see implemented. The partocrats are
still in a strong position to make sure that his power remains limited and
checked. Gorbachev has not recovered the presidency denied to him by his
selectors in 1985 despite the tradition established since 1977 to combine it
with the General Secretaryship. He has also failed to promote to the Politburo any of the real "Gorbachev's men." In the whole top leadership of the
country there are only two people—Vsevolod Murakhovsky, one of the
several first deputy chairman of the U.S.S.R.'s Council of Ministers and the
Chairman of Gosagroprom (the recently-created giant superministry for the
agricultural-industrial complex); and Georgy Razumovsky, the man in charge
of the CPSU's CC Department of Party Organs—who closely worked with
Gorbachev in his Stavropol days and were in fact his personal promotees
and devotees. Although Razumovsky was promoted at the Party's 27th
Congress to the CPSU's CC Secretaryship, his entry into the Politburo, as
well as Murakhovsky's, has been firmly blocked.

Indeed, in the Politburo Gorbachev is surrounded not by cronies or even
trusted allies but either by suspicious supervisors, such as Andrei Gromyko,
the President, and Mikhail Solomentsev, another septuagenarian in charge
of the Party's Control Commission, or by envious rivals, such as Ligachev
and Ryzhkov. If in these circumstances Gorbachev not only retains the
driver's seat but feels quite comfortable in it, it is because the single largest
group dominating the present-day Politburo—the so-called KGB-MVD
group, consisting of the former KGB General Geidar Aliev, former MVD
General Eduard Shevardnadze and the present Chairman of the KGB,
General Viktor Chebrikov—lends him its powerful support.

Their support to Gorbachev is, however, far from unconditional. It will,
no doubt, last only as long as Gorbachev is prepared to do their bidding in
preference to his own. Hence, he has to behave himself, e.g. to keep his
deeds and even words within the limits of his mandate.

That the KGB-MVD group's support for Gorbachev is not to be taken for
granted was quite clearly signalled by Aliev at the unprecedented "free"
press conference that he held during the 27th Party Congress, when he took
on Gorbachev on two accounts.[84] In the first place, he let it be known that
the "anti-alcohol campaign" was conducted too rapidly by Gorbachev.
Having stated that before the anti-alcohol campaign liquor sales accounted

for about half of the annual retail trade turnover worth 346 billion rubles, he complained that the sudden reduction of these sales by 30 percent had deprived the state of about 60 billion rubles in revenue. Since the state did not have the capacity to replace liquor by other consumer goods in high demand, a heavy cash crisis broke out in the country. Aliev concluded that it would perhaps have been wiser to conduct the anti-alcohol campaign more gradually, without exposing the treasury to such heavy losses—an open snub to Gorbachev. It seems, however, that KGB General Aliev was much more concerned about the mounting mass discontent that the anti-alcohol campaign had provoked and the rising popular hostility to the authorities that launched this campaign than about purely fiscal interests. The warning to Gorbachev to be more careful in pursuing agreed changes was, on Aliev's part, unmistakable.

Aliev's second warning to Gorbachev concerned the latter's attacks on the privileges of the *apparatchiks*. In contrast to Gorbachev's report to the Congress, Aliev staunchly defended the entitlement of "responsible workers" to the privileges they "lawfully enjoy" and outrightly dismissed the "egalitarian tendency" (*uravnilovka*). (Typically, El'tsin, whose speech at the Congress was devoted to fighting corruption and denouncing privileges as one of its forms, inconsistently toned down some of his remarks on the topic, in one place condemning the system of special shops altogether, and, in another, only their use by people who were not entitled to such privilege—"did not deserve it.")[85] Here again, Aliev seemed to be more concerned about preserving the stability of the system against the discontent of the "deprivilegized" *nomenklatura* (justly called by the people in the Soviet Union "privilegentsia") than anything else.

The significance of these remarks by Aliev is not only in their showing that Gorbachev's power is still strictly limited but also in their indicating a growing rift within the Soviet leadership over the scope and pace of implementation of the egalitarian and disciplinarian policies associated with the name of Gorbachev.

The power situation in the Soviet Union was once more exacerbated during the Congress by the appointment of the veteran Soviet ambassador to the United States, Anatoly Dobrynin, to the Secretaryship of the Central Committee of the Party, instead of the veteran Comintern worker, Ponomarev. Dobrynin is, no doubt, Gromyko's man, and through him Gromyko's control over Gorbachev's functioning in the foreign policy field will be substantially increased. It seems that through Foreign Minister Shevardnadze, the KGB-MVD group in the Politburo is now quite firmly teamed up with Gromyko and Dobrynin in order to exercise effective control over Gorbachev and the rest of the leadership. It is, I repeat, the support rendered at present by this Politburo team to Gorbachev and Gorbachev's basic compliance with that team's demands that make him an effective leader, not his mythical personal power as too many people, both in the East and the West, tend falsely to believe.

The Congress, having confirmed the consolidation of power within the Politburo of the "KGB-MVD-Gromyko team," as well as the continuous support of this group for Gorbachev's frontmanship (Gorbachev was allowed, as a bonus for his compliance, to bring Razumovsky into the Central Committee's Secretariat), saw at the same time a certain decline in the power of the second secretary of the Central Committee, Ligachev, a formidable man and one of Gorbachev's main rivals. This was evidenced not only by the appointment of Zaikov to full membership in the Politburo on a par with Ligachev, but most of all by the strengthening of Gromyko's position through Dobrynin's appointment. Together, Gromyko, Shevardnadze, and Dobrynin are easily able to overrule Ligachev in his own field of foreign policy and thus take it out of his effective control. In policy terms this will most likely mean that priority is attached to interstate relations as opposed to interparty ones.

Because of the above correlation of forces in the top echelon of Soviet rulership, Gorbachev finds himself in a very difficult situation indeed. On the one hand, if he overplays his hand on a specific reform, let alone launches a revolution from above, the partocrats could still easily dispose of him. On the other hand, if he does not engage swiftly enough into significant reforms, eventually leading to such a revolution, and continues to play the partocratic game for much longer, his credibility among the technocrats may be irreparably damaged, if not altogether lost. In the end the technocrats may abandon all hope of having in Gorbachev their champion and potential leader, and when the time comes for them to move against the partocrats, this move will have to be directed, in the first place, against Gorbachev as their official leader. Gorbachev has to beware of being thus compromised and identified by the technocrats with the rest of the partocratic establishment. He has to do everything in his power to avoid such a fate. Gorbachev is thus engaged in a tough race against time with some very narrow scope left for him to win that race. Is he aware of this situation and is he dealing with it adequately? I think he is, and he does whatever he can.

There is a special quality to the vocabulary Gorbachev uses in policy pronouncements since he has become the General Secretary of the CPSU's CC. It is a vocabulary that deliberately makes for inconsistency, confusion, and, sometimes, even direct self-contradiction. On the one hand, for example, Gorbachev constantly praises the achievements of the past and stresses the Party's full commitment to continuity of its policies. On the other hand, however, and almost in the same breath, he denounces that same past in the strongest possible terms, saying, for example, that "we cannot procrastinate any longer, we cannot wait, for there is no time left for bestirring (*raskachka*), it has all been spent by the past."[86] Yes, it has, because in the past "we have not. . .been insistent enough in reconstructing structural policies, the forms and methods of management, the very psychology of economic activity."[87] The main paradox of this statement consists, however, in the fact that Gorbachev himself does not offer any measures that, if taken, could lead to such restructuring, but, at least, he has indicated what his real long-term intentions are. Gorbachev also, on the one hand, constantly praises the qualitative advantages of the socialist planned economy over all other economic systems, and urges strengthening centralized control over plan discipline (e.g. strict fulfillment of the plan indices by the enterprises), but, on the other hand, he denies the very possibility of effective centralized planning altogether, by saying, for example, that "to hope that the Gosplan" (the State Planning Committee) "is able to work out all the chains of interbranch linkages and find an optimal solution—means to live under an illusion. Even a ministry cannot do that."[88] At some other point, he, somehow suddenly and almost out of context, throws in even the idea about transforming the Gosplan into a "scientific-economic organ consisting of outstanding scholars and leading specialists." Attributing this idea to Lenin, he declares that such a new Gosplan would be preoccupied with qualitative indices, . . . innovation of production, labor productivity growth."[89] Having thus, in passing, done away with Gosplan as a central body of state authority, and also with the whole system of economic planning in the form it was always practiced in the U.S.S.R., he abruptly turned to another subject which, paradoxically, was the improvement of central coordination of and control over research in science and technology.

The enterprise, the basic productive unit, occupies a special place in Gorbachev's policy pronouncements. When discussing the plans for further raising its independence and responsibility, he inevitably has to put that whole problem into the context of the enterprise's subordination to ministries and other state planning and management bodies. By doing so he makes clear that in no way could one expect the enterprise to acquire a really independent status now. But, at the same time, he hints at the *desirability* of an entirely different situation. "One ought to give," he says, "the productive associations and enterprises the possibility of earning money themselves, . . . and of free disposition of it, of widely using credit."[90] In the Soviet context that reads as a really revolutionary proposal. Furthermore, in another place of the same report, he suggests that "one should take measures that would strengthen the consumer's impact on the technical level and the quality of production,"[91] thus tacitly acknowledging the desirability of introducing something approximating a free-market direct relationship between the producer and consumer.

Gorbachev stresses as often as possible his desire to move in that "free socialist enterprise" direction, however limited and nonexistent his practical proposals for that may be today. For example, without in any way assessing the results of the limited experiment introduced by Andropov to test how the enterprises would work if left on their own, he directly declared that such experiments were not enough and one had to start "moving from them to the creation of the whole system of the economy and management,"[92] based on the principles introduced by that experiment (i.e. the principles of "freedom of socialist enterprise"). Hence, an entirely new economic and management system based on the independence of the socialist enterprise, is what Gorbachev tells his constituents he wants to see introduced in the country at large. No hint, however, is given that one really is about to start moving in this direction. In Gorbachev's present vocabulary, desirability and possibility are two distinct and separate things. And as we have seen, the policies Gorbachev deems as desirable are in direct opposition to the actual policies that he introduces and advocates.

Analyzing the speeches and pronouncements of General Secretary Gorbachev (including the Report to the April Plenary Session of the CPSU's CC, but excluding the later ones), Archie Brown has made a profound observation that 'space' (*prostor*) and 'innovative' (*novatorskiy*) as well as. . .'self-management' or 'self-government' (*samoupravlenie*) "are key words in Gorbachev's vocabulary."[93] "Though words," he rightly adds, "are not yet deeds, they should be taken seriously when they come from the lips of the Party General Secretary."[94] But in what sense should they be taken seriously, if they are, at least as yet, entirely divorced from deeds? It seems to me that Gorbachev, by using these words and deliberately making all the above confused, inconsistent, self-contradictory and out-of-context statements, seeks to achieve one aim and one aim only. He wants the technocrats, his natural constituents, to know that he is their man, that he entirely shares all their ideas as well as their aspirations and goals for the future. By being so inconsistent, he, on the one hand, begs for their understanding of the limits imposed upon his ability to act and, on the other hand, signals to them that his desire for change is as limitless as theirs and that whenever an opportunity for him to act freely arises, he will take full advantage of that opportunity and do exactly what they wish and expect him to do.

Summing it all up, one could say that Gorbachev in his speeches pleads constantly with the technocrats for their trust in him and for patience with what he is saying and doing at the given moment. It is, indeed, a complex balancing act. Walking the difficult tightrope of Soviet power, Gorbachev tries to make sure that he does not fall to either side and behaves extremely carefully with regard to both those sides—the partocrats and the technocrats alike.

Will he succeed? It all depends on whether he will be able to establish and properly consolidate personal power. His main tactical goal cannot be other than the abolition of oligarchy and the restoration of autocracy. Without gaining truly autocratic power, any Soviet leader is bound to continue with the procrastinating policies of the Brezhnev years and cannot even think of embarking on the road to innovation and change. Therefore the main battle between Gorbachev and the partocrats will take place first (and is taking place already) not in the realm of policies but in that of power relations. The measure of success here is the progress of the contender for absolute power in changing the personnel on all levels of power and management. It is crucial for Gorbachev to create around himself a formidable "technocratic coalition of leaders" and proliferate it so that the partocrats would be deprived of the means that allow them ultimately to exercise overall control.[95] There is no doubt that the partocrats will staunchly resist any such attempts on Gorbachev's part, and he will have to be extremely careful and canny in order to outwit and outmaneuver those inveterate political dealers who still dominate the Kremlin's corridors of power, without losing his own head in the process.

This battle is still in full swing, and nothing is, as yet, decided. If, however, Gorbachev succeeds, then indeed "these. . .who think. . .that he will be hamstrung, may be in for a surprise."[96] But only then, for he may equally fail or, which is one and the same thing, settle for a compromise, and in this case not the skeptical disbelievers but the hopefuls sharing the optimism of the author of the above quotation could be in for a surprise themselves.

In any case, as the situation now stands, the scenario of change by the means of a technocratic revolution from above (as opposed to Stalin's partocratic revolution from above) is much more likely to be the one that will eventually materialize. Only if the revolution from above proved to be abortive or failed altogether, could the scenario of smooth technocratic succession again become its rival.

The demands for a revolution from above are by now clearly audible even on the surface of Soviet society. The works of such influential official scholars as Abel Aganbegyan, Evgeny Ambartsumov, Fedor Burlatsky, Anatoly Butenko, Boris Kurashvili, Tatyana Zaslavskaya, to name but a few,[97] all to some extent point in this direction. Perhaps the most clearly pronounced call for launching such a revolution came in the by now famous

Novosibirsk Memorandum prepared in April 1983. Although the author of this document was academician Tatyana Zaslavskaya, there is very little doubt that it was written on behalf of a large group of leading Soviet economists and social scientists as a discussion document for a seminar organized by the top scientific and administrative bodies dealing with the Soviet economy, including the economic departments of the CPSU's CC themselves.

The thrust of this document is rather unusually straightforward. Already in the opening paragraph, the author of the document states that the underlying cause of all Soviet economic troubles is "the lagging of the system of production relations, and hence of the mechanism of state management of the economy which is its reflection, behind the level of development of the productive forces."[98] "Instead of enabling their accelerated development, it is becoming more and more of a brake on their progressive advancement."[99]

For a Marxist to state that in a certain society there is such a "contradiction between productive forces and the system of production relations" equals his saying that in this society social revolution is inevitable and ripe to take place in the very near future. But this is only a general statement.

The document then goes on to say that "a radical reorganization of economic management" (a euphemism used in the document for the word revolution) "essentially affects the interests of many social groups, to some of which it promises improvements, but to others a deterioration in their position. By virtue of this, attempts at improving production relations, bringing them into greater correspondence with the new demands of productive forces, attempts undertaken by the higher organs of power, *cannot run their course without conflict*" (emphasis added). "The successful resolution of this task is only possible on the basis of a well thought-out socialist strategy being brought into play, a strategy that would simultaneously stimulate the activity of groups interested in changing present relations and block the actions of groups capable of obstructing this change."[100]

The document thus makes no bones about a conflict being inevitable, as is the case in all revolutions, but urges the leadership ("the highest organs of power") to take the revolutionary initiative upon itself and play out the conflict implicit in such an undertaking by employing in a determined manner a "socialist strategy," whereby the activities of the groups interested in change would be maximally stimulated (under the leadership of the powers that be) and those of its opponents effectively blocked. The document, in other words, suggests that, if a revolutionary change is both inevitable and necessary, let us best of all have a revolution from above, i.e. not a spontaneous and chaotic, but a well-coordinated and controlled, revolutionary process, based on a strategy elaborated beforehand by the authorities themselves.

The document also quite explicitly states which groups in society would be the greatest beneficiaries of that revolutionary change. It says, "Logically speaking, the group which must be most interested in the transition to economic methods of management is the managerial 'staff' of the enterprises (associations), whose rights it has been proposed to widen sharply, and, in the second place, the ordinary workers and ITR (Engineering and Technical Workers), who could use their individual capabilities more fully, work more effectively and receive a higher salary."[101]

It tries to present the very top stratum of society as a beneficiary of such change, too. However, the author of the document, in order to prove this point, had to employ a differentiated approach. She had to admit that "a good number of workers in the central organs of management, whose prospective role ought to be increased, is afraid that its responsibilities will become substantially more complicated, as economic methods of management demand much more of highly qualified cadres than do administrative methods. The guarded response of this group of workers to the idea of a transition to and a consistent implementation of economic methods of management often manifests itself in unfounded assertions, as though such transition was going to undermine the centralized motive power in the development of the socialist economy, or to reduce the real importance of the plan."[102]

Here the document, of course in a roundabout way, brings out the issue of the conflict between the partocrats and the technocrats in the top stratum of the land itself. What the above reasoning implies in terms of strategy should be rather clear; a change of systemic proportions cannot be accomplished without employing revolutionary means and without using them to the effect of quashing the inevitable resistance of the strata that are bound to oppose such change by all means in their power. Hence, the technocratic part of the top leadership, drawing support from the managers, specialists (ITR), and workers at the bottom of the social ladder, should not hesitate to set itself against the medium level of that ladder, "the workers in departmental ministries and their organs"[103] as well as against the partocratic "anti-change" group in the top leadership itself, with the view of "liquidating them as a class." The author thus implies that the necessary systemic changes can be introduced only in this forceful way of a full-fledged "class struggle," and that one would be able really to start introducing them only after all opponents of change were definitively deprived of their power and influence.

There is on the whole nothing unusual about such radical views. In private, Soviet intellectuals readily express opinions that are much more radical than those put in rather careful language by Zaslavskaya in the Novosibirsk document. The unusual thing is that such views were presented in a document prepared for an official though not public discussion.

The origins and the fate of this document are as revealing about the present state of the Soviet Union and the fluctuation of opinion within its rulership, as its content. It was commissioned under Andropov's auspices for discussion,[104] as mentioned above, at a special seminar called in April 1983 by the U.S.S.R.'s Academy of Sciences, economic departments of the CPSU's CC, and Gosplan. The available information suggests that the seminar took place and received the document, on the whole, favorably. The initiators and the authors of the document expected some positive practical conclusions to be drawn from it soon. However, after the June 1983 ideological Plenary Session of the CPSU's CC, it became apparent to all those involved that their hopes had been misplaced. By July 1983, when Andropov was already practically unable to exercise control and the Party apparatus was effectively managed by Chernenko, academician Abel Aganbegyan was strongly reprimanded for allowing such a document to come out of his Institute. This reprimand apparently caused anger and frustration among the people involved in the venture of preparing the document and, as a result, in the beginning of August it was leaked by one of them to Dusko Doder, the *Washington Post* correspondent in Moscow.[105] The sensation that it caused in the West and later, when through Western radio channels the information was received there, in the U.S.S.R. itself, deterred the authorities from taking any further reprimanding action against Aganbegyan, Zaslavskaya, and their associates. They were simply silenced altogether on this subject and, for some time, on other less controversial subjects, too.

Suddenly, shortly after Gorbachev was put in charge of the Party apparatus as its General Secretary, came an unexpected breakthrough. A special interview with Tatyana Zaslavskaya with her picture was published by the official governmental paper *Izvestiya*.[106] In this interview Zaslavskaya was, for the first time, given an opportunity publicly to restate her views expressed in the Novosibirsk document. Without ever referring to the document, she briefly summarized its content showing that she adhered to every word that was written there. At times, in the interview, she was even more scathing with regard to the official system than in the original document itself. There was in this interview also a significant change of emphasis. In the original document Zaslavskaya was hesitant about the massive and determined support for the changes that she proposed, among the people in whose best interests such changes would be; in the interview, however, she was already absolutely positive and decisive on that issue. "An overwhelming majority of people (90 percent of managers (*rukovoditeli*) and 84 percent of ordinary workers)," she declared, "are conscious that under different economic and organizational conditions they could work much more efficiently."[107] She also stressed very strongly that enterprises have always struggled to get more rights for themselves, to exercise more initiative, but so far to no avail. "One used to punish (*bili*) initiative. And by inflicting much pain (*i bol'no*)," she explained.[108] But the striving for enterprises' independence by those working in them has, according to her, not diminished, although because of these painful punishments, there are, among their managers, a few people who "are only able to fulfill the directives issued from above."[109] Hence, now, even clearer than in the original document, Zaslavskaya sees the troops of the two opposing camps of Soviet society lined up for the decisive battle about changing the system on a scale amounting to a social revolution, through an action initiated from above.

What was, however, most amazing was that now, unlike in 1983, she got the opportunity to state such a radical revolutionary view publicly, in an authoritative governmental paper with a mass circulation.

Zaslavskaya did it once again in January 1986 when her article on the same subject was published by another authoritative Soviet daily in the most prominent space usually reserved for leading articles.[110] Here she repeated her field work-based research conclusion that "the overwhelming majority of people—90 per cent of managers and 84 percent of workers—hold that in different economic conditions they could work with much greater efficiency" and explained that by "different economic conditions" these people mean a situation "when a human being is in possession of the right to independence and initiative, when his income is directly dependent on the quality of his work."[111] It is creative independence in one's work or "initiating economic behavior" that in Zaslavskaya's opinion is the main social resource for the country's all-round development, as yet largely untapped. In her view, the idea of the collective contract has the potential of putting this resource to work but not in the way this idea is being applied now. To make the idea of the collective contract really workable, she asserts, one has to apply it not selectively but *universally* (emphasized by Zaslavskaya), and also free it from the excessively detailed regimentation which curtails workers' initiative and thus does not provide the necessary space for their independence and creativity.[112] What Zaslavskaya in fact advocates is independence of economic enterprises from the state with whom they would be entering, when necessary, into a contractual relationship that by its very nature excludes administrative subordination and control. Her proposal also stipulates the right of individuals and groups to create and run their own independent enterprises. In other words, Zaslavskaya's suggestions clearly go against the grain of the present official Soviet economic and social policies briefly described above. Nevertheless, they have received high-profile publicity and are officially discussed as possible policy proposals.

Has this got to do with the "invisible hand" of Gorbachev? I think it has. What we have seen here is not simply a redress. It is a drastic reinstatement into the range of legitimate subjects for public discussion of the most acute and sensitive problems of Soviet society and economy. Although in a round-about and much more careful way, today Gorbachev himself contributes a lot to this kind of discussion by making all those ambiguous statements about desirability, which we have discussed above in some detail. And in what Gorbachev is thus saying one can detect many things that directly echo, sometimes almost literally, the Novosibirsk document.

Zaslavskaya's case is by no means unique. An analogous, but yet un-resolved, case was that of Evgeny Ambartsumov, another prominent Soviet social scientist. It all started with Ambartsumov's article on NEP (Lenin's 1921 New Economic Policy giving green light to small-scale private enter-prise) which he tried to consider as a viable model for launching an all-round drastic reform in the Soviet Union of today.[113] The article was prepared during Andropov's incumbency but appeared in print in April 1984, i.e. when Chernenko was already in charge, and provoked a strong reprimand from the Party. In July 1984, the Party's theoretical magazine, *Kommunist*, severely attacked Ambartsumov together with the editorial board of *Voprosy istorii*, the magazine that published his article.[114] The editorial board of *Voprosy istorii*, after having discussed the *Kommunist* article at its "enlarged meeting," duly repented and acknowledged the criticism directed against it as entirely justified.[115]

Thus far, there has been no redress for Ambartsumov. But there are signs that it may soon come. For Ambartsumov's ideas were recently taken up and developed by another prominent Soviet scholar, Fedor Burlatsky, in a lengthy article published in the prestigious weekly, *Literaturnaya Gazeta*, under the very rubric "Decisions of the 27th Congress of the CPSU—into life."[116] Burlatsky goes even further than both Ambartsumov and Zaslav-skaya. He demands "radical economic reforms, aimed at making the whole economy work dynamically, as if in a self-regulating régime." According to Burlatsky, nothing short of total reorganization, along the ideas of Lenin's NEP, could achieve this goal. He calls for the full implementation of self-sufficiency (*khozraschet*) in all enterprises without exception, "not of the sham self-sufficiency, wrapped in the spider's web of administrative regula-tions, but of the full and genuine one, with all the benefits and losses for each enterprise and worker that follow from it." Burlatsky wants to develop the "socialist market" to its full scale and, when he alludes to the necessity of soliciting private investment into the Soviet economy and of making "the ruble an internationally convertible currency," one is able to conclude that he means it in both domestic and international terms. Economic competition (not the sham socialist emulation) should become, according to Burlatsky, the foundation of the functioning of each enterprise, be it "a factory, a cooperative, a scientific center, a cinema or a television studio, a publishing house, a newspaper or magazine." Burlatsky does not directly call for legalization of private enterprise. He concentrates instead on cooperatives that individual people should be able to form in towns for engaging themselves in independent economic activities and then says that, along with the cooperatives, families and individuals may also perform similar functions. As for agriculture, he does not see why the whole relationship between town and country should not become exclusively commercial, equivalent-exchange based, and goes out of his way to say that the family-based autonomous link "is no less a legitimate form of socialism than the usual cooperative."[117]

Thus, in spite of the upsetting policy trends, confirmed by the 27th Congress of the Party, the discussion on wide-ranging and deep-cutting decentralizing reforms is still in full swing. The representatives of the Soviet technocrats still find official outlets for publicizing their highly controversial proposals and by continuing to do so show that they have not given up hope. This to me is a reliable symptom of the revolution from above still being very much in the offing. Only time will tell whether it will one day, against all odds, materialize, or whether some other events could overtake its course and precipitate change that would develop along entirely different scenarios. It is to these other scenarios that I will be turning my attention in the chapters following the Postscript to this one.

Making Sense of *Glasnost'* and Democratization: Postscript (May 1987)

Glasnost' (openness) and *demokratizatsiya* (democratization), the latest additions to the catalogue of Soviet domestic policies conceived under Gorbachev, were introduced when the Soviet leadership began to realize that its 1985-beginning of 1986 policies of mere *uskorenie* (acceleration) and *perestroyka* (restructuring) were inadequate for the tasks these policies were supposed to accomplish and on their own totally lacking the capacity of bringing the Soviet Union out of its entrenched impasse. *Glasnost'* took shape by mid-1986 and democratization was sanctioned as official policy only in January 1987 by the controversial Plenary Session of the CPSU's CC which, after being three times delayed, when finally assembled was still very reluctant to approve the whole range of "democratizing" measures proposed by Gorbachev on behalf of the top leadership.

By no means, however, did the introduction of *glasnost'* and democratization spell a change in the tenor and overall direction of Soviet policy pursued previously under the catchwords of acceleration and restructuring alone. As in 1985-1986, the possibility of going for at least a relative decentralization has been firmly ruled out, and the Soviet top leadership's unbending commitment to solving the country's problems by more centralization and all-round invigoration of the Party's and state's control over all walks of Soviet life was unequivocally emphasized once more. Indeed, despite the liberal connotations that the words openness and democratization invoke, the policies introduced under the guise of these words were meant to serve only as additional devices designed not to change but merely to prop up the same overall policy aimed at invigorating the Soviet system as it exists today without resorting to innovation or structural change, in the hope that by being thus propped up that policy may, after all, work.

When in the 1860s, under Tsar Alexander II, the policy of *glasnost'* was introduced in Russia for the first time, the oppositionally-minded Russian writer Nikolai Chernyshevsky remarked that *glasnost'* is a word specially invented by bureaucrats to deny people the freedom of speech. (I am indebted to Professor Alec Nove for bringing this remark to my attention.) This remark applies to *glasnost'* today perhaps even more aptly than it did in Chernyshevsky's time. Indeed, among the "no go" areas for present Soviet *glasnost'* are, to name but a few, Marxist-Leninist ideology, socialism and communism, Lenin's personality and record, the leading role of the Party, the principle of democratic centralism, the Russian Revolution of October 1917, the whole record of Soviet international politics, all the policies approved by the current Soviet leadership, or, to sum it up, all the fundamental issues and subjects still considered to be the "sacred cows" that only outright enemies may dare to challenge or even question. And with enemies, *glasnost'* or not, one does not discuss; one fights them till they are beaten to the ground.

The single and specific target of *glasnost'* is in fact the so-called "human factor." It is not the system but the quality of functioning on its behalf by particular individuals that, under *glasnost'*, has become the legitimate subject of more or less free discussion. With *glasnost'*, the Soviet media and ordinary people have acquired, for the first time in decades, a real possibility of criticizing, severely and with impunity, the slack performance, abuse of power, nepotism, corrupt practices, and other sins violating the "lofty principles of communist morality" of particular officials in the lower, middle, and, in some specially approved cases, also higher ranks of the Soviet hierarchy. So far the highest living official exposed to such public criticism was the former full member of the Politburo and First Secretary of Kazakhstan's CP's CC, Dinmukhamed Kunaev. It is worthwhile noting that Kunaev was exposed to public criticism only after his formal removal from office.

It follows from the above that the whole *glasnost'* campaign in ideological terms boils down to an attempt at channeling the blame for all the failures and deficiencies of the Soviet system on its inept and corrupt officials. In other words, whatever is wrong is, under its terms, due exclusively to the failure of particular individuals properly to perform their duties, despite the system's perfectly socialist qualities. Politically, however, this ideological scapegoating is supposed to provide the top leadership with new radical means of more effectively controlling the behavior of its subordinates at all levels of the hierarchy. By trying to become able freely and knowingly to dismiss and indict or restore and promote leading personnel in accordance with the real quality of their work, the top leadership not only seeks to increase its discretionary powers but also hopes significantly to improve the performance of the system and thus substantiate its claim that it is not the systemic but the human factor that is at the root of all trouble.

Although, in essence, mounted as a rather vigorous attempt at exonerating the Soviet system from whatever was or is negative in Soviet life in general, and at defending its re-centralized, post-Khrushchevian structure in particular, *glasnost'* is nevertheless a very dangerous policy, as it has certainly set the Soviet top leadership on a collision course with the lesser partocratic *nomklats*, a very powerful stratum as Khrushchev's demise showed quite eloquently. Not only are these lesser partocrats losing under *glasnost'* the cherished security of tenure of office, granted to them under Brezhnev, but they also, on an ever-increasing scale, become subject to criminal and disciplinary investigations and charges. According to the U.S.S.R.'s Procurator General, A. M. Rekunkov, during 1986 alone indictment proceedings were instigated against as many as 200,000 officials and the numbers of officials thus treated steadily continue to grow, albeit, as he noted, a great many still manage to escape deserved punishment.[118]

No doubt, the partocrats situated below the top leadership will do their utmost to reconsolidate their privileges so severely endangered by *glasnost'*. If they were unable by their collective effort to block *glasnost'*, and if the top leadership were reluctant with the passage of time practically to abandon the *glasnost'* related anti-establishment policies altogether, these lesser partocrats may attempt to stage against it a palace coup, as they already once did with regard to Khrushchev, and install in its place another top leadership that would be willing properly to protect the partocratic establishment's vested interests. It is, by the way, in the partocratic establishment that the song "*otkopaem Brezhneva, budem zhit' po prezhnemu*" (we are going to dig up Brezhnev and live as usual) was born and is getting ever more popular. The fact that the lesser partocrats are consolidating their opposition to *glasnost'* and closing ranks to defeat the "awesome changers" at the top has been powerfully stressed by one of the most influential Soviet journalists, Alexander Bovin. Calling the opponents of *glasnost'* after the writer Sergei Zalygin's

definition "homegrown bureaucratic Soviet socialist conservatives," Bovin
warns his readers that

> "THEY are on the offensive . . . THEY have not lost hope of burying us . . .
> THEY have twice thrown US back, succeeded twice in barring the way to long
> overdue changes . . ." (here Bovin refers to the "destalinizing" 20th congress of
> the CPSU in 1956 and the abortive economic reform of 1965) ". . . THEY are
> again hoping to outlive US."[119]

The lesson of Khrushchev's demise has not been lost on the present Soviet
top leadership either. It is only too well aware that standing on its own it has
practically no chance of prevailing over the lesser partocrats' opposition.
Therefore it desperately tries to get the support for its policies from the strata
outside the Party's and the state's apparatuses, which it badly needs, as this
is the only realistic means that may prevent it from being thoroughly
defeated at the hands of the lesser partocrats. With the view of harnessing
the intelligentsia's (e.g. also the technocrats') support, the Soviet top leadership decided to extend *glasnost'* to include quite a significant relaxation of
ideological censorship over cultural heritage and contemporary creative endeavors in the arts and sciences. It was also with the view of beefing up the
support of the workers (and of the technocrats, too) that it preferred democratization to other policies that would equally have provided more discipline
among, and a higher degree of responsibility carried by, the officials.

Let us begin with democratization, the most recent policy under which
elections of various officials, in multi-candidate slates and by secret ballot,
are to be introduced. The electors under this policy will not get the freedom
to choose for office their own candidate. As Gorbachev made crystal-clear in
his Report to the January (1987) Plenary Session of the CPSU's CC, the
Party is not at all considering a relaxation of its leading role in the field of
"selection and distribution of personnel." As before, he stressed, "the decisions of higher organs [of the Party] are obligatory to all lower-level party
committees, including also the decisions on personnel."[120] This means that
the *nomenklatura* system, under which the appointments of the leading
personnel were made in the past, is to remain intact. However, under the
policy of democratization, the same *nomenklatura* system, instead of putting
up only one candidate for an elected post, will select for a post two or even
more candidates, all equally suitable for the job from the Party's point of
view, from among whom the electors must choose. The idea here is to entitle
the people to get rid of the officials they most deeply dislike, for no one
would cast a vote for an unknown boss if one did not think that any boss
would be better than the present one.

This policy endows the leadership with more flexibility in disposing of the dead wood in the *nomenklatura* lists. In order to remain in their *nomklat* positions, officials will now have to please not only their superiors, but also their subordinates, which is an extremely difficult task. The mass of electors are supposed to develop a sense of meaningful participation in public life. By removing from office dishonest and inept officials, and thus actively helping the top leadership to weed out corruption and slackness, the masses are expected to close their ranks with the top leadership, lending the latter their full support in fighting those sections of the partocratic officialdom who, in order to protect their vested interests, would like to remove this leadership from office and, consequently, also deprive the grassroot electorate of their newly-acquired participatory and decision-making roles.

Now, when democratization has already become official policy, the battle within the officialdom rages not so much over the principle of "democratic elections" as over the extent of its practical application. The January (1987) Plenary Session of the CPSU's CC in fact rejected (by not including it into the Resolution) Gorbachev's proposal about submitting to the new electoral process Party officials, but agreed to apply this process to managers of enterprises, thus making the technocrats who occupy a significant proportion of managerial posts, and also some of the most junior partocrats in these same posts, bear the brunt of democratization in the first place. The battle about who in the hierarchy should be submitted to the "democratization-style" elections is far from over. But even if the top leadership has its way and multi-candidate elections under secret ballot are introduced on a broad scale, and the double goal assigned by the leadership to democratization—that of more effectively disciplining and centrally controlling the officials on the one hand, and getting in that process the cooperation and support of the masses on the other—can not easily be achieved. The resistance of partocratic *nomenklatura* is bound to be formidable, and the electors, as long as the selection of candidates for office is predetermined by the *nomenklatura* system that keeps the Party apparatus in overall charge of everything that is going on, are likely to remain very skeptical and profoundly apathetic. The combination of both these factors may cause the natural demise of the whole process of democratization even after its initial success. On the other hand, if the electors show too much enthusiasm for democratization and start to demand really free elections, the top leadership itself might be induced to revoke its democratization campaign before the whole process got out of hand and became uncontrollable. To sum it up, Soviet-style democratization hardly has a bright future. It is a typical half-measure; and, as history tells us, half-measures either never take off or, when and if they do, invariably produce destabilizing effects and never the intended positive results.

The latest extension of *glasnost'* to include some relaxation of ideological censorship is also a typical half-measure, bound either to end in demise (as did its previous edition under Khrushchev) or to have in the end a profoundly destabilizing effect. The new cultural thaw, however, is for the time being a reality, although it proceeds cautiously and at a slow pace.

Let us take, for example, the issue of cultural heritage. For the magazine *Ogonyok* (Little Light) to receive permission to print a few politically innocuous poems by Nikolai Gumilev—one of the classical representatives of the Silver Age in Russian literature who was executed by the Bolsheviks in 1921 for allegedly plotting a monarchist coup and whose poems therefore never have appeared in Soviet Russia before—a preface, stating that Gumilev never wrote any anti-Soviet poems (which he indeed did not, since he was dead within a few months of the Bolshevik seizure of power), had to be published together with the poems themselves. Anna Akhmatova's *Requiem*, a much more controversial poem, emotionally depicting the atmosphere of the years of Stalin's terror and previously banned in the U.S.S.R., appeared, however, in the same magazine without any such explanations: Gumilev's widow, Akhmatova, was, after all, a recognized *Soviet* author, which her executed husband was not. So was Mikhail Bulgakov, whose *Dog's Heart*, unflatteringly depicting Russian life in the aftermath of the Revolution, was also recently published for the first time by another literary magazine. Some works of a few émigré Russian writers—Vladimir Nabokov and Vladislav Kbodasevich among them—saw their first appearance in the U.S.S.R., too, but, again, only the politically innocuous ones and on condition of being introduced by explanatory prefaces, as in the case of Gumilev. For example, to justify the publication of a few lyrical poems by Khodasevich, the popular Soviet Russian poet, Andrei Voznesensky had to invoke in the preface the authority of the founder of "socialist realism," Maxim Gorky, who on several occasions spoke very highly of Khodasevich's poetry.

Such caution applies not only to publication of cultural heritage, but also to the public release of contemporary works, be they books, films, plays, pictures, or sculptures, that were previously either banned or withheld from the public not because they challenged the Soviet system or the Party line, but because the authors expressed in them their own authentic personal positions with regard to life, history or art itself, which did not always exactly correspond to those of the Party. It goes without saying that works challenging the Soviet system or questioning the Party line remain banned under *glasnost'* as they have always been before.

As many participants and witnesses to the Soviet cultural scene report, none of these concessions to cultural freedom were volunteered, let alone initiated, by the authorities themselves. Before any of the recently published controversial works of past or present authors were allowed to appear, members of the intelligentsia interested in their appearance had to fight the authorities tooth and nail. Such fights bore positive results in some cases, and in some they did not. There are many cases in which the authorities remained unyielding, refusing public release point blank. The best known such case was the authorities' refusal to allow the magazine *Novy Mir* to publish Solzhenitsyn's *Cancer Ward*, a novel that in the late 1960s had already been formally accepted for publication by that same magazine, but was then, at the last moment, banned by the censors. However, to soften the blow of this blunt refusal, the authorities granted the new editor of *Novy Mir*, Sergei Zalygin, permission to publish in his magazine instead the *late* Boris Pasternak's novel, *Doctor Zhivago*, although for some mysterious reason, not before 1988.

This example illustrates how firmly committed the authorities are to being in full control of each move within the new cultural thaw and, at the same time, how eager they are not to annoy excessively or too much to upset the intelligentsia's sensitivities.

As the same sources have also indicated, for the authorities to begin to consider a plea for publication or release of a controversial work, it is necessary to present that plea in politically submissive terms, claiming, for example, that the work in question, although unorthodox in the form of its presentation, is consistently Soviet in substance. A typical case of such necessary mimicry is the petition submitted by the actors of Moscow's Taganka Theatre to Gorbachev, asking him to allow the founder and artistic director of their Theatre, Yuri Lyubimov, to return to the U.S.S.R. from his exile in the West. In order to receive the authorities' hearing of their petition, the actors had to vouch in it for Lyubimov being personally and artistically a true Soviet man. Only after thus having given the assurance of their political loyalty did the actors receive the authorities' permission to start talking to Lyubimov about the possibility of his return to Moscow. However, as soon as Lyubimov, together with a group of other émigrés, signed a memorandum of the Resistance International criticizing the inconsistencies in current Soviet policies, the negotiations with him were abruptly terminated, and it was publicly announced in Moscow that by signing this "anti-Soviet" document" Lyubimov had himself finally forfeited the possibility of returning to his native land.[121]

All these facts exemplify the elaborate strategy the Soviet top leadership has developed in the framework of *glasnost'* with regard to the intelligentsia. Having in principle decided to satisfy some demands of the intelligentsia for more cultural freedom, it is making concessions in this respect only under pressure and on certain carefully selected issues which, being least politically controversial, are at the same time those on which the members of the intelligentsia have the strongest feelings, as the amount of pressure exercised by them demonstrates.

In following such a line the Soviet top leadership hopes to co-opt the intelligentsia without much loosening, let alone losing, the ideological grip. Concurrently, these token concessions made by the present Soviet leadership to the intelligentsia's demands are designed to establish that leadership's liberal and "pro-intelligentsia" credentials which in turn would entice the intellectuals, and the technocrats in general, to lend it their support in the struggle against any opposition from within the apparatus which, having no such credentials, would be automatically deemed as representing the "forces of Stalinist reaction."

The ultimate goal of this strategy is to channel dissent into the appropriately widened systemic framework and then finally to eliminate it altogether with the Soviet officialdom achieving as a result ultimate and effective control in the U.S.S.R. over the limits of public debate of all the relevant issues concerning the past, present, and future of the country and the world. Typically, the Soviet press started to print specially solicited articles by prominent members of the intelligentsia with a solid dissident record, calling people to abandon their dissident posture and unreservedly join the system under the conditions of its restructuring. For example, Len Karpinsky, a well-known journalist and scholar who in the mid-1970s was expelled from the Party "for views incompatible with Party membership" and consequently lost his job, in an article solicited by, and published in, *Moscow News*, stated that although dissent was in the U.S.S.R. "a mass-scale frame of mind," it need not be anymore, as

> "the opposition [to the former state of our society] . . . (if it were honest) must turn into active participation in the practical building of new life. The criticism addressed to the old state is to get blended with the work on the consolidation of the changes. It is ridiculous to waver before an open door. One should enter as soon as he or she hears the invitation—come in. . .I do not envy those," he continues, "who still hope to get self-determined outside the common historic destiny of their compatriots."[122]

Literaturnaya Gazeta took an interview on the same subject from Andrei Sakharov as soon as in December 1986 he was allowed to return from Gorky to Moscow, undertaking to publish whatever he said, but since Sakharov apparently took a different stance from Karpinsky's, deciding thus to remain one of those who, according to Karpinsky, have opted to get self-determined outside that awesome historic destiny, his interview has never been printed in the columns of that literary weekly, ironically nicknamed "socialism's Hyde Park."

As we see from the above, also in this, the most liberal and spectacular aspect of *glasnost'* spelling a new cultural thaw, the Soviet top leadership's real aim is further invigoration of its rule and consolidation of the pattern of centralized political and ideological control over society and the state.

When embarking on the policies of *glasnost'* and democratization, the present Soviet top leadership seems to have followed T. Zaslavskaya's 1983 recommendation about the leadership initiating and achieving change in the U.S.S.R. by simultaneously stimulating the activity of groups interested in changing present relations (most of the rank-and-file workers, the technocrats, intellectuals, and their likes) and blocking the actions of groups (such as the partocrats in below-the-leadership sections of the Soviet hierarchy) capable of obstructing this change.[123] The problem, however, is that the policy for which the activity of change-minded groups is now being cautiously stimulated by the leadership is not a policy of change but merely that of an invigorated status quo. The present Soviet top leadership is determined to keep the re-centralized post-Khrushchevian system of power and management in the U.S.S.R. intact, wishing only to eliminate from it the disintegrative feudal elements that crept into it with the guarantee of tenure of office, extended by Brezhnev to the top officials in provinces and branches, and that made the established centralized systemic pattern slack and difficult to coordinate and control.

The partocratic leaders of provinces and branches, with their cronies, are bound strongly to oppose any top leadership determined to deprive them of their feudal privileges, regardless of whether this is going to be done by changing the system or by merely redressing in an effective manner its centralized structure. But the grassroots population, from the workers to the top intellectuals—those who, according to Zaslavskaya, are interested in changing the "present relations"—can hardly be effectively and on a long-term basis mobilized to support a leadership that, instead of striving for real change, merely seeks to reconsolidate the centralized pattern of the same "present relations."

Many Soviet officials and commentators are already bitterly complaining about the people's sluggish response to the leadership's appeal for support. They indicate that the people do not yet trust the leadership's ability to stick to change and see it through, remaining rather skeptical about the whole endeavour of *glasnost'*, at least too skeptical to stick out their necks and abandon their traditional fear-informed cautiousness. Most people, in Alexander Bovin's words, "are waiting, hesitating; they want change but they do not believe in it."[124]

The Soviet top leadership finds itself therefore practically in a "no win" situation. It is bound to fail in its endeavor to gain a committed and lasting support from the society at large, unless it changes course altogether, forgets about the gimmicks of limited *glasnost'* and democratization under the Party's control, and decisively embarks on the road of full-fledged decentralization, amounting to a revolution from above. Insisting on the continuation, though in an amended form, of the present course, the Soviet top leadership will finally have either to bow to the partocratic opposition and revert to the Brezhnevite rot or, alternatively, to concede the battlefield with the partocrats to the social forces themselves, thus precipitating the outbreak of a revolution.

This is to say that *glasnost'* and democratization are dangerous policies not only because they are bound to split the partocratic establishment, setting its central section (the so-called *direktivnaya* [directive-issuing] *nomenklatura*) in conflict with the provinces and branches sections (the so-called *ispolnitel'naya* [executive] *nomenklatura*), but also because the intelligentsia and the workers, becoming ever more frustrated with the 'no change' attitude of the leadership, may start using even the meager facilities provided to them by *glasnost'* and democratization as the springboard to press for real reforms of the system or even to assume the reformist path independently of the powers that be. There is no way the authorities could reliably control *glasnost'* and democratization all the time, effectively preventing these policies from acquiring a moment of their own, which, having swept aside all the controlling devices, would start shaping the policies of real change from below. They can either suppress *glasnost'* and democratization before this process starts, and even at its outset, or otherwise witness the revolutionary consequences of their unsuppressed continuation. This is the fate of all half-measures, and *glasnost'* and democratization, pursued in the Soviet Union today, would hardly represent an exception to that rule.

Soviet intellectuals already have started to voice their protests against the limits of *glasnost'*. For example, the Russian writer Vladimir Dudintsev, whose novel *Not By Bread Alone* marked the beginning of Soviet open dissent in 1956 and who in 1986, after 30 years of almost total silence, published in the magazine *Neva* another highly controversial and previously "unpublishable" novel, *The White Clothes*, in his recent interview with *Literaturnaya Gazeta*'s correspondent Igor Gamayunov, stated that limited *glasnost'* is a contradiction in terms. As there is no limited justice, there cannot be limited *glasnost'*. In his view, as long as *glasnost'* is not "limitless," the

"secret and open opponents of restructuring will be pushing the 'borderline' of *glasnost'* in the direction that will make it safe for them. They will do so until *glasnost'* is done away with altogether. . .Whoever is in favor of limited *glasnost'* exposes his covered desire to stop the process of restructuring."[125]

It is difficult to disagree with this analysis. *Glasnost'* in its present limited form is indeed unviable. The situation is such that either the limits imposed upon *glasnost'* will prevail, abolishing *glasnost'* altogether, or *glasnost'*, having decisively overcome these limits, will turn into authentic freedom of speech and thus become a true vehicle of revolutionary change in the U.S.S.R. This is what Bovin has in fact stated in his *New Times* article even more strongly than Dudintsev. According to his analysis, the conservatives have twice won the battle against change, because of "our indecisiveness, the half-measures we took, our inability to carry things to completion. . .We began to speak the truth, but did not go beyond half-truths. And every half-measure, every decision that remains on paper is a bastion, a stronghold for the opponents of change." THEY, the opponents of change, he believes, may again win their battle against US, its proponents, for, as he states, "today, too, we have not everywhere broken through the barrier of semi-openness and half-truths. Today, too, we have our eye on the brakes even before we have picked up speed." According to Bovin, the only way to ensure change is to break the "barriers of semi-openness and half-truths," or, in other words, to institute "limitless *glasnost'*." Bovin wants the people to take the initiative to achieve this goal. He writes: "Let us then muster our courage and see to it that the moment of truth should not be merely a fleeting instant, but should become an integral part of our life."[126]

At this stage of its existence, the Soviet system has obviously exhausted its inner resources for renovation and redress to such an extent that its leadership is left without any 'safe' policy options. Whatever course the Soviet leadership were to take, this course would be inevitably fraught with consequences undermining the Soviet system's very ability to survive.

One such course that the partocratic leaders of provinces and branches would prefer is the continuation of Brezhnevite procrastination, leading to the system's gradual decay and, finally, to its disintegration. The specter of Solidarity in Poland haunted the Soviet top leadership when it decided to abandon this course. Another such course that the intelligentsia, the techno-crats generally, and the rank-and-file workers would gladly opt for is decentralization, which in its present state the Soviet system is no longer able to accommodate to any, even the minimal, degree, and which therefore would irrevocably undermine its basic foundations. The third course that the present top leadership has actually chosen is invigoration of the existing centralized structure of the system, entailing the mobilization, by half-measures such as *glasnost'* and democratization, of support for this course by social forces from without the ruling apparatus, who, having acquired the potential actually to use their increased strength for their own purposes, may take the destiny of the country into their own hands, sweeping away the Party apparatus and the whole Soviet system of rule with it.

Faced with only such alternative policy courses, the Soviet leadership finds itself today in the situation of the hero of a popular Russian folktale who had to choose between three roads, one of which led to his beheading, another to the loss of his horse and no return, and the third to the swamps no living creature could cross. When the Soviet leadership has, however, chosen one of these roads, namely that of invigoration (leading to the swamps?), it has done so because in terms of the system's survival it deemed this course to be the safest. Indeed, from the point of view of the partocratic *apparatchiks* at the top of the Soviet hierarchy, and, especially, the police generals who form today the core of the ruling Politburo, it is much easier to keep in check the social processes taking place within the framework of *glasnost'* and democratization—as they are all related either to the functioning of the official media or public bodies—than the effects of decentralization that would unleash the spontaneity of the country's whole population and transform most of the present public bodies into autonomous enterprises. Another specter, that of the 1968 Prague Spring, tells the Soviet leaders what consequences they may face if they were to opt for decentralization. *Glasnost'* and democratization are in their view different. Even if they got out of hand, the partocrats at the top are sure that by using the coercive and other administrative means at their disposal, they would not have too much difficulty suppressing whatever "overspills" may occur and either bring *glasnost'* and democratization back into the officially controlled framework or, if necessary, eliminate them altogether, to the joy and with the enthusiastic support of the leadership's partocratic underlings. After all, in the early 1960s, they successfully did exactly that when the cultural thaw initiated under Khrushchev acquired a menacing dimension (there is a strange feeling of *déjà vu* about the new 1986-1987 cultural thaw in the U.S.S.R.) and the 1987 Chinese experience of cutting down the renewed (1986) "Hundred Flowers" experiment confirmed to them that they could do it again without too much trouble. It however remains to be seen whether the Soviet *apparatchiks*' present sense of security could stand up to the test of time. This is, at least to me, most doubtful.

Glasnost' and democratization, as we have seen, are not independent policies. They are part and parcel of the previously conceived policy of restructuring which in its turn was introduced as a package of measures designed to achieve the so-called acceleration. Acceleration, that is, faster, better, and more productive performance of all the same functions that the Soviet system has always been performing, so far remains the declared main Soviet policy goal to which everything else in the U.S.S.R. should be subordinated. As an authoritative leading article in the Party's theoretical and political magazine *Kommunist* has explained, "restructuring . . . is the

creation of a reliable and effective mechanism of social-economic acceleration of the Soviet society," whereas the measures of which restructuring itself
consists are "all-round development of democracy and socialist self-management, invigoration of dicipline and order, widening of *glasnost'* and of
criticism and self-criticism."[127]

Restructuring is indeed a policy under which everything in the Soviet
system has to remain basically unrestructured. Its idea is that technological
modernization under the conditions of intensive development of the Soviet
economy will automatically take care of the restructuring insofar as the systematic elements are concerned. Policywise, restructuring should be restricted
to measures assuring the invigoration of discipline and effective enforcement
of law and order. With regard to the enhancement of work discipline, one of
the basic constituent elements of the policy of restructuring is the anti-
drunkenness campaign. Another is the introduction of the collective contract,
according to which the workers are to be remunerated not for the individual
operations each of them performs but for the whole product they collectively
produce. The idea here is to make the amount of pay every worker receives
dependent on the work of every other worker in that particular workers'
collective, an arrangement that is supposed to induce the workers' intolerance
to their fellow-workers' slackness and breaches of work discipline. Each
worker would thus become his fellow-workers' keeper and the workers'
collective as a whole, a conscientious mutual enforcer of work discipline of
all its members. Yet another disciplining device was instituted in the form of
state commissions for the quality control of the goods produced. If these
commissions that are now constituted as bodies independent of the productive units refuse to release a particular product to the consumer, the workers
involved in its production will receive no payment, let alone bonuses for the
work they expended on producing it.

Glasnost' and democratization, complex devices as they are, basically
seek, as it was shown above, to enforce discipline and order, too, but in the
first place among managers and other officials. One should not be fooled
apparances but recognize *glasnost'* and democratization for what they are.
However, there is no way of denying that without having changed the tenor
and direction of Soviet policies, *glasnost'* and democratization have made
them much more of a mixed bag, which has rendered the whole situation in
the Soviet Union visibly less stable and much more unpredictable. The fact
that the Soviet top leadership, in order to preserve the status quo, went for
the introduction of such ambiguous and risky policies as *glasnost'* and
democratization, is a clear indication that the régime is neither willing nor
able to go at this stage for a revolution from above. Having thus decreased
the probability of such a revolution, the policies of *glasnost'* and democra-

tization have, however, significantly increased the chances for the change in
the Soviet Union to come about in the form of confrontation.

Political Change Through Confrontation

Technocratic Reaction to Partocratic Relapse

In the previous chapter I have briefly considered the possibilities for a
partocratic relapse. I tried to show that it may happen either as a reaction to
Gorbachev's reformist overdrive or as a gradual process of advancing stifling
"counter-reformism" over which Gorbachev himself may opportunistically
choose to preside. Such a partocratic relapse as the present policy trends
indicate, could be accompanied by some drastic measures aimed at a radical
reconsolidation of the political status quo. These measures could even
amount to a kind of "neo-Stalinist" spell. But whatever these measures were,
it is certain that they would be bound to provoke a strong resentment and
discontent among all the élites, to say nothing of the masses. Even without a
pronounced partocratic relapse, the situation in the Soviet Union may grow
extremely tense and grave if the revolution from above simply failed to
materialize soon enough and thus partocratic procrastination continued
unabated for much longer. The Soviet Union is today in such an all-round
critical state that the partocratic policies may, by their mere continuity,
provoke the outbreak of a nationwide crisis, with all the extremely grave
consequences that it may entail.

It is the necessity of finding a solution to such a crisis that may induce the
technocrats to rise against partocracy and, in an open confrontation with
the partocrats, try to assume supremacy. We have already witnessed events
of a similar type in at least two countries of the Soviet bloc which took place
at different critical periods of time. One such event was the initiation of
change by the technocratically minded part of the Czechoslovakian Party's
Central Committee at the December 1967 Plenary Session of that body. The
analogy here consists in the fact that the rebellion of the majority of the
members of the Central Committee against Novotny's leadership of the
Party, which took place at that session, was provoked by the excesses of the
inflexibly dogmatic and ruthlessly oppressive (outdated even by international
communist, e.g. Soviet, standards of the time) policies of that leadership
rather than by a positive drive for the system's liberal reformation per se.
The latter came later, in the spring of 1968 (hence, "Prague Spring"), with
the search for alternative policies to the ones which were refuted—a search
in which the "intrastructural" dissidents acquired an unexpectedly prominent
and, in the end, decisive role, spelling the breakdown of the totalitarian rule
in Czechoslovakia altogether.

Another analogous development took place in 1956 in Poland when the Party's Central Committee was, for several months, virtually divided into two warring factions: the one uniting "reactionary" hardline Stalinists, called, according to the name of the palace they made their meeting place, "Natolinians," and the other, uniting "progressive" reformists, called, according to the name of the leader they were seeking to reinstate at the helm of the Party, "Gomulkians." The "Polish October," of which the "Prague Spring" was an almost exact replica, started by a full victory of the "Gomulkians" over the "Natolinians" at the October 1956, Plenary Session of the Party's Central Committee—the first such session after the split. There was, however, no need for Soviet intervention to put the Polish October down, since, differently from Dubček, Gomulka had been able to suppress it all by himself. "What did change in Poland after October 1956? Nothing but Gomulka." This Polish joke explained the situation in a nutshell. Before 1968, I would refer to this experience as to a model of what I am trying to project here. After 1968, this experience was overshadowed by the Prague Spring and Poland gained new "change experience" to which I shall refer later. Hence, I will stick in this instance to the Czechoslovakian example or to what one may call the *Czechoslovakian model of change.*

The Czechoslovakian model of change could be set in motion in the Soviet Union by the rapidly deteriorating economic situation alone, but a partocratic relapse would strongly strengthen the chances for its materialization.

Popular Reaction to Economic Demise

It is common knowledge that since the early 1970s the rate of economic growth in the Soviet Union has been steadily declining. It is this phenomenon that Zaslavskaya and her associates undertook to explain and try to remedy in the Novosibirsk document. This document opens by stating the following: "Over a number of decades, Soviet society's economic development has been characterized by high rates and great stability. This automatically suggested a notion about the organic nature of its features for the management of a planned socialist economy. However, in the past 12-15 years a tendency toward a noticeable decline in the rate of growth of the national income began to make itself felt in the development of the economy of the U.S.S.R. If in the eighth five-year plan the average annual increase was 7.5 percent and in the ninth it was 5.8 percent, then in the tenth it fell to 3.8 percent, and in the first years of the eleventh it was about 2.5 percent (with the average population growth at 0.8 percent per annum). This does not provide for either the rate of growth in living standards that is required for the people, or for the intensive technical retooling of production."[128] Then, after having refuted the "partial character" of the current explanations of this "sad tendency," Zaslavskaya stated that "there is a more general reason at the foundation of this phenomenon,"[129] and proceeded to the formulation of her radical conclusion about the contradiction between the productive forces and the Soviet system of production relations. When Gorbachev engages in a critique of the weaknesses of the Soviet economic performance, he, like Zaslavskaya, starts his exposure of these also by referring to the same phenomenon, in terms almost literally copying those of Zaslavskaya. His opening phrase usually sounds like that: "From the beginning of the 1970s, certain difficulties in the economic development made themselves felt."[130]

Unofficial estimates assess Soviet economic performance as being even slacker than the official figures and statements would suggest. In the Soviet Union "the almost universal belief" is that the rate of economic growth has long been even below zero and that it is still "steeply falling."[131] Although only a belief, it is not entirely without foundation in reality. This belief is based first on the fact that Soviet officials tend, as a rule, to present statistical reports greatly exaggerating the real results of their office's performance,[132] and is based also on the everyday experience of each person of the ever more acute shortages of supplies and goods.

The fact that Soviet citizens en masse are, in spite of official reassurances, convinced that the Soviet economy is in such a deep recession should be considered as the most important factor providing for the possibility of a crisis breaking out into the open and provoking mass unrest. In such a psychological climate, as we know from the Polish experience of 1980, every trivial conflict can turn into a major confrontation. In Poland, after all, the "Solidarity" movement started with the sacking of Anna Walentinowicz from her menial job as crane operator in Gdansk's Lenin Shipyard, and a certain deterioration in meat supplies—events that, by any standards, were rather trivial, but in a given psychological atmosphere proved to be able to trigger a major crisis.

Since in a Soviet-type socialist society all economic shortages as well as breaches of justice are automatically considered by the people as the fault of the government and the manifestation of the inherent inability of the system to provide for the elementary needs of the working people, an economic crisis is virtually inseparable from a political one. In that sense the population's conviction that the Soviet economy is in deep demise becomes tantamount to a latent crisis of the overall credibility of the government as well as of the whole system over which this government is presiding. Hence, partocratic procrastination, with the inevitably slackening economic performance and constant drop in living standards that it entails, is prone to bringing about at any point in time a situation of total anarchy and disarray. Strikes, riots and insurrections could spontaneously break out, as was already the case in the late 1950s, 1960s, and 1970s, but on a much larger scale.[133] The mood for that is already more than ripe.

All foreign observers of the Soviet Union, as well as private Soviet citizens visiting the West or writing uncensored letters abroad,[134] are quite unanimous in stating that the appalling shortages of food and other commodities are creating an atmosphere of universal resentment and animosity, "swelling a 'reservoir' of popular aggression and hopelessness."[135] The element of hopelessness here, perhaps, is especially important. As George Feifer witnesses, *bezizkhodnost'* (literally exitlessness) was "the word most people" (in the Soviet Union) "used to sum up their condition."[136] And when such a feeling becomes dominant, rebellious outbreaks are most likely to happen. It has been reported that popular protests and strikes took place in the 1980s in Tula, Sverdlovsk, Volgograd, and in the Siberian coalfields. The May 1980 strikes, "the largest in modern Soviet history—at the major auto works in Tolyatti and Gor'kiy, were not unexpected: workers told me that the general sense of grievance was very high."[137] Solzhenitsyn reports about a general strike in Perm', which was put down by military force, the operation being started by a parachute landing of the troops on the rooftops of the factories occupied by the strikers.[138] There is no doubt that the Polish unrest has also made its impact on the already disturbed Soviet workers, and one should wait and see what the long term consequences of that will be. All this brings me to the conclusion that the change in the Soviet Union could start from the workers' unrest along the lines of what has been constantly happening in Poland (Poznan in 1956; Gdansk in 1970; Radom, Warsaw, and other places in 1976; Gdansk and then the whole country in 1980). In Poland, however, the threat of Soviet invasion did not allow these events to be brought to their logical conclusion,[139] whereas there is no such restriction in the case of the Soviet Union itself. This is to say that there is also a strong possibility that it will be the *Polish model of change* which, when applied to the Soviet Union, will start the process of political change there.

But even if the Polish model failed to materialize in the Soviet Union and if the partocrats were able effectively to suppress the technocrats, thus preventing also the Czechoslovak model from being set in motion, the situation with regard to change in the Soviet Union may still not remain reliably steady. At a certain point of the country's plunging into economic chaos and social anarchy, the Soviet Army, as a "natural partisan of order," will most likely be induced to interfere and to assume political power.[140] Hence, the situation in the Soviet Union could also develop along the lines of the *Portuguese model of change*.

The Military Takeover

There is a lot of controversy in the specialist literature with regard to the role of the Army in Soviet society. One view argues that a full cohesion exists between the Party and the military, whereby the military fully accepts its role of a mere "executant" of policies initiated by the Party from above. This "division of labor" view, applied to the whole Soviet system (and ignoring the divisions between partocratic and technocratic elements within that system's particular institutions themselves), is based, in the case of the military, on a special admission that there is in the Soviet Union a particular "party-military consensus" which places the military ideologically closer to the Party leadership than other divisions of the Soviet establishment.[141]

Some scholars and journalists go even further, claiming that Soviet domestic and foreign policy is dominated today not solely by the Party apparatus but by a "military industrial complex" composed of the Party, the military, the KGB, the managers of heavy industry, etc.[142] It is only natural that those who are holding such views think that a military coup in the Soviet Union is "quite unlikely."[143]

Here again we are faced with the unwillingness of the West to admit the "superbureaucratic" position of the Party apparatus within the Soviet establishment and with the tendency of too many Western scholars to see the institutional consensus within the Soviet system as either self-sufficient (with no need to go beyond the surface of the institutions themselves) and, as such, reflective of the conflictless totality of the system's whole structure, where each part (the Party, the Army, etc.) only plays a functional role accorded to it,[144] or as a give-and-take consensus between different, institutionalized interest groups with the Party kept on top in as far as it properly serves them all by aggregating their various interests.[145] In fact the problem is neither institutional nor inter-institutional but purely intra-institutional, since all Soviet institutions, e.g. the Army, are run by the Party apparatus and, in addition, in the great majority of cases, directly by partocrats, which explains why all Soviet institutions so nicely aggregate into the monolithic total structure, with the Party at its helm. (Because of the Party's policy priorities, this structure might as well be termed the military-industrial complex, but since this wrongly implies an analogy, or even sameness, with the American military-industrial complex, I would strongly object to it.) What really matters in the Soviet Union is not how institutions get on with one another but what relationship exists between partocrats and technocrats within the institutions themselves. The question, in other words, is how would a certain professional group organized as an institution behave, if, when rid of partocratic domination, it could act on its own as a proper interest group (as defined, with Lodge's help, above in Chapter III).

The scholars who, on the contrary, admit that the military as such is a group whose interests differ from and in many respects contradict those of the Party,[146] are again divided in their views on what the specific interests of the Soviet military might be. The most popular one, shared also by the media, is the view according to which the Soviet military is even "more Catholic than the Pope" (i.e. more totalitarianly Communist than the Party itself) and that, therefore, if it staged a coup d'état it would do so not for the sake of introducing political change, but for the removal of a flabby (e.g. détente-minded) Party leadership and the restoration of an orthodox, hard-line Stalinist totalitarian dictatorship.[147] This view, reflecting the instinctive Western fear of "black colonels" or "white generals," as opposed to any kind of civilian authority (a view which again exemplifies the inadmissible bias towards basic identification of the U.S.S.R. with normal countries, i.e. those of the West), was, strangely enough, most explicitly articulated in the writings of a recent Russian émigré, Alexander Yanov,[148] especially in his article entirely devoted to a polemic with Solzhenitsyn,[149] *inter alia*, with what Yanov interpreted as Solzhenitsyn's direct appeal for a military coup.[150] The evidence substantiating this view consists of various reports on international negotiations at which the representatives of the Soviet military allegedly took the hardest line, various Kremlinological assessments (always dubious) and occasional public pronouncements of some Soviet generals in praise of Stalin.

Let us try to interpret this evidence which, on factual grounds, I do not intend either to challenge or question. It seems to me that the duly recorded hawkish attitudes of the Soviet military establishment[151] do not at all indicate its communist orthodoxy or devotion to the totalitarian partocratic régime. In my view, by thus behaving, the military (in alliance with their partocratic bosses) are trying to uphold and promote the relative strength and influence of their office within the system with all the benefits and privileges which come with it. In other words it is the natural way for the military to express their office patrimonial interests and to compete with their rivals for the share of the cake.

Moreover, the heavier the Soviet rulership's reliance on confrontational and expansionist policies is, the more dependent it becomes upon the military in overall terms. And not only because the military is the most important executioner of such policies but also, and mainly, because these policies, being likely to alienate other establishments, make the Party heavily dependent for its survival in power on the Army's support (which may one day turn from unconditional into a very conditional one indeed, thus undermining the authority of the Party and establishing the military's supremacy). Hence, not only immediate gains in terms of finance and status are thus achieved by the Army, but also long-term advantages of drastically increasing the professional military stratum's political weight. (I used the word *professional* here to distinguish the genuine military from the political officers of the Army and to emphasize that the growth of the military's influence will inevitably be accompanied by a proportional diminution of partocratic control over it.)

The experience of history shows that if a government becomes dependent for its survival on the exclusive support of one particular force outside the government, that supporting force acquires more power than the government itself and finally replaces it altogether. This, for instance, was the case with Kerensky's Provisional Government in Russia after September, 1917, when, in its confrontation with General Kornilov and under the menace of a military coup (known as Kornilovshchina), it relied entirely on Bolshevik support, thus making itself completely dependent upon the Bolsheviks who then only had to decide about the time of their own coup formalizing their ascendancy, which in essential terms had already been achieved before that coup. This was also the case in Chile in September, 1973, when President Allende, trying to strengthen his government without allowing the extreme left to enforce its supremacy by breaking the Constitution, called upon the military to join him and made General Pinochet his Minister of Interior. It was from this position of actual power that Pinochet and his associates staged a coup against Allende, thus removing the last stumbling block on the way to their full control over the country. This actually shows that, along with the Portuguese, the *Chilean model of change* (both being merely variations of basically the same model of a military takeover) can also be envisaged as applicable for the beginning of the process of political change in the Soviet Union. It will actually develop in the U.S.S.R. if the Party, in the pursuit of its expansionist policies, becomes entirely dependent on the Army or if it, in a situation of crisis and ensuing anarchy and disarray, tries to call on the Army to assume greater powers (by joining the government or otherwise) in order to help the Party to restore order.

In my view, the professional military stratum, as well as other specialist élites, has no vested interest in maintaining the Soviet system of rule. Its authentic (but, of course, latent) stand is, perhaps, even more "anti-Soviet" than that of other such élites.

The military, more than any other Soviet establishment, was always and continues to be a virtual prisoner of the Party. The system of close supervision of every commanding officer by a political commissar, introduced by Trotsky in 1918, has never been dismantled or significantly altered and is still in full operation. The main Political Directorate (MPD) of the Soviet Army, whose representatives are assigned to every military detachment as political deputies of the commanding officer (*zampolit*), is officially a department of the Party's Central Committee and not solely of the Ministry of Defense, which puts the Party, even formally, in direct control over every military unit and not only over the Army as a whole. It is difficult to interpret this cumbersome institutional arrangement of "double command" on all levels of the Army as an expression of real cohesion between the Party and the military; it rather indicates the opposite, namely that the Party deeply distrusts the military and treats it as a potentially hostile force needing to be kept under vigilant check. Or shall we as usual dismiss the Party's judgment as paranoic, only because it does not fit in with our own rational ways of thinking, or, what sometimes amounts to the same, our assumptive prejudices?

Whatever the answer, there is sufficient evidence to suggest that the military commanders do not like this arrangement at all. Marshal Zhukov, the most popular Russian military commander of the Soviet time and a person who could be justly considered a genuine spokesman for the whole military stratum, as soon as he was appointed Minister of Defense in 1955, started undermining this arrangement by curtailing the controlling powers of the political officers and concentrating the authority in the Army exclusively in the hands of the military commanders. The whole officer corps was overenthusiastic about these developments and, because of them, the already highly popular Zhukov was unanimously hailed by the military as its genuine leader. This is clear not only from many witness accounts but even from the Party documents accusing Zhukov of "Bonapartist tendencies to seize power,"[152] "to tear off the Armed Forces from the Party, to counter-oppose the Soviet Army to the Party's leadership,"[153] etc. For some time the Party, because of the internal skirmishes of that period (1955-57), was unable to react "properly" (meaning suppressively) to these developments in the Army (each of the warring factions in the Party needed Zhukov's support, and it was quite significant that he gave it to the Party's "liberal wing," headed by Nikita Khrushchev, whose course towards destalinization he fullheartedly upheld), but as soon as the hardline "anti-Party group" was smashed by the so-called liberals and Khrushchev became the Party's undisputed leader in June 1957, Zhukov was expelled from the Politburo and removed from his post as Minister of Defense in October 1957.[154] The inevitable increase after Zhukov's dismissal of the military animosity towards the Party and the appropriate growth of the Party's constant mistrust of the military was reflected in the fact that from 1957 till 1973 neither the Minister of Defense nor any other military man held a seat in the Politburo, which precluded the military of having a direct influence on the political decision-making process (e.g. on purely military problems; this made the military entirely dependent on the central apparatus of the Party which thus became the sole intermediary between it and the Party's Politburo and Secretariat, where all vital decisions, especially on military matters, are taken).

The post of the Minister of Defense after Zhukov was subsequently occupied by two military men, Marshals Rodion Malinovsky (1957-1967) and Andrey Grechko (1967-1976), both of whom as the Party's promotees (from soldiers to marshals) were typical partocrats, making their careers within the Army. Grechko, however, was the last such partocrat among the senior generals of the Soviet Army and after his death in 1976 there was apparently no professional military man who was at the same time a partocrat and whom the Party could therefore trust as Grechko's successor. Hence, the Party decided to break with the long-standing tradition of having a military man appointed to the post of Minister of Defense altogether (this tradition has been upheld since Trotsky's replacement by Mikhail Frunze in 1925, with a relatively short interval for Stalin's and Bulganin's occupation of this post) and dispatched its own Secretary, Dimitry Ustinov, a civilian, to assume that position, promptly giving him the rank of a general of the army, and after three months promoting him to that of a marshal. It is rather symptomatic that by 1976 there was no one left among the professional military men whom the Party could have fully trusted to be its plenipotentiary representative in the armed forces, although General Kulikov and Marshal Yakubovsky were obvious contenders for this post.[155]

It was only after Ustinov's death in December 1984, that a rather obscure military man, Marshal Sergey Sokolov, was given the post of the Soviet Minister of Defense. Maybe by then that Ministry was already reliably put under the Party apparatus's control via channels surpassing those connected with the Minister personally, and there was not much danger any more in having a professional military man as Minister; maybe, the Party, in the aftermath of the Ogarkov controversy and after having knocked out in a dramatic move this military strongman from the line of succession to Ustinov's post, wanted, in compensation, to demonstrate to the military, by making this appointment, some kind of good will; and, maybe, the Party tried to accomplish both these goals by Sokolov's appointment, in one go. Only in April 1985, however, was Sokolov elevated to the candidate membership in the Politburo and, as the Plenary Session of the CPSU's CC on July 1, 1985, confirmed (by dropping Romanov from the Politburo and promoting in his stead, to its full membership the prospective Minister of Foreign Affairs, Eduard Shevardnadze, but not Sokolov), he will not be allowed to rise above that level. This is a clear indication that the Party's traditional mistrust of the military has not significantly abated. The professional military remains within the Soviet power establishment today, as it always has been, a second-rate group—a fact strongly emphasized on the day of Chernenko's funeral by the conspicuous absence of the representatives of the military on the reviewing stand on the Lenin Mausoleum and their much reduced representation on that stand during military parades and official demonstrations that have taken place since.

Apparently something extremely serious, from the Party's point of view, happened in the Army in 1976—so serious that the Party found it impossible then to make a Sokolov-type appointment to the Ministry of Defense. For some reasons, of which we as yet know nothing, the Party was then obviously extremely suspicious of the military and clearly afraid of losing its grip upon it. It even deemed Ustinov's appointment to the post of Minister of Defense not a sufficient deterrent from the Army's getting out of the Party's control. Did Brezhnev remember the experience of Napoléon who, having dispatched his brother, Louis, to rule the Netherlands on his behalf, very soon found out that he was dealing not with his own emissary but with a proper king ready to defend the interests of his country to the bitter end? I do not know, but I doubt it. Probably something more practical exercised the Politburo's mind when in May, 1976 (Ustinov was appointed in April) it decided to bring into public existence a special body, the Defense Council (*Soviet Oborony*), charged with overall responsibility for policymaking on and supervision over all military matters, and to officially announce that the General Secretary of the Party, L. Brezhnev (at that time not yet the head of the Soviet state), himself promoted on that occasion to the rank of a marshal (before Ustinov), was to be appointed as its Chairman. Why was it done? What forced the Party, during the two months after Grechko's death in 1976, to introduce so suddenly a "three line Party Whip" in addition to all the formidable means of control over the Army of which the Party was already in possession? Apparently the military, the old and most vigilantly-guarded prisoner of the Party,[156] started to show signs of restlessness again, forcing the jailer to take new, urgent and drastic measures to increase the security of his prison accordingly. I know that this is not a precise answer but who, except the then mèmbers of Politburo, could answer this question more accurately.

There are, of course, those who say that by taking these drastic measures the Party was protecting its "moderate" policy line from the military extremists. But what are the rational grounds for such a contention? On what kind of an analysis of the real situation in the U.S.S.R. can this contention be based? Why on earth should one assume (assume, since there are no exact facts proving this point) that professional military men are more partocratic than the partocrats themselves and seek to enforce the partocratic hard line against the will of their partocratic rulers?

I already mentioned that Marshal Zhukov, who is generally considered a typical representative of the Soviet military and its natural leader, was a staunch supporter of Khrushchev's line on destalinization. It was actually Zhukov and the Army who played the decisive role in making this line prevalent. It was also Zhukov and the Army who wanted to proceed with destalinization farther than Khrushchev and his partocratic colleagues would consider safe for the system, actually causing Zhukov's fall. If the Army was for destalinization in the 1950s, could it be the case that during the last three decades it has changed its mind so drastically that it is now prepared to engage itself into a struggle for restalinization? Some people would answer "yes" and say that in the 1950s the military did not praise Stalin (they praised Zhukov instead) and that now they do (out of absence of a strong leader still alive). But is it a convincing answer? Is it not ironic that it was Marshal Zhukov himself, the champion of destalinization, who on various occasions in his lifetime publicly praised Stalin and his leadership during the war? His memoirs also contain an extended eulogy of Stalin's high qualities as a leader, world politician, organizer, and military commander.[157] Is that an inconsistency? I do not think it is. As a patriot and one of the main heroes of Russia's Great Patriotic War against Hitler, Zhukov was adamant not to let the image of the Chief Commander of the victorious Russian Army, under whom he and other generals loyally served their country, be tarnished for expedient political reasons (these mainly being to blemish a person and by that to try to whitewash the system). Whatever the objections to that stand of Zhukov and some other generals (and there could be many), one cannot deny that it contains some moral integrity. Moreover, Stalinist purges and terror can be unequivocally refuted without necessarily denying Stalin a good record over the conduct of the war or some positive leadership qualities. (Positive leadership qualities and military talents are in no way inconsistent with a Mafia gang leader's character; on the contrary, they are rather its requisites.) After all, the tragedy of Russia under Bolshevik rule is not the result of Stalin's bad character but rather of the bad character of the Bolshevik system that produced Stalin as its legitimate leader. (Actually, under a different system, Stalin would have had to exercise leadership in an entirely different manner, whatever his personal inclinations.) In the war, however, he was a worthy national leader of Russia and that is what very many generals, including Zhukov, were and are keen to stress—not as good Stalinists but as good Russians.

There is no doubt whatsoever that the ideology of an important section of the Soviet military, and especially of its highest command, is straightforward patriotism and Russian nationalism. Marshal V. Chuikov was, for instance, one of the founding fathers and moving spirits of the notoriously nationalistic (one could even say, chauvinistic and anti-Semitic) Society for the Protection of Ancient Monuments. According to A. Yanov's information, Soviet Marshals Chuikov and Kulikov were the people who secured the permission for the publication in Moscow of the controversial and explicitly chauvinistic and anti-Semitic novels of a certain Ivan Shevtsov.[158] However, much as one could and should oppose chauvinistic and anti-Semitic exaggerations of Russian nationalist ideology, one should not confuse that ideology with Stalinism or any programs for the enhancement of totalitarian Communism.

Russian nationalism is incompatible with Soviet communism for reasons whose explanation lies far beyond the limits of this paper. Whatever unpleasant aspects Russian nationalism may have (as has any other nationalism, especially in its exaggerated chauvinistic and/or jingoistic forms), it is a much more humane and popular ideology than abstract and a-national communism. The political victory of Russian nationalism over communism would therefore be welcomed; for the polity that would be created on its basis could be able to establish peace with its own people and substantially to reduce international confrontation, limiting it to those issues only which have a bearing on Russia's genuine national interests in contrast with the global communist ones. And there are no such genuine Russian national interests that would be in real conflict with those of the U.S.A. or most West European nations.

The removal of communist totalitarianism and its replacement with Russian nationalist authoritarianism (e.g. in the form of a military dictatorship) would certainly introduce into Soviet society, at least to some extent, political pluralism,[159] in itself sufficient to change the country's whole social outfit from a static, and rotting, to a dynamic, and improving via adjustment, one. It will also put an end to the expansionist communist policies of the U.S.S.R. now threatening mankind on a global scale.

Patriotism and Russian nationalism are, however, not the only dissident ideologies which are spread among the military, including also some sections of the Army's high command. The Army, in general, is a representative cross-section of the Soviet society, and all the alternative ideologies which are present in that society are, no doubt, represented in the Army too. That liberal-democratic ideas, explicit pro-Western sympathies, and genuine aspirations for safeguarding peace are quite widely spread among top military people is proved by the case of Oleg Penkovskiy, a senior officer of the Soviet Army's General Staff, who because of his fervent anti-Communism and strong commitment to democracy and peace, worked, until arrested in 1962, for the British and American intelligence. (He was convicted of treason, sentenced to death and executed in 1963.) In spite of his relatively modest rank of colonel, attained at 31, Penkovskiy can be considered as representative of the highest Soviet military stratum not only because of his extremely sensitive position in the Military Intelligence Service (GRU) but also because of his close personal relations with "ministers and marshals,[160] generals and senior officers, members of the Central Committee of the Communist Party of the Soviet Union," whom he vividly described in his memoirs.[161] He was perhaps exceptional among them in his heroic decision to join "the ranks of active fighters for a better future for my people,"[162] but, as he himself witnesses, not exceptional as far as his hatred for Communism and the whole "harmful system" is concerned.[163] His democratic pro-Western views and his commitment to peace were not unique for his milieu either. "There are many people," he writes, "who think and feel as I do, but they are afraid to unite for action."[164]

Another solitary heroic deed of a senior Soviet Army officer was recorded during the workers' uprising in Novocherkassk in 1962. The commander of the troops sent to put down the rebellion (it is rumored that he was a colonel, too) refused to fire at the people and, having thus disobeyed orders, subsequently committed suicide.[165] Here again, the loyalty of a senior Soviet Army officer to himself and to the people took precedence over his loyalty to the government. And no one knows how many similar cases went unnoticed.

That the mood of the military is not different from that of the rest of Soviet society is even more true in the case of middle rank and junior officers. In this respect, it is characteristic that the democratic dissident movement, which spread in the U.S.S.R. in the second half of the 1960s, encompassed from its very beginning not only civilians but also Army officers. We know, for instance, quite a lot about one group of dissident Navy officers in the Soviet Baltic Fleet, G. Gavrilov, A. Kosyrev and G. Paramonov, who organized a secret "Union of Struggle for Political Rights" (*Soyuz Bor'by za Politicheskie Prava*) and produced an extremely interesting document suggesting a program for democratic change which started to circulate in *samizdat* in 1968. We know about these officers and do not know of many others who were probably acting like them because they, in order to get their documents in circulation, dared to contact the prominent civilian dissidents in Moscow (P. Yakir and his group) and were subsequently arrested in May 1969 by the KGB (which was keeping Yakir under constant surveillance). The civilian dissidents (e.g. Sergei Soldatov) were interrogated in this case and all details, known to them, were made public, via *The Chronicle of Current Events*.[166] These officers were typical members of the democratic dissident movement concerned with political liberties and human rights. The document they produced echoed, though not uncritically, the ideas of Andrei Sakharov's 1968 *Memorandum*.

Every observer of the events of the Hungarian Revolution in 1956 knows that several detachments of the Soviet Army, led by their officers, joined the Hungarian insurgents. Less known is the fact that a great number of Soviet officers who have "bravely fulfilled their duty to the socialist cause" in Hungary to the end, came back home accomplished dissidents. This is what one of them, a former Soviet Army captain, Evgeny Shiffers, who with his tank detachment, himself participated in the suppression of the Hungarian revolution, tells us.[167] E. Shiffers, after this experience, left the Army and established himself as a dissident religious writer, which shows that the military contributed to Soviet religious dissent too.

The only reported terrorist act against L. Brezhnev was committed on January 22, 1969, by a Soviet Army officer, A. Il'in, who missed Brezhnev but killed the chauffeur of a governmental car and wounded the astronaut T. Beregovoy. As we see again, a representative of the Army took a share in the kind of "extrastructural" resistance activities outside the mainstream of the dissident movement, which were manifested in civilian life by the activities of VSKhSON[168] or the explosion on Moscow's underground. But also the Soviet mainstream overt dissident movement included from its very early days some professional military men. The late General Petro Grigorenko, one of the leading figures of Soviet overt dissent, is such a case.

The genuine mood of the middle rank officers of the Soviet Army was again brought out into the open with the November, 1975 mutiny on the Soviet battleship (T.B.D.) "Storozhevoy" (250 man crew) and the 1976 defections of two Soviet military pilots, V. Belenko (who flew with his MIG-25 to Japan) and V. Zosimov (who defected to Iran and was immediately extradited by the Shah to the Soviet Union). The aim of the mutineers of the "Storozhevoy" was actually the same as that of the pilots—they simply wanted to emigrate from the Soviet Union to the West and did it in toto by staging a mutiny and taking over the ship. This was actually a direct rebellion against the system (it was rumored that the leader of the rebels was the chief political officer of the ship)[169] carried out with the full awareness that one destroyer ship cannot destroy the whole Soviet system but can at least offer its crew a means of liberation from this system by defection. An important feature of the rebellion was that a crew of one of the aircraft bombers sent to dispose of the ship refused to throw bombs at it.[170]

Belenko's case is here of special importance. He had planned his defection for two years; he specially secured for this purpose a copy of a Soviet strategic plan for attacking China, with maps and other supplements, intending to bring it all to American attention (a mini-Penkovskiy sort of case); most interesting is, however, his description of the mood of his fellow officers as being not simply anti-system but "on the verge of patience" with it.[171] After the statements of Belenko, which clearly show how and to what dangerous extent "the resistance to the CPSU ripens in the Army,"[172] there is nothing surprising about the extraordinary measures that the Party had to take in 1976 in order to ensure the continuity of its grip over the country's military force.

It is a bit surprising when people who are well aware of these facts still assess the Soviet military as a totally reliable pillar of the partocratic régime or, even more so, as a force which is representing the extreme totalitarian (Stalinist) wing of the so-called "Coalition of Fear,"[173] allegedly determined to enforce that régime by all means in its power. It is even more surprising to me when similar views are held by scholars, who do not merely know the facts but have themselves most precisely indicated the key for the right assessment of the military's role in Soviet society and its relationship with the Party. That is, for example, what George Breslauer did when he wrote "that the importance of new technologies has brought into the army young professionals whose training and outlook resemble those of scientific personnel in other areas of the specialist communities"[174] and thus precisely defined the military as a basically technocratic force. He also stressed here the most important aspect of the problem by showing that the professional military personnel, who today form the core of the army, are not essentially different from other technocratic communities and that "together they form a strong block," able to exercise pressure and achieve common goals.[175] To him, however, this does not spell any conflict or difference of interests with the Party. On the contrary, he is convinced that "the military and the Party-state have a common interest" and that together "they are attempting to integrate the military, industrial, educational, and scientific communities into a vast complex that focuses on national goals." He would even go so far as to say that "in all these respects, civil-military relations (in the contemporary Soviet Union—A.S.) are. . .analogous to Germany under Bismarck and the Kaisers."[176]What an idyllic view of the Soviet reality is thus presented! One could think that G. Breslauer writes here not about the present Soviet situation but projects a futurological vision of Russia, freed from partocratic rule and already developing along nationalist lines. Unfortunately this is not yet the case, although G. Breslauer's conclusions about the technocratic nature of the Army clearly spell out that sooner or later it will indeed be the case.

The technocratic nature of the present military, so generously acknowledged by G. Breslauer, is in my opinion the basic fact which brings together all the odd pieces of evidence discussed above and enables us to come to a definite conclusion that (a) it is likely that the Army will be the force which is going to initiate political change in the Soviet Union; (b) that this change will be basically aimed at the same goals as the change initiated by any other part of the Soviet technocratic establishment; and (c) that therefore both the

Portuguese and Chilean models of change could be indicative of the course of political change which is going to take place in the Soviet Union.

I have discussed the issues concerning the Army at such great length because they are of central importance to the whole problem of political change. For as long as the Party can retain the control over the Army and use its force at discretion, no change in the Soviet Union can be successfully initiated. Therefore the problem of change in the Soviet Union is largely the problem of the Army's readiness for change, of its ability to either start the change itself or to align in the course of change with the forces other than itself who are going to start it.

For summing up my arguments I would like to adduce the following words of one of the most prominent living Russian novelists, the recently exiled Georgy Vladimov: "I believe, and have been saying so for quite some time, that it is the military which will overthrow the present régime. . . Of all the forces that could do this job I single out the Army because it is only the Army that has its own noble national task—the defense of the fatherland. . . The military officers do not build their careers on the suffering of other people. Maybe this is why their way of thinking is so much freer than, let us say, that of the Party and KGB men. I used to meet in Russia high-ranking military people. . .who were profoundly, in a non-trivial way, contemplating the fate of Russia, her economy, her ecology; who thought about what may happen and what is to be done. I am sure that. . .in this milieu there are many sensible people who are ready to make an effort in order to bring Russia into the community of civilized democratic powers."[177]

The Régime's Inner Collapse

For the reasons stated above, the Party could well prefer to take a different approach to the imminent or actual crisis facing the country, i.e. the one which would reliably exclude the Army from interference in politics. In this case, the Party would have to take certain positive steps in coping with that crisis and thus assure that things in the country would not deteriorate to a degree that could provoke the Army to take the reins of power into its own hands (prevention of the Portuguese model). On the other hand, the Party, in the course of taking such steps, would have to avoid calling upon the Army to ensure its power's security (prevention of the Chilean model) and instead call upon other sections of the Soviet techno-cratic establishment to help it in this enterprise, granting them in exchange some independent powers to deal with the outstanding economic problems.

If the Party accepted this approach, it would find itself in a situation similar to that of Louis XVI, king of France, during the fifteen years of his prerevolutionary reign (1774-1789). When Louis XVI succeeded to the

French throne France was in a terrible economic condition which the young king, differently from his predecessor and grandfather, Louis XV (who knew better and therefore, like Mr. Brezhnev, decided to live on without even trying to cure the country's ills), was determined to sort out by introducing some "within-system" reforms. One of his first royal acts was the appointment of the famous French economic thinker and local government reformer, Anne-Robert-Jacques Turgot, to the post of comptroller general (minister of finance and virtually prime minister), who was given the necessary powers to implement this task. In two years Turgot prepared, and in 1776 issued, his famous Six Edicts containing a whole program of reforms including the abolition of a number of dues and offices as well as the whole traditional institution of *corvée*. Turgot's reforms were, however, in direct opposition to the plans of the king and the establishment. They wanted slight "within-system" changes and what Turgot proposed amounted to a "system-rejective" change. Asked by the king to moderate his plan, Turgot refused to do so, prophetically pointing out that anything less than what he was proposing would not only fail to solve France's problems but would also confuse and deteriorate the situation even more. The result was predictable. Turgot was dismissed and his Six Edicts abolished. It seems to me symptomatic that Soviet intelligentsia called Kosygin, after the Party refused to go ahead with his 1965 economic reform, "*ublyudochnyi Tyurgo*" (the poor man's Turgot), because his reform program, far from being as bold as Turgot's, was also much lower in economic quality, and also because, differently from Turgot, Kosygin remained in office.

Turgot's dismissal did not mean, however, that the king had changed his mind and renounced the reformist path. On the contrary, after having dismissed Turgot, Louis XVI put another reformist, Jacques Necker, who seemed to be much less radical and much more amenable than Turgot, in charge of the country's finances. Necker's impeccable anti-Turgotist credentials—in 1775 he published a pamphlet directed against Turgot, which was especially critical of his policies of free trade in grain—also encouraged the king to make Necker his choice as Turgot's successor.

Although a moderate and a compromiser, Necker was the person who actually engineered the outbreak of the French Revolution (by the way, it was his dismissal on July 11, 1789, which provoked the storm of the Bastille on July 14). Turgot was right. Reforms lesser than those proposed by him (and such were the reforms which Necker was trying to implement) got France into even bigger trouble. Extraordinary measures were now needed, not gradual reforms. In 1787, the king summoned the Assembly of Notables, asking it to approve of such extraordinary measures and close ranks around him to save the country, but was faced with a plain refusal. Instead the Notables asked the king to recall Necker to solve the country's outstanding problems (in 1781 Necker had also been forced to resign, having been accused of financial mismanagement) which, after some hesitation, the king did in 1788. It was Necker who persuaded Louis XVI that there was now no way out of the financial crisis other than to call the Estates General, a representative institution which had not been assembled since 1614, to approve of the necessary extraordinary measures and insisted on double representation therein of the Third Estate (without which, he rightly argued, the whole enterprise would be void of any meaning). The rest of that story is well known and was briefly referred to above—the "second pivot" was thus introduced and the French Revolution began.

I have recalled here that piece of French 18th century history because it gives us a classical example of the fall of a system whose ruling stratum considered the system's preservation their highest commitment and dealt with every arising crisis not with a view to its genuine solution but only to the system's survival. As one sees from this example, if the system is so outdated that it has no room left for a "within-system" change, even the most rigid policies are unable to save it; at the end of the day it is bound to collapse economically and, subsequently, socially and politically too. One used to say about the Bourbons (though after the revolution; the saying originated in 1795) that they forgot nothing and learned nothing. This is even more true of the Soviet partocrats. Until recently they still tried to follow the "no move" line of the old Bourbon king, Louis XV. Now, at least the top leadership with Gorbachev at its helm, decided to change this procrastinating line to the reformist path that Louis XVI followed with Necker's help. Allegedly introduced to solve the acutest developmental problems the country faces, this path has, in fact, been chosen only for the sake of increasing the system's chances for survival. It remains to be seen whether the results of these attempts to save the unviable system at whatever cost, will not be like those which Louis XVI himself witnessed in 1789.

I am far from suggesting that the change in the Soviet Union could follow the 1789 *French model of change* exactly. It is difficult to imagine that the Party would ever even consider calling any sort of a representative assembly of the type of the Estates General (or *Zemskiy Sobor*). It is rather more likely that the Soviet Turgots, Neckers, and Calonnes (another reformist comptroller general of France who held this office in 1783-1787; it was he who persuaded the king to call the Assembly of Notables in 1787 but, having failed to get the latter's approval for the measures he thought necessary to introduce, resigned in despair) would have no choice but to preside over the process of their own institution assuming the position of a "second pivot," thus splitting the Soviet political system in order to get things really moving.

In its vain but insistent pursuits of a "within-system" solution of the aggravating economic crisis (which is of a permanent nature in the Soviet Union), the Party could, for instance, establish a new institution of economic management endowing it with large autonomous emergency powers. This institution could even be constructed as a quasi-representative body, for instance as a system of economic councils operating on all administrative levels—local, republican, and All-Union. The seats on these councils would probably be distributed between the economic managers as well as some workers (the Soviet third estate) on the one hand and the representatives of the Party on the other, the latter intending to use the councils as a forum for reaching a new consensus, i.e. not one of stagnation but one of "within-system" change, with the civilian technocrats. A similar body, the Collective Farms Council (*Sovet Kolkhozov*), was already instituted by the Party in 1969, to solve, on the basis of such a consensus, some of the most acute problems of Soviet agriculture,[178] but this arrangement did not work as the Party expected it to and, shortly after its creation, this institution disappeared into oblivion (by 1973 there was no further mention of it). Hence, I am not referring here to idle fantasies but to something which, though abortive and shortlived, has already taken place in reality as a certain way of dealing with acute economic situations. On the other hand, the Party could prefer to avoid creating any new bodies and try to use an institution of state economic management already existing within the system for the same purposes, for example, Gosplan, which is the most general and senior economic office in the whole system. The result would hardly be any different one way or another. As F. Znakov pointed out, "any institution, new or old, if endowed with sufficient autonomous powers, could (and most certainly would) after some time of frustrating attempts to get the Party's approval for necessary reforms, turn into the 'second pivot,' splitting the Soviet political system and starting in the vast country of the Soviets the process of so much needed (and desired) change."[179]

Of course, for those in whose view interest groups in Soviet society are identical to the offices operating in it (and who therefore refuse to admit that each Soviet office is an arena of latent confrontation between partocrats and technocrats, in fact the real interest groups operating in the Soviet society on an overall scale) the suggestion that Gosplan might be the potential Soviet "second pivot" seems to be not simply nonsensical but "breathtaking."[180] Indeed, Gosplan is one of the most "reactionary" Soviet institutions and, if one considers the Soviet Union as a system whose only constituent elements are internally coherent offices, the idea that, of all such offices, Gosplan should be considered as a likely "second pivot," must sound odd to say the least. It is exactly this "institutional" approach which was demonstrated by Jerry Hough, who, when refuting the idea about Gosplan's "revolutionary" potential, wrote that "although all technocrats are not so conservative as Gosplan, my sense is that the top governmental *apparatus* is rather more resistant to change than the Central Committee *apparatus*" (emphasis added).[181]

Since I have once already replied to these arguments, I shall allow myself to repeat them here once more:

"I do not think that Hough was fair when he presented. . .the conflict between the partocratic and the technocratic strata in Soviet society as" (being, in my view) "one between the Party apparatus and all the other apparatuses of authority and management in the U.S.S.R. For . . . this conflict is not related to structural divisions of power and management in the Soviet system, but is of a socially ubiquitous character. Its manifestations could be identified within any single office as well as within any field of 'unstructured' social activities. To me, all the apparatuses of the U.S.S.R. without exception—not only the Party apparatus itself but the Soviet apparatus, the army, the security forces, the trade unions; in short, every single structure right down to the Red Cross and Crescent Society— are still dominated by partocratic forces. On the other hand, technocratic forces not only are present in all the apparatuses—inclusive of the Party apparatus itself—but growing more prominent and are making their presence felt to a greater extent in all of them. That is why it should have been evident that . . . 'the tens of thousands of engineers and agronomists with managerial experience who work in the Party apparatus,' if progressive, are progressive not only when they work elsewhere, as Hough wants me to believe, but wherever their work is done, e.g. in the Party apparatus itself . . .

I completely agree with Hough that, as an office, Gosplan is one of the most conservative structures in the power apparatus of the U.S.S.R., which is only natural since under different circumstances Gosplan would doubtless be the first office to be dismantled. In my view, office interests as such, however, are not of paramount importance. Without discounting them altogether, one should take into account the differing social and political interests of various strata within the Soviet establishment on a wider scale, as in all bureaucracies, e.g., inside Gosplan too. Looking from this perspective, one must at least theoretically admit that in the U.S.S.R. every major office could become a field of intensive struggle for dominance between the technocrats and the partocrats, and thus could turn into a stronghold of the technocrats from which they could launch an attack against partocratic rule. In this respect, one should bear in mind that Gosplan is by its very nature an office whose gates are open wider for technocratic penetration than the gates of other offices of equal influence and importance, which, by the way, makes Znakov's point" (about the possibility of Gosplan becoming the 'second pivot') "more sensible than at first glance it seems to be."[182]

There is yet another possibility for the Soviet political system's split and thus for the "second pivot's" appearance in the Soviet Union. The one suggested above (creation of new institutions of economic management or endowment of old institutions, for example Gosplan, with new powers) is distinguishable by a regular pattern of "transfusion of power" from one "pivotal" institution to another which thus becomes "pivotal" itself (a process developing within the framework of the French model of change). This other possibility, on the contrary, is related to a process of a much more sudden nature.

In 1956, when the Party denounced Stalin and promised to introduce reforms, people from all walks of Soviet life were strongly stimulated to bring their criticism of the system's performance and proposals of change into the open. Meetings discussing the decisions of the 20th Congress of the Party, debates on Vladimir Dudintsev's controversial novel, *Not by Bread Alone*, and other similar public events, began to turn into a genuine mass movement which, although too shortlived to acquire an organized pattern, made an impact of lasting nature on Soviet society by giving birth to the overt dissident movement. The 1956 history may repeat itself if the Party stayed long enough on its newly adopted course of *glasnost'* (openness) and continued to encourage the intelligentsia and the grass-roots population to speak their critical mind publicly. There is no guarantee that *glasnost'* could be reliably controlled by the Party all the time, for in the long run the Soviet population, at present still very skeptical and extremely reluctant to stick its neck out, may, after all, take *glasnost'* seriously, transgress the narrow limits set for it by the Party today, and use this newly found freedom of expression for system rejective purposes. Such a turn of events is much more likely at present than in 1956, since during the last "lenient" three decades people's fear of the regime has greatly diminished, while their trust in the rulers' good will has totally evaporated. It is also very likely that certain institutions might become the centers of these debates. Some clubs and academic institutions in Moscow are already showing signs of assuming this role by regularly organizing controversial lectures and discussions, for the time being only on cultural and historical topics, which the Party, wanting to keep the intelligentsia appeased by satisfying at least some of its cultural needs, reluctantly tolerates.[183] (By the way, that is how the Petöfi Club in Budapest was started in the early days of 1956.)

The Party would probably seek to suppress such spontaneous manifestations by people, as it did in 1956-57, and would insist on keeping the discussion of all controversial issues exclusively within the official framework of the media and institutions supposed to deal with these issues under the Party's direct control. In most drastic or specially selected cases of such grassroot manifestations, the Party would have to resort to "exemplary" repressions of some of the new overt dissidents which, in the troubled situation of an "opened-up" crisis, could bring the organizations to which these repressed people belong to their defense. An unexpected and uncontrolled controversy can thus start between these organizations and the Party whereby the former, especially if supported by any of the discussion centers mentioned above, could assert itself as the "second pivot," thus splitting the system before any other office could assume this role in a more regular way. This is actually what happened in Hungary in 1956 when, by having rallied in defense of its members Tamas Aczel and Tibor Dery against the CC, the Writers' Union's primary Party organization (in association with the Petöfi Club) assumed its independence from the Party apparatus and started to challenge its policies.

Hence, the *Hungarian model of change* can be added to all the others as the one along whose lines the change in the Soviet Union might be incepted.

The Relevance of the "Second Pivot"

We preceded the review of the various scenarios of political change in the Soviet Union by contending that whatever the concrete way in which change in the Soviet Union could materialize, it would inevitably start by the split of the established totalitarian political system into two pivots. Indeed, in the latter two sub-scenarios, developed along the lines of the French and Hungarian models of change, the centrality of the "second pivot" issue is quite explicit. The same, I think, though not as explicitly, is also quite obvious in the first two scenarios, to which the Spanish and Czechoslovakian models of change appeared to be the closest. There, the split of the Party's Central Committee (or of any other highest decision-making body—the Politburo, the Secretariat, etc.) into two separate pivots, with the second pivot thus being formed on the basis of a part of a previously whole institution, was implicitly suggested as the prerequisite for starting the process of change.

More complicated is the question of the same general rule of the second pivot operating in the cases of the scenarios of change based on the Portuguese and Chilean models. The fact that the army stages a military coup does not necessarily mean that it thereby assumes the role of the second pivot. In Portugal in 1974, it did indeed assume such a role; as it did in the Spanish Civil War of 1936-1939, as well as on some other similar historical occasions when the army revolted against the system, of which it was supposed to be a subordinated element, by staging a coup aimed at fundamental changes of a *permanent* nature amounting to the replacement of one political system by another. On most occasions, however, the army, when staging a coup, does not challenge the system within which it functions at all. On the contrary, it tries to consolidate that system, making it more cohesive and better able to withstand any attempts directed towards its split and subsequent destruction. The change it introduces in these cases amounts to a reinforcement of the same system's sole pivot by *temporarily* altering the mode in which it operates and the composition of the personnel which are running it. In fact, by staging such a coup, the army is continuing to act as a constituent element of the old system and not as its second pivot at all.

Most of the military coups, so often taking place in Latin America, the coups which brought the military to power in Greece in 1967 or in Turkey in 1980 (as well as previous such coups in that country) or in many other places (Thailand, Pakistan, etc.) are of exactly such a "system-preserving" nature.

Of that same nature was also the so-called military coup in Poland staged on December 13, 1981, under the command of Party Chief and Prime Minister, General Woiciech Jaruzelski. The whole substance of this coup was preservation of the crumbling system of partocratic supremacy. It was, in fact, organized not by the military but by the ruling Party apparatus which just used for that purpose its own military branch operated by the Party's envoys to the Army, such as Jaruzelski, Siwicki, Kiszczak, et al., i.e. by pure partocrats dressed up in Polish generals' uniforms. The military branch of the Party apparatus, as the one least disintegrated and best equipped with means of suppression, was rushed onto the scene to fortify all the other parts of this apparatus that were about to fall apart, and to crush at the same time "Solidarity" and all other public outlets able to provide the Polish people with independent power and influence.

It is worthwhile to note that the main Polish military force—its conscript army, together with the professional military officers that are in charge of it—were safely locked up in their barracks during the whole duration of that "military" coup. The coup was in fact perpetrated by the special security and police forces (the so-called ZOMOs). The regular military force could not be trusted with the performance of such a task. Only later were some regular troops brought in to help the ZOMOs to enforce "martial law." But they were always attached to the ZOMOs in a supplementary capacity and were put under their strict command.

There is little doubt, too, that the whole "military" operation started on December 13, 1981, was carefully planned during the entire period of Jaruzelski's occupation of the highest offices in the country, if not before, and not only in Warsaw but also in Moscow, which explains the numerous trips the Soviet Marshal Kulikov, the Chief Commander of Warsaw Pact forces, was making to Warsaw during the last months before the "military" rule was imposed.

I greatly doubt the possibility of an authentic military coup being staged either in Poland or, for that matter, in any other Soviet dependency. For the Polish Army, as well as the armies of all other Soviet satellite states, are not self-sufficient entities, but elements of the united forces of the Warsaw Pact run by Soviet generals and their Party supervisors. These Soviet functionaries are in fact the real supremos over the whole Polish military establishment, and over Jaruzelski himself.

Since the Party and the Army of the Soviet Union are in full control of the Party and, to no lesser extent, of the Army of Poland, any genuine rebellion of the Polish Army would have to be directed in the first place against its superior foreign authority, not against the Polish people, who in this event would wholeheartedly support their Army and join with it in this liberatory (though desperate and, most likely, self-destructive) venture.

I do not exclude that in the event of Soviet intervention in Poland such a rebellion of the Polish Army could still take place, but then it would be led by genuine military people (colonels rather than generals) against not only the foreign intruders, but in the first place against Jaruzelski and his "military" establishment themselves. One should not overlook, however, the difficulty of realizing such a plan. The main problem here is that each separate army unit (e.g. the Polish Army) within the united forces of the Warsaw Pact has at its disposal only three days' combat supply of ammunition, the rest being controlled and supplied exclusively by the Soviet commanders of the Warsaw Pact forces themselves.

Since the Soviet Union is politically and militarily independent of any outside force, the situation with a military coup there would inevitably assume an entirely different character. Even if the Party apparatus itself did engineer there a "military" takeover, like they did in Poland, it would become extremely difficult for it to keep the thus elevated marshals and generals in proper check and effectively prevent the Chilean model of change from being set in motion. The same would be true also for Jaruzelski, Siwicki and Kiszczak if there were no supreme Soviet command over them. But the Soviet Jaruzelskis, Siwickis and Kiszczaks, after having staged a successful coup, would have nobody above them, which makes for a qualitatively different situation indeed. This is to say that in Soviet conditions if the Army rose to take independent political action, it would inevitably assume the role of the "second pivot."

Indeed, in both my "military coup" sub-scenarios (based on the Portuguese and Chilean models of change) the Army was considered as the force actually splitting the system with a view to its fundamental change and thus putting itself into the position of the system's second pivot. Hence, the rule of the second pivot was here fully observed, too, without implying any crude assumptions that the Army, every time it seizes power, actually acts as the system's second pivot.

The second pivot issue is even more complex in the Polish model of change. Here we were confronted with a spontaneous grassroot movement developing outside the official system and therefore with one that by its own effort should have been unable to either split this system and produce its second pivot or directly affect it in any other way. In the light of F. Znakov's theory, such a spontaneous grassroot movement, whatever its form—strikes, riots, or demonstrations—is in itself unable to become the vehicle of political change; it could serve only as an indication of the degree to which society is ready for such a change. Indeed, in F. Znakov's opinion, the quite popular romantic view of revolutions as spontaneous mass up-risings, barricade battles between the insurgents and the government's armed forces, etc., is totally erroneous and anti-historical. "After the *second pivot* of society's organization had emerged, the fate of the revolution would be decided in the confrontation of forces representing the old system of power and the second pivot"; before that, spontaneous confrontations between unorganized grassroot rebels and the government would be either no more than symptoms of some wider "change-inducing" issues or, at best, powerful outside impulses for the second pivot to form itself within the system and start initiating the real process of revolutionary changes, e.g. by organizing the disenchanted masses for an active support of those changes.[184]

It follows from the above that the Polish model seems to be relevant in terms of change only insofar as it could initiate developments within the official system leading to its split into "two pivots" in accordance with the other previously considered scenarios of change. Indeed, the Central Committee (or the Politburo) could split into two pivots on the grounds of the differing views of its members as to how one should deal with rebellious grassroot manifestations or which policies one should adopt in order to prevent the occurrence of such manifestations in the future. In a similar way such manifestations could serve as a pretext or stimulus for the Army or any other public body to challenge the authority of the Party's leadership and thus become second pivots themselves.

Grassroot manifestations are therefore able to trigger off latent tensions within the official system and could be used by certain forces there as a proper, and probably long-awaited, opportunity for making their decisive bid for power, but by and in themselves they do not represent an independent and self-sufficient model of change. If that is really the case, why should one then consider the Polish model as a basis for a separate scenario of change at all? Is it not more correct to regard it as merely one of the many possibilities for the initiation of any proper scenario? The answer to that is "no," simply because the Polish situation of 1980 differed from other as far as the striking workers in Gdansk's Lenin shipyard managed to develop a coherent organizational structure not simply on a local scale, but in the form of a United Strike Committee which very soon established its authority on a national scale. (One should note that the existence in Poland of a strong, and at that time yet unsuppressed, overt dissident movement was in this respect of decisive importance, especially insofar as the process of formation of the United Strike Committee's authoritative leadership was concerned.)

This organizational structure, being at its inception an "outside body" to the system, was, of course, not yet a proper second pivot, since it could neither have split the system nor have immediately acquired a recognized place within it, in order to be able to produce such a split. But as soon as it emerged *beside* the official system it became an important force to be seriously reckoned with by the Polish communist government. Faced with an outside public body of such magnitude and strength, this government had only two choices: either to crush it as an unauthorized (and thus, in official terms, illegitimate) creation or to grant it official recognition, at least to a certain extent. The latter alternative for which, after some hesitation, the Polish authorities temporarily opted when they accepted this United Strike Committee as a valid partner for the negotiation of a settlement with the strikers, meant nothing else but the institutionalization of this Committee within the official system. This Committee, and later the "Solidarity" trade union, by being thus institutionalized shook the foundations of Polish communist totalitarianism and assumed in it automatically the role of the second pivot.

There were no inner constraints preventing this newly-established and officially recognized public body from fully realizing its immense potential. Without the external constraint of possible Soviet intervention, the whole official totalitarian system in Poland would have been toppled by this second pivot immediately and irreversibly. But the presence of this external constraint, of which all the forces comprising the Polish second pivot were only too well aware (not least because of the Catholic Church and the dissident Workers' Defense Committee, KOR, constantly drawing the workers' attention to it), restrained operations of this second pivot to an extent which allowed the official system to survive, remain essentially unaffected, and then redress itself by the means of the "military" coup.[185]

At any rate, the Polish model is just one more way in which the second pivot can be formed in society, with all the implicit consequences (and in the

Soviet Union's case, with no artificial constraints to prevent it from fully developing, these consequences, as far as the régime is concerned, can only be fatal). The only difference is that here the second pivot emerges not as a result of the system's split from inside but because of the system's attempt at incorporating an outside body, unmergeable with it; the split is thus produced in the system by the incorporation of that body into it.

In conclusion, one should note that a power crisis in Poland or in any other satellite country can produce a profound destabilizing effect on the Soviet Union itself. After all, the Soviet bloc is an integral empire and everything which happens on its outskirts is bound directly to affect the center. In other words, a part of the empire setting itself firmly against the center and the center, in response, setting itself against that part of the empire also produces a "two-pivotal" situation with all the possible consequences that this situation may entail.

Poland, where the crisis is far from being settled, is still the strongest contender to produce such a two-pivotal situation again and thus strongly challenge the stability of the Soviet system itself. For everybody, in Poland and elsewhere, has now understood that no change will be possible in Poland or any other part of the Soviet bloc until changes occur in Moscow. Hence, any move worthwhile undertaking in Poland or in any other Soviet dependency, should be precisely timed and have sufficient strength to make a real impact on stability in Moscow.

Concluding Remarks on the Next Step in
Russia's Political History

The "second pivot" is an issue of crucial importance insofar as it is the only reliable indication of the beginning of political change either in the Soviet Union or in any other authoritarian system. With the second pivot theory, Soviet watchers are acquiring a reliable instrument for a proper assessment of the significance of different events in their relation to political change. This applies especially to Kremlinologists whose criteria of evaluation of changes are now so confused and grossly lacking in methodology. But what kind of political change should we expect in the Soviet Union if the second pivot finally appeared there and started functioning? What are, in other words, the possible alternatives to the present Soviet political system?

Having explored the possible ways of, and positively assessed the prospects for, political change in the Soviet Union, one must also consider its foreseeable consequences. Western scholars usually discuss this problem in the context of a simple opposition between dictatorship and democracy or hegemony and polyarchy.[186] In other words, for them, change becomes a real issue only insofar as a hegemonic order can be replaced by a polyarchic one (or vice versa), or at least insofar as one can envision such a replacement. No wonder these scholars assess chances for political change in the Soviet Union as extremely grim. Indeed, if one identifies political change in the Soviet Union with the establishment there of a Western liberal democracy, one is bound to come to pessimistic conclusions. After nearly seventy years of effective suppression of political freedom, all the requisites of political society in the U.S.S.R. have been rooted out, and it will take some time for them to reappear in that country.

In this context, the arguments about the inevitable replacement of partocrats by technocrats in the position of power also lose for a Western scholar all their impressiveness. As Walter D. Connor pointed out, the professionalization (or technocratization) of the Soviet élite is not necessarily linked with political change because technocrats are not necessarily democrats.[187] "The technical intelligentsia has essential skills, but most of its members cannot be numbered among the dissidents."[188] The broad masses of Soviet people, according to Connor, are also not a serious factor of change because, as he points out, they "do not demand legality, representative institutions, freedom. . . The interest in freedom and the rule of law is not broad enough, is not sufficiently a 'mass' interest, to make its accommodation critical."[189] Both these points about the technocrats and the masses are perhaps true, but political change in the U.S.S.R. does not necessarily imply the establishment of "legality, representative institutions, freedom." Political change in the Soviet Union is indeed unlikely to involve the establishment of democratic rule, but it is very likely to establish a *rational* and nationally-minded government as opposed to the present *irrational*, single-ideology-based, and clique-minded régime. In fact, while the new rational government that would emerge from political change in the U.S.S.R. would have the full support of the technocrats, as well as of the overwhelming majority of people, it may also be authoritarian for a significant period of time.

But, as I have argued elsewhere, "authoritarianism is not totalitarianism, because authoritarian rule does not necessarily encompass in a rigid framework all spheres of human life and activity."[190] Any new political régime in the U.S.S.R., authoritarian or not, will not only be compatible with a pluralistic economic pattern and with considerable autonomy for the economic system *vis-à-vis* the state (i.e., with the re-emergence of an autonomous civil society) but, if it is to command the support of the technocrats, must be explicitly based on these principles. Such a régime, authoritarian or not, will do away with the sole official ideology (in a framework of national ideology, quite a few political, social and religious ideologies can co-exist) and thus provide conditions for the emergence of a pluralistic ideological pattern in social life. Ideological pluralism, in its turn, implies more freedom for creative work and for expression of different interests, including those now represented by civic, national, and partially religious dissent (partially, because any degree of ideological tolerance would automatically solve the problems of most religious groups). Under such a régime, the necessary preconditions for creating a democratic system of government could evolve in due course, too, but the establishment of a democracy (polyarchy) is indeed not the most immediate and realizable task in the struggle to bring about political change in the U.S.S.R. The most important task here consists of liquidating totalitarianism and this is what political change in the U.S.S.R. is going to mean in the first place.

The first post-Soviet government of Russia may be, in a way, similar to the Bonapartist régime in France after Napoléon's 1799 18th of Brumaire coup, but without its Jacobin flare. (I am referring here to the authoritarian form of Bonapartism which Napoléon I successfully used for building up a modern administrative system for the French state and for introducing a body of codified law, marking the borderline between France's civil society and her polity, rather than to Napoléon's ideologically-motivated plans of conquering Europe and establishing "progressive" France as the leading power on the continent.) This first post-Soviet government of Russia, whatever its character or ideology (although there is little doubt that it will be technocratic in character and nationalist in ideology) and whatever the mechanism of the formation of the "second pivot" by which it will be created, before doing anything else, will have to solve the following three main problems:

1. The first is that of separating the civil society from polity—that is to say, dismantling totalitarianism and creating a comprehensive legal system that would provide the necessary conditions for effective functioning of social and economic institutions not under the discretionary rule of the Party-state but under the rule of law, i.e. in an autonomous and basically self-sufficient way. Some could call it the reinstitution of private enterprise and free market.

2. The second is that of sorting out the complex network of tense, hostile and, in some cases, directly antagonistic intra-national relations within the Soviet Union, as well as in Soviet-dominated Eastern Europe, in order to create some organic ground for peaceful cooperation between Russia and other nations involved. It seems to me that any post-Soviet government will try to reach a consensus with the non-Russian nations of the area by conceding to their respective demands of either sovereignty or genuine

autonomy in exchange for firm guarantees on the part of those nations of the inviolability of Russian national interests within respective national territories.

3. The third problem is that of putting an end to more than sixty years of artificial, purely ideologically-motivated and, by no rational standards necessary, confrontation between the East and the West, and of establishing, in accordance with the national interests of all parties involved, a pattern of Russia's genuine cooperation with the Western world, above all with the other superpower—the U.S.A. This problem will be of special importance and its settlement of paramount urgency as it will, among other things, create the pattern of international stability and cooperation between major powers of the world, without which it would be virtually impossible to achieve a reliable settlement of the second problem of settling intra-national relations within the present Soviet realm of rule, as well as of other international issues in which Russia has a vital interest (e.g. the Sino-Russian conflict), and also very difficult to accelerate adequately Russia's economic development.

With Russia busy settling the above issues, both the present Soviet realm and the entire world should become much safer and better to live in.

NOTES

The fundamental research for this section was carried out when the author was a Visiting Scholar at the Hoover Institution, for whose generous support he wishes to acknowledge his profound gratitude.

1. "Left-Wing Communism—An Infantile Disorder" (1920), quoted from Robert C. Tucker, ed., *The Lenin Anthology* (New York: Norton, 1975), 602. Lenin repeated here the idea he had first formulated and elaborated at greater length in his longish article, "The Downfall of the Second International" (Summer 1915). There, however, he talks, in the same terms, about the symptoms of a revolutionary situation only, whereas in "Left-Wing Communism," he unequivocally declares the quoted formula to be "the fundamental law of revolution."
2. *Republic*, 545d, (quoted from J. Adam's edition of *Republic of Plato*, Vol. II).
3. Ibid. (quoted from A.D. Lindsay's edition of *Plato, The Republic*).
4. The term "great revolution" was used by many theorists and philosophers, inclusive of de Tocqueville and Marx, but was defined as "reconstitution of the state" by George S. Pettee with a special view of providing a taxonomical distinction between revolution proper and all other political change brought about by drastic and/or violent means (such as putsch, coup d'état, etc.). For further reference, see George S. Pettee, *The Process of Revolution* (New York: Harper & Brothers, 1938), 3ff.

5. *Revolution* (Oxford: Basil Blackwell, 1975), 102.

6. *Treatise on General Sociology,* §2054, but also §2057 and §2058.

7. *Revolutionary Change,* 2nd ed. (London: Longman, 1983), 108.

8. This is Max Weber's shortest and most general definition of legitimacy. (Quoted from Max Rheinstein, ed., *Max Weber on Law in Economy and Society* [Cambridge, Mass.: Harvard University Press, 1954], 328.)

9. This idea permeates the whole of Marx's work, especially *The Class Struggles in France* (1848-1850), *The Eighteenth Brumaire of Louis Bonaparte* (1852), and *Civil War in France* (1871).

10. *Manifesto of the Communist Party* (1848); quoted from Robert C. Tucker, ed., *The Marx-Engels Reader,* 2nd ed. (New York: Norton, 1978), 490.

11. *Democracy in America* (1835-1840). Especially relevant here is p. 274 of the Simon & Shuster (New York, 1964) edition.

12. Ibid.

13. The term "millenarianism" to characterize such movements and their rule was introduced and elaborated by Chalmers Johnson in *Revolution and the Social System* (Stanford: Hoover Institution Press, 1964), especially 35-39.

14. "Left-Wing Communism," 602. Popular revolt may cause such a "nation-wide crisis" and/or be an expression of it.

15. For Chalmers Johnson's discussion of different kinds of courses of action open to the ruling élite during "power deflation. . .from conservative change to its poiar opposite, complete intransigence," see his *Revolutionary Change,* 96-100 (the above quotation is on p. 96).

16. F. Znakov, *Pamyatnaya zapiska* (Memorandum), in Radio Liberty's *Arkhiv Samizdata* (Samizdat Archives), No.374 (1966): 21-22.

17. "*Nomenklatura*: The Soviet Communist Party's Leadership Recruitment System," in *Canadian Journal of Political Science* 2, No.4 (December 1969):493-512. See also his *Political Elite Recruitment in the Soviet Union* (London & Basingstoke: Macmillan, 1984).

18. *The Soviet Prefects* (Cambridge, Mass: Harvard University Press, 1969), esp. 114-116 and 150-170.

19. *Nomenklatura: Die herrschende Klasse der Sowjetunion* (*Nomenklatura*: The Ruling Class of the Soviet Union) (Vienna-Munich-Zürich-Innsbruck: Fritz Molden Verlag, 1980). The German edition was first, the French followed soon, and in English this book was published by Bodley Head (London) in 1984, the same year in which the Russian original appeared (Overseas Publications Interchange, London). Not everyone agrees with Voslensky's definition of the *nomenklatura* as the ruling class. Some even take strong issue with that contention. See, for example, John F. Miller, "The Communist Party: Trends and Problems," in Archie Brown & Michael Kaser, eds., *Soviet Policy for the 1980s* (London & Basingstoke: Macmillan, 1982), 21.

20. Out of the population of 274 million and of the Party membership of just above 18 million. Not all *nomklats*, however, are card-carrying members of the Party. Maybe about 10-15% of them on the lowest level, and some, though very few, on the higher levels, are not. The figure of not less than 2 million *nomklats* is arrived at by John F. Miller, "The Communist Party," 21. In my estimation

there should be about 5 million *nomklats* in the whole of the U.S.S.R.

21. This is the term by which the members of the Politburo and the CPSU CC's Secretariat are mockingly referred to by people in the U.S.S.R. In private communications it is used universally—a fact duly reflected in Vasily Aksenov's novel, *Ostrov Krym* (The Crimean Island) (Ann Arbor, Michigan: Ardis, 1981).

22. For a recent comprehensive review and profound analysis of the state of discussion of "interest groups" in Soviet politics by one of the founding fathers of the "interest-group" approach to the study of the U.S.S.R., see H. Gordon Skilling, "Interest Groups and Communist Politics Revisited," *World Politics* XXXVI, No. 1 (October 1983): 1-27.

23. Jerry F. Hough, "The Soviet System: Petrification or Pluralism," *Problems of Communism* XXI, No.2 (March-April 1972): 41-42; repeated by the same author in Jerry F. Hough & Merle Fainsod, *How the Soviet Union is Governed* (Cambridge, Mass.: Harvard University Press, 1979), 554-555; 567.

24. A. Shtromas, *Political Change and Social Development: The Case of the Soviet Union* (Frankfurt a/Main-Bern: Verlag Peter Lang, 1981), 70.

25. Ibid., p.71

26. Milton C. Lodge, *Soviet Elite Attitudes Since Stalin* (Columbus, Ohio: Charles E. Merrill Publishing Co., 1969), 34.

27. Ibid.

28. Ibid., 40.

29. Ibid., 115. Milton C. Lodge rightly includes the military into the specialist élite, too.

30. In fact, Lodge includes all these strata into the specialist élite broadly defined by him.

31. "Group Conflict and Political Change," in Chalmers Johnson, ed., *Change in Communist Systems* (Stanford, Calif.: Stanford University Press, 1973), 217 and 220.

32. "Dissent and Social Change in the U.S.S.R. and Poland," *Studies in Comparative Communism* XII, Nos. 2 & 3 (Summer/Autumn, 1979): 250.

33. The term "colored markets" (meaning different kinds of unofficial markets of which the black market is only one) was introduced by Aron Katsenelinboigen who also gave a brilliant analysis of their operation in the U.S.S.R. and proved the involvement in these "colored markets" of the whole population. (See his *Soviet Economic Planning* (White Plains, N.Y.: M.E. Sharp, 1978), 165-201. For some elaboration on that subject see also A. Shtromas, *Political Change and Social Development* (in note 24), 71-74; and A. Shtromas, "Crime, Law and Penal Practice in the U.S.S.R.", in *Review of Socialist Law* 3, No. 3 (September 1977): 297-324, but especially 298-301.

34. For the richest collection of cases of economic crime and corruption involving high officials, from within all layers of *nomenklatura*, see Konstantin M. Simis, *U.S.S.R.: Secrets of a Corrupt Society* (London-Melbourne-Toronto: J.M. Dent & Sons, 1982).

35. "To Fight Communism: Why and How?" *International Journal on World Peace* 1, No. 1 (Autumn 1984): 20-44, but especially 27-28 and 37-39.

36. See: "Dissent and Political Change in the U.S.S.R.," in *Studies in Comparative*

Communism XII, No. 2 & 3 (Summer/Autumn 1979): 212-244, but especially 222-235.

37. The term was coined by Abdurakhman A. Avtorkhanov; see his two volumes *Proiskhozhdenie partokratii* (The Origins of Partocracy) (Frankfurt a/Main: Posev Verlag, 1973); and in English, *The Communist Party Apparatus* (Chicago: Henry Regnery & Co., 1966).

38. Igor Yefimov (Moskovit), another prominent Soviet author (both official and samizdat) now in exile, thinks that the term "technocrats" is inapproprate since skills in technology characterize only a part of this category of people. Henceforth, he proposes to call them the "informstructure," in analogy with J. K. Galbraith's "technostructure." (See his contribution to the present series Vol. II, *The Economy and Society,* Part 3 [New York: Paragon House, forthcoming]). One could indeed call the Soviet counter-élite "informstructure," or "specialists," as M. C. Lodge does, or any other way. I personally prefer the term "technocrats" because it has acquired in social science literature (particularly in the French one) "citizenship rights" for describing specialists whose political ideas and goals are determined by what they see as optimal conditions for application of their professional skills, whatever these skills may be. It is also in my view the most convenient term to be used as an antonym to "partocrats."

39. "Totalitarian Rule and Social Change," in Z. Brzezinski, ed., *Dilemmas of Change in Soviet Politics* (New York & London: Columbia University Press, 1969), 77.

40. London, Unwin Books, 1972; 146-147.

41. *Die Totengräber des Kommunismus* (Stuttgart: Steinbrüben Verlag, 1964), 150.

42. *Pamyatnaya Zapiska,* 12.

43. Ibid.

44. Ibid., 7. For F. Znakov's whole reasoning on this subject, see ibid., 7-12.

45. "Co-optation as a Mechanism of Adaptation to Change: The Soviet Political Leadership System," in Roger E. Kanet, ed., *The Behavioral Revolution and Communist Studies* (New York: Free Press, 1971), 138; and "System Attributes and Career Attributes: The Soviet Political Leadership System, 1952 to 1965," in Carl Beck, ed., *Comparative Communist Political Leadership* (New York: David McKay Co. Inc., 1973), 57-58.

46. This decline established by Seweryn Bialer in *Stalin's Successors: Leadership, Stability and Change in the Soviet Union* (Cambridge: Cambridge University Press, 1980), 117–122. He explains it by high levels of continuity in the middle and upper leadership posts, but he also notes the increase in promotions from within the Party apparatus as substitute for ''co-optation of specialists.'' This, to me, is indicative of the partocrats' fear of ''technocratic infiltration'' and their desire not to allow their control to be weakened or challenged by any outsiders.

47. See S.A. Kugel', ''Izmenenie sotsial'noy struktury sotsialisticheskogo obshchestva pod vozdeystviem nauchno-teknicheskoy revolyutii,'' (The change of the social structure of the socialist society under the influence of the scientific-technical revolution) in *Voprosy Filosofii,* No.3 (1969): 18–19.

48. *Itogi vsesoyuznoy perepisi naseleniya, 1970* (Results of the All Union Population

Census), 111, (Moscow: Statistika, 1971); 6–7.

49. *Vestnik Statistiki,* No. 6 (1980): 41.

50. See, for instance, Fedor M. Burlatsky, "Notion of Ideological Régime," a paper presented to the Tenth World Congress of the International Political Science Association, Edinburgh, August 1976.

51. This information is based on published short memoirs on Gorbachev by his former student colleagues, now émigrés residents in the West. One such memoir is Lev Yudovich's published in *Time* magazine; another is by Zdenek Mlynarz, "Il mio compagno di studi Mikhail Gorbaciov," *L'Unita*, April 19, 1985: 9.

52. His first very well documented positive assessments of Gorbachev are: "Leadership Succession and Policy Innovation," in Brown & Kaser, *Soviet Policy for the 1980s*, 223-253; "Postscript: July 1982," Ibid., 267-272; but, more importantly, "Gorbachev: New Man in the Kremlin," *Problems of Communism* 34, No.3 (May-June 1985): 1-23; and "Can Gorbachev Make a Difference?" *Détente*, No.3 (May 1985): 4-7.

53. The Information Report on the CPSU CC's Plenary Session that selected Gorbachev to the General Secretaryship (as published in *Pravda* of 12 March 1985) refers to this selection as *edinodushno* (in a united spirit) instead of *edinoglasno* (unanimously).

54. See Stephen Milligan, "Time-Check on Gorbachev," *Sunday Times*, 16 June 1985, 17; and "Inside Moscow," by the same author, *Sunday Times*, 23 June 1985, 22. Milligan's information was confirmed by many independent sources during 1986 and 1987.

55. From reliable sources I learned that during the selection of Gorbachev, some members of the CPSU's CC stated their case in Gorbachev's favor by saying that it is high time for the U.S.S.R. to project to the world a vigorous image again and thus "rub the noses" *(uteret' nos)* of those imperialist enemies who expect us to grow weaker.

56. Romanov was brought to Moscow as an ideal compromise figure, equally unsuitable and equally acceptable both to the Andropovites and Chernenkoites. Andropov knew that Romanov was his arch-enemy but he had enough compromising material against him to keep him in check, either by making him to behave or, alternatively, by ousting him from office, and ending his career for good. Chernenko did not like or respect Romanov, but, as an arch-anti-Andropovite, Romanov was, at the moment, entirely acceptable to him. Both were pleased to bring in an outsider to Moscow's power network and thus a Politburo weakling unable seriously to challenge any of its strongmen, and also avoid controversy about choosing either a new member of the Politburo or strengthening the hand of any of the existing members, all of whom were stronger than Romanov and established as either Andropov's or Chernenko's men.

57. See "V Politburo TsK KPSS," (In the Politburo of the CPSU's CC) *Pravda*, 22 March 1985, 1.

58. The Report states that the Politburo has also discussed the CPSU's relations

with other "communist, socialist and national-democratic parties," but it does not refer to any decisions taken in this field.

59. For the acceptance speech, see *Pravda*, 12 March 1985, 3; for the funeral speech—*Pravda*, 14 March 1985, 1.

60. See, for example, his Report to the April Plenary Session of CPSU's CC in *Pravda*, 24 April 1985; his Report "Korennoy vopros ekonomicheskoy politiki Partii," (The key problem of the Party's economic policy) delivered to the meeting called by the CPSU's CC to discuss the problems of the acceleration of the scientific technical progress, in *Pravda*, 12 June 1985; his speech in Dnepropetrovsk metal factory, in *Pravda*, 27 June 1985; as well as the Political Report of the CPSU CC to the 27th Congress of the CPSU delivered by Gorbachev on February 25, 1986 (the full official text published in *Pravda* 26 February 1986).

61. *Pravda*, 27 June 1985, 1; exactly the same line of argument he presented in the Report to the 27th Congress of the Party (*Pravda*, 26 February 1986, 5).

62. *Pravda*, 27 June 1985, 2.

63. Ibid. It is interesting to note that for the first time here Gorbachev discussed the problems of improving quality in such a "reduced" context. In his Report to the April Plenary Session of the CPSU's CC (*Pravda*, 24 April, 1) as well as in the Report to the meeting called by the CPSU's CC to discuss the problems of the acceleration of the scientific technical progress (*Pravda*, 12 June 1985, 1), Gorbachev gave quality a much higher and more independent profile by putting it before quantity in the context of changes in economic planning, material incentives, etc.

64. *Pravda*, 26 February 1986, 5.

65. Ibid., 6.

66. *Pravda*, 24 April 1985, 1. It is worthwhile noting that at the 27th Congress of the CPSU the decisions of the April (1985) Plenary session of the CPSU's CC were constantly referred to as the main landmark setting the pace of the U.S.S.R.'s development into the next century. Since the April (1985) Plenary Session of the CPSU's CC, Gorbachev has frequently referred to *perestroyka* (restructuring) as being equal to revolution.

67. See M. Gorbachev, "Sel'sky trudovoy kollektiv: puti sotsial'nogo razvitiya," (Rural Working Collective: Ways of Social Development) *Kommunist*, No.2 (January 1976): 29-38. For a detailed but rather more skeptical analysis of Gorbachev's policy pronouncements during his First Secretaryship of the Stavropol Provincial Committee of the CPSU (the Party's *kraykom*) see G.G. Weickhardt, "Gorbachev's Record on Economic Reform," in *Soviet Union/Union Soviétique* 12, Part 3 (1985): 251-276; esp. 253-259.

68. See his "Kolektivnomu podryadu na sele—shirokuyu dorogu" (For the Collective Contract in Rural Areas—A Wide Road), in *Pravda*, 20 March 1983, advocating these popular ideas and, at the same time, never voicing support for official policies such as the Brezhnevite Food Program or Chernenkoite expansion of arable lands; in fact, he was thus implicitly challenging these policies and, at the same time, cleverly disclaiming responsibility for the failing harvests and the notorious general malfunction of Soviet agriculture of which he was officially in charge. I think that George Weickhardt clearly underestimates Gorbachev when

he says that his attitudes to reform prior to his appointment as General Secretary were "neither new nor radical nor were they his original ideas" ("Gorbachev's Record,": 276). Although, agreed, his ideas were neither new nor original, in the given circumstances they certainly were bold and non-conformist. Weickhardt rightly stresses that the "collective contract" is not identical with the autonomous link because the "collective contract" could be concluded also with the larger, mostly specialized, brigade, and that it in practice does not "key link members' compensation entirely to the volume of their harvest" (Ibid., 265). What he, however, disregards, is the fact that in the context of Gorbachev's pronouncements to which he refers the "collective contract" is merely a codephrase for the advocacy of the "autonomous link"—a codephrase that Gorbachev had to use in order to be able publicly to discuss unconventional ideas within the conventionally acceptable framework (for "collective contract," in contrast with the "autonomous link," was then too within the range of agricultural policies acceptable to the Party).

69. For a partial confirmation of this, see John N. Hazard, "Legal Trends," in Brown & Kaser, *Soviet Policy*, 102.
70. "Leadership Succession and Policy Innovation," in Brown & Kaser, 241-242 and 244-245.
71. *Pravda*, 26 February 1986, 4.
72. Ibid. Prominent Soviet economists V. Belkin and V. Perevedentsev, the two main proponents of the experiment with family-based productive links mounted by Ivan Khudenko in the late 1960s in Kazakhstan's state farm Akchi, managed to publish a page-long article in April 1987, highly praising Khudenko's initiative and calling it "not the past, but the future of Soviet agriculture" (see their "Drama Akchi" [The Akchi Drama], *Literaturnaya Gazeta,* 1 April 1987, 12). There was, however, no word in this lengthy article on how Khudenko managed to increase the Akchi farm's productivity six times and the farmers' earnings threefold in one single year, other than stating that he had used the now fashionable principle of the "collective contract" creatively. The article seems to be aimed not so much at propagating the Akchi experiment as at accusing the now disgraced Kazakhstan's CP CC's then First Secretary, Dinmukhamed Kunaev, of viciously destroying the Akchi experiment and of putting Khudenko into jail under false charges, all in an effort to protect his and his cronies' vested interests against the interest of the Party and the state. The fact that the advocates of family link based organization of Soviet agriculture, trying to resuscitate the debate on Khudenko's experiment, have to take advantage of the Kunaev bashing campaign, and even then limit their remarks to hints and unsubstantial issues, is a clear enough indication that the Soviet rulers do not consider going for an agricultural reform along the Chinese path or Khudenko's (which is one and the same thing), deeming the whole subject of family links taboo, despite *glasnost'*. It, furthermore, demonstrates the limits of both *glasnost'* and Gorbachev's personal power, which appears to be insufficient even for putting to full-scale debate an issue about which Gorbachev is on record as having very strong and positive feelings. It is, nevertheless, very significant that *Literaturnaya Gazeta* (probably with Gorbachev's personal connivance) had the

courage to bring Khudenko's name back into circulation, first, by briefly and modestly questioning the legitimacy of his conviction some fifteen years ago on criminal charges (see: A. Vaksberg, "Komu eto nuzhno?" [Who needs it?], *Literaturnaya Gazeta,* 21 January 1987, 10) and now, by defending him outright, though without explicitly disclosing what is being defended.

73. Published by the way of summary in *Pravda,* 29 March 1986.

74. Ibid., 1.

75. Ibid., 2.

76. In fact a series of decrees: the CPSU's CC Decision, "On Measures to Strengthen the Struggle Against Unearned Incomes"; the Decree of the U.S.S.R.'s Council of Ministers under the same title; and the Decree of the Presidium of the Supreme Soviet "On Strengthening the Struggle Against the Extraction of Unearned Income," all published by the way of summary in *Pravda,* 28 May 1986, 1-2.

77. Ibid., 2. As reported in *Izvestiya* (2 April 1987, 2), the CPSU's CC and the USSR's Council of Ministers have issued a Joint Decree "On Measures to Improve the Work of Collective Farms' Markets," according to which the management of the collective farms' markets in the country is being transferred to *Potrebkooperatsiya* (consumers' cooperatives' agenies) with a view of making the official consumers' cooperatives (operating on the basis of state-fixed prices) the only sellers on these markets to individual customers of agricultural products, which they will be buying wholesale from collective farms and individual producers. This decree marks the end of whatever was left of free market activities in the U.S.S.R. during the post war years.

78. For the full text of the Law "On Individual Working Activities" see *Pravda,* 21 November 1986; 1–2.

79. See O.S. Ioffe's contribution to the present series, Vol. II, *The Economy and Society,* Part 1 (New York: Paragon, forthcoming). Earlier a similar idea was put forward by the prominent French historian Alain Besançon, according to whom "there exist two, and only two, general models of Soviet politics. Since both of them have been applied during the very early years of the régime, I will define them by their inaugural names of *war communism* and *NEP." (Court traité de sovietologie à l'usage des autorités civiles, militaires et religieuses* [Paris: Hachette, 1976], 23).

80. "But now the situation is such that one cannot limit change to partial improvements—a *radical reform* is necessary." (emphasis added). See *Pravda,* 26 February 1986, 5.

81. For more details on how Andropov's anti-corruption campaign lost momentum, see my contribution to the Symposium on Soviet Law After Brezhnev, in *Soviet Union/ Union Soviétique* Vol.11, part 3 (1984): 319-320.

82. For an elaboration on the theme of the transformation of the Soviet system from totalitarian autocracy into totalitarian oligarchy, see A. Shtromas, "Does Andropov Matter?" in *Hoover Institution Newsclips,* No.82 (March 1984): 820055-56.

83. A.P. Fedoseyev, *O Novoy Rossii: Al'ternativa* (On New Russia: The Alternative) (London: Overseas Publications Interchange, 1980); a shortened and up-

dated version of this program is presented in Fedoseyev's contribution to this volume.

84. Screened on BBC-2 *Newsnight* TV program on 27 February 1986.

85. See El'tsin's speech in *Pravda*, 27 February 1986; 2-3.

86. "Korennoy vopros ekonomicheskoy politiki partii," *Pravda*, 12 June 1985, 2.

87. Ibid., 1.

88. Ibid., 2.

89. Ibid., 1-2.

90. Ibid., 2.

91. Ibid.

92. Ibid., 1.

93. "Can Gorbachev Make a Difference?" in *Détente*, No.3 (May 1985): 5.

94. Ibid.

95. That Gorbachev is busy doing exactly that has been rightly observed in a leading article of the *Times* which, however, had no sympathy for such a kind of endeavor as Gorbachev's at all. According to that article, Gorbachev "appears to be concentrating on eliminating potential opposition, rather than setting out to eliminate the major difficulties, domestic and foreign, with which he should be coping." (*Times*, 1 July 1985, 13). What the *Times* does not appreciate is the fact that without eliminating the opposition and acquiring autocratic power, Gorbachev will not be able to set out to change the policies to the effect of eliminating difficulties at home and abroad.

96. Archie Brown, "Can Gorbachev Make a Difference?" *Détente*: 7.

97. For an analysis of E. Ambartsumov's, A. Butenko's, and B. Kurashvili's views, see Rolf H.W. Theen, "Nomenklatura in the U.S.S.R.: Instrument of Policy and/or Obstacle to Reform," in this series, Volume II, *The Economy and Society*, Part 3 (New York: Paragon, forthcoming). I shall deal here, in more detail, with the views of T. Zaslavskaya and F. Burlatsky.

98. For the full text of the Novosibirsk document in the original, see Radio Liberty's *Arkhiv Samizdata* (Samizdat Archives) (No.5042, 1983). This quotation (as well as the ones which are to follow) is from the English translation, "The Novosibirsk Report," published in *Survey* 28, No.1 (Spring 1984): 88.

99. Ibid., 92, where the same formula as quoted above is in fact repeated but contains this one more sentence which was missing from the opening statement.

100. Ibid., 98.

101. Ibid., 99.

102. Ibid.

103. Ibid.

104. Academician Abel Aganbegyan, then the direct boss of Zaslavskaya in Novosibirsk and a person without whose authority and approval this document could not have been produced, was for many years closely associated with Andropov and acted as his adviser on economic affairs. Aganbegyan enjoys an established reputation of a leading "progressive" Soviet economist advocating radical economic reforms for more than two decades.

105. The first report on that document by Dusko Doder appeared in the *Washington Post* of August 3, 1983.

106. T.I. Zaslavskaya, "Vybor strategii," (The Choice of Strategy), an interview conducted by *Izvestiya*'s special correspondent E. Manucharova, in *Izvestiya*, 1 June 1985, 3.

107. Ibid.

108. Ibid.

109. Ibid.

110. T. Zaslavskaya, "Sotsial'nyi resurs," (The Social Resource) *Sovetskaya Rossiya* (Soviet Russia), 7 January 1986, 1.

111. Ibid.

112. Ibid.

113. "Analiz V.I. Leninym prichin krizisa 1921g. i putey vykhoda iz nego", (V.I. Lenin's Analysis of the 1921 Crisis and of the Ways Out of It) *Voprosy istorii* (Problems of History), No.4 (1984): 15-29.

114. In an article by E. Bugaev, "Strannaya pozitsiya," (A Strange Position) *Kommunist*, No.14 (July 1984): 119-126.

115. See "Posle vystupleniya 'Kommunista'," (After *Kommunist* Spoke), *Kommunist*, No.17 (September 1984): 127.

116. F. Burlatsky, "Lenin i strategiya krutogo pereloma," (Lenin and the Strategy of Drastic Change) *Literaturnaya Gazeta*, 16 April 1986, 2.

117. Ibid. Burlatsky has stated the same objectives in his more recent article, 'Perestroyka: Filosofskyi aspekt'' (Restructuring: the Philosophical Aspect), in *Sovetskaya Kul'tura* (Soviet Culture), 2 April 1987, 3.

118. See G. Ovcharenko's and A. Chernyak's interview with Rekunkov, published under the title "Zakon est' zakon" (The Law is the Law), in *Pravda,* 25 March 1987, 3.

119. Alexander Bovin, "Memory: A Factor to Be Set in Motion", *New Times,* No. 5, March 1987; 9-10.

120. M.S. Gorbachev's Report to the Plenary Session of the CPSU's CC on 27 January 1987, "O perestroyke i kadrovoy politike partii" (On Restructuring and the Personnel Policy of the Party), *Pravda,* 28 January 1987, 3.

121. See "The Crisis of Conscience," in *Moscow News* No. 15 (12 April 1987): 8–9; V. Orlov, " 'Poborniki svobody' trebuyut repressiy'' ('Champions of Freedom' Demand Repressions), *Sovetskaya Kul'tura,* 11 April 1987, 6.

122. *Moscow News,* No. 9, 1 March 1987; 11-12.

123. See n. 100.

124. A. Bovin, op.cit., 9.

125. Vladimir Dudintsev and Igor Gamayunov, "Dialog. O 'mekhanizme tormozheniya' i problemakh psikhologicheskoy perestroyki'. Vse 'ZA', kto zhe 'PROTIV'?" (Dialogue. On the 'Mechanism of Stoppage' and the Problems of Psychological Restructuring. All Are 'FOR', Who Then is 'AGAINST'?), *Literaturnaya Gazeta,* 25 March 1987, 12.

126. A. Bovin, op.cit., 10.

127. "Uchitsa demokratii, utverzhdat' zakonnost'" (To Learn Democracy, to Assert Legality), *Kommunist,* No. 5, March 1987, 3.

128. "The Novosibirsk Report," 88.

129. Ibid.

130. "Korennoy vopros ekonomicheskoy politiki partii," *Pravda*, 12 June 1985, 1. This is, by the way, one obvious example of the affinity between Gorbachev's and Zaslavskaya's way of thinking and presenting arguments for change.

131. Reports by travelers and émigrés are incredibly unanimous about it throughout the last 15 years. The most incisive and detailed analysis of such attitudes is given in George Feifer's "Moscow's Angry Silence," *Sunday Times* 20 July 1980, from which the quotations are taken.

132. In Soviet parlance this is called *pripiski* (additions). According to official policy pronouncements and critical articles appearing in the Soviet press, *pripiski*, in spite of them being made a criminal offense, are still practiced by all Soviet enterprises and offices without exception. This is understandable since the greater the figure in the statistical report the bigger the prestige of the office and the bonuses of its personnel. The magnitude and persistence of the problem of *pripiski* and *ochkovtiratel'stvo* (eye-wash) was once again emphasized in the Decree of the U.S.S.R.'s Council of Ministers "On Measures to Strengthen the Struggle Against Unearned Incomes" published on May 28, 1986, and referred to in the preceding section (see note 76). The Decree introduces additional measures to be applied by the state bodies in order to combat this phenomenon (see *Pravda*, 28 May 1986, 2).

133. For example, to name a few most prominent and best publicized instances: the strike turned into a riot in Temir-Tau (1959); workers' riot in Groznyi (1961); the famous Novocherkassk workers' uprising (1962), and Dneprodzerzhinsk workers' rebellion (1972). For more details on and sources substantiating these events, see Roland Gaucher, *L'Opposition en URSS 1917-1967* (Paris: Albin Michel, 1967), 359; Jean Chiama & Jean-Francois Soulet, *Histoire de la dissidence: Oppositions et révoltes en URSS et dans les démocraties populaires de la mort de Staline à nos jours* (Paris: Seuil, 1982), 286-288; Joseph Godson, "The Role of the Trade Unions," in Leonard Schapiro & Joseph Godson, eds., *The Soviet Worker: From Lenin to Andropov*, 2e (London & Basingstoke: Macmillan, 1984), 123-124, and note 22 on p. 134.

134. The Russian émigré magazine *Posev* (Sowing) regularly publishes letters from the U.S.S.R. which reached the West and in which the situation in the country is frankly, and often emotionally, reviewed. For detailed evidence on Soviet manual workers' anger and frustration with the Soviet régime and the whole Soviet way of life, see Max Ralis, "Workers' Social Perceptions," Schapiro & Godson, eds., *The Soviet Worker*, 237-257; especially 252-257. It is interesting to note that Ralis and his researchers did not come across any Soviet worker who had anything favorable to say about the political, social and economic circumstances of the U.S.S.R. And they have interviewed only those workers who were travelling abroad, i.e. a specially trusted and privileged group.

135. G. Feifer, "Moscow's Angry Silence."

136. Ibid.

137. Ibid. For a summary and sources substantiating the mentioned strikes as well as for some more instances, see: Joseph Godson, "The Role of the Trade Unions,"

in Schapiro & Godson, eds., *The Soviet Worker*: 108-134 and especially 123-124, and note 22 on p.134; and Fyodor Turovsky, "Society Without a Present," Ibid., 162-199, especially 180-182.

138. "Misconceptions About Russia Are a Threat to America," in *Foreign Affairs* 58, No.4 (Spring 1980): 811.

139. Jadwyga Staniszkis, a prominent Polish sociologist and a "Solidarity" activist, succinctly defined the Polish events of 1980-81 as an "auto-limited (or self-limited) revolution." See her *Pologne: La révolution autolimitée* (Paris: Presses Universitaires Libres, 1982) for a briefer summary of her views in English, see her article, "The Evolution of Forms of Working Class Protest in Poland: Sociological Reflections on the Gdansk-Szczecin Case, August 1980," *Soviet Studies* XXXIII, No.2 (April 1981): 204-231, especially 226ff. (in the "Postscript").

140. F. Znakov's expression, and also his idea. See F. Znakov, *Pamyatnaya zapiska*, 23.

141. See William E. Odom, "The Soviet Military: The Party Connection," in *Problems of Communism* XXII, No.5 (September/October 1973): 12-26. For the most detailed, book-length presentation of that position, see Timothy J. Colton, *Commissars, Commanders and Civilian Authority: The Structure of Soviet Military Politics* (Cambridge, Mass. & London: Harvard University Press, 1979). A summary of Colton's views is presented by him in "The Party-Military Connection: A Participatory Model," in Dale R. Herspring & Ivan Volgyes, eds., *Civil-Military Relations in Communist Systems* (Boulder, Col.: Westview Press, 1978), 53-75.

142. See Morton Schwartz, *The Foreign Policy of the U.S.S.R.: Domestic Factors* (Encino, Calif.: Dickenson, 1975), 184; also Michel Tatu, "Decision Making in the U.S.S.R." in Richard Pipes, ed., *Soviet Strategy in Europe* (New York: Crane, Russak & Co., 1976), 53.

143. Stanley Rothman & George W. Breslauer *Soviet Politics and Society* (St. Paul, Minnesota: West Publishing Co., 1978), 253.

144. Odom, "The Soviet Military."

145. Schwartz, *The Foreign Policy of the U.S.S.R.*

146. The leading exponent of this view is Roman Kolkowicz. For a detailed, book-length presentation of his position, see his, *The Soviet Military and the Communist Party* (Princeton, N.J.: Princeton University Press, 1967). A summary of Kolkowicz's views on the subject is given in his, "The Military," in H. Gordon Skilling & Franklyn Griffiths, eds., *Interest Groups in Soviet Politics* (Princeton, N.J.: Princeton University Press, 1971), 131-169. Apart from him, this view is upheld by Mathew P. Gallagher, "Military Manpower: A Case Study," *Problems of Communism* XII, No.3 (May-June 1964); Thomas W. Wolfe, *Soviet Strategy at the Crossroads* (Cambridge, Mass.: Harvard University Press, 1964); and, for a summary, "The Military," in Allen Kassof, ed., *Prospects for Soviet Society* (New York: Frederick A. Praeger, 1968), 112-142; Herbert Goldhammer, *The Soviet Soldier* (New York: Crane, Russak & Co., 1975).

147. A typical representative of such a view among Western scholars is Michael J. Deane; see his *Political Control of the Soviet Armed Forces* (London: Macdonald & Janes, 1977).

148. See his *Détente After Brezhnev: The Domestic Roots of Soviet Foreign Policy* (Berkeley, Calif.: Institute of International Studies, University of California, 1977); *The Russian New Right: Right-Wing Ideologies in the Contemporary U.S.S.R.* (Berkeley: Institute of International Studies, University of California, 1978).

149. "Dyavol menyayet oblik (SSSR: Liberalizatsiya ili Stalinizatsiya)," [The Devil Changes His Image (U.S.S.R.: Liberalization or Stalinization)] *Sintaksis*, No.6 (1980): 88-110, especially 97; 107-109.

150. In a broadcast for the Russian service of the BBC in February 1979, Solzhenitsyn said that he believes that among the people in key positions within the Soviet Army and administration, there are "genuine sons of Russia. And Russia waits for them to fulfill their filial duty." See "Intervyu s. I.I. Sapietsom, BBC" (An Interview with I.I. Sapiets for the BBC) *Vestnik RKhD* (The Messenger of the Russian Christian Movement), No.127, IV (1978): 295.

151. E.g. most exhaustively by Deane, *Political Control of the Soviet Armed Forces.*

152. As quoted from Marshal Rodion Malinovsky's speech at the 22nd Congress of the Party on 23 October 1961; see: *XXII S'ezd Kommunisticheskoy Partii Sovetskogo Soyuza: Stenograficheskyi Otchet* (The 22nd Congress of the Communist Party of the Soviet Union: Stenographic Report) Vol.2 (Moscow: Gospolitizdat, 1962), 120. The main Party document on Zhukov's case is the Decision of the Plenary Session of the CPSU's CC of 29 October 1957, but its content was more fully revealed in various speeches at the 22nd Congress of the Party than in the brief published information on it specifically.

153. As quoted in Nikita Khrushchev's Report to the 22nd Congress of the Party on 17 October 1961 (see Ibid., Vol.1, 107). For a view on the meaning of Zhukov's intentions and actions that is opposite to mine, see Timothy J. Colton, "The Zhukov Affair Reconsidered," in *Soviet Studies* XXIX, No.2 (April 1977): 185-213, and his *Commissars, Commanders*, 175-195.

154. In a popular joke of the time, Zhukov was likened to the carrying rocket and Khrushchev to the space module carried by it to the orbit (the carrying rocket after fulfilling its mission is rejected by the module and its remnants burn out in the atmosphere when falling back to earth).

155. M.J. Deane has convincingly shown that in the last years of Grechko's tenure of office he fell out with the rest of the Politburo on a number of significant issues taking on them a professional military, as opposed to a party-political, stand. Deane argues that this may have played a role in the Politburo's decision to appoint as Grechko's successor a civilian man (see *Political Control of the Soviet Armed Forces*, 268-269).

156. Kolkowicz wittily depicted it, "an up-to-date military machine that is forced to wear a horse-collar of ideological and political controls" (*The Soviet Military*, 341-342).

157. See G.K. Zhukov, *Vospominaniya i razmyshleniya* (Memoirs and Thoughts) Vol.1-2 (Moscow: APN, 1974), especially 1: 314-353.

158. See A. Yanov, "Dyavol. . .", 102.

159. Roman Redlikh has convincingly explained that the national-patriotic ideology easily lends itself to different interpretations because its central concept, the

country's common good, is so broadly based that it inevitably produces a plural pattern of public opinion (i.e. what the best thing for the country today is, what the policy priorities should therefore be, and how policy targets should be achieved is not predetermined but a subject for free discussion) inconceivable under communism with its absolute ideological stereotypes; see his, "Poraboshchenie slovom" (Enslavement by Word), *Posev*, No.7 (July 1980): 38.

160. Especially with artillery Marshal Sergei Varentsov who was his close friend (almost a foster father) from the years of World War II.

161. Oleg Penkovskiy, *The Penkovskiy Papers* (Garden City, N.Y.: Doubleday, 1965), 56. I am convinced that Penkovskiy's papers are genuine and totally dismiss the allegations of them being faked, which deter so many authors from using them for reference.

162. Ibid.

163. "I happened to marry a general's daughter," Penkovskiy writes, "and I quickly found myself in a society of the Soviet upper classes. I realized that their praise of the Party and Communism was only in words" (Ibid., 55).

164. Ibid., 56.

165. For more details, see Gaucher, *L'Opposition en URSS*, 359; Chiama & Soulet, *Histoire de la dissidence* 71-72; 286-288. In a footnote the latter two authors explain that it is not entirely clear whether the cause of the suicide of the commander of the troops that were ordered to put down the rebellion in Novocherkassk was the fact that he received the order to fire at the workers or that the soldiers under his command refused to obey such orders (Ibid., 470). These authors do not refer to the sources substantiating this thesis, but all reports available to me unequivocally suggest that the commander committed suicide after having refused to carry out the received orders. See also Joseph Godson, "The Role of the Trade Unions," in Schapiro & Godson, eds., *The Soviet Worker*, 108-134, especially 123-124.

166. The first report on their arrest appeared in *The Chronicle*'s Issue No.5 (10) of 31 October 1969, under the heading, "Arrests of the officers of the Baltic Fleet" (see in *Posev, Tretiy Spetsial'niy Vypusk* (Posev's Third Special Issue), April 1970: 10). More details of the case were published in *The Chronicle*'s next issue, No.6 (11) of 31 December 1969 (Ibid., 37-38). See also "Eshchio ob areste ofitserov Baltiyskogo flota" (More on the Arrest of the officers of the Baltic Fleet) *Posev* No.1 (1970): 3; and Peter Reddaway, ed., *Uncensored Russia: The Human Rights Movement in the Soviet Union* (London: Jonathan Cape, 1972), 171-183.

167. I have not come across E. Shiffer's work in the West but I read them in samizdat publications in Moscow.

168. VSKhSON (Vserossiyskiy Sotsial'no-Khristyanskiy Soyuz Osvobozhdeniya Naroda—All-Russian Social-Christian Alliance for Liberation of People)—a clandestine organization that aimed at overthrowing the Soviet régime, if necessary, by force. It made its first appearance in Leningrad on February 2, 1964, and was uncovered and destroyed by the KGB in 1967. For the most comprehensive treatment of VSKhSON, see John B. Dunlop, *The New Russian Revolutionaries* (Belmont, Mass.: Nordland, 1976).

169. See Aleksandr Milits, "Esminets 'Storozhevoy'," (Battleship "Storozhevoy") *Posev*, No.6 (June 1967): 4.

170. Ibid.

171. For more details, see Yury Chikarleyev, "Ukradennye leitenanty," (The Stolen Lieutenants) *Posev*, No.10 (October 1976): 24-25.

172. Ibid.

173. The expression is A. Yanov's; see his *The Russian New Right*, where the concept of three coalitions—the "Current" one, the one "of Hope" and the one "of Fear"—is elaborated throughout the book but is most concisely presented in a chart given in Appendix 1 to the book (p. 169).

174. Rothman & Breslauer, *Soviet Politics and Society*, 225.

175. Ibid.

176. Ibid.

177. "Iz-za chego my vernemsya? Beseda s Georgiem Vladimovym" (Why Are We Going to Return? A Conversation with Georgy Vladimov) *Strelets* (The Archer), No.2 (February 1986): 35.

178. The decision to create this Council was formally adopted by the 3rd All-Union Congress of Collective Farmers; see *Tretiy Vsesoyuznyi S"ezd Kolkhoznikov, 25-27 noyabrya 1969 goda. Stenograficheskiy Otchet* (The Third All-Union Congress of the Collective Farmers, 25-27 November 1969: Stenographic Report) (Moscow: Kolos, 1970), 270-272. The details of its organization (from the Union Council to the district councils) and functions are given in its Rules published in *Sbornik Postanovleniy Soveta Ministrov SSSR* (Collection of Decisions of the Council of Ministers of the USSR), No.12 (1971), Art.90.

179. F. Znakov, *Pamyatnaya zapiska*, 23.

180. Jerry F. Hough, "Thinking About Thinking About Dissent," in *Studies in Comparative Communism* XII, Nos.2 & 3 (Summer/Autumn 1979): 271.

181. Ibid.

182. A.Y. Shtromas, "Rejoinder," in *Studies in Comparative Communism* XII, Nos.2 & 3 (Summer/Autumn 1979): 275-276.

183. A recent example is Yuri Borisov's lecture, "Stalin: the Man and the Legend," at the State Institute of History and Archives in Moscow, which was followed by an extremely sharp debate. For a vivid report on this event, see: Elfie Siegel, "Die Moskauer kommen zusammen um Stalin zu kritikieren: in *Frankfurter Rundschau*, March 31, 1987, 4.

184. F. Znakov, *Pamyatnaya zapiska*, 22.

185. Hence, Jadwyga Staniszkis's concept of the "self-limiting revolution" (see note 129). For my more detailed account and assessment of the Polish events of 1980-1981, see: A. Shtromas "Poland: What Next?," Free Life 2, No. 4 (Winter 1981/1982): 14-25.

186. The terms "hegemony" and "polyarchy" were introduced and elaborated by Robert A. Dahl with the view of making the usage of the terms "democracy" and "dictatorship" more differentiated and precise. See his *Polyarchy: Participation and Opposition* (New Haven & London: Yale University Press, 1971).

187. This point is argued at great length in a special section, "Present and Future," of

his article, "Differentiation, Integration and Political Dissent in the U.S.S.R." in Rudolf L. Tökes, ed., *Dissent in the U.S.S.R.: Politics, Ideology and People* (Baltimore: Johns Hopkins University Press, 1975), 152-156.

188. Ibid. 156.
189. Ibid. 155.
190. Alexander Shtromas, "Dissent and Political Change in the Soviet Union," in Erik P. Hoffmann & Robin F. Laird, eds., *The Soviet Polity in the Modern Era* (New York: Aldine Publishing Co., 1984), 740.

2

How the End of the Soviet System May Come About

A Commentary on Section 1

R. V. BURKS

On the whole, I find Professor Shtromas' paper helpful and enlightening. In my view it provides us with three potentially significant additions to our understanding of Soviet affairs. At the same time, however, I also think the paper tends to underestimate the complex and stubborn character of the set of problems that we have all come here to Geneva to struggle with, by way of a conference which, I might add, has been convened largely owing to Dr. Shtromas' dedication and organizing ability.

Let me first summarize the three potential additions to our understanding as I see them.

To begin with, Dr. Shtromas' paper makes clear to me for the first time a possible connection between the professional composition of the Soviet new class and the problem of marketization. His argument runs to the effect that without central planning the élite element he refers to as partocratic could not maintain its position at the apex of the totalitarian pyramid. Contrariwise, the skilled professionals, whom he refers to as technocrats, have an eminently political interest in market reform since under market conditions, their skills and their talents would give them a greater competitive advantage in their inherent conflict with the partocracy. In a market society the technocrats would tend to displace the partocrats, making for more rational governance. Those who read my contribution to this volume (Part II, Section 1) will have observed that my own argument has been strongly influenced by the Shtromas view.

Secondly, the Shtromas paper paints a new picture of General Secretary Mikhail Gorbachev—new at least to me. The Secretary is presented as essentially a technocrat, the first ever to rise to the supreme position in the Kremlin hierarchy, enthroned by aged partocrats to save their rule from the crisis situation to which their own policies had brought it. Thus, the new General Secretary must tread a tricky path until, if ever, he can establish his own personal domination of what Shtromas characterizes as an oligarchic totalitarianism. Gorbachev's need to deal with two constituencies in conflict with each other accounts, according to Shtromas, for the special nature of the Secretary's public utterances. On the one hand, he praises the system built by his senior partocratic colleagues, while, on the other, he woos the technocratic constituency by hinting at rational improvement of that same system.

I find this portrait appealing, especially since it relies heavily on the scholarship of Archie Brown of St. Anthony's College. Whether it is a true portrait I do not venture at the moment to judge, but certainly it provides us all with an hypothesis that should help in sorting out leadership developments in the future.

In the third and last place, Shtromas' paper argues at length and with considerable force for the candidacy of the Soviet army as the second pivot. By this he means that the military would serve as the base of a revolution from above which, while carrying through a market reform and in the process liberating Soviet society from the embrace of a totalitarian state, would govern as a Russian national, but nonetheless rational, autocracy. I am impressed with the paper's evidence in support of the thesis that the Soviet military leaders are not necessarily passionate advocates of Communist totalitarianism but are instead fundamentally technocratic in outlook. At the same time, these leaders constitute, as do the forces they command, a representative cross section of Soviet society, even though they themselves are ethnically Russian and undoubtedly patriotic in that sense.

Nonetheless there is inherent in all three of these potentially valuable contributions to our understanding of Soviet politics a coloring of optimism that may be disturbing to some of us, and mayhap particularly to the historians here.

This brings me to my final point. Let us assume that, in accordance with the Shtromas scenario, the military has taken the role of the second pivot and, after an internal crisis of some duration, has replaced the Party apparatus and the *nomenklatura* as the government of Russia and its dependencies.

Thereupon, asserts Shtromas, the new military dictatorship would be faced with three main tasks: 1) the introduction of the rule of law and, accordingly, the marketization of the economy; 2) the solution of the national problem, in Eastern Europe as well as in Russia; and 3) the termination of 60 years of artificial, ideologically motivated, and irrational confrontation between East and West, together with the establishment of a Russian pattern of genuine cooperation with the Western world.

Let me attempt to examine briefly the second of these, the national problem. Would it not be true to assert that the outer limit of within-system change in the satellite states would be defined by the political situation obtaining at the metropolitan center, i.e., in Moscow? If that is so, then are we not entitled to assume that the crisis that replaced the Party apparatus with the military leadership in Moscow was neither so severe nor so protracted that Solidarity was able to capture control of the Polish government or that the GDR and the FRG were able to unite. Presumably what we would have to deal with would be an Eastern Europe that had become a set of Moscow-oriented military dictatorships. For it does seem to me that if the Soviet military could not retain its hold on the satellites in Eastern Europe, it would encounter difficulty in retaining its hold on power in Moscow. The loss of the satellites, and particularly of East Germany, would shift the military balance sharply in favor of NATO, and I question whether the new dictatorship could survive so severe a blow to Russian national security. By the same token, military Moscow could no more tolerate the Finlandization of the European satellites than Communist Moscow could accept socialism with a human face; in either case the effect on the Muscovite polity itself would be destabilizing.

Furthermore, we must ask ourselves if the new military dictatorship could agree to withdraw its troops from Afghanistan. Could the dictatorship abandon a régime so clearly dependent for its existence upon Moscow at a time when the whole of the socialist community was in turmoil and Third World dependencies, régimes such as the Cuban, were at risk? I, for one, am inclined to doubt it.

This brings us to still another aspect of the national problem, namely, that of the Soviet minority republics. Shtromas suggests that they should be granted either autonomy or sovereignty, at their choice, so long as Russian interests were protected by "firm guarantees on the part of those nations of the inviolability of Russian national interests within [their] respective national territories."

If, for example, the Ukraine should opt for sovereignty, how would Russian maritime egress through the port of Odessa and thence to the Straits, the Mediterranean, and the great outer world be secured? Would Odessa become a Russian free port? Would such an arrangement satisfy the Russian national interest? Would it be acceptable to the Ukrainians?

To take another prominent case, would the Soviet naval and radar facilities located in the Baltic republics be turned over to newly sovereign states? Or would Russian use of these facilities be guaranteed by long-term leases? And, if so, how much would the sovereignty of the restored Baltic states be worth?

Again, I am not sure of the degree of flexibility a Russian military dictatorship could have on issues like autonomy and sovereignty for minority republics. Even less, I should think, than in the case of the satellites. Because, for example, granting sovereignty to such republics as the Ukraine and the Baltic states would mean not only a loss of military advantage vis-à-vis the West, but also a surrender of territories that traditionally have been Russian.

Let us hope that the military dictatorship would at least be willing to settle for a genuine degree of minority republic autonomy. But somehow I do not associate grants of political autonomy with military autocracy. In the event of marketization, furthermore, autonomy granted to minority republics could be used to foster the growth of uneconomic but politically useful heavy industries, as has been the case in Yugoslavia, much to the woe of that Federation.

In thinking of these problems we should, I suppose, remember that the universal mission of world communism, tattered as it may have become, did provide a justification for minority republics, satellite states, and socialist Third World dependencies. For these were way stations on the road to a world government in which war would be unnecessary, poverty banished and . . .—we are well aware of the remainder of this litany. Abandonment of the communist ideology would put on the political agenda of the quondam socialist community such questions as autonomy and sovereignty.

The cases of the Baltic republics and of the Ukraine remind us of the long struggle waged first by Muscovy and then by tsarist Russia to reach the sea, so as to establish a viable connection with that outer world from which it was, unfortunately, necessary to import such devices as gunpowder, warships, and railroads, in order that the country might survive. I am reminded of the fact that the failure of the British effort to seize the Straits in 1915 probably made inevitable the revolutionary upheaval of 1917, for with that failure Russian troops had to be sent to attack enemy positions without sufficient rifles to go 'round.

I would point out also that the recent submarine incidents off the great Swedish naval base at Karlskrona, together with the recent maneuvers of Soviet blue water naval forces off the coast of Norway, strongly suggest that the Muscovite high command intends to occupy the Scandinavian peninsula in the event of conventional war between East and West. Only in this fashion would the Russians be able to base their submarine fleet on the Norwegian fjords, so as to mount an effective attack upon American shipping bound for the European theatre of operations.

Perhaps we should remind ourselves of the fact that even today the Russian superpower possesses maritime outlets to the seas of the world not dominated by potentially hostile states only by way of the White Sea and the Sea of Okhotsk.

One could marshal other arguments in support of the thesis that there inevitably would be some substantial continuities in the policies and outlook of any post-Soviet government, whether military dictatorship or not. The conflict between East and West is, in my view, not primarily a product of an historical accident that brought Communism to power in Russia. Communism is also to some considerable extent the Russian ideology because it is a useful means of promoting Russian national interest in, I would argue, an inherently conflictual situation. Surely no one would contend that the Russians could have turned Cuba communist by occupying it with an expeditionary force!

What concerns me is not so much whether the Communist régime would be followed by a military dictatorship. Indeed, if it were I should think it would be in the Western interest to offer such a dictatorship whatever assistance it would be able to accept.

Rather what concerns me first and foremost is that the economic impasse in which Soviet Russia now finds herself may lead to a system breakdown, even an outbreak of anarchy, that could induce a desperate leadership deliberately to raise the level of international tension—for the present high level of which it must accept major responsibility—in the hope of bringing its citizenry to rally around and restore internal order, and that in conjunction with this maneuver, either through escalation or through accident, a nuclear holocaust could ensue.

3

A Realistic Vision of Change

A Commentary on Section 1

ALEXANDER J. MATEJKO

There is a tendency among many Western sovietologists to "accommodate" themselves to the object of their investigations and take for granted the existence of the Soviet empire. The vested interest of keeping alive the object of professional interest plays here a certain role. However, things change in history and the continuation of human institutions is never a matter of fact. Of course, any investigator should strive to remain free from wishful thinking and, in the case of studying the U.S.S.R. from the Western perspective, we should be careful not to indulge ourselves in making judgments that actually are projections of our feelings and wishes. On the other hand, there is also another danger: to try so hard to be objective that our perspective becomes much too narrow and actually eliminates any courage to consider the possibility of a radical change. In the modern world there are many factors that accelerate the socio-economic, cultural, and political change and make predictions particularly difficult.

Alexander Shtromas in his paper offers a realistic and well documented vision of radical changes in the U.S.S.R. originating mainly from internal developments. The moral collapse of the system and its inability to appeal to a sense of duty and justice is one of the major failures of Soviet communism. The Polish events since 1980 actually give insight into decay of the system in which people do not have enough chance to apply their abilities, improve their standard of living, and self-actualize themselves. Solidarity movement has capitalized on the indignation of working people against the system of reinforced injustice, non-authorized privileges, and waste of human and material capacities.

The Polish revolution has an obvious moral background. People reject the system based on manipulation, oppression, neglect of human dignity, widespread bureaucratization, and self-perpetuation of the ruling élite. In other countries of the Soviet bloc there are similar reasons for mass dissatisfaction, and sooner or later they will activate the oppositional tendencies. These Western politicians, businessmen, and intellectuals who assume the permanence of Soviet communism and even try to take advantage of its rigidity obviously are not well disposed to consider seriously the alternatives discussed by Shtromas and other critics of the Soviet system. In the West this may seriously handicap understanding of various scenarios of Soviet development. We need badly a vivid imagination in this respect in order to be intellectually well prepared to face potential changes.

I appreciate the intellectual imagination and courage of Shtromas in considering possibilities widely denounced by many sovietologists as totally unrealistic and therefore not worthy to be given attention. Radical social change was ignored in the past regarding Iran and several other countries; the cost to the West of this neglect was very considerable. For many people in the West it is difficult to acknowledge the fact that the Soviet system may be *permanently* unbalanced, which badly affects the quality of any calculations regarding the subject of the East-West relations since these calculations are done without taking properly into consideration the Soviet structural disequilibrium. Shtromas takes for granted the weaknesses of this system, and the power demonstrations of the Soviet élite do not impress him; in this respect his position is diametrically opposed to that of those Western experts who just take for granted that the Soviet military and political presence in the world is and will remain unshakable. It is the historical practice of Russian foreign policy to use widely the illusion of power in order to take advantage of their partners and adversaries. Of course, it would be naive to ignore the Soviet military might or the tragic experiences of Soviet people with the foreign invasions, but one should always remember that the overestimation of the Soviet potential is not less misleading or even dangerous than the underestimation of it.

The moral factor is formally recognized within the Soviet communist system in the sense of a collective mobilization of individuals towards official goals. People are expected to be sensitive to "social debt" owed by them to the community and repaid by devoted work and loyalty. This type of morality actually functions effectively in the Israeli kibbutzes, monasteries, religiously oriented collective farms, and other communities willing and able to take care of their members. The Soviet social organization is mainly oriented to the exercise of power and *not* to the welfare of its members. Soviet institutions are understood as sources of oppression and bargaining and not as sources of moral inspiration. The morale of Soviet citizens is low and proof of it may be found in the official pronouncements of political leaders who for years have complained about the low discipline of workers, shoddy products, labor turnover, absenteeism, and stealing of public property.

The major value of this conference is in the substantial extension of developmental alternatives regarding the Soviet bloc. Why ignore the internal contradictions of the system or diminish their significance? The political consequences of the thesis that the Soviet system is stable and permanent are quite obvious. For example, West Germany for years tolerates the aggressive spying activities originating from East Berlin and Moscow; the rationale is that it is acceptable at any cost in order to keep intact good relations with the German Democratic Republic. As long as any alternative to the present system in Russia is voluntarily excluded as impossible, the West is ready to pay heavily for maintaining the status quo. A major extension of political alternatives and the acknowledgement of the possibility of a systemic change in the Soviet bloc would allow the Western decision makers to escape from these self-imposed limits.

There is no reason to identify this greatly enlarged perspective with a "war monger" orientation. The West actually does not have any decisive interest to conquer Russia or even to destroy the Soviet bloc. Things may develop peacefully and total world war is in nobody's actual interest. It is a well-known fact that the Soviet's talking about Western aggressiveness is a basic measure to justify the absolute Soviet rule over many nations. By accepting the Soviet language of peace propaganda the Western mass media unwillingly pay a service to a cause opposed to genuine Western interests. To look for chances of world peace by ignoring the actual Soviet internal situation is definitely not effective in handling the very delicate and complicated network of international relations.

I do not think that it would necessarily be good for the West to destabilize the Soviet bloc; chaos in that part of the world may be very dangerous for world peace, and the Western powers actually have only a limited chance to act effectively in order to promote peace and order outside their own terrain. Several papers presented at this conference show how many factors inside the Soviet bloc actually act for the sake of destabilization: ossification of the ruling élite and the loss of touch with reality, conflicts of interests (between various nationalities, branches of the economy, rural and urban people), inadequate standard of living, inequalities between various strata, suppression of civil rights, heavy burden of external help, low work efficiency, mismanagement of national resources. I agree with Shtromas that present-day U.S.S.R. is already well on the way to destabilization; the unavoidability of a major reconstruction of power relationship is a matter of fact. New developments will happen and it is up to the West to be prepared for them and to act accordingly.

It is very difficult to gain a clear insight into the Soviet affairs, and therefore there is grave danger of misjudgment. The Western democratic framework does not necessarily prepare experts to understand the mechanism of struggle within the Soviet élite, the defense by Polish workers of their collective interests, or the position of local east European élites versus the top Soviet élite. The systemic pressure existing in eastern Europe at all levels of the hierarchy and the collectivistic nature of communist societies both make obsolete many refined and scholarly Western insights. Unexpected developments are possible: oppressed strata and nations may revolt; there may be a major institutional split at the top; military may disobey the orders; the ruling party may be effectively challenged by other groups; the economic inefficiency may inspire reforms undermining the present rulers; some suppressed nations may change alliances.

My image of future events in eastern Europe is the growing confrontation between reformers both inside and outside of the ruling establishment on the one hand, with the people who are objectively and subjectively endangered by the destabilization on the other: *apparatchiks*, leading military circles, various categories of privileged people, lazy bums living at the expense of hard working people, surplus people in the enterprises, employees of the socially useless branches of the economy. There is no chance to implement any reforms without pain and high social costs. Too many people have to be redirected, exposed to the necessity to change their occupational profile, prevented from playing games at the expense of public well-being, deterred from exploiting others and being themselves useless or even harmful. The confrontation of myths with reality must become a matter of fact. So far people in eastern Europe blame each other for economic failure and misconceptions prevail, much reinforced by unreliable statistical data. It will be very difficult to achieve peace and order under such conditions of distrust of everything that looks official.

A major moral revival seems a necessary remedy because without it the reconstruction of East European societies would not be possible. Who will inspire and promote this revival? Marxism is a dead doctrine in eastern Europe and any moral reconstruction based on it is improbable. Orthodox Christianity represents some potential, but its church hierarchy in the Soviet bloc has been much penetrated by secret police in order to make it subservient to Marxist rulers. Roman Catholicism represents a major power only in Poland. Secular humanism is widely spread among the East European intelligentsia, but this does not necessarily mean that this kind of humanism actually may have a large appeal outside the ranks of the intelligentsia. It seems to me that the ideal of self-growth related to the tradition of the great Russian moralistic literature will play a major role in the spirituality of Eastern Europe and that in this particular respect we will witness in the near future substantial development. This actually happens under the somewhat relaxed cultural policy promoted by Gorbachev and his supporters from the ranks of intelligentsia. Several Russian writers and poets have expressed their hopes that the moral message would have now much more chance to escape the official censorship so far pushing Soviet literature and arts into mediocrity and propagandism.

The reality of contemporary eastern Europe is an enigma because only a limited testimony in this respect is available. Probes done by various people and institutions are quite often heavily influenced by particular interests and insights or even biases of the people doing them. This is particularly evident in the Soviet sociology so far limited mostly to praising the official policies. There is much important to be done in order to learn about the Soviet reality and to improve the administration according to the acquired knowledge. Constructive criticism is badly needed in social sciences that are expected to contribute more than just being the obedient servents of the official authority.

Social forces released from the official pressures may be quite different from expectations. For example, it was a major disappointment for many Western leftists to acknowledge the fact that in Poland during sixteen months of relative freedom, Marxism appeared of no real significance among the blue collar workers as well as among intelligentsia. The communist system is probably very superficially rooted in the mentality of people and the relaxation of official pressure may lead in other East European countries to results similar to those in Poland. This would not be very surprising when considering how little was left from the totalitarian movements in Italy, Portugal, Spain, and Germany after the collapse of their rule.

The major future problem will probably be to secure a necessary minimum of cooperation between various nations so far forced to coexist within the Soviet bloc. Goodwill and mutual assistance have to be established in order to rescue the common well-being. These nations badly need each other and it would be against their collective interest for each of them to involve itself in major confrontations. Much has to be done in this respect. For example, Poles and Russians distrust each other and mutually accuse one another of exploitation. International cooperation and assistance in eastern Europe has to be based on new principles which would reinforce trust and mutual satisfaction of nations—something missing under Soviet Communism.

The revival of civil rights in eastern Europe is the necessary condition of any successful reform, but the learning of democratization needs time and much patience. [1] Any new establishment will have major difficulties to overcome in order to improve the work discipline, employment loyalty and commitment to tasks. No miracles can be expected in this respect.

NOTES

1. On this subject see my books *Comparative Work Structures: Ideologies and Reality in Eastern Europe* (New York: Praeger, 1986), as well as *The Self-Defeating Organization* (New York: Praeger, 1986).

PART

IV

THE ALTERNATIVE

A. THE VISIONS

1

Images of the Soviet Future

The Western Scholarly Debate

TERRY McNEILL

Who shall decide, when doctors disagree
And soundest casuists doubt like you and me?
Alexander Pope

Writing on the same theme some seven years ago, George Breslauer identified five recurring images of the future of the Soviet Union in Western scholarship. These range, at one extreme, from the view of the Soviet system as basically stable and capable of coping with the demands placed upon it, to the diametrically opposite view, according to which some kind of fundamental transformation is in the offing. This transformation may be impelled by circumstance, action from above, or insoluble crisis and could take a number of distinctively different political forms.[1]

Since Breslauer offered his analysis events have not stood still. Research has added new insights to our understanding of the Soviet political process. Social and economic problems that existed ten years ago have not lessened but become markedly more acute in the interim. On the other hand, how-

ever, the logam of gerontocracy has at last broken. A younger leadership
has come to the fore and policy options that were previously ruled out of
court are now under active consideration. Given these developments, it is a
good time to take stock once again of our thinking about the U.S.S.R. and
our anticipations about what is likely to be its fate.

The analysis that follows will chart the main trends in Western scholarly
thinking about how the U.S.S.R. is changing. In particular, three frequently
recurring and central projections will be singled out for special attention.
One is the idea that the U.S.S.R. is following an evolutionary course
involving gradual softening and liberalization, leading ultimately to an
obliteration of the contrasts between itself and the Western democracies.
The other is the notion that the system is bound for self-destruction impelled
by its inherent defects and a constituent inability to resolve mounting
problems. The third is, what has been called, "the muddling through" belief.
This sees the party-state system continuing more or less as it is for the
foreseeable future while adapting in a piecemeal way to problems and
difficulties as they arrive.

In a sense, the issues before us are still those posed by Trotsky as the
subtitle of his *Revolution Betrayed*: "What is the Soviet Union and Where is
it Going?" The persisting topicality of these questions may be read as a
manifestation of the intractability of the problem they address and maybe,
too, as a comment on the progress made in fifty years of attempts to
decipher the Soviet enigma. Let us begin with the issue of what the Soviet
state is, for, without knowing what it is, it is difficult to say where it is
going.

The Sui Generis View: The Totalitarian Cul-de-sac

Until the late 1950s, controversy, except among political axe-grinders,
about the nature of U.S.S.R. and its likely future was minimal. Most
scholars accepted the characterization provided by the totalitarian conceptual framework. The totalitarian state, it was held, represented a new,
distinctively twentieth-century political phenomenon, analytically distinct
from other authoritarian or autocratic systems. It was a system where the
power of the state was absolute, civil rights absent, life politicized, society
atomised, and autonomous groups non-existent.

Totalitarianism was seen as the ugly spawn of the fusion of a messianic,
utopian ideology and modern techniques of communication, command, and
control. Totalitarian orders were typically ruled by a dictator operating
through subordinate agencies, the most important of which was a monop-

olistic political party. Purges, terror, and arbitrariness were used to keep everyone in a state of petrified quiescence. The goals of government were dictated by an ideological creed that legitimated the system, prescribed policy, and signposted the future. Mass campaigns and war hysteria were frequently employed as aids to social transformation and to justify repression and privation. A centrally controlled command economy, monopoly of the avenues of social and career mobility, and control of information networks deprived everyone of the possibility of independent livelihood, professional autonomy, or alternative perspectives. The possibility of change other than of a catastrophic type was not provided for. The future was stark. Either the totalitarian state would perpetuate itself in more or less the same form or it would collapse in a self-induced crisis. Evolutionary possibilities towards something more normal were not provided for. The totalitarian state was in a cul-de-sac of its own making, incapable of engendering real support or acquiring legitimacy.[2]

Few challenged the contention that as a description of the Stalin period, this portrayal closely approximated the known facts. But by the late 1950s there was a growing feeling that, with the changes wrought since Stalin's death, this image of the U.S.S.R. was failing to keep step with reality. New developments had taken place that were incongruent with the model. These included reduction in terror, the transition to a more collegial form of rule, the re-emergence of political institutions, and evidence of at least the beginnings of rudimentary observation of the rule of law.

Carl Friedrich, who provided the archetypal statement of the totalitarian model, modified his "syndrome" to allow for the changes. He substituted psychic for physical terror and de-emphasized the centralilty of one-man dictatorship. But the critics were not satisfied. Some said that the model was still only capable of answering "how" questions but not "why" ones. Others claimed that it had failed to generate empirically testable hypotheses. It was said that it could not explain social problems—juvenile delinquency, crime, family instability and the like (did it seek to?). Others said it encouraged moral smugness and unjustified self-righteousness. Many said that the model focussed exclusively on régime output and was insensitive to the possibility of political supports. It was accused of being blind to evolutionary and developmental processes, save those that were in line with its own assumptions. The identification of Nazism and Stalinism as variants of a common type was held to be an oversimplification which obscured the vast differences between them. T. H. Rigby warned that totalitarianism had acquired such misleading and conflicting connotations and become embedded in such dubious social attitudes that its use was obscuring the reality behind it.[3]

In all—with influential exceptions—it was widely felt that totalitarianism as a concept had lost its explanatory power; that it over-simplified; that it was too narrow in focus; that it unduly magnified Soviet peculiarities such as Marxist ideology. As a result, analysis of the Soviet Union was being artificially separated from the mainstream of political science and, consequently, from the benefit of the conceptual insights generated by comparative studies. Fresh thinking was called for, specifically, thinking along comparativist lines which would integrate the study of the U.S.S.R. with political science generally and take account of evolutionary processes within the system.

The Normalising View: Modernizers in Disguise

An influential figure among early critics of totalitarianism was John Kautsky. Kautsky held that communist régimes could best be understood when placed within a developmental framework. The revolution that had brought the Bolsheviks to power, he observed, had taken place in a traditional society disrupted by the strains of early industrialization. It was led by politically westernized intellectuals whose aim was rapid industrialization. In this they were far from unique. Theirs was a goal virtually universal among Third World modernizing intellectuals. For analytical purposes the Bolshevik revolution could therefore be placed in the context of nationalist revolutions in underdeveloped countries, particularly those where régimes had embarked on politically directed development. The differing symbols that appeared to contrast the two types of revolution, such as communist internationalism/national independence, were, it was claimed, of lesser significance than their shared goal of modernization. This goal transcended symbolic differences and steered them towards similar policy options. Thus, just as Third World modernizers find it necessary to rely heavily on the state and sometimes on coercion as instruments of economic transformation, and hence are pulled in a broadly socialist direction, so communism finds it increasingly necessary to assume a nationalist front as a means of legitimization.[4]

Kautsky did not reject totalitarianism entirely. Rather, he relegated it to a phase in the historical evolution of the U.S.S.R.—the phase of "mobilization." Strict centralization of power, terror, coercion, and the creation of a siege mentality were to be explained as transitional instruments, reflexes of (forced) development. Similarly, ideology was recast as no more than an energizing myth of limited operational significance for policy determination. Like other aspects of totalitarianism, it was best understood as a feature of the development process whose function became clear when the factor of economic development was held constant.

While the Kautskian approach, in shifting attention to change as the determining factor, seemed to some analysts to be a welcome advance over the apparently static picture provided by totalitarianism, others found the new model in its application to the U.S.S.R. to be too reductionist. They felt too that it employed dubious assumptions, one such dubious assumption being the degree of Russian backwardness at the time of the revolution. More critically, Kautsky was seen to have grossly mistaken the significance of ideology. Development for the Soviet régime, it was objected, has never been an end in itself; it was but an element within a transcendant normative framework which, while it certainly included the goal of development, had more far-reaching purposes. To reduce communism simply to a type of development strategy would not explain many key features of the régime nor the persistence of such irrationalities as collectivized agriculture.[5]

Richard Löwenthal argued that the similarities Kautsky pointed to between communism and revolutionary nationalism in power were very superficial. In practice, communism and Third World-type modernization were very different, tending to lead to different strategies of politically forced development, different kinds of imposed social change, and different unforeseen effects on the evolution of the régimes themselves. For instance, he noted, Third World nationalist modernizers might resort to the one-party state as an antidote to tribalist separatism; the incumbent leader can be a dictator and may be made a demigod; torture, suppression of civil rights and censorship may be rife. Such régimes do not, however, usually feel it necessary to impose collectivization or create a command economy; and while they may covet their neighbors' goods, they do not as a rule seek to impose on them their own social system.[6]

Logically, it follows from the developmentalist line that, when economic development is attained, the need for coercive instruments diminishes, and the system evolves towards more benign forms. Hence, while in its initial phase the appropriate context within which to view the U.S.S.R. is the Third World, as it progresses towards modernity and is acquiring all the social and political concomitants that modernity implies, in a later phase the point of reference must shift to advanced industrial society of the Western type. This is presumably what Kautsky meant when he said: "Just as communism must not be a barrier to the comparative analysis of underdeveloped or developing countries, so it must not prevent the development of models that can be usefully applied to the study of both communist and non-communist advanced countries."[7]

Convergence: The Airport Lounge Syndrome

From Kautsky's thesis it is but a short step to the idea of system convergence and the notion of universal industrial society—the culmination of
the development process—characterized by broadly similar cultural, political,
and economic patterns.

In itself this is not a new idea. It is prefigured in a number of thinkers,
explicitly in Sorokin who wrote in 1944 that if war could be avoided, the
Soviet Union and the United States would converge into a society of an
integrated type based on the best features of capitalism and communism.[8] At
that time, however, such opinions were rare. It was not until the 1960s, and
in large measure as a result of the work of the developmentalist school, that
the idea began to attract significant numbers, perhaps the most influential of
whom were Daniel Bell and J. K. Galbraith. According to Galbraith:

> The nature of technology, the nature of the large scale organization that
> sustains technology, and the nature of the planning that technology requires,
> has an imperative of its own, and this is causing a greater convergence in
> all industrial societies. In the East European societies it is leading to a
> decentralization of power from the state to the firm; in the West European
> societies, it is leading to a kind of ad hoc planning. In fewer years than we
> can imagine, this will produce an indistinguishable mélange of planning
> and market influences . . . The requirements of deep scientific perception
> and deep technical specialization cannot be reconciled with intellectual
> regimentation. They inevitably lead to intellectual curiosity and a measure
> of intellectual liberalism.[9]

In a fuller statement, the argument runs something like this: Totalitarian
methods that had come into force during the Soviet mobilization phase
become increasingly "dysfunctional" as the communist state develops a more
complex economy. Social changes, rising skills and qualifications, emerging
professionalism, growing popular expectations and the like constrain and
mould the régime. Pressures from key groups for a better quality of life,
more participation, and responsible government increase. The authorities
eventually recognize that running a complex and technically sophisticated
economy requires managerial and workforce initiative incompatible with
traditional forms of central control, just as it imposes rationality in economic
decision-making and resource allocation.

Often linked with this view is the argument that the pace of régime
adaptation can be hastened by appropriate external actions, especially by
détente, expanded trade, and a friendly Western posture. Put together,
pragmatic considerations and political demands fuse to produce irresistible

pressure for structural and systemic change. The old values of unquestioning obedience, party primacy and unrelenting centralization of control functions wither; élite outlook softens and comes into line with social and economic realities.

Adherents of this view found confirmation of such a trend in the disappearance of overt terror, the emergence of a technocratic element in party and state élites, the Kosygin economic reforms, the growing openness to the idea of some degree of marketization of the economy, and the appearance of political dissidence. Ideology was on the wane and the Soviets were becoming just like the rest of us. In short, the imperative of technology was moving the U.S.S.R. towards assimilation to the West, developmentalism had stretched to become determinism and, miraculously, out of it all would spring liberty.

It is sometimes difficult to know whether facts prompt theory or theory invents facts. Whichever way it was, not surprisingly—with the appearance of the emollient anticipations of developmentalist/technology-determinist trend—analysts began to be struck by just how similar the U.S.S.R. and the West, particularly the United States, really were, rather in the way that airport lounges transcend cultural barriers and acquire a barely distinguishable sameness the world over.

Alex Inkeles wrote that whereas in the past he found it necessary to stress that the similarities between the American and Soviet economic systems should not be allowed to obscure the basic differences, he now felt it necessary to reverse the emphasis and urge that "certain differences between the two systems not be allowed to obscure the basic similarities."[10] In a roundup of writing on the convergence theme, Alfred G. Meyer discovered material suggesting: (a) "ideological convergence"; (b) growing similarity in social problems in the U.S.S.R. and the West—delinquency, alcoholism, generational conflict, environmental and ecological degradation; (c) cultural similarities—striking resemblances in trends in art and entertainment supplied (both in the direction of cultural sterility); (d) structural similarities, e.g. the Komsomol and American Greek-letter fraternities; (e) psychological convergence through the attraction of persons of similar personalities into élite positions.[11] Likewise, many studies of Soviet image, behavior, and policy abroad (which is not a subject of direct concern of this paper, and hence may only be mentioned), especially those of the 1970s "détente" phase, discovered in this domain too a crop of what was claimed to be strong resemblances between the U.S.A. and U.S.S.R. The "logic of superpower status" was thus harnessed to "the logic of industrialization," together buttressing the idea of the emergent supra-ideological, transcultural, transpolitical, homogenized industrial society.

All Bureaucrats Together

If industrialization is one path to convergence, for others the highroad is bureaucratization. This perception has two variants—the leftist and, for want of a better term, the structural. Parenthetically, it may be added, that for some on the left (and also for a number on the right) the common ground of the two systems is more likely to emerge as a result of statist hypertrophy in the West than through liberal adaptations in the Soviet Union. Inspired originally by the highly negative portrayal of Western society advanced by Herbert Marcuse and several of the zanier figures of the pop/pot/flower-power cults of the late sixties, they construe the logic of industrialism to be ever-increasing state domination of society. Hence totalitarianism is an emerging phenomenon of Western societies as well and is becoming evident in the form of the leviathan state, bureaucratic control, and corporatist regulation.[12]

A further variant of leftist-perceived convergence is the idea of convergence through Soviet "reversion to capitalism." This contention survives today mostly in polemical form in pockets of the European left but intrudes to a degree into the scholarly debate through such journals as *Critique* and the works of Ernst Mandel, Charles Bettelheim, Tony Cliff, and others.[13] Though the provenance of this idea belongs with Menshevik and other early Marxist forebodings about the likely outcome of a socialist revolution implanted in conditions of economic and social backwardness, the canonical reference for most proponents is Trotsky's theory of revolutionary degeneration, developed by him in outline form in a number of publications in the 1920s, but most fully in *The Revolution Betrayed* (1936). In the footsteps of the master, this school (if Trotsky's fissiparous followers may be called a school) sees the Soviet bureaucracy as a "degenerative" element which has usurped proletarian prerogatives, is poised to undo "the gains of October," and turn the clock back to capitalism. Whether this has already happened or is yet to happen as a result of marketization of the economy is a major source of contention. Interlinked with this is the question of whether to describe the bureaucracy as a caste, class or stratum—an interminable argument that runs from Trotsky through James Burnham, Milovan Djilas, Tony Cliff and onwards.[14] Such ponderings may make for interesting disputation and indeed have some intellectual merit, but they are not widely accepted as advancing very far our knowledge of the direction the U.S.S.R. is headed. The case for thinking that our understanding of the U.S.S.R. will be enormously enriched by labelling it with the right class tag, is, to say the least, not obvious. Besides, it takes some word bending to find much evidence of capitalism in the U.S.S.R.

The version of the convergence via bureaucratization theme which had most impact among scholars is one whose roots run back to its classical formulation in Weber and whose application to the U.S.S.R. has been developed by Barrington Moore, by Alfred Meyer, and others.[15] The convergence implied here does not in the first instance claim to be a whole system convergence, in that it does not involve values, policies or culture. For Meyer, to take the leading figure of this group, the key factor is structure. Soviet bureaucracy is viewed, not primarily as a political or social phenomenon, but as an organizational, managerial form. Using this perspective, Meyer finds arresting parallels between the Soviet bureaucracy and a large Western corporation. He acknowledges, however, that in contrast to its Western equivalent, Soviet bureaucracy is all-embracing. According to Meyer every Soviet citizen is in a sense a civil servant; "all organized life, political, economic, cultural goes on within the framework of institutions created and managed by the party."[16]

In employing this approach Meyer is trying to get away from excessive ethnocentrism in approaching the Communist world. He was convinced that it was mistaken to use concepts and models whose applicability was limited to communism alone, or to it and at best one or two other systems. In their place he offers a scheme which not only has the apparent advantage that it is more empirical—its subject matter exists in various organizations; but also more comparative, in that bureaucracy might be examined in different national contexts and in different ages using insights drawn from a variety of studies.

While superficially attractive, Meyer's theory seems to be making the mistake of substituting one form of ethnocentrism for another. As Paul Hollander has said: "To apply without reservation the concepts and models developed in the context of Western political institutions and traditions to Communist and other non-Western societies might be a good deal more ethnocentric than the practice criticized by Professor Meyer. By following his advice we would project terms and perspectives which derive from a particular and limited historical experience and scholarship and which may have little relevance to the new phenomena they describe."[17] Hollander also suggests that Meyer's concept of the Soviet bureaucracy is far too bland and simplistic. Reducing it to little more than a variant of a general, world-wide phenomenon tends to diminish its most distinctive feature—its political character.

Actually, Hollander is doing Meyer a slight disservice. Meyer was not oblivious of the Soviet bureaucracy's political character. Indeed, he expressly says that an important distinction (between Soviet and Western bureaucracies) is that communist systems are "sovereign bureaucracies," whereas other bureaucracies exist and operate within larger societal frameworks and con-straints.[18] In contrast to a democratic society, the communist state is really one single bureaucratic system extended over the entire society, or "bureauc-racy writ large."[19]

But this distinction is easily lost. In any case it does not go far enough. It leaves out the issue of power and the ends of power. Meyer's over-concern with structure and structural similarity is at the expense of func-tional dissimilarity and the vastness of the divide that separates an open, pluralist society from a closed, collectivist one. And what further clouds matters is his rather peculiar rendering of the goals of communist govern-ment. It is all somehow reduced to the idea of management and system maintenance.

Maria Hirszowicz translates this rather anodyne picturing of Soviet communism into more robust language. Power rather than system manage-ment is the crucial thing. This is what distinguishes Soviet bureaucracy from those in the West. "The maintenance of power has become the pri-mary goal and most spectacular feature of the communist administration. The administrative and managerial functions continue to be performed but superimposed over them as a dominating aim is the consolidation of power."[20] Starker still is the view of Michael Voslensky. In his devastating critique of the Soviet master class, the *nomenklatura,* he paints the picture of a corrupt, malfeasant, selfish, morally debased and self-serving clique interested in little other than the preservation of their power and privi-leges,[21] a view to which the émigré Soviet lawyer, Konstantin Simis, has added a wealth of documentation and for which the émigré Hungarian philosophers Ferenc Feher, Agnes Heller and Gyorgy Markus, have sup-plied a penetrating theoretical explanation.[22] To be sure, neither the facts nor the theoretical explanations that the above authors use when dealing with communist bureaucracies are suggesting any kind of convergence between Communism and Western democracy, between the East and the West. On the contrary, they stress the uniqueness of the Communist bureaucratic system and its total incompatibility with anything that may artificially look similar to it in the West.

The problem with all the variants of the convergence theory cited above is that they are at heart deterministic. They either assume that economic and technological forces will, irrespective of differences of politics and culture, mould a common future for all societies; or they see the future as prefigured in growing bureaucratization and the trend towards the administered society. What they leave out is political choice and consideration of the divergent forces at work. Thus they foreclose possible alternatives.

There has always been a Westernizing pull in Russia, both tsarist and

Soviet. As is well known, the great debate in the political currents of the last century was between the Westernizers and the Slavophiles. The split in Bolshevik circles in the 1920s between the affiliates of "socialism in one country" and their Trotskyite opponents is in some sense a continuation of that issue. Indeed Russian history can be seen as a struggle between two contrary forces: the Asiatic and the European. The former inclines to isolation, fixity and collectivism; the latter—towards contact, development and individualism. This has meant, as Andrei Amalrik has observed, that Russia has been characterized by long periods of political stagnation broken by periods of convulsive movement—revolutions and reforms—after which everything congeals again for a long time. The longer the period of stagnation, the greater the rigidity of the régime, the more violent the convulsion when the "convulsive movement" comes. Convergence is not therefore a steady and consistent process, but an element in a zig-zag movement that takes Russia now closer to, now further away from the mainstream of Western development.[23]

But to return to the theories considered above, while it must be acknowledged that they merit consideration in their own right, with hindsight one can see that they are very much creatures of their time. Their emergence corresponds closely with the shift in a number of Western countries in the 1960s towards greater government interventionism, marked by attempts in Britain and some other countries at national economic planning and in the United States by an apparent growing acceptance of the ideas of social justice and welfare as legitimate concerns of government. On the other side, their stimulus was the apparent acceptance in the U.S.S.R., Czechoslovakia, and Hungary in particular of types of economic reform which seemed pointed towards reducing statization of the economy and at accepting an enlarged role for the private sector. For those looking to getting the confirmation of a political counterpart to the trend towards a more liberal Soviet stance on economic matters, such a confirmation was found in the appearance of political dissent, which at first seemed an unstoppable force, and in the easing of emigration policies in the U.S.S.R. during the early 1970s. Naturally, pluralization and liberalization fitted particularly well into the technology development-driven vision of convergence.

It is notable that a decade later, with the return to East-West confrontation and the conspicuous shift in a number of Western states away from government interventionism in economic matters, and with the apparent rejection in the U.S.S.R., especially in the later Brezhnev years, of any real attempt at economic reform, serious consideration of convergence as a likely trend fades from Western scholarly publications. If past patterns hold, it will hardly be surprising if, with the present apparent renewal of Soviet interest in reform, resumption of détente and, at the same time, with the West turning back to a more Keynesian economic stance, convergence will be once more center stage of the fashionable theories' parade.

Let us turn now to a contrasting scenario—the idea that the future of the U.S.S.R. lies not in convergence with the West but in systemic crisis and in a struggle to retain integrity against disintegrative forces born of inner decay and loss of control over social groups and imperial possessions—a crisis which could have several distinct political outcomes.

Crumbling Communism?

In a 1966 *Problems of Communism* article whose echoes are still with us, ("The Soviet System: Transformation or Degeneration?")[24] Zbigniew Brzezinski powerfully argued that the CPSU was no longer capable of innovatory leadership and had become a brake on domestic social progress. He saw the U.S.S.R.'s potential as stymied by bureaucratic and dogmatic restraints. A gap was opening up between society and the political system reminiscent of the late tsarist period. This condition was aggravated by the decline in the quality of the political élite, unable to deal with the worsening situation either by reform or terror. The rigidity of the political system made it incapable of responding to the demands of social groups. Youth, consumers, professionals, and minority nationals were becoming increasingly alienated. In the absence of a profound transformation aimed at breaking the power of the Party apparat and making the system more responsive to social demands, he foresaw further alienation and decay that could lead eventually to rebellion and a breakdown of order. Broad support for the Brzezinski view came from Robert Conquest, who maintained that the political system had become radically and dangerously inappropriate to its social and economic dynamics.[25]

Doubt, however, was cast on the Brzezinski thesis from a number of quarters. Prominent among those expressing doubt was Jerry Hough. In contrast with the closed, rigid, petrified order pictured by Brzezinski, Hough saw in Brezhnev's Soviet Union a process of gradual devolution of power from the leader or inner collective to a "differentiated leadership echelon," a perception he formulated in the concept, "institutional pluralism."[26] By this he meant that key social and political groups were acquiring a measure of functional autonomy from Party control and greater say in decision-making. The policy making process was increasingly characterized by bargaining between groups, albeit within a framework of limited demands, and policies themselves were seen to alter incrementally in response to the interplay of group pressures. Although Hough made no predictions concerning the possibility of crises, nor did he assume the irreversibility of the trends he witnessed, he emphasized the existence of social supports for the régime and contested the assertion of an ever-widening gulf between régime and people.

In the debate that followed, criticism of Hough's position focussed not so much on the substance of his argument as on the terms in which it was couched. For many of his opponents "pluralism" was the sticking point. The close connection between that term and liberal democracy with all the connotations implied about minority rights, lobbying, a free press, group autonomy, and so on, ruled out the possibility of its having any application to the U.S.S.R. Others felt that Hough was obscuring important differences between the various stages through which communist states have passed. As Archie Brown remarked, if personal rivalries, competition between different branches of the bureaucracy and consultation with specialists are to be the hallmarks of pluralism then, for instance, the Czechoslovakia of today may be as legitimately called pluralist as the Czechoslovakia of 1968, with KAN, K231 and all the other manifestations of independent group proliferation.[27] In hindsight, Hough himself concedes that the term "pluralism" was not the most felicitous choice. It led his readers to suppose an identification between the Soviet and Western political systems that was not intended. Instead, he now concedes, the normatively negative expression "bureaucratic domination" would have been preferable, or, perhaps, even the term "corporatism."[28]

In fact, the latter notion has begun to attract quite a following mainly through the work of Valerie Bunce, John Echols III, and Blair Ruble.[29] Proponents of corporatism argue that the superiority of it over pluralist approaches lies in its avoidance of the latter's assumptions about group multiplicity, passive state behaviour, and systemic stability. Maybe so, but on the other hand it seems to rely too heavily on projecting as indelible systemic features what may be an ephemeral pattern of institutional balances or what are in fact the characteristics of a particular style of leadership. To take an example of what is meant: there is little question that under Brezhnev the major bureaucracies, their subsections, territorial interests, and various kinds of alliances were major actors in the policy process. But, how much did this owe to Brezhnev's placatory disposition and tendency to act as broker in the middle rather than leader in front and how much actually to corporatist systemic transformation? Even if one were to concede that something like a corporatist form of rule has taken root, this would in no way diminish the reality that there is one corporation that remains overwhelmingly preeminent, namely the party *apparat*. Under Brezhnev that *apparat* was not only reunited (Khrushchev had split it into two rings, differentiated by economic responsibility for either industry or agriculture) and restored to primacy but also significantly enlarged in function. To portray it as little more than one interest among others or just as an agency operating the ring for institutional bargaining is surely a profound mistake.

In addition to these points, it also has to be said that it is by no means certain that the political prominence which some incorporated institutions acquired in the Brezhnev era will remain with them. The demotion of Marshal Ogarkov and the foisting of the septuagenarian Sokolov on the military as Minister of Defence, coupled with the decision to deny the latter political status normally associated with the post of Minister of Defence, may, for instance, indicate that Gorbachev, upon coming to office, was seeking to push the military down a rung in the institutional pecking order (a Soviet response to the Polish situation or, what might be termed, the working of the Jaruzelski factor?).[30] This in turn raises the issue, what criteria determine whether or not an institution is incorporated? Is it possible to say that the trade unions were more "incorporated" when their chief, Shelepin, was in the Politburo than they have been since when his successors are not? Do the slight changes that have taken place in weighting of the various bodies in the Central Committee really tell us all that much about their respective political influence? The status of institutions and the standing of the individuals who head them are not as easily distinguished as corporatism implies. Whether the Brezhnevian board of management style survives under a more forceful leader in a system driven by canine compulsion to top-dog dominance must be seen as problematic.[31] But this is taking us away from the main issue of system stability.

On this issue the contributions of two scholars are particularly noteworthy, and from different sides of the fence. Walter Connor was prominent among those who took issue with the Brzezinski view.[32] In particular, he contested Brzezinski's assertion about the régime's failure to meet social demands. In contrast, Connor held that the régime was reasonably successful here, if only because of the relatively undemanding nature of Soviet society. Job security, elementary welfare and incremental improvement in consumption were adequate, he thought, given the inertia and political passivity of the Soviet population, to produce a basis of consensus and acquiescence. Mass passivity, élite privilege, and establishment self-interest operated to subdue unrest. Like the Soviet dissident writer, Andrei Amalrik, he felt that in the absence of externally induced crises (such as war with China or military entanglements in the Middle East) the régime would probably remain immune to serious internal challenge.[33]

Without access to opinion surveys it is difficult to gauge the accuracy of Connor's reading of the Soviet public. Emigré interviews and the works of some recent insiders do certainly give his thesis a degree of credibility. The sociologist Viktor Zaslavsky, for instance, argues that such little things as the "closed enterprise," manipulation of privilege and career channels, and various tactics of workers' compartmentalization are effectively used by the régime to dampen disaffection.[34] He also underlines the importance of the army and other instruments of socialization in inducing compliant attitudes. Such opinion samples as he was able to carry out indicate a considerable measure of régime acceptance and policy approval. Likewise, Andrei Amalrik has pictured the specialist and establishment elements of the Soviet population as pervaded by a self-protective, cautious psychology, while the masses experience no more than passive discontent; neither element is seen as a threat to the régime's stability.[35]

From a different tack Alexander Zinoviev also lends support to the idea of social quiescence.[36] He sees this quiescence as deriving from the atomized, cell-like structure of communist society where the individual is bound to the larger social organism by collective psychology, collective consciousness and collective ideology. In this world of what might be called sructural coercion, the individual is controlled by his colleagues, relatives, friends, administration, local authorities, special government bodies, and institutions.[37]

Of course, public moods can shift with dramatic suddenness, as the volatility of Russian history itself well demonstrates. But maybe the crucial factor is not the mood of the mass but rather the temper of minorities. As George Breslauer has observed, "social turmoil has usually been initiated by a very small proportion of the population which has not had to spread its influence very far in order to paralyze or transform a régime."[38] Furthermore, when Connor was arguing the case for social quiescence he was not to know that a spate of agricultural disasters was just round the corner, accompanied by severe food shortages, rationing in provincial towns, and enforced purchasing on the relatively expensive *kolkhoz* market. Had he known this and had he taken greater cognizance of the growing problems in the economy generally, he might have been more hesitant in assuming the possibility of continuing incremental improvement in living standards, upon which his prognosis of stability is based. Although it is true that no disturbances on the scale of the outbursts of 1962-63, of which Novocherkassk was the most violent example, have been reported so far, the sporadic wildcat strikes of recent years (Togliatti works, Donetsk coal mines, Kama River truck plant, etc.) suggest a restiveness in workers' circles that may portend something quite different from that projected in the picture of the endlessly patient Soviet masses. Even without such foreknowledge there were plenty at the time who thought Connor was being over-sanguine.

Responding to Connor's arguments in an essay published in 1976, Richard Löwenthal conceded the possibility that over the short run Connor's view about the prospects for stability based on the existence of broad consensus on values between régime and people might have some substance.[39] He also accepted Hough's point about the emergence of a degree of high level intergroup bargaining consonant with the notion of "institutional pluralism," though not at the expense of continuing apparat dominance. But as to these providing a basis for long term stability he had grave doubts. With regard to long term prospects he was at one with Brzezinski and Conquest. Like them he found a growing dysfunction between the dynamics of society and the nature of the régime. The ruling élite, he suggested, has an inherent incapacity for the kind of political and economic reform necessary to restore economic performance and public confidence. The *apparat* acting out of narrow self-interest was likely to block all such attempts. The likely consequence would be protracted stagnation of living conditions and progressive alienation of the masses. Given the absence of open discussion and effective feedback channels, the régime would consequently be likely to misread the situation. Eventually what legitimacy it had would erode. State and society would then polarise and crises would occur with increasing frequency, culminating in a dénouement which could be anything from a reactionary retrenchment to system overthrow or even possibly some kind of thoroughgoing reform. The one thing that might save the régime, Löwenthal thought, was the establishment of radically different institutional procedures for choosing leaders and making decisions. What the public needed most of all to be assured of was not that the régime had all the answers but that the set-up was such that there was a reasonable chance that the right answers could be found. "In modern conditions," as he put it, "there is no alternative to legitimacy based on institutional procedures."[40]

Löwenthal's insistence on the paramountcy of procedural legitimacy, as he admits, derives from Talcott Parsons' theory of the indispensability of democratic forms in modern society. This seems somewhat formalistic. Indeed, Breslauer has argued that adopting a Parsonian approach leads Löwenthal into a deterministic, mechanistic image of the Soviet future, as a concomitant of which he underestimates the possibilities of political choice and exaggerates the ruling élite's incapacity for reform. In actuality, as Breslauer admits at one point, Löwenthal is much less deterministic than he (Breslauer) initially makes out.[41] In fact, Löwenthal claims no more than to have identified a tendency, not an inevitability.

The stasis that Brzezinski identified in "Transformation or Degeneration?" became even more marked in the latter days of Brezhnev. The old Soviet joke about the aged inhabitant of the Kremlin pulling down the blinds and rocking the carriage to give the passengers the impression that they were going somewhere had more than a grain of truth. During Brezhnev's interminable dying the senescence that was settling upon him seemed to pervade the whole system. Positive leadership was abandoned in favor of ritualistic noises. Meanwhile, bearing out the dictum that tragedy in history repeats itself as a farce, the sick man of the Kremlin was regaled with a personality cult, decked out with absurd achievements and invented literary accomplishments. The brief interregna of Andropov and Chernenko did little to change the overall picture. As a result the problems that have accumulated are not far more acute than when Brzezinski first identified them. The decline in GNP growth and factor productivity; shortages of capital and labor; the burgeoning black market; the serious worsening in male and infant life expectancy; the alcoholism and related disease problems; the housing, food, and service deficiencies; the gradually worsening energy situation; the problems in eastern Europe (now an economic liability, rather than the asset it once was); the tensions between nationalities; the rampant corruption; the emergence of diverse forms of deviance and dissidence; the incompetence of management and the indolence of workers; the rise in divorce, marital stress, and abortion; the decline in public health care; the problems of technological backwardness and obsolete planning; not to mention a dragging foreign war, and the mounting drain of bailing out indigent dependencies, are too well known to need rehearsing.[42] Put thus, they are certainly a damning indictment of communist misrule, but do they make the case for assuming some catastrophe is unavoidable?

Before leaping to such a conclusion one needs to bear in mind that many of the problems the régime faces are not aggregative and that some even negate each other. For instance, disintegrative trends in eastern Europe can actually have an integrative effect upon the Soviet Union itself. The crushing of the Prague Spring may have evoked condemnation elsewhere, but within the Soviet Union, with a few notable exceptions, it elicited at least tacit approval. Likewise, while Poland's Solidarity movement caused a few sympathetic ripples in some contiguous parts of the U.S.S.R., the bulk of Soviet citizenry seem to have been at one with the repressive stance of the Kremlin. And again, whereas it might be thought that consumer privations resulting from the military's insatiable appetite would provoke an antimilitary backlash, this has not happened, at least not on any threatening scale. So far, the outpouring of Manichean anti-Western propaganda has been an effective sales pitch for whatever sacrifices the régime sees fit to impose. Possibly too the grandeur of globalist power is adequate compensation for empty stores, just as the paupers of Victorian Britain were jingoistically entranced by the onward march of empire despite the wretchedness of their own condition.

While sounding a cautionary note, however, it must be said that to many observers the evidence pointing to problems of crisis proportion is overwhelming. Of all the problems, that involving the nationalities is the one most often seen as crucial. Interethnic tension is regarded by some as a widening faultline threatening the very integrity of the Soviet state. Proponents of this thesis point to pentup anti-Russian animosity among the minorities, aggravated by policies of Russification, colonization, and political exclusivism. They point to a gathering backlash against Russians in the outlying republics. They note the general rise in national frictions and the lack of any constitutional machinery for resolving them. Incidents are related about discrimination against Russian nationals in the ethnic areas, about their being repressed and unfairly treated in the non-Russian lands, from Kazakhstan through the Volga to the Baltic and elsewhere. There are complaints about job dismissals and other forms of injustice. We hear of provincial leaders refusing to listen to the grievances of Russians in their localities and blocking their attempts to alert Moscow about their mistreatment. Republican *apparatchiki* engage in shady maneuvers to exclude Russians (and other non-natives) from the local *nomenklatury*. Instances are recorded of leaders in the Baltic states deliberately blocking development projects lest they bring with them further influxes of Russian skilled labor. And much is made by the proponents of the crisis-through-ethnic-conflict idea of anti-assimilatory manifestations. They focus on the fierce attachment of the stronger nations to their native traditions, language, literature, and other features of identity, and on the occasional violent reaction against one or other repressive action of central government—as occurred within the last decade in, for instance, Georgia and Lithuania.[43]

While all this is no doubt in the main true, it is not exactly new. Such things have gone on for a long time. What is sometimes forgotten is that ethnic animosity is not only anti-Russian but also to a degree multilateral. In Georgia the anti-Armenian variety prevails. In Armenia the target is the Azerbaidzhanis. Among the Azerbaidzhanis it is directed at both Georgians and Armenians. There are the well known Polish-Ukrainian frictions and many others too. As far as régime stability is concerned, however, the important thing about the nationalities problem is that the elements of it are not aggregative. They are discrete, compartmentalized and fragmented, and this gives the Kremlin great scope for handling each aspect of it separately. Overall, the evidence that nationality tensions are on a sharply steepening curve is hard to find. The present mixture of police measures, censorship, buying-off of potential national liberation champions with career inducements, development investment, and the constant barrage of pro-Soviet, antibourgeois nationalist propaganda seem to be a pretty successful recipe for keeping the problem at a manageable level. It is difficult, therefore, to envisage minority nationalism in itself presenting insuperable problems unless the régime has already been gravely weakened by some other cause—splits within the élite, serious worsening of the economy, military humiliation, or whatever.

In the past, outsider expectations of separatist-inspired upheaval usually centered on the Western borderlands, sometimes on the Caucasus. Today they focus more on the Asiatic, Muslim regions. Two forces are seen as triggering agents—demographic upsurge and fundamentalist overspill. Specialists are somewhat divided, however, over whether this can actually happen. While Yaacov Ro'i can find evidence in the press of the Asiatic Soviet republics of serious anxieties about the "Islamic problem," and Alexandre Bennigsen sees the rise of concern in specialist journals about the destabilizing potential of the Islamic upsurge finding also a great deal of other evidence of intense national/religious activity among Soviet Muslims,[44] others, such as Viktor Zaslavsky and Martha Brill Olcott, are less convinced. They would argue that Soviet programs of modernization and secularization have bitten deep and that, as a result, Islam is no longer a vital constituent in the make-up of Soviet Muslim élites, although Zaslavsky concedes, still a force among the peasant masses.[45]

Itis a difficult argument, sometimes further confused by simplistic judgments. Too much is probably being made of mere demographic factors. Of course the dramatic growth of the Muslim population in comparison with the low reproductive rates of Slavs and other European groups is a fact. Neither is it to be denied that the economy of the Muslim regions as it stands is insufficient to absorb their swelling numbers. And what makes the situation worse is that Muslims, even the young men whose geographical and other horizons have been expanded by military service, are extremely loath to migrate to labor deficit areas. Fewer than three percent of Central Asians live outside their homelands or the immediately adjacent territories. Nor can it be denied that there are many signs of estrangement between Muslims and non-Muslims, as may be seen in the low rates of intermarriage between the two groups and in the perpetuation of exclusivist Islamic cultural patterns. But it is too hasty to leap from premises about demography and culture to political conclusions. Zaslavsky warns that the social impact of a group derives not just from size but from its level of organization and the degree of control it exercises over its resources. Sociological research, he says, demonstrates that predominantly rural populations where families are large generally tend to be socially inactive and politically passive. Consequently, his judgement is that if the Central Asian population should remain prevailingly agricultural, maintain high birthrates, and show little inclination to migrate, its growth from 50 to even 100 million will not in the least affect its social behavior or seriously threaten the régime.[46]

However, Zaslavsky is probably too readily dismissive of those who see political activism stemming from Islamic revivalism, whether imported from Iran or through indigenous reawakening. His argument is that projecting religion as a political force in Soviet society is a case of mistakenly transposing Western values. And so he scorns the notion that a sociocultural expression of developing nations could have a determining influence on an advanced country such as the U.S.S.R. This, however, begs the question—is Central Asia advanced? It also seems to indicate a rather naive faith of the restraining power of GNP on fanaticism. Zaslavsky may be faulted too for failing to consider the possibility of Muslims being aroused, not necessarily as a result of ideological overspill from Iran, but by Soviet persecution of their co-religionists in Afghanistan—which, according to Bennigsen's information, is a particularly incendiary issue for them.[47] It would indeed be ironic if the Afghan invasion, believed to have been impelled by Moscow's fear of its Kabul dependency falling to insurgent Islamics, should be the catalyst domestically of the unrest that was feared so much abroad.

In the long run, a pivotal factor upon which political stability in Central Asia—as in the U.S.S.R. generally—will turn is the state of the economy. Over the past two decades the central government has poured considerable development funds into the Asian republics. Though the increment to output of such investment seems to have been modest, it has given some substance to régime claims of evenhandedness in its nationalities policy. The contrast between the living standards of the Asian republics today and a generation ago is well marked. These people now have many of the appurtenances of development and have considerably outpaced the material progress of their cross-border neighbors. These things plus the kudos of associate superpower membership must in some measure help offset feelings of political and national deprivation. But what will be the outcome, if, as a result of a straitened econmy and the ever-rising demands in other sectors, investment were to be cut back? What will then compensate for denial of national rights?

Some would argue that this is all looking in the wrong direction, that the decisive, and for some potentially the most divisive, force in the Soviet Union is centripetal rather than centrifugal nationalism, i.e. the nationalsim of its Russian core. This phenomenon is now beginning to attract attention among outside scholars and considerable efforts have been given to analyze it.[48] In a sense, of course, Russian nationalism has all along been a major force in the U.S.S.R. Did not Lenin warn: "Scratch a Russian communist and you'll find a great-power chauvinist"? And, as someone has said, "Stalin (who was not even Russian) didn't even have to be scratched."

Needless to say, the argument about the role of nationalism, and especially about its relationship to ideology in the Kremlin's consciousness, is not a new one. Mikhail Agursky, for instance, has charted an extensive literature on this, stretching back over many years, arguing that Marxism is only a cover for the real driving force of the Soviet system, namely Russian nationalism.[49]

Carlton Hayes was putting forward this view as early as 1931.[50] In more recent times Robert Tucker and Zbigniew Brzezinski have argued along broadly similar lines.[51] According to those of this persuasion, since at least the 1930s, Russian chauvinism has been the covert (and not so covert) substance behind much that is avowedly Soviet. They would say that the supposedly ideologically inspired, supra-national, homogenized state that communism portends is essentially a generalization of attributes presently identified with the dominant nationality. In the foreign domain they see imperial ambition rather than communist mission as the enduring impulse behind Soviet expansionism.

This view of the relationship of Russian nationalism to the Soviet state is hotly contested. Alexander Shtromas takes a very different position. With Frederick Barghoorn, he is of the opinion that nationalism is simply exploited by the cynics of the Kremlin for their own ends. Shtromas contends that the Soviet Union is "first and foremost an ideological state whose very substance is communism and whose rulers have at heart only one single interest, that of communist domination, not only over Russia and its vicinities, but over the entire world." Russia is to them "only the means to their globally conceived ends." Similarly, Barghoorn believes that the régime has turned to nationalism because of the impelling need to find a broader base of support.[52]

Be this as it may, in some ways the social and political ground for a Russite, nationalist transmutation of the régime has already developed. The support for it is there in the tendency to blame excessive solicitude for the minorities and foreigners for the poor state of affairs in the economy and society. With all the endless propaganda about the egalitarianism of the "Leninist nationalities policy" and the "fraternal" handouts given to this or that needy dependent, such attitudes are not surprising. In most countries it is the stratum of low-skilled workers that is most likely to respond to narrow nationalist bigotry; there is evidence that their Russian counterparts are no exception. Notably, it is among them that the cult of military victories, nostalgia for Stalin and feelings of alienation most openly combine into a chauvinistic brew.[53]

Not just the Russian masses but the specialists too, driven by professional frustration and lack of career opportunities, could be pulled on to a nationalist bandwagon. And besides these all those who hanker for discipline, obedience, and the verities of a more isolationist, authoritarian order could well find their answer in a nationalism that draws its substance mainly from an older sense of Russian national mission and imperial greatness. This would include not only the groups mentioned but also, perhaps, elements among the military and the literati reacting against the political and ideological vacua left by the withering of communist ideology.

An assertion of Russianness, of course, does not all have to be negative. Russian national pride has a healthy and wholesome side, as manifest in the rekindled literary interest in peasant themes, Old Russia, Slavic culture, and in the general search for national self-respect through moral, cultural and philosphic introspection.

Russian nationalism is indeed a mixture of many different elements ranging from the moderate and commendable *vozrozhdenchestvo* (national revivalism or, broadly speaking, the Solzhenitsyn-Osipov wing), which advocates introspection, outrightly renounces Soviet imperialism and supports the cause of independence for non-Russian nations now under Soviet rule, to chauvinistic extremism (of the Shimanov-Fetisov-Skurlatov type) that is imperialistc, colonialistic, xenophobic and anti-Semitic. In this, Russian nationalism is not different from the nationalisms of other nations. The difference consists in the fact that in the non-Communist (or, generally, non-theocratic) systems, nationalism in whatever form—less or more extreme—normally shapes the ideology and policies of the state, whereas in Russia, officially at any rate, it does not. If it were different, Russia would stop being a Communist ideocracy and become a nation-state in the proper sense of this word, or, in other words, would undergo a radical systemic change.[54] According to Amalrik, the ground is already being laid for the emergence of a right-wing, Russite military dictatorship, which means that a fascist-like "national Bolshevism" may be a possible next step in the development of Russia's statehood. Yanov is also envisaging such a perspective and, like Amalrik, is extremely alarmed by it.[55] However, John Dunlop, Darrell Hammer, Alexander Shtromas, Vladislav Krasnov, and some other scholars, whilst sharing the view that nationalism most probably will shape the next post-Communist Russian state, see in it, on the contrary, the springboard for the development of genuine pluralism and, eventually, of a Russian democratic political system.[56]

Whoever is right, Russian nationalism has to be recognized as the most potent factor forming Russia's political future.

A Gorbachevite Regeneration?

The scenarios projecting systemic degeneration, centrifugal nationalist disintegration and/or Russite reaction, discussed above, gained their largest following in the Brezhnevian twilight. They assumed the perpetuation of economic stagnation and the inability or unwillingness of an aging élite to allow necessary changes. The alternative, and one that is now being seriously considered since the emergence of Gorbachev and a younger cohort of leaders, is that in different hands the moribund U.S.S.R. will assume new life.

Indeed, the possibility of some such regeneration under a successor leadership is presently being envisaged by quite a number of commentators. Hough, for instance, argues that the pro-change element in the U.S.S.R. is larger and more influential than we imagine.[57] He believes that the conventional assumption about the bureaucracy's vested interest in the perpetuation of the existing system must be set beside their knowledge that many of the things they hanker for, such as a higher standard of living, foreign travel, and the better things in life, are not possible as things are. Even the military, which is probably the main beneficiary of the present system of centrally determined resource allocation, in Hough's view, has no necessary commitment to the system should it prove no longer capable of meeting their needs. Hough would go so far as to say that under Gorbachev there is a good chance that Russia will resume the road to modernization lost sight of since the time of Pyotr Stolypin and as a result of being hijacked by the Khomeini-style Leninist revolution of 1917.

Hough's view that there are significant elements within the top *nomenklatura* who would be open to new ideas for achieving economic recovery, if only to preserve their privileges and to secure good prospects for their children, seems plausible enough.[58] Anyone who has been following the recent writings of such prominent academics as Abel' Aganbegyan, Fedor Burlatsky, Tatyana Zaslavskaya, Boris Kurashvili—to name but a few— must accept this.[59] It is abundantly clear that the spirit of reform may have become dormant under Brezhnev, but it was far from being dead. However, if, as the majority of Western economists seem to think, a real economic upsurge, and with it all the things that Soviet bureaucrats are said to desire, is not feasible without largely abandoning central planning for a marketized system, then, for a large number of top and middle-rank *apparatchiks* it means that the price of progress is their power. The circle of *nomenklatura* monopoly cannot be squared simply with the goal of economic efficiency.

Unquestionably, the ultimate logic of a market-based reform is to push the party and state to the sidelines of economic management by denying them the right of arbitrary interference in managerial matters. It also must mean that the policy of full employment, one of the U.S.S.R.'s few genuine achievements, would have to be sacrificed for the sake of rationalizing labor usage. Marketization would also probably mean bankruptcy and the closedown of inefficient plants; it would mean, too, the emergence of inflationary pressures, as the pent-up pressure of enforced savings burst out into the marketplace. All these things must surely inflame social passions. Given the loss of power and the attendant very real political dangers, it is difficult to assess how really significant is the constituency among the Soviet establishment willing to take such risks. Furthermore, it is hard to see how such a radical change could possibly come about incrementally. Almost certainly, it would mean an outright political confrontation between reformists and the Party conservatives and their diehard affiliates within the military-industrial complex.

So much for the possibilities. How do they square with what is happening? The successor government is now in place. After two false starts the long awaited generational transition is taking place. In which direction is the Gorbachev administration pointed? Gorbachev has made economic regeneration the top item on his policy agenda. How does he propose to achieve it? Is his programme for recovery slanted in a liberalizing direction or is it something more modest?

Clearly, the measures adopted so far fell well short of the urgings of the more ardent internal reformers, some of whom point to Hungary, others to China, some back to NEP as the signpost to follow. So far Gorbachev has made sympathetic noises but failed to act upon their advice. It is still early days and the reform movement is still relatively weak, but maybe too, Gorbachev is more conservative than he has presented himself. A further problem is that those who are for reform are divided on what is needed and dispersed in such a way as to make it difficult for them to act cohesively. In Hungary there was much greater unity of purpose among reformers, and this naturally made their task that much easier.

As things stand, it would appear that Gorbachev is not harking to the more radical camp. Rather, his drive is for efficiency through discipline and hard work. Here he is taking a leaf out of Andropov's book rather than Zaslavskaya's. But Andropov, as he himself admitted, had no recipe for putting the moribund system to rights. Whether Gorbachev has remains yet to be seen. All that can be said at this point is that while his initial steps have been quicker than Andropov's, they seem to be headed in a very similar direction. Given the scale of his purge and the tally of the mighty that have fallen, the argument that the new Party leader is not in a position to legislate radical actions at this stage because of residual collegial restraints, a holdover Central Committee of Brezhnevites and bureaucratic impediments does not stand up. There is a peculiar but recurring tendency in the Western literature to account for the failure of Soviet leaders to pursue systemic reform in terms of the obstructive role of the bureaucracy. But, as Igor Birman has caustically noted, can this really be true when it is the case that these obstructive bureaucrats "cannot even defend their seats?"[60]

A more probable explanation of the absence of radical change is that this leader, like all his predecessors since Stalin, has not tried to introduce it. Even Khrushchev's efforts did not add up to much more than organizational juggling; in no way did he seek to alter the basic principles of centralization, party monopoly and the right to arbitrary interference from above. Gorbachev may be in the same mold. Indeed many of his actions are very evocative of Khrushchev's. If he continues along present lines, one will have to conclude that the former Stavropol *apparatchik* is intending to settle for creating greater efficiency within present systemic parameters rather than trying to change them.

It also must be added that although the scale and rapidity of his personnel changes have resulted in a noticeable rejuvenation of the bureaucratic tier, as men in their fifties phase out the Old Guard of septuagenarians with a few notable exceptions (such as Ryzhkov the new prime minister) the replacements seem to be remarkably similar in background and, as far as one can tell, outlook to those they replaced. If it is the case, as is so often argued, that there can be no significant reform of the Soviet system until there is a major shift in the pattern of recruitment to high office, then it is difficult to see how a radical transformation could be realized with such people at the helm.

Seweryn Bialer once wrote that the Brezhnev generation of Soviet leaders represented a specific type of modernizing mentality, one that was thoroughly conservative in that it sought to combine incremental material progress and welfare without disturbing the social and political relations and organizational framework on which material production is based. In other words, they strove to compartmentalize the process of modernization, to seal it off from other things. This Bialer aptly dubbed "the Saudi Arabian mentality of modernization."[61] The case for saying that their successors are in any significant sense different is not yet obvious.

Of course, temperament and disposition are but one factor; circumstances may impose their own rhythm. The postwar revolution in consumer expectations has yet to hit the U.S.S.R. No one knows what will be the effect when it does. Neither can it be confidently predicted how a people accustomed for some time to a slow but perceptible rise in living standards might react should these standards suffer a prolonged downhill slide. Nor ought any leader to be sanguine about the repercussions were workers to be deprived of job security as a consequence of the régime's attempts to achieve efficiency through labour shake-outs.

In the eyes of a number of prominent Soviet analysts Gorbachev would make a grave mistake if he tried to get away with itsy-bitsy changes. The situation is so grave, they feel, that further procrastination is not an option.

This, for instance, is the view of Richard Pipes. In a very thought provoking article published shortly before Gorbachev's accession, Pipes addressed the issue of reform.[62] Like many of the contributors to this volume and such recent commentators as Carl Linden, Lewis Gann, and Mikhail Bernstam,[63] Pipes sees the U.S.S.R. as in the throes of a serious systemic crisis demanding decisive action. And with them, too, he sees the crisis as two-sided. On the one hand, it is a political crisis induced by a self-serving privileged class, "that in its highest echelons, the so-called *nomenklatura*, has turned into a completely parasitic stratum. Corrupted by privilege and peculation, estranged from its own people, ruling an overextended empire, and devoid of any sense of service or obligation, it is in grave danger of losing control." Paralleling this is an economic crisis resulting from inadequate productivity that is caused by "excessive centralization of economic decision-making . . . and inadequate incentives offered to workers and farmers."[64] Conditions exist which correspond to Lenin's concept of a revolutionary situation. All that is missing is the subjective element, the organized social or political force able and willing to turn an objective possibility into a reality.

This subjective element is missing, Pipes argues, because through bitter experience Soviet people have long since shed any romantic illusions about revolution and recoil from the fratricidal mayhem it would unleash. This means that the constituency for violent change is negligibly small. Ways of escaping from crisis, therefore, reduce to the following possibilities: reversion to Stalinism, intensified aggression leading to a world war, and internal reform. The first he rules out, if only because there could be no reversion; Stalinism would have to be recreated and reimposed. The second he would not preclude but thinks unlikely because of the risks entailed. So, by elimination, he settles for reform. While he does not attempt to spell out all the details of such a reform, he insists that it would have to involve legal as well as economic elements. The establishment of a rule of law is as important as the decentralization of industrial decision-making and the extension of private enterprise to bridging the gap between régime and people. Turning the fictive federalism of the U.S.S.R. into something closer to reality, he also sees as a possible accompaniment to such reform. The greater the failure of the present system the better he feels the chances of such a reform are. This conclusion holds obvious implications for Western policy:

> The implications which these observations hold for Western policy should not be difficult to draw. The West would be well advised to do all in its power to assist the indigenous forces making for change in the U.S.S.R. and its client states, forces that are eating away at the Stalinist foundations of communist régimes. By denying to the Soviet bloc various forms of economic aid, it can help intensify the formidable pressures which are being

exerted on their creaky economies. This will push them in the general direction of liberalization as well as accommodation with the West, since this is the only way of reducing military expenditures and gaining access to Western help in modernization.[65]

Pipes' belief that stick rather than carrot is the way to induce reform of the U.S.S.R. aligns with the thinking of a significant, though probably a minority, view among specialists such as Jeane Kirkpatrick, Aaron Wildavsky, and Alexander Shtromas.[66]

This is not a view to which Alec Nove would subscribe. He is steadfast in his belief that a more cooperative relationship is in the interest of both sides and that the policy of agreeing to sell to the Soviets only those things that they have no wish to buy is pointless.[67] Nor would Jerry Hough share Pipes' view. While in the final chapter of his book, *Soviet Leadership in Transition*, he argues very cogently for a more purposeful and less reactive and oscillating Western policy towards the U.S.S.R., he parts company with Pipes on the question of how reform may best be encouraged. In Hough's view there has to be an incentive—stick maybe but carrot certainly. We should encourage and bolster up the progressive element within the leadership and, for this, confrontation will not do. On the question of just how much carrot the West should dangle, there would be presumably even more parting of company. Hough would go so far as to offer "a comprehensive American-Japanese program to assist in the development of the Siberian oil fields."[68] Pipes would see this as precisely the kind of policy that would relieve the Kremlin of its dilemma—perish or reform.

The idea that the future of the U.S.S.R. is as much in our hands as it is in their own is, of course, not new. It has been around for a long time and it comes in many forms. One—and one that featured significantly in Western (wishful) thinking during the détente of the 1970s—is the belief that trade leaps all barriers and that commerce will soften the Soviet police state and sow the seeds of eventual liberalization. Or, as Lloyd George has put it, the "sobering influence of trade" will "bring an end to the ferocity, rapine and the crudity of Bolshevism surer than any other method."[69] Another aspect of the same conviction is the contention that closer association with the democratic world will create an unquenchable yearning within the U.S.S.R. for greater liberty and the advantages of a free society. Up to a point, of course, this is right. It is true that the Soviet people feel this way. But the assumption that what the people want the régime also wants is totally without foundation.

Perhaps the most recurrent, and, from the point of view of Western interests, the most dangerous type of illusion about Western influence upon the U.S.S.R., is the belief that Western restraint in military matters will necessarily strengthen the position of "dovish" voices in the Kremlin against their "hawkish" rivals and make the Soviet Union more amenable in its behavior in the world.

The tenacity of this thinking evidently represents the triumph of hope over experience. Recall the naive expectations that followed the story that Andropov could read English (untrue) and liked whiskey (maybe)—presumably his favorite reading was *The Rights of Man*, mulled over as he sipped his malt. Recall too that Britain and Germany traded heavily with Russia in the 1920s and '30s without any perceptible impact on the emerging edifice of Stalinist totalitarianism. Note that the flow of technology throughout the détente of the 1970s evoked neither reform nor liberalization, nor did it abate Soviet expansionism abroad. Soviet troops were ferried to Kabul in trucks built with Western know-how and American microchips went to improve the accuracy of Soviet missiles. Conversely, bear in mind that Reagan's hardline neither jeopardized the triumph of the purportedly liberal Gorbachev over his hawkish rival Romanov nor did the NATO decision on INF deployment and force modernization prevent the Soviets returning to the negotiation table.

The lesson seems to be that, while concessions to the U.S.S.R. are certainly a factor in Kremlin considerations, they do not necessarily have the consequences their advocates suppose. Goodwill may sweeten the atmosphere just as self-disarmament may lessen the likelihood of conflict, but self-delusion is neither a sensible recipe for transforming the Soviet system nor one for containing Soviet designs.

Conclusion

In the light of the analyses discussed in the course of this paper, what is the answer to the question posed at the beginning—whither the U.S.S.R.? It is at this point that the note of skepticism borrowed from Alexander Pope returns.

First, the models and conceptualizations of the direction of political change discussed at the beginning of this paper were not found to provide a convincing basis for predicting the shape of things to come. The totalitarian model is largely silent on the issue. The totalitarian régime, as Pipes has said, is "by definition incapable of evolution from within and impervious to change from without."[70]

Second, developmentalist approaches turned out to be too mechanical and deterministic. Also, the argument for assuming inevitable convergence between East and West left out too many important considerations of culture, tradition, and belief—not to mention the self-interest of the Soviet élite.

Third, as far as fundamental reform initiated from above is concerned, while there are some grounds for optimism, the signs of this coming to pass soon are few. The conviction that what the Soviet Union needs is profound change *of* the system rather than improvements *to* it still seems more obvious to foreigners than to the bulk of the Soviet establishment. The fact that economic reform has been accepted in Hungary or that China has turned in a big way to market forces—in both cases with considerable success—will not necessarily convince the Kremlin that it has no choice but to follow. What works in a small, homogeneous, economically compact nation like Hungary may not be deemed appropriate under the very different conditions of the U.S.S.R. Decentralization of economic decision-making in the U.S.S.R. that entailed passing power to the authorities of the non-Russian republics could give them a potentially dangerous independence from central control. This problem does not arise in Hungary. And with regard to China's reform, it should be recalled that this reform followed a period of prolonged upheaval that had already seriously weakened the power of the governmental and party bureaucracies, hence making it easier for a reformist leadership to have its way. In spite of the Gorbachev purge, in the U.S.S.R. both are institutionally intact.

Fourth, the view that a collapse of the Soviet system is in the immediate offing was not found compelling either. Most arguments along such lines tend to underestimate the possibilities for remedial measures and overstate the chances of mobilizing and converting the feelings of discontent, un-doubtedly present among social and ethnic groups, into an effective anti-régime force were to come into existence, that by itself would not necessarily spell the collapse of the Soviet régime. For, in the last resort, stability in the U.S.S.R. depends on the régime's willingness and ability to use force. When all else is said, this is still the agency that keeps the Soviet empire in existence. The U.S.S.R. was created by force, is held by force and needs force to survive as an integral state.

No doubt, grave problems that are increasingly menacing the stability of the Soviet régime loom large. Although the immediate future of Eastern Europe seems tranquil and, from a Soviet perspective, probably a good deal more reassuring than it was a short time back, the present quiescence could be the lull before the storm. Disintegrative forces are not extinguished. Storm clouds are gathering. The seeds of freedom are springing up again. Solidarity is down but not out. The East European economies, with some partial exceptions, are feeble and continue to fall behind their Western neighbors. The communist régimes have long since exhausted what little credit they ever had and exist only as impositions underwritten by Soviet power.

Another major problem of the not too distant future is certainly energy shortage. The U.S.S.R. is no longer able to meet its clients' needs. Oil purchases abroad (excluding the arms-for-oil deals with Libya) require hard currency and consequently mean an increased debt burden. This will severely add to the economic strain the Soviets already experience. Ultimately it will feed through in the form of foregone development opportunities and an even more depressed standard of living. Rumania and Bulgaria have already had to impose stringent austerity measures because of energy shortages. In the case of the former there have been major incidents of industrial unrest.

In view of this situation it would be spurious to expect the Kremlin to take a more indulgent attitude towards any kind of dissent. Although Gorbachev may have made friendly noises about his old student friend and later luminary of the Prague Spring, Zdenek Mlynar (noises, incidentally, reciprocated by the latter),[71] no more than that other well-known, lately deceased "closet liberal" and "secret ally of dissidents" is he prepared to let dissidence become a threat. Here there is no let up. Shcharansky may have been let out, but at the same time the arrests continue, the harrassment goes on as usual and the Serbsky Clinic has opened a branch in Kiev.[72]

There has been speculation at times that the régime's policy of outright suppression of dissent will ultimately backfire. That in denying protest any legitimate outlet the Soviet rulers will eventually push it in a more violent direction (as seems to be happening in Bulgaria), creating conditions similar to those that gave rise to the revolutionary underground in nineteenth century Russia. This may yet be the case, but so far, apart from a few isolated acts, there is no evidence that the remnants of the dissident movement are turning in this direction. And if they did, it would simply provide the régime with the pretext it needs for an even more brutal repression, rather than further their political aims. Whatever the long-term prospects for dissent may be, it is most unlikely that it will in the immediate future get out of hand and represent a direct threat to the régime's stability. And if dissent and protest are kept under control, all other problems will be deprived of the muscle that breaks and makes political systems.

Reverting to the main theme, in the immediate future then—and it is only the immediate future one can speak about with any degree of confidence—the probability is that the U.S.S.R. will not collapse, converge, or initiate a major systemic transformation. More likely, the Kremlin will try to muddle through much as before. Instead of a marketizing reform, carrot and stick methods will probably be the approach, only the stick will probably have a good deal more whack and the carrot a bit more bite. After all, this is the line Andropov followed and, if the statistics are to be believed, it enabled him to wring some extra return from the economy. It must not be forgotten that there is still enormous slack in terms of unused or underused resources in the U.S.S.R. Almost certainly, even small changes such as enlarging household plots, expanding the role of autonomous work units, opening areas of retail trade and the service sector to private initiative, and better use of material incentives in the factories, would make a marked improvement to general economic performance and living standards. And some steps in this direction are already in progress. The limited experiment in economic decentralization initiated by Andropov is being extended to the rest of the economy and is, reportedly, producing some modest dividends. If this is enough to arrest the decline and take the edge off popular discontent—which it may do, given the relatively modest expectations of Soviet consumers—Gorbachev may be satisfied, though the reformers will be keenly disappointed.

In *Present Danger* and in a number of other seminal works, Robert Conquest cautions against failing to recognize the profound gulf that separates despotic from civic cultures and in particular of the foolishness of imputing to Soviet leaders Western sensitivities and ways of thinking.[73] By extension this caution applies to their respective political universes as well. Problems that democratic societies (civic cultures) could not withstand do not represent the same threat to despotism. On any yardstick, the whole Soviet farrago ought to have fallen apart long ago. Indeed, predictions of imminent collapse have been a recurrent theme in Western publications ever since 1917. Winston Churchill records that British emissaries to wartime Russia reported back in panic that so chaotic and ill-managed was everything that the Soviet war effort was bound to collapse in no time. But systems of the totalitarian type seem proof against most threats. Stalin's power did not crack despite terrible military humiliation, mass desertion, and enemy occupation. Likewise, Hitler's Germany remained loyal to the last gasp. In contrast, the Hohenzollern and tsarist régimes caved in before far lesser pressures. Admittedly, Franco's falangism did not outlast him but his was largely a personal power. Communism is a system of power that can survive its creators.

The coercive power of the Soviet state, the strength of its repressive agencies have not diminished. Whether, as with dissidents, this is done as the death of a thousand cuts, rather than in the more nakedly brutal methods of Stalin, is largely a distinction without much difference. The face of the contemporary Kremlin may wear a smile but, to draw on Gromyko's accolade in nominating Gorbachev, it still "has teeth of iron."

Nonetheless, all empires eventually die. Precedent suggests the process begins with rot at the center and disintegration at the edges. Evidence of the former and to some extent the latter are visible within the Soviet imperium.

But precedent also shows that such processes can be long drawn out. The Ottoman Empire was the "sick man of Europe" for nearly two centuries; Austria-Hungary lived in a lingering twilight long after the days of grandeur of its Holy Roman Empire days. Rome itself went through a process of decay that extended over many centuries. In most previous cases the dénouement, when it came, was the result of an unsuccessful war.

The Soviet Union clearly shares some of the symptoms of its imperial forerunners and in the longer term must follow the same course, unless it opens itself to change before pent-up pressures overwhelm it. But in the short run the countervailing trends should not be underestimated. Besides, weakness at home can in part be offset by achievements abroad. Unlike dying empires in the past, the Soviet Union shows no inclination to retreat into a defensist posture or to overreach itself in risky military adventures. Its foreign policy shows prudence, calculation, and tenacity in the pursuit of objectives, the chief of which is to attain dominance in the world. The older generation strove hard to attain such a position but were inhibited in their efforts by relative military weakness, a sense of ingrained insecurity and memories of past humiliations. The new generation of leaders have inherited a country with enormous military power. They seem to be much less burdened by the fears that afflicted their forefathers and much more confident in their dealings with the outside world. They may be less hesitant than previous leaders in using military power to tip the "correlation of forces" more decisively in their direction.

But whether or not further foreign gains do occur, domestically the Soviet Union faces a troubled future. In many ways the system is living on borrowed time: a faltering economy, a corrupt élite, a society that is pulling steadily away from the mental fetters imposed upon it, restive minorities at home and within the wider imperium, a rotting ideology, increasingly unreal, and littered with broken promises. It is tempting to see in all this the death-knell of the extremely vicious Soviet experiment in forced social transformation. But this is to anticipate. There is as yet no indication of the existence of the "second pivot," to use Shtromas' expression, or, in more conventional parlance, of the emergence of a counter-élite. The coercive organs remain fully at the disposal of the régime (which is hardly surprising when the lion regularly gets the lion's share), and the differences evident within the ruling group seem to be more in the nature of variations on a theme rather than deep divergencies over policy. The partocratic/technocratic divide, which Frederick Fleron and others have made so much of, seems still more an analytical distinction than a political divide.[74]

In short, the processes at work have not yet gone far enough for anyone to say with conviction that this or that evolutionary or revolutionary line is inevitable. The U.S.S.R. may be weak in some respects, but it retains powerful means of blocking undesired forces and enforcing obedience among its subjects. In addition, it now has a leadership that is much more energetic than those that went before in its readiness to tackle problems and flexibility of approach. The Gorbachev régime has not yet foreclosed all options, even the more daring ones. Some improvements have already been made. An important one is that the trend towards bureaucratic ossification and élite stagnation has been arrested, though it is not yet clear to what extent new people mean new policies.

We should not forget that the Soviet régime has weathered many difficulties in the past. The Party has shown itself surprisingly able to adapt to new demands. It is too soon yet to write it off. If catastrophe eventually overtakes the régime, it is unlikely to be as the result of any one issue but rather through the accumulation of strains stretching the system to breaking point. But this is further than we can foresee.

The writings cited in the paper—and they are far from exhaustive—show that a great deal of speculating about the Soviet future has been taking place. The track record on predictions about the U.S.S.R. is, however, not very inspiring. Social science is a very inexact affair, its Soviet offshoot certainly no better. As is so often the case, we are stronger on theories than we are on facts to support them. It is true that we know a great deal more about the U.S.S.R. than we once did; the iron curtain is much leakier than it used to be and the flood of émigrés released during the seventies has added inestimably to our knowledge. But the dark areas are still vast. A crucial generational change is taking place, yet we have barely begun to study it. The rash of data-based analyses that appeared during the enthusiasm for empirical approaches in the late sixties and early seventies has dwindled, perhaps because too often their methodology was more impressive than their findings. But such studies, though one would hope of a much broader scope, are needed again. It is vital to know more about the emerging generation. They are the human substance upon which the abstraction of system and the projections of future turn. Their willingness whether or not to make changes is the key to what will happen. If they are no better than replicas of their predecessors, the cataclysmic prospect becomes likely. But should they be prepared to initiate reform, or at least not to impede it, less drastic possibilities open up.

The experience of Russia indicates that radical change, for good or ill, comes from above, as an act of autocrats using their unchallengeable authority to break down the obstacles before them. In an otherwise pessimistic scenario, the Yugoslav dissident politician and former confidant of Tito, Milovan Djilas, has seen this as the one hope for the U.S.S.R. "The only possibility of change in the Soviet Union lies in the creation of some kind of enlightened absolutism which could initiate reforms. . . .Even for such an enlightened autocrat to emerge, it is imperative that there be some sort of a national crisis: a military crisis or revolutionary crisis, or both at the same time. Such a perspective, it must be noted, is in accord with Russian history."[75] According to many of those cited in these pages, the crisis Djilas spoke of has arrived. If they are right, is Gorbachev the man for such times? Has he the stuff of a Peter the Great, an Alexander II, or a Stalin? Or is he just another transitional figure, trying to halt the final dissolution of a system that has outlived its time? Time will tell. In the meantime, the ice has begun to shift a little. While we may prepare contingency obituaries for Soviet communism, it would be premature to publish them.

NOTES

I owe a debt of gratitude to a number of scholars who provided most useful comments on a draft of this paper, presented at the PWPA Conference, Geneva. These include the official discussants David Gress, Alexander Matejko, and Helena Richter; also to my former colleague Franco Rizzuto, who made helpful comments on an earlier draft of this essay. I should also like to thank Keith Bush who has made available to me a great deal of material on contemporary Soviet personalities and developments. To Alexander Shtromas I am particularly indebted. His courteous editorial guidance, his insight and vision as a Soviet scholar have been invaluable.

1. G. W. Breslauer, *Five Images of the Soviet Future: A Critical Review and Synthesis*, in the series of *Policy Papers in International Affairs*, No. 4, published by the Institute of International Studies, University of California, Berkeley, California, 1978. For a later consideration of the issues involved, see Breslauer's "Images of the Future and Lessons of the Past," in R. Wesson, ed., *The Soviet Union: Looking to the 1980s* (Stanford, Calif.: Hoover Institution Press, 1980); R. F. Byrnes, ed., *After Brezhnev* (London: Frances Pinter, 1983); J. L. Nogee, ed., *Soviet Politics: Russia After Brezhnev* (New York: Praeger, 1985); R. W. Wesson, *The Aging of Communism* (New York: Praeger, 1980); A. H. Brown & M. Kaser, eds., *Soviet Policy for the 1980s* (Bloomington: Indiana University Press, 1983); and E. P. Hoffmann, ed., *The Soviet Union in the 1980s* Proceedings of the Academy of Political Science, Vol. 35, No. 3 (New York: The Academy of Political Science, 1984), are a sample of particularly interesting works by leading figures in the field on trends in Soviet development after Brezhnev and on possible futures for the régime.

For a stimulating and closely argued anticipation of possible Soviet futures, see A. Shtromas, *Political Change and Social Development: The Case of the Soviet Union* (Frankfurt/Bern: Verlag Peter Lang, 1981). For some of his ideas on this subject matter, see also his contribution to the present volume. In a similar vein is C. A. Linden's *The Soviet Party-State: The Politics of Ideocratic Despotism* (New York: Praeger, 1983), where underneath the crust of ideocratic despotism exercised by the present-day Soviet Party state a spectrum of twelve distinct political ideologies that are opposed to official Marxism but genuinely held by the Soviet peoples is discerned and projected as providing a viable foundation for an alternative political future.

2. The literature on totalitarianism is too large to cite in detail here. The classic statement on the concept is C. J. Friedrich & Z. Brzezinski, *Totalitarian Dictatorship and Autocracy* (Cambridge, Mass.: Harvard University Press, 1956). An important later reappraisal by Friedrich and other scholars is C. J. Friedrich, M. Curtis & B. R. Barber, eds., *Totalitarianism in Perspective: Three Views* (London: Pall Mall Press, 1969). A useful bibliography of the main writings about or employing the totalitarian approach may be found in L. Schapiro, *Totalitarianism* (London: Macmillan, 1972), 133-139.

3. In R. Cornell, ed., *The Soviet Political System* (Englewood Cliffs, N.J.: Prentice Hall, 1970), is reproduced a series of articles voicing the main criticisms of totalitarianism published in the 1960s. See also the views of the contributors to C. Johnson, ed., *Change in Communist Systems* (Stanford, Calif.: Stanford University Press, 1970). References are drawn from these articles.

4. See J. H. Kautsky, *Communism and the Politics of Development* (New York: Wiley, 1968) and other works by the author, including "Communism and the Comparative Study of Development" in Cornell, *The Soviet Political System*.

5. Reference here is to the arguments of Daniel Bell ("Ideology and Soviet Politics") and Roy D. Laird ("The New Soviet Myth: Marx is Dead, Long Live Communism") in Cornell, *The Soviet Political System*, and in particular to R. Löwenthal ("Development vs. Utopia in Communist Policy"), in Johnson, *Change in Communist Systems*.

6. Löwenthal, *Ibid.*, passim.

7. Kautsky, "Communism and the Comparative Study of Development," in Cornell, *The Soviet Political System*, 58-59.

8. A view expressed in P. Sorokin, *Russia and the United States* (New York: Dutton, 1944); and in his "The Mutual Convergence of the United States and the U.S.S.R." reprinted in his *The Basic Trends of Our Times* (New Haven: Yale University Press, 1964).

9. J. K. Galbraith, "The World Through Galbraith's Eyes," *New York Times Magazine*, 18 December 1962, quoted in J. Seroka & M. D. Simon, eds., *Developed Socialism in the Soviet Bloc* (Boulder, Col.: Westview Press, 1982), 22.

10. A. Inkeles, *Social Change in Soviet Russia* (Cambridge, Mass.: Harvard University Press, 1968), 408-409. For a brief summary of the main points of his argument, see his "Models and Issues in the Analysis of Soviet Society," in Cornell, *The Soviet Political System*, 14-24.

11. In A. G. Meyer, "Theories of Convergence," in Johnson, *Change in Communist Systems*, 313-341, Meyer provides a roundup and critique of existing writings on the convergence theme.

12. H. Marcuse, *One Dimensional Man: Studies in the Ideology of Advanced Industrial Society* (London: Routledge & Kegan Paul, 1964).

13. Reference here is to E. Mandel, *On Bureaucracy: A Marxist Analysis* (London: International Marxist Group, Pamphlet No. 5); Mandel, *From Class Society to Communism* (London: Ink Links, 1977); Mandel, *The Leninist Theory of Organization: Its Relevance Today* (London: International Marxist Group, 1971); Ch. Bettelheim, *Class Struggles in the U.S.S.R.* (New York: Monthly Review Press, 1976); Bettelheim, *The Transition to Socialist Economy* (Hassocks: Harvester Press, 1975); T. Cliff, *State Capitalism in Russia* (London: Pluto Press, 1974); Cliff, *Party and Class* (London: Pluto Press, 1971). Many of the issues raised in these works have been examined in the journal *Critique: A Journal of Soviet Studies and Socialist Theory* (Glasgow). See, for instance, H. Ticktin, "The Contradictions of Soviet Society and Professor Bettelheim," *Critique*, No. 6 (Spring 1976): 17-45.

14. See M. Djilas, *The New Class. An Analysis of the Communist System* (London: Unwin Books, 1966); J. Burnham, *The Managerial Revolution* (London: Penguin, 1945); T. Cliff, *State Capitalism in Russia*.

15. See in particular Barrington Moore Jr., *Terror and Progress in the U.S.S.R.* (Cambridge, Mass.: Harvard University Press, 1954); and A. G. Meyer, "U.S.S.R. Incorporated," in D. W. Treadgold, ed., *The Development of the U.S.S.R.* (Seattle, Washington: Washington University Press, 1964).

16. A. G. Meyer, as quoted in R. Clifton, M. Glenny & P. Lewis, eds., *Options in Soviet Government and Politics* (Milton Keynes: Open University Press, 1976), 28.

17. P. Hollander, "Observations on Bureaucracy, Totalitarianism, and the Comparative Study of Communism," in Cornell, *The Soviet Political System*, 63.

18. A. G. Meyer, "The Comparative Study of Political Systems," in Cornell, *The Soviet Political System*, 48. At a later point in the same essay he defines communism as "the application of the corporate pattern of entrepreneurship and management to modernizing countries. . . .so that one might define communism as corporation writ large." *Ibid.*, 52.

19. Ibid., 48.

20. M. Hirszowicz, *The Bureaucratic Leviathan* (Oxford: Martin Robertson, 1980), 17. As Hirszowicz also rightly notes: "The concept of the sovereignty of the bureaucracy is meaningless, however, so long as it is not related to the institutional framework that in communist countries is one-party rule." *Ibid.*

21. M. Voslensky, *Nomenklatura*, trans. E. Mosbacher (London: The Bodley Head, 1980).

22. K. Simis, *U.S.S.R.: Secrets of a Corrupt Society* (London: Dent, 1982); F. Feher, A. Heller & G. Markus, *Dictatorship Over Needs* (Oxford: Blackwell, 1983).

23. A. Amalrik, "The Soviet Union—Approaching 1984," in R. Wesson, *The Soviet Union*, 250.

24. Z. Brzezinski, "The Soviet System: Transformation or Degeneration," *Problems of Communism* XV, No. 1 (Jan.-Feb. 1966): 1-16. The analysis given here is presented in a more extended fashion in Z. Brzezinski, ed., *Dilemmas of Change in Soviet Politics* (New York: Columbia University Press, 1969). For this article and the series it triggered, see the various issues of *Problems of Communism* following the publication of the Brzezinski article. The chief contributors to this debate were F. Barghoorn, A. Schlesinger Jr., W. Leonhard, M. Beloff, E. Lyons, R. Conquest, B. Meissner, M. Levine, A. Nove, H. Seton-Watson, D. Treadgold, M. Tatu, M. Fainsod, and others. A selection of these contributions is included in the aforementioned *Dilemmas of Change in Soviet Politics*.

25. See R. Conquest's "Immobilism and Decay," in Brzezinski, *Dilemmas of Change in Soviet Politics*, 65-72.

26. For a very closely worked exposition of the strengths and weaknesses of pluralist, corporatist and related approaches, see J. F. Hough, "Pluralism, Corporatism and the Soviet Union," in S. G. Solomon, ed., *Pluralism in the Soviet Union* (London: Macmillan, 1983), 37-60. In this essay Hough proposes a set of statements about the U.S.S.R. which he says would be acceptable to all the various schools of interpretation—totalitarian, pluralist, etc. It highlights how artificial the debate has often been, so often about labels rather than substance. A more extended exposition of some of the issues raised in the essay may be found in J. F. Hough, *The Soviet Union and Social Science Theory* (Cambridge, Mass.: Harvard University Press, 1977).

27. A. H. Brown, "Pluralism, Power and the Soviet Political System: A Comparative Perspective," in S. G. Solomon, *Pluralism in the Soviet Union*, 70.

28. J. F. Hough, "Pluralism, Corporatism and the Soviet Union," in S. G. Solomon, *Ibid.*: "It does not take a highly sophisticated scholar to recognise that the reality of the Soviet political system corresponds far better to the corporatist model as presented here than to the pluralist model" (39); and: "From a tactical point of view, it clearly would have been better to label the new developments of the Brezhnev period with a normatively negative phrase such as 'bureaucratic domination' rather than one containing the normatively positive word 'pluralism', however qualified" (52).

29. For instance, V. Bunce and J. Echols III, "Soviet Politics in the Brezhnev Era: Pluralism or Corporatism?" in D. R. Kelly, ed., *Soviet Politics in the Brezhnev Era* (New York: Praeger, 1980); and B. Ruble, "The Applicability of Corporatist Models to the Study of Soviet Politics: The Case of the Trade Unions," in *The Carl Beck Papers in Russian and East European Studies*, No. 303, (published by the University of Pittsburgh, 1983). See also B. Harasymiw, "Application of the Concept of Corporatism to the Soviet Political System," *Newsletter on Comparative Study of Communism*, No. 5 (November 1971): 40-54.

30. The demotion of the former Soviet Chief of the General Staff, Marshal Ogarkov, in September 1984, is still a murky business. Various rumours were put about, including that he had offended against party ethics by too insistently pushing for a redirection of resources away from nuclear weaponry and into modernizing conventional arms. There is an obvious basis for this interpretation in his article "The Defence of Socialism: The Experience of History and the Contemporary

Era," in *Krasnaya zvezda*, 9 May 1984. Gorbachev's failure to have Marshal Sokolov brought into full Politburo membership was made particularly glaring by the promotion of Ryzhkov and Ligachev to this position and the upgrading of KGB Chief, Chebrikov, while at the same plenary session Sokolov was accorded only a candidate's rank. Military representation took another knock the following July 1985, when their overseer, Grigorii Romanov was ousted from the leadership.

31. The disposition of Politburo places in Gorbachev's first year as leader is remarkably different from the pattern associated with Brezhnev. This underlines how much less institutionalized the Politburo is in terms of posts represented than, say, a British or American cabinet, where there is a high degree of continuity in representation from administration to administration.

32. See W. Connor, "Dissent in a Complex Society," *Problems of Communism* XXII, No. 2 (March-April 1973), and "Generations and Politics in the U.S.S.R." *Problems of Communism* XXIV, No. 5 (September-October 1975).

33. A. Amalrik, *Will the Soviet Union Survive Until 1984?* (New York: Harper & Row, 1970).

34. See V. Zaslavsky, *The Neo-Stalinist State* (Brighton: Harvester Press, 1982).

35. A. Amalrik, "The Soviet Union—Approaching 1984," in R. Wesson, *The Soviet Union, 259.* Amalrik argues that as a result of a mistaken projection of Western experience, there is a tendency among Western scholars to overestimate the significance of the opinions of the Soviet "man in the street." During times of stability what he thinks, Amalrik says, has no significance. Only in the event of a crisis at the top, when disoriented masses would clutch at any destructive demagogic idea, would he become a significant political force.

36. A. Zinoviev, "*1984* and 1984," in Shlomo Giora Shoham & F. Rosenstiel, eds., *And He Loved Big Brother* (London: Macmillan, 1985).

37. Ibid., 67-68.

38. G. W. Breslauer, *Five Images of the Soviet Future*, 15.

39. R. Löwenthal, "The Ruling Party in a Mature Society," in M. Field, ed., *Social Consequences of Modernization in Communist Societies* (Baltimore: Johns Hopkins University Press, 1976).

40. Quoted in Breslauer, *Five Images of the Soviet Future*, 37.

41. Ibid., 40. But, in making his argument more open-ended, Löwenthal, as Breslauer rightly points out, raises serious questions about the utility of the Parsonian framework of "evolutionary universals" in the first place.

42. For a succinct overview of the problems facing the U.S.S.R., see G. Warshofsky Lapidus, "Social Trends," in R. F. Byrnes, ed., *After Brezhnev*; and R. V. Burks, "Die nahende Krise in der Sowjetunion," *Osteuropa* XXXIII, Nos. 6, 7 & 9 (June, July and September 1983). See also R. V. Burks' contribution to this volume.

43. References here are drawn from the very extensive literature on the nationalities issue. The literature itself is too vast to cite in detail, but attention may be drawn to a comprehensive review article on the subject by G. Warshofsky Lapidus, "Ethno-movements and Political Stability: The Soviet Case," *World Politics*

XXXVI, No. 4 (July 1984): 555-580; and to a recent essay on the subject by A. Shtromas, "Language, Culture and Ethnic Entity in the Soviet Socialist System," *Plural Societies* 15, No. 3 (October 1984): 220-238. Both authors are critical of the view, best epitomized in the title of Hélène Carrère d'Encausse's best selling book, *L'Empire Eclaté*, that rising nationalism on its own may undermine the Soviet system's stability and conclude that the system of authority in Moscow has to be directly destabilized first for the nationalities to start playing an active disintegrating role. In the words of Warshofsky Lapidus "rising nationalism, in the absence of a major military conflict on Soviet territory, is unlikely to pose a serious threat to the stability of the Soviet system" (580). For Shtromas, "national issues to start playing a decisive role in the U.S.S.R.'s disintegration, the authority in the centre of the Union must collapse first. Of course, national unrest, if sufficiently widespread, could precipitate such a collapse, provided the disruptive factors within the system of central authority itself were mature enough to burst out if thus incented" (237).

44. See Yaacov Ro'i, *The U.S.S.R. and the Muslim World* (London: George Allen & Unwin, 1984); A. Bennigsen, "Mullahs, Mujahidin and the Soviet Muslims," *Problems of Communism* XXXIII, No. 6 (November-December 1984). See also, M. Rywkin, *Moscow's Muslim Challenge* (New York: Sharpe, 1982).

45. M. Brill-Olcott, in "Soviet Islam and World Revolution," *World Politics* XXXIV, No. 4 (July 1982): 487-505, argues that secularization and development have bitten sufficiently into Soviet Muslims as to make them impervious to fundamentalist revivals. Zaslavsky (in *The Neo-Stalinist State*), with some qualifications, shares this view. Bennigsen, of course, disagrees.

46. V. Zaslavsky, *Ibid.*, 119-121.

47. A. Bennigsen, "Mullahs, Mujahidin and the Soviet Muslims," 34. Bennigsen's information and arguments have recently been confirmed in a perceptive article on this issue by M. Frankland, "Moscow Purges Islamic Tendency," *Observer* (London), 26 January 1986.

48. The meaning of Russian national reassertion is a highly charged subject. For some, such as Alexander Yanov, it is a retrograde development; for others, such as John Dunlop, it is a positive step. [See: A. Yanov, *The Russian New Right: Right-Wing Ideologies in the Contemporary U.S.S.R.* (Berkeley: Institute of International Studies, University of California, Research Series, No. 35, 1978); and J. Dunlop, *The New Russian Revolutionaries* (Belmont, Mass.: Nordland Press, 1976); as well as his more recent books: *The Faces of Contemporary Russian Nationalism* (Princeton: Princeton University Press, 1983); and *The New Russian Nationalism* (New York: Praeger, 1985)]. For other views on the subject, see D. Hammer, "Russian Nationalism and Soviet Politics," in J. L. Nogee, *Soviet Politics*; A. Ulam, "Russian Nationalism," in S. Bialer, ed., *The Domestic Context of Soviet Foreign Policy* (Boulder, Col.: Westview Press, 1980); and E. Allworth, ed., *Ethnic Russia in the U.S.S.R.: The Dilemma of Russian Dominance* (Oxford: Pergamon Press, 1979).

49. See M. Agursky's contribution to Vol. III of this series, "Soviet Communism and Russian Nationalism: Amalgamation or Conflict?"

50. C. J. H. Hayes, *The Historical Evolution of Modern Nationalism* (New York: Russel & Russel, 1931), 166-167. This work is also mentioned in M. Agursky's contribution to Vol. III of this series.

51. Z. Brzezinski, "The Soviet Past and Future," *Encounter* XXXIV, No. 3 (March 1970); and R. Tucker, "Communist Revolutions, National Culture and Divided Nations," *Studies in Comparative Communism* VII, No. 3 (Fall 1974).

52. A. Shtromas, *To Fight Communism: Why and How* (New York: Professors World Peace Academy, 1985), quotation on p. 2; F. Barghoorn, *Soviet Russian Nationalism* (New York: Oxford University Press, 1956).

53. V. Zaslavsky, *The Neo-Stalinist State*, 126-129.

54. As A. Shtromas has put it, "Russian nationalism has always been and still is essentially anti-Communist, and thus should be considered as a force basically opposed to the Soviet political régime . . .The more the present system depends on nationalist support, the more vulnerable it becomes and the more likely it is to envisage a nationalist take-over of power from the Communists, thus bringing the period of Communist rule in Russian history to an end." ("Dissent and Political Change in the Soviet Union. Rejoinder by A. Y. Shtromas," *Studies in Comparative Communism* XII, Nos. 2 and 3 (Summer/Autumn 1979): 275.)

55. According to Amalrik, such a nationalist state would be tantamount to "a sort of Russian fascism, with great explosive potential in a multiethnic state." (See his "The Soviet Union—Approaching 1984," in R. Wesson, *The Soviet Union*, 255). For Yanov's almost analogous views, see his *Russian New Right*.

56. For the relevant works of Dunlop and Hammer, see note 48, for Krasnov's, his contribution to this volume, and for A. Shtromas' "The Building of a Multi-National Soviet Socialist Federalism: Success and Failures," *Canadian Review of Studies in Nationalism*, XIII, No. 1 (Spring 1986): 79-97, as well as "Language, Culture and Ethnic Entity," *To Fight Communism*, and "Dissent and Political Change."

57. See J. F. Hough, "Gorbachev's Strategy," *Foreign Affairs* 64, No. 1 (Fall 1985).

58. For my analysis of Gorbachev's views and promises, see: T. McNeill, "Mikhail Gorbachev—Just Another Apparatchik?" *RL/RFE Research Bulletin*, Rl 464/84 (December 10, 1984); and *Prospects for East-West Relations* (London: British Atlantic Publications, 1985). For an excellent background study of Gorbachev, see A. H. Brown, "Gorbachev: New Man in the Kremlin," *Problems of Communism* 34, No. 3 (May-June 1985).

59. The most widely remarked upon, and most radical, piece of reformist advocacy in Zaslavskaya's so-called "Novosibirsk Report." For the full text of this, see Radio Liberty's *Arkhiv samizdata*, AS 5042 26, August 1983; or *Survey*, 28, No. 1 (Spring 1984); and for a penetrating analysis of its contents, see P. Hanson, "Discussion of Economic Reform in the U.S.S.R.: The 'Novosibirsk Paper'," *Radio Liberty Research Bulletin*, 28 September 1983. For a reiteration by Zaslavskaya of the gist of her criticism of the failings of Soviet economic planning, see her article "Sotsial'nyi resurs," (Social Resource) *Sovetskaya Rossiya* 7 January 1986.

60. I. Birman's contribution to Vol. II of this series, "Economic Reforms for the Future: Possibilities and Probabilities."

61. S. Bialer, "The Political System," in R. F. Byrnes, *After Brezhnev*, 22-23.

62. R. Pipes, "Can the Soviet Union Reform?" *Foreign Affairs*, 63, No. 1 (Fall 1984).

63. C. A. Linden, *The Soviet-Party State*; L. Gann & M. S. Bernstam, "Will the Soviet Union Stay Communist?" *The Intercollegiate Review* 20, No. 1 (Spring/Summer 1984).

64. R. Pipes, "Can the Soviet Union Reform?" 50.

65. Ibid. 61.

66. See the lengthy interview between George Urban and Jeanne Kirkpatrick, "American Foreign Policy in a Cold Climate: A Long Conversation," *Encounter* LXI, No. 3 (November 1983): 9-34; A. Wildawsky's several contributions in A. Wildawsky, ed., *Beyond Containment: Alternative American Policies Toward the Soviet Union* (San Francisco: ICS Press, 1983); and A. Shtromas, *To Fight Communism: Why and How?*

67. A remark made by Alec Nove on a number of public occasions.

68. J. F. Hough, *Soviet Leadership in Transition* (Washington, D.C.: The Brookings Institute, 1980), 163.

69. Quoted by H. Smith in *The Russians* (London: Sphere Books, 1976), 609.

70. R. Pipes, "Can the Soviet Union Reform?" 49.

71. Mlynar, a former senior Czechoslovak party figure and theoretician of the "Prague Spring," who was acquainted with Gorbachev at university, wrote a rather complimentary piece about the Soviet *jeune* premier in a Vienna newspaper, in which he ventured the opinion that Gorbachev would be likely to introduce reforms. On being told of this during a conversation with the Italian prime minister, Bettino Craxi, Gorbachev is reported to have said: "Ah yes, Zdenek, his judgment, coming from an intellectual of the Prague Spring, is something that would merit discussion." (Reuter's dispatch of 29 May 1985.)

72. As an illustration of Gorbachev's position on civil rights, we may quote the following: "In my view, the importunate 'attention' given by anti-communist and Zionist propaganda to the fate of Jews in the U.S.S.R. is nothing but hypocrisy which pursues far-reaching political objectives . . . which, moreover, are far removed from the true interests of Soviet citizens of Jewish nationality." On the question of political prisoners, he had this to say: "They do not exist in our country. Just as persecution of citizens for their beliefs does not exist. People are not tried for their beliefs in our country." And on Sakharov: "It is well known that illegal actions were committed on his part . . .Measures corresponding to our laws have been applied regarding him." "Plus ça change . . .!" Quotations drawn from an interview granted by Gorbachev to the French communist newspaper *L'Humanité*, see *Pravda*, 8 February 1986.

73. R. Conquest, *Present Danger. Towards a Foreign Policy* (Oxford: Basil Blackwell, 1979). See also Conquest's, "The Soviet Order," in R. Wesson, *The Soviet Union*, 225-247.

74. F. J. Fleron Jr., "Representation of Career Types in Soviet Political Leadership," in R. B. Farrell, ed., *Political Leadership in Eastern Europe and the Soviet Union* (London: Butterworths, 1970), 108-139.

75. Quoted by R. Pipes, in "Can the Soviet Union Reform?", 54.

2

Images of the Soviet Future

The Émigré and Samizdat Debate

VLADISLAV KRASNOV

The purpose of this paper is to review the main images of the Soviet future—or, rather, of Russia's post-Soviet future—that have emerged in the *samizdat* and émigré polemical writing, to evaluate them, and to suggest which one is most desirable and has the best chance to be realized. The topic is so vast that I will have to limit myself only to the main images produced in the past two decades or so. Realizing that my selection is open to the charge of subjectivity, I can only say that I have tried to cover the largest possible ideological spectrum and the full range of futuristic imagination. Regretfully, I had to limit myself only to those documents that were originally written in Russian and thus may be presumed to reflect various Russian viewpoints rather than those of other nationalities of the U.S.S.R.

At first, I will give a brief history of the debate, understood as one involving not only actual polemic between authors, but also polemic between documents that "debate" each other implicitly. While outlining the main contours of the debate, I will indicate its participants, their work, and the issues discussed. The connection between the debate and historical events of the time will be kept in mind but only occasionally mentioned. In the conclusion, I will summarize the main images emerging from the debate, analyze the debate as a whole, and suggest my own preference for the development beyond the present Soviet régime.

Blossoming of the Debate (1968-1974)

The beginning of the futurological debate may be dated June, 1968, when Andrei Sakharov, a prominent nuclear physicist reputed to be the father of the Soviet hydrogen bomb, wrote his memorandum, *Progress, Peaceful Coexistence and Intellectual Freedom*, and released it for circulation in *samizdat* and for publication abroad.[1] Based on the theory of convergence, then popular in the West, the memorandum suggested the following alternative to present global conflict between communism and capitalism: while in the communist countries, the combined "realistic forces" of the "Left Communist Leninists" and the "Left Westernists" prevail over the dogmatic forces of Stalinists and Maoists, and institute reforms aimed at democratization of the communist system, in the capitalist countries the "left, reformist wing of bourgeoisie" prevails over reactionary forces opposed to peaceful coexistence and enact a series of reforms aimed at greater social justice. As a result, the U.S.S.R. and the U.S.A. would enter an era of cooperation. By the year 2,000 they would eliminate poverty and assure intellectual freedom throughout the world, and then move toward establishing a "world government." Sakharov's hopeful vision provoked a sensation in the West and contributed to creating an atmosphere conducive to the West's adoption of détente in later years.

In the U.S.S.R., however, the only official response to Sakharov's memorandum was the beginning of his persecution. Although Sakharov became a champion of all dissidents, his hopeful vision of convergence was soon countered by two very different *samizdat* authors. One was Andrei Amalrik, a young dissident and former history student who had been expelled from Moscow University and spent some time in exile in Siberia. The other was Aleksandr Solzhenitsyn.

In his provocatively entitled pamphlet, *Will the Soviet Union Survive Until 1984?*, written in April-June, 1969, Amalrik predicted a war with Communist China in which, after a series of defeats on the battle field, the Soviet Union would disintegrate and Russia herself would cease to be a Eurasian power. Without naming him, Amalrik completely discounted Sakharov's vision of convergence by calling "naive" a belief that "a certain 'humanization of Socialism' will take place and the inert and oppressive system will be replaced by a dynamic and liberal one."[2]

Solzhenitsyn responded to Sakharov's memorandum in an article entitled

"As Breathing and Consciousness Return." Even though he wrote it some-time during 1969 and showed it to Sakharov, the article was not released to *samizdat* until 1973 when it appeared at the lead of *From Under the Rubble*, a collection of eleven *samizdat* articles written by seven authors, initiated and edited by Solzhenitsyn.[3] Solzhenitsyn paid Sakharov a tribute by calling his memorandum a "fearless public statement" and an "important event" signifying the return of "breathing" to the revived Russian public opinion. He also praised Sakharov for the nobility of his purpose. But Solzhenitsyn disagreed with just about everything else. Acknowledging that Sakharov himself no longer held the same views, Solzhenitsyn nonetheless found it necessary to discuss the memorandum point by point because "in our country a massive section of educated society is still stuck fast in the way of thinking which Sakharov has passed through and left behind."[4] Solzhenitsyn reproached Sakharov for worship of the "undethroned idol" of progress in the sense of scientific and technological development; questioned his belief in the ability of socialism to acquire a human face; objected to his proposal to introduce a multiparty system and suggested that an authoritarian form of government would be a better way to get the country out of its present impasse. He also repudiated Sakharov for identifying the progressive forces of the U.S.S.R. with the "Left Communist Leninists" and the "Left Westernists" and for not believing in the vitality of "national spirit."

In his second article, "Repentance and Self-Limitation in the Life of Nations," Solzhenitsyn enlarged the debate by focusing on the nationalities issue. He attacked two extremes which have surfaced in *samizdat* and émigré writings on that issue. One extreme is to absolve the Russians for whatever sins they might have committed before and after 1917. The other extreme is to view the Communist system as an expression of national aspirations of the Russian people and, consequently, to blame the Russians for whatever misfortunes that befell other nationalities under communism. Solzhenitsyn identified the first extreme as "National Bolshevik" and the second as "russophobe," and denounced both. Insisting on the international character of the communist affliction, he proposed that all nations suffering from it should repent for succumbing to the communist temptation. He explained that "repentance must be expressed not so much in articles, books and broadcasts as in national *actions*," and then told exactly what the Russians should do once they are free: "With regard to all the peoples in and beyond our borders forcibly drawn into our orbit, we can fully purge our guilt by giving them genuine freedom to decide their future for themselves."[5]

Solzhenitsyn's third article, "The Smatterers," dealt with the question of what social class is likely to lead the country out of its present impasse.

Solzhenitsyn's answer was unequivocal: the atheistic Soviet intelligentsia or, as he calls them, "the smatterers" (*obrazovanshchina*) and "philistines," should have no claim to the leadership role because, even though they are intelligent enough to see the faults of the régime, they lack the moral strength to refuse to participate in official propaganda, and therefore engage in doubletalk. Solzhenitsyn rather puts his faith in the ordinary Russian workers and peasants, "because the people on the whole take no part in the official lie, and this today is its most distinctive feature, allowing one to hope that it is not . . . utterly devoid of God."[6] Sharing his negative view of the atheistic intelligentsia with the authors of *Vekhi (Landmarks*, 1909) and *Iz glubiny (De Profundis*, 1918) who had blamed it for precipitating the revolution, Solzhenitsyn called for the formation of a new intellectual and self-sacrificial élite. Only by sharing the interests and spiritual values of the Russian people, the new élite should become "the backbone of a new nation." In "The Smatterers" Solzhenitsyn reproached dissident intellectuals for not proposing any better course of action than "a program of *cautious enlightenment*," that is, as he put it, "philosophize in one's burrow, hand the result over to *samizdat*, and the rest will happen *automatically!*"[7] According to Solzhenitsyn, intellect alone cannot solve the problems. What is needed most is moral strength and a belief in the Russian people, both of which presuppose a religious faith.

Among other authors who contributed to *From Under the Rubble* were Mikhail Agursky, a cyberneticist who later emigrated to Israel, and Igor Shafarevich, a prominent Soviet mathematician. In his article, "Contemporary Socioeconomic Systems and Their Future Prospects," Agursky rejected both communism and capitalism as "profoundly flawed," and envisioned the emergence of a new socioeconomic system which would be founded on "the principle of social justice for all," but, unlike both capitalism and communism, would not use productivity growth as "the yardstick of progress." Agursky refused to call this new system socialist because "[socialism] rejects spiritual and moral values" and "preaches violence."[8]

In one of his articles, "Socialism in Our Past and Future," Shafarevich likewise rejected any form of socialism as an alternative. But his argument against socialism is different from that of Agursky. Shafarevich rejects socialism not so much as a nineteenth century economical theory, but primarily as an expression of an instinctual death-wish which, he alleges, has afflicted various cultures over the span of thousands of years. In the teachings of socialism, says Shafarevich, "Mankind is being opposed by a powerful force which threatens its very existence and at the same time paralyzes its most reliable tool—reason."[9]

In his second article, "Separation or Reconciliation: The Nationalities Question in the U.S.S.R.," Shafarevich took to task the Russian chauvinists, particularly for the one "vice that is typically Russian: the inability to see the line that divides us from other nations, the lack of inner conviction in their right to exist within their own national identity."[10] At the same time he questioned separatism as a cure to the nationalities problem and argued that "Whatever the ultimate solution may be, the only healthy path to it is through the rapprochement of peoples."[11]

In his third article, pointedly entitled "Does Russia Have A Future?" and placed at the end of the collection, Shafarevich challenged Amalrik's prediction that "Russia is nearing the end of her historical journey" and is already "dead and about to decompose." Praising Amalrik for "following one possibility through to its logical end," Shafarevich faulted him for the failure to appreciate "the idea of justice as a force capable of influencing history."[12] Yes, Russia is dead, Shafarevich seems to argue, but precisely because "she has passed through death [Russia] may hear the voice of God" and be reborn. Since "the whole of mankind has now entered a blind alley," says Shafarevich, "the path to Russia's rebirth is the same as the path that will enable man to find a way out of his blind alley, to find salvation from the senseless race of industrial society, the cult of power and the darkness of unbelief."[13] Thus, Shafarevich extended our debate about Russia's future to a debate as to whether the world has a future. His ultimate answer to Amalrik is: "Russia's fate is in our hands; it depends on the personal efforts of each and every one of us. But the essential contributions to the cause can be made only through *sacrifice*."[14]

All in all, *From Under the Rubble*, remains one of the most striking landmarks in the development of the debate about Russia's future.

Almost simultaneously with his work on *From Under the Rubble* Solzhenitsyn wrote his celebrated *Letter to the Soviet Leaders* which became another landmark in the development of our futurological debate. Although the *Letter* was mailed to the addressees on 5 September 1973, it was not made public until shortly after Solzhenitsyn's expulsion from the U.S.S.R. in February, 1974. The *Letter* is a daring attempt to offer a positive and constructive program of peaceful and orderly exit from the impasse, a program which, Solzhenitsyn hopes, would be acceptable to at least some Soviet leaders in a not so remote future. Alerting them to the two "chief dangers facing our country in the next ten to thirty years"—a war with Communist China and the impending global ecological crisis—Solzhenitsyn urged them to renounce the Marxist-Leninist ideology, the principal "roadblock on the path to our salvation."

Remarkably, he did not ask them to relinquish their power or disband the party. Nor did he ask for free election "at which people might not vote you in."[15] Dismissing the eight-month period after the February revolution as "chaotic caricature of democracy," he suggested that the Soviet leaders could best conform to Russian historical tradition by leading the country out of its present totalitarian stage to a form of authoritarian rule, in which the party would share power with the local soviets that are presently totally subservient to the party in spite of the fact that they gave their name to the Soviet Union. Solzhenitsyn also proposed "free art and literature" and giving "your fellow countrymen the chance to move up the rungs *without* having to have a Party card."[16]

Appealing to their latent Russian national patriotism, Solzhenitsyn urged Soviet leaders to take charge of a new bold initiative of switching the country's resources from promoting a world revolution to the development of the Russian Northeast, a development which would help both to avert the ecological crisis and provide a better defense against Communist China. Acknowledging his debt to the efforts of the Teilhard de Chardin Society and the Club of Rome in alerting to the danger of global ecological crisis, he urged Soviet leaders to abandon the Western (both the capitalist and the Marxist) belief in progress as a "steadily expanding economy" and called instead for "a zero-growth economy, a stable economy." While proposing to renounce Marxism as state ideology, Solzhenitsyn insisted that a "competition between all ideological and moral currents, in particular between all religions," should be allowed. Parenthetically, he stated his own belief in Christianity as "the only living force capable of undertaking the spiritual healing of Russia."[17]

Solzhenitsyn's *Letter* has remained unanswered by those to whom it was addressed. But it greatly furthered the debate about Russia's future by provoking a number of *samizdat* responses from widely different segments of the political spectrum: Sakharov's pro-Western liberal, Roy Medvedev's self-proclaimed Marxist, and Vladimir Osipov's Russian nationalist.

In his *samizdat* article signed on 3 April 1974, Sakharov welcomed Solzhenitsyn's contribution to the debate and endorsed some of the most important of Solzhenitsyn's proposals, such as turning the country away from expansionism to domestic democratization, disarmament, and economic reform. But he strongly disagreed with Solzhenitsyn's argument in favor of "the authoritarian system of law and Orthodoxy" and rejected his condemnation of the West for relying on scientific and technological progress. Sakharov also felt that Solzhenitsyn overestimated the threat of war with China, and found his Northeastern idea "doomed to failure from the start." He traced Solzhenitsyn's errors to his overestimation of the role of Marxist-Leninist ideology as a tool of oppression and to his belief in Russian Orthodoxy. "I am convinced that the nationalistic and isolationist direction of [Solzhenitsyn's] thought and [his] religious-patriarchal romanticism," said Sakharov, "lead him in fact, to very fundamental mistakes and make his proposals utopian and potentially dangerous."[18]

Roy Medvedev, a dissident Soviet historian who calls himself a Marxist and "democratic socialist," responded to Solzhenitsyn's *Letter* in a *samizdat* article, "What Awaits Us In The Future?" While sharing Sakharov's apprehensions about Solzhenitsyn's "nationalism" and "isolationism," Medvedev conceded to Solzhenitsyn that "the national life of Russians is hampered to a far greater degree than that of, say, Armenians, Georgians, and the Uzbek peoples."[19] Nonetheless, Medvedev reproached Solzhenitsyn for allegedly excessive concern with the Russians, and at the same time rejected his proposal that the "border nations" should be allowed to secede. Like Sakharov, Medvedev defended technological progress, dismissed Solzhenitsyn's Northeastern ideas as utopian, and discounted the possibility that the Orthodox Church might play a significant role in the future. Above all, Medvedev disagreed that Marxism is dead and should be removed as a roadblock on the way to a healthier society. While admitting that Marxism has been abused, Medvedev maintained that "all the shortcomings and vices that exist in the Soviet Union cannot be blamed on Marxism-Leninism," and that, for example, "Marxism never asserted that there can be no individual proprietary initiative in a socialist country [or] that under socialism there can be only one party and that no opposition should be allowed."[20] Medvedev denied that Marxism has anything to do with the Sino-Soviet conflict, and insisted that all problems of the U.S.S.R. can be best solved on the basis of "genuine Marxist thinking." He envisioned the emergence of "a new socialist party that differs from current social democratic and communist parties," a party that "could create a loyal and legal opposition to the existing leadership and help to renew and revitalize the CPSU."[21]

Solzhenitsyn's *Letter* found its most enthusiastic supporter inside the U.S.S.R. in Vladimir Osipov, my friend and fellow history student at Moscow University from which he was expelled in the late 1950s.[22] During the 1960s, Osipov spent seven years at hard labor. He is best known as the founder and editor of the Russian nationalist *samizdat* magazine *Veche* (1971-74). In his article, "Five objections to Sakharov," written in April 1974, Osipov praised Solzhenitsyn for a "clear and sober evaluation of the situation" and for offering a realistic "program of salvation." Suggesting that Solzhenitsyn's proposals might become acceptable to Soviet leaders within the foreseeable future, Osipov proclaimed his *Letter* the "manifesto of the century." Osipov's five objections to Sakharov's were:(1) underestimation of the threat from Communist China; (2) Sakharov's alleged "cult of science" and "progress"; (3) not understanding that "other, nonauthoritarian path" is still "unsuitable and premature" for Russia; (4) philosophic bias against Slavophilism; and (5) the failure to empathize with the plight of the Russian people who not only suffer under the yoke of an alien ideology like all other nations, but are also accused of being willing oppressors of others.

Contrasting Sakharov's own proposals with those of Solzhenitsyn, Osipov said that while Sakharov himself does not believe that his proposals would be ever accepted by Soviet leaders, Solzhenitsyn proposes "neither despair, nor revolution, but the *power of the Soviets*," which Soviet leaders would be hard put to reject.[23]

In his other article, "On the goal and the methods of legal opposition," written in May 1974, Osipov focused on the need for a coalition of all opposition. Noting deep ideological divisions among dissidents, Osipov suggested that they can do without a single common ideology, as long as they are bonded together by being equally persecuted for their heterodoxy. But he urged all oppositional forces to unite around a single goal, forcing the government to accept three demands: (1) Respect your own Constitution; (2) Respect the Universal Declaration of Human Rights; and (3) Demand genuine reforms. He explained the latter by urging "the Communist Medvedev, Social Democrat [Anatoly Levitin-] Krasnov, and the liberal Sakharov" to rally around Solzhenitsyn's proposals because "[they] are realistic, constructive, can be acceptable to the government, and because they stem from a person who is profoundly tolerant to all sorts of heterodoxy."[24] Although in the beginning of the article he reproached Sakharov, Medvedev, and Krasnov for "unjustified sharpness" of their responses to Solzhenitsyn's *Letter*, Osipov maintained a conciliatory tone in the rest of the article which he concluded by calling for adherence to legal methods of opposition.

The Debate Goes On and Abroad (1975-1980)

In spite of Osipov's dedication to legal methods, he was arrested on 28 November 1974, convicted of "slandering the Soviet system," and sentenced to eight more years of labor camps which he has now served out. Also in 1974 the magazine *Veche* ceased to be published, and Solzhenitsyn was expelled from the country. Several other prominent dissidents were either expelled or allowed to leave the U.S.S.R. during the 1970s: Valery Chalidze, Amalrik, Levitin-Krasnov, Vladimir Maksimov, and Vladimir Bukovsky, to name just a few. It is no surprise that from 1975 on the center of the futurological debate has shifted to *tamizdat*, including such émigré periodicals as *Kontinent* and *Vremia i my* founded by the newcomers to the West. Nonetheless, *samizdat* has continued to serve as a vital source for *tamizdat* and a receptor of the works written in freedom. To outline the development of the debate after 1974, we shall start with the works produced inside the U.S.S.R.

One such work was Sakharov's book, *My Country and the World*. Although Sakharov prefaced it by saying that "I have not basically changed the views formulated [in the Memorandum of 1968]," the new book reflects a much more critical evaluation of the Soviet system, and conversely, takes a more positive view of the West. Whereas in the memorandum he mostly blamed the "reactionary circles" of the West for the threat of a global war, now he depicts Soviet totalitarianism as the chief suppressor of human rights, the chief perpetrator of violence, and the chief threat to world peace. Condemning the "Leftists" for their contribution to the Communist victory in Vietnam and for their advocacy of unilateral disarmament, Sakharov calls for international defense of human rights. He implores Western intellectuals to get rid of their "Left-Wing faddishness," including the belief in "inverted Slavophilism," that is that the peoples of the Communist countries do not care for human rights because they lack a democratic historical tradition. "I am convinced," says Sakharov, "that the defense of Soviet political prisoners and other dissenters . . . is not only the moral duty of honest persons throughout the world but constitutes a direct defense of human rights in their own countries."[25] In an apparent concession to Solzhenitsyn, he called the Marxist-Leninist "ideological monism" one of the main causes of "an unrelenting persecution of dissidents."[26]

Describing the U.S.S.R. as a country of social injustice, low living standards, moral deprivation, and economic inefficiency, Sakharov suggested a program of reforms that is much more specific and radical than the one in the memorandum. It includes twelve proposals: (1) economic reforms, including full automony for factories; (2) partial democratization of industry and agriculture; (3) full amnesty for all political prisoners; (4) freedom to strike; (5) freedom of conscience and information; (6) public accountability of officials; (7) freedom to choose residence and employment; (8) freedom to emigrate and to return; (9) equal rights for all citizens, beginning with the abolition of *nomenklatura* privileges; (10) right of Soviet republics to secede; (11) a multiparty system; (12) limitation of state monopoly on foreign trade and currency reform. Sakharov emphasized that such reforms are urgently needed "in order to bring our country out of a constant state of general crisis, and to eliminate the consequent danger to mankind."[27]

In November 1975 Sakharov, who declared himself "a confirmed evolutionist and reformist, and an opponent, as a matter of principle, of violent, revolutionary changes of the social order," was awarded the Nobel Peace Prize.[28] The award meant international recognition of not only Sakharov's personal courageous struggle for human rights but also of the whole dissident movement. Characteristically, Solzhenitsyn was among those who nominated Sakharov for the award. The award boosted the debate about alternatives and encouraged Western scholars to pay more attention to the debate.[29]

Two other books written inside the U.S.S.R. were soon published in the West. One was Shafarevich's *Socialist Phenomenon*,[30] the thesis of which we have already discussed in conjunction with his contribution to *From Under the Rubble*. Another was Valentin Turchin's *The Inertia of Fear and the Scientific Worldview*, a shorter original version of which had circulated in *samizdat* since 1968. Turchin, a prominent Soviet mathematician and dissident, after emigrating to the West enlarged the original version in such a way as to challenge both Solzhenitsyn and Shafarevich. While admitting that "the rise of totalitarianism is unquestionably part and parcel of the scientific-industrial era,"[31] Turchin argued that the cure for totalitarianism should be sought not in religion but in the improvement of scientific methods in dealing with social problems. "For me a return to Christian fundamentalism is impossible," says Turchin, "and I am deeply convinced that it is impossible for the great majority of our contemporaries."[32] According to Turchin, only modern scientific methods can engender in modern men an "antitotalitarian conscience capable of vigorous social action."

While endorsing Shafarevich's approach to socialism as a worldwide historical phenomenon rather than a product of nineteenth century industrial revolution, Turchin totally disagrees with Shafarevich's contention that socialism is an expression of an instinctual drive to self-annihilation. For Turchin, socialism is rather an intuitive and life-affirming drive for common good. Despite his insistence on application of scientific methods to social problems, Turchin sees socialism not in Marxist economic terms but as a sort of secular religion of common good. Taking strong exception to the already existing forms of socialism, Turchin believes that his yet unborn socialism alone "will give the Free World the necessary minimum of unity and firmness" that is necessary to prevent the world from going the way of Soviet totalitarian socialism.[33]

Turchin sees Russia's future in the context of global evolution toward a new scientific worldview of which the religion of socialism would be an integral part. He believes that his Soviet contemporaries will play a very special role in the emergence of a new global civilization, but that "we must begin from scratch" simply because too few "filaments of old Russia" remain intact and "it is not in our power to graft on dead tissue."[34]

Notwithstanding what Turchin says, his compatriot in exile Solzhenitsyn has continued to work on the rediscovery, cleansing, and restoration of, perhaps, not so few "filaments of old Russia" in whose vital power he still believes. Ironically, Solzhenitsyn's chief contribution to the debate about Russia's future lies in his work on the novelistic cycle *The Red Wheel* about

Russia's past. By deliberately and steadfastly focusing on the past, Solzhenitsyn seems to be saying that Russia's future can be neither divined nor
prepared for, unless the true image of her past is fully restored. But while
devoting most of his time and energy to his novels, he also made a few
public statements, such as the Harvard University Commencement Address
titled "A World Split Apart," and "Misconceptions About Russia Are a
Threat to America."[35] While he became a controversial figure in the West,
he managed to stay in the center of our futurological debate. In his new
pronouncements Solzhenitsyn stuck to his original proposals, but clarified
some points. In his Harvard Address, for instance, he refused to accept "the
West, such as it is today, as a model to my country." At the same time,
praising Shafarevich's book, he rejected socialism, presumably in any form,
as an alternative, and denounced it as "a false and dangerous current."[36]

In "Misconceptions" he accused some of the recent émigrés, most notably
Alexander Yanov, author of *The Russian New Right*, of "an unabashed
blurring of distinction between Russian Orthodoxy and anti-Semitism" and
of depicting the current rebirth of Russian religious and national consciousness as a threat to the West. He took Yanov to task for his "extraordinary theory according to which the rising forces of national and religious
consciousness and the declining, cynical communist leaders have but a single
dream—to merge together into some sort of 'New Right.'"[37] While reiterating
his authoritarian vision, he explained it as a necessary stage to make the
descent from the "cliff of totalitarianism" orderly and peaceful, and added:
"As concerns the theoretical question whether Russia should choose or
reject authoritarianism in the future, I have no final opinion, and have not
offered any."[38]

An examination of Yanov's work would indeed show that he indis-
criminately lumps together both the "National Bolsheviks" (whom Solzhenitsyn has condemned) and the religiously oriented Russian *vozrozhdentsy*,
such as Osipov and Solzhenitsyn, into a mythical New Right coalition
aiming at "the gradual construction of an ideological base for the possible
transformation of the regime in the U.S.S.R. and the restoration of
Stalinism."[39] After seizing power in the Kremlin, the New Right coalition
would attempt to subjugate both Yugoslavia and China in order to create "a
new ascetic civilization closed to the West."[40] "To prevent the triumph of the
New Right, [the U.S.A.] would have to use, in addition to armaments . . .
the intellect of the nation, its political talent, its enterprise and inventive-
ness," Yanov concludes.[41]

Yanov's book was not the only example of the émigré debate spilling over
into Western scholarship. Alexander Shtromas, a dissident of Lithuanian
background who emigrated to England in 1973, in 1981 published, in

English, a book-length study devoted to the prospects of political change in the U.S.S.R. Disputing Yanov's thesis, Shtromas argued that "Russian nationalism has always been and still is essentially anti-Communist, and as such, should be considered as a force basically opposed to the Soviet political regime." Shtromas suggested the inevitability of eventual transfer of power from the totalitarian "partocrats" to the nationally and rationally-minded "technocrats." Considering a variety of ways in which political change in the U.S.S.R. may come about, he attaches high probability to the process of change being initiated by the nationally-minded professional (and thus technocratic) military stratum. Although, according to Shtromas, the new post-Soviet government may remain authoritarian "for a significant period of time,"[42] it would accomplish "the most important task . . . of liquidating totalitarianism," and thus clear the way for an eventual establishment of "polyarchic democracy."[43]

Among émigrés who have disputed Solzhenitsyn's belief in the Russian national and religious rebirth as the basis for a new Russia, was Valery Chalidze, the founder of *The Chronicle of Current Affairs*. Chalidze wrote several anti-Solzhenitsyn articles, in which he denounced "Ayatollah Solzhenitsyn." In his *Kontinent* article, "About certain tendencies in emigré journalism,"[44] Chalidze deplored the dominance of Solzhenitsyn's ideas in Russian emigré publications, and maintained that the Soviet régime is "stable" and "flexible," and "would, possibly, survive all of us." He denied that there is hatred of communism among ordinary people or that there is any significant religious revival in the U.S.S.R. Chalidze also denounced Solzhenitsyn's authoritarianism and endorsed Yanov's thesis that the rebirth of Russian nationalism may lead to neo-Stalinism.

In his rebuttal to Chalidze, "Why do the Russians quarrel?" published in the same issue of *Kontinent*, Vladimir Bukovsky accused Chalidze of conducting a "politically motivated campaign" against Solzhenitsyn whom he defended as a "symbol" of all opposition. Nevertheless, Bukovsky spelled out his own disagreements with Solzhenitsyn. Treating Solzhenitsyn as an artist rather than a "politican," Bukovsky finds his *Letter* "astonishing in its naive faith in the power of words that is so typical for writers."[45] Bukovsky also disagrees with Solzhenitsyn's emphasis on authoritarianism and Christianity. "Christianity has existed almost two thousand years, and yet it saved us neither from communism, nor fascism, and one certainly cannot expect salvation from the corrupt and controlled Orthodox Church," says Bukovsky.[46] Reproaching both Chalidze and Solzhenitsyn for polemical excesses, Bukovsky ended his article with an appeal for unity of opposition.

Vladimir Maximov, editor of *Kontinent*, made his contribution to the futurological debate in "Reflections on democracy," published in the weekly

Russkaia Mysl'.[47] Like Solzhenitsyn, Maximov suggests a "third way" as a solution of "the dead-end dilemma: Western democracy and Eastern totalitarianism." To implement that "third way," Maximov urges reviving the commune as a fundamental self-governing unit of the future "Russian Federated State." As to the future form of government, he would leave the decision up to the Constituent Assembly to be elected in a free, but indirect election. Putting little trust in the Western multiparty system, Maximov would allow political parties only on a local level. He also urges economic and administrative decentralization, separation of state and church, and otherwise limiting central authority.

The Anti-Solzhenitsyn Collections

In 1976 there were published in the West two collections of *samizdat* and émigré writings, *Samosoznanie* (Self-awareness) and *Demokraticheskie al'ternativy* (Democratic alternatives),[48] that sought to present alternatives to the present régime different from those suggested in Solzhenitsyn's *Letter* and *From Under The Rubble*. In fact, both collections, especially the latter, appear to be as anti-Solzhenitsyn as they are anti-régime.

The first collection, *Samosoznanie*, was published by Chalidze's Khronika Press in New York. It was compiled and introduced by three former activists of the human rights movement—Pavel Litvinov, Mikhail Meerson-Aksenov, and Boris Shragin, now emigrated. The compilers define the "trend of thought" that underlies the collection as "liberal-democratic." They emphasize the continuity of their ideas with the tradition of Russian liberalism that originated at the end of the nineteenth century and found its political embodiment in the party of Constitutional Democrats (1905-1917). When the human rights movement began in the mid-1960s in the U.S.S.R., say the compilers, it was inspired by such authors as Nikolai Berdiaev, Sergei Bulgakov, Pavel Miliukov, and Petr Struve. The compilers also proclaimed the continuity of the struggle for human rights in the U.S.S.R. with the struggle against "the arbitrariness of Tsarism" that had been going on since Radishchev (1749-1802).[49] As a token of their willingness to cooperate with the West, they included in the collection a chapter from Richard Pipes' book, *Russia Under the Old Regime*.

In his contribution to the collection, the article about the human rights movement in the U.S.S.R. ("O dvizhenii za prava cheloveka v SSSR"), Litvinov reproaches both Solzhenitsyn and Osipov for favoring "authoritarian" alternatives to the present régime.[50] While admitting that "besides humanistic slogans, the [human rights] movement has neither political nor economic programs,"[51] Litvinov argues that the most urgent task of the opposition consists not in formulating new programs but in educating people to have a greater respect for legal process and for the rights of individuals *(pravosoznanie).* Unlike the revolutionary movement in tsarist Russia, says Litvinov, "the human rights movement has focused its attention on the defence of individuals against the arbitrariness of the state, not on the creation of a new polity or social structure."[52]

However, there was at least one contributor to the collection who dealt head-on with the question of alternative economic system.[53] Yury Orlov, a physicist and one of the founders of the Moscow group for monitoring the Helsinki Accords, was later imprisoned. Orlov pointedly entitled his article, "Is socialism of a non-totalitarian type possible?" Although many Western intellectuals would not hesitate to answer positively, "the facts, so far, have convincingly testified to the existence and considerable stability of only the totalitarian type of socialism," says Orlov in reference to his country.[54] Disputing the belief that all problems can be solved with the help of social reforms, Orlov warns the West against succumbing to reforms that "may unexpectedly throw the West into the abyss of totalitarian socialism."[55] At the end Orlov cautiously endorses the possibility that non-totalitarian type of socialism might emerge, and suggests his preference for a "decentralized socialism" which would rely on private initiative but which would allow only limited private property. However, that type of socialism cannot be realized, says Orlov, unless all opposition to the present régime unites into a single anti-totalitarian organization based on ethical principles. The main principle should read, "A physical coercion of people who do not coerce others must be absolutely rejected and treated as a crime."[56] According to Orlov, only decentralized socialism based on solid ethical foundations can assure both prosperity and individual liberty.

Unlike *Samosoznanie,* the other collection, *Demokraticheskie al'ternativy,* is chiefly concerned with socio-economic alternatives to the present régime. Compiled by Vadim Belotserkovsky, formerly a Soviet journalist and now an émigré, this is a collection of ten authors: eight Soviet émigrés, one Yugoslav (Mihajlo Mihajlov), and one German (Jan Elberfeld). All the authors profess, or at least sympathize with, one or another variety of non-totalitarian socialism—from Leonid Pliushch, who favors a multiparty Euro-communist system, to German Andreev, who is apparently no more social-ist than the late Lev Tolstoy whose brand of Christianity he advocates. As Belotserkovsky explains in his introduction, the collection has a dual pur-pose. First, anticipating "grave crisis" of the present régime, it aims at providing a practical and positive program of action so that opposition could move into the emerging political vacuum. Secondly, it aims at preventing the "reactionary and chauvinist right" from instituting an alternative that Belotserkovsky considers even worse than the present régime.[57] The second purpose inevitably heightens the polemical thrust of the collection.

Belotserkovsky variously describes the common political and ideological denominator for the collection as being "new left," "liberal-left," a "synthesis," and a "third way." He welcomes the publication of *Samosoznanie*, and particularly praises Orlov's search for a "synthesis" between the best features of capitalism and socialism. However, even though he sees himself and his confederates as a "left stream" within a larger "liberal-democratic flow," his predominant concern with social reform issues occasionally puts him at odds with the other authors of *Samosoznanie*. Still, the chief polemical thrust of his collection is unmistakably against the Russian nationalist "right," most notably Solzhenitsyn, whom he describes as a "fierce proponent of clerical authoritarianism."[58]

Among the more interesting contributions to the collection,[59] is German Andreev's essay "Christianity, Tolstoy, and the collection *From Under the Rubble*." Andreev reproaches Solzhenitsyn for a "narrow partisan approach," as well as for an anti-Tolstoyan nationalist thrust. According to Andreev, Tolstoy's brand of Christianity may become a unifying force for all religiously thinking opposition. It ought not be criticized but urgently needs to be saved "from under the rubble." "The world, and consequently Russia, can be saved only on the condition that all believers unite in their struggle against atheism (in the Tolstoyan sense of this word)," says Andreev.[60] Elsewhere he suggests that Tolstoyan ideas may even bring together believers and atheists in their opposition to the present régime. Agreeing with Solzhenitsyn that a moral revolution is urgently needed in the U.S.S.R., Andreev claims that Solzhenitsyn understands such a revolution only in a narrow sectarian sense. Instead, Andreev proposes a moral revolution that would be open for both the Orthodox and other Christians, for the humanist intelligentsia and non-believers, for the proponents of "democratic socialism" and anti-socialists, the émigrés and the "fighters" inside Russia. For all of them Lev Tolstoy could serve as a guiding star in the search for God and the truth, says Andreev.[61]

Belotserkovsky himself directly challenges Solzhenitsyn in his "Letter to the future leaders of the U.S.S.R.: an alternative to Solzhenitsyn's proposals." His chief objection to Solzhenitsyn is that the "compromise between totalitarianism and authoritarianism" that Solzhenitsyn proposes, would hardly make the present régime better. At any rate, it would render meaningless all the sacrifices that were made in the struggle against that régime. Belotserkovsky does not rule out the possibility that Solzhenitsyn's proposals might be accepted by Soviet leaders, but then, he warns, they would become "the shortest way to a *physical* revolution." Apparently realizing that the peaceful, evolutionary, and practical elements of Solzhenitsyn's proposals constitute their chief strength, Belotserkovsky seeks to show that they do not. However, he fails in his task because he does not demonstrate the connection between Solzhenitsyn's proposals and the "physical revolution," except by saying that Solzhenitsyn's proposal to abolish the Marxist-Leninist ideological monopoly is analogous to the cancellation of the oath of allegiance to the tsar that caused anarchy in the army. Anyhow, Belotserkovsky counters Solzhenitsyn's proposals with his own *"peaceful* way to a rejuvenation of the Soviet Russia . . . on the basis of continuity of socialist ideals . . . that (contrary to Solzhenitsyn) have not lost their attractiveness to large categories of Soviet society."[62]

In his other contribution to the collection, the article "The contours of a synthesis: a new left worldview," Belotserkovsky spells out, perhaps unwittingly, just how much his ideas differ from what is known in the U.S.S.R. under the name of socialism. He envisions, for example, a synthesis between the best features of capitalism, such as incentives to work and a free market, and the best features of socialism, such as concern for the common good; or, as he puts it in Hegelian terms, between the "capitalist thesis" of private ownership and the "socialist antithesis" of total nationalization of property. This synthesis would create a collective ownership and self-management of industrial enterprises by groups of workers who would then compete with their products on a free market. Belotserkovsky also envisions a rejuvenation of the "Soviets without the party" that would be elected at the factories and would directly represent the interests of the workers on local and national levels. (He would not forbid the formation of political parties but would limit their activities to the domain outside the factories.) Reproaching the Westernizers ("our liberals") for wishing to emulate the West to the point of being ready to fully restore capitalism, Belotserkovsky promises to "synthesize" them with the Slavophiles.[63] Belotserkovsky admits that he has been influenced in this thinking by the European Third Way movement, headquartered in Achberg, West Germany, in which a number of émigrés from Czechoslovakia play an important role and which sponsored the publication of the collection.[64]

As to Solzhenitsyn, who was the main target of criticism of the above two collections, as well as of numerous magazine and newspaper articles, he largely ignored the attacks until 1982 when he gave a general rebuttal to all of his opponents in his article, "Our pluralists," published in *Vestnik* in 1983. For lack of space I must forego his counter-arguments. Suffice it to say that he lumped his opponents all together under one title. Using it in a derogatory sense, he equated "pluralism" with moral relativism, indifference, and confusion.[65]

The Books of the 1980s

During the 1980s the debate branched out into a number of books written by Soviet émigrés devoted almost exclusively to speculations about the Soviet future. Among these books are Anatoly Fedoseyev's *O novoi Rossii: Al'ternativa* (About a new Russia: an alternative), 1980; Aleksandr Zinoviev's *My i Zapad* (We and the West), 1981; Valery Chalidze's *Budushchee Rossii* (Russia's Future), 1983; Sergey Soldatov's *Zarnitsy Vozrozhdeniia* (The dawn of rebirth), 1984; the late Igor Glagolev's *Post-Andropov Kremlin Strategy*, 1984; and Vadim Belotserkovsky's *Samoupravlenie* (Self-management), 1985.[66] Each of these books deserves more attention than that permitted by the scope of this paper; therefore only a few words about each might be in order.

Fedoseyev, a prominent Soviet electronics specialist, Lenin Prize Winner, and Hero of socialist labor who defected to the West in 1971, envisions a new Russia as a land of free enterprise that should be even "freer" than the West because, as Fedoseyev alleges, the state and trade unions in the West currently exercise too much "monopolistic" control over private enterprise. Fedoseyev's book is appended by a remarkably detailed blueprint for a future Russian constitution. The blueprint has a number of affinities with the Swiss constitution which Fedoseyev obviously admires. Another appendix is entitled "A Project of Transition from Socialism to a New Russia." In it Fedoseyev envisions a coup d'état by "non-Marxist" but patriotic elements of the Party, the KGB, and the army as the most likely prelude to the development of a free enterprise system.

Finding himself at odds with just about everyone in the Soviet emigré community, Zinoviev devotes his book to the proposition that, as much as he hates it, Communism has come to Russia to stay. Since he proposes no alternatives, his works are outside the scope of this paper.

Chalidze, on the other hand, puts his faith on the convergence theory which stipulates that the conflict between the West and the U.S.S.R. will diminish as the system of free enterprise acquires more and more "socialist" features, in the form of state controls, and as the socialist economic monopoly in the U.S.S.R. becomes undermined by the so-called second economy. While Chalidze is not too sanguine about the prospect of greater state controls in the West, he argues that the existence of the semilegal "second economy" in the U.S.S.R. is a clear indication that the country "wants to live under capitalism,"[67] at least as far as service industries are concerned. But for the convergence theory to be put into practice, the expansion of Soviet influence throughout the world must be contained, says Chalidze.[68]

Soldatov's book is chiefly remarkable for the insights it provides into his activities as one of the founders of the clandestine "Democratic Movement of the Soviet Union" and the principal author of its program (which will be discussed later).

Glagolev, who like Fedoseyev defected from the ranks of the Soviet élite, also strongly favors a system of free enterprise. However, unlike Fedoseyev, he prefers to model Russia's political system not on Switzerland, but the U.S.A. Although both Fedoseyev and Glagolev worked for a time with the NTS, later both of them criticized the NTS program (see below) for being too "socialistic."

In his new book, *Samoupravlenie*, Belotserkovsky elaborates on ideas of the "third way," "synthesis," and "self-management," which he first presented in the collection *Demokraticheskie al'ternativy* and then developed in his book *Svoboda, vlast' i sobstvennost'* (Freedom, power, and property), as well as in a collection of his own articles, *Iz portativnogo Gulaga Rossiiskoi emigratsii* (From the portable Gulag of the Russian emigration).[69] The new book is just as polemical and, perhaps, even more abrasive in tone. Belotserkovsky now complains that his ideas are being shunned by both the conservatives and the liberals who allegedly predominate in the emigré publishing. The book's chief value lies in the author's attempt to put the question of "self-management" into a broader historical perspective. Admitting that he was inspired by the anarcho-syndicalist ideas that his father had espoused before he became a Bolshevik, he discusses the experience of self-management in Poland during the Solidarity movement, in Yugoslavia (however, only cursorily), and in such capitalist countries as Spain and the U.S.A. The book is appended with a draft of a law on self-management of Polish factories that was proposed by the trade union "Solidarity" in July 1981. It also contains interviews with two Solidarity activists and an American researcher of self-managing enterprises in the U.S.A. According to Belotserkovsky, not just the "authoritarian nationalists," but the majority of Soviet dissident intellectuals, including such liberals as Shragin, Pomerants, and the late Amalrik, suffer from "hatred of the people" (*narodofobiya*)[70] and therefore do not believe that the Russian workers are capable of freeing themselves from the grip of totalitarianism by switching to self-management

"The Last Hope to Survive"

We shall conclude our review of major individual contributions to the debate with a discussion of Lev Timofeev's essay, "Poslednyaya nadezhda vyzhit' " (The last hope to survive) written inside the U.S.S.R. during Andropov's rule and first published in the emigré magazine *Vremya i my* (Time and We) (Nos. 75-77, 1984) and then as a book in 1985. Timofeev's essay deserves special attention not only because it is a comprehensive discussion of the future coming from inside the country but also because its author is a talented, passionate, and articulate writer, who had the courage to write it even though he anticipated being punished for it.[71]

Timofeev is described as a typical Moscow intellectual of Jewish background. Born in 1936 in Moscow into a prominent Soviet military family, he grew up in the carefree lifestyle of a member of Soviet *priviligentsiya*. He graduated in 1960 from the prestigious Moscow Institute of Foreign Trade and for a while worked for the Ministry of Foreign Trade. However, he soon abandoned his privileged job in order to learn more about life in the U.S.S.R. He worked as a fisherman and served in the army where he used his knowledge of English and Spanish to train the Cuban officers. After he was demobilized from the army in 1964, he bought a summer house in a Russian village for recreation. During his visits there he learned first hand about the hard life of Soviet peasants, which he later described in his first *Samizdat* essay.[72] For the last two decades Timofeev worked mostly as a journalist, a job which afforded him an opportunity for extensive travel across the U.S.S.R. He advanced to the position of literary consultant for the Soviet magazine *Molodoi kommunist* (Young communist). But after his son emigrated to the U.S.A. in 1978, Timofeev and his family (wife and two daughters) experienced considerable hardships. Formerly a Party candidate, Timofeev left the party several years ago.

In "The Last Hope" Timofeev focuses on the question of the Soviet future in the opening paragraph:

> We live in a country the future of which is hidden in the fog. Where are we going? What is going to happen to us in three to five years? Nobody knows an answer to these questions, not even the leaders of the country . . . The future has vanished, as it were, from the political lexicon of our leaders.[73]

This lack of perspective is all the more striking because the present state of affairs in the country augurs nothing but "the stagnation and impoverishment on a country-wide scale." According to Timofeev, Khrushchev was at least able to inspire people with his vision of the Soviets catching up with America in food provisioning, even though nobody believed in his vision of a perfect communist society. Brezhnev and his successors, on the other hand, offered no alternative to the present stagnation, and only promised more of the same. For their inability to solve domestic problems, says Timofeev, Soviet leaders are trying to compensate by "an ambitious and agressive foreign policy aimed at squeezing in their fist not only their own people but also Poland, Afghanistan, and, whenever there is an opportunity, any other country."[74]

Polemicizing with many Western observers' conclusions that there is no significant opposition to the present régime because Andropov did away with the most vocal dissidents, Timofeev describes the current political situation of the country in terms of deepening polarization between the government and the governed. "Today one can confidently say that the most important social spiritual process . . . consists in the growth of society's awareness of its own opposition to authorities," says Timofeev.[75] He explains the confusion of Western observers by the fact that they look for such conventional forms of discontent as workers' strikes, mass demonstrations, and public statements of protest by individuals, that is, the forms of opposition which they are used to seeing in the West. But, since the Soviet state itself is highly unconventional, argues Timofeev, one should be looking harder for unconventional forms of opposition. The fact that Andropov managed to have Solzhenitsyn expelled, Sakharov exiled, Orlov imprisoned, and the Helsinki groups dissolved, does not mean that there is no longer opposition, says Timofeev.[76]

What are those unconventional forms of opposition in the U.S.S.R.? According to Timofeev, opposition is now expressed not so much in words as in actions, such as the resistance of workers to the official drive to increase labor productivity.[77] Moreover, the very fact that the government maintains a "colossal propaganda machine" and tries to suppress even token dissent, suggests that it is fully aware that things can get out of hand at any time. As Timofeev argues, even bribery in the U.S.S.R. must be considered not so much an illegal or unethical activity, but rather as a form of resistance to the régime. "If we were strictly to follow the [official] doctrine, we would die. We can survive only by defying the doctrine, only by resisting it," says Timofeev.[78] In fact, he contends that beating the régime is a way of life for popular masses of the country, and this contention, coming from "inside," seems to vindicate the appropriateness of Shtromas' broad definition of dissent as "refusal to assent."[79]

Comparing the present Soviet régime to the Roman Empire during its period of decline, Timofeev eschews giving any well-defined alternative to it. But if he is cautious about long-range alternatives, he is very firm in his rejection of any revolutionary, radical, and theoretical "quick-fix" solutions. He also doubts the ability of the régime to democratize itself. Somewhat paradoxically, Timofeev puts his faith in the common sense of the people as expressed in the maturation of both public opinion (obshchestvennoe mnenie) and public reason (obshchestvennyi razum). However, his faith in common sense of Soviet people becomes perhaps less paradoxical when he points out the latent respect for religious values among Soviet citizens. Thus, according to Timofeev, family life in the U.S.S.R. would be unthinkable, if people did not instinctively cling to Moses' Ten Commandments.[80]

Timofeev's emphasis on the necessity of a spiritual approach to the present ills of Soviet society is especially significant because he is an economist by education and training. Just as significant is the fact that, Timofeev finds inspiration chiefly in Christianity. Apparently sympathetic to all religions, Timofeev seems to think that a return to Christianity would be the most practical way out of the impasse of the totalitarian society. Pointing out that Christianity originated as the religion of the slaves, Timofeev argues that, among all religions, it is best suited to the present conditions of the U.S.S.R. "Today we, the slaves of the communist doctrine, accept the teaching of Christ as a voice calling us to a spiritual liberation from political and economic conditions of our existence," says Timofeev.[81] Timofeev's respect for the traditional Christian values of the Russian people extends to Russian history. He strongly disagrees with those who trace the origin of Soviet totalitarianism to the autocratic despotism of Ivan the Terrible, Peter I, and Nicholas I. According to Timofeev, the chief source of totalitarianism lies in the "bloody idea" of "The Communist Manifesto."[82] As to the predictions of a future preponderance of Muslim people in the demographic structure of the U.S.S.R., Timofeev counters it with the observation that Muslim immigrants to the Slavic and other traditionally Christian districts of the country are very susceptible to the influence of Christian values.

Referring to Solzhenitsyn's well-known article, "Don't Live According to a Lie," written on the eve of his expulsion, Timofeev says that that admonition struck a deep chord among many Soviet people, especially intellectuals, for whom duality of consciousness is a fact of life. However, Timofeev thinks that the appeal of Solzhenitsyn's admonition is limited to those who can tell the difference between a lie and a truth.[83] As to the popular masses, Timofeev argues that even though they may not exactly know the difference because Soviet propaganda continues to confuse them, they nonetheless feel the difference intuitively and resist the imposition of lies. Soviet people cannot yet live according to truth, Timofeev seems to be saying, but they have largely refused to *think* in the categories of the Communist doctrine.[84]

Timofeev does not predict that "morality and reason will necessarily triumph over the radical madness in politics," as he calls the communist doctrine.[85] But he is convinced that as long as people in the U.S.S.R. are not physically dead, there is a hope. Moreover, he believes that Russia's "monstrously negative experience" might serve as a source for the creation of an "*ideal* civic order" (*ideal'noe grazhdanskoe ustroistvo*) of the third kind, that is the one that is qualitatively different from both Soviet totalitarianism and Western democracies:

> Wouldn't the very process of rejection of the communist idea create in the future . . . the new kind of social community and public institutions that will overcome both the dull inhumanity of totalitarianism and the moral fickleness of democracy that is forever ready to give in to anyone who knows best how to deceive the simple-minded majority of the voters?

As he himself admits, Timofeev's prediction may not come to pass, but he seems on a surer ground when he speculates that the resistance of Soviet people to the régime may have prevented Europe from succumbing to the Communist idea, "just as in the past we protected Europe from the Tatars." He insists that any alternative to the present régime must take into account the country's "monstrously negative experience."[86]

Timofeev does not advocate a social revolution. In fact, he warns against it, saying that "Freedom cannot be obtained by violence."[87] Timofeev calls for a spiritual overcoming of the régime, and for a return to religious values instilled in people by centuries of tradition. He also calls for the formation of a united front of opposition to the totalitarianism régime, "the front of common sense."[88] He is aware, however, that that task is extremely difficult because the government has been successful in dividing the forces of opposition and would not allow "any sort of united front of resistance in any sphere of societal life, particularly, in the economic sphere where the societal counter-pressure has been especially strong."[89]

Programs of Oppositional Groups

Our roundup of the futurological debate would be incomplete without saying a few words about those images of Russia's future that emerge not from individual viewpoints but from programmatic statements issued in the name of various oppositional groups. Although they do not necessarily engage in polemics, the programs of oppositional groups must be considered an indispensable part of our general debate due to the mere fact of their existence. Below I will limit myself to just three such programs: those of the NTS, VSKhSON, and DDSS.

National Labor Union of the Russian Solidarists, better known by its Russian acronym NTS, was founded by Russian émigrés in 1930. Headquartered in Frankfurt, West Germany, it currently draws it membership mostly from the second wave of emigration. The NTS presents itself as an organization whose main body clandestinely operates in the U.S.S.R., whereas its headquarters abroad serve as a coordinating center. Be that as it may, the NTS has been known in the U.S.S.R. for a long time and some of its documents were circulated in *samizdat*. In its Program the NTS proclaims its adherence to the new ideology of solidarism rooted in the philosophy of Christian "personalism" and the ideas of syndicalist social organization (hence "labor union").[90] The NTS Program presents the solidarist ideology as an alternative to all main contemporary ideologies: liberalism (capitalism), socialism (which tends to become totalitarian), fascism and communism (both unacceptable as totalitarian). As its historical objective, the NTS Program sees the completion of the revolutionary process that started with the February 1917 revolution but was aborted by the communists. It promises popular representation, social justice, the rule of law, and equality of all before the law. On the nationalities issue, it promises self-determination through a plebiscite as to whether a nation should stay in a free confederation with Russia or choose independence. As far as the economy is concerned, the NTS Program favors three forms of property: national, collective, and private. The nationalized sector would include natural deposits, energy resources, the defense industry, and countrywide transportation and communication. The NTS Program also stipulates separation of state and church, goodwill to all religions, but no discrimination against nonbelievers.

The NTS Program considers hopes for a "positive evolution" of the régime "unfounded" and advocates its elimination through a "People's Liberation Revolution." However, it sees that revolution not as a "spontaneous explosion of the forces of destruction and revenge," but as "the change of ideas," not an "instantaneous overthrow" but as a "complex and multi-faceted process."[91] That process may include three options: (1) gradual disintegration of the party monopoly on various fields of social life; (2) direct coup d'état carried out by key figures of the party and the army disillusioned with the system; and (3) open confrontations of the populace with the "organs of oppression," confrontations that might turn into a general uprising. According to the NTS Program, it is likely that at some point the three options might coalesce.

In recent years, the NTS sponsored, on the pages of *Posev*, a number of debates in which it sought to explore whether disillusioned key members of Soviet establishment could play a positive and constructive role in the elimination of the dictatorship through reforms.[92] However, Ernst Neizvestny, a renowned sculptor and one of *Posev's* authors, while agreeing with the NTS proposition that there are some "thinking" leaders who are fully aware of the "malaise" of the system, nevertheless doubted the possibility of "bloodless reforms," simply because that malaise has gone too far.[93] Dismissing Sakharov's and Solzhenitsyn's proposals as "purely humanitarian,"

Neizvestny seemed to endorse the NTS approach which seeks to confront the régime with more specific proposals, as well as with the "alternative authority" embodied in an organization.

The All-Russian Social-Christian Union for the Liberation of the People, better known under its Russian acronym VSKhSON, was an underground organization which proclaimed the overthrow of "the Soviet dictatorship" as its goal. VSKhSON was founded on 2 February 1964 by four Leningrad University students. Headed by Igor Ogurtsov, an orientalist, it grew to a membership of twenty-seven people, and was supported by a larger network of sympathizers, before it was uncovered by the KGB in 1967. Seventeen VSKhSON members were sentenced to various terms. Ogurtsov received the harshest, fifteen years, which he has by now served out, although he still remains in exile. Since the history of the VSKhSON was described, and its various documents, including the Program, were translated into English and analysed in John Dunlop's excellent book, *The New Russian Revolutionaries*,[94] I refer the reader to that book for details. Here I would just summarize the most essential points of the Program, written largely by Ogurtsov.

Rejecting Communism for both its "striking similarity with Fascism" and for being a "sickly offspring of materialist capitalism,"[95] the Program suggests a "third way" and envisions that "tomorrow's world will be founded in Christian ideals," including "the freedom of the individual, the sacredness of the family, brotherly relations among people and the unity of all nations."[96] Economically, "VSKhSON seeks to find a middle ground between collectivism and laissez-faire capitalism," says Dunlop, who also points out that the program stipulates that syndicalist associations would play a considerable role in the management of the economy and the government.[97] It is noteworthy that the program seeks to provide checks and balances by the separation of powers into four branches. In addition to the usual three—legislative, executive, and judicial—the Social-Christian government would have another major check on its power in a supervisory (*bliustitel'nyi*) Supreme Council (*Verkhovnyi Sobor*) in which one-third of the seats would be reserved for the Christian hierarchy. As to the executive branch, Dunlop thinks that a constitutional monarch seems to be indicated, but admits that the program does not clearly spell it out. "A revitalized monarchy, enjoying the respect and support of the populace and ruling in conjunction with syndicalist unions and corporations—this would seem to be VSKhSON's vision," says Dunlop.[98]

Dunlop also points out a "great similarity" of VSKhSON's ideas with those of Solzhenitsyn, except that the latter rejects the use of revolutionary violence. It should be kept in mind, however, that even though VSKhSON envisioned a forcible overthrow of the régime on the model of the 1956 Hungarian revolution, its members had but one rusty revolver at their disposal, and they neither engaged in nor advocated terrorism. As they counted on the emergence of opposition inside the party, their commitment to violence can be considered as only conditional.

Finally, a few words must be said about the image of the Soviet future that emerges from the Program of the Democratic Movement of the Soviet Union (henceforth referred to as DDSS, the organization's Russian acronym) which began circulating in *samizdat* in October, 1969, and in 1970 was published in the West.[99] Recently, Sergei Soldatov, a Soviet dissident who had spent six years in Soviet jails before he was allowed to emigrate in 1981, took credit for writing it.[100] Politically, the DDSS Program envisions a multiparty representative democracy, with free elections, separation of powers, trial by jury, and amnesty for all political prisoners. It also proclaims economic "pluralism" founded on three forms of ownership: national, collective, and private. On the nationalities issue, it proposes the creation of "The Union of Democratic Republics," after each nation had a chance to ascertain its wishes through a referendum under the auspices of the U.N.

Although, on the whole, the DDSS Program is close to that of Sakharov, it radically differs from it in two respects: (1) it presupposes the use of illegal and conspiratorial methods to achieve liberation from communism; and (2) it advocates a religious revival. In these two respects the DDSS is similar to the VSKhSON, although it recommends only nonviolent means. According to Soldatov, due to the fact that the DDSS was formed as an underground organization, its program and activities were largely ignored by *The Chronicle of Current Events*.[101] Osipov, on the other hand, reproached the DDSS Program for its "anti-Russian statements" and the condemnation of socialism.[102] Soldatov himself was not quite satisfied with the program, and after "spiritually tearing it apart," in 1972 he wrote for a group of coconspirators *The Program of Ethical and Political Rebirth* in which he emphasized that political liberation is meaningless unless it is accompanied by moral standards higher than those of the oppressors.[103] For that he was soon arrested.

Conclusion

As we have seen, the Russian *samizdat* and émigré debate on the Soviet future has produced a considerable body of literature that has not yet been assembled, sorted out, translated, analyzed, and assessed. It is beyond the scope of this paper to analyze and evaluate each of the many contributions to the debate. The most I can do is try to assess the significance of the debate as a whole, to identify the areas of agreement and disagreement among various visions of the future, and to determine their chief thrust. I shall start with a number of general observations pertaining to the debate as a whole.

First of all, one cannot overestimate the fact that the debate took place at all, and continues to the present day, in defiance of the totalitarian state that has used every means to project to Soviet citizens, and the outside world, the one and only image of the country's future—that of its dismal present. To those who have witnessed the spiritual and intellectual wasteland, "the rubble," that was left behind at the time of Stalin's death in 1953, the debate itself must seem a miracle indeed. Secondly, one is impressed with the multitude, variety, and the wide ideological range of the images of the future that were produced as alternatives to the only permissible official image. This shows that the present régime is thought to be moribund by people of the most diverse backgrounds and persuasions: from pro-Western liberals, Russian nationalists, and Christians to Marxists, para-Marxists, and a variety of socialists. Thirdly, the debate makes it abundantly clear that it springs forth from the very heart of the Soviet experience, is deeply rooted in the actual conditions of the U.S.S.R. and responds to the most urgent needs of the country. Virtually all of the participants in the debate used to be exemplary Soviet citizens, and some of them formerly were convinced Communists. All of them are genuine products of the system, and they discuss its future as insiders. Fourthly, one should not underestimate the fact that the debate went across Soviet state borders and was clearly enriched by the experience, knowledge, and perspectives that some of its participants, the émigrés and defectors, had acquired while living in freedom outside the U.S.S.R.

Lastly, the debate as a whole is distinguished by the fact that none of its participants is a professional futurologist, nor does any one of them pretend to be. Although some of them are outstanding scholars, writers, artists, and scientists, they do not debate Russia's future from a detached, objective, and scholarly viewpoint. On the other hand, one cannot accuse them of indifference and relativism, as they clearly demonstrate a great passion for truth and an uncommon courage to speak up when they know that such outspokenness in the U.S.S.R. would certainly invite punishment. One can hardly blame them for being amateurish visionaries who advocate their visions as much as they predict them.

A methodological question naturally arises: Can we take seriously visions of the future that are obviously influenced by the subjective personal inclinations of visionaries? Of course, my answer to this question is positive; otherwise, I would not have endeavored to write this paper. In fact, I believe that my group of visionaries, taken as a whole, deserves as much attention as any group of professional futurologists, even though the latter could justifiably claim objectivity as their forte. In the final account, Russia's future—as any other country's future—depends more on the will of its most dedicated citizens than on any theoretical construct of outsiders, no matter how logical or objective.

Another methodological question is this: Even if one would readily acknowledge the dedication of my visionaries to their country, to what extent do they represent the aspirations of the Soviet people at large? This question cannot be conclusively answered until the country is free enough to have meaningful elections or, at least, opinion polls. However, there could be little doubt that the above images of the future do reflect a very wide range of dissident opinion, and that dissent, broadly defined, reaches far beyond the small dissident circles of intellectuals who come in direct contact with Western media, and thus are better known to the West.

Besides the above methodological uncertainties arising from the necessarily speculative nature of the subject, there are two other obstacles which contribute to the difficulty of evaluating the debate, as they hindered the debate itself. For one thing, more often than not, the debaters did not have easy access to the works of their opponents. Osipov, for instance, responded to Sakharov's critique or Solzhenitsyn's *Letter* solely on the basis of what he had heard on a Deutsche Welle Radio broadcast in Russian.[104] The other obstacle has to do with the fact that the debaters were inevitably influenced by the Soviet *newspeak*, that is by distortion of the meaning of words through arbitrariness and deliberate imprecision of their definitions. As a result, the debate often suffers from purely emotional response to such notions as "socialism," "Soviet," "pluralism," and "democracy."

Let me now try to classify all the images of the Soviet future that were discussed in this paper into broader categories. Roughly, all the images can be divided into two distinct categories as to whether their authors are positive or negative, optimistic or pessimistic about Russia's future; in other words, as to whether they were produced by "believers" or "non-believers" in a better future for the country which presently finds itself in the firm grip of totalitarianism. Among the images produced by the "non-believers" are: (1) the late Amalrik's prediction of Russia's historical death, that is a zero-future image; (2) Zinoviev's more-of-the-same image; (3) Yanov's the worst-is-yet-to-come prediction of a coalition between the Stalinists and the Russian nationalists, unless (4) Yanov's own vision—that of the West helping the current Soviet leaders to maintain the status quo in the spirit of détente and with the hope that the régime would eventually mellow by itself—is put in practice.

Although I think that an awareness of the above negative images is necessary, as a "believer" myself I may be presumed too biased to even attempt their evaluation.[105] Therefore, it is best to forego their discussion altogether. Both as a Russian who has a faith in his country and as an American who is far from being satisfied with the present global situation, I would rather concentrate on the images that not only offer solutions to Russia's problems but also imply that a better future for the whole world would follow.

So, the remainder of the images that have emerged in the debate represent positive thinking, and they may be summarized in the following twelve distinct types, named after their principal sponsors:

(1) Sakharov: Westernist, liberal orientation; favors Western parliamentary democracy; mixed, mostly socialized economy; self-determination for border republics; counts on a convergence with the West; and urges resistance to Soviet expansion.

(2) Roy Medvedev: Marxist philosophy; favors "democratic socialism" within a multiparty system; believes that Marxism can best solve Soviet problems; would allow some privatization of agriculture, but retain basically socialist economy; no secession for border republics; foresees no role for orthodox Christianity or religion in general.

(3) Turchin: Secular, Westernist, "scientific worldview"; foresees the emergence of a new socio-economic system embracing the "religion of socialism," but until then urges resistance to Soviet expansion.

(4) Orlov: Apparently secular inspiration; advocates a "synthesis" between socialism and capitalism in the form of "decentralized socialism"; emphasizes a need for ethics of nonviolence; and urges an antitotalitarian alliance of all oppositional forces.

(5) Belotserkovsky: Secular, anarcho-syndicalist and Marxist philosophy; advocates a "Third Way" both in government and economy, based on workers' "self-management"; foresees no role for religion; wants to minimize "physical revolution" by stressing a continuity of a future Russia with the present system.

(6) Fedoseyev: Apparently secular inspiration; favors the Swiss constitution as a model; advocates an unrestrained free market economy but land must be nationalized; would allow national self-determination including secession, but favors federation of autonomous republics; goodwill to all religions; counts mostly on a coup by patriotic forces from within the establishment as a trigger of fundamental transformation.

(7) NTS: Solidarist ideology inspired by Russian religious philosophy; advocates a new, solidarist, polity; mixed economy, based on syndical-

ism; professes national self-determination but favors a confederation of autonomous republics; professes goodwill to all religions but no privileges over atheists; envisions a popular revolution but also counts on the "constructive" forces within the government to start the process of change.

(8) VSKhSON (Ogurtsov): "Social-Christian" ideology; an emphasis on a need for a Russian national and religious rebirth; may favor constitutional monarchy based on the division of powers, including a Church hierarchy; favors a mixed, mostly syndicalist, economy; would agree to a secession of "occupied nations"; relies on conspiratorial methods leading to a popular revolution, but also envisions a coup by patriotic forces from within the establishment.

(9) DDSS (Soldatov): Believes in universal religious and spiritual revival; advocates a "Third Way" in polity; mixed economy based on three forms of property—individual, collective, and state; urges consolidation of ethnic Russians through secession of border nations; emphasizes a need for interreligious ethics; favors conspiratorial but nonviolent methods of change; envisions disengagement of a future Russia from meddling in other countries and cooperation with Europe.

(10) Solzhenitsyn: Believes in the necessity of a Russian national and religious rebirth; envisions an authoritarian transitional stage, perhaps, under the tutelage of the party, until a new polity, based on Russia's historical heritage, is created; apparently favors a mixed economy with a prevalence of private enterprise; professes national self-determination including the right to secede; hopes for a preeminence of Russian Orthodox moral authority but asks for no privileges; emphasizes the need for an evolutionary, nonviolent path of reforms, perhaps, with the party in charge but on the condition that the Marxist-Leninist ideological monopoly is abolished.

(11) Maximov: Religiously inspired; urges a "Third Way" in polity with some elements of Western multiparty system; a mixed economy, including voluntary village communes; and basically supports Solzhenitsyn's emphasis on the need for Russian national and religious rebirth.

(12) Timofeev: Apparently inspired by Christian ethics; envisions the emergence of a new polity from the bitter experience of totalitarian rule; professes nonviolence; believes that opposition to the régime is all-pervasive; urges the formation of an anti-totalitarian alliance of "common sense."

As will be seen, more graphically, in the Appendix, the above twelve types of futuristic imagination represent a rather wide "spectrum of positive alternative visions of Russia's future."[106] I have listed them in no particular order, except that the first half seems to be secularly inspired while the latter half emphasizes a need for religious and spiritual revival, be it individual, national, or universal. In other words, the first six visions are produced by secular "believers" in Russia's better future, while the latter six are authored by religious believers. This disparity undoubtedly reflects deep ideological divisions existing within Soviet society. The basic division seems to be between those who, like Sakharov, Medvedev, Turchin, and Belotserkovsky, describe the ills of totalitarian society in secular terms, and prescribe a secular cure; and those who, like Solzhenitsyn, Ogurtsov, Soldatov, and Timofeev, diagnose Marxist ideology itself as a spiritual disease, and recommend a cure accordingly. This philosophical division has naturally resulted in different specific suggestions for the future, especially, in such categories as form of government, economy, and the role of religion (See Appendix).

However, all the differences notwithstanding, there exist large areas of consensus that stretch across all ideological and political divisions.[107] The greatest area of consensus that unites all twelve types of visionaries is that all of them find the present system moribund. All of them want either to replace the system entirely or change it fundamentally. All of them aim at the same primary goal of democratization, liberalization, humanization, and, if I may use a "poli sci" word, detotalitarianization of the present régime. For that reason, the régime persecutes and suppresses all of them. To be sure, our debaters disagree on the specific form of government. However, even then they tend to agree that a future Russia cannot simply adopt a ready-made Western-style parliamentary system but needs to find its own "Third Way." The same applies to the search for a new economic system: the consensus is that the Soviet economy cannot satisfy the needs of the country unless a certain degree of private ownership, private enterprise and market economy are allowed. The prevailing thrust seems toward a mixed economy with various degrees of individual, collective, and state enterprise. This thrust is significant because a mixed economy can serve as a foundation for political pluralism.

Another area of consensus is in the approach to nationalities problem. Virtually all of our debaters agree that democratization of Russia proper cannot take place unless various national minorities have an opportunity to exercise the right of self-determination. With the exception of the Marxist Medvedev, all seem to accept the possibility that several border republics might wish to secede. As to the nationalities which might wish to stay with the Russians, all seem to agree that they should be given a genuine autonomy within a federation.

A third area of nearly complete consensus pertains to the category of future foreign policy. All debaters envision the withdrawal of Soviet troops from Afghanistan and Eastern Europe, the cessation of Soviet support to the so called "National Liberation" (in fact, mostly terrorist and Marxist) movements, the end of the nuclear arms race with the West, and the establishment of friendly cooperative relations with the U.S.A., Western Europe, Japan, and other peaceful countries.

Finally, a large area of consensus can be seen in the category of methods of attainment (of the goal of the detotalitarianization of the present régime), where virtually all authors emphasize evolution and reforms rather than revolution, and advocate nonviolent methods of pushing the government on the path of reforms. Even when the NTS and VSKhSON call for revolution, they emphasize that it is not a revolution of hatred, wanton destruction, and revenge, but a revolution as a change of the value system. Evidently, Lenin has taught at least one lesson to Russia very well—that a violent revolution, no matter how justified it may appear, ultimately fails, even when it succeeds. Against the background of universal violence and terrorism our Russian "futurists" do not seem to belong to this world. Their attitude to violence and revolution makes one wonder how they hope to get rid of Lenin's creation without using Lenin's means. One may think, perhaps, that they would preach nonviolence as long as they would not have at their disposal *his* means. But I do not think so. I believe they really do represent a new kind of thinking that seems "other worldly," and yet alone has a chance to pull Russia, and the world, out of its present dead-end.

After having praised all these visionaries as a group, I feel free to admit that, on the whole, I find myself more in agreement with those who emphasize the spiritual approach in general, and the Russian national and religious rebirth schemes, such as Solzhenitsyn's, Ogurtsov's, and Timofeev's, that is with the mainstream *vozrozhdentsy,* in particular.[108] One does not have to be a Russian to realize that Solzhenitsyn's approach has the best chance to succeed and thus to benefit all. For one thing, among all others, Solzhenitsyn's approach is the one that has the potential to appeal to the largest possible democratic constituency—the Russian people of Orthodox background, that is about half of the population. All negative demographic trends notwithstanding, ethnic Russians will continue to be the largest block of potential voters for the foreseeable future. When combined with the millions of Ukrainians and Belorussians of Orthodox background, that block would command if not a majority then an overwhelming plurality for a long time.

I am not saying that all Soviet citizens of Slavic Orthodox background are against so-called "Soviet power," but then Solzhenitsyn does not ask them to be. The emergence of the All-Russian Society for the Preservation of Historical and Cultural Monuments (*VOOPIK*) and the Rodina Club, as well as the popularity of the Russian ruralist writers (*derevenshchiki*) indicate that there is a growing realization among the Russians that Marxist-Leninist ideology and the goals of the Soviet state are contrary to, or incompatible with, the national values and aspirations of historical Russia.[109] A potential clearly exists for the formation of a broadly based Russian national opposition, an opposition that is all the more dangerous to the régime because it would find support not just at low layers of society but would penetrate it vertically up to the top of the Soviet hierarchy. The government knows about this potential source of opposition, but it also knows that as long as the free world, including many Soviet émigrés, fears Russian nationalism more than it fears communism, there is little need to worry.

I think the Soviet government would worry much more if all oppositional groups, especially those in emigration, took seriously the appeals of Osipov, Orlov, and Timofeev to stop bickering about non-essential issues and strive instead for a single anti-totalitarian alliance. I believe Solzhenitsyn's proposals can best serve as a basis for such an alliance. By virtue of his contribution to Russian literature, he occupies the highest moral ground and can stand above narrow partisan views. It is no accident that in *The Red Wheel* he portrays Stolypin as a "liberal-conservative" reformer and, particularly, praises him for steering the ship of state along a "new and for Russia unusual middle course" (*vesti Rossiiu novym neobychainym srednim farvaterom*).[110] This does not mean that Solzhenitsyn is calling for a return to the time of the tsars. It rather means that he suggests Stolypin as a model of patriotic, but non-partisan and essentially centrist, "liberal-conservative" statesmanship for future Russian leaders.[111]

I see no reason why Solzhenitsyn's own proposals cannot be modified in such a way that they would be more centrist and thus more acceptable to other segments of anti-totalitarian opposition and to the West. To do so Solzhenitsyn could, for example, tone down his anti-socialist rhetoric and treat non-totalitarian forms of socialism in the same manner that he accords to the local soviets, drop his objections to the formation of political parties, leave the decision about the future form of government to a freely-elected Constitutent Assembly, and balance his nationalist appeal with an internationalist appeal, similar to the one cultivated by Maximov and Bukovsky. Solzhenitsyn's program can incorporate not only Belotserkovsky's ideas about using the Polish Solidarity experiments with "self-management," but also Orlov's suggestions for "decentralized socialism" as well as the NTS' and Ogurtsov's ideas about syndicalism. I think Solzhenitsyn made it clear enough that he is *not against* those opponents of the Soviet régime whose ideological, political, and religious beliefs differ from his own. But, perhaps, he could make it clearer still that he is *for* and *with* them, at least, as long as they strive for the primary common goal of pulling the U.S.S.R. out of its present totalitarian dead-end. Conversely, Solzhenitsyn's opponents should recognize that without the Russian national and religious rebirth movement any anti-totalitarian coalition would have little chance to succeed.

All in all, the debate about the Soviet future clearly demonstrates that virtually all alternatives to the present régime are not only compatible with the interests of the free world, but promise to eliminate exactly those features of the present régime which inherently make it an enemy of peace, freedom, and human dignity. A future Russia may never become a copy of Western democracies, but it will certainly be their friend and partner in creating a better world.

NOTES

1. Andrei Sakharov, *A. Sakharov v bor'be za mir* (A. Sakharov in the struggle for peace), a collection incl. "Razmyshleniia o progresse, mirnom sosushchestvovanii i intellektual'noi svobode" (Thoughts about progress, peaceful coexistence, and intellectual freedom), (Frankfurt am Main: Posev, 1973), 9-65. Since it was originally published under the title, *Memorandum Akademika A. Sakharova* (Posev, 1970), I refer to Sakharov's work as the memorandum. One of the early English editions was *Progress, Coexistence and Intellectual Freedom* (New York: Norton, 1968). Quotations are from English language publications, if available.
2. Andrei Amalrik, *Will the Soviet Union Survive Until 1984?* (London: Penguin, 1970), 26. For the Russian original see *Prosushchestvuet li Sovetskii Soiuz do 1984 goda?* (Amsterdam: Herzen Foundation, 1970).
3. Alexander Solzhenitsyn et al., *From Under the Rubble* (Boston, Toronto: Little, Brown and Co., 1974).
4. Ibid., 3-4.
5. Ibid., 135. In "Repentance and Self-Limitation" Solzhenitsyn chiefly polemicizes against the anonymous NN's article "Metanoia" and the pseudonymous Gorsky's article "Russian Messianism," both of which were published in the *Vestnik Russkogo Khristianskogo Dvizheniia* (Paris, France), No. 97.
6. Ibid., 268.
7. Ibid., 257. In "The Smatterers" Solzhenitsyn polemicizes against Altaev's article "The Dual Consciousness of Intelligentsia and Pseudo-culture" and Chelnov's "What Is to Be Done?" (both in *Vestnik*, No. 97); L. Ventsov's "Think!" (*Vestnik*, No. 99), as well as against several *samizdat* articles by Semyon Telegin and G. Pomerants.
8. Ibid., 81.
9. Ibid., 66.
10. Ibid., 102.
11. Ibid., 104.
12. Ibid., 280 and 281.

APPENDIX

Spectrum of Positive Alternative Visions of Russia's Future

	Categories of Ideas / Authors	Philosophical Inspiration	Form of Government (transitional/ultimate)	Economy	Approach to Nationalities Problem	Future Foreign Policy	Role of Religion	Methods of Attainment
1	Sakharov	Secular Liberal Westernist	Western democracy	Mixed	Self-determination Autonomy	Disengagement; cooperation with West	No role	Convergence evolution reforms
2	Medvedev	Secular Marxist Westernist	Democratic socialism, Multiparty	Mostly socialist; private initiative	No right to secede but more autonomy		No special role but more religious tolerance	Reforms from above
3	Turchin	Secular "Scientific worldview" Westernist	New Polity	Socialist		Disengagement	"Religion of socialism"	Evolution resistance to Soviet expansion
4	Orlov	Secular	"Synthesis"	Decentralized socialism; Third Way		Disengagement	Need for ethics	Anti-totalitarian alliance; nonviolence
5	Belotserkovsky	Secular Anarcho-Syndicalist Marxist	"Third Way"	Self-Management Syndicalism			No role	No "physical revolution," Continuity
6	Fedoseyev		Western democracy; Swiss model	Free market but nationalized land	Self-deter. Autonomy; Federation	Disengagement	Goodwill to all religions	Coup

7	NTS	Solidarist Russian religious philosophy (Berdiaev)	New Polity	Mixed, based on syndicalism	Self-determination Confederation; Autonomy	Disengagement	Goodwill to all rleigions but no privileges	Mixed: Coup, reforms popular revolution
8	VSKhSON (Ogurtsov)	Russian religious philosophy (Berdiaev)	"Third Way" perhaps, Constitutional monarchy	Mixed, based on syndicalism and "Social Christianity"	Secession for occupied nations	Disengagement	Christian hierarchy as fourth power	Conspiracy, popular revolution, and/or coup from above
9	DDDS (Soldatov)	Universal religious revival	"Third Way"	Mixed	Consolidation of Russia thru secession	Disengagement, Cooperation with Europe	New interreligious ethics	Conspiratorial but nonviolent
10	Solzhenitsyn	Russian National/ Religious rebirth	Authoritarian transitional state including the party)	Mixed	Self-determination	Disengagement	Russian Orthodox moral preeminence	Evolution, nonviolence; concessions from above
11	Maximov	Religious	"Third Way" Authoritarian/ democratic; multiparty on low level	Mixed, incl. village communes	Self-determination	Disengagement	Religious ethics	Evolution, Pressure of world opinion
12	Timofeev	Christian ethics	New Polity	Mixed		Disengagement	Christian ethics	Anti-total. alliance of "common senses;" nonviolence

13. Ibid., 293-94.
14. Ibid., 291.
15. Aleksandr I. Solzhenitsyn, *Letter to the Soviet Leaders* (New York: Harper and Row, 1974), 15.
16. Ibid., 78 and 74.
17. Ibid., 77-78.
18. Andrei Sakharov, "On Aleksandr Solzhenitsyn's *Letter to the Soviet Leaders*," in *The Political, Social and Religious Thought of Russian 'Samizdat': An Anthology*, eds. Michael Meerson-Aksenov and Boris Shragin (Belmont, Mass.: Nordland, 1977), 291-301, esp. 300. This anthology also contains articles by Gorsky, Pomerants, Altaev, and Ventsov, that were mentioned in note 7.
19. Roy Medvedev, "What Awaits Us In The Future?" in *The Political, Social and Religious Thought of Russian 'Samizdat,'* 76-96, esp 77.
20. Ibid., 88.
21. Ibid., 93.
22. Wladislaw Krasnow, "Vladimir Osipov: From Atheism to Christianity," *RCDA (Religion in Communist Dominated Areas)* XVIII, Nos. 1-3 (1979): 9-13.
23. Vladimir Osipov, "Piat' vozrazheniy Sakharovu" (Five objections to Sakharov), in *Tri otnosheniia k rodine* (Three attitudes to motherland), (Frankfurt: Posev, 1978), 73-80. I have not capitalized the initial letters in English titles to indicate that it is my own translation from the original. Osipov admits in the article that he responded to what he had heard about Sakharov on a *Deutsche Welle* radio broadcast.
24. Ibid., 186.
25. Andrei D. Sakharov, *My Country and the World* (New York: Random House, 1975), 37.
26. Ibid., 31.
27. Ibid., 100.
28. Ibid., 102.
29. See, for instance, F. J. M. Feldbrugge, *Samizdat and Political Dissent in the Soviet Union* (Leyden: Sijthoff, 1975); Peter Reddaway, *Uncensored Russia: Protest and Dissent in the Soviet Union* (1972); George Saunders, ed., *Samizdat: Voices of the Soviet Opposition*; Rudolf Tökes, ed., *Dissent in the U.S.S.R.: Politics, Ideology, and People* (John Hopkins Univ. Press, 1975); and John B. Dunlop, *The New Russian Revolutionaries* (Belmont, Mass.: Nordland, 1976); and Donald R. Kelley, *The Solzhenitsyn-Sakharov Dialogue: Politics, Society and the Future* (Westport, Conn. and London, England: Greenwood Press, 1982). See also Ludmila Alexeyeva, *Istoriia inakomysliia v. SSSR: noveishii period* (New York: Khronika Press, 1984); and its English translation, *Soviet Dissent: Contemporary Movement for National, Religious, and Human Rights* (Middletown, Conn.: Wesleyan Univ. Press, 1985).
30. Igor Shafarevich, *The Socialist Phenomenon*, transl. William Tjalsma (New York: Harper & Row, 1980), first published in Russian under the title *Sotsialism kak iavlenie mirovoi istorii* (Paris, YMCA Press, 1975).
31. Valentin Turchin, *The Inertia of Fear and the Scientific Worldview* (New York:

Columbia University Press, 1981), first published in Russian as *Inertsiia strakha* (New York, Khronika Press, 1977), 108.

32. Ibid., 109.
33. Ibid., 284.
34. Ibid., 288.
35. Aleksandr Solzhenitsyn, "A World Split Apart" (Harvard University Commencement Address, June 1978), in *Solzhenitsyn at Harvard*, ed. Ronald Berman (Washington, D.C.: Ethics and Public Policy Center, 1980); Idem, "Misconceptions About Russia Are A Threat To America," *Foreign Affairs* 58, No. 4 (Spring 1980).
36. Solzhenitsyn, "A World," 12.
37. Solzhenitsyn, "Misconceptions," 809.
38. Ibid., 827.
39. Alexander Yanov, *The Russian New Right, Right-Wing Ideologies in the Contemporary U.S.S.R.* (Berkeley, Calif.: Institute of International Studies, University of California, 1978), 7.
40. Ibid., 151.
41. Ibid., 160-161.
42. Alexander Shtromas, *Political Change and Social Development: The Case of the Soviet Union* (Frankfurt am Main, Bern: Peter Lang, 1981), 81.
43. Ibid., 132.
44. Valerii Chalidze, "O nekotorykh tendentsiiakh v emigrantskoi publitsistike" (About certain tendencies in émigré journalism), *Kontinent* 23 (1980): 151-75.
45. Vladimir Bukovsky, "Pochemu russkie ssoriatsia?" (Why do the Russians quarrel?) *Kontinent* 23 (1980): 176-99, esp. 191.
46. Ibid., 193.
47. Vladimir Maksimov, "Razmyshleniia o demokratii," (Reflections on democracy) *Russkaia Mysl'*, 23 August 1979, p. 6. This article is summarized in my text on the basis of John B. Dunlop, *The Faces of Contemporary Russian Nationalism* (Princeton, N.J.: Princeton University Press, 1983), 248-49.
48. *Samosoznanie: Sbornik statei* (Self-awareness: a collection of articles). Compilers P. Litvivov, M. Meerson-Aksenov, and B. Shragin (New York: Khronika Press, 1976); and *Demokraticheskie Al'ternativy: sbornik statei i dokumentov*, compiler Vadim Belotserkovsky (Achberg, West Germany: Achberger, 1976).
49. *Samosoznanie*, 7.
50. Ibid., 70.
51. Ibid., 80.
52. Ibid., 86-87.
53. Among other contributors, in addition to the compilers, are Yevgeny Barabanov, Lev Kopelev. Dimitry Nelidov, Richard Pipes, Grigory Pomerants, and Valentin Turchin. Barabanov also contributed to Solzhenitsyn's *From Under the Rubble*.
54. *Samosoznanie*, 279. In 1986 Orlov was released and allowed to emigrate as part of the Daniloff exchange deal.
55. Ibid., 296.
56. Ibid., 299.

57. *Al'ternativy,* 165-166.
58. Ibid., 89.
59. Other contributors to the collection are Leonid Pliushch, Mihajlo Mihajlov, Jan Elberfeld, Yulia Vishnevsky, Alexander Yanov, Anatoly Levitin-Krasnov, Efim Etkind, and Evgeny Kushev.
60. *Al'ternativy,* 165-166.
61. Ibid., 167.
62. Ibid., 263.
63. Ibid., 86.
64. Ibid., 91.
65. A Solzhenitsyn, "Nashi pliuralisty," *Vestnik* II, No. 139 (1983): 134.
66. Anatoly Fedoseyev, *O novoi Rossii: Al'ternativa* (London: Overseas Publications Interchange Ltd., 1980); Aleksandr Zinoviev, *My i Zapad* (Lausanne, Switzerland: L'Age d'Homme, 1981); Valerii Chalidze, *Budushchee Rossii: Ierarkhicheskii analiz* (New York: Chalidze Publ., 1983); Sergei Soldatov, *Zarnitsy Vozrozhdeniya: Opyt politicheskoi bor'by i nravstvennogo prosvetitel'stva,* intro. by Abdurakhman Avtorkhanov and Martin Dewhirst (London: OPI, 1984); Igor Glagolev, *Post-Andropov Kremlin Strategy* (Washington, D.C.: Association for Cooperation of Democratic Countries, 1984); Vadim Belotserkovsky, *Samoupravlenie,* intro. by Jiri Pelikan (Munich: 1985).
67. Chalidze, *Budushchee,* 185.
68. Ibid., 195-196.
69. Vadim Belotserkovsky, *Svoboda, vlast'i sobstvennost'* (Achberg, West Germany, 1966); an *Iz portativnogo Gulaga Rossiiskoi emigratsii: sbornik statei* (München, West Germany, 1983).
70. Belotserkovsky, *Samoupravlenie,* 108.
71. Lev Timofeev, *Posledniaia nadezhda vyzhit'* (P.O. Box 410 Tenafly, N.J. 07670: Hermitage, 1985). Besides the essay, pp. 115-177, the book contains Timofeev's previous *samizdat* work, "Tekhnologiia chernogo rynka ili krest' ianskoe iskusstvo golodat'" (Intricacies of the black market, or the peasant art of going hungry), 7-111. For his writing, Timofeev was arrested on 19 March 1985, and on 30 September 1985 sentenced to six years in a labor camp. In early February 1987 he was released as part of Gorbachev's "openness" campaign.
72. See note 71.
73. Timofeev, *Nadezhda,* 115.
74. Ibid., 115-116.
75. Ibid., 117.
76. Ibid., 121.
77. Ibid., 122.
78. Ibid., 128.
79. Shtromas, *Political Change,* 21.
80. Timofeev, *Nadezhda,* 131.
81. Ibid., 136.
82. Ibid., 168-169n and 149n.
83. Ibid., 171.

84. Ibid., 175.

85. Ibid., 177.

86. Ibid., 176.

87. Ibid., 169.

88. Ibid., 153.

89. Ibid., 152.

90. See the NTS program in a Russian pocket edition, *Programma Narodno-Trudovogo Soiuza (rossiiskikh solidaristov)* (Frankfurt am Main: Posev, 1975). For a description in English of the NTS Program and of several other *samizdat* programs see Feldbrugge, *Samizdat and Political Dissent in the Soviet Union.*

91. Ibid., 62.

92. For alternatives to Soviet foreign policy, see, for instance, *Posev*, No. 3 (1981); for economic alternatives, No. 4 (1982); for constitutional alternatives, Nos. 5-6, and for a debate about them, No. 8 (1984), and Nos. 1 and 3 (1985).

93. Ernst Neizvestnyi, "Budushchee rezhima" (Future of the régime) *Posev*, No. 5 (1984), 30-35, esp. 33. This is a chapter from his book, *Govorit Neizvestnyi* (Frankfurt: Posev, 1984).

94. Dunlop, *The New Russian Revolutionaries.*

95. Ibid., 244.

96. Ibid., 247.

97. Ibid., 186.

98. Ibid., 190.

99. *Programma demokraticheskogo dvizheniia Sovetskogo Soiuza* (Program of the democratic movement of the Soviet Union) (Amsterdam: Herzen Foundation, 1970).

100. Soldatov, *Zarnitsy*, 193.

101. Ibid., 196.

102. Osipov, *Tri otnosheniia k radine*, 185.

103. For complete text see Soldatov, *Zarnitsy* 359-84.

104. See note 23.

105. I am indebted to the late Amalrik for making me think of Russia's historical death as a possibility. Zinoviev likewise has a point when he says that the attractiveness of communism throughout the world does not seem to diminish. As to Yanov's prophecy of the Nationalist/Stalinist conspiracy, I find it groundless; nonetheless it serves to remind that a growth of nationalist sentiments among large nationalities makes their small neighbors worry, and it is incumbent upon the former to reassure the latter.

106. Carl A. Linden, an American sovietologist, in his penetrating study, *The Soviet Party-State: The Politics of Ideocratic Despotism* (New York: Praeger, 1983) devotes a whole chapter, "Repressed Political Potentials" (Chapter 4), to alternative visions. In his "Spectrum of Political Orientations in the Post-Stalin Period," presented in the form of an ingenious circular diagram, he also lists a dozen alternatives to the present régime. Although his selection somewhat differs from mine, I certainly agree with his contention that the present Soviet rule is "under hazard of replacement by another form of rule through either gradual

change or sudden overthrow" (p. 87) and that the "alternative" authors should not be seen as "a small coterie of courageous individuals, but as the expression of a long-suppressed and long-submerged civil culture" (p. 109).

107. C. A. Linden, in *The Soviet Party-State*, likewise concludes that there exists "a consensus in support of a non-despotic order" (p. 109) among the main alternative visions. He particularly sees "the Sakharov-Solzhenitsyn counterpoint" not as "a mutually exclusive opposition" but as "the germ . . . of a 'two-party' politics of a nondespotic Russian civil order of the future," 103.

108. Dunlop uses the term, *vozrozhdentsy*, in his *Faces of Russian Nationalism* (see note 47) and in *The New Russian Nationalism* (The Washington Papers/116, publ. with The Center for Strategic and International Studies, Georgetown University, by Praeger, 1985), 88.

109. About the VOOPIK and the Rodina Club, see Dunlop, *Faces of Russian Nationalism*, 63-87. My own study of the responses of the Soviet populace to the art of the nationalist painter Ilya Glazunov indicates that the majority of ethnic Russians are fed up with Marxist-Leninist ideology and long for many things of the past that the régime abhors. See Vladislav Krasnov, "Russian National Feeling: An Informal Poll," in *The Last Empire: Nationality and the Soviet Union*, ed. Robert Conquest (Stanford, California: The Hoover Institution Press, 1986), 109-130.

110. Aleksandr Solzhenitsyn, *Avgust chetyrnadtsatogo* (Paris: YMCA Press, 1983), 2: 179.

111. Incidentally, the example of Deng Xiaoping's reforms in China gives credence to Solzhenitsyn's counting on the possibility of an orderly transition to a non-totalitarian rule under the tutelage of the party.

B. THE PROPOSALS

Introduction to Section 1

ALEXANDER SHTROMAS

Anatoly Fedoseyev's piece is unique in this volume—as, indeed, in the entire series—because of it being a personal rather than a scholarly statement. In contrast to the preceding works by Terry McNeill and Vladislav Krasnov, it does not owe anything to the study of relevant literature, most of which our author has never read anyhow; and, unlike the follow-ups by Alice E.S. Tay, Georg Brunner, and Olympiad Ioffe, it is not based on professional expertise in any of the social science disciplines. For Professor Fedoseyev is not a social scientist but a radio engineer who rose to the top of his profession in the Soviet Union (earning there his doctorate, a full professorship, and many scientific distinctions, including the title of Hero of Socialist Labor and the Lenin Prize) and who claims no other expertise than that in his own field. It is from this particular perspective of a leading radio engineer who in Soviet conditions was deprived, despite his prominence, of the possibility properly to apply his skills and realize his creative potential, that Fedoseyev delivers his judgment on the Soviet system and elaborates a projection of what, in his view, would be a desirable and realizable alternative to it.

It would therefore be wrong to assess Fedoseyev's work by applying to it standard academic criteria. They simply would not fit. For his is solely and exclusively the work of a *participant observer* trying to arrive at a view of what to change in his observed system, and how to change it, in order to make his participatory activities satisfactory and fulfilling. Attempts at associating Fedoseyev's views with any school of thought within the spectrum of Soviet dissent would also be futile. For his views are outside that spectrum altogether. A typical high-ranking Soviet official scientist, Fedoseyev had never been associated with dissidents, and before his defection to the West did not even come across any *samizdat* or *tamizdat* works. Neither were there among his personal friends any with whom he could or would freely discuss social and political matters. To the West, however, Fedoseyev came with his concept of the Soviet system and his views on the alternative that should replace it, firmly established. These views have not substantially changed since.

One can agree or disagree with Fedoseyev's particular ideas and proposals, find some of them more and some less attractive, but there is no way of denying that he speaks for the entire stratum of Soviet technocrats of which he is a typical and also a leading representative. This stratum should not be identified with that of the Soviet successors to the traditional Russian denying that he speaks for the entire stratum of Soviet technocrats of which he is a typical and also a leading representative. This stramus should not be identified with that of the Soviet successors to the traditional Russian intelligentsia which has always been the main breeding ground for dissent and for which the numerous prominent dissidents, from Alexander Solzhenitsyn to Andrei Sakharov, are the natural spokesmen. With that kind of intelligentsia Fedoseyev and technocrats like him have very little in common. Born in 1910 in a poor St. Petersburg working-class family, Fedoseyev managed to elevate himself to the professional stratum only by using to their full extent the spectacular opportunities for upward mobility prized highly by the Soviet régime for people of his social background. Having worked so hard for his promotion from a lower social stratum to a higher one, Fedoseyev fully concentrated on his official job, diligently trying to make the best of it. Because of that, all kinds of side currents that may have been fashionable among the traditional intelligentsia left him practically unscathed. He was one of those Soviet technocrats who, by trying to be as effective and useful in the functions performed as the unconducive Soviet conditions allowed, are seen as being, together with the partocrats, one of the most reliable pillars of the Soviet system. Now we know that this is only a shallow appearance. What the typical Soviet technocrats really think behind this appearance, Fedoseyev told us in absolutely unequivocal terms. In contrast to the vociferous intelligentsia, the Fedoseyev-type hard-laboring technocrats are a remarkably silent group. It is with Fedoseyev's voice that they have clearly spoken, perhaps for the first time.

Whatever one makes of Fedoseyev's work otherwise, it is extremely significant as a testimony on the way in which the minds of the Soviet technocrats really work. That this testimony adequately reflects reality was confirmed by the Soviet Academician's Tatyana Zaslavskaya's field work-based research data, according to which over 90% of Soviet managers are dissatisfied with the system in which they have to perform their functions, and desire its qualitative change to make them fully autonomous in, and responsible for, what they do.[1]

The technocrats, as the most influential and numerous Soviet professional stratum, are poised to replace the partocrats as the Soviet Union's ruling élite in not so distant a future. There is very little doubt that in their program of social and political change the technocrats would be to a large extent guided by Fedoseyev's ideas, even if they had had no chance to study his work beforehand. For Fedoseyev's concepts and recommendations are not simply congenial to, but, in most respects, precisely reflect and formulate the innermost ideas and plans of the whole Soviet technocratic stratum. This is why I find Fedoseyev's work to be so uniquely valuable an insight into the future of Russia and thus also so central for the "Alternatives" part of this volume and the series as a whole.

Fedoseyev's concept of the Soviet system and his vision of an alternative one that in his view would serve his country best, have previously found scattered expression in two of his books[2] and scores of articles published only in the Russian language. It is for the first time here that his concept and vision are presented in a systematic manner within one, though quite lengthy, paper. It is also for the first time here that Fedoseyev's ideas will be made available in English and thus introduced into the international professional debate on the problems of the Soviet future. I believe this to be one of the most valuable contributions that the present series makes to scholarly and strategic thinking on the Soviet Union and its destiny.

With these words I will leave the reader to ponder over Fedoseyev's own text and the challenging testimony it contains.

NOTES

1. See her articles in *Izvestiya* of 1 June 1985, and *Sovetskaya Rossiya* of 7 January 1986.
2. A. Fedoseyev, *Zapadnya: Chelovek i sotsializm* (The Trap: The Man and Socialism) (Frankfurt a/M: Posev, 1976); A. Fedoseyev, *O novoy Rossii: Al'ternativa* (On New Russia: The Alternative) (London: Overseas Publications Interchange Ltd., 1980).

1

The Passage to New Russia and Some Thoughts on Its Alternative Constitutional Order

ANATOLY P. FEDOSEYEV

The Unique Stability of "Mature Socialism" and Its Extraordinary Resistance to Change

Changes of government and even changes of state systems are now happening very frequently. Nowadays, there is no stability of authority. However, at the same time, even down-and-out socialist countries, which are multiplying at a high rate, are extraordinarily stable. They display exceptional resistance to any change, and attempts to change them internally, from above, from below, or from the outside, are quickly exhausted without any results.

The U.S.S.R. is the first and foremost of the socialist countries. Its stability is exceptional in comparison to any other country, including imperial Russia. Even the change of a top leader does not make much difference. The cause of this exceptional stability is actually very simple. *The U.S.S.R. as a whole is the property of the State. It is managed by a single authority which is called the Politburo.* Despite its origin as an organ of the Communist Party, the Politburo is the actual government. Exactly the same structure of power exists in all other socialist countries. All the money and all means of life and activity are under the control of the Politburo and its apparatus. Any kind of organized opposition requires some material base for its activity: accommodation, means of communication, publishing equipment, and of course, money; but since it is impossible to get all these facilities without permission from the government, any attempt to obtain them without such permission will be uncovered and the opposition immediately eliminated.

Any form of organized opposition ("second pivot" or an alternative center of power, to quote the terms used by A. Shtromas) is very harmful to the system of socialist management. The Politburo cannot permit it. But if there is no organized opposition there will be no change of the system of governments either. As a rule, the Politburo itself frequently attempts to introduce some reforms in order to increase the efficiency of the extremely ineffective socialist economy; for example, the attempts at introducing some kind of market relations between state enterprises, some degree of decentralization of management, some kind of privatization, and so on. However, very soon after such attempts are undertaken it becomes apparent that, as a result, the centralized management grows weaker without a corresponding benefit for the economy being achieved. Also, these reforms show a tendency to develop beyond control and threaten to destroy the whole system of socialism. Sooner or later the reforms must be abandoned.

The extraordinary stability of the socialist system leads many people to the conclusion that socialism is here to stay forever and that it is useless to work on the development of an alternative. Of course, this is wrong. However, in order to understand why it is wrong, it is necessary to recall the origin of the idea of socialism, and the history of its development into a mature state. It is also necessary to understand some fundamental properties of mature socialism. I shall discuss these below.

A Short History of Mature Socialism. Ethics of a Human Society

The family and the tribe were the first collectives of people with a better living standard, made possible by the specialization of labor and functions. A member of such a small collective sees clearly the advantages of collective labor and life for himself. Personal interest is in harmony with the interest of the collective as a whole.

The family and the tribe called into life such new qualities—of people and for people—as honesty, justice, equality, brotherhood, freedom, and so on. These qualities were necessary for the survival and the prosperity of these small collectives. The totality of these qualities is the essence of the ethics of a collective or, in general, a society. *It is important to understand that all these qualities have no meaning at all for a human being living alone without any contact with other human beings.* These qualities may be even detrimental in a fight between human beings, families, tribes, since they do not contribute to victory.

Increasing numbers of people in a society led to still greater advantages for its members because of further development in specialization of labor and functions. The large society itself created a completely new human being, highly intellectual and highly efficient, able to live in a sophisticated and varied cultural environment which he created himself. It was completely senseless and even inconceivable to live alone and refuse to use the fruits that only society could produce.

However, in a large society the tribal harmony between personal and collective interests started to wane. The former direct and clearly seen connection between personal and collective interests became an abstraction. It became even advantageous to neglect society's ethics. In tribal life, the instinct of self-preservation (egoism) had dictated—live and work honestly. Now the same instinct of self-preservation dictated—do not live and work honestly, because otherwise you may starve to death. This attitude became the greatest obstacle to the proper and efficient functioning of human society.

The history of human society is full of ideas and attempts to create a noble society that could eliminate this disharmony between personal and collective interests. Because most religions teach honesty and dignity, it is not surprising that most of these ideas and attempts used some religious tenets. However, their success invariably depended on the number of people involved. If the number was small enough and everybody's labor was clearly seen and readily measured, there was a modest success. The kibbutz in Israel is a modern example of this. Over-large collectives, sooner or later, were governed by force and finally disintegrated. To transform Israel as a whole into a kibbutz is impossible.

The Birth of the Idea of Socialism

The astonishing and remarkable scientific discoveries made three or four centuries ago formed a solid base for the whole of our modern science and technology. Philosophers and great thinkers of the time were tremendously impressed. They were suddenly made to feel that humanity could be the lord of its own fate. They became suddenly aware of the tremendous might of the human mind. They even began to think it had no limits at all. The human mind was transformed into a new God, whom one could trust and worship. Two significant consequences were the result of the new "cult of reason":

1. The old God and religion became redundant. Religion teaches that humans and their minds are completely insignificant in comparison to

the wisdom of God. The old God and religion became enemies of the new cult.

2. The omnipotence of the human mind makes the creation of a perfect society possible, a society run according to the ethics we already know. That society has been a human dream for centuries.

The idea of socialism was born. Socialism was to be a highly rational, highly benevolent, highly organized society.

It is easy to see the great difference between socialism and previous collectivist ideas. Socialism was not intended for a group of people; it was intended for the whole of humanity. Socialism had acquired a new tool—the omnipotent human mind—to build a new society, and had found new enemies of God and religion, which had to be liquidated (or subjugated and used for the same purpose, as it was much later invented by Khomeini in Iran).

The Development of the Idea of Socialism

It took a few centuries for the idea of socialism to ripen to maturity. In the West there were several attempts at socialist revolutions, including the great French Revolution of the eighteenth century. However, it was only the Bolsheviks who brought the idea to maturity. What does this mean?

1. In abstract terms, everybody agreed to the society's ethics. However, each particular case is controversial. Honesty and justice are one thing to a buyer; to a seller they are quite the opposite. "Why are his wages high and mine low?" And so on. There are as many interpretations of honesty and justice in a particular case as there are people. It is a manifestation of the diversity of the instincts of self-preservation (egoism). To build the perfect socialist society on millions of different interpretations of society's ethics is impossible. Faced with a specific case, different people will take different decisions and act in different ways. The perfect organization of socialism is incompatible with such chaos. It is impossible to persuade everybody to accept a single line of action, which is necessary in order to achieve the perfect socialist society. The Bolsheviks understood that:

   a) socialism must be a society which is managed by a single will; it must be a complete unity.
   b) the correct interpretation of society's ethics and all decisions must be given by a single authority.
   c) these interpretations and decisions must be forced upon the people.
   d) after socialism has led the people to unprecedented prosperity, the instinct for self-preservation will die and force will be redundant.

e) the great goal justifies any means used to reach it—even monstrous lies, inhumane and dirty means, mass terror.

2. People who are independent economically are also independent ethically and politically. It is impossible to force millions into doing anything to which they do not agree. It is even impossible to organize mass terror in order to force them into submission. So it was necessary at first to deprive people of their means of existence and of their economic independence.

To this end it was necessary to nationalize all means of production, all means of life, and to eliminate the free market. This was also deemed to be beneficial in eliminating greed, selfishness, and other evils. (It is worth noting the cause of the failure of the great French Revolution. At that time the population of France consisted mostly of peasants. To deprive them of their means of existence and of their independence was impossible. The idea of collectivization was as yet unknown.) Now the Bolsheviks knew the real meaning of their goal (socialism) and knew the means to reach it. The idea of socialism was now mature.

Socialism and Its Development in Russia

Under the influence of socialist ideas the intelligentsia of Russia had engaged itself into demoralizing and undermining the tsarist régime and was successful in this. World War I completed the disintegration of that régime. But except for the Bolsheviks, no other party had a clear goal, a clear strategy, and the necessary flexibility of tactics. The power was lying about, abandoned. The Bolsheviks took it without much effort, but in order to make their nominal power real, they wanted to attract millions of activists. They issued the famous decrees: "About Land," "About Peace," "Against Speculation" (the free market's prohibition), "About Nationalization," which presented the incentives known for millenia: legalized robbery, the possibility to square accounts, to obtain revenge, to transform oneself from dirt to a local dictator, and so on. Millions did swallow the bait and began to serve the Bolsheviks, thus assuring them real power. Over the great expanses of Russia great numbers of little Lenins and Stalins appeared everywhere. They were acting like real Bolsheviks even without any orders from the center. Under the leadership of professional Bolsheviks these millions of activists liquidated the press, the leaders, and the rank and file members of all oppositional parties. They destroyed the whole apparatus and economy of the tsarist régime, and liquidated all its organizers. *The point of no return was reached.* Simultaneously, everything was nationalized and everybody was deprived of his own independent means of existence, including, of course, all those millions of Bolshevik activists themselves. Everybody's means of existence fell into the hands of the Bolshevik power apparatus which became the master over everybody's life and death. *The Bolsheviks thus acquired the capacity of conducting mass terror.*

Of course, all across the great expanse of Russia, there were even more millions of people prepared to fight the Bolsheviks to the last drop of their blood. But they were doomed. They could not propose a clear and popular alternative to Bolshevism, nor could they provide good enough incentives. Finally, they were not as unscrupulous as the Bolsheviks as far as their methods of struggle were concerned. They suffered a shattering defeat at the hands of the Bolsheviks. *Civil war, devastation, and hunger had created in the souls of the shattered population a real craving for some strong régime to bring order to their lives. Since there was no authority except that of the Bolsheviks, most of the population, under these circumstances, were forced to serve the Bolsheviks.*

The next step (in logic, not in chronology) towards the final goal of socialism was the liquidation of all the different movements, factions, and leaders within the Bolshevik party itself, except for one. Different Bolshevik factions and leaders had advocated their own ways towards socialism, but it was impossible to implement real leadership of the masses in such circumstances. *The masses themselves were confused and they wanted to have a single leadership; they had lost their independence and now they could not live without being fully cared for by authority.* Stalin happened to become the Bolshevik who eliminated that confusion and who created the necessary single authority. *Under his sole leadership he created the socialist structure, and a very solid one at that.*

Of course, the masses themselves were not uniform. There were still millions upon millions of people who were thinking and acting independently, and who represented a real or potential obstacle to the unity of socialism. Other millions upon millions were, however, incapable of thinking or acting independently, and hated those who were capable of it. Under Stalin's leadership the latter liquidated the former. *The construction of socialism was complete; the whole population was made to conform to the will of the single greatest leader and his crew.*

The peasants were also deprived of their independence by means of collectivization (this process, much later, was to be finalized by the transformation of kolkhoses into state farms, making peasants into state employees like everyone else).

The cost of the construction of socialism in Russia was, according to certain estimates, as high as 67 million dead, the best and most active part of the population. It was the same story in all the other socialist countries.

Mao, according to some estimates, liquidated more than 100 million Chinese to achieve conformity to socialism in China.

The next step was to realize all the promised enormous advantages of the highly organized socialist society—to create the real, unprecedented prosperity promised by the theory of socialism. Stalin and his crew were professionally incapable of doing it. Their profession was mass terror and other dirty methods necessary to build socialism. This next step was postponed until Stalin's death and until a proper change of the crew had taken place.

Under Stalin the masses had lived in a state of constant terror and fright. They had become weary of it. Khrushchev cleverly used this situation and obtained strong support from the masses with his denunciation of Stalin's terror. *In any case, the need for mass terror had disappeared; complete conformity of the people had been achieved already.*

Khrushchev earnestly believed in the goodness of socialism and the future prosperity it promised. He even created a new program for the Bolshevik party pledging the success of communism in only twenty years. The statement was sincere and unambiguous. He boasted in advance about future bright prospects. However, Khrushchev's expectations failed to materialize. The reasons for this are fundamental and I shall speak about them later.

All the suggested advantages of socialism turned out to be mere fiction. Everybody, including the leaders and the masses, was disappointed. What was left of the socialist idea was a monster of power over the whole population of the great country. Of course, the monster wanted to keep its power by any means. The exact similarity between the structure of socialism and a war machine also became clear. It was quite easy to transform the U.S.S.R. into a very powerful, totalitarian, industrial and military complex. The complex was devoted to military blackmail and to spreading socialism all over the world.

The leaders of the U.S.S.R. learned that, say, a billion rubles, invested in civic needs, disappeared like a whiff of smoke. The same billion invested in weaponry created a beautiful aircraft carrier. Socialism was good at producing swords, but it was very bad at producing ploughshares. The U.S.S.R. was transformed into a total war machine. There, of course, lay the basis of great trouble; a bad civic economy will sooner or later lead to the destruction of the war machine, too. Thus the time factor became very important.

I shall now turn to the failures of socialism.

The Failures of Socialism

Three Ways to Manage a Society

The first one is self-regulation. Private property is prevalent and there is a highly competitive free market. Strong competition is absolutely necessary. This type of economy is managed by millions of the people themselves.

The second one is full state management. Everything is state property and is under government control and planning. Both production and distribution are planned. *In fact, all aspects of life are planned.* The economy is managed by a very restricted group of people. This type of management is used not only under socialism but also under nazism, fascism, or any other kind of totalitarianism.

The third one is mixed management, where state and public corporations coexist with private property. The market is restricted and is regulated in a complex way. The state (government) partially controls and plans the distribution of resources.

It can be seen in the West that mixed management tends to get closer to complete socialist management. This trend is quite natural; the tasks of mixed management are extremely demanding, but the means a Western government has at its disposal to meet these demands are always restricted and certainly insufficient. Hence, the government will want to spread its powers.

It is very important to understand that the laws of economics, and even of life, are completely different under self-regulation and under full state planning. Cost, price, earnings, wage, salary, profit, income, tax, efficiency, gross national product, budget, and so on, *have completely different and incompatible meanings in these two systems.* So have upbringing, education, housing, feeding, transportation, manufacturing, enterprise, servicing, and so on.

Full State Planning

Let us now look at some of the traits of mature socialism.

1. State planning in the U.S.S.R. has to encompass all the millions of units and all the millions of mutual ties in the enormous economic network. It is impossible for any human brain or any collection of human brains, as well as for any present or future computers to survey and understand this network in detail, especially taking into account the unpredictability and lack of uniformity of the millions of different human beings operating this network.

2. Therefore, real state planning is actually concerned only with the main economic balances. (This is far from complete, but it is the only way to manage a socialist economy.) These economic balances are: the balance between production, prices and wages; the balance between new working hands, new work places, and investments; the balance between produc-

tion and resources; and so on. There are millions of other factors which cannot be taken into account. The risk of error is great, and as a result, the state planning is frequently reduced to chaos. However, as a rule, everybody is punished (must be) severely if the plan is not fulfilled.

3. Every enterprise or institution in the U.S.S.R. has a five-year plan for wages or salaries and for the number of employees. This means that everybody's income is fixed in advance for the next five years. Otherwise, it would be impossible to achieve the very important economic balance.

This also means that higher productivity, which is not planned in advance, cannot be paid for. *State planning makes it impossible to pay more for higher productivity. Many different wage systems have been tried to stimulate productivity. All have been in vain because of the necessity of preserving, by the plan, the balance between production, prices, and wages. (This makes any wage bargaining in socialism impossible.)* There is a saying: "They pretend to pay us, and we pretend to work."

4. In the planning net every unit depends on the other units. If you wish to raise productivity in any one of them, a great many (if not all) units must do the same, because they supply to each other materials, tools, energy, and so on. The chances of such universal enthusiasm or simply universal feasibility are practically nil. *The planning network resists any positive changes. (Negative changes do happen frequently.) State planning decreases productivity definitely and greatly.*

5. The probability of getting to any unit the necessary supply of materials of the right quality and quantity at the right time in such a huge planned network is also practically nil. Because of this there has always been a great army of "fixers" who are sent by one unit to another to squeeze from them the supply allocated by plan. Several years ago it was unofficially decided to have production plans but not to specify the plans for the necessary supplies. Obtaining supplies was up to the units' initiative and ingenuity. State planning was in decline.

6. *This inability of state planning to secure the correct interflow of goods, services, and materials between units created a climate of universal deception and fraud in the fulfillment of plans in which the Politburo was also involved. It would be a great embarrassment to the Politburo if the overall state plan was not fulfilled, since that could put its prestige at stake.*

7. These natural deficiencies of state planning create a universal neglect of quality and variety of goods produced because even planned quantity is extremely difficult to achieve and in many cases this demands deception.

8. The laws of common sense and the laws of natural economics are in complete contrast to the laws of an economy that is fully managed by the

state. This creates a *false* impression of incompetence and stupidity on the part of the managers of a socialist economy.

9. *The fundamental defect of full state management is that it deprives millions upon millions of ordinary people of any possibility of realizing their individual creative capabilities. The tremendous creative potential of millions of people is left untapped. At the same time, the creative potential of the supreme managers is quite negligible compared with that of the population at large.* It is impossible to correct this defect without destroying socialism and without the Politburo losing its power. Socialism is self-destructive because there is only one way in which it can manage its economy—the way of socialist state planning.

Society and the Working People

Everything in any country is created and produced by working people: by engineers, scientists, technicians, workers, artists, teachers, and so on. The whole spiritual and material culture of any country is created by them. A low living standard, a low level of spiritual and material culture in any country is the result of low quality and low quantity of mental and physical labor of the working people of that country. This may be due to the fact that working people may suffer bad health, may have little energy, little basic education, poor skills, or may even have no desire to work properly.

There may be a great many different motives for working people to do their work: public recognition, honor, vanity, ambition, the need to achieve something, etc. Work can even be a simple habit. However, there are universal motives for that obligatory labor without which no country can exist: to earn money for food, clothing, housing, and so on, including the satisfaction of spiritual and all other needs, on an ever increasing level. These universal personal interests of working people can be reduced to the single wish to get higher wages or salaries for less labor in the best conditions. It is not hard to see that these interests are destructive for society as a whole. They lead to inflation, unemployment, poverty; and if these working people are not opposed in their drive to assure the fulfillment of their interests, the total quantity and the quality of goods and services produced are liable to decrease and to deteriorate. This in its turn leads to an inevitable decline in living standards for the working people themselves.

In a society of self-management the selfish interests of millions of working people are opposed by the selfish interests of millions of owner-entrepreneurs. These owner-entrepreneurs strive to wring out of working people more and better labor for lower wages or salaries. A positive balance between those opposing masses consisting of millions of people would lead to spiritual and material prosperity for all. (It is worth noting that managers of corporations in the West are themselves hired working people. They cannot exert proper opposition to the selfish interests of other working people.)

In a socialist country everybody is a working person. There are no owner-entrepreneurs at all. Even supreme managers and the Politburo itself are hired working people. But everybody wants a higher wage or salary, or other privileges, for less and worse labor.

In the U.S.S.R. nobody manages his own property, or spends his own money. Everybody, including the supreme managers and the Politburo, is robbing and bankrupting the country to get the most for themselves. Of course, the more they do this the less they get. Corruption, theft of state property, deception, idleness, the underground economy, and the black market are prospering under these conditions. State planning offers the ideal opportunity for this.

Socialism is a unique society where the interests of the abstract state (cheaper and better labor) are opposed to the personal interests of the whole population (higher wages and privileges for less and worse labor). *There is no social balance. Socialism is a unique society with an extreme social imbalance, scarcely corrected by the extreme power of the state.* According to *The Economist*, the living standard of the U.S.S.R., compared to that of other nations, shifted from N56 in 1976 to N70 in 1982. The U.S.S.R. is now behind Spain (N62), Ireland (N59), Greece (N68), Puerto Rico (N69), Singapore (N49), and Hong Kong (N56) ("The World in Figures," 1984 edition).

Some Other Interesting Properties of Socialism

1. *Everybody is everybody's enemy*

In the process of fulfilling the plan, the working man unavoidably comes into conflict with any of his subordinates or consumers, because the state's interests are alien to all of them.

Customers demand goods and services, quality goods and services, but the salesman is completely powerless to supply them. The state supplies him with shoddy goods and services which are also insufficient in quantity besides. So, the salesman considers any customer as an enemy to be despised and insulted. When, in his turn, the salesman becomes a customer, he feels himself an insulted nonentity.

The same relationship exists between a bus driver or conductor and the passenger, between a chief and his subordinates. The working man, when he works, tends to be a despot to any outsider, be he a subordinate or a customer. When he himself is a customer or subordinate, he too is despised and feels worthless. This situation is a result of socialism and state planning which are inseparable.

2. *Everybody depends upon the state and state planning*

Everything people need for living comes from the socialist state and the authorities. Therefore, people must court authorities, not their own neighbors. That is another reason why everybody is everybody else's enemy. Cooperation and mutual respect among people are discouraged by socialism.

3. *Foreign policy of socialist countries*

To repair the social imbalance is virtually impossible. It is extremely difficult for the Politburo to maintain its power over the millions of people it rules. The Politburo should do everything to make the maintenance of its power possible. The interests of the country and of its population are very low on the Politburo's list of priorities.

The foreign policy of a socialist state becomes a policy to maintain the power of the Politburo. This policy is, of course, in absolute contrast to the foreign policy of any ordinary country. It certainly confuses any foreign diplomat who has been taught to pursue the interests of his country and its population.

The foreign policy of any socialist country is a policy of spreading instability first and then establishing socialism everywhere. Socialist countries and socialism have now become the main sources of instability and conflict in the world.

4. *Material and spiritual failure of socialism*

I have considered the fundamental reasons for the failure of socialism. It is easy to see that these reasons cannot be removed without a conversion to private property and to a competitive free market. Under socialism, the instinct of self-preservation (egoism) became even stronger. It did not die. *Socialist dictatorship, the most powerful in the world and in history, has been unable to force the most deprived and miserable working people in the world and in history to work properly for their own benefit.* The citizens of a socialist country happen to be much further away from high moral principles —forming the necessary foundation to a good society—than even the most evil capitalists themselves. The real ethics of socialism are actually much worse than the real ethics of self-regulated capitalism.

It is also important to note that religion is right: the human mind is definitely nothing compared with the complexity not only of the universe but even of its smallest part—human society. Socialism has revealed the enormous, extreme limitations of the human mind and human science; these limitations will stay with us forever.

How Will Socialism and the U.S.S.R. Collapse?

It is possible now to draw the following conclusions:

1. The U.S.S.R. will not be able to maintain the full potential of its

industrial military complex until the promise to achieve the victory of socialism over the whole world is fulfilled.

2. The state power in the U.S.S.R. will gradually be weakened and disintegrate, with this process beginning in its lower echelons. These lower echelons have already lost their power to fulfill their duties properly. *Not one decree of the Politburo is fulfilled now.*The crew has lost its previous strength and yields to universal indiscipline. Already Mr. Brezhnev was complaining in private about this. If one reads any decree carefully, one can see that it is but a repetition of a series of previous decrees; this may be an excellent caricature of management, but management it is not.

3. The weakening of state power and the spreading of chaos will lead finally to the rise of organized opposition. Human rights will eventually, de facto, be assumed by people. Of course, human rights and socialism are completely incompatible. So the degree of that assumption will be directly proportional to the degree of the state's weakening.

4. The population of the U.S.S.R., obviously, is very reluctant now to take its fate into its own hands. A return to tsarism would not be viable. Neither would the Western way of life with inflation, unemployment and increasing poverty, crime and decadence. As yet no acceptable alternative to socialism has been evolved, and there exists among the people a definite fear of getting into an even worse situation after socialism has collapsed. *However, the understanding that nothing can be worse than socialism is gradually spreading among the population.* The availability of an acceptable and credible alternative to socialism would be a decisive factor in the process leading to the collapse of socialism.

5. It is important to note that *the West, in the name of the balance of power and other self-perceived advantages, is actually trying to help the Politburo to maintain its power.*

   However, the main force which will eventually destroy socialism is socialism itself, with the country's population being the main tool of its final destruction. The West cannot change this fact. Western help to the Politburo may somehow delay events but it cannot stop them altogether.

6. *The final period in the life of the U.S.S.R. will be characterized by a gradual collapse of state planning and state management as well as by the corresponding expansion of independent underground economy and private enterprise activity.* One could even envisage that some remote regions of the U.S.S.R. will become uncontrollable by and independent from the center—a situation which could easily spread.

7. The Politburo will be forced to seek some new, non-socialist, solutions. The refusal to do so may threaten their ability to survive. They are

certainly even now considering some variants of NEP. However, these variants do not promise to offer a viable solution. In the GDR, in Hungary, in Poland, in Yugoslavia, where there are NEPs, the results are quite unsatisfactory.

Making the underground economy and commerce legal cannot be a radical enough solution either. Such a decision, just like the NEP, would not work because the state sector would still be prevalent. The efficiency of the whole economy depends on the efficiency of heavy industry and big state enterprises for producing consumer goods. *That is a reason why new NEPs are not working; the inefficient state sector is still oversized and dominant. The underground economy, when, and if, legalized, is bound to lose its efficiency.* Now it does not pay taxes. It does not comply with any regulations. Legalization will remove all these advantages from the underground economy and thus deprive it of its present efficiency. Of course, the introduction of some kind of NEP, or measures legalizing the underground economy, accompanied by the corresponding expansion of independent private enterprise, can improve matters, but not much. *The big state sector will still be very wasteful.* However, such a first step can sooner or later lead to a second, and to a third. This tendency is quite probable.

8. It is, of course, impossible to predict the exact chain of events which will lead to the collapse of the U.S.S.R. It may be a gradual disintegration. It may be a "palace coup." It may be an army coup. It may even be a KGB coup; the KGB, as the best informed part of the socialist system, is especially aware of the authentic feelings of the population and of the real situation in the country.

It is important to understand that at present, to the whole population, from the rank and file up to the Politburo itself, socialism no longer is the beautiful rising star it used to be. It has grown old and arthritic.

9. It is also important to understand the great difference between the socialist revolution and the conversion from socialism to democracy, even if this conversion is revolutionary. After the October Revolution, something like 67 million dead were necessary to achieve the complete conformity of people to socialism. The new conversion would not demand conformity and would not need mass terror. Many deaths from illness and hunger after the October Revolution were the result of political prohibition of individual activity seeking self-preservation; individual self-preservation had to yield to the preservation of socialism. The new conversion will not need this prohibition. Human beings, if left alone, are extremely inventive in the pursuit of self-preservation. The only cause of death will be revenge and crime. But revenge cannot lead to mass killing

because human beings, as a rule, are repelled by killing. In the event of a power vacuum they would take justice into their own hands and might resort to lynching serious criminals taking advantage of the unruly situation. Thus, the possibilities for criminal bacchanalia would also be limited. The conversion will hardly be completely bloodless, but the bloodshed will not be on a scale which could be even remotely compared with that which followed the October Revolution.

The Sources for the New Russia Alternative

What are the sources from which the alternative for new Russia could be shaped? The first such source is, of course, the logic of the very processes of disintegration of socialist management. The second is some still preserved historical traditions and mentality coupled with new traditions and mentality developed during the Soviet period. The third is based on lessons drawn by the Soviet intellectuals from the Western history and way of life. In the second and the third my own personal experience and mentality are unavoidably included. I am a native Russian and lived almost all my life in Russia and the U.S.S.R. I certainly represent a large part of the people in the U.S.S.R.

It is important to state from the outset that I bear no grudge against the U.S.S.R. I graduated from the Electrotechnical Institute in 1936, and went on to a very successful career. I even had my own laboratory. In the course of my research and developmental work I obtained two science degrees— candidate's (1949) and doctor's (1959). I was awarded Lenin's prize for my military inventions (1960), and the title of Honorary Worker in Science and Technology (1970); the Order of "The Red Labor Banner" (1950), and two "Orders of Lenin" (1960, 1971) were bestowed upon me. I was a member of many important scientific bodies in the U.S.S.R., and in May 1971, just one month before my defection, I was awarded the highest distinction—the title of "Hero of Socialist Labor," with gold star.

I also want to stress that I do not consider the leadership of the U.S.S.R. as senile, dogmatic, or stupid. Quite the opposite; for over sixty-eight years the Soviet rulers have been capable of fooling the world. They keep a great people—270 million of them—under their control, and many other people, too. It is the socialist system that is senile, dogmatic, and stupid, although it is extremely effective in suppressing people and in depriving them of all means of resistance.

My writings are the result of cool, rational thoughts, not of hatred. My whole personal story is open to anybody who can read Russian—*Zapadnya* (The Trap), published in Frankfurt/Main by Possev Verlag, in 1976.

Gradual Collapse of State Management in the U.S.S.R. and a Choice for the Future

Even a small cell of the Soviet society contains in itself (as in a hologram) most of the characteristics of the whole socialist society. Let us consider one such cell chosen at random. The Soviet newspaper *Izvestia* of 15 July 1979 tells us about the bad state of affairs in a most modern bus garage, N 11, in Moscow. I will summarize the story as follows:

1. Bus drivers are the best paid workers in garages, earning 200-400 rubles per month.
2. However, every time a bus is out of order, inoperational, the driver will be idle and will get only a miserable wage.
3. If the driver puts his bus into the special, very well-equipped, repairing division of garage N 11 for repair, he will get himself in big trouble. The bus will be mysteriously stripped of all removable parts and will thus be completely ruined. Not only will the driver have lost his bus, he will also lose his job (no bus to drive), and his wage.

   The newspaper refers to this situation (the ultimate theft) as something almost normal.
4. So, in order to safeguard their jobs and wages, drivers are forced to repair their buses themselves, working infinitely long and unpaid hours, even during the night.
5. But, as a rule, there are no spare parts available; there is only one way to get them—the black market. Drivers are thus forced to buy spare parts to repair their buses on the black market, and they have to pay for these parts with their own money.
6. There are other facets to this story. All employees, particularly drivers, also take part in quite common practices of deceiving the state in order to get some additional benefits for themselves. This is because even the high wages drivers are paid are quite inadequate for a family to live on.

Let us draw the following conclusions from this typical example of real Soviet life and from our general experience:

1. The planning system of socialism is unable to provide this particular garage (and all others) with what it needs for its normal operations.
2. Material things (spare parts, parts in general, tools, equipment, petrol, and so on) disappear continuously (and on a very large scale) from the state enterprises to reappear on the black market.
3. The mode of operation of garage N 11 (and others) does not at all correspond to what can be called the socialist mode of operation. It is,

perhaps, nearer to the operational mode of cooperative enterprise in the state service. The happenings at garage N 11 are certainly a typical example of how selfish interests are satisfied by their adaptation to the given circumstances. This situation is characteristic of any cell within the socialist society. The garage of course does not really care about the quality of its service to the public, or its efficiency. The main aim of the garage's management and the employees is to get from the state more benefits for less work. (I have found the same phenomenon to exist in public bus services in the West; they represent not so much a service to the public as the public's service to the drivers and conductors, which allows them to be kept on the payroll.)

Imagine that this Soviet garage became a full cooperative (or corporative) enterprise without paper shares but with shared power of command, exercised without *any* intervention from the state. Efficiency would certainly improve. There would be less theft. However, to prevent bus fares from rising excessively, the state still would have to subsidize the garage. Other great obstacles to raising the efficiency will be the mutual envy, suspicion, and fighting typical within genuine cooperatives. Nevertheless, the state management will be relieved of a great burden, and the bus service will be somewhat improved.

Imagine now that this garage became the personal property of some really independent entrepreneur. Envy and suspicion, naturally, will not disappear. However, since the gratification of one's efforts will be decided by the owner, mutual fighting among employees will become useless and will eventually disappear, thus bringing team work into existence. Supervision will be much better; so will accounting; and public service in itself will improve considerably. The egoism of employees and owners will be moderated by their mutual interaction and the necessity to reach general consent. There will be no waste of public money on subsidies. I have personally experienced how much more efficient and good the private bus service is, for example, in Hong Kong (better almost than everywhere else where the bus service is public).

I would like to show by this example that this way of solving the crisis in the Soviet economy can be very tempting, but, obviously, politically it is quite unacceptable. However, the process of this uncontrollable gradual transfer of managerial power into the hands of working people themselves is spreading. It is, of course, not a way for strengthening socialist structures, but rather a radical change to a completely different, non-Soviet, structure. It leads to a gradual and uncontrollable loss of the Politburo's power to manage the country.

Let us look a little further. The present Soviet taxi service works on the same lines as that garage, N 11, or any other Soviet garage. A great many Soviet enterprises manufacturing consumer products operate using the same mixture of operational modes: socialist and private (cooperative or corporative) modes. There are groups of travelling craftsmen (*Shabashniki*) who appeared after Stalin's times and who work privately for kolkhoses, and earn good money. Progressively, these groups become better equipped, better organized, and are doing business on a bigger scale.

It is interesting how the Soviet practice of socialism itself creates new avenues for independent private business activities. Formerly, students were obliged to work in teams for kolkhoses on the construction of pigsties or cowsheds. Now, teams of students are doing the same work, but they do it privately, earning very good money during their vacation. The knowledge they acquired during the previous involuntary work provided them with the basis to start their own new enterprises.

Under the pressure of unending shortages, Soviet newspapers carried out campaigns to encourage working people to work privately after hours. There was of course no need for such encouragement. Millions already were working in this way. What the newspapers really wanted was to explain to some Soviet administrative officials that the Politburo actually approved of this practice. As it is, many millions (if not all) are at present engaged in two modes of operation: one is the involuntary and unproductive state socialist mode (negligible reward), and the other is the voluntary, desirable, private mode (good reward).

The scale of that non-socialist, private activity, started to grow progressively after Khrushchev's times of mass disappointment in socialism. Now this private activity commands quite a sizable part of the country's resources and manufacturing capacity, and it is developing even faster. It is closely connected with the also expanding free market ("black market"). Money, materials, labor, are taken out of the state sector and are transferred into this private sector by millions of people in millions of ways. "Very well!" some people will say, "It produces the same mixed economy as in the West; there is no danger in it for the Politburo." However, there is a snag: it destroys socialist management, and it destroys socialism. Full state management (planning) was always in principle incapable of providing the correct interflow of goods and services between state enterprises, which is the necessary basis for their normal work and production. Now this interflow was completely disorganized. In desperation, the Politburo decided to continue to plan the main balances and production volumes, but to drop the actual planning of this interflow, and hand it over to state enterprises themselves. (This was done unofficially.) In this way, barters, unofficial connections, bribery, black market, private activity, were involuntarily accepted as a normal element of socialist management.

It is interesting that, a long time ago, Gosplan tried to introduce direct consumer-supplier connections, but without success. However, it is not hard to see that the planning of main balances cannot be isolated. It directly depends on how the interflow is actually performing. A disorganized interflow will result in the disorganization of the planning of the main balances.

Corruption, which is the inevitable result of this process, will reach ever wider echelons of state management. *It means that the Politburo is losing its power to manage and that the apparatus of socialist management itself is disintegrating.* There is no doubt that the Politburo realizes its growing managerial impotence and feels frightened. This explains why the position of the Greatest Leader has lost its attraction. It explains the Politburo's readiness to hand this position to a young, unexperienced person like Gorbachev. They hope that this undoubtedly clever, energetic, and active man will be able to work miracles, and will be able to restore their socialist power structure. Of course, this is impossible. *The temptation to resolve the crisis of the economy and of socialism by handing Soviet enterprises over to self-management will be very great.* It would provide an opportunity for the Politburo to retain some managerial power by the means of taking the lead in the process of transformation. *The Politburo could thus hope to be able to adjust to the newly emerging structure of management.* Of course, this will not be simple.

Self-Management

In the West, dreams about establishing workers' self-management abound; there have been many unsuccessful attempts at implementing it. To be sure, among working people there are some who have ambitions to become managers without putting in the necessary effort and without having the required qualifications. They make a lot of noise about this and stir "the movement," but real working people are not interested in it. It is not their profession. They have another one. They want higher wages, less working hours, lighter work, better conditions, and so on. However, they need more muscle to get all this. So, they may favor the movement and support their fellows with managerial ambitions. But they themselves do not want to manage or to be responsible for any kind of management. They vaguely feel that their interests may be counterproductive to those of good business, and thus that self-management would make them worse off. Actually, in the West, hundreds of enterprises would already be self-managed by working people if it were not for their quite correctly felt reluctance to engage in such a venture. In the U.S.S.R. people are the same as in the West. They are managing their unofficial cooperatives because they have only one, even worse, alternative: state management. I am sure that they would prefer the corporative mode of operation: to have shares (of value proportional to the wages), and a professional management whom they can push, and pull, and criticize, and change. I am sure that they would like to have the possibility to sell their shares and to make their enterprise completely private in the future, or maybe to start their own small private businesses.

Not Big, Not Small, But Good Is Beautiful

In the course of this disintegration of full state management and self-managerial transformation the over-large, cumbersome, unmanageable Soviet enterprises will be split into much smaller units. The Politburo feels already that their policy—the bigger, the better—must be revised. Over the last few years they have begun to split some giant kolkhozes into smaller ones to make them more manageable and more efficient. The Western economic experience also exemplifies the inefficiency of giant corporations. These Western giants too consume state subsidies, use special state privileges and the privileges of monopoly. They focus on themselves the blackmail practices of trade unions and the so-called class struggle. They are a source of great instability.

Nomenklatura

There is also another important reason for the Soviet working people to be against giants and monopolies. Indeed, the giants and monopolies are the breeding ground for the rising of the *nomenklatura* class, the class which Soviet people hate deeply. The West has already created its own very big and very prosperous *nomenklatura* class, the class of the managers of the state, the corporations, trade unions, parties, financial institutions, a class which is quite isolated from the rest of the population. This class also rules the population of their respective Western countries, increases economic contrasts, enhances social instability. For example, the *Times* of 17 May 1985 informs us: "British industrial managers spend on their travel and entertainment £17.4 billion." (The whole defense budget is only £18 billion.) This is on top of extremely generous perks they have given to themselves. Compare this frivolous spending with other corporation spendings. The rate payments amount to only £6 billion, corporation taxes to only £8.4 billion, and even expenses on advertisements only reach £4.05 billion. Entertainment thus seems to be the paramount item and certainly the most expensive one. *Nomenklatura* is the same everywhere.

I think our people are fed up with giants, monopolies, enormous concentration of any kind of power and *nomenklatura*.

The Shaping of New Russia's Alternative Constitutional Order

Direction of Change

I foresee the following course of events:

1. Transformation of state enterprises into self-managed cooperative or corporative enterprises. Transformation begins with enterprises manufacturing consumers' products.
2. Appearance of a great number of small, completely private enterprises.
3. Division of giants and monopolies into smaller, and less complex units, with a great improvement in efficiency and manageability.
4. Dissipation of other kinds of concentration of power: economic, trade union, party, financial, and so on.
5. Kolkhozes, freed from outside intervention, will be left alone to continue or to dissolve.
6. Sovkhozes, also freed from outside intervention, will be transformed into either cooperative or corporative enterprises.
7. A greatly expanded black market will finally be transformed into a proper free market.
8. Intended future: transition from state property to public property (cooperatives and corporations) and then to private property in the real sense of the word. The final goal—to have millions of efficient owner-entrepreneurs, a decrease in the number of cooperatives and corporations, and extinction of state enterprises.

I would suggest including in the Constitution the following norms:

1. Prohibition of monopolies and other centers of concentration of power over people or over the country. Criteria: a) staff is more than 5,000 or, together with blue-collar workers, 10,000; b) the share of market or other activity is more than 5%; c) assets are bigger than 0.01% of national assets.
2. A special state inspection—with access to books and other sources of information concerning any enterprise or institution in order to check against the above criteria—should be decreed by constitutional law.
3. Enhancement of competition in all fields of people's activities should be one of the state's main obligations.
4. The management system of the country must be self-regulating and consist preeminently of private enterprise functioning in a really free and strongly competitive market; this would mean the regulation of millions of people by millions of people themselves. It would also mean the

highest internal social stability (no class struggle) because all those millions of contradictory selfish interests would be resolved in millions of mutually advantageous compromises. These selfish contradictions would then not concentrate themselves into the contradictions of interests among gigantic power concerns.

Decentralization of the Country's Political Management

Of course, the passage to the self-regulating system of management by private enterprise and a free, strongly competitive, market in New Russia will bring with it full economic decentralization. However, there is a very important additional aspect to decentralization. Beside the needs which can be satisfied by people themselves in the free market economy, there are still many public needs requiring governmental management. This governmental management will be faced with the same disharmony between public and personal interests which is characteristic of modern society (except, to some degree in Switzerland). There will be no success if that which is ethically necessary to make the society prosperous will be seen as contrary to the personal interests and to the instinct of self-preservation (egoism). *We should create a structure of governmental management conducive to a situation in which the personal instinct of self-preservation would dictate compliance with the society's ethics as much as possible, to be honest and to work and live properly.*

Actually, such a desirable structure must consist of cells like a family or a tribe (which I have mentioned before) that are, to the necessary extent, autonomous, but still sufficiently cohesive to make the society function like a very good orchestra. It is very much like the cells in the human body: they function completely independently but still comply with the needs of the whole body and are orchestrated within it; the interests of the cells are inseparable from the interests of the body, and vice versa. The structure of Swiss communities is, in my opinion, near to this desirable structure. Swiss communities on average consist of 2000 persons. In our specific case, the size of communities must be bigger but not so big as to lose the important properties which make it something like *a large family.*

It is important that these communities be self-governed and *self-financed* but still coordinated into and subordinated to society. I think *they must collect all taxes* (state revenue) on their territory and *use part of it (to be defined by constitutional law) for themselves.* Another part must be paid to the higher echelons of the governmental structure. It is important that these communities should not look to the central government for handouts, as is the case everywhere now.

In this instance the public interest (community's interest) will be seen as the personal interest of everybody, too. *The personal interest of self-preserva-tion would dictate to the individual to comply with the society's ethic for his own good.* I have found that this works quite well in Switzerland which has led it to become, on the one hand, the most prosperous country in the world, and, on the other hand, a country with the best record as far as the enforcement of law and order is concerned. The quality of life in Switzerland is the highest in the world, so high that the life span since 1982 reaches 79 years.

The next echelon of government, the one above the community, can be something like a canton, or district, or region. It would coordinate com-munities and arbitrate between them. A still higher echelon could be the national autonomous state, coordinating the cantons and arbitrating between them, and also issuing the state laws.

It is interesting to note that the collapse of the government of the Soviet Union, or of any central government in general, leads indeed unavoidably to the creation of such cells or communities. The history of the creation of societies out of primeval families thus repeats itself. I think it will be the very natural way for New Russia to follow. The task will be not to return, after this initial step, back on to the road of centralization, the road inevitably leading to disharmony between public and personal interests; the task will be to repeat history, not in full but only in its first part.

It is absolutely natural for New Russia to become a confederation of sovereign national states. It means that *the Parliament of this confederation must consist of the authorized delegations from the national parliaments.* The number of representatives in such delegations to the Confederal Parlia-ment must be proportional to the population of the individual national states. At the same time it must not be bigger than 1:N part of the Confederal Parliament's membership, where N is the number of national states. This condition would prevent any one state from dominating the Confederal Parliament. It is important that laws and regulations issued by national parliaments would deal only with the national states' internal affairs, but *these laws and regulations could not be annulled or altered by laws issued by the Confederal Parliament. All these laws are and must be in different fields of activity and must not interfere with each other.* The Confederal Parliament should deal with foreign affairs, the monetary system, the organization of defense, the rules of relations with the outside world, customs and other activities which are not strictly within the competence of national states. Obviously, coordination of the national states and arbitration between them must be also the business of the Confederation. I presume that the Confederation will also provide a standardization service which will *recommend* certain standards in goods and services to the national states;

such service is necessary to produce out of a conglomeration of different cells something like a unity of character. I suppose too that the principle of self-determination of the national states simply cannot be ignored and must be written into the Constitution. The criterion for exercising self-determination should be defined, I think, as the will of at least two thirds of the national state's electorate expressed in a public referendum held within the national state. Two thirds, of course, not of the number of participants in the referendum, but of the number of electors. In my view, this rule must be applied to any kind of suffrage in New Russia because the other way leads to crimes of manipulation and to erroneous representation. It seems to me that such a structure of political management (of course without a parallel structure of party leaderships or centralized trade unions organization) will work out quite naturally.

I think that our people are really weary of over-centralization and the flow of incomprehensible directives issued from far above. The shift of state management to the communities, closer to the grassroots people will prove very beneficial for society's stability and prosperity.

Limits of State Power

No government has enough power or money to manage any country properly. Therefore, in the course of time, all governments are unavoidably set to increase their power and the rate of taxation by legislation. There are no natural boundaries that could limit this process. Socialist managers hold all the possible power and dispose of all available taxation (achieved actually not by tax procedures but through allocating the lowest possible wages and salaries), yet they still cannot manage properly. The Soviet population hate their greedy and wasteful managers—their "Big Brother." They are the victims of the very negative experience of the exercise of this extreme power by the authorities, and of their own extreme powerlessness. They are conscious also of all the tricks used to increase bureaucracy constantly (it is never reduced) and to take from them the fruits of their labor (which they know will be wasted). I think that the following suggestions for New Russia will be welcomed by the Soviet population:

1. The state's revenue (of all echelons of the state apparatus put together) must be limited to a certain portion of the national income. (I have calculated that 30-35% would be quite enough for all reasonably defined public needs.)
2. The number of people employed by the state (all echelons of the state apparatus put together) must be limited to a certain percentage of the

total population (a reasonable figure would be about 0.5%, but certainly not more than 1%).

3. The state's spending must not be higher than the state's revenue. There must be no deficit.
4. The functions of the state must be limited to those which cannot be performed by the population itself. There must be no state intervention into the free market's self-regulating mechanism. There should be no wages, salaries, or price control.

The most important functions of the elected government must be:

1. Strict enforcement of law and order.
2. Strict enforcement of strong competition in all fields of economy and social life.
3. Strict enforcement of the limits placed on any kind of concentration of financial, industrial, social, or political power over people.
4. Strict enforcement of and arbitration for the fulfillment of voluntarily concluded contracts between employer and employee, seller and buyer, other individual contractors, individual members and their associations, users of services (for example, passengers) and service organizations and companies, and so on.
5. Introduction of a code recommending the observance of certain rules of honesty and morality, and engagement in propaganda of this code. Censure of pornography, perversiveness, the glamorizing of violence and propagation of antisocial behavior.
6. The performance of certain public services which cannot be operated by the private sector.

This, of course, must be written into the Constitution. Any constitutional change should be made only by the means of a referendum held on each question separately. A majority of two thirds of the votes—of the electorate, not of the actual participants in the referendum—should be necessary to introduce such a change.

It should be noted that the limited state power briefly described above will not lead society to develop into anarchy. Quite the opposite: state power will be effectively concentrating on the enforcement of law and order. In this field our "limited state power" will be much stronger than what we have today in the U.S.S.R., and also in the West. The same is true for foreign affairs and defense; our "limited state power" in these fields will be also stronger than anywhere else without losing its flexibility and efficiency.

Non-Party Government

It is interesting that among the emigrants from the U.S.S.R. there are only very few who want to create a political party, or to become a member of a political party in order to fight for freedom in Russia. Most of them do not like to be party-men, even in general. Many are against parties even as an institution. Actually, in the West, among Russian émigrés, there is only one political party—the NTS, *Natsionalny Trudovoy Soyuz*. But even this organization avoids using the word "party" in its name or in its program.

Dislike of the CPSU is very strong within the population of the U.S.S.R., and this dislike, to a degree, spreads to any party aspiring to get itself in office. I was not surprised to find some native Westerners who, for that same reason, do not like political parties either. A party represents the interests of only a small part of the population. In actual fact, no party ever represents the majority of the population. All parties, naturally, have some kind of ideology and, as a rule, this ideology is alien to the ordinary people. People tend to change their allegiance from one party to another, not necessarily because that particular party represents their interests in a better way, but because the previous government proved to be bad, and because there is no other choice. Parties fight each other, not better to represent the interests of the people, but to get power for themselves. However, a change of ruling party may lead to extreme instability in government policies. (One party, for example, will nationalize, whereas the other will denationalize.)

I am sure that the non-party system suggested below will be more suitable and better acceptable for New Russia:

1. Any association of citizens, including parties or trade unions, or any sizable group of people, can propose any citizen as a candidate for election.
2. Any candidate must have his own personal political program, presented in a clean, written form. He must also produce a written autobiography, with a portrait. His telephone number and home address must be made available so that any member of the electorate may easily contact him. The sponsoring group must present all this material with a list of all the candidate's supporters *to the election committee*. This list will show the supporters' addresses and will be signed by them.
3. The election campaign must be based on the written individual political program, the written autobiography, the presented portrait, and other relevant information. There can be publicity through newspaper articles, television and radio programs. All expenses for all candidates must be equal and must be paid by the state. No other expenses must be allowed.

4. Elections must be based on universal suffrage, equal, proportional representation, and should be exercised in the form of direct vote and secret ballot.
5. It should be particularly stressed that any elected candidate should win the majority of the electorate, not just the majority of the participants in the election.
6. No person can hold an elected office for more than two terms.

Separation of Powers

In the U.S.S.R., the structure of power or management, created by Stalin and further streamlined by consecutive Soviet leaders, is extremely complicated, strictly centralized and very well protected from the loss of power by the Politburo. Outside observers can see in the U.S.S.R. the usual triad: the hierarchical "trees" of the legislative, executive, and judicial powers—the "tree" of the Soviets, the "tree" of the ministerial executive, and the "tree" of the judiciary. The hierarchical structure within the "trees" in such bodies as the army, the KGB, trade unions, and so on, look very much like the corresponding hierarchical structures in any other country. There is, however, a radical difference. None of these "trees" has independent power. They are just empty shells, into which power flows from an outside source, namely the hierarchical system of the party apparat. If I compare power to water, this party *apparat* system looks like a large reservoir with a big pipe gradually branching down into a net of smaller and smaller pipes. At each branching off there is a valve which can be closed or opened. All other "trees" are fed by "water" from this party-power distribution system.

It goes without saying that all valves are operated by vetted and trusted party men. The "water" supply is always carefully measured, and there will be no "water" reserves. Crucial elements of life like food and military ammunition are exactly distributed by such a system. Any rebelling cell will be immediately isolated by the closure of valves. It will get no more food and no more ammunition. The party system is continuously improving its efficiency in the exercise of this controlling function. No official in any of the "trees" ever has a complete set of means at his disposal to fulfill his duty. To be able to act, he must always get additional "water" from the main "tree," i.e., the party. At any time, any official in any "tree" can be isolated and thus made inoperational (cut off from the "water" supply).

A very interesting fact is that frequently "water" is given to the executive "tree" to make judicial decisions, or to the Soviet "tree" to make industrial (i.e., executive) decisions. All trees, except the party one, have a somewhat vague, insecure existence; their duties are not clearly defined; everything is in the hands of the Politburo; everybody is under "the God's will." Some "valves" and branches are secret.

In this way, the Politburo regulating the main "valve," and with the controlling power over all other party "valves," in fact manages all the "trees" together.

I have not yet said anything about the media and propaganda "trees." They are controlled in the same way.

The failure to act properly with regard to a small "valve" does not necessarily present a danger for the system. Rebels will be immediately isolated, dismissed, and punished. However, a similar failure in the case of a big "valve" can be very dangerous. Very strict vetting and checking reduce this hazard, but not sufficiently. Stalin again provided the means of protection against this pitfall by a primitively simple method: continuous change of the party people operating big valves and, of course, keeping them under continuous surveillance. If any "valve operator" shows signs of over-independent thinking or acting, he is dismissed, or transferred to some other job. This movement of personnel makes the organization of conspiracy at all important "valves" almost impossible. A keen observer can see this continuous movement. Last year, for example, we witnessed Marshal Ogarkov's dismissal. The more important a man is (bigger valve), the more closely he is watched, and at his first attempt to act without proper directive, he will be immediately dismissed.

I am absolutely sure that such a perfect system of centralized power has never been in existence before. Unfortunately for the Politburo, under the pressure of millions of unsatisfied people, even perfect systems will eventually accumulate destructive effects, and will not be able to save socialism from destruction.

It is evident that this perfect system is absolutely unsuitable for New Russia, and it must be completely dismantled. The new structure of power must consist of three independent "trees": legislative, executive and judicial.

It is very interesting that in the West judicial positions are held by specialists (lawyers) but that executive positions are not. Any elected person can become a minister of this or that without any professional knowledge. It seems that everybody in the West thinks that the management of a country is so simple that no professional knowledge is required. Something along the lines of Lenin's dictum: every kitchen maid can manage the state. I think that this is just an obsolete tradition dating from the times when human societies were smaller and simpler. I think that state executives must be chosen from professional people, even if they are not members of the elected parliament. The procedure for their appointment and dismissal must, of course, be decreed by the legislative power of parliament.

In the West there are also signs pointing to the transformation of the three separate powers into one; personally, I think this is dangerous for the future of democracy. In Britain there is no written constitution, and the likelihood of changing the whole constitutional order is far from being equal to zero. In Britain also there is no separation of executive and legislative powers. Elected (sometimes for life) members of Parliament, i.e., of the legislative branch of state power, are becoming ministers—members of the executive branch of state power. In the U.S.A., on the other hand, Congress gradually takes upon itself the power of legislating over every possible decision of the executive and judicial powers. If every step of a judge or a president is controlled by laws issued by legislature then the whole concept of separation of power goes to pieces. Congress will rule everything. There is also a tendency in the U.S. Congress to change the American Constitution simply by legislating a series of new laws, virtually abrogating the Constitution. It means that the written constitution of New Russia must impose some limits on the legislative power, too. These limits should protect the population from the unexpected advent of legislative dictatorship, and thus the disintegration of constitutional order. There must be protection, for example, against military juntas' attempts at taking over. This kind of protection can be achieved by obligatory changes from time to time within the military leadership, for example by some kind of rotation (Stalin's method).

I think the same must be done in the fields of executive power.

The independence of judges should be protected by their appointment for life. However, some procedure must be provided in order to make it possible to remove a "mad judge" from office. I suggest that no less than 80% of the community's council vote and a consecutive no-less-than 80% vote of the national Parliament would be sufficient to have a judge removed. Besides, there must be definite constitutional provisions prohibiting any judge from having any other job or vested interests in anything liable to influence or bias his impartial judgment. Furthermore, the holding of a judicial office should be made incompatible with membership of political or professional associations, for such membership can also make a judge biased and partial. The judges of the supreme court, the protectors of the constitution, also must be appointed for life; they should not hold another job, have vested interests, or be members of political or professional bodies. That is the only way to preserve their independence and the integrity of their judgment. A "mad" supreme judge can be removed by a near-to-unanimous vote of the respective national parliaments or the Confederal Parliament.

Judges should be appointed, I think, by a not-less-than 80% vote of the respective national parliaments, on the advice of the councils of the communities.

It seems to me that after the painful experience of Soviet bureaucracy our people will prefer a much simpler and less expensive form of parliament, especially so because the functions of the parliaments of New Russia will be very limited and will have much less influence on the day-to-day life of the population. The self-regulating free competitive market will drastically decrease the need for governmental intervention.

I think it will be naturally desirable to have single-house parliaments. The second house was meant to be less dependent on the winning of votes because of the longer or even life terms of service of its members, and therefore it was meant to look better after the country's interests. The modern experience of this system's work shows that the above purpose has never been achieved and that any two or even three house parliaments still are, as a rule, pursuing policies aimed at winning votes, policies which usually are detrimental to public good. The multi-house system is also very expensive (high taxes are necessary), very bureaucratic and very rigid.

For New Russia I suggest single house parliaments.

Need for a Great Leader

Any dictatorship needs a Great Leader. Any unstable country craves for a Great Leader. A population which has lost its bearings requires a Great Leader. Everywhere there are leaders. But does it make people happier or more self-assured? No, it does not. Switzerland has no Great Leader. It is the only country whose president is almost unknown to his countrymen. And yet Switzerland is the most orderly, self-assured, rich and happy country in the world. The Swiss people have found their bearings; they know how to live and how to work. I think it will be the same in New Russia. There will be no need for the spectacles provided by presidents, prime ministers, party gensecs, and so on. The chairman of the Federal Parliament can be the head of the Confederation. He can even be called the President. However, the population of New Russia will not need political leaders as such. There will be plenty of spiritual and religious leaders of all kinds. Nobody in New Russia will need a Great Leader who will show the population that has lost its bearings how to work and how to live. The population of New Russia will have found its bearings.

Perhaps I should note that in New Russia, over the suggested alternative structure, a monarchical superstructure can be established, as is the case in Britain. Such a monarchical superstructure would not be able to change the substance of this suggested alternative.

The Legal and Judicial Systems

Our people are certainly sick of the so-called Soviet justice. They crave for something which is impartial and really just. The quality of justice in prerevolutionary Russia was defined as fast, just, and merciful. If we qualify "merciful" as merciful to victims, then it will be what people want.

The Western system of justice has, unfortunately, completely failed to protect people. For example, in the U.S.A. crime is practically free for all, and it is very profitable. Myriads of lawyers, organized into extremely powerful cartels, make justice a very slow and very expensive process. Ordinary people cannot afford to go for justice in such a system.

Millions of laws and rules, many of them contradictory, obsolete, or simply ridiculous, make real justice almost impossible. Quite the opposite may happen: innocent people can be framed. In the single year of 1976 the U.S. Congress issued about 100,000 new laws and regulations. In England twenty thick volumes of new laws are published every ten years. In such legal jungles how is it possible to sort out who is innocent and who is guilty? I think that there is a possibility of finding a law according to which any one can be made a criminal. It is really surprising that the common sense of the Western people still prevails and that in many cases justice is properly done. *It means that the judgment of the judges becomes more important than the laws themselves.*

In New Russia the judicial system must be completely renewed. We know that freedom cannot be limitless. For example, there cannot be freedom to kill. Freedom of legislation certainly needs some limitations and restrictions as well:

1. The number of laws must be in accordance with the ability of the human mind to grasp them. I suggest that fifty laws for the general public and fifty laws for every profession should be a limit.
2. There must be more room for judges to use their discretion, as the name judge itself suggests. The definition of fraud, for example, should not be limited to a certain way of deceiving. Any fraud which results in deprivation of property, loss of status, health, life, must be defined as a crime of fraud. One law should be sufficient to deal with any fraud bearing in mind that there is also *the judge*.
3. Laws must be written in language that is clear to anybody with a school education.
4. All judges (specialists) should be appointed for life by national parliaments. Judges must be given much wider rights to use discretion in their judgments.

Only such matters that can lead to capital punishment should be decided by a jury. All other matters should be decided by a single judge, or a few of them. There must also be a special court of justice for all labor conflicts (no strikes nor violence). The most important principles of the judicial system should be: a) the highest probability of punishment for any crime; b) the full compensation of the victim by the criminal; c) the complete removal from society (capital punishment) of all *intentional* murderers, *successful or unsuccessful*—sex, age, or motive should not be taken into consideration; d) since long imprisonment is expensive and useless, the longest term of imprisonment must be three to five years, but it must be a real *punishment*, not a pleasant rest from criminal activity, and prisoners must work and be taught a profession; e) punishment must take into account the financial conditions of criminals; for example, fines must be based on a percentage of their income, so that rich and poor should be punished equally; f) punishment must also take into account the criminal's character: for hooligans, who humiliate people, do not understand morals and words, and see common punishment as something like a medal for heroism; punishment, in order to be a real deterrent, must be humiliating.

It is necessary to support the judicial system with an adequate system of crime prevention. In this the government must play an important role. The state should not dictate to us how to live, how to do things, how to work, how to interact with other people, *if we do not break criminal laws*. Nevertheless, the state should be allowed to recommend and to propagate rules of good behavior and rules of social ethics. A special, elected parliamentary commission must be set up with the power to prohibit such items destined for spiritual consumption, which advertise and propagate violence, perversion, and pornography. It is recognized that it is right for the state to ban poisonous and unhealthy products destined for material consumption. So why not do the same with poisonous items destined for spiritual consumption?

Placing a murderer or a rapist behind bars is not considered a restriction of personal freedom; neither should the prohibition of spiritual murder or rape, which can be much more evil, be considered as such.

I am sure that the majority of our people will approve of such a system.

Organized Crime

Of course, the builders of New Russia should take into account the evils plaguing Western society. One such plague is organized crime. For example, the U.S.A. experience shows:

1. Organized criminals keep an army of very experienced lawyers on their payrolls.
2. To get evidence against organized criminals is almost impossible.
3. The laws themselves provide very good covers for organized criminals, stressing their rights in particular, and much less those of the victims.
4. Organized crime continues to prosper and flourish.

In my opinion, in New Russia there must be a special legal arrangement to deal with organized crime. I would suggest the following. Police, in such cases where it is helpless to eliminate organized crime, will turn to a special parliamentary commission for help. Together they will study the case and may decide to involve the public to whom a description of the members of the criminal organizations and their deeds will be issued. A local referendum will then be conducted about the desirability of deportation of local gangs to another locality. If the gangs continue their criminal activity in the other location a referendum is conducted there. After three referenda, gang members are put into prison for three to five years. Perseverance in their criminal activity after that, and a further referendum, will mean capital punishment. This means that in cases of organized crime the general public as a whole will be the judge. Through the combined involvement of the police, a parliamentary commission and the general public, the danger of framing innocent people will be eliminated.

Also it will be necessary for any adult person in New Russia to have a special identity card, which must be presented on authority's demand. This would greatly reduce criminal activity. Honest people need not be afraid of disclosing their identity. The need for identity cards in the West is clearly demonstrated. To identify a person in the West there are a lot of "surrogate" identity cards: driver's license, special credit cards ("American Express"), "green cards," and social security cards in the U.S.A., police permits, and so on. How, otherwise, could complete strangers be trusted with valuable goods or services, even on a temporary credit basis? So, people need these "surrogate" identity documents almost every day. However, their use presents evident shortcomings: they are easily forged, and they do not really provide sufficient identification. It is thus very easy to avoid being identified, and criminals certainly use this situation—which suits them—to the full while honest people suffer.

It seems to me that our people will support these measures, too.

Monetary System

In any socialist country (as in many countries of the world in the nineteenth century) money is printed and minted by the state. Over-printing of money will create inflation but not debt. Inflation can be quite quickly cured by rise in productivity.

The common modern Western monetary system seems to be absurd. Money is printed by a private bank ("Federal Reserve Bank" in the U.S.A.), and is lent to the government, sometimes at very high rates of interest. The fact that there are two or three representatives of the finance ministry (out of up to twelve private persons) on the board of the bank does not change anything. The bank remains a giant "private" monopolistic *corporation* which not only commands the state's finances but also acquires extraordinary power over the country as a whole, including, in the first place, the country's economy. In its turn, this financial corporation is enormously enriched by taxpayers' money.

I do not think that this absurd system will be accepted in New Russia. Actually, the Soviet monetary system will be acceptable with, evidently, some substantial changes. The printing of the money and its distribution to the various echelons of government must be done according to a special decree issued by the Confederal Parliament of New Russia (like that in the U.S.A. at the end of the nineteenth century). The money of New Russia, of course, must be freely convertible. However, as in Soviet times, exchange rates must be established by the finance ministry for sufficiently extended periods of time. Great expertise will be needed to do that, but the new system will be conducive to making New Russia's economy stable. It will also, to some extent, suppress money speculators, so common in the West.

It means that *in New Russia the country's government will not share its power in the management of the country with any other unelected body,* as happens in the West, where it is hard to judge who governs the country—the elected government or a giant financial monopoly.

Defense and Foreign Policy

There is no doubt that New Russia will not keep its army contingent anywhere but on its own territory. Our people do not want to oppress other people. The first step on the road to New Russia will be, without doubt, the removal of all our military forces from abroad. Also, all aid to other socialist dictatorships and to other subversive forces in the world will stop. There will be much more stability in the world after that. Mutually advantageous trade and cultural relations, and cooperation will be the basis of our foreign policy. New Russia will free the world from the sinister source of instability, wars, and other threats which the U.S.S.R. now represents. It will give new hope to the world. Our people, like any other people, do not want war. Wars in modern times are wanted only by governments and generals who are not responsible to the people. Unfortunately, even after the creation of New Russia, there will still be quite a number of countries similar to the U.S.S.R. around. Therefore, New Russia will have to maintain adequate military forces. I would like to point out that these forces cannot have a democratic structure. An efficient military force must be centralized and subordinated to the single will of its command. A really democratic New Russia will thus need that undemocratically organized military force. But the military will be under the strict supervision of the state. They will have a new code of conduct and behave according to new ethical values; they really will be the force of defense, not offense. We have already pointed to the precautions needed to prevent the rising of a military junta, and the loss of the army's subordination to the democratic government. The same precautions should apply to the intelligence services without which the military force, as indeed the whole security of New Russia, could be jeopardized and made powerless. The essential secrecy laws also must be maintained. Our people certainly do not approve of the Western inability to maintain their freedom from subversion by the KGB. They can appreciate the difference between the Soviet way of keeping everything secret from the population and the necessity to keep certain things secret *from the enemy*. The first way is directed against the population. The second against the enemy and to the benefit of the population.

Separatism

The whole world at present is everywhere experiencing flareups of bloody separatism. It is a quite natural reaction to the trend of ever higher and higher centralization of management in the countries involved, and the ever stronger and increased powers of central governments in modern times. The point is very simple: How can the central government really decide what people living in places thousands of miles away from the center should do, how they should live, what they should spend, how they should work? Local people, no doubt, know their business much better than the central government does, but they are not allowed to decide for themselves, and their money flows to the center to be arbitrarily spent and wasted there.

The self-governed and self-financed communities suggested for New Russia, and the sovereignty of national states, will certainly lead to the natural extinction of separatism. People will manage their own finances and have the power to decide how to run their own affairs.

Once more, a good example is Switzerland, with its four distinct regions, each inhabited by a different nationality, and where there is no separatism at all. Every region is free to live as they wish.

The National Question

My personal experience shows that the overwhelming majority of our people have no racial prejudices or national hatred. These negative feelings have always been inspired and organized by the government and are part of its policy. In New Russia there will be no need for majority rule of any nationality in the questions of day-to-day life. Everybody will be able to live according to his wishes, to his traditions, to his culture, speak his own language, respecting, of course, the same wishes of other people(s). It means that all nationalities, even very small ones, will be able to live as they wish, and to develop their own cultures and languages as much as they wish. It would be possible to have self-governed and self-financed national communities. It would also be possible to have fully sovereign national states—members of the Confederation.

The very important question of the language can be solved if everywhere three languages are taught in schools and other educational institutions: 1. the common language of the Confederation (probably Russian); 2. the national language; 3. an international language (probably English). Any person or any group of people will be free to speak, study, propagate any other language beside these three.

I am sure that the national question will disappear in New Russia. Switzerland has four official languages, and even more nationalities, but there is no "national question" in that country. On the other hand, a small country like Belgium has only two main nationalities, yet they are fighting each other. Switzerland is decentralized and Belgium is not.

Land

I think that the nationalization of land is one of the very few good things that socialism has introduced. It is interesting though that this good thing did not do any good for socialism. But it will certainly benefit New Russia.

The fact that in the West land is private property and the object of most immoral speculation that is utterly destructive as far as the interests of the country are concerned, reflects not the natural human laws, but the results of war, conquest, and theft. How can land, on which people are living, walking, working, be someone's property? It is not a product of human labor. So, how can it be sold or bought? Of course, it is possible to do trade in everything, even in sunlight. However, the conditions under which all this is possible cannot be termed otherwise than criminal, unlawful, inhumane.

The nationalization of land was, without doubt, a right measure to take. However, nationalization as such does not completely solve the question of land. Land that is communal property is neglected, wasted, spoiled. It is not properly cultivated. It produces no adequate harvest. In the present situation, everybody knows that the land given to him may be taken back at any moment. So why waste one's labor cultivating it? To repair this defect it is necessary to include the following clauses into the Constitution of New Russia:

1. Land is distributed free or let by community councils.
2. Every citizen or family are entitled to get a limited plot of land free, or to rent a bigger, but also limited, plot for commercial purposes.
3. The free plot or rented plot are *given for life and hereditary usage*. Rent

charges can be changed only according to changes in the value of money. Thus, rent will not be cancelled by the user because of economic pressure from the state authorities.

4. This land cannot be taken back if it is used. If, however, it is not used for a substantial length of time, or if it is used for unlawful purposes, then it can be taken back by a court's decision.

5. The land itself cannot be bought or sold. Of course, it can be voluntarily returned if not needed.

6. Everything which is produced or built or arranged on the land by means of human labor (harvest, irrigation arrangements, buildings, machinery, and so on), can of course be bought and sold freely. The right to the land itself can be simultaneously transferred from one person to another, also freely. One could ask: What is the difference? Who can prove that the price does not include a fee for the land itself? The difference is that there will be no speculation on empty land. The land will not be wasted or neglected. At the same time, agricultural cultivation of the land will be stimulated in the same degree as in the case of land ownership.

Of course, there will be land in public use: parks, public gardens, national parks, wildlife reserves, and so on.

The same applies to the natural resources, whether they be under ground, above ground, in the air, in waters, and so on. They too may be rented for exploitation, in the above manner. Natural resources in themselves are not the product of human labor *until they are explored and then put into exploitation.* They too cannot be someone's property, to be bought and sold. When they are explored and extracted, that extracted part is the product of human labor which then can be bought and sold.

I am sure that the famous idea to return land to its prerevolutionary owners now looks absurd, and anyway it cannot be realized.

Housing

All state authorities know that state (council) housing is a source of big losses. It is also a source of slums; councils are not able to maintain properly their housing estates.

It also prevents the free movement of working people around the country, thus contributing to the open or hidden unemployment. State housing is also the subject of the most nagging criticism about authorities. All this is the U.S.S.R.'s reality. The burden of state housing for socialist managers is very great. It thus seems to be very natural, in the course of the passage to New Russia, to declare that *all Soviet housing is to become the property of the people who live in those houses,* of course, with the right to sell or to let them to others, and also with the necessity to maintain them and to pay for water, gas, electricity, and other services. Obviously, there will be great inequality: some will have luxury flats, others will have just a dog's hut. Nevertheless, it is the best and shortest way to future housing distribution according to one's financial abilities or merits.

Other kinds of housing, like communal living quarters or hostels, can become the object of commercial tendering or can be transformed into shareholders property.

Education and Religion

Everything is created and produced by working (as defined before) people. It means that prosperity depends not only on people's desire to work but also on their skill and knowledge. The desire to work will be secured by the social balance between the egoism of both the working people and the competitive owner-entrepreneurs. Professional and academic education must serve the important purpose of giving the necessary skills and knowledge to working people.

No government in the world can know and predict new needs in education. Neither can they know or predict particular circumstances for educational needs, arising from the peculiarities of every pupil. Our people and teachers have felt the need for freedom in education for a long time. In the U.S.S.R. there are actually a great many semi-private special schools in disguise to fill these needs.

Our people certainly will want private and diversified education which will give parents the freedom to choose the most suitable education for their children. They can come to grips with the diversity of free market requirements much better than any government can. Primary and secondary education must be basically free. It can be done by the state issuing vouchers for every child to pay in this way for his education in any private school. The money value of these vouchers must be equal for all children. If parents want to send their child to some extraordinary and expensive school, they can do it by supplementing the vouchers with their own money.

Children's education must not be obligatory. It is no use to force a person to be educated.

In my opinion, education must be permeated also by the teaching of moral standards and social ethics forming a certain code of proper behavior, just like in Soviet schools they teach the ethics of socialism and Marxism. I am sure the majority of parents want to have this kind of teaching. Of course, this moral education must be preceded by the moral upbringing of children in their families and in preschool institutions. One cannot feed small children with all the reasons to behave well known to oneself, and one cannot invent for oneself the best moral code. To fill the gap, religion provides a splendid basis since it contains all the principles necessary for correct moral and social upbringing, as well as for education. Religion is a powerful tool for correct upbringing, and it must assume a proper educational role, with the encouragement of the state authorities. Science and religion are considered enemies only in the minds of the socialists and immature people, including immature scientists. Science is very useful for making our life more comfortable and efficient. It is, however, completely useless at providing any integrated code of beliefs. And it certainly is quite incapable of serving as a tool in children's early upbringing. It is important to understand that in an individual's behavior, science and knowledge in general play quite a small part—I would say about 20% of the whole. One's emotions, and individual codes of belief, based on personal experience, define the prevalent part of one's behavior. This means that *science (knowledge) and a code of belief (faith) are complementary to each other.* Religion gives us a very good and a very integrated code of belief. This code, extremely simple and abridged, nevertheless leaves a lot of space for imagination. Its scales of time and events are God's scales, not exactly human. Science decodes and expands some small parts of the biblical picture of the universe, but it will never render a complete, integrated picture of it, or a picture which is sufficiently simple for a layman to grasp. *Religion is conducive to social ethics. It is very important for society's life.* In the U.S.S.R. the need for religion is felt very strongly by the population. Of course, there must be no state religion, and people must be free to follow their own religious faith.

Higher education also must be private, and diversified; it must be assisted by state loans to students which they must repay with a small interest, after graduation, over a period of, say, twenty years. This system will be quite naturally acceptable after the experience of the Soviet system of higher education. Students must not take part in political activities; failure to comply with this ruling will result in expulsion, and the immediate refunding of the loan. Students' business is to be taught, not to teach others. After graduation they can undertake any political activity they choose and teach others.

The Media

Our people are craving for "human" means of communication. The Soviet media propagate naturally everything that corresponds to the ethics of socialism. This cannot be, in principle, the media for proper communication between human beings (not socialist robots).

Evidently, the media in New Russia must be greatly diversified which means that it must be mostly private. However, again, unlimited freedom for the media will be extremely dangerous. In the West the media are extremely monopolized though not to the same degree as in the Soviet Union. Lately, Mr. Murdoch has bought out almost all the main American press organs for $1.5 billion. How can parliaments in the West give such enormous power over people's minds to one individual or corporation? The media can rule parliaments, can overthrow them, can rule countries. I do not think that our people will approve of such a sinister and dangerous thing after their Soviet experience. I suggest the following:

1. No owner or corporation can own more than one vehicle of communication; they will be allowed one radio station, one television channel, one newspaper, one magazine, and so on. Of course, the state must also own one such part of the media in order to channel its own point of view.
2. Radio and television can be financed by compulsory fees which everybody possessing a radio or television set must pay to the station of his choice (not to all of them). In this way stations that are not acceptable to the general public will not be able to survive.

Naturally, there must be restrictions on the advertisements on radio or television. Every emigrant from the U.S.S.R. hates the advertisement system on Western radio and television. I suggest the following:

1. No advertisement can interrupt programs.
2. Advertisements must be restricted to certain times by a *set schedule*.
3. Advertisement must be considered an obligation to the customers. If, for example, an advertisement states that people, by using some kind of furniture, will lose weight, then it must be so. If this is not true, then a firm is liable to prosecution, which must be brought not only by persons from the public, but also by special state attorneys. Western advertising is absolutely wild and deceitful. Advertisements must reflect the true properties of goods and services. Not products of fantasy and "consumer coercion."

Welfare

Old-age pensions, the value of which must be equal to a proportion (say 50%) of the wages or salary over the last few years, must be paid basically by the state. They should not be index-linked, but increased at certain intervals to keep in step with the general living standard. Reaching pensionable age should not mean automatic dismissal. Retirement must not be obligatory. I think that the pensionable age must be raised to seventy for both sexes, and that pensioners should be allowed to work in any way they want. Insurance companies, but not employers, can be another source of pensions. Employment is most precious. To suppress it by taxes or by some other obligatory payments replacing taxes is unwise.

All able-bodied people *must* work, "must" in this case meaning that state unemployment or sickness benefits must be low enough so as not to be competitive with wages or a salary, and should only be paid over a limited period of time. Invalids must be treated like pensioners. I am sure that in the New Russia's proposed constitutional order there will be enough suitable work, even for invalids. Of course, such a welfare service will be much better than the Soviet one. Furthermore, New Russia (a much more efficient society) could well afford it.

Health Service

An unhealthy population and unhealthy working people can be very strong obstacles to the material and spiritual prosperity of a country. Social balance and social stability also may well depend on the health of working people. There is a proverb: A healthy body keeps the spirit healthy.

In the U.S.S.R. health services are free but extremely bad. There are shortages of nurses, equipment, beds, linen, clothes, drugs—shortages in virtually everything. In most cases patients must care for themselves. Hospitalized patients, in many instances, are cared for and fed by their relatives. Bribery is rife everywhere. If one compares the results achieved by the Soviet health service against the actual expenses incurred (including bribes), it is probably a very expensive kind of health service. More popular than the free clinics are the paid-by-patients clinics, but these do not change the general picture of a very bad health service.

It may not come as a surprise to learn that in the U.S.S.R. there are different kinds of special health services but these much better services are only accessible to key Soviet managers, not to the ordinary people. For top Soviet rulers there exists a top health service which is the best and favorably compares with the Western health service. It is, of course, hidden and secret. This deplorable situation has led to the emergence of very large numbers of different kinds of private unorthodox underground health services, sometimes very expensive and entailing long waiting queues because of their popularity. I am sure that the Soviet population has a high esteem for paid health services because they understand that it cannot be but better and more reliable.

The British health service is free. It is certainly incomparably better than the Soviet one, but is still far from adequate and is now almost bankrupt. My experience of the American health care shows that it is also acutely wanting. It suffers from extreme monopolism, gigantism, and wrong ideas. Some corporations have up to 150 gigantic hospitals with up to 1,000 beds each where medical personnel are members of great cartels, where patients are mass-handled, just like cars on a conveyor belt, and where the medical staff are also extremely specialized, like workers on a conveyor belt. Nobody knows anything about the patient who, eventually, is wired to some electronic equipment and is completely deprived of any personal attention. General practitioners (doctors) are also members of great professional cartels; they are very expensive but quite inadequate. They can deal with some standard illnesses by some standard means, mostly by standard strong and poisonous drugs. The great exception, of course, is surgery which in the U.S.A. is excellent though very expensive.

The cost of such a monopolized, standardized, impersonal and inefficient monster is so gigantic that it can bankrupt the whole nation.

The lessons to be drawn for New Russia are the following:

1. Health services must be mostly private.
2. Hospitals must be limited by law to, say, 100 beds.
3. Cartels (associations) of the medical profession, like all others, must be prohibited or limited by law to, say, 500 members.
4. Medical corporations must be limited by law to one hospital or clinic.
5. There must be strict enforcement of strong competition in the medical service.
6. The state must reimburse, say 50% of the cost of medical services to the patient.

Poor people should pay only a token price. Insurance companies must pay, say 80% of the costs. No service should be completely free. Free services are not respected, and are frequently wasted. Even a small contribution from the patient makes him look for a competitive price. This will help keep medical costs from excessive increases.

The Question of Inflation

To start with, one should note that the price of any goods or services ultimately consists of three parts: the sum of taxes, the sum of wages or salaries, and the sum of profits. The sum of profits rarely exceeds 10%. When prices inflate it means that the culprits are taxation, wages and salaries, which were increased without a corresponding increase in productivity.

In conditions of private property of millions of owner-entrepreneurs being prevalent and of compromises between the interests of employees and employers unrestricted by anything, except criminal law and norms of communal life (assuming, of course, that strong competition is also such a norm), inflation will be practically impossible. The owner-entrepreneur allowing wages or salaries to be higher without higher productivity will be bankrupt. Other competing owner-entrepreneurs will not permit him to be that licentious. This would provide a very good barrier against this part of the mechanism making for inflation.

Taxation

Though taxation in the U.S.S.R. is even much higher than in the West, it is hidden in the form of low wages and salaries. That part which is open is actually very small (the maximum is 13%). So I am sure that our people will object to anything which is close to the Western taxation. Western taxation in modern times intends to squeeze as much money as possible out of the population, and to redistribute incomes in order to make them more equal.

All governments always need much more money than they actually have. Direct and indirect taxes tend to become more numerous, higher and higher in their value, and finally very complicated and very expensive to collect.

Direct redistribution is achieved by "progressive" taxation; higher incomes are taxed more highly. However, progressive taxation does not remove the usual great differences in incomes; the rich stay rich. *Progressive tax is never successful in providing for redistribution.*

Who pays taxes? The rich, the poor? Taxes on profit, on corporations, on property, on legacies, on income, on goods, on services, on dividends, on energy, and so on—*all taxes are actually paid by the consumer.* All taxes end up in prices of goods and services. Nobody can print money to pay them. They are paid by raising the prices of goods and services, and extracting money to pay for taxes in this way. *The fact is that the complexity of the taxation system (which is very costly to administer) is a very expensive cover for the government's greed. This complexity does not serve any other useful purpose.*

The above consideration shows that it is cheaper and better to abolish all taxes except a tax on certain goods and services at a single flat rate. All other taxes must be prohibited by the Constitution.

The Question of Unemployment

Many people think that unemployment is the result of overproduction and new technology. They say that it will stay with us forever from now on. This is absolute nonsense. Overproduction means in reality overpricing (low productivity) or production of unnecessary goods and services. Decrease prices enough (increase productivity enough) and everything useful will be bought. *The needs of people and society are boundless.* Of course, they constantly change—demand for some kinds of goods and services will diminish or vanish altogether, whereas other demands appear and increase—but they always expand in scope. New technology increases productivity; it reduces prices and expands the market. The introduction of cars and the elimination of horses did not result in decreased employment. On the contrary, employment was greatly increased. New technology has been with us for centuries. It does not create unemployment. Unemployment is created by laws against owner-entrepreneurs, by laws promoting monopolies and big business, by laws regulating prices, wages, salaries, by many restrictions on the movement of labor, by hundreds and thousands of rules regulating small businesses and self-employment, by high and very complicated taxes, by restrictive trade union practices, by too much imbalance "in favor" of working people which in fact gratifies their egoism only. If all these were removed, as is suggested in the alternative for New Russia presented here, full employment would become a normal state of affairs. *Full employment is perfectly possible.* Even invalids will have, if they wish, suitable employment. And suitable jobs will be available for elderly people to improve their life and decrease the burden of their welfare on the younger generation.

Mental and Physical Labor as a Main Source of Right Social Ethics

Creative and efficient mental and physical labor is the only source of spiritual and material prosperity of any human society. In socialist perception, its role is absolutely crucial. According to the socialist idea, in order to eliminate greed and selfishness, it is necessary to reach an unbelievable level of prosperity allowing to satisfy all possible needs of every member of society. This demands lots and lots of physical and especially mental labor. Nothing drops free from the sky. The most important slogan of socialism is: labor must be an affair of honor, valor and heroism. In this greatest and most important task socialism has failed abysmally. The hard reasons for this have been explained already. However, this failure does not compromise the role of labor as the greatest asset and most important factor in human society. Creative labor is still the source of:

1. Good social ethics. A person brought up in conditions of useful labor respects his own and other people's effort. He never will be a vandal or a destroyer. It is impossible to produce useful things or useful thoughts by deceiving nature. Honesty, the desire to work, skill, and knowledge are necessary for any productive activity. *Useful labor produces all those human qualities which make for the essence of ethics of a prosperous society.*
2. A tranquil and happy society, because *any person who has achieved his creative goals by his mental and physical labor is happy.*

3. *Mutual cooperation (instead of a class struggle) and team work.* I am sure that any member of the team which created the space shuttle, or of any group that just built a good house, a member who contributed personally to any creative team effort, is certainly proud of it. He also anticipated the satisfaction derived from such an endeavor.
4. Spiritual and material prosperity.

It is a socialist paradox that the majority of decent Soviet people are actually craving for all these things (1, 2, 3) yet still produce "lousy" labor. In socialist society there is no agency which can resolve this paradox. The sole agency who could do so is the network of millions upon millions of owner-entrepreneurs who, by their selfishness, acting in conditions of strong competition, would moderate the antithetic selfishness of millions upon millions of working people. The millions upon millions of interactions between and compromise reached by owners and workers are capable of solving the task, which socialism cannot.

Conditions which could lead to this creative social balance between the opposite selfishness of millions are:

1. Prohibition of monopolies and giants.
2. Prohibition of any excessive concentration of power over people or over the country.
3. Enforcement of strong competition in all fields of human activity.
4. Abolition of laws favoring or discriminating against anyone or any body.
5. Abolition of all taxation of owners' income.
6. Abolition of all regimentation of businesses, except or the limits set to their activity by criminal law.
7. Equal opportunity for everybody to pursue any kind of noncriminal activity, freely, without any restriction by taxation, noncommercial charges, licensing, regulations, anticompetitive practices, and so on.

These conditions will produce those millions upon millions of owner-entrepreneurs (out of working people themselves) who will engender so many jobs that there will be suitable employment for everybody: young, old, pensioners, invalids, housewives, and so on; and all kinds of jobs: permanent, temporary, part-time. This is the only way to a happy and prosperous society and also a society with the highest standards as far as good spiritual values are concerned.

Perhaps this is the right place to state that our people's experience of socialism is the greatest contribution to this new alternative to socialism. I think that without this socialist experience, the new alternative would be impossible to develop.

Manifestations, Demonstrations and Riots

There are some happenings in the West of which our people would not approve. I mean demonstrations and manifestations which end up in riots, in violence, and the destruction of property; in damage to the health of people, and not seldom in loss of life. I do not think we would like it.

I suggest the following:

1. Organizers of demonstrations must be fully responsible for maintaining peace and order. Under the criminal law of New Russia they must be responsible for all violence, destruction, loss of health and life. They must compensate the victims of demonstrations, and go to prison if necessary.
2. In many instances it is youths who start throwing stones, who set fire to everything. Their parents must be made responsible for these misdeeds (under criminal law) as well as the youths themselves.

I am sure that our people do not like violence, and the constitutional order of New Russia will give everybody abundant means to express their will and to influence events in a democratic, nonviolent way.

Résumé on New Russia's Alternative Constitutional Order

In short, New Russia will probably be a country in which:

1. Personal interests will be recognized as the basis to the interests of the society as a whole and the country at large.
2. All possible classes and groups of people with their contradicting interests, by acting lawfully, will be called to contribute to the achievement of social equilibrium.
3. These contradicting interests will provide for such a natural social equilibrium because there will be no giants, no monopolies, no excessive concentrations of financial, economical, political, trade union, or social power over people or the country as a whole, and they could easily be moderated into millions of mutual interactions. Social equilibrium in a classless socialist society is impossible.
4. This social equilibrium eliminates the need for extreme and cruel state power to compensate for a lack of internal social equilibrium.
5. The creative potential of millions of individuals will be freed to create the greatest spiritual and material prosperity.
6. There will be no rule of the majority over the minorities either, because everybody (including any minority) will be equal under the law and will be free to build their own life according to their wishes and their capabilities—of course, with the safeguard for equal freedom for others.

7. I think that it will be the country in which the same set of norms of social ethics will be fully accepted by everybody and will be to the highest possible degree in accordance with everybody's instinct of self-preservation (egoism). It will be a country where religious values will be held in the highest esteem by most.

In general, I see New Russia as:

1. A society in which the most important and main task of any human society, that is, greatly to improve the quality of human life in both material and spiritual senses, and continue to improve it for all times, will be fulfilled to the maximum degree.
2. A society which will be able to maintain its social equilibrium internally, that is without needing any external coercive forces, such as the state, to enforce it.
3. A society without coercive giants and monopolies and without much contradiction between the interests of individual members and the interests of society as a whole. The interests of New Russia's society will be, ultimately, tantamount to the totality of the interests of its citizens.
4. A society in which every member has something to achieve and will be proud of his achievement.

Problems of Transition to New Russia

Full State Management and Détente

The majority of Russian emigrants of the first and the second waves consider any leader of the U.S.S.R. and his command as representatives of Satan. Stalin, in their mind, certainly was Satan himself. The best labels would be "lunatics," "gerontocrats," "dogmatists," "senile," and so on. The massive destruction of people's lives, the mountains of corpses, the excessive misery and slavery, which the construction of socialism and mature socialism brought to the world, completely justify even much stronger emotions and hatred. All it means is that people not only very strongly disapprove of the builders and rulers of socialism, but also that they are unable to explain their motives. This situation is of course very dangerous for the cause of freedom. It gives those "satanists" and "lunatics" a very big advantage in their intention to conquer the world. It is indeed impossible to overcome the powerful enemy whose motives you do not understand. Détente is, of course, a splendid manifestation of this absolute misunderstanding. However, the matter of motives is actually very simple, as in the proverb which says: Simplicity is quite enough to fool the wise man.

This matter is the full state management:

1. Everything is state property.
2. Production and distribution are centrally managed by the state. Actually, all aspects of life are centrally managed by the state.
3. There is a very great and very complicated power structure which allows management of such a great country as the U.S.S.R. from a single center—the Politburo.

It is not surprising that non-uniform, unpredictable, irrational, individually extremely complicated human beings just cannot comply with that uniform, predictable, extremely rational, extremely monolithic system of full management by the state which is socialism.

It was necessary to destroy sixty-seven million of the best, active human beings just to achieve conformity with the system of full state management. After that, in order to keep full state management intact, it has been *necessary* to maintain the colossal system of intimidation, mutual spying, and elimination of potential rebels; to suppress everything which is human, even inside people's minds. But even this colossal system of fear and intimidation has been incapable of forcing human beings to work and to live up to the standards required by the socialist full state management system. Yes, the power of full state management is there, people are not yet rebelling. But it is only power without the ability to bring about productive results; people defy the system in its most important task: getting the greatest material and spiritual prosperity for human beings. Instead the system causes extreme material and spiritual poverty, and misery. The perfect organization that full state management claims to represent is completely alien to the basic properties of human beings.

Now, put yourself into Mr. Gorbachev's shoes. He is certainly completely innocent of all the horrors of socialism. He is by all standards a common human being but a clever and smart one. He now presides over that system which we have just described. I think he already knows how vulnerable the full state management system is. He (as a great many Western politicians do) thinks, however, that bad things (low productivity, idleness, absenteeism, theft, black market, and so on) are the net result of bad management and of the bad behavior of people, which as such can be corrected by improving certain methods of management, fighting corruption, tightening discipline and taking other similar measures. What Mr. Gorbachev obviously cannot understand is that no such measures will achieve anything positive as *the system of full state management suffers from the fundamental and incorrigible fault of being inherently incompatible with natural human instincts and hence peo-*

ple's normal behavior. I suspect that you, my reader, are also sure of the ability of the human mind to correct everything, especially if that what is to be corrected is so evident to you yourself. Nevertheless your idea, my reader, is false; you can correct any particular fault to a certain degree through your special effort, but you will not be able to correct all the faults altogether. It is like Heisenberg's famous principle of uncertainty: By improving something you will make something else worse. Now, Mr. Gorbachev of course will try to improve state management and to win over the hearts of the working people to make them work better (for their own benefit). The Old Guard has already lost faith in state management, but he is young and full of life. However, in two or three years he will understand that the Old Guard are right in their skepticism and their impotence to change things. He will find out that he, too, is impotent to improve matters. Then, what is to be done? Any reform in the right direction (to free humans to be humans) will take away a part of his power to manage. Considerable reform will bring about his complete loss of power to manage.

Being no fool, Mr. Gorbachev will try not to allow this to happen and thus will have to resort to all the stupid, lunatic measures that will maintain state management with all its inhumane features intact.

There are a great many people who nudge the U.S.S.R. to go the "Hungarian way" or, in general, to NEP. (They greatly overestimate the "goodness of life" in Hungary—it is actually only slightly better.) Unfortunately, the "Hungarian way" without the orthodox U.S.S.R., will lead automatically to the complete disintegration of full state management, with Kadar and his command unable to survive this disintegration. It is only the "orthodox" and powerful U.S.S.R. that can save the Hungarian Party leadership from this danger. If Gorbachev were to go the "Hungarian way," in a short time there would be no socialist Hungary nor any other socialist satellites left. Everywhere in the Soviet Empire the socialist full state management would disintegrate automatically. And where would Mr. Gorbachev be?

So, all this is very complicated. The eventual collapse of full state management is unavoidable. However, the Gorbachevs of this world must find some ways to loosen the power of state management and at the same time keep a certain control over the events so that they do not perish in the very stormy transformation from an inhumane into a humane society.

There is still another option. Mr. Gorbachev, like many socialists, may think about the conquest of the world by socialism. Maybe, if the whole world were under full world state management, human beings would change their behavior and become uniform, rational, predictable, manageable? The socialist idea is that a complete transformation of human nature under the influence of the rational, perfect full state management is entirely possible. Human beings will lose their instinct of self-preservation (egoism) and become perfect saints.

In this case Gorbachev and his likes will be on top of the world. They will be the saviors of the human race. They will be Gods. Could one not argue that this, yet unchecked possibility, is very attractive to them?

Now, what about détente? It seems to Western people that they could have a way to mutual understanding and friendship between the U.S.S.R. and the West, which would eventually lead to disarmament on both sides, convergence of the two systems, and thus the beginning of eternal peace. They do not understand that such arrangements would heavily aggravate the task of maintaining full state management in the U.S.S.R.; for these arrangements would greatly induce human beings in the U.S.S.R. to take up independent initiatives and thus to form themselves into a force destructive of full state management. These arrangements would also mean that the option of conquest of the world by socialism and of establishing a perfect, full state management system on a worldwide scale, would be eliminated.

The Gorbachevs of this world would be complete fools to go for détente in this way. On the contrary, they must use whatever détente they can achieve to consolidate full state management and keep it over millions of human beings in the U.S.S.R. and also to spread socialism (and instability and conflict) everywhere in the world where there is an opportunity to do so. The Gorbachevs of this world would be fools to allow the U.S.S.R. to disarm because it means that they would lose their grip over the Soviet population and also lose an important tool for the conquest of the world.

Détente can be real only in the case of the complete collapse of full state management in the U.S.S.R. and of its complete transformation into New Russia in accordance with the alternative presented in this paper. Until that time détente will be always against the interests of all human beings in the entire world.

Détente between the U.S.S.R. and the West is exactly the same as détente between wolf and sheep. The idea of détente shows that the West, not Gorbachev and his likes, completely fails to understand the very important things that the latter understand fully. So, who are the lunatics?

This chapter is a balancing piece to the next one on the vested interest in New Russia.

Everybody in the U.S.S.R. Has Some Vested Interests in the New Russia's Alternative

It is evident that ordinary people will be much better off in New Russia. Better off both materially and spiritually. Happier, too. Material and spiri-

tual advantages will be quite considerable because millions will become free
to exercise their individual talents and capabilities in creating their own
individual material and spiritual wealth and, consequently, the wealth of the
society as a whole. Spiritual advantages will be especially significant. Socialism is actually spiritual vacuum, because all individuals, including Politburo
members, must act and think along socialist lines, maintain socialism, which
is an extremely hollow and boring exercise. Sometimes it is even repelling.
Socialism is spiritual vacuum because the satisfaction and the development
of spiritual needs are very expensive and demand very high material investment which socialism cannot afford.

It may sound surprising, but the ruling echelons, including Politburo
members, can have personal advantages in New Russia as well. I knew
personally quite a number of members of the ruling élite. Of course, their
material well-being (good for socialism but not in general) is connected
directly with the socialist system which endows them with power. Hence,
they would certainly fight for socialism to stay, but only to a point. Their life
too is exceedingly boring and dull. They also live under very heavy and
extensive constraints which are contrary to their human common sense and
insulting to them as creative and active human beings. Very often they too
find their "socialist duties" rather repelling despite the fact that they have
acquired the habit of discharging these duties. They certainly are not happy
people. Of course, there are, among them, dull robots, who are quite
satisfied with their life and "activity," but they are a minority.

Even for the socialist élite, brains (say, special) and energy are necessary
to be able to get to the top. It is a myth that they are all stupid and lazy.
Evidently, socialism demands some special capabilities which would not
serve any good in a free society. However, brains and energy are necessary in
any case. Actually, in New Russia they will be able to use their abilities
much better and much more, to their own advantage.

Socialist robots could be worse off in New Russia. However, it would not
be up to them, in this case, as in many others, to decide. On the other hand,
one could argue that in a free society human robots could be very useful,
too. The most important question is, of course, what will prevail: the
pleasure of power or the creative urges which every human being has?
Disorganization of the power and management structures can decrease the
pleasures of power, transforming them into displeasures.

The above also applies to socialist military and KGB generals. Their
abilities can be adjusted to the new moral climate and to the new great
possibilities that New Russia would offer, even more easily than would be
the case for the socialist rulers. I would not say that all of them will do well
in New Russia, but the best, the most talented and valuable amongst them

certainly will. They are professionals and are necessary in any modern society (I do not talk here about those responsible for criminal acts). Actually, for the great majority of the socialist managerial élite, the chances in New Russia would be very good. The decline in their socialist managerial power and the dangers that go together with that decline may force them to rethink their position. They could get a great advantage even during the transitional period because they could deliberately take on a leading role in it.

Possible Course of Transition in the Case of an Orderly Transformation

I would like to underline some very important goals to be reached in the course of the transformation of the U.S.S.R. into New Russia.

1. To suppress revenge. Millions of Soviet people were involved in improper actions not through their own free will. Socialism cannot leave anybody alone. In Hitler's Germany nobody was left alone either. The U.S.S.R. now, however, is different; almost all the main murderers and torturers who were building socialism, including Stalin himself, are dead. They have thus escaped their Nuremberg trials, which they deeply deserved. The number of new murderers and torturers is much smaller, and their trial must be postponed until matters have settled.

2. It is important that every citizen, good or bad, should be involved in the transformation of socialism into New Russia. Even members of the Soviet apparatus up to the Politburo level itself. *It is important to explain and to show that everybody has an acceptable future in New Russia as is indeed the case.*

3. It is important to provide an occupation for everybody, and the means for some kind of existence during the transformation. Anybody who is ill, incapable, or too old must be cared for by state welfare. *Transitional inflation would be unavoidable.*

4. It is necessary to abolish immediately all taxes and restrictions on any private enterprise, and to free trade and commerce. This will certainly reduce unavoidable transitory hardships.

5. Kolkhozes and state farms must be immediately freed from control from above. The fate of kolkhozes must be decided by meetings of the *kolkhozniks. Kolkhozniks* would have to decide whether to dissolve the kolkhozes and to get from them a piece of land and some property for their private use. State farms must be made the property of their employees.

   All restrictions on the free sale of the agricultural products of kolkhozes, state farms or individuals, must be immediately lifted.

6. It is necessary to hand over all dwellings to the dwellers themselves. This would be their property.
7. Gradually, starting with the consumer products industry, all the economy should be transferred to the ownership of the employees. The same should be done with all other institutions including schools, hospitals, and clinics. Every employee must receive a number of shares proportional to the value of his wage or salary. These shares can be sold and bought. During the first couple of years the wages and salaries must still be paid by the state. For the first two to three years the old management must be maintained. After that period a new management can be elected. I think this is the best possible road to introduce private ownership in the future.
8. Everybody who wishes it should be given a piece of land (from the kolkhozes' land funds). In times of upheavals and stress such plots of land have been extremely helpful against the threat of mass hunger.
9. All army contingents should be immediately withdrawn from all satellites and occupied countries. Some of the military forces should be gradually demobilized.
10. For the first one to two years some administrative restrictions should be maintained on movements of the population.
11. The CPSU, the ministries, the structure of the army, the KGB and the militia should not be abolished before the end of the transformation. It is necessary to use them to keep order and, most importantly, to cooperate in achieving the goals of the transformation.
12. A Constituent Assembly should be called to issue the Constitution.
13. A referendum should be held on the Constitution of New Russia.
14. An election for the new organs of government should then be called.
15. The previous, now unnecessary, power structures should be gradually dissolved, with some parts of them being transformed into a part of the new state structure.

Some details concerned with the discussion of the above problems can be found in my book, *New Russia, An Alternative,* published in Russian by Overseas Publications Interchange Ltd. (London, 1980).

I would like to express my gratitude to Alexander Shtromas for his encouragement, help and advice, and also to Françoise BonKain for decoding my rather messy manuscript.

2

Law and the Soviet State

Some Thoughts About the Future

ALICE ERH-SOON TAY

Nineteenth century socialism, of which Marxism-Leninism is an ideological offshoot, was above all a critique, in the name of general social and collective interests, of the commercial-individualistic society of laissez-faire capitalism, of its emphasis on property and private law. It proclaimed property to be a social function and not a private right. It saw state and law as destined to wither away or at least to lose their preeminently coercive function. The government of men would give way to the administration of things; the self-ordering community would take over from the State and its functionaries; rational planning would replace class interests and class power. By and large, socialists were hostile to law as a social institution and not only as the mainstay of particular social orders. If they accorded any place to law under socialism, they did so by seeing law as a passive instrument, as a means of steering society or of elevating social interests over private interests.

The socialist vision in the nineteenth century and much of the twentieth has been both backward-looking and forward-looking. Socialists have had a strong hankering for and have projected into the future an idealized version of the organic community, the village *Gemeinschaft* of face-to-face relations, allegedly spontaneous harmony and fellow-feeling, informal and substantive justice, and full or comparative equality. They have contrasted this with the atomism, individualism, Hobbesian war of all against all of the modern *Gesellschaft*, the civil society of the economists, which Rousseau called a desert populated by wild animals. But they have also seen themselves as heirs of the eighteenth century Enlightenment, using science in the cause of human self-determination, progress and welfare, replacing irrational conflict by rational administration, private law by public law, class interest by the socio-technical norm. They have attacked the *Gesellschaft*, in short, not only from the *Gemeinschaft* side but from the bureaucratic-administrative side, in the name not only of community but also of rationality. The tension between these two criticisms and their ultimate incompatibility with the concept of human self-determination and human liberty that was supposed to be the point of it all explains both the constant bifurcation and schisms in the ideologies of socialism and the ultimate failure of the socialist utopian ideal.

Neither laissez-faire capitalism nor liberal democratic ideals—private right, private interest and private law—now command the respect or entertain the hopes for an ever brighter future of liberalism and individualism that they once did. Both *Gemeinschaft* and bureaucratic-administrative strains command widespread support and have important impact in western societies. These are unquestionably undergoing various forms of socialization from within, and a constant extension of the public at the expense of the private. In one sense, many socialist attitudes and demands grow stronger and stronger within western societies—egalitarianism, elevation of the alleged social interest over private interests, and the power and authority, indeed the ubiquity, of the State. On the other hand, some of the most central socialist hopes and beliefs are rapidly losing authority and plausibility in all modern societies, whether communist or western. No one serious believes that the State and Law, let alone all forms of human coercion and conflict, will wither away under socialism. Few believe that public ownership of the means of production, distribution, and exchange makes them work more efficiently than private ownership. No one believes that such public ownership inevitably inaugurates or leads to an era of freedom or of prosperity. The ultimate goal of socialism, especially in its Marxist formulation, has visibly disintegrated—at best, socialism has become, not the higher way, but an alternative one. For many of us, though not for all, it may seem clear that life under Marxist-Leninist governments is much more nasty, brutish, and short than under democratic ones and that there is no question of treating the two great highways into modern industrial and post-industrial societies as *equally* attractive or unattractive routes. But we have become increasingly aware that at least some of the major problems of modern mankind appear independently of the route we take, that they are not tied to the choice between State or private owner-ship of the means of production.

Central to the nevertheless overwhelmingly important difference between western democratic and communist societies is the concept of the rule of law as an expression of constitutionalism, of the open and public control of government and adjustment of interests, of a distinction between the manipulation of "palace politics" and the free public discussion and social and electoral action of democratic politics as the science of freedom.

The great achievement of Western European civilization lies in its uniquely sharp and self-conscious delineation and working out of a concept of private law to be distinguished from and counterposed to public law, public policy, and public administration. That concept stands at the very foundation of any effective justice and freedom-loving conception of the rule of law and of the State as itself subject to the rule of law. The concept is faced by new problems and tasks through the creation of the welfare state, problems and tasks that threaten the clarity and specificity of our concept of law and devotion to the rule of law, but remains central to liberal democracy and to that which distinguishes the *Gesellschaft* from the managerial, bureaucratic State.

A properly worked out and historically based conception of the ideal of the rule of law sees it unapologetically as a specific historical product. That product subsumes within it the development and great achievement of Roman law and the judicializing of human affairs in the legalistic democratic or bourgeois revolutions of the eighteenth century that spread the principles of democracy throughout the world, in principle if not always in practice. It subsumes the elevation of equality, liberty, and ultimate control of government by the people and of law as a regularized, humane, impartial and intellectually honest way of dealing with relations between people, and with relations between people and their government, in the light of general, and morally infused, depersonalized principles of conduct.

The rule of law in this sense is an immense historical achievement, carrying implications that go far beyond the formal principle of justice as equality before the law, and promoting and strengthening demands for equality and fairness wherever they occur. It is a rule of law that is not easily or readily exportable as an instantly transferable commodity. Such a rule of law is seen in sections of western society today as not entirely appropriate for the twenty-first century or alternatively as gravely threatened by the development of the *active* state, engaged in the business of creating mass public bureaucracies for the purpose of instituting and maintaining deliveries of social services to mass populations. It is a rule of law desperately longed for though not yet fully understood or realized by millions under communist rule. Its appeal is increasingly recognized, at the level of lip service, by communist rulers themselves.

At the international level, a host of United Nations conventions and declarations have sought to make some of the most important ideological principles of the rule of law in this specific sense matters for universal respect and application, by converting them into rights (human, political and civil), independent, in principle, of particular states or legal systems. This implies what many states have unhappily recognized and hence overtly or covertly rejected—that international law is not just a series of arrangements between states but an extension of the rule of law and of all the implications of the western ideal of law (as a general human ideal) into world affairs. It is remaining ineffective in all except Western democracies because of the cynical selectivity with which both communist and Third World states proclaim and apply these rights and insist on exempting themselves from their operation.

The nature and functions of law and public perceptions of its social importance are changing in both the communist world and the free world. In the Western democracies, the rule of law does not command the same degree of widespread public support, at least among the educated, as it once did. In communist societies, the earlier emphasis on mass mobilization, politicization, informal procedures, and flexibility has been replaced, to a significant extent, by emphasis on regular procedures, clear demarcation of authority, and bases for social stability and predictability. This is summed up in increasing emphasis on "socialist legality" and the positive social function of law and on the State as representing and protecting, in socialist society, the State and the interests of all the people. To consider these developments seriously we need to recognize that the word *law* can be used in different senses, that there are different and competing "legal" traditions and that not all properly enacted laws and legal procedures are evidence of the "rule of law."

II

Eugene Kamenka and I, in writing about law and legal ideologies in the modern world, especially in societies ruled in the name of Marxism-Leninism, have elaborated what we see as three paradigms of law and social organization that compete with each other in most modern societies. These are the *Gemeinschaft* paradigm, the *Gesellschaft* paradigm and the bureaucratic-administrative paradigm.[1] According to the German sociologist Ferdinand Tönnies,[2] in the *Gemeinschaft* type of social regulation, punishment and resolution of disputes, the emphasis is on law that expresses the will, internalized norms and traditions of an organic community, within which every individual member is part of a social family. Here there tends to be no sharp distinction, if there is any formal distinction at all, between the private and the public, between the civil wrong and the criminal offense, between politics, justice, and administration, between political issues, legal issues, and moral issues. There is no theory of law as a distinct, autonomous social institution. The village is ruled by custom, the city—in its *Gemeinschaft* character—by religion and authority. There is little emphasis on the abstract, formal criteria of justice. The person at the bar of judgment is there, in principle, as a whole man, bringing with him his status, his occupation and his environment, all his history and his social relations. He is not there as an abstract right-and-duty-bearing individual, as just a party to the contract or as owing a specific and limited duty to another. Justice is thus substantive, directed to a particular case in a particular social context and not the establishing of a general rule or precedent. Its symbols are the seal and the pillory. The formalisms of procedure in this type of justice, which can be considerable, are linked with magical *taboo* notions, are emotive in context and concrete in formulation; they are not based on abstract rationalistic concepts of justice and procedure. Punishment, as Michel Foucault has stressed, is public, is a social drama, symbolizing the awesome power of the social unity.[3] The almost overwhelming strength of this *Gemeinschaft* strain in traditional Chinese legal procedure, with its emphasis on the emperor and the magistrate as the father of his people, and in popular Chinese concepts of the political order, justice, morality, and the place of the individual in society, is widely recognized. It was very much the medieval world picture in Europe (though in conflict with the strongly contractual foundations of feudal rights and privileges). It was also characteristic of proceedings before the early English jury and in the Russian peasant *mir*, for instance, as envisaged in the 1497 *Sudebnik* of Ivan III, where men were to be freed or convicted not as a result of investigating the specific crime they were accused of, but on the basis of their general reputation in the community, to which the jury testified. It remains characteristic of aspects of justice in communist societies, with their emphasis on the general social behavior of the accused, and in Moslem, community and revolutionary courts and tribunals.

The *Gemeinschaft* is not a description of an actual existing society in all its aspects; it describes a dominant or strong *moment* (in the Hegelian sense) or tendency of a society. It is a Weberian ideal type, linking actual institutions and the historical ideologies or perceptions on which they rest and which they mould, and showing how these presuppose and tend toward a particular view of man and society and the relations between them. There are in any society countervailing trends to the dominant world view, institutions that do not fit, beliefs that do not square—sometimes very powerful or important institutions or beliefs. The King's Common Law in feudal England was one such institution that, in certain respects, quite fundamentally did not square and stood in contradiction with baronial justice. So were elements of Roman private law (as opposed to Roman public law) in the Republic, and Principate and the Empire, even if the concept of *ius* was backed by the *Gemeinschaft* philosophy of the Stoics. For the *Gemeinschaft* as *Gemeinschaft* does not have a specific legal tradition. It brings together law, justice, and morality and fuses them with politics and administration.

It is central to an understanding of the initial attitudes of communist régimes to law that they begin in the hour of revolution by elevating such *Gemeinschaft* conceptions of law against "the rule of law" and that they continue in varying degrees to appeal to *Gemeinschaft* conceptions and ideologies in their rejection of "bourgeois" formalism and legalism, relying at crucial periods on terror, political direction, and authority and "extra-legal measures" to maintain authority and submission to it.

The *Gesellschaft* type of law and legal regulation is in all respects the very opposite of the *Gemeinschaft* type. It arises out of the growth of individualism and of the protest against the status society and the fixed locality; it is linked with social and geographical mobility, with cities, commerce and the rise of Protestantism and the bourgeoisie. (Communist revolutions, so far, have not been successful as internally-based revolutions in any society in which *Gesellschaft* traditions were dominant; they have been dependent on the imposition of external force.) The *Gesellschaft* view assumes a society based on external as opposed to internal links, made up of atomic individuals and private interests, each in principle equivalent to the other, capable of agreeing on common means while maintaining their diverse ends. It emphasizes formal procedure, impartiality, adjudicative justice, precise legal provisions and definitions, and the rationality and predictability of legal administration. It is oriented to the precise definition of the rights and duties of the individual through a sharpening of the point at issue and not to the day-to-day *ad hoc* maintenance of social harmony, community traditions, and organic solidarity; it reduces the public interest to another, only *sometimes* overriding, private interest. It distinguishes sharply between law and administration, between the public and the private, the legal and the moral, between the civil obligation and the criminal offense. Its model for all law is contract and the *quid pro quo* associated with commercial exchange, which

also demands rationality and predictability. It has difficulty in dealing with
the State or state instrumentalities, with corporations, social interests and
the administrative requirements of social planning or a process of production
unless it reduces them to the interests of a "party" to the proceedings
confronting another "party" on the basis of formal equivalence and legal
interchangeability.

The *Institutes* of Justinian already elevate this conception of "private" law
as concerned with the individual. The American Constitution and Bill of
Rights and the French Declaration of Rights of Man and the Citizen are the
fundamental ideological documents of the *Gesellschaft* type of law, which
reached the peak of its development in the judicial attitudes of nineteenth
century England and of German Civilians, and in the actual legal system of
the United States. It is enshrined, at least in part, in the concept of the
Rechtsstaat and the rule of the law, *i.e.* of a specifically legal conception of
the foundations and core of the operation of justice and legitimacy in
society, as a demand for government by law, not men. It is at home with the
social contract theory of society, with individualism and abstract rights. This
view is also enshrined in the United Nations Covenant on Civil and Political
Rights—the Covenant that nondemocratic states are most concerned to
denigrate and make subordinate by elevating instead social, economic and
collective rights as alternatives to rather than as extensions of civil and
political rights. This view again elevates a specific, historically shaped conception of law and justice, closely linked with the individualism and a
specific legal tradition grounded in the private law of the Romans and
focusing on law and justice as conflict-resolution according to broad general
principles and rules applying to all persons in that situation. But while this
view of justice, too, elevates one particular function—that of conflict-resolution—it has its characteristic views of the social ordering and resource-
allocation functions. It assimilates the former, as far as possible, to the
minimum framework necessary for orderly and effective pursuits—*i.e.,* to the
rules of the road or the basic regulations of buying and selling necessary to
make a market possible. Resource allocation it leaves to the efforts of
individual enterprise, at least in principle. (In fact, of course, no society has
been a pure *Gesellschaft* and no relations or institutions have ever been
based solely on the cash-nexus or individual interest.) But the *Gesellschaft*
conception of law and justice is especially suspicious of the attempt to derive
these from the social whole; it sees the state as resting on law and serving the
pluralism of private interests, rather than imposing a superior and independent universal interest or conception of justice.

Whether we treat individualism and the ideology of *Gesellschaft* relations
as preceding and facilitating, or following and reflecting, the development of
bourgeois capitalist society (and the former view is more plausible), there is

no doubt that Tönnies' contrast helps to dramatize and illuminate (show what is involved in) the social revolution that overtook Europe after the Industrial Revolution. It helps especially to bring out sharply the conflict between classical liberalism and early socialism, explaining the nature of their confrontations and of their sympathies, the basis of their enmities and alliances. Nor is there any doubt that the *Gemeinschaft* strain has remained strong in the socialist and other critiques of capitalism and liberalism, that it is an active force today.

Nevertheless, the contraposition of *Gemeinschaft* and *Gesellschaft* as the two fundamental social traditions smacks unmistakably of the nineteenth century. It ignores the ever-increasing scope and power of the state and its bureaucracies that have become so evident in the twentieth century. It ignores the increasing emphasis on bureaucratic rationality, on planning and administration within the capitalist firm itself, and the widespread impact that planning goals and values elevated by research and development have had on modern society. That phenomenon, not much noticed by Tönnies, constituted a fundamental theme in the work of Max Weber and much earlier, through the scientific optimism of the French Enlightenment and the technocratic interests of the Saint-Simonians, had become a central part of socialism as the ideology of rational planning. For socialism and, for that matter, much wider social sentiments today, do not represent mere attempts to bring into being a new secular *Gemeinschaft*. We are forward-looking where the *Gemeinschaft* was backward-looking, progressive where it was traditional, rational and scientific where it was emotional and familial.

The opposed paradigms of *Gemeinschaft* and *Gesellschaft*, then, require a third distinct paradigm, that of the bureaucratic-administrative society and "legal" system. It is within that paradigm, indeed, that the conception of law as social control, as a means of general administration, receives its fullest development. Where *Gemeinschaft* elevates community and common tradition, religion or ideology, human relationships, and organic bonds, where *Gesellschaft* elevates the abstract individual and his abstract rights and duties in a social contract and a system of abstract and impersonal law, the bureaucratic-administrative elevates or pretends to elevate what the Soviet legal theorist E.B. Pashukanis called the socio-technical norm—the rational requirements of a social province, field or activity, the implications of a policy, the regulations required to alter consciously a society and its ways of living, in short, its concept of law.[4] Where the *Gemeinschaft* thinks of justice as the *justitia communis*, oriented to particular cases in a particular social context, where the *Gesellschaft* sees justice as commutative, determining rights and duties on abstract, impersonal and universal principles of law, independent of status, the bureaucratic-administrative society elevates the concept of legality, of action according to regulations to which human beings are subject, by which their status and their consequent rights and duties are determined.

Bureaucratic-administrative regulation, thus, is quite distinct from both *Gemeinschaft* and *Gesellschaft* law, but it does not stand in quite the sharp uncompromising opposition to them that they do to each other; pursuing different aims, it nevertheless finds points of contact and affinity with each of the other forms. The bureaucratic-administrative emphasis on an interest to which individuals are subordinate, on the requirements of a total concern or activity, brings it to the same critical rejection of *Gesellschaft* individualism as that which is characteristic of the *Gemeinschaft*; it gives it a similar interest in maintaining harmonious functioning, in allowing scope for *ad hoc* judgment and flexibility, in assessing a total situation, and the total effects of its judgment in that situation. This is why the growth of corporations has produced *Gemeinschaft*-like features in the internal direction of the corporation, even while the corporation maintains *Gesellschaft* relations with its external counterparts. At the same time, bureaucratic-administrative regulation is a phenomenon of large-scale, non-face-to-face administration, in which authority has to be delegated. As the scale grows, bureaucratic rationality—regularity and predictability, the precise definition of duties and responsibilities, the avoidance of areas of conflict and uncertainty—becomes increasingly important. This requirement of bureaucratic rationality in the bureaucratic-administrative system stands in tension with *Gemeinschaft* attitudes, unless they are strictly limited in scope. It finds a certain common ground with the distinguishing features of *Gesellschaft* law in the emphasis on the universality of rules and the precise definition of terms, in the important role ascribed to the concepts of *intra* and *ultra vires*, in the rejection of arbitrariness and of the excessive use of *ad hoc* decisions to the point where they threaten this rationality. In the Soviet Union the bureaucratic-administrative strain has been very strong indeed, imperfect as the execution may often have been. While earlier Soviet theoreticians saw law being replaced by the revolutionary consciousness of justice, which would strengthen the *Gemeinschaft* side of socialism, in fact the influence of plan and of bureaucratic requirements in the Soviet Union has been notably in the direction of strengthening the presuppositions of bureaucratic rationality and of thus strengthening, at least to some extent, the respect and need for *Gesellschaft* law.

Much of the argument in jurisprudence has been concerned with judging the merits of competing prescriptions for the use of the term *law*, though the dispute has rarely been purely verbal. There is a strong tradition which wants to reserve the word *law* for use in a narrow sense (as in "the rule of law") to refer to what we have called the *Gesellschaft* type. Others would say that *Gemeinschaft* law is also law and some use the word *law*, at least in one sense, broadly enough to include bureaucratic-administrative regulation, even in its pure ideal type form, as well.

Domination-submission, however, is clearly extra-legal and supra-legal in that it neither implies nor requires a structured system of regulation incorporating certain values and moral or socio-political assumptions; gangsters can and do rule by terror and the imposition of force and they need not ideologize their pretensions. Domination-submission therefore does not inevitably confront the *Gemeinschaft*, the *Gesellschaft*, and the bureaucratic-administrative form as a fully blown rival pattern of a social structure of value system; it can, to some extent, live above or within all of them, modifying or shaping the conditions in which they operate. It is also, to some extent, implied by each of them. The ideals of *Gemeinschaft*, in their classic formulation, incorporate domination-submission in so far as it can be plausibly presented as voluntary exercise of parental responsibility and voluntary submission to parental will. As such, they are particularly susceptible to degeneration into naked relations of personal domination and helpless or hopeless submission. The French Revolution and the ideals of the *Gesellschaft* were, in fact, a protest against precisely this sort of degeneration, an attempt to create a political and legal system that was by its very nature inimical to the institutionalization of status, of dependence, of relations of personal dominance and submission. It was an attempt to replace the government of men by the government of law. *Gesellschaft* law as a pure ideal type is indeed inimical to the recognition of social hierarchies; it does presuppose the equality of all the parties before it, and it operates best when those parties are in fact equal and do not stand, one to the other, in a relation of pervasive dependence or subordination. (The elevation of the abstract rights of women and rights of children is an attempt to turn the family into a *Gesellschaft* and not a *Gemeinschaft* institution recognizing implicitly the bias of *Gesellschaft* law toward freedom and equality and against status-dependence.)

The bureaucratic-administrative form, on the other hand, lends itself much more readily to an institutionalization of domination-submission. In communist countries, including China, the domination-submission relation has been institutionalized, or at least ideologized, in the doctrine of the leading role and historical infallibility of the Communist Party and in the proclamation of "democratic centralism"; a vast range of legal and extra-legal measures have been taken to ensure that the domination remains secure. The overwhelming basis of domination is, in the narrower senses of law, extra-legal. Though *Gemeinschaft* attitudes and bureaucratic-administrative structures are more easily manipulable in the interest of domination than *Gesellschaft* attitudes and structures, *Gemeinschaft* can produce dangerously uncontrollable popular enthusiasm or resistance through its implicit elevation of fellowship, of popular participation, and non-impersonal relations, and its stress on the mutual ties between rulers and ruled. On the other hand, bureaucratic rationality can produce attitudes highly critical of irrational bases for domination and "inexpert" personnel in control. The history of the Soviet Union in the past sixty years confirms all of these points; the Soviet régime has been able to manipulate all three of the ideal types in the interest of its domination, but it has also been confronted by limited challenges from each. The Soviet government, indeed, has not committed itself exclusively to any of the three types. It has kept all the options open and has quite skillfully balanced *Gemeinschaft* and bureaucratic-administrative attitudes and procedures with appeals to socialist legality and limited but patent *Gesellschaft* guarantees and assurances.

III

Developments in the Soviet Union since 1966 are not encouraging for the earlier liberal hope that breaches in the Iron Curtain, increasing emphasis on the role of law under socialism and more sophisticated legal enactments, as well as the increasing education of leaders and public alike, would lead to the strengthening of *Gesellschaft* attitudes and arrangements and of the rule of law. On the contrary, the *Gesellschaft* structure and concepts of the Stalin Constitution and the earlier codes, ineffective as they may have been in practice, have been "integrated" into more subtle and dangerous constitutions and codes that subordinate law to the central concern of "steering society" and that frankly continue to make all rights dependent on the fulfillment of social duties and their tendency to help strengthen the socialist system. Insofar as the Soviet Union elevates law, it does so in the name of bureaucratic correctness and of obeying state commands. Totally lacking from Soviet legal theory is a concept of justice as an ideal embodied in and striven toward by the legal system; totally lacking is any positive appreciation of the legal tradition as having independent social value and social values.

In China, paradoxically, the situation at present bears more similarity to the Khrushchevian thaw (when we all looked to Olimpiad S. Ioffe and some of his colleagues to bring Soviet rulers to an appreciation of the values of civil law) than to the Soviet Union under Brezhnev, Andropov, Chernenko, and Gorbachev. Deng Xiaoping's bold move in proclaiming the rule of law and legal education to be part of the Four Modernizations goes far beyond present-day Marxist-Leninist theory elsewhere; it shows rather an appreciation of the historic role of bourgeois economies and of their legal systems in making people more productive, more competent, more capable of dealing with and living in a complex and forward-looking society, and it has been accomplished by a formal recognition, limited though it may be, of a distinction between law and politics, crime and ideological error. But as Ioffe rightly remarks in his contribution to this volume, the tension between the requirements of political domination and economic reform and achievement is intolerable for the communist system of government—these subsystems tend to destroy each other. That is why in China we see thaws and frosts, why the elevation of family and individual enterprise today is accompanied by campaigns against spiritual and material pollution, why the elevation of law is already becoming the elevation of *economic law* and why economic law is seen, as in the Soviet Union, as a means of steering society and defining the proper place of each activity within it—even if such definition is no longer seen as exclusively carried out by political campaigns and direct normative commands.

It is one of the professional deformations of people working on communist societies that they can grossly overrate the extent to which the comparatively more subtle and flexible ideology of the current régime is actually internalized by its subjects or its ideologues. Thaws end because each time they bring out the extent of dissidence, of demand for freedom and honesty, for justice and independent formulation and application of law, to be found in these societies. Marxism as either a *Gemeinschaft* or bureaucratic-administrative ideology commands no solid support in Marxist-Leninist societies among those who think, except as a defense against the emergence of economic oligarchies, of great and visible economic inequalities publicly justified and promoted, and against foreign economic domination. Leninism as the ruthless and centralized political control of everything that is socially significant flourishes with or without benefit of ideological justification. If it is undermined, it will not be, I believe, by the gradual growth of counter-ideologies. Régimes collapse; they are not overthrown. They collapse through incompetence and loss of nerve, defeat in war or financial or economic disaster, a sudden and sharp reversal at a time of previously rising expectations. Nationalism, religious sentiments and beliefs, economic reversals and war, including war between no longer fraternal socialist states, are real dangers for the régime, but legal traditions, independent social institutions and the strength of liberal sentiments are not. The *Gesellschaft*, as ideology and as reality, has been far too weak in the Soviet Union to confront the régime on the basis of liberal democratic demands.

If the Soviet régime were to collapse, the most immediate likely result, in the absence of external military threat not supported by some nationalities in the Soviet Union, would be the break-up of the Soviet Empire, the hiving off of at least some national republics—the Baltic States, perhaps the Ukraine—and the growth of distinctive law, politics and administration in Georgia, Armenia, Azerbaijan and Central Asia. In all of these, existing All-Union and Union Republican legislation could provide, with gradual amendment, the basis and indeed the reality of a western type legal system, which would no doubt quickly become rich and complex in the Baltic Republics and remain comparatively crude and simple in the RSFSR and Central Asia. But the formal structure and the fundamental concepts and procedures of Soviet law are those of the western legal traditions. It is the political setting in which they operate, the lack of any judicial independence, the cynicism and dishonesty with which legal provisions are applied and guaranteed rights violated that constitute the evil of the Soviet system. This is made possible by pervasive censorship and the successful suppression of all significant protest or independent action. Remove these, and the basis for moving toward a genuine rule of law for the peoples of the Soviet Union, through comparatively simple amendments of legal provisions, is made perfectly possible. The provisions that have to be removed or inserted—the elevation of safe-guarding the socialist system against any criticism or exercise of otherwise guaranteed rights—the need to give citizens power to initiate constitutional action, for instance, are glaringly obvious. Most of the evils of the Soviet Union, even today, are extra-legal and contra-legal. It is political hegemony, not law, that has to be overthrown. The *Gesellschaft* forms are there; it is their spirit that is missing.

IV

This is to some extent confirmed, if not always wittingly, by the important and moving contribution to this volume by Anatoly Fedoseyev, "The Passage to New Russia and some Thoughts on its Alternative Constitutional Order." Fedoseyev is a good man and a sensitive one. He recognizes, correctly, the extraordinary stability of the Soviet system in comparison with all other countries, inside and outside the Soviet bloc, and with Imperial Russia. He sees, too, that the basis of this exceptional stability is actually very simple: "The U.S.S.R. as a whole is the property of the State"— managed by a single authority called the Politburo. The commands of the Politburo may not all be executed effectively or even always be meant to be executed; there are limits to the commands it can give. But on anything that is politically important as a direct challenge to its power and authority, the Politburo has effectively imposed its will. It is able to do so because Bolshevism, in contrast with earlier revolutionary movements such as those of the French Revolution, destroyed completely, through nationalization, the economic independence of all social groups. On that basis, coupled with the capacity for conducting mass terror, uniformity and conformity could be and were created in the Soviet Union.

The extraordinary success of Bolshevism in establishing total ownership and control over a society, Fedoseyev argues, has to be balanced against failures of the socialist system that many have drawn attention to. These are the impossibility of economic reform to ensure higher productivity without destabilizing the system and the very idea of state planning, and the inability to ensure a correct interflow of goods, services and materials, and individual identification and satisfaction with state regulated economic activity. Bolshevism creates hostile relations between citizens, powerless to cooperate sensibly; it undermines their self-respect and allows the population to see its interests rank very low on the list of priorities of the Politburo, which is primarily interested in maintaining its power internally and externally.

So far, we have Fedoseyev, the sensitive and perceptive critic of or even portrayor of the Soviet Union as it is. When he turns to the question of how socialism and the U.S.S.R. will collapse, he becomes the good man, convinced for no very good reason, that evil cannot survive. People in the U.S.S.R., especially at the lower echelons, he believes, are losing their power to fulfill their duties properly; there is universal indiscipline, failure to fulfill economic tasks, which is undermining the power of the state in the U.S.S.R. This, Fedoseyev argues, not distinguishing economic growth from military and political capacity to destroy internal opposition, will result in chaos, in the rise of organized opposition, and in human rights being eventually, *de facto,* assumed by the people. The understanding that nothing can be worse than socialism is already spreading among the population, he argues. An acceptable and credible alternative to socialism would be a decisive factor leading to the collapse of Bolshevik power. Such collapse would in any case be approached through the growing ineffectiveness of state planning and state management and through the corresponding expansion of independent underground economies and private enterprise activities. Countervailing factors— the fear of most Soviet citizens of the more demanding life of enterprise, responsibility, choice and uncertainty, the pride in Soviet power, the dislike and fear of other nationalities and foreign neighbors—are ignored, as they have largely been ignored by most of the contributors to this series of volumes.

Personally, I wish Fedoseyev were right, but his account is too sketchy and too full of unanalyzed terms to convince me. He pays homage to Shtromas's interesting and historically based conception of a "second pivot," but he produces no reasons for thinking that one will emerge in the Soviet

Union. He does not examine the relationship between economic effectiveness in the sense of efficient management and military and political effectiveness. He gives no reason for suggesting that the Politburo is weakened or weakening in its capacities for military and political control, in its capacity to stamp out opposition in time. He leaves open the question whether the collapse of the U.S.S.R. he envisages will result from gradual disintegration or from a palace coup, such as an Army or KGB coup. He bases both possibilities on the growth of widespread disillusionment.

I do not mean by this that Fedoseyev's scenario is impossible. Many of us are agreed that the inability of the state-run economy to deliver the goods and to create an adequate level of continuing material and psychological satisfaction is the Soviet leadership's main weakness and one that it cannot remedy effectively without threatening to undermine its political power. What we are doubtful about is whether widespread but diffuse dissatisfaction, offset by a picture of patent political and military power and determination and of major power and standing in the world, is enough to lead to collapse. Such collapse, I suspect, will require a split in the ruling group, a major miscalculation or loss of nerve—events that are by their very nature contingent. One can only say that the Party created by Lenin has proved an extraordinary instrument for weeding out from its own ranks the indecisive, the insufficiently brutal, the adventurous, and unstable. The rigidity that is its weakness is also its strength. Nor is there any reason to suppose that a decisive shift of power to the military or to the KGB would not result in the new rulers using the old methods of ensuring adequate control.

Like many good men, though in a less extreme form, Fedoseyev sees virtue arising out of the collapse of systems and states, out of a return to the individual as the point of social activity and the harmonizing of individuals through small groups, and good but few laws. To that extent, the disintegration of the Soviet system rather than a palace coup is important to his argument—yet a palace coup seems to me initially more likely.

Once the authority, working style and concrete domination of the Communist Party and of the Politburo had by some not easily envisaged route almost totally collapsed, I have little difficulty in seeing how to set the Soviet Union on the path to democracy. But I believe the measures needed to be almost precisely the opposite of those advocated by Fedoseyev—they need initially to be subtle political and legal measures rather than moral and formal constitutional proclamations as such. They will have to be piece-meal emendations and increasing elaborations and complications of the existing formal legal and political structures. They will have to be taken against the background of fear, crisis, possible disintegration, and great uncertainty; they will require a statesman of the caliber of Lenin or Kemal Pasha

Atatürk—a person who never loses sight of the end but who is capable of using existing *forces* and opportunities.

The first formal step would be provision for genuinely free elections, for the formation of political parties and their capacities to receive voluntary contributions and to lease or own and control property and means of communication, for regular meetings and genuine legislative activity of the Supreme Soviet of the U.S.S.R. and of the republican supreme soviets, which of course could be and probably should be renamed. There should also be provision for the continuation of the Communist Party with the abandonment of democratic centralism and of nomination or ratification from the top down, and for open and contested elections within the Party and the possibility of multiple endorsement of Party candidates for public office—in short, a democratic Communist Party based on the practical smashing and legal abrogation of its authoritarian structure. The aim would be to free the existing membership of the Communist Party from authoritarian control and to encourage the formation of competing factions or even successor parties. Nationalist parties in the Republics, religious parties, etc. should be allowed to emerge and to resume the task, begun in the first two decades of the twentieth century, of educating the Russian public into political democracy. Executive power, however, could not be immediately surrendered to a *still* inchoate legislative body—the welding of executive decisiveness and efficiency with emerging democratic legislative authority is the task calling for a real statesman.

The great political danger would be that which made possible the Bolshevik coup in October 1917—political instability, fragmentation, inability to work together. The political provisions necessary would have to be played by ear in the light of the situation and a fairly strong and comparatively authoritarian leadership would have to manipulate the foundations for democracy in the way, say, that Kemal Atatürk did in Turkey, ensuring stable government while also encouraging and stabilizing the emergence of a responsible opposition and of other parties representing major interest groups. The electoral law—which must be based on regional rather than proportional representation, or a mixture of the two—will need to balance democracy and stable, workable government. One must envisage and accept the possibility that secessionist parties could and should gain dominance in certain areas of the Soviet Union and reconsider the nature of their links with the remainder of the former Soviet Empire.

Second in importance to the working out, by trial and error, of a modern democratic political system nevertheless geared to stable working majorities and the formation of large but broadly-based parties, is the creating and strengthening of an independent judiciary and legal profession and of legal provisions that will protect in a real way the right of the citizens, the independence of trade unions and professional organizations, a system of court conducted and sanctioned industrial arbitration, etc. This can easily be done on the basis of reasoning and amending the existing Soviet Constitution and codes of law and should in fact be done over a lengthy period of time in the light of experience. A Bill of Rights, specific rather than grandiose, will be necessary in Soviet conditions and a special constitutional court—consisting of people like Olimpiad Ioffe—should be given authority to hear and determine constitutional matters. The Procuracy in Soviet conditions is an institution that might well be abolished. The KGB needs not only to be abolished but its leaders, or some of its worst thugs and campguards, tried with careful emphasis on the difference between criminal acts and political errors. Of course, institutions to carry out some of the legitimate functions of the Procuracy and even of the KGB will need to be reestablished, but it is best to break all historical continuity here.

It would be silly for me here to attempt to set out hard and fast plans for a democratized Soviet Union, in the event of such plans becoming possible, when so much depends upon the form of the collapse and the forces ready to take over at least provisional and transitional government and to organize the foundations of the new society. But I do not believe that Fedoseyev, in his characteristically Russian preference for honesty, truth, decency, and simplicity over law and politics, has pointed in the right direction. One cannot dissolve society back into decent individuals or small groups; one must work with the institutions and social traditions that are here. Churches and religious communities need to be legalized and their social significance and tendencies gauged after such legalization. Parties need to emerge and their tendencies and social bases observed.

The possibility of democratizing the Communist Party is part of the process, unless the circumstances in which the Soviet government collapses or is overthrown are such that there is irresistible widespread popular demand for the dissolution and banning of the Communist Party—though, in such an eventuality, an alternative political home or homes will need to be found for the great mass of rank and file party members willing to work under the new conditions. Union republics need to be given freedom and control and the pluralism thereby created be used as a brake on central government power. Initially, a genuine federal system with residual power in the union republics seems advisable; secession on the basis of referendum should be made possible, but it will probably be important for the new rulers not to be seen as presiding over an instant, uncontrolled disintegration of the Soviet State in which secessions or the contemplation of secessions are not accompanied by cordial working agreements between recognized equals who, nevertheless, are not strangers.

The loosening up of the economy similarly cannot be done in one grand gesture; here the Chinese distinction between economic sectors subject to mandatory planning, economic sectors given discretion within more flexible advisory means, and economic sectors privatized where demand exists is a starting point that will of course lead to new complications and difficulties.

NOTES

1. I draw, in the paragraphs that follow, on E. Kamenka and Alice E.S. Tay, "Social Traditions, Legal Traditions," in Eugene Kamenka and Alice Erh-Soon Tay, eds., *Law and Social Control* (London: Edward Arnold, 1980), 3-26, especially pp. 15-16, 17-19, and 20-23. The Western concept of the rule of law is integral to, grew up as part of, and cannot be totally divorced from, the *Gesellschaft* paradigm.

2. Ferdinand Tönnies, *Gemeinschaft und Gesellschaft* (Kiel, 1887), in English translation by P.V. Loomis, *Community and Society* (New York: Harper and Row, 1957), is the source for the references to this author that are to follow. For the discussion of Tönnies's concepts of *Gemeinschaft* and *Gesellschaft* and their application to forms of law and the legal system, see: Eugene Kamenka, "*Gemeinschaft* and *Gesellschaft*," *Political Science* (New Zealand), No. 17 (1965): 3-12; E. Kamenka and A.E.S. Tay, "Beyond the French Revolution: Communist-Socialism and the Concept of Law," *University of Toronto Law Journal*, No.21 (1971): 109-140; and E. Kamenka and A.E.S. Tay, "Social Traditions, Legal Traditions," and "'Transforming' the Law, 'Steering' Society," in E. Kamenka and A.E.S. Tay, eds., *Law and Social Control*, 3-26 and 105-116.

3. See: Michel Foucault, *Discipline and Punish: The Birth of the Prison*, translated from the French by A. Sheridan, (New York: Pantheon Books, 1977).

4. E.B. Pashukanis, *Obshchaya teoriya prava i marksizm* (*Opyt kritiki osnovnykh yuridicheskikh ponyatii*) (Moscow, 1924; 2nd ed. Moscow, 1926; 3rd ed.—with a few additions to the text—Moscow, 1927); translated into German from the 3rd edition by Edith Hajos, with a special preface by Pashukanis, as *Allgemeine Rechtslehre und Marxismus: Versuch einer Kritik der juristischen Grundbegriffe* (Vienna, 1929); and into English by Hugh W. Babb as E.B. Pashukanis, "Marxism and the General Theory of Law," in J.N. Hazard, ed., *Soviet Legal Philosophy* (Cambridge, Mass.: Harvard University Press, 1951).

3

Soviet Constitutional Law

*What Must Be Abolished or Changed
and What Can Be Retained?*

GEORG BRUNNER

By its very nature, the future has always been and will always be uncertain. This simple fact intimidates every scholar invited to answer the question in the subtitle of my paper because of the obvious danger of getting lost in speculation. Even in democratic societies, whose future development might be influenced by proposals for reform made by scholars living in the societies concerned, there is ample evidence for the futility of scholarly endeavors to foresee and shape the future. How much more must this be the case with the Soviet Union, whose future will be framed by as yet indiscernible social and political forces outside the sphere of this author's influence?

Nevertheless, there is a starting point of departure into the uncertain future on the assumption that the question asked is reasonable. If this is so, one has to presume that constitutional law will play a certain role in the Soviet future. That this presumption is not a mere truism but involves fundamental changes in the present constitutional law is the point I will be elaborating upon in the first part of my paper. The second part will be devoted to particular points of stress in the present constitutional system of the Soviet Union, in order to make some guesses as to their possible effects on constitutional developments in the future.

That the Constitution Be the Supreme Law of the Land

According to Article 173 of the Soviet constitution of 1977 "the Constitution of the U.S.S.R. shall have supreme legal force." This sounds good but says nothing—under the prevailing circumstances. Should this constitutional sentence become a real legal provision and not merely represent words strung together, the prevailing legal conditions are to be changed fundamentally.

Theoretical Considerations

It is well known that official Soviet political and legal theory adheres to the concept of the instrumentality of law. This traditional line was stressed by Brezhnev in the concluding remarks of his speech "On the Draft of the Constitution of the U.S.S.R." on 4 October 1977, when he called upon the deputies of the Supreme Soviet of the U.S.S.R. to adopt his Constitution in order to "arm the Soviet people with a new, mighty means of building communism."[1] If, however, law in general and the constitution in particular are nothing else but means to an end, they cannot have any real binding force. An instrument does not bind but serves its lord who uses it at will. Of course, this contradicts the very nature of law, which is a set of rules that may be created but, once created, are not supposed to be used for political purposes. A legal norm that is considered to be valid only in the cases in which it is expedient, is not a legal norm at all. But this is exactly what the legal concept of the Soviet constitution is all about—its provisions are subject to the proviso of political expediency. This has been also reflected from the very beginning in the Soviet constitutional practice where from the Soviet point of view even the most blatant violations of the text of the constitution have been considered perfectly constitutional.

Examples for this are numerous and go much beyond the wide limits of the constructional problems that often arise in constitutional law. Here are some such examples taken from the time when the Constitution of 1936 was still in force: the constant practice of establishing and abolishing ministries by *ukazy* (decrees) of the Presidium of the Supreme Soviet, disregarding Articles 77, 78, and 146, according to which changes in the system of ministries were to be brought about by a procedure providing for constitutional amendments; Malenkov's appointment as Chairman of the Council of Ministers by the Central Committee of the CPSU on March 5, 1953, though according to Article 56 appointing the government belonged to the exclusive jurisdiction of the Supreme Soviet; the change at the top of the Council of Ministers from Khrushchev to Kosygin, effected by the Presidium of the Supreme Soviet on October 15, 1964, that had thereby exceeded its constitutional powers that comprised—according to Article 49 lit. 7—the appointment of individual members but not of the Chairman of the Council of Ministers. There have been numerous similar examples under the present Constitution, too. One of these was the sacking of N. Tikhonov from the post of Chairman of the Council of Ministers, and his replacement by N. Ryzhkov, that were, contrary to the constitutional requirements (Articles 122 lit. 4 and 129 of the 1977 Constitution), also effected by a mere decree of the Presidium of the Supreme Soviet of September 24, 1985.

It follows from all this that the main function of the Soviet constitution is not a normative one; it is rather to be found in the field of ideology and propaganda. In the first place, the Soviet constitution is expected to help to produce the teleologically motivated idea of legitimacy of the existing political power structure, symbolize the political unity of the Soviet people by evoking a feeling of togetherness, and deceive the non-communist world about political realities in the Soviet Union.[2] If the constitution is supposed to gain legal significance in the Soviet future, the communist concept of constitutional law is to be changed. From an instrument of political power, the constitution has to be reversed into a lord over that power; or, in other words, the primacy of politics has to be replaced by the primacy of law.

Main Consequences: Banishing the Basic Contradictions

Establishing the normative function of the Soviet constitution as supreme law of the land requires the banishment of some basic contradictions, called "dialectical" in theory, that are rendering possible political manipulation in practice. Two of them should be dealt with.

a) The first contradiction concerns the relationship between Article 2 and Article 6, stating the supremacy of the people and that of the Communist Party respectively. In the prevailing ideological context the solution to this obvious contradiction points to the *supremacy of the Communist Party*, since achieving the ultimate goal of a communist society is not a matter of accidental majorities produced by popular elections but a matter of the best insight into the requirements of social development embodied by the Communist Party *per definitionem*. It is for this pretension to utmost wisdom that the constitution cannot exert any binding effect on the Party, and the Soviet political system cannot be a government of laws, but of men. A solution to the contradiction in question, in favor of the normative function of the constitution, must renounce the Communist Party's ideological and political supremacy and lead to the deletion of Article 6 without reservations.

Some Western scholars are contemplating the possibility that the Brezhnev Constitution has taken a first step in this direction by inserting a Section 3 into the final version of Article 6 to the effect that "all Party organizations shall function within the framework of the Constitution of the U.S.S.R."[3] It seems to me that this view is far too optimistic and not even in accordance with grammatical rules for construing legal provisions. For Soviet terminology thoroughly differentiates between Party organizations to be found on the regional level and below on the one hand, and the Party as a whole on the other—the latter's highest organs on the national level do not belong to any organization.[4] Consequently, Section 3 does not cover the Party leadership, whose power of defining the "framework of the Constitution" has not been restricted anyway. Apart from that, immediately after the adoption of the constitution, leading party and state officials pointed out that what the framers of the constitution had in mind was the traditionally propagated but not always observed division of labor between party and state apparatuses, according to which the party should guide and control the state without intervening in its everyday administration.[5] The 27th Congress of the Party reversed this situation to some extent by inserting in the Party statutes a new provision (Article 60) that, varying from the constitutional formula, states that the "Party"—the qualifying word "organizations" was omitted here—shall function within the framework of the Constitution.

b) The second basic contradiction is inherent in the principle of "socialist legality" and proclaimed on the constitutional level by Article 4. This principle is composed of two contradictory elements. On the one hand it comprises the binding force of law ("strict observance of laws and other legal acts"), while on the other it orders the politically expedient application of law ("conformity with the objective requirements of social development"). Which element is to be preferred in case of conflict is again a matter of political expediency to be solved on the basis of current Party policy. It must be admitted, however, that Soviet legal writings in the post-Stalin period have been showing a tendency to emphasize the first and to pass over the second element. From time to time the reader may come across passages stating the inadmissibility of refraining from applying a legal norm for reasons of expediency,[6] but, in spite of these encouraging tendencies, in legal practice systematic violations of legality appear to occur up to the present day. In connection with the repression of the dissident movement, numerous violations of the rules of criminal procedure have been committed by Soviet authorities,[7] but it has never been said that this practice was not in accordance with the socialist legality.

Banishing the second element from socialist legality for the sake of the simple rule of law (in the sense of an unconditionally binding force of the law) would entail serious changes in the idea of law as it is used by the Soviet constitution regarding the legislature (Article 108, Section 4), the executive (Article 133), and the judiciary (article 155). The provision saying that laws shall be made by the Supreme Soviet (and the People) exclusively and shall be binding for administrative agencies and judges makes sense only when by law an abstract and general rule is meant that concerns an unspecified number of cases and persons. From this idea of law, which in German is called *Gesetz im materiellen Sinne*, a fundamental principle follows which emerged already in ecclesiastical controversies of the fourteenth century as the formula *quod omnes tangit ab omnibus approbetur*, and was later incorporated into Rousseau's theory of the *volonté générale* in a more radical way. In modern times this principle claims that laws, as a rule, are made by the legislature (i.e., an assembly representing the people), and that subordinate legislation may be admitted with express authorization by the constitution or the legislature only. In Soviet constitutional law there is no rule like that. Whether a certain legal rule should be adopted in the form of a *zakon* (law) of the Supreme Soviet, of a *postanovlenie* (decree) of the Council of Ministers, or of a simple *prikaz* (order) of an individual minister, is a question to be answered on the grounds of political expediency. In Soviet legislative practice the absence of the substantive notion of law results in a reversal of the hierarchy of sources of law: the most important regulations are included in those sources that are placed at the bottom of the hierarchy. As the constitution is located at the top of the hierarchy it comprises the less important norms. Should the constitution become the supreme law of the land the substantive notion of law has to be introduced into it first.

Precedents and Prospects

The development sketched above was already experienced by Plato. In the ideal state depicted in the *Republic* there is no room for law. In the view of a philosopher-king blessed with the virtue of knowledge, law appears simply superfluous. After having had disillusioning experiences with bringing up a philosopher-king for Syracuse, Plato moderated his views and in the *Statesman*, and even more so in the *Laws* (both works were written during and after the kingship's failure in Sicily), he contented himself with the "second-best state," held together by the "golden cord of law."[8] The rule of law, although providing a foundation only for the second-best state, is nevertheless to be striven for considering the evidence about human intelligence being insufficient for making the philosopher-king a real alternative.

For Western Europe it took several centuries full of blood and tears to realize this "second-best state." It was the period of constitutionalism that bestowed upon Englishmen at the end of the seventeenth century, and upon the continental peoples of Western Europe in the course of the nineteenth century, a political system in which a constitution became the supreme law of the land, guaranteeing an independent judiciary and reducing the formerly unlimited power of the monarch, ruling by the grace of God, to merely that of the executive branch (with some prerogatives) of government. Opposite the monarch was placed a representative and independent legislature, and its power steadily grew. Tsarist Russia followed this process at a distance of about a hundred years, and, when she was approaching the threshold of constitutionalism, she did it hesitantly and with an afterthought. The Fundamental Laws of 1906 clung to the Byzantine concept of *samoderzhavie* (autocracy) and did not advance to the substantive notion of law completely, for legislative power assigned by Articles 7 and 86 to the Emperor, the Council of State, and the Duma as a joint authority was sapped by too many royal prerogatives.[9]

The Bolsheviks interrupted constitutional developments in Russia and pushed the country back into a political status where belief in the unlimited wisdom of the Party concentrating all temporal and spiritual power in its hands was justified on pseudoscientific grounds and imposed upon the nonbelievers by force. Is there any probability of change from sophocracy to nomocracy in the Soviet Union in the foreseeable future? An outstanding analyst of the Soviet system, Boris Meissner, has been contemplating a systemic transition from autocratic to constitutional one-party rule,[10] implicitly suggesting the possibility of repetition in the U.S.S.R. of the Western European process of constitutionalizing an absolute powerholder. But where are the *Kadety*?* Despite more law oriented interpretations of socialist legality, Article 6, Section 3 of the Brezhnev Constitution referred to above, the current project of publishing a *Svod Zakonov* (Code of Laws), and other signs of assigning to law a greater role in administrative life, I can hardly see social or political forces powerful enough at present to succeed with the idea that laws are preferable to party wisdom. Undoubtedly, among the Soviet intelligentsia there are more than a few people who think so; especially the lawyers are striving for the enhancement of the role of law. But even within the narrow limits of influence the intelligentsia can exert the lawyers' share is rather small. The social reputation of Soviet lawyers is low, and when they acquire political status they are called Lenin and Gorbachev.

Particular Points of Stress and Their Possible Effects on Constitutional Development

Let us assume that at a certain stage of future development the Soviet constitution will really gain binding force in the strict sense of a supreme law. Would, in this case, the Soviet Constitution of 1977 be able to cope with

---

* *Kadety*—The Constitutional Democrats, a political party in preBolshevik Russia that above all sought the introduction of the rule of law, considering it to be central to all other changes and reforms in the country.

the most important challenges stemming from the vital points of stress in the Soviet system? Four areas should be singled out for closer examination: (1) the nationality issue, (2) economic stagnation, (3) political rigidity, and (4) the monocratic power structure. These areas of tension, if differently formulated, i.e. for (1) federalism/autonomy, for (2) satisfactory living standards, for (3) civil rights, and for (4) democratic participation, would correspond— in this particular order—to the main expectations of people living in the Soviet Union.

The Nationality Issue

For well-known reasons the nationality issue may be considered the most serious and durable problem of the multinational Soviet state. Since Lenin's days the Soviet constitution has been trying to solve this problem on a territorial basis by means of Soviet federalism and autonomy. The territorial principle, however, could be applied only to ethnic groups living in more or less compact territorial settlements. This is so because under the territorial principle the point of reference in granting legal status to an ethnic group is the territory and not the group itself as such. Scattered minorities are therefore discriminated against of necessity. The most striking examples of such discrimination are the Jews and the Germans with about 2 million members each. Stalin's attempts to settle the Jews traditionally scattered over the whole of the Soviet Union in their own autonomous region in the Far East proved to be a complete failure. Today, about 11,000 Jews are living in Birobidzhan, constituting about 5.5 percent of the regional population and 0.6 percent of all Soviet Jews. Since the destruction of their Volga autonomous republic by Stalin in 1941, Soviet Germans do not comprise any territorial unit. These cases, as well as some others, vividly illustrate the limitations of the territorial principle and constitute a direct violation of Article 27 of the International Covenant on Civil and Political Rights, to which the Soviet Union is a party. Under the cited provision, the Soviet Union is obliged by international law to grant the members of its ethnic, religious, and linguistic minorities the rights to enjoy their own culture, to profess and practice their own religion, and to use their own language. In order to fulfill this international obligation the territorial solution offered by Soviet constitutional law has to be supplemented by arrangements for these minorities on a group basis.

The Jewish autonomous region illustrates another defect in the Soviet system of federalism and autonomy. The territorial solution of the nationality problem presupposes the establishment of such territorial units in which the ethnic group concerned constitutes the majority. Otherwise that ethnic group would be subjected to the will of the real majority and could not effectively participate in the political and administrative matters of the territory formally assigned to it, let alone make that territory its own domain. An analysis of the ethnic composition of the individual union republics shows that there, by and large, the majority requirement is fulfilled. The only exception to that rule is the Kazakh SSR where the Kazakhs represent only thirty-six percent of the republic's population, thus being a minority, while the Russians with a share of 40.8 percent constitute the relative majority.[11]

Quite a different picture emerges on the level of the autonomous units. At first sight, there are forty-two ethnic groups organized in thirty-eight autonomous units of their own (twenty autonomous republics, eight autonomous regions, ten autonomous districts), the difference between the number of ethnic groups and territorial units resulting from the fact that in four territorial units there are two titular nationalities. A closer look at the national composition of these thirty-eight units reveals, however, that only nine out of the forty-two titular nationalities command in them the absolute (six cases) or relative (three cases) majority of the population,[12] and thus are in a position enabling them, theoretically at least, to determine the political and administrative management of their respective territories. In twenty-two autonomous units Russians dominate even numerically,[13] and in the Abkhazian ASSR Georgians outweigh the titular nationality. In merely ten autonomous units the nationality concerned constitutes the absolute (6 cases) or relative (four cases) majority of the local population,[14] while the remaining five territorial units represent special cases that cannot be comprehended in terms of nationality.[15] The conclusion that follows from the above data is that Soviet autonomy, at least in its present form, is highly deceptive. If federalism and autonomy are to be retained as the main, but not an exclusive, constitutional means for solving the nationality issue in a future multinational state, federal and autonomous units are to be restructured in such a way that ethnic groups, if possible, be granted a territorial unit where they have a majority share of the population.

Federalism and autonomy by their very nature imply decentralization as opposed to deconcentration. Decentralized entities must have a precisely defined area of their responsibilities and exclusive jurisdiction, that would be barred from any interference by higher authorities, except for the cases of unlawful activities. Decentralization of this type is incompatible with the Soviet concept of federalism and autonomy. This incompatibility has been made much clearer than it was before by the new Constitution of 1977.[16] In its Article 70 the Soviet Union is presented as a unitary federal state (*edinoe soyuznoe gosudarstvo*), which logically is nonsense. A state may be either a unitary or a federal one, but not both at the same time. The insertion of the word "unitary," which was missing in the corresponding Article 13 of the Constitution of 1936, reflects the growth of centralizing tendencies during the last two decades. Their theoretical foundation is to be found in the principle of "democratic centralism" that has been expressly elevated to the rank of a constitutional principle by Article 3 of the Brezhnev Constitution. In recent Soviet writings it has been very plainly stressed that socialist federalism and autonomy are based on the principle of democratic centralism.[17] As democratic centralism involves the obligation of the lower bodies to observe and execute the decisions of the higher ones, there is no room left under it for decentralization of any kind. Federalism and autonomy in the true sense of these words require the abandonment of democratic centralism, its elimination from the set of constitutional principles of the state structure.

Decentralization of any kind requires a clear-cut division of responsibilities and jurisdictions. The systems of federal and autonomous jurisdiction, as set out in the Soviet constitution, fall far short of this requirement, and it would not come much nearer to it even after the deletion of Article 3. Obscuring responsibilities has always been a striking feature of Soviet legislation, whose main points of reference have been tasks rather than functions. Article 73 of the Constitution of 1977 stands in this traditional line, by enumerating the powers of the union without clearly stating whether the individual tasks listed are to be undertaken by legislative or administrative authorities. What makes things even worse is the concluding Point 12, a constitutional novelty which empowers the union to settle "all other matters of all-union importance." Thus, the presumption of competence in favor of the union republics, included into Article 76, Section 2 of the Constitution, is practically disproved and reversed into the following general rule: the jurisdiction of the union shall cover all matters the union thinks it should.

One could go on citing further constitutional defects of a more technical nature. This is, however, unnecessary because the above analysis is sufficient for drawing this conclusion: federalism and autonomy may be considered as appropriate constitutional devises for solving the nationality issue—and they are being discussed for such a purpose even in the West today[18]—on condition that they be developed further in both legal and organizational respects and reach the stage of decentralization with a precise division of powers. But this alone will not do either; territorial decentralization along ethnic lines ought to be supplemented by group-oriented minority rights.

Economic Stagnation

The traditionally deplorable state of the Soviet economy is one of the main causes of the low standard of living and social services. The general dissatisfaction of the population with the performance of the Soviet system originates from here. Unfortunately, the constitution cannot do very much for improving social and economic conditions beyond laying down some general principles. In any case, these principles should not hinder social and economic reforms thought fit by competent authorities to improve the situation.

As to the compatibility of reasonable economic reform with the Soviet constitution, two complications seem, at first glance, to constitute an obstacle.

The first one is the socialist system of ownership, set out in Articles 10-13, and in particular the privileged position of state ownership within it. Though I would not deny that relations of ownership do have some relevance to economics, I feel that the fascination of Soviet ideology with the question of ownership is somewhat outdated. It originates from the Marxist perception of economic conditions in the nineteenth century, when private ownership of the means of production conceived as a comprehensive property right of particular individuals was indeed prevalent. However, during the last hundred years, conditions in the developed countries of the Western world have fundamentally changed. Different forms of associate ownership (joint-stock companies, limited-liability companies, public corporations, etc.) of the huge mass of the most important means of production have come to the fore, which should have been welcomed by Soviet ideologists as prominent landmarks on the way of collectivizing private property. However, Soviet ideologists refrain from praising this new plurality of owners, because they are bound to believe in the superiority of state and cooperative forms of ownership only. Nevertheless, "capitalist" and "socialist" forms of associate ownership have evident similarities, since both of them are characterized by a separation between the legal status of respective owners and the property rights of possession, use and disposition mostly exercised by other persons. Owners and managers are today two distinct groups in all societies. State ownership is therefore a highly abstract concept which is in need of concretization by legal rules. The state as such cannot act in the economic sphere directly, and thus its property rights must be exercised by a number of administrative and economic units acting on the state's behalf. Economic decentralization has as its inevitable consequence the increase of power of state enterprises to exercise property rights with the jurisdiction of state administrative authorities waning accordingly. So the question arises, at what point of decentralization this major, qualitative change will occur, making the sacred dogma of state ownership untenable?

It must be said that Soviet economic reforms have yet never come near this point of change, and therefore Soviet jurisprudence has not yet felt the necessity seriously to question the concept of "operative management" developed by A.B. Venediktov at the end of the 1940s in order adequately to interpret the enterprise's managerial powers.[19] On the other hand, more far-reaching economic reforms in Eastern Europe, especially in Hungary, have led to remarkable theoretical controversies about state ownership and even initiated proposals favoring the concepts of relative or dual ownership.[20] Developments have progressed even further in Yugoslavia where legal scholars engaged in the search of the missing owner of "social property" gave up all hope of finding one long ago.[21] What can be deducted from this East European experience is the fact that constitutional dogma of socialist, and especially state, ownership of the means of production complicates, but does not prevent economic decentralization. To find a way to get around it was proved in the last analysis to be only a matter of the jurists' legal imagination and intellectual capacity. Thus, the present constitutional norms are strictly speaking not obstructing the way to decentralizing economic reforms; however, it would be advisable, though not imperative, to throw overboard the whole constitutional theory of socialist ownership before starting such reforms.

Having accorded the primary importance to associate ownership one should not overlook either the small-scale ownership of the means of production. In this field private ownership has kept its significance in the West and should also be extended in the East. In this case again, the present constitutional state of affairs in the Soviet Union is bothersome but not prohibitive. Article 17 of the Constitution permitting individual economic activities in principle and referring the matter to the legislature for further elaboration may serve as a starting point for appropriate legislative measures.

The second constitutional obstacle to reasonable economic reforms may be found in Article 16 of the Constitution providing for a planned economy. But what does planning mean? Does it necessarily mean imperative planning or may it also be conceived of as merely indicative planning? To be sure, nothing else but imperative planning has, as yet, been on the agenda of Soviet economic reforms. Hungarian economic reforms, however, show that transition to indicative planning that is not too far removed from what is known as *planification à la francaise* is possible without renouncing the concept of planned economy altogether. As a consequence, in this case, too, the point is not the wording of the constitution but its interpretation. As to economic administration, Article 16 is ambiguous, for it combines elements of both centralization and decentralization in a "dialectal" way, i.e., it is free to shift the emphasis according to considerations of expediency. On the whole, the present wording is more in favor of centralization because it characterizes the Soviet economy as an "integral economic complex" and mentions the "sectoral" before the "territorial" principle, and "centralized direction"—before "managerial independence and initiative of individual enterprises." Nevertheless, these semantic subtleties are primarily indicative of the economic conservatism that was prevailing at the time of the Constitution's adoption. It is true that this attitude has not changed much since, but it could change without getting into conflict with the Constitution.

Finally, a word should be said about the extensive constitutional catalogue of social and economic rights that Soviet ideologists are so proud of. I have tried to explain elsewhere why I do not believe in the usefulness of social and economic rights and why I am opposing their insertion into Western constitutions.[22] In contrast to individual liberties, social and economic rights, in order to be properly defined for their precise content, need further elaboration by detailed legislation. By no means can this be done in the constitution itself. Furthermore, the effectiveness of social and economic rights depends, first of all, on economic performance and public wealth that cannot be created by legal orders. For this reason, proclamations of social and economic rights on the constitutional level run the risk of degenerating into shallow propaganda slogans. Presently, this is in complete conformity with the Soviet Constitution, whose primary function is propaganda, but this would not fit a genuine supreme law of the land. Therefore, in the future, it would be better to do away with the whole catalogue of social and economic rights.

Civil Rights

The absence of effective civil rights in the Soviet Union is felt and deplored most by the intelligentsia, while for the broad masses of the population civil liberties are, presumably, of secondary importance as compared with material well-being.[23] Apart from that, however, the unwillingness of the Soviet rulers to respect human rights, to say nothing about ensuring them to all Soviet citizens, clearly violates the Soviet Union's international obligations under the International Covenant on Civil and Political Rights of 19 December 1966. Therefore, adjusting Soviet constitutional law to the requirements of international law should be envisaged as one of the most urgent tasks in the future.

A comparative study of the catalogue of human rights included in the International Covenant on Civil and Political Rights and of its counterpart in the Soviet Constitution shows that the problem with such adjustment is not merely quantitative. Almost all freedoms enumerated in the Covenant are embodied in the Soviet Constitution. The most important exception concerns Article 12, Section 2 of the Covenant guaranteeing the right of free movement of people, including the right of their freely leaving the country and returning to it. It goes without saying that this right must be introduced into Soviet constitutional law. The essential point, however, consists in the fact that the qualitative Soviet concept of civil rights is at variance with the international concept of human rights.[24] From the logical point of view, the only solution to this contradiction is the acceptance of the international concept by Soviet national law. On the theoretical level, this solution presupposes the acknowledgement of the existence of human rights binding the national legislator and the endowment of the constitution with a proper normative function as has been suggested above, in the first part of this paper.

Apart from that, several corrections of the constitutional design of civil rights will be on the agenda. They would concern the existing constitutional reserves attached to specific civil rights and to these rights as a whole. First of all, one would have to abolish the general constitutional reserve, contained in Article 39, Section 2, according to which the interests of society and the state constitute the inherent limits of the individuals' exercise of their civil rights. Such a clause undermines the very substance of civil rights even if there were no longer a Party authoritatively to define what the interests of the society and state are. Exactly the same applies to Article 59, Section 1, stating the inseparability of the exercise of citizens' rights from the performance of their duties and obligations, though some sort of a reasonable legal interdependence between citizens' rights and duties may be thought of even in the future. Special constitutional reserves restricting the political liberties also must go. The freedoms of speech, press, and assembly under the present Soviet constitution are supposed to be exercised "in accordance with the interests of the people and in order to strengthen and develop the socialist system" (Article 50, Section 1); the freedom of association is confined to "the aims of building communism" (Article 51, Section 1) as is the case with the freedom of scientific, technical, and artistic work (Article 47, Section 1). It is evident that within these constitutional limits no freedom whatsoever can flourish.

Another technique of restricting civil rights at will is represented by legislative provisos. Constitutional provisions that in one form or another transfer the power of determining the scope of civil rights to the ordinary legislator, are numerous in the field of personal freedoms and particularly insofar as the individuals' property rights are concerned.[25] In this way the real meaning of the proclaimed rights is reduced to a mere reference to the current legislation. This has to be changed. The technique of legislative provisos has gained special momentum in connection with Article 58, Section 2, which contains one of the most remarkable provisions of the Constitution of 1977. According to it, the Soviet citizens are granted the right of judicial review of administrative acts infringing upon their rights "in the manner prescribed by the law" (*v ustanovlennom zakonom poryadke*). In the lively debate that had ensued after the adoption of the Constitution, the majority of legal scholars, as well as the Institute of State and Law of the Academy of Sciences of the U.S.S.R. itself,[26] interpreted the phrase cited above as being related to procedural arrangements only. Such an interpretation rendered the introduction of a general clause imperative but, alas, this proved to be of no avail—later Soviet legislation retained the sheer enumeration principle anyway.[27] In order to prevent the possibility of legislative events taking a similar course, and to keep the legislature within the limits of its proper functioning, that should be aimed for in the future, restrictive and precise use of legislative provisos is strongly advisable. Civil rights should be de-limited and limited by the interests of the public good and other citizens' rights, but such delimitation and limits should be prescribed with utmost legal precision by the constitution itself and in such a way that a fair balance between public and personal interests is achieved. It should be admitted, however, that getting the desired legal precision on the constitutional level is rather difficult. The best tried method of preventing endless controversies about the "true" contents and scope of individual civil rights and their judicial protection has been found in the introduction of some sort of constitutional judiciary. In the beginning a thorough study of current ex-periments in Hungary and Poland may be as useful as analyzing two decades of experience of Yugoslavia's constitutional court. One may even start by reviving the memories of the 1920s when the Supreme Court of the U.S.S.R. exercised some modest powers of "constitutional supervision." Of course, the few examples of judicial shaping of constitutional provisions under socialism neither had nor have very much to do with civil rights. But why shouldn't the embryos be capable of becoming full-fledged organisms?

Democratic Participation

The desire for democratic participation seems to be nourished by Soviet Russian political culture even less than are demands for civil rights. Tsarist or communist autocracy had a long and deeply rooted tradition in Russia that was hardly interrupted by the elections of the abortive Constituent Assembly held in November-December 1917. In view of the traditionally prevailing political attitudes, democracy in Russia cannot be brought about by constitutional means alone; participatory attitudes tempered by a sense of responsibility can develop, but only as the result of a long-term process of political maturation. In this respect, a future Soviet constitution can be expected only to avoid hampering the process. By and large, even the present constitution, as the analysis of its provisions suggests, is able to live up to these expectations. John Hazard was quite right when he observed that since Stalin's death evolution within the Soviet system has taken place without any amending of the constitution or the institutional structure and that this has been possible "because institutions offering the prospect of activity more closely approximating that of Western systems were available to be put to other purposes than those for which they were originally conceived."[28] The basic departure from inequality as a determinant of political participation and from the indirect system of elections was indeed accomplished by Stalin's Constitution of 1936. Since then very few constitutional provisions have been open to criticism on the grounds of their being in the way of a democratic evolution.

The present electoral system, as it is outlined by Articles 95-102 of the Constitution and concretized by several electoral laws, meets the standard requirements of democratic participation. Some uneasiness may be evoked by Article 100, Section 1, which grants the right to nominate candidates to the Communist Party and certain types of organizations and meetings. This provision implies a one-party system but it does not necessarily exclude competitive elections. At least it envisions various nominating bodies that could act simultaneously and to the effect of proposing more than one candidate for each office of deputy. Neither is the possibility of competitive elections precluded by electoral laws in force. Hence, under the assumption that in the future Constitution there will be no Communist Party monopolizing all political power, the possibility of competitive elections may be realized without much difficulty. Nevertheless, the existing restrictions on the right to nominate candidates, whereby only certain organizations are entitled to exercise it, may hinder democratic initiatives from below, as was demonstrated by the failure of two dissidents, Roy Medvedev and Liudmila Agapova, to get themselves registered as candidates for the election to the Supreme Soviet of the U.S.S.R. in 1979. Registration of their candidacies was refused by the district electoral commissions with reference to Article 42 of the Electoral Law of 6 July 1978, on the grounds that the group nominating them, "Election 79," was neither a properly registered public organization nor a workers' collective. The preceding application for having the above group registered as a public organization had been turned down on a legal pretext by the executive committee of the Dzerzhinsky Raion Soviet in Moscow. In order to avoid such abuse of power by administrative agencies, it would be expedient to admit candidacies on the condition of their being supported by a certain number of signatures, rather than according to the requirements that exist in the electoral law today.

As to the legal status of deputies, the fiction of the imperative mandate was abandoned by the Constitution of 1977 in favor of the limited-imperative mandate containing elements of representation. This change is expressed most clearly by Article 103, Section 3 where, as a point of orientation for the deputies' activities, the "interests of the state" are listed first; the needs of the constituencies have merely to be "taken into account," and then by the deputies only, and the "electors' mandates" (*nakazy*), given before the election, produce no other effect than the newly elected soviet's obligation to examine them (Article 102).[29] Although at present the Soviet's deputy, according to constitutional theory, is not yet a free representative of the people independently appraising the public good, he may come nearer to this ideal should the political environment change at some time in the future. Without the power-monopolizing Communist Party, the limited-imperative mandate does not much inhibit democratic participation.

A final point to be considered here concerns the legal power of the Soviets as representative bodies. It is well known that in Soviet constitutional doctrine Rousseau has gained a victory over Montesquieu as the separation of powers has been displaced by their unity. It is also well known that there is hardly any field in the Soviet system where constitutional practice is in such sharp contrast to constitutional doctrine. Soviets on every administrative level are empowered to do anything they like but, apparently, they like doing nothing. This situation could only have developed without infringing upon the constitution because the latter lacks effective constitutional devices compelling the Soviets to exercise their powers. The real power of the state rests instead with the various executive authorities responsible to their Soviet theoretically but deputizing for it almost completely in practice. The exclusive jurisdiction of the Union and republican supreme soviets described by the Constitution (Article 108, Section 3; Article 137, Section 3; Article 143, Section 2), as well as of the local soviets, is rather limited—it is virtually restricted to general planning and to the formal making of some "non-delegatable" decisions. Instead of proclaiming a utopian omnipotence that cannot be materialized, it would be wiser to delineate exactly the sphere of competence where action can be taken exclusively by the soviets themselves or with their express authorization. In this case, as in many others, less would be more.

Conclusion

What constitutional changes are to be initiated if the present Soviet system is to adapt to the challenges stemming from the main points of systemic stress? In answering this question the paradox suggests itself: Not the text but the spirit of the constitution needs basic changes. Constitutional provisions may be changed here and there, but greater institutional changes seem unnecessary. The common denominator of minor changes would consist in the endeavor to make constitutional provisions more precise. From the technical point of view, lack of precision is a preeminent feature and a general defect of the present Soviet Constitution. This is quite understandable because that Constitution's main function is window-dressing. The Soviet Constitution is expected to propagate lofty ideas while at the same time concealing a profound disregard for them. For this purpose, inaccuracy of constitutional formulae is the most suitable state of legal affairs—the more imprecision there is in it the better.

Basic changes must take place in the whole political and ideological system within the boundaries of which the present Soviet constitution operates. It is the Communist Party pretending supernatural wisdom and not any specific legal provisions that must disappear in the first place if the constitution is to start fulfilling its proper normative functions.

NOTES

1. *O proekte Konstitutsii (osnovnogo zakona) Soyuza Sovetskikh Sotsialisticheskikh Respublik i itogakh ego vsenarodnogo obsuzhdeniia* (Moscow: Politizdat, 1977), 15.
2. See in more detail, G. Brunner, "The Functions of Communist Constitutions," *Review of Socialist Law* 3, No.2 (1977): 121 ff. (146 ff.).
3. B. Meissner's contribution to M. Fincke, ed., *Handbuch der Sowjetverfassung* (Berlin: Duncker u. Humblot, 1983), 177 ff.
4. For this common usage in connection with Article 6 section 3, see, among other sources, the authoritative *Konstitutsiia SSSR. Politiko-pravovoy kommentariy*, edited by B.N. Ponomarev, the Secretary of the Party's Central Committee and a candidate member of its Politburo at that time (Moscow: Politizdat, 1982), 38.
5. See I.V. Kapitonov, "KPSS v politicheskoy sisteme razvitogo sotsialisticheskogo obshchestva," *Kommunist* 55, No. 6 (1978): 29 ff. (36 f.); also: M.P. Georgadze's contribution to *Osnovnoy zakon nashey zhizni* (Moscow: Politizdat, 1978), 127.
6. See, among other sources, V.V. Lazarev's contribution to *Osnovy sovetskogo gosudarstva i prava* (Kazan: Izdatel'stvo Kazanskogo Universiteta, 1974), 94; *Konstitutsiia SSSR*, 31; S.E. Zhilinsky's contribution to *Sovetskoe gosudarstvennoe stroitel'stvo i pravo* (Moscow: Mysl', 1984), 89.
7. Typical violations are listed in Ch. Osakwe, "The Process of Law and Civil Rights Cases in the Soviet Union," in D. D. Barry, G. Ginsburgs, P.B. Maggs, eds., *Soviet Law After Stalin,* Vol. I, *The Citizen and the State in Contemporary Soviet Law,* (Leyden: A.W. Sijthoff, 1977), 179 ff. (209 ff.).
8. *Laws*, 644e: "it is the leading string, golden and holy, of 'calculation,' entitled the public law of the State."
9. V.V. Ivanovskiy, *Uchebnik gosudarstvennogo prava*, 3rd ed. (Kazan: Kazanskii Imperatorskii Universitet, 1910), 354 ff.; A. Palme, *Die Russische Verfassung* (Berlin: Dietrich Reimer, 1910), 97 ff.; M. Szeftel, *The Russian Constitution of*

April 23, 1906 (Brussels: Edition de la Librairie Encyclopédique, 1976), 123.

10. B. Meissner, *Das Sowjetsystem und seine Wandlungsmöglichkeiten* (Bern: Verlag Schweizerisches Ost-Institut, 1976), 25.

11. This and the following data are based on the results of the all-Union census of 1979.

12. These are the following nationalities: 1. Volga Tatars (relative majority in the Tatar ASSR) 2. Chuvashes (absolute majority in ASSR) 3. Chechens (absolute majority in Chechen-Ingush ASSR) 4. Ossetes (relative majority in North Ossetian ASSR, and absolute majority in South Ossetian aut. region) 5. Buryats (absolute majority in Aginsk-Buryat aut. district, but minority in the Buryat ASSR and the Ust'-Ordyn Buryat aut. district) 6. Kabardians (relative majority in Kabardian-Balkar ASSR) 7. Karakalpaks (relative majority in ASSR) 8. Tuvins (absolute majority in ASSR) 9. Komi-Permyaks (absolute majority in aut. district).

13. This is the case in nine Autonomous Republics (Bashkir, Buryat, Kalmyk, Karelian, Komi, Mari, Mordovian, Udmurt, Yakut ASSRs), five autonomous regions (Adygei, Gorno-Altai, Jewish, Karachai Cherkess, Khakass aut. reg), and eight autonomous districts (Koryak, Nenets, Taimyr/Dolgano-Nenets/, Ust'Ordyn Buryat, Khanty-Mansi, Chukot, Evenk, Iamalo-Nenets aut. dist.).

14. See note 12. There are nine nationalities in a majority position but ten territorial units with a national majority because the Ossetes have a majority position in two autonomous units.

15. These are the following: 1. The Dagestan ASSR has no titular nationality in the strict sense of the word because by the term "Dagestan" various North Caucasian tribes are embraced, ten of which are listed separately in demographic statistics. These tribes constitute a majority in the ASSR taken as a joint group only. 2. The Adzhar ASSR situated in Georgia is named after Georgian Muslims whose share in the population is not known. 3. The Nakhichevan ASSR is legally part of the Azerbaijan SSR and has a compact Azeri population but is situated within the territory of the Armenian SSR; so, in fact, it is an Azerbaijan enclave in Armenia. 4. The Nagorno-Karabakh autonomous region belongs to the Azerbaijan SSR but the majority population is Armenian; as it borders the Armenian SSR it could be united with it, but unification has been denied by Soviet authorities persistently. 5. The Gorno-Badakhshan autonomous region is part of the Tajik SSR and has a Tajik population; its autonomous status can be explained in historical-geographical terms only.

16. For further details and a comparison with the regulations of the 1936 Constitution, see A. Shtromas, "The Legal Position of Soviet Nationalities and Their Territorial Units According to the 1977 Constitution of the U.S.S.R." *The Russian Review* 37, No.3 (1978): 265 ff.

17. A. Ya. Lepeshkin, *Sovetskiy federalizm* (Moscow: Yuridicheskaya Literatura, 1977), 191 ff.; E.I. Kozlova's contribution to V.S. Shevtsov, ed., *Sovetskoe gosudarstvennoe pravo* (Moscow: Vysshaya Shkola, 1978), 212; and E.I. Kozlova, ed., *Sovetskoe gosudarstvennoe pravo* (Moscow: Vysshaya Shkola, 1983), 254 and 261; M.G. Kirichenko's contribution to M.G. Kirichenko, ed., *Sovetskoe gosudarstvennoe pravo* (Moscow: Vysshaya Shkola, 1983), 154.

18. See G. Héraud, "Fédéralisme et groupes ethniques," in Th. Veiter, ed., *System eines internationalen Volksgruppenrechts*, pt. 1 (Vienna: Braumüller, 1970), 61 ff.; Th. Veiter, "Territoriale nationale Autonomie," Ibid., pt. 2 (1972), 238 ff.; G. Héraud, "Ethnischer Föderalismus—zur Vermeidung ethnischer Konflikte," in F. Esterbauer, G. Héraud, P. Pernthaler, eds., *Föderalismus als Mittel permanenter Konfliktregelung* (Vienna: Braumüller, 1977), 73 ff.

19. For the current state of legal discussion, see Ph. Aubert de la Rüe, "Das operative Verwaltungsrecht sowjetischer Staatsunternehmen," *Osteuropa-Recht* 25, No.4 (1979): 207 ff.; B. Dutoit, "The Law of Property in the Socialist States," in F.J.M. Feldbrugge, W.B. Simons, eds., *Perspectives on Soviet Law for the 1980s* (The Hague: Nijhoff, 1982), 229 ff.

20. See G. Brunner, "Die Wirtschaftsreformen und die Reformen des Wirtschaftsrechts," in H.H. Höhmann, M.C. Kaser, K.C. Thalheim, eds., *Die Wirtschaftsordnungen Osteuropas im Wandel*, vol. 2 (Freiburg: Rombach, 1972), 225 ff. (270 ff.); Gy. Eörsi, *Comparative (Private) Law* (Budapest: Akadémiai Kiadó, 1979), 331 ff.; T. Sárközy, *Die Theorie des gesellschaftlichen Eigentumsrechts im Verlauf der sozialistischen Wirtschaftsreformen* (Budapest: Akadémiai Kiadó, 1980), 134 ff.

21. For want of a more recent study, see, even today, A.G. Chloros, *Yugoslav Civil Law* (Oxford: Clarendon Press, 1970), 161 ff.

22. G. Brunner, *Die Problematik der sozialen Grundrechte* (Tübingen: J.C.B. Morh/Paul Siebeck/, 1971).

23. On the basis of interviews conducted with Soviet émigrés in Israel, this impression has been confirmed in St. White, *Political Culture and Soviet Politics* (London: Macmillan, 1979), 102.

24. For an elaboration on this point see G. Brunner, "Civil Rights," in F.J.M. Feldbrugge, G.P. van den Berg, W.B. Simons, eds., *Encyclopedia of Soviet Law*, 2d ed. (Dordrecht: Martinus Nijhoff, 1985), 124 ff.: *idem*, "Recent Developments in the Soviet Concept of Human Rights," in F.J.M. Feldbrugge, W.B. Simons, eds., *Perspective on Soviet Law*, 37 ff.

25. This is the case concerning the privacy of citizens, their correspondence, telephone conversations, and telegraphic communications (Article 56), the inviolability of the home (Article 55), personal property (Article 13), the rights of authors, inventors, and innovators (Article 47, section 2).

26. "Konstitutsiya SSSR i rasshirenie sudebnoy zashchity prav grazhdan," *Sovetskoe Gosudarstvo i Pravo* 49, No.11 (1978): 63 ff.

27. In fact, the decision was taken quite early and passed unnoticed. Article 4, section 3 of the Fundamentals of Civil Procedure of the U.S.S.R. and the Union Republics was altered by decree of the Presidium of the Supreme Soviet of the U.S.S.R. of 9 October 1979 (*Vedomosti SSSR*, 1979, No.42, item 697) to the effect that in the field of administrative law application to the court is admitted "*in cases* and in the manner" (*v sluchayakh i v poryadke*) prescribed by law. No such law had, however, been in existence. At present, apparently, a law on judicial review of administrative acts is being prepared, which might improve the situation (see the interview with Professor Valery Savitskii in *Izvestiya* of 9 April 1987).

28. J.N. Hazard, *The Soviet System of Government*, 5th ed. (Chicago: University of Chicago Press, 1980), 12.

29. The legal diminution of *nakazy* has been made quite clear by the Decree of the Presidium of the Supreme Soviet of September 1, 1980, "On the organization of the work with electors' mandates" (see *Vedomosti SSSR*, 1980, No. 36, item 736).

4

Prospects for the Reception of Soviet Law After the Collapse of the Soviet System

OLIMPIAD S. IOFFE

Introduction

The Soviet system, in its most abstract aspect, is characterized by (1) the unlimited political power of the ruling summit which (2) concentrates the economic monopoly as (3) the real source of its domination over the country and (4) relies upon propagandists and suppressive means, including law with its declarative rules and compulsory regulations.[1] This system is inherently contradictory, and therefore it must inevitably collapse. Any suggestion as to when and where this collapse might occur belongs to the realm of conjecture. At any rate, not legal scholars but sociologists and futurologists should deal with such predictions.[2] As for legal research connected with the possibility of reception of Soviet law, at least to some extent, by a new society which will replace the Soviet system, it is sufficient to deduce from the structural limitations of that system the inevitability of its collapse. In this regard the following circumstances seem especially important.

First, the Soviet state as a political organization cannot pursue economic activity directly. Such activity must be imposed by the Soviet state upon economic entities either recognized as state organizations (economic associations, state enterprises, etc.) or disguised as non-state economic units (collective farms, consumer cooperatives, etc.). Thus, the economic monopoly of the political rulers exists in the U.S.S.R. in the form of an inevitable separation of economic activity from economic domination. This is the determinative contradiction of the Soviet system which, in the final analysis, leads to all its other insoluble conflicts.

Second, in order to pursue economic activity directly, Soviet economic entities need a certain economic independence from the Soviet state. If the necessary independence is not assured, the state is bound to become a substitute for these entities by assuming direct economic activity itself. This, when it has happened, has always resulted in economic failures because political organizations are inherently unable to pursue economic activity directly themselves. Conversely, if economic entities attain the necessary independence, then the state itself is bound to lose its economic monopoly, which, in the end, amounts to an absolute, not simply a relative, loss of governmental control over the economy. Such a loss of control has always resulted in political failures, because the unlimited political power is incompatible with the economic independence of those who are under political domination of that power.

Third, the permanent attempts by the Soviet leadership to find a way out of this *circulus vitiosus* have always necessitated maneuvering between economic centralization and economic decentralization. Economic centralization (Lenin's war communism, Stalin's rigid planning, Brezhnev's economic and industrial associations) by supporting an economic monopoly as the primary source of unlimited political power, corresponds to the nature of the Soviet system. But, at the same time, it entails an economic crash and thus threatens the entire system with collapse. Economic decentralization (Lenin's NEP, Khrushchev's *sovnarkhozy,* Kosygin's 1965 reform), by undermining the state's economic monopoly and weakening, as a result, its unlimited political power, contradicts the nature of the Soviet system. But the need to the economic crash makes economic decentralization a necessity that has to be implemented although it threatens the entire system with political collapse.

It goes without saying that the potential of such maneuvering is not inexhaustible. Sooner or later it will have to come to an end, even if one takes into account propagandistic and suppressive measures, both legal and illegal, which strengthen the unlimited political power based primarily upon the economic monopoly of the governing élite. Therefore, the Soviet system seems to be doomed, and the final collapse of that system can be accelerated or decelerated but not decisively prevented by whatever actions of the state. Nevertheless, along with adamant foes, the Soviet system also has good natured critics who, though they do not deny certain defects within the system, believe that these defects can be eliminated not only without fundamental change in, but with definite advantages for the system itself. To avoid obsolete illustrations and to remain within the limits of a legal, as opposed to a general discussion, let me use this opportunity to answer the points made by Harold Berman in his paper delivered during the Conference "Soviet Law and Soviet Economy" at the University of Connecticut School of Law in September, 1984.[3]

First of all, the speaker expressed his doubts as to the reliance of unlimited political power in the U.S.S.R. upon the state's economic monopoly. In his opinion, this monopoly is illusory as can ostensibly be evidenced by the existence of a so-called second (underground) economy. It probably never occurred to the speaker that the second economy is underground just because the first economy is monopolistic. Moreover, Berman contended that it is not the State's economic monopoly but rather the support of the people that gives political strength to the Soviet régime. If such a bold assertion were combined with arguments explaining the GULAG Archipelago, punitive psychiatry, the actual annihilation of political rights and freedoms, then meaningful polemics with the author would at least be possible. However, neither the possibility nor the necessity of polemics arise, as the postulate of the people's support formulated in one place is disproved by Berman himself in another place, where, according to him, the same people characterize their relations with the Soviet state by the formula: "The State pretends to pay us, and we pretend to work for it."

Further, unlimited political power, in Berman's view, is derived not only from ownership of wealth but from wealth itself, which by definition includes economic efficiency: the less efficiency, the less wealth; the less wealth, the less power. Actually, however, it is not wealth itself but rather its further increase that encompasses economic efficiency "by definition." As the owner of the entire country's economy, the Soviet state has already become the wealthiest entity in the world. Its interest in enlarging its wealth by means of economic efficiency is beyond doubt. However, the Soviets accept only such ways of making for economic efficiency which do not weaken the state's economic monopoly through material stimuli, leading to the independence of economic entities and, subsequently, to economic self-sufficiency of Soviet citizens. Berman, on the contrary, thinks that the very stimuli which would entail these results must be used by the Soviet régime to its advantage. Then, in order to bring to light the substance of his idea, the formula—"the less efficiency, the less wealth," etc.—must be expressed in a different way: "the more wealthy the citizens, the stronger their support for the government; the stronger this support, the more power." Is this logical? Yes, it is, but, unfortunately, not in the context of historical logic. In real history only the opposite situation can be observed: "The more democratic the state, the higher the scale of the citizens' political freedom; the stronger the citizens' general freedom, the higher the level of their economic well-being." And vice versa: "the lower the level of the citizens' economic independence, the broader their political subordination; the stronger the political obedience of citizens, the more dictatorial the political power of the state." Although Berman speaks with unfeigned seriousness about continuous improvement of the citizens' welfare in the U.S.S.R.,[4] his assessment is based only upon certain limited periods of Soviet history—directly after the Second World War, the post-war restoration, the contemporary period, etc. Comparison with the well-being of Western citizens is carefully passed over. Were it not, it would be necessary to come to the conclusion, on the basis of the same logic, that in the U.S.A. or in the Federal Republic of Germany political power must be far more unlimited than in the U.S.S.R.

Then, Berman agrees that Soviet rulers periodically switch from economic centralization to economic decentralization. He asserts, however, that this reveals not a cyclical but a spiral development, because certain results attained during each decentralization survive the subsequent centralization. His only illustration seems persuasive, but only at first glance: in the early 1960s Khrushchev gave the right to enterprises-purchasers to refuse to enter into planned contracts of delivery, and this right has been retained, notwithstanding the subsequent centralization in 1973-1974. Yes, the right was really retained, but who functioned as the rightholder? Not the enterprises, which being included in production associations, have practically lost the status of juridical persons. And not the production associations, if their higher industrial association, having assumed the functions of supply itself, executed the contracts of delivery. But industrial associations are administrative agencies, not economic entities. Does the acquisition by administrative agencies of the right given to economic entities demonstrate a cyclical or spiral development of economic management in the U.S.S.R.?

Lastly, according to Berman, all of the economic difficulties of the U.S.S.R. stem, not structurally from the Soviet system but from the lack of courage on the part of the Soviet leaders. If they were sufficiently courageous, they would abandon rigid centralized planning, introduce reasonable economic freedom, develop rational economic incentives, and the entire complex of economic problems would consequently be solved in the best way, without involving even an insignificant modification of the Soviet system. But in this case, the author's contention does not seem very original. How many people have addressed to the Soviet leadership various projects and recommendations that were intelligent and based on experience, knowledge, and even courage. The reaction of the Soviet leadership has always been the same: deafness and silence. Does this occur accidentally? By no means! The Soviet rulers understand their actual interests better than any of their unsolicited advisers. They know quite well what corresponds to the interests of the Soviet system and what would destroy it forever. It is not the lack of courage that restrains them from an abrogation of centralized planning as the principal obstacle to the country's and citizenry's well-being, but rather it is the absolute certainty that they will lose their political power as soon as the economic monopoly slips out of their grasp. Despite all of its economic difficulties, the Soviet leaders support the existing system, because only this system can support them. They must be touchingly naive dreamers and not extremely realistic Soviet rulers to believe that the Soviet system can be changed and simultaneously preserved just as the Soviet system. Either change or preservation. *Tertium non datur.*

What, however, about Chinese reforms? Do they not prove that the system can be modified and remain the same in principle? The time has not yet come to answer this question with the necessary certainty. If the mentioned reforms are temporary, and their goal is to prevent an economic crash, then the system has not truly changed, and it reveals only the symptoms of cyclical development, not of economic or political revisionism. If, however, the same reforms are directed toward permanent modification, they can mean nothing but the replacement of one system by another. The future will show which of these assumptions is right and which is wrong. However, one thing seems beyond doubt even now: a modification of the system cannot be neutral as far as its identity is concerned, and, vice versa, the identity of the system cannot survive its modification. This principle must be taken into consideration in order to correctly assess not only Chinese experiments but also Gorbachev's reforms, at present expressed by propagandistic declarations and certain legal provisions which will be checked in the future by the actual practice.

Thus, the Soviet system as such precludes essential improvements or fundamental perfecting. Its final hour in human history has not yet come, but, owing to its own peculiarities, this system is historically doomed. Does this mean that, along with the system itself, everything that has been connected with it must disappear completely and for good? This question may be asked with reference to any component of Soviet society. Our analysis, however, is restricted to only one component—Soviet law.

Prerequisites of Reception

The issue of the reception of legal systems is not a new problem in jurisprudence. The example of Roman law seems the most striking but by no means the only one of its kind. However, until now, jurisprudence has dealt with legal reception exclusively as with an historical phenomenon, while the reception of Soviet law must be analyzed from a futurological point of view. At the same time, it is well known that futurological predictions are relatively dependable only if they rely upon the appropriate historical experience. Thus, it seems very important to recapitulate the most essential causes of the reception of Roman law in order to find the necessary prerequisites for the future reception of Soviet law. To be brief, these causes are the following.[5]

On the one hand, Roman law reflects the economic, political and other peculiarities of Roman society or of the historical epoch coinciding with the existence of Roman society. This character is typical for legal rules on slaves, their sale and purchase, liberation from and the restoration to slavery, etc. All rules of mentioned and similar kinds became obsolete with the transition to a new historical epoch, and they disappeared together with the Roman Empire or at least together with the slave-owning period of human history. Reception in no way applied to them. On the other hand, the ancient Romans elaborated an entire system of rules, without which no human society with relatively developed economic circulation and stable property relations could function. Insofar as these rules retained specific Roman peculiarities (like these which dealt with *nexum*, for example) not only were they not objects of reception, but frequently they were abandoned in ancient Rome itself. On the contrary, the more abstract were the rules (like these which dealt with *mutuum*, for example) the more easily they were incorporated by the legal systems of future generations.

In contrast to its predecessors, contemporaries and a great number of successors, Roman private (not public) law was abstract, i.e. deprived of attachment to a specific country or historical time. In its abstractness it was also comprehensive—the overwhelming majority of legal rules possessed this quality—and, in its comprehensiveness, logically interdependent, i.e., co-ordinated among equal and subordinated precepts within the limits of the established hierarchy of legal provisions. All these circumstances predetermined the distinctions between Roman law and other legal systems of the past from the viewpoint of their historical fate. Future generations, in creating legal systems of their own, used not only the legal achievements of ancient Rome—Greek law, and to a far broader extent, Canon law have also left significant traces in the general development of legal history. However, while other legal systems have enriched the legal achievements of all humanity only by certain components, reception as a comprehensive approach was applied only to Roman law. In addition, Roman lawyers, these *juris conditores*, proved to be inimitable in their role as creators of legal culture, including legal vocabulary, legal technique, legal principles, and even legal language. Reception of Roman law meant simultaneous reception of the legal culture of Roman jurisprudence which proved to be of primary significance not only in legal-theoretical but also, and first of all, in legal-practical activity.

In assessing the prospects of reception of Soviet law with reference to the Roman historical model, one comes to the conclusion that Soviet law has no chance of achieving a similar record after the collapse of the Soviet system. This conclusion derives from fundamental properties inseparable from the very essence of Soviet law. In a great number of their widely proclaimed declarations, the Soviets have announced the decisive rupture with all other legal systems. They pretend to have nothing in common with those legal rules that are already known to all of humanity and with those legal orders that can be created upon any social basis other than the socialist one.[6] If these declarations are considered as representing a serious program and not as propagandistic verbosity, the only imaginable deduction leads to the mutually exclusive alternative: either the reception of Soviet law is impossible, since the construction of socialism belongs to the realm of utopia, or its reception must be all-embracing, since socialism is the solely acceptable organization of future societies. It seems, however, that of the two assumptions, the former is closer to the reality and the latter resembles a fairy tale. As the experience of China demonstrates, even countries that call themselves socialist and which initially borrowed much from Soviet law eventually began to replace this law with their own gradually elaborated regulations. Nevertheless, if not a comprehensive reception, then, at least, a retention of certain components of Soviet law by the future society that will replace the Soviet system seems not only possible but at the same time quite desirable. This must inevitably be the case because of a number of circumstances.

As is generally known, Soviet law and legal reality established in the U.S.S.R. differ significantly from one another. In legal declarations, the Soviets tirelessly vow their faithfulness to the interests of the whole people, and this not infrequently results in legal rules that are formulated as if they really must be accepted by all mankind. Article 39 of the Soviet Constitution reads, for instance, "Citizens of the U.S.S.R. possess in their entirety the socio-economic, political, and personal rights and freedoms proclaimed in and guaranteed by the U.S.S.R. Constitution and Soviet law. The socialist system ensures the expansion of rights and freedoms, and the continuous improvement of the conditions of life of citizens through the fulfillment of programs of socio-economic and cultural development."[7] This would be a salutary regulation, from the viewpoint of any human society, if, instead of "socialist system," one were to use an abstract term—"social system"—in order to designate the principal source that is to assure the reality and expansion of human rights and human freedoms. However, Soviet citizens do not possess, either in full or even partial measure, the rights and freedoms enumerated by the cited article. To some extent, this incontestable fact can be documented by the Soviet Constitution itself which, in the second paragraph of the same article, decrees that "the use of rights and freedoms by citizens must not harm the interests of society and the state or the rights of other citizens." Relying upon such a restriction, the Soviet rulers manage, even legally, to justify the reduction to nil in practice of that which has been so grandiosely promised by law, thus assuring the genuine conformity of Soviet law with rulers' interests, not with the interests of the Soviet people. However, at issue is the reception of Soviet law, not of Soviet legal reality. The legal reality peculiar to the Soviet system will disappear together with this system, and detached from Soviet legal reality, Soviet law may be to some extent an attractive rather than a repulsive phenomenon. Certain of its rules seem even more alluring if the corresponding legal texts are cleared of elements which pave the way for the dubious reality, as, for example, by substituting for the words "socialist system" some other term, and by rejecting (or substantially revising) the second paragraph of Article 39 of the Soviet Constitution. Under such conditions, some components of Soviet law would be better used than ignored by the future society.

Although the U.S.S.R. as a political organization engenders different assessments, on one point the divergence of opinions gives way to definite unanimity: this organization is a new, or at least extremely peculiar institution in comparison with other political organizations known to human history. The peculiarities of a system alone, however, do not guarantee its longevity. As a whole, the Soviet political organization is doomed to collapse just as are all of the substantial components of the Soviet system. However, certain separate elements, if removed from this organization and adjusted, if necessary, to modified circumstances, can prove to be independently viable. For example, federal states existed before the U.S.S.R. was created. However, all of the former federal states in the world, including the U.S.A.—one of the most striking illustrations—were based upon the territorial principle.

In contrast, the U.S.S.R. is the first federal state in the world which relies upon the national principle. "The Union of Soviet Socialist Republics," says Article 70 of the Soviet Constitution, "is a unitary, union and multinational state formed on the basis of the principle of socialist federalism as a result of the free self-determination of nations and the voluntary association of equal Soviet Socialist Republics." In this quotation, Soviet law proves to be perhaps more remote from legal reality than in the majority of other cases. The soviet federal state appeared not because of nations' free self-determination but as a result of the victory of Lenin, who supported federalism, over Stalin, who insisted upon unitarianism. The sovereignty of national (union) republics, including first of all their right of free secession from the U.S.S.R., has been fictitious since the very beginning.[8] And even this fictitious sovereignty suffered further restrictions after Stalin had established his personal dictatorship and acquired the possibility to implement his unitarian beliefs, though without a formal renunciation of the word "federalism." Later, Khrushchev and then Brezhnev restored some of the republican rights which had been annihilated by Stalin. But this changed only Soviet law, not Soviet legal reality. Nevertheless, national federalism as a legal idea could be absolutely necessary for political creativity in the future, when the Soviet system will be replaced by a new political organization. This idea must, of course, be adequately formulated in law and precisely observed in practice, especially inasmuch as one deals with national sovereignty, equality and self-determination or with the constitutional review and other legal guarantees of genuine federalism. However, it might be that after the Soviet political organization collapses, not all the nations that are now members of this organization will wish to create their own separate states. Owing to historical traditions, initially compulsorily imposed but maintained over a long period, some nations might express their desire for mutual cooperation in the legal form of state federalism. Then, despite the collapse of the Soviet system as a whole, national federalism, though invented by creators of this system, could be preserved by proselytes of other political ideals.

In addition to possessing political unity, the U.S.S.R. can also be considered as a vast but united economic entity. With some relatively unimportant exceptions, the entire economy of the country belongs to the Soviet state. Bearing in mind the economic failures that have always accompanied economic development in the U.S.S.R., it is most probable that no one will strive to imitate this broadly compromised model. However, the economic shortcomings of the Soviet system stem not directly from the Soviet economy but from its subordination to Soviet politics. If the Soviet economy were not the principal source of unlimited political power, planned centralization would no longer be politically necessary, and cyclical development, in the form of periodic transitions from centralization to decentralization with the following restoration of centralization instead of decentralization, could be replaced by another, more rational, managerial regulation. The new society, constructed on different principles, would certainly dispense with the typically Soviet dependence of economy upon politics. However, this does not mean that it would return to a system where small and separate industrial enterprises and individual agricultural plots are the only admissible forms of economic activity. As the experience of the most progressive Western countries proves, side by side with small industrial enterprises, significantly stronger state economic entities do exist, and vast economic associations, which accumulate private capital, are the ones that are most compatible with the exacting contemporary demands on economic development. In the agricultural area individual farming also coexists and cooperates with huge sale and supply associations. Then, why should one assume that a new system, which will be established on the territory of the present U.S.S.R., must return to economic disunity, instead of striving toward economic integration? And if integration, though essentially modified, survives, then Soviet experience in the legal organization of economic activity, will, no doubt, be of some help in directing the new economic system, though that system will then consist of genuinely separate economic units. This experience will allow to put to good use the historically accumulated advantages while at the same time avoiding what historically proved to be a failure.

Because of the priority of politics over economy, and because of the subordination to politics of all other components of the Soviet system, including law, Soviet jurisprudence has always been deprived of the opportunities that would make it genuinely creative in correlating legal theory and the law in force. In this area, legal scholars in the U.S.S.R. must restrict themselves to purely commentatorial work. Theoretical criticism of newly adopted laws is entirely forbidden. When a Soviet professor of criminal law once tried to criticize certain recently issued criminal regulations that in his opinion were absolutely unacceptable, he lost all his positions except his post as a teacher, and this was still viewed as a very lenient sanction for the violations he had committed. Comparatively older legal rules, which do not touch upon fundamental principles of the Soviet system, but deal rather with less important, secondary subjects of legal regulation, are within the permissible realm of critical analysis. But this analysis cannot, of course, be as fruitful as that which would exceed the limits of allowed criticism. Therefore, in order to express their creative demands in fuller measure, those legal scholars who cannot be satisfied with mere commentaries on Soviet laws, or with purely political "legal propaganda," attempt to find a less dangerous point of application for their intellectual capacities.

In this respect, Soviet jurisprudence follows the example set in other branches of creative activity. Perhaps, the situation of poetry most closely resembles that of jurisprudence. It was once remarked that Soviet poetic translations exceeded in quality the poetic translations of a number of other countries, since the most talented Soviet poets (Pasternak, Akhmatova, etc.), deprived of the poetic freedom necessary for their own creativity, concentrated on the poetry of foreign authors as the only area where freedom of thought could be disguised as faithfulness to the original. *Mutatis mutandis*, analogous conclusion appears to be applicable to Soviet jurisprudence in the works of its most capable representatives. These scholars are primarily absorbed by legal constructions, legal categories, legal terminology, legal techniques—in a word, by that which can be generally typified as legal culture in its broadest interpretation. It certainly does not mean that any Soviet scholarly innovation in this field deserves to be adopted by non-Soviet jurisprudence. Some of these innovations, as, for instance, the one related to the contradistinction and interdependence of legality and legal order, continue to be unclear to Soviet lawyers themselves. Others, as, for instance, the innovation concerning legal rules which determine concrete tasks rather than generally prescribed behavior, are specifically Soviet in that they are meant to be applied to economic planning and analogous state task-setting activities. It goes without saying that innovations of both these kinds would not readily assimilate in a system different from a Soviet one.

Soviet jurisprudence has, however, elaborated theoretical instruments, which, because of their abstractness, could be applied with much profit anywhere and therefore should not be consigned to oblivion. Categories of legal regulation, legal relations, legal system and system of legislation, legal sanctions and sanctions of responsibility, legal fault and legal causality—such is by no means an exhaustive enumeration of the Soviet innovations among which one can seek, and perhaps may be fortunate enough to find, something more valuable than that which has no worth outside the limits of Soviet law and Soviet jurisprudence.

Thus, if not on a grand scale, then in a number of components, Soviet law does possess the necessary prerequisites for future reception. Moreover, there are no obstacles to the reception of these components even now, while the Soviet system remains in existence. Other countries, both with similar as well as opposite systems, may borrow certain Soviet institutions, rules or ideas that are compatible with their structures and that correspond to their needs. In order to render the indicated prospects less abstract and more palpable, the necessary attention must be paid to the principal areas of legal regulations.

Outlines of Reception

In depicting the Soviet system in its united and divided aspects, one easily distinguishes the three most important constituent parts: politics, economy, people. Therefore, in order to outline more specifically the potential reception of Soviet law, it seems reasonable to consider this problem in direct connection with legal regulations in the enumerated areas. Along with them and from the same point of view, legal culture as a general topic must be the subject of a similar analysis.

Legal Reception and Soviet Politics

According to the official Soviet point of view,[9] and especially judging from Soviet practice,[10] in the relationship between politics and law, the former plays the leading and the latter the subordinate role. This means that law does not regulate politics but, on the contrary, politics direct law. Nevertheless, major political undertakings require appropriate legal forms. In this sense, it is possible to speak about legal regulations in the realm of political activity.

Since the mid-1950s, the U.S.S.R. has accompanied its relatively significant new statutory rules with preambles in order to define the political targets of legislative novelties and to dictate the permissible directions of the future interpretations of these rules in theory and practice. One cannot, of course, contend that this approach is exclusively Soviet. The American Constitution, adopted in the late eighteenth century, contained an appropriate preamble. Later on, similar sections occasionally appeared in the most substantial normative acts of other countries. In addition, preambles are not the only means of achieving the mentioned objectives. The issuance of so-called Motives to the 1896 German Civil Code (the BGB or *Bürgerliches Gesetzbuch*), owing to their greater size, helped to determine law-applying politics with stronger efficiency than the necessarily brief legal preambles possibly could.

Motives, however, in contrast to preambles, are not legally binding, and in part, where differences during preliminary discussions of a prospective law are reflected, contain no clear directives for law-applying agencies at all. One resorts to preambles only sporadically, for the U.S.S.R. the latter represent almost a permanent method of legislative activity. As a matter of course, Soviet preambles deal not so much with reality as with demagogy, rather distorting than expressing the actual goals of the statutes introduced. Hardly anyone treats seriously the Preamble to Fundamental Principles of Civil Legislation,[11] when it proclaims as the aim of the law "actively to promote the resolution of the tasks of the construction of communism," or the Preamble to Fundamental Principles of Labor Legislation,[12] when it asserts that "the socialist system creates the material and moral interest of the people to achieve the best results of their labor and constantly to develop and improve their social production." Nevertheless, even these preambles, distant from reality as they are, prove to be quite instructive for judges and other officials who have become accustomed through their extensive experience to the translation of senseless demagogy into a working instrument. How many contracts detrimental to the Soviet system have been deemed invalid because of their nonconformity with "the construction of communism," and in what number reasonable systems of payment for labor have been rejected because they were found contradicting the principle of correct combination of material and moral stimuli for achieving "the best labor results" and/or the interests of "the constant development and improvement of social production."

As for legal systems which do not manifest a divergence between legal regulations and legal reality, they need not distort the preambles to their laws. In these cases, preambles must not be used less often than in the U.S.S.R., but, in contrast to their application in the U.S.S.R., the exactitude of preambles, their veracity as well as their concision, will excise from legal regulations the verbal demagogy so incompatible with the very idea of law. As a result, the significance of preambles would be inestimable. With this technical approach, the legislator's target would be brought to the attention of those officials who put legal rules into effect, and in such a way the politics of legislation would become also law-applying politics—an important unity without which there is no true legality.

In the politics of law-making and law-applying, the U.S.S.R. appeals for the participation of non-state (non-governmental) organizations, sometimes only in words but not infrequently also in practice. Thus, Article 113 of the Soviet Constitution enumerates those agencies and organizations which hold the right of legislative initiative, i.e. the right to introduce bills that the legislator must discuss, though not necessarily accept. First, the Constitution mentions state agencies, beginning with the two houses of the U.S.S.R.'s Supreme Soviet, its Presidium, the Council of Ministers, etc., and ending with the U.S.S.R.'s Supreme Court and Procurator General. Along with these, the Constitution also lists the non-state (non-governmental) entities, stating in the second paragraph of the same article that "public organizations through their all-Union agencies also enjoy the right of legislative initiative." The cited article bears no relation to reality, not only in the second, but even in the first paragraph. It is well known that no bill may be considered by the U.S.S.R. Supreme Soviet, unless this bill either issues from the Politburo or has received the Politburo's approval. If not the Politburo, then most often the Council of Ministers and sometimes the Presidium of the U.S.S.R. Supreme Soviet function as agencies that actually use their right of legislative initiative, relying upon the Politburo's support. In practice none of the other state (governmental) agencies mentioned by the Constitution has ever functioned in similar capacity. It is all the less surprising that non-state (non-governmental) so-called mass public organizations have even fewer opportunities to transform their right of legislative initiative from *nudum jus* into *jus vestitium*. This right remains only on paper, it does not exist in reality. Nevertheless, the Soviets appeal to the discussed constitutional rule in order to illustrate the genuine democracy of socialist society in contrast to the fictitious democracy of the corrupt and decadent West. Actually, however, democratic countries have more reasons than the U.S.S.R. to grant the legislative initiative to certain non-state organizations, endowing them in this respect with genuine, not fictitious, rights.

Another example of citizens' participation in state affairs, more realistic than the right of legislative initiative, belongs not to constitutional but to procedural law. According to Article 41 of Fundamental Principles of Criminal Procedure,[13] "representatives of social organizations of working people may, by ruling of court, be permitted to participate in the judicial examination of criminal cases as social accusers or defenders." As for "social defenders," they take part sometimes in examination of insignificant cases, especially if the accused has positive references and official support. On the contrary, "social accusers" are more frequently won over to the state's side especially when this is necessary for the sake of propaganda in political cases. For example, the Union of Soviet writers sent its representative Kedrina as a social accuser in the case of Siniavsky and Daniel, who, because of publishing their books abroad, were accused of anti-Soviet propoganda and were subsequently punished with long prison terms.[14] It was very noteworthy that in a country of almost undisguised anti-Semitism a person notorious for her reactionary writings included in her speech as social accuser a charge of anti-Semitism against Andrei Siniavsky only because he used the name Abram Terts as a pseudonym. However, since the criminal case against this writer was so obviously preposterous, the Soviets were compelled to employ in it all possible means in order to tone down the truly arbitrary nature of the proceedings and to assure at least an appearance of legality. Under the circumstances, the appointment of a social accuser was a rather convenient method.

If a country of genuine legality considers the legal reception of Soviet institutions of social accusers and social defenders to be useful, it certainly will not apply these institutions as a trump in a political play but exclusively as a means of justice. Of course, the structure of the given country's judicial system, or the dominant ideas of its legal profession, or, finally, its legal traditions might be incompatible with the participation of social accusers and social defenders in the judicial examination of criminal cases. Then the mentioned reception would be out of the question. However, if these or other obstacles do not exist, the institutions of social accusers and social defenders could be adopted with positive results. At any rate, these institutions are not inseparable from the Soviet system. As peculiar expressions of the scale of democracy they are more befitting of democratic countries than of totalitarian régimes. This is why they are well-suited to outlive the Soviet system in the form of reception by the new or by a contemporary society, despite the fact that the initial establishment of these institutions gravitated not so much to judicial activity as to the legal dressing-up of the ways in which arbitrary political goals are achieved.

Legal Reception and the Soviet Economy

The Soviet system, analyzed not from a political but from an economic point of view, appears as a purposefully organized vast economic entity. And, since the twentieth century is the epoch of the creation and dominance of huge economic associations, total disregard of Soviet economic experience would be unforgivable. As is generally known, a great many of the organizational approaches invented and employed by the Soviets with regard to their economy have proved to be inefficient. The principal cause of this inefficiency can be found in the subordination of the economy to politics with the transformation of the thus established economic monopoly into the primary source of unlimited political power.[15] Under the influence of poor economic results, sometimes the entire economic organization of the U.S.S.R. is negatively assessed without making an exception for those organizational methods which by themselves, not as components of the existing system, are entirely positive. In my opinion, at least two institutions belong to such positive exceptions that should not be ignored by the future as well as by contemporary Western economists and jurists. These institutions are economic accountability (*khozraschet*) and the property right of operative management.

No large economic entity can function as a single unit. In order to be economically functional it must create separate organizations (enterprises, associations, etc.) as subordinate and at the same time independent units. Without subordination, the large economic entity as such would lose its property rights and the supremacy of rule over its components. Without independence the separate organizations of which this large entity consists would be deprived of material incentives and freedom of decision-making that is the prerequisite for any sensible economic activity. Both conditions, which at first glance seem mutually irreconcilable, could be easily implemented by using the methods of economic accountability and operative management. If the Soviets had not distorted their own legal-economic inventions, that would indeed be the case. For taken in their purest form, without Soviet distortions, economic accountability and operative management are apt devices of efficient economic management that may doubtlessly prove to be useful long after the Soviet system has been relegated to past history.

Economic accountability as it is theoretically characterized in the U.S.S.R. consists of three features.

First, all economic organizations must cover their own expenses without subsidies from the state. But this principle is completely abrogated for certain privileged economic organizations in such areas as, for example,

military or metallurgical production, which operate under a régime of planned losses and state subsidies. This dispensation allows privileged organizations to sell their output at artificially low prices and thus encourages the
expansion of their production. Conversely, the ability of other economic
organizations to cover their expenses is consistently undermined by the
state's practice of withdrawing funds from their accounts to cover other
needs. In addition, local Party agencies, ignoring legal restrictions, frequently
finance construction and other projects with money squeezed from economic
organizations. Furthermore, the ability of economic organizations to plan
and meet their expenses is weakened by the mandatory priority given to any
unexpected governmental order, regardless of the magnitude of disruption
thus caused to the organizations' routine production.

Second, economic accountability presupposes equivalence: an economically
independent organization must pay and be paid for everything in full. It goes
without saying that this feature is also inapplicable to subsidized organizations. But it undergoes significant limitations in many other cases too. On
the basis of the annual account, all surplus financial resources not needed to
fulfill the following year's plan are withdrawn by the state without compensation. Buildings and installations can be withdrawn in the same way by
a decision of the competent agency at any time of the year, even if they were
constructed by economic organizations using their own revenue. Within the
limits of established prices, actual equivalence finds application only to the
sale of the product. But once surplus money not needed for the next year's
plan is doomed to be lost at the end of the current year, in the final analysis
equivalence stops being observed in this area as well.

Third, economic accountability assumes profitability; the income of an
economic organization must exceed its expenses. The exceptions to this
principle are legion too. By definition, this principle cannot apply to the
numerous subsidized enterprises. On the other hand, if a non-privileged
economic organization sustains losses because the planning agencies suddenly
shifted its production facilities to a new task, it will not be reimbursed. The
régime of contract law, which is supposed to protect profitability, undergoes
a similar subversion. Generally speaking, an economic organization that
breaks a contract must pay full expectation damages. However, all payments
for damages received by an economic organization are transferred to the
state budget at the end of the year. As a result, economic organizations
resort to contract suits only with reluctance and, to compensate for the
elimination of any incentive to sue, Soviet law imposes a positive duty to
bring suits.[16]

Thus, economic accountability differs in Soviet theory and Soviet practice.[17] But even in its curtailed form economic accountability plays the role
of the most essential prerequisite of economic autonomy in the U.S.S.R.

One can imagine how this role would increase if the same method were used uncurtailed under the régime of free economy. Reject the Soviet distortions, take the idea of economic accountability in its primeval state, cut away all legal regulations that weaken or undermine this managerial method, and the ensuing positive economic results will soon prove this institution worthy of reception.

Operative management, as the second Soviet institution of economic regulation, which deserves to be assessed with regard to its potential reception, deals with the property rights given by the Soviet state as an owner to state economic entities as participants in the direct economy activity.

Ownership means the right of possession, use and disposition.[18] Operative management also includes possession, use and disposition of that property which has been either given to state organizations by the state or was legally acquired by these organizations as a result of their own economic activity.[19] However, ownership is broader than operative management. Moreover, operative management appears to be derivated from ownership and subordinated to it. Ownership, comprised of the three enumerated rights, may be restricted only "within the limits established by law." Operative management, although including these same rights, does not in fact entail their usage with respect to all kinds of property given to state organizations. These organizations possess and dispose of their product but may not use it, or they possess and use their enterprises but may not treat them as an object of disposition, etc.[20] On the other hand, possession, use and disposition as ingredients of operative management are restricted not only by the law but also by the objectives of the activity of each state organization, by planning tasks which emanate from the state, and by the purposes of various parts of property (such as fundamental funds, circulating funds, etc.).[21] Only those who do not notice these distinctions strive to characterize operative management as *sui generis* ownership.

In Soviet doctrine, this occurs very seldom. Only a few Soviet scholars support the idea of divided ownership, i.e. ownership which belongs to some extent to the state as well as to state organizations.[22] They forget, however, that postglossators, introducing the concept of divided ownership, envisioned a situation in which no particular owner would have supremacy over any other one, and in which the rights of every participant in such ownership would be restricted by the rights of other participants.[23] Operative management has nothing in common with this situation, because the state may withdraw any property from state organizations *ad libitum* or even liquidate certain organizations at any time. The state, of course, can act thus as the only owner, not as a subject that divides its ownership with that of its own organizations.

Even more widespread is such a misinterpretation in Western literature.

At the same 1984 conference in Connecticut, Berman, when discussing ownership and operative management, said: "I had always thought that the genius of this legal invention was that it gave the actual benefits of ownership—what lawyers call the 'incidents' of ownership, namely, possession, use, and disposition—to the enterprises, while not disturbing the theoretical ownership, the fictitious unitary ownership of the state as such."[24] Thus, Berman went even further than do the Soviet adherents of the theory of divided ownership. The latter consider the state and state entities as concurrent owners. The former proclaims the state to be only a theoretical owner and the state entities to be actual proprietors. One would be hard pressed to deviate further from Soviet reality than does the author of a conception that views the entity which can do anything with the property involved as only a theoretical owner and considers as actual proprietors those whose rights are so severely restricted in favor of that so-called "theoretical" owner.

The real meaning of operative management can be properly explained only if the concept of operative management is not confused with the concept of ownership rights. Derived from state ownership, operative management economically assures the legal subordination of state organizations to the Soviet state. However, if the property rights encompassed by this Soviet invention were strictly observed by the higher governmental agencies, the economic independence of state organizations from the Soviet state would also be assured to an extent necessary for their meaningful participation in economic activity and, consequently, for the normal functioning of the Soviet economy as a whole. Unfortunately, rather than observing, the Soviet Government and especially the Communist Party, practically disregards the property rights of subordinate economic entities.

Actually, all of the violations of economic accountability, already described above, are at the same time violations of the right of economic entities to exercise operative management. Therefore the positive potential of this right has not resulted in the kind of achievement that could be attained under more favorable circumstances. But the collapse of the Soviet system would mean the creation of such favorable circumstances. These circumstances also exist in those contemporary societies that are based on political democracy and economic freedom. If these contemporary or future societies should find themselves in need of economic decentralization within the limits of a united ownership, and if such a decentralization should demand the creation of separate enterprises subordinated to one economic entity but relatively independent from it in the realm of economic activity, operative management, in its undistorted state, would prove to be no less efficient than a consistent application of economic accountability would be. Thus, the contours of the potential reception of Soviet law reveal themselves even more distinctly in the realm of legal regulation of economic activity than this was the case with political activity.

Legal Reception and the Status of the Person

From the viewpoint of finding areas of potential reception, the legal status of the person in the U.S.S.R. seems substantially more difficult to assess than are legal regulations connected with the Soviet economy or even with Soviet politics. The Soviet system is, first of all, a system in which the person is suppressed by all possible means. Then how can one expect any reception in this area after the collapse of the very system of such suppression? Strange as it may seem, reception here nevertheless remains possible.

Sometimes in Soviet law, quite positive regulations concerning the interests of individual citizens are introduced. This happens mainly because of obvious oversights by Soviet rulers which they themselves eventually admit. Since abrogation of these regulations would be rather inconvenient, once thus adopted they are simply not being applied. But the regulations themselves remain intact and, if necessary, they can become the object of reception. For example, during the codification of Soviet civil law in the early 1960s, the Soviets were sufficiently vigilant to prevent the issuance of the chapters of the union-republican civil codes containing an entire complex of elaborated rules on the protection of personal non-property rights (the right to privacy, the right to name, etc.) However, one all-Union rule, protecting honor and dignity, was left in,[25] and very soon it became a source of trouble, especially for the Soviet media. Contrary to their established practice incompatible with any retraction, the media under this rule could now be ordered by the court to publish retraction of materials defamatory in their substance and untrue in their assertions. However, by means of multifarious forms of pressure (through Party organizations, managers of entities where a potential complainant worked, etc.) the Soviets made sure that in judicial practice cases of civil law protection of the person's honor and dignity were reduced almost to nothing. However, this in no way reflects or affects the quality of that legal regulation itself. In fact, in terms of such quality this regulation in Soviet civil law has certain indisputable advantages in comparison with Western legislation, and it would be unforgivable to disregard these advantages in future legislative activity. In most Western countries that have established civil law protection of honor and dignity, the complainant has the duty to prove that the defamatory rumors spread by the defendant do not correspond to reality. Otherwise his suit has to be dismissed.

Such a legal treatment of these cases seems strikingly unjust, because it relies upon a presumption that each person is as bad as follows from any gossip directed against him, unless he manages to prove the groundlessness of his calumniator's assessments. It appears obvious, however, that human relationships must be based on the opposite presumption: each person is honest and decent, unless proved otherwise. Under such a principle the defendant would bear the burden of proving the correctness of his claims, and if he could not do so, then the victim's suit would be successful. The Soviet regulations, being formulated in accordance with this model, are therefore preferable to the analogous Western regulations. It is true that in Western countries the complainant may demand punitive damages which are not admitted by the Soviet protection of honor and dignity. But theoretical assessments of this difference do not appear to be unanimous. There are proponents and opponents of monetary compensation of *dommage moral.* At any rate, *onus probandi* must not depend on the existence of this compensation. The principles of morality should play here the determining role in fairly distributing the burdens of proof between the complainant and the defendant. The complainant must prove that certain rumors debasing his personality have been spread by the defendant. Otherwise the suit would have no legal ground. In his turn, the defendant must prove that these rumors correspond to reality. Otherwise, the complainant's honor and dignity should receive full legal protection, that is, it should be protected to the extent to which the defendant failed to prove the truthfulness of his allegations concerning the complainant.

Sometimes, similarly positive regulations that strengthen the status of citizens appear because of internal or international circumstances which are stronger than the Soviet reluctance to establish these regulations. For instance, when the process of rehabilitation was in full swing after Stalin's denunciation, the question of monetary compensation for harm caused by the wrong actions of agencies of justice became for the Soviet régime extremely acute. It was unthinkable, on the one hand, to criticize judicial arbitrariness, but, on the other hand, it was just as impossible to avoid giving some protection to the property interests affected by the denounced violations, especially taking into account the fact that Poland, a neighboring "socialist" country, had included rules for dealing with this problem in its civil legislation of the late 1950s. And as at that time a new codification of the U.S.S.R.'s civil law was under way, this problem had to be solved by appropriate rules. Therefore, Fundamental Principles of Civil Legislation, adopted in 1961, established in the second paragraph of Article 89 that "the respective state agencies bear financial liability in the instances and within the limits specially provided for by the law for harm caused by the improper actions of officials of the agencies of inquiry, preliminary investigation, procuracy, and court." As one will immediately notice, the cited article has peculiarly Soviet characteristics: in principle, the problem has been solved, but in practice the proclaimed solution will acquire actual force only after instances and limits of its applicability will be specially provided. As a result, for almost twenty years this rule was a "dead letter" in Soviet law. However, having signed the 1975 Helsinki Declaration, which focused its attention upon human rights, the Soviets could not continue with their tactic of foot-dragging. The preparation of special regulations has begun, and in 1981 the appropriate normative act was at last promulgated.[26] This time it was proved once again that the second paragraph of Article 89 had been pure sub-terfuge, and because the "special" regulations of 1981 formulated a definite solution, the mentioned paragraph was replaced by a clear and simple formula.[27] Now the second paragraph of Article 89 reads: "Harm caused to the citizen as a result of illegal conviction, illegal criminal prosecution, illegal application of confinement under guard as a measure of restraint, illegal imposition of an administrative penalty in the form of arrest or corrective labor, is compensated by the state in full measure independently of the fault of the officials of the agencies of inquiry, preliminary investigation, procuracy and court, in the order established by law."[28]

It would seem that now the entire issue was legally exhausted. But one thing provokes suspicion: although four years have passed, judging from the published records of judicial practice of the U.S.S.R., not a single case has been heard by the court on the basis of these revised regulations. This enigma can be unraveled only in one way. For decades, Soviet justice has been based on the principle: if a citizen was arrested, he should be accused; if he was accused, the court should convict him; if he was convicted, the entire rehabilitation should not take place in the way of appeal or review. Some measure of punishment must be always applied and preserved. Other-wise, Soviet justice would be compromised, and its corresponding agencies would be shown to have "defects in their work."[29] Now, the same principle must be strengthened by material stimuli. Since each "defect in work" of agencies of justice can lead to monetary losses for the state, all shortcomings must be skillfully concealed in order to avoid these losses. And who knows? Perhaps the very favorable new regulations will actually be more disadvan-tageous to the citizenry than was the old rule: instead of compensation for harm caused by illegal justice, all cases of judicial wrongdoing will be even more artificially proclaimed legal.

However, beyond the limits of the Soviet system and independently from the actual policy of the Soviet state in this area, the legal regulations which are formally in force seem to be deserving of reception. The state must protect its citizens by all possible means, mainly relying upon agencies of justice. But if these agencies infringe upon citizens' interests, no one but the state shall be responsible for the result, including the harm caused. It does not matter that the officials of justice are not guilty. The state is guilty in its inability to assure irreproachable activity of its agencies of justice. If it can not achieve this, not the citizens but the state itself must bear the responsibility for all results entailed by judicial inefficiency. It is also irrelevant that the heavy burden of monetary expenses will be imposed upon the state by the described regulations. The damage done must be completely compensated regardless of the burden entailed. If the state would like to lessen such a burden, it should concentrate its efforts upon the perfection of the activity of judicial agencies rather than shifting property losses to the citizens' shoulders. The U.S.S.R. has established appropriate rules and formally has done this with strict consistency. Therefore, their reception is desirable, despite the contradiction between reality and law in the U.S.S.R. today. Such a reception should be accomplished by means of separating the legal rules favorable to the person from the Soviet system that suppresses the person by ignoring and/or breaking these rules.

Legal Reception and Legal Culture

In contrast to legal regulations embodied in either statutory or case law, legal culture is also reflected by jurisprudence.[30] But even in its jurisprudential part, this culture retains its importance for legal practice, to say nothing of legal theory or legal education. To understand law correctly and to apply it properly one must rely upon various components of the legal culture (categories, vocabulary, technique, etc.). This is why the reception of legal culture can and shall be discussed as directly pertaining to the general problem of the reception of legal systems. The legal system of the U.S.S.R. does not present any exception in this regard either.

As for Soviet law, one question of legal culture connected with the federal structure of the U.S.S.R. is of special interest—that of the technical correlation between federal and republican legislation. In countries of genuine federalism, this correlation seems at first glance to be quite simple: federal and state legislative agencies develop their activity in conformity with their respective jurisdictions and in accordance with the federal constitution. However, some complications manifest themselves even in these cases. Not infrequently a lack of coordination in the realm of legislation can become a serious obstacle to normal human activity in federal states. This is why they sometimes resort to special methods of securing legal unity without violating the federal principles. One such special method consists in the issuing of additional model codes or model statutes, not by legislative agencies but by research institutions. This is aimed at stimulating the members of the federation to adopt them and thus to achieve the desired unification.

The U.S.S.R. does not belong to the class of genuine federations. In essence, it is a unitary state disguised by a federalist label. As a result, its legislation, though formally decentralized between all-union and republican legislators, is actually unified, with the exception of certain insignificant peculiarities that are preserved for the sake of camouflage in various union republics. Therefore, the Soviets have elaborated certain new legislative forms which, while serving the goal of uniformity, nevertheless possess a federal coloring: in cases where the promulgation of codes pertains to republican jurisdiction (civil codes, criminal codes, etc.) the jurisdiction of the U.S.S.R. encompasses the promulgation of all-union fundamental principles (of civil legislation, criminal legislation, etc.). This gives the central authority the opportunity to establish unified regulations, even if they belong to republican jurisdiction, and ensures the *verbatim* duplication of all-union fundamental principles by the appropriate acts of republican codifications. If one takes into account the fact that such a publicly legalized method is combined with the secretly introduced obligatory approval of republican codes by a special all-union agency before these codes may be adopted by republican legislators, one will understand the otherwise incomprehensible occurrence that the codes of all fifteen republics look more like legislative twins than independently adopted laws. As a matter of course, genuine federal states do not need to borrow an experience that represents a caricature of federalism.

At the same time, the adoption of federal fundamental principles and state's codes seems by itself to correspond to the nature of federalism. In the form of fundamental principles, the federal legislator is able to express the rules which pertain to federal jurisdiction and therefore must be binding upon all members of the federation. This would assure a unity of legislation within the limits of actual legality. Such legality also would not be violated, if, along with generally binding regulations, fundamental principles contained model rules, which, though exceeding the federal jurisdiction, could be either accepted or rejected by members of the federation. In case of rejection the differences of legal rules concerning the same subject would be unavoidable in various federally united states. However, within the limits of acceptance, which should occur at least to some extent, the unified regulation, necessary under contemporary circumstances as often as not, can be achieved despite the federal structure of the given state and without violating either federal or state jurisdiction. In the outlined direction, the Soviet experience might be subject to the reception by other social systems.

Looking to Soviet jurisprudence, one encounters broader sources of cultural achievement than in Soviet legislation. Nevertheless, here too, it seems sufficient to restrict the appropriate illustrations to only one example. In any country the branches of law dealing with legal responsibility for the result of illegal behavior assume the existance of a causal link between the latter and the former. Among the concepts of causality suggested by Western jurisprudence on the basis of Western judicial practice, three are most often applied: the concept of direct and remote causes, the concept known by the title *conditio sine qua non*, and the concept of adequate causality. Each of these has its advantages and disadvantages, but, unfortunately, no one can be proclaimed invulnerable. Therefore, research of the discussed topic by Western scholars is still in the process of development.

Soviet jurisprudence, which initially borrowed Western concepts of causality, has never shared the theory of direct and remote causes. In criticizing this theory, legal scholars of the U.S.S.R. have been always pointing out that a cause could be remote but at the same time more important than the direct one. The two remaining theories were temporarily adopted. Criminalists supported the concept of *conditio sine qua non*, while civilists preferred the concept of adequate causality. Such a difference is quite understandable. Criminal law does not provide for strict liability, and, relying upon the criterion of fault, may break the endless chain of causality which stems from *conditio sine qua non* at the point of guilty conduct, provided that without such conduct the indictable result would not have occurred. On the contrary, civil law, in certain cases, deals with strict liability. Therefore, the civilists, instead of *conditio sine qua non*, which, if nobody is guilty, allows to extend the chain of causality *ad infinitum*, have concentrated on adequate causality, which considers human conduct that generally, not only in the given case, would engender analogous results to be the legally relevant cause.

The described situation was preserved until the late 1940s, when new concepts of causality were elaborated by Soviet scholars. The process of elaborating such new concepts of causality is not yet finished; however, a number of theories have already been suggested.[31] In contrast to the past, Soviet scholars no longer refer to different causalities in criminal and civil law. Instead they strive to attain a unified solution for the entire area of legal regulation. The suggested solutions, however, are far from unanimous. The divergence among them can best be illustrated by a comparison of the following two concepts: the necessary and the accidental causal links, on the one hand, and, on the other hand, causality which creates the reality or the possibility of the result. According to the first concept, circumstances which entail a certain result do not play the same role in its causation. Some are necessary, others are accidental causes. A person may be held responsible only if his conduct produces the necessary causes of the result. If he causes the same result accidentally, he should not be held responsible. However, adherents of this theory either neglect to formulate the criteria for making distinctions between necessary and accidental causation or argue for the adoption of different criteria. Thus, under the same title, instead of one there are, in fact, many theories.

According to the second concept, human conduct can lead to the reality or to the possibility of a certain result, and the possibility, in its turn, is either concrete or abstract. The creation of the reality or of the concrete possibility is considered as a causality that is sufficient for holding a person legally responsible for what he did, whereas the creation of the abstract possibility relieves from responsibility those who have caused it. However, since the criteria for distinguishing between the three types of causation are differently formulated by different authors, the concept of the reality and the possibility consists of different variants, as numerous as are the variants of which the concept of necessary and accidental causal links consists.

Thus, the Soviet concepts of causality are as far from perfection as are those of their Western counterparts. But they have their own advantages which deserve to be studied by foreign and future scholars with a view toward their potential positive use. This is so because the question of causality belongs to the realm of abstract theoretical ideas, not to that of theoretical support for a peculiarly Soviet doctrinal posture. The reception of certain facets of legal culture developed by Soviet jurisprudence is possible and should at least not be precluded in all cases where pure theoretical thought, rather than particular doctrinal demands related to Soviet reality, is reflected.

Conclusion

In summing up the foregoing analysis, the following deductions can be made.

In the event of the unavoidable collapse of the Soviet system in the historical future, reception of Soviet law seems possible and even desirable to a certain degree. Such reception is possible on condition that the borrowed rules and categories be 1. extremely abstract and, as a result, separated from a specifically Soviet socio-political context, or 2. progressive insofar as the legal text itself is concerned although not necessarily so within the context of Soviet legal reality, or 3. suitable, despite Soviet distortions, to be beneficially employed after reasonable purification, or 4. important as technical achievements and thus as positive contributions to the general development of legal culture. The reception of Soviet law to a certain degree is also desirable because 1. the positive legal experience accumulated by any country belongs to all of humanity, and 2. historical continuity is best served not by waste, but rather by economic usage of all the positive achievements of the past, however generally negative the past experience may have been.

But if, at least a restricted reception of Soviet law is possible and desirable, does this not mean that the Soviet legal system, with all of its defects, also reveals some indisputably positive capacities? In no way! Only certain abstract legal rules and techniques or certain legal regulations which contradict the true substance of Soviet reality should not be precluded from reception, and even those on condition that they were purified of Soviet specificity. In other words, reception should be limited to some tangible results of individual creativity. Everything related to the regular functioning of the Soviet legal system should be definitely excluded from reception.

The negative attitude toward the Soviet system should not be extended to a negative assessment of the people living under the Soviet régime and of their creative deeds performed despite and in defiance of that régime. After all, the Soviet system is bound to collapse, not just because of its substantive unviability but first and foremost because the invincible force of the creative human spirit will eventually make people refuse to be reconciled with the domination and slavery imposed upon that spirit by the Soviet régime. And, thus, it will be the people that ultimately will reject the régime and create in its stead a new socio-political and legal system.

NOTES

1. For elaboration, see O.S. Ioffe, "Law and Economy in the U.S.S.R." in *Harvard Law Review* 95, No.7 (May 1982): 1501-1625.
2. So far, these predictions have, without exception, failed to materialize. Amalrik's is one such striking case in point. See A. Amalrik, *Prosushchestvuet li Sovetskyi Soyuz do 1984 goda* (Amsterdam: Herzen Foundation, 1964).
3. H.J. Berman, "The Possibilities and Limits of Soviet Economic Reform," in O.S. Ioffe, M.W. Janis, eds., *Soviet Law and Economy* (Dordrecht-Boston-Lancaster: Martin Nijhoff Publishers, 1986), 59-77.
4. *Newsweek*, 9 May 1983; p. 86.
5. For a detailed discussion, see C. Sherman, *Roman Law in the Modern World* (New York: Columbia University Press, 1937).
6. These assertions are not, of course, true. Not only French and German, but even ancient Roman law affected Soviet law during its creation and continue to influence it at present. See, for example, O.S. Ioffe, "Soviet Law and Roman Law," *Boston University Law Review* 62, no.3 (May, 1982): 701-730.
7. Here and hereinafter references are to the 1977 Soviet Constitution, in the author's translation.
8. The 1977 Constitution, Article 72.
9. See V.I. Lenin, *Sochineniia* (Works) (Moscow: Gospolitizdat, 1964), 24, 36.
10. E.g. *SP SSSR*, 1976, No.21 item 104.
11. They were adopted in 1961 under the title Fundamental Principles of Civil Legislation of the U.S.S.R. and Union Republics, in *Vedomosti SSSR*, 1961, No.50, item 325 (with further numerous changes).

12. They were adopted in 1970 under the title Fundamental Principles of Legislation of the U.S.S.R. and Union Republics on Labor, in *Vedomosti SSSR*, 1970, No.29, item 265 (with certain further changes).

13. They were adopted in 1959 under the title Fundamental Principles of Criminal procedure of the U.S.S.R. and Union Republics, *Vedomosti SSSR*, 1959, No.1, item 15 (with further numerous changes).

14. See M. Hayward, ed., *On Trial: The Soviet State Versus "Abram Tertz" and "Nikolai Arzhak"* (New York: Harper and Row, 1967).

15. As outlined in more detail in the Introduction to this chapter.

16. *SP SSSR*, 1981, No. 9-10, Part I, item 62.

17. See O.S. Ioffe, P.B. Maggs, *Soviet Law in Theory and Practice* (London-Rome-New York: Oceana, 1984), 142-144.

18. Fundamental Principles of Civil Legislation, Article 19.

19. Fundamental Principles of Civil Legislation, Article 26-1.

20. See *supra,* note 18; O.S. Ioffe, P.B. Maggs, *Soviet Law in Theory,* 162-171.

21. See *supra,* note 19.

22. For example, see V.P. Shkredov, *Ekonomika i Pravo* (Moscow: Ekonomika, 1967), 102-105.

23. E. Landsberg, *Die Glosse des Accursius und ihre Lehre vom Eigentum* (Leipzig: publisher not indicated, 1883).

24. See *supra,* note 3 and text accompanying note 3.

25. Fundamental Principles of Civil Legislation, Article 7.

26. *Vedomosti SSSR*, 1981, No.21, item 750.

27. *Vedomosti SSSR*, 1981, No.44, item 1184.

28. As noted, this order has already been established; see *supra,* note 26.

29. This expression is broadly used not only as a phrase of Soviet professional legal slang but even as language of official instructions of the Procurator General, of the U.S.S.R.'s Supreme Court, etc.

30. I put aside legal regulations implemented by jurisprudence when, as in ancient Rome, certain of its representatives had *jus respondendi* generally binding in the way similar to that of interpreted law itself.

31. For a review of these theories, see G.K. Matveev, *Osnovaniia Grazhdanskoi Otvetstvennosti* (Moscow: Yuridicheskaya Literatura, 1970).

APPENDIX

American Research and Instruction on the Soviet Union

Some Reflections

ROBERT F. BYRNES

Introduction

The nature and quality of American research and instruction in Soviet studies lie at the foundation of our understanding of the Soviet Union and therefore of our judgments concerning likely future developments. Just as the Soviet system has changed over the years, so have our knowledge and understanding. An analysis of American research and instruction in Soviet studies can therefore illustrate both the nature of change in the last third of this century and the relationship between those changes and our comprehension of them. Finally, while the connection between our knowledge and understanding of a state's leaders and the electoral process of that state and the state's actual policies is not direct, some relationship does exist. All of us appreciate that Western policies can have only a limited effect upon Soviet actions, but we also assume that sound information may lead to sensible activities that may help move the Soviet government toward providing more free and prosperous arrangements for the Soviet peoples and lead to a more peaceful world.

I speak as an American scholar-teacher concerning research and instruction carried on within the United States, with the hope that we Americans will profit from reviewing our programs and that others will appreciate the strengths and shortcomings of our research and instruction and can revise their programs, whether established before or after ours. American analysis and teaching concerning the Soviet Union reflect in many ways the role the United States occupies in the world as well as the character of higher education in the United States. We must introduce basic changes in the spirit and character of our educational system as a whole before we can produce substantial improvements in this small part of it.

I am a product of the system of research and instruction that I seek to describe and analyze. As a scholar-teacher of the now older generation, I accept a share of the responsibility for creating the flaws I discuss.

Although we are all human beings living on the same shrinking planet at the same chronological time, we must begin by recognizing that understanding any other people and their culture is difficult, simply because others' values, beliefs, traditions, and institutions are to some degree different. That we are all human, that many of our goals are similar, that our institutions often bear identical names and seem to resemble each other, that we face many similar domestic and international problems, and that our futures are more closely tied together than our pasts have been, complicate our understanding because the apparent resemblances often obscure the fundamental distinctions.

With regard to the Soviet Union, the difficulties are especially great, because Soviet history, tradition, basic political values, and attitudes toward the individual and the state are so distinct from those with which we are familiar. In addition, the Soviet government severely restricts access to the Soviet Union and to materials about Soviet life and politics, increasing the barriers and creating an additional one in the form of suspicion and fear. Finally, American knowledge of the Soviet Union has only a recent base and has grown in circumstances that deeply affect the glasses through which we view the Soviet Union. In effect, American programs began after World War II, on a very small foundation. No one can therefore expect the same level of understanding, inadequate though it is, that Americans possess of the English, the French, or the Germans.

Advantages

Research and instruction concerning the Soviet Union in general has grown and we have profited from the most beneficent of circumstances, above all the right of each scholar-teacher to choose his own subject, utilize research materials throughout the Western world, and express his conclusions in whatever way he wishes. Research in this area rested originally on the great breadth, sweep, and quality of Russian culture that Americans began to discover a century ago in the novels of Tolstoy, Dostoevsky, and Turgenev, the plays of Chekhov, the music of Tchaikovsky, and the glories of Russian ballet. In the 1930s the excitement of the early Communist effort to destroy an old culture and to create a new civilization based on a scientific and planned approach won the sympathetic interest of many informed Americans, as the purges created a sense of fascinated horror. Later, the massive Soviet contribution to military victory over the Nazis, the expansion of Soviet power over the peoples of Eastern Europe, and the confrontation of two powerful political and social systems created popular interest in learning more about the Soviet Union. Scholar-teachers could hardly have sought more propitious circumstances.

After World War II, most American educational leaders and members of the informed public began to appreciate the changing nature of the shrinking world, the new position in world politics the United States suddenly occupied, and the massive changes in spirit and curriculum that education had to therefore undertake. At that time support for expanding research and construction concerning other parts of the world, particularly the Soviet Union, was strong throughout society. The enormous explosion of higher education because of the general recognition that education was the key to progress, the GI program that encouraged hundreds of thousands of veterans to continue their education, and the wave of encouragement to ambitious and intelligent young men and women from all levels of society to enter colleges and universities together provided massive funding increments and splendid opportunities to revise and expand curricula. Education became a growth industry, providing administrators opportunities to add new faculty members and fields of study. At the same time, the leaders of the great private foundations, with more funds at their disposal than ever before, decided to help universities launch new programs with funds for scholarship, fellowships, faculty appointments, research, travel, and rapid expansion of library collections.

Another bonus, one that we have not appreciated properly and that may not recur, was the flood of millions of refugees from the Soviet Union and Eastern Europe, including many highly-trained scholars and teachers in all fields of study. This flow, which supplemented a smaller increase of the same nature in the 1920s and 1930s, provided informed specialists on the geography, history, literature, politics, sociology, and cultures of the Soviet Union, scholars who contributed their knowledge and understanding as well as an insight that produced judgments different from those of native Americans. In addition, other capable and experienced men and women from these areas who were not specialists on the Soviet Union helped educate their faculty colleagues as well as their students, whether they were teaching mathematics, chemistry, or music.

The openness and ease with which American colleges and universities welcomed these new immigrants and enabled them to contribute their knowledge and insight is one of the glories of American society. Michael Karpovich, who helped more than thirty young men and women obtain Ph.D degrees from Harvard after 1945, and his colleague and friend, George Vernadsky of Yale, who trained fewer scholar-teachers but whose publications constituted fundamental resources for thousands of Americans trying to comprehend the Soviet Union, were only the most visible of this large and fascinating group. David Dallin, Michael Florinsky, George Florovsky, Roman Jacobson, Naum Jasny, Nicholas Timashev, Sergei Yakobson, and Avraham Yarmolinsky are only a few of those born in Russia who contributed greatly to the growth of American educational resources.

In short, American higher education faced a splendid opportunity, with abundant resources, to introduce changes just at the moment public interest and scholarly excitement concerning the Soviet Union was flourishing. We then discovered a crucial additional blessing: the existence of small but sound academic bases on which to expand research and instruction and, above all, of a small number of able and dedicated scholar-teachers superbly qualified to organize and direct new programs.

The personal and professional qualities of the Americans who launched the expansion of Russian and Soviet studies in the decade or two after World War II were crucial. This handful had received sound basic training in their disciplines, often supplemented by further study in universities in Western Europe. Knowing French and German and both the scholars and scholarship of those countries, they also benefited greatly from the opportunity of having lived and worked in the Soviet Union in the 1920s and 1930s. In 1958 the Soviet government restricted access to American scholars for the first time since 1936. But the scholars who were able to get into the country before that time lived with Soviet families, came to know their colleagues in institutions in Moscow and Leningrad, travelled quite freely about the country, and enjoyed access to almost every aspect of Soviet life. They emerged with a command of Russian, a knowledge of and an affection for the peoples that cannot be obtained from books or from the controlled arrangements in which foreign scholars now study in the Soviet Union, and an understanding of Soviet society which only life in the circumstances they enjoyed can provide. In addition, the turbulent times through which they had lived and their awareness of the critical need to expand enormously the level of American knowledge and understanding led them to dedicate their lives not to producing scholarly tomes so much as to helping train the first dozen and then hundreds of young scholar-teachers to continue the work they had begun. Thus, Gerold T. Robinson, who in 1932 published the classic, *Rural Russia under the Old Régime*, did not complete and publish the two research projects on agriculture under Soviet rule and on Soviet Marxist thought he began after 1932. Instead, he devoted his time and energies to helping train others. Similarly, Philip E. Mosely, whose knowledge of the Soviet Union and of Soviet policies and politics I have always thought unsurpassed, helped train the next generation of scholar-teachers on Soviet politics and Soviet foreign policy, producing only a number of insightful essays and articles rather than the scholarly volumes he could have written. They were written later by those whom he helped educate.

The founders of Soviet studies in the United States contributed in another important but less appreciated way. Aware of the deep political controversies within the United States that Soviet domestic policies and the zig-zags of Soviet foreign policies created, and out of a crucial need that scholarly work remain free from involvement in political debate, these scholars helped train young men and women to obtain and describe the facts as objectively as they could by their own example and work and, while remaining citizens, to stand removed from the political controversies that divided the American public. Robinson was the founder and first director of the Russian Institute at Columbia University, the mother institute for Soviet studies in the United States, and Clyde Kluckhohn was the first director of the Russian Research Center at Harvard University. These were the first and second most important institutions in Soviet research. Their colleagues recognized the need for keeping these institutions free from politics and political disputes and unaffected by the oscillations—from fear to enthusiasm—that often sweep over the American public. Robinson was particularly explicit: he established the Russian Institute not only to provide expert training for specialists in education and government service but also to create a group of scholar-teachers and a body of knowledge on which the public could rely for objective facts and judgments as a check against information the Soviet government and its supporters would distribute. The public could also rely on the Institute to be objective about the views of an American government that for any reason any time might advocate policies not based on the most careful analysis of the evidence. As a consequence, American specialists on the Soviet Union during the decade or two after 1945 remained above political controversy and acquired a deserved reputation for thorough and careful analyses, regardless of the directions in which political winds blew. This helped enormously to create a calm atmosphere in which American statesmen and political leaders could wrestle with the extremely complicated problems that Soviet policies often create.

One can appreciate the significance of this contribution by examining briefly the activities of American specialists on China during the bitter controversies in the late 1940s and the 1950s over developments within China and over American policy toward China. Many specialists on China became engaged in the controversy and fought bitterly with each other and with the government. These disputes among individuals and then between groups from the major institutions led some to level charges before Congressional committees concerning the personal, professional, and political positions of their colleagues. The deeply divided field of American specialists, therefore, not only failed to provide our policymakers and public with the kind of objective information they needed, but contributed to the bitterness and destructiveness of the disagreements. The politicalization of the field of Chinese studies is less apparent than thirty years ago, but the country and Chinese studies both paid a high price for the failure of the senior scholars to demonstrate the same responsibility and dedication as their contemporaries in the Soviet field.

Disadvantages

Soviet studies after World War II also suffered from some handicaps. One was the newness and smallness of the number of specialists, compared, for example, with the number in Chinese studies, already a century old. In 1940, American universities possessed only four departments of Slavic languages and literature. Only a dozen trained scholars taught Russian history in American colleges and universities. Ignorance of things Russian and Soviet was almost total. Libraries were small and usually consisted only of books and journals in Western languages, and interest in strengthening these collections was limited.

The United States was so predominantly an English-speaking country and had enjoyed such a long period of splendid isolation from the rest of the world that interest in teaching and learning foreign languages, even French and German, was very low. Moreover, these and other languages were usually taught as mere academic exercises.

Finally, when the Soviet Union opened its doors for research in 1958 with the first Soviet-American cultural agreement, the two governments established a controlled artificial arrangement under which Americans could undertake research there only in the same small number that Soviet scholars wished to study in the United States. The barter agreement, in which up to twenty and then up to fifty young American scholars could work in Moscow and Leningrad in return for the same number of Soviet scholars to be allowed to study in institutions throughout the United States, provided conditions for research and for understanding Soviet life far inferior to those the founders of Soviet studies enjoyed in the 1930s. Limited almost entirely to dormitory life in the two major Soviet cities with promised access to archives often withheld, denied the right to interview Soviet officials, restricted from mingling informally with citizens beyond the university, and often prevented from having any significant opportunities to discuss their work and Soviet life with Soviet specialists, they received a narrow view of the Soviet Union. These restrictions, as well as the constant effort necessary to obtain the opportunities that the cultural affairs agreement assured them, created a limited knowledge and produced a sense of hostility to the Soviet system (albeit not to the Soviet people) that has ever since affected these scholars' views of the Soviet Union. Perhaps conditions have improved somewhat over the years, or Americans may have become inured to the inequities, even to the point of "attempting archival work without access to the archives."

Achievements

The outstanding achievement of American research and instruction on the Soviet Union in the last four decades is the establishment of a large national base for continued expansion and improvement. The United States now has at least ten major university centers and dozens of minor ones scattered throughout the country, with well-trained and experienced faculties in the major disciplines, such as geography, economics, political science, languages and literature, and history, and often with specialists as well in fields such as law, fine arts, music, sociology, education, business administration, religion, philosophy, and journalism. Indiana University, for example, has more than fifty faculty members who specialize in Russian and East European studies. Some are natives of the Soviet Union. Virtually all the other men and women have studied for months at a time on several occasions in the Soviet Union and/or Eastern Europe. They have mastered Russian and sometimes other languages as well. They are members of departments and institutes or centers that provide understanding, support, stimulation, and an interested community of scholars.

For the past twenty years, the American Association for the Advancement of Slavic Studies has constituted a national organization which helps bring together scholars from all disciplines, publishes a professional journal and newsletter, obtains research and travel funds, helps arrange participation in international conferences, and represents the interests of this field of study before the federal government on such issues as funding for national programs and the continued free flow of materials from states under communist control. The number of publishers eager to produce volumes on the Soviet Union and of journals established to publish articles is almost overwhelming. Above all, the scholarly and teaching achievements have won the understanding, respect, and support of the American academic community and of the central pillars of American life. Russian studies now constitutes a visible and accepted part of the academic scene.

In addition, the facilities necessary for scholarship and teaching are abundant and efficient. The number of large, well-organized libraries in the United States is the envy of scholars throughout the world, and the ease of access to materials of all kinds is astounding for anyone used to Soviet libraries. Collections such as those of the New York Public Library and the Library of Congress are probably the largest and best centers for Soviet research in the world outside of Moscow, and all the materials within these great libraries are freely available to anyone. The large and well-organized collections at Harvard, Columbia, Illinois, and Berkeley rank with any others in the world, and most major institutions have large, accessible, and rapidly growing resources. The Hoover Institution is only the largest and best-known of the institutions with libraries that specialize on particular aspects of Soviet studies. In short, the easy availability of research materials constitutes a tremendous advantage.

A revolutionary expansion in bibliographical tools, from the published catalogues of most of the important libraries of the Western world to a rich variety of special bibliographies, makes locating significant research materials much easier and simpler than just twenty years ago. Interlibrary loans provide scholars access to materials anywhere in the United States and in parts of Western Europe. Microfilming and photocopying, which earlier generations would have considered miraculous, are now standard equipment, and computer networks add another remarkable increment.

Measuring the quality of American research is impossible, even for a team of responsible scholars, but it constitutes one of the glories of the past four decades. The flood of books and articles in fields such as the intellectual history of nineteenth century Russia, or national minorities, or personnel changes within the Soviet party and government is so vast that even the most diligent scholar is pressed to read the essential volumes and the reviews of the others, unless he is willing to ignore Soviet and other scholarship, abandon his research, and neglect his teaching.

We have no doubt achieved more in terms of quantity than in quality, in part because Soviet studies still constitute a fledgling field, without the depth and experience that studies established earlier have acquired. Nevertheless, some tests of scholarly achievements provide positive results. American scholars who visit the Soviet Union are not surprised by their experiences, demonstrating that the scholarly works they read and the instruction they received were accurate. Those who specialize in ancient Greece or medieval France will (presumably) never enjoy the opportunity to test the validity of their scholarship against reality, but studies of the Soviet Union have admirably met this test. Papers by American scholars at international conferences compare favorably with those that scholars from other countries produce. Foreign reviews and analyses of American scholarship, often even in the Soviet Union, are generally well rated. Analyses of the Soviet economy by Americans twenty or thirty years ago, when information was scanty and fragile, and again today, when it is more abundant, have proved remarkably sound when compared with Soviet figures published long after these studies were computed using today's official statistics and scholarship. In every field of study, from Dostoevsky to mortality rates to Russian policy during the Crimean war to the Stalin purges in the late 1930s, Americans young and old have produced volumes of distinguished merit.

In short, the American contribution to the worldwide study of Russia and the Soviet Union rests on solid bases and is impressive. When Soviet scholars acquire the opportunity to freely study Russian history and culture and developments within the Soviet union since 1917, they will surely appreciate the resources preserved and made easily available and the spirit and care with which Western scholars have analyzed Russia and the Soviet Union.

Flaws

American Higher Education

Progress creates fewer problems than does stagnation, but every rise to a new plateau creates new difficulties. Moreover, advancement often exposes unstable foundations, creates new fissures, and stimulates the need for review and revision. Thus, the achievements in American research conceal flaws and shortcomings that require repair to maintain their bases and to advance.

Basically and inevitably, the field of Soviet studies reflects the strengths and weaknesses of American higher education. Almost everyone concerned about American education is convinced that it has serious faults, particularly in terms of the quality of instruction, the level of effort and progress required, and the absence of stimulation and vitality. Courses in Soviet studies reflect these shortcomings, in the students and the faculties in the curricula, in the decline in a sense of challenge, and in the decline of standards.

Role Within the University

Perhaps the most fundamental problem is the peripheral position Soviet studies occupies in some universities. Soviet studies is considered a kind of luxury, a department that the university accepts and even endorses but does not consider so essential that the institution should sustain and support it as it does organic chemistry or business administration or macroeconomics. Some major institutions, especially state universities, have decided that the function of the university is to promote research and instruction concerning the world, not just the North Atlantic part of it, and that the university should therefore sustain and support Soviet and other studies as they do the more traditional cirriculum. However, others agree that while the study of Russian language, literature, history, and politics should be a fundamental part of the undergraduate curriculum, sustaining a multidisciplinary program and providing scholarships, fellowships, research and travel funds, and enlarged resources are beyond their resources and therefore feel that Soviet studies should be the responsibility of private foundations or the federal government. Consequently, graduate study on the Soviet Union and other so-called non-Western areas is often peripheral and dependent on outside support. Thus, when most foundations turned to other interests and government support declined in the 1970s—as they no doubt will again—Soviet studies in these centers declined precipitously.

The spirit of many institutions, which tolerate and even endorse Russian studies but endure them in an indifferent or even hostile atmosphere, also reflect this position. Many faculty members have little knowledge of or interest in other parts of the world, except for the information they acquire from the daily press. Consequently, the framework and spirit in which they teach remains the familiar North Atlantic spirit of decades ago. As one disillusioned reformer exclaimed, "What does it profit the university if it changes the entire curriculum but is stuck with the same old faculty?" Since the spirit of our colleges and universities has remained substantially unchanged from the prewar period, even with numbers of new courses devoted to Russia and other parts of the so-called non-Western world, these additions have affected only those students who participate in the new courses. The great bulk of our students receive the same narrow Anglo-Saxon view of the world as their parents did forty or fifty years ago. Indeed, most students and most Americans probably learn more—and this is not a great deal—from the mass media about the Soviet Union than they do in colleges and universities or from the publications of our highly trained scholars.

Moreover, revising the collegiate curriculum is very difficult; an institution can add courses and faculty quite easily, especially if it obtains complementary funds, but a faculty will defend an established curriculum as though it were the last bastion of freedom. The words of David Starr Jordan, president of Indiana University a century ago, when he sought to introduce new science courses and the scientific method into the curriculum, have a familiar ring today: "It is as difficult to change a curriculum as it is to move a cemetery." In short, a university is one of the most conservative institutions in the world and resists change with great skill and success.

Training

Another basic flaw is the character and quality of the graduate training most universities provide. Those who have launched major American research and training centers recognize that the Soviet Union is a culture different from ours—not necessarily superior or inferior, but different. No historian can be appropriately trained if he concentrates solely upon history; he needs an immersion into the total culture, an interdisciplinary approach through other basic disciplines such as political science, literature, and economics, as well as philosophy, religion, art, music, sociology, and anthropology. The programs in the 1940s and 1950s therefore required that each graduate student study in five basic disciplines, with an additional inter-disciplinary seminar or colloquium. As each student completed this broad training, used the research methods and information acquired in the various disciplines in his research, and then continually broadened and deepened his knowledge as he advanced in his career, those who established the training centers assumed that the need for formal inter-disciplinary study would disappear.

Alas, this "area approach" for training specialists in Soviet studies never was effective and has disintegrated in the last two decades. Except for some of the early scholar-teachers, such as Mosely, Robinson, and Fainsod, who had studied for long periods of time in the Soviet Union and who used the methods and insights from several disciplines in their research, few faculty members possess the breadth of knowledge necessary for helping to educate their graduate students to the value of the interdisciplinary approach. Moreover, instruction in each discipline still remains quite separate from that of other disciplines, and the scholar-teachers do not attempt to coordinate their courses and to demonstrate the utility of the "area" system. In short, the area programs are at best multidisciplinary, not interdisciplinary. The traditional disciplines quickly overcame this imaginative but of course difficult approach and reasserted their authority over each graduate student's training, making programs one dimensional. First, the course arrangements resemble "independent pillars of knowledge," with the disciplines unrelated to each other in the mind of both the faculty and the students. Finally the entire structure collapsed as institutions no longer required study in five disciplines and in interdisciplinary colloquia and seminars. The majority of students in most disciplines now concentrate their training in one discipline, under scholar-teachers whose knowledge and interests both are restricted to that discipline. The original basic disciplines remain strong but independent, while those fields of study outside the basic disciplines have withered away or become weak. Consequently, our training concerning other cultures has become remarkably narrow, often limited to one "pillar." Unfortunately, as universities have swollen in size, the sense of intellectual and social community that brought together faculty members and graduate students from different departments in lively social and intellectual sessions has broken down, especially in those universities located in large cities, which are now in the majority. Educational institutions have become atomized, precisely at the time when the unity of knowledge is ever more visible and important.

Intellectual training during the last fifteen or twenty years has also become increasingly shallow, as knowledge has exploded and most scholar teachers have concentrated on their students' "learning more and more about less and less." Thus, for almost all Americans, the Soviet Union means Russians and European Russia; most courses about the Soviet Union, except those in geography, concentrate upon Russia west of the Urals. One of the reasons for the American delay in recognizing the force behind the religious and national minority movements in the Soviet Union is that even our specialists know little about peoples other than Russians and almost nothing about the Moslems in Central Asia or the vast expanses and numerous peoples of Siberia. American specialists failed to recognize the Sino-Soviet split for almost a decade, as did our government, in part because of the specialists' blindness—because we knew virtually nothing about the long history of Russian-Chinese relations, little about their disagreement over their roles in the international revolutionary movement, and almost nothing about the arcane philosophical issues over which they wrangled.

For most specialists other than historians, and for those historians interested largely in the twentieth century, the history of Russia and the Soviet Union begins in 1890. Many programs provide no instruction on Russia before 1800, and even fewer provide advanced instruction on the period before Peter the Great. Indeed, many specialists are totally illiterate concerning Russia before 1890. The inevitable concern about current affairs in this dangerous era has brought a concentration in both research and instruction since 1945. The number of recent books and this conference itself indeed illustrate a growing interest in the future, even over the present time. Imagine a French specialist on the United States whose knowledge of American history began with 1945, or even with 1865.

Most programs now provide effective training in Russian and in the other languages of the Soviet Union important for research there, except for the general neglect of Ukrainian. However, the American national weakness in mastery of other languages has had an especially destructive impact upon Soviet studies. I believe that fewer than half of the most able American specialists on the Soviet Union can read and speak German and French or have the capability of using research published in those languages. I think a poll of the American participants in this international conference would demonstrate this, as it would also indicate that the scholars from the other countries are fully acquainted with research published in English.

An even more serious point is the fact that only a small minority of the youngest scholar-teachers and those now in training even recognize this as a shortcoming. Consequently, bright and able young men and women publish books now that neglect large numbers of primary sources and scholarly studies published in German and French because they are unaware of these works. What limited, parochial scholarship in the last third of the twentieth century! What arrogance and ignorance this reflects! What a blight upon other academic achievements!

The final two weak aspects of American training programs are, first, the failure to require that every student who intends to become a scholar-teacher in the Soviet field, or a government analyst, should spend at least a semester in the Soviet Union as part of his graduate program and secondly, the inability, indeed the failure to seek scholars' right to travel freely throughout the Soviet Union, to undertake research on almost any subject, and to obtain easy access to all research resources necessary. In 1985, any sensible scholar-teacher would assume that any well-organized graduate program would require travel and study in the Soviet Union for all graduate students interested in that country—but not one does. Imagine the eagerness with which scholars on ancient Greece would welcome the opportunity to spend several months in the Athens of Pericles! Witness the eagerness with which foreigners come to the United States to study it!

After more than twenty-five years of academic exchanges with the Soviet Union, one would assume that American officials, administrators, and scholars would be determined to abolish the restrictions under which senior and junior scholars can live and work in the Soviet Union. Some minor improvements have occurred since 1958, but they have been trifling and often temporary. The Soviet government no longer limits Americans to Moscow and Leningrad but allows some whose special research interests require study in other cities to continue their work in these centers; it sometimes allows easy travel beyond the major cities, especially in European Russia, but it maintains firm control and restricts access to most of the country. The government denies access to archives which it had previously promised, and it denies visas to Americans interested in subjects which the Soviet government considers delicate or sensitive, usually the very areas in which large numbers of American scholars are interested, such as foreign policy (even prerevolutionary), minority problems, party personalities and politics, and economic problems. In short, the Soviet government controls the admission and conditions of study of American scholars (and of others as well) in an arrangement that violates the principles of free movement fundamental to a free society. Yet Americans quietly accept and tolerate the sacrificing of their principles to obtain limited opportunities. By this, they accustom new generations of American scholars to accept controls that earlier generations would have immediately rejected.

Second, because of the concentration upon a single discipline, the weakness in foreign languages, and the shallow and hasty character of American graduate training, the "explosion of knowledge" in recent years has over-emphasized recent scholarship. Americans neglect the centrally significant books, the classics that every specialist on the Soviet Union should read, whether written in Russian, French, German, or English, whether published fifty years ago or a hundred years ago. Most scholars go through a complete course of graduate study, and even their careers, without studying many of the most important books that everyone interested in the Soviet Union should read carefully. I recently reread the books and articles the late Hugh Seton-Watson had produced. I discovered from his footnotes and bibliographies that this fine British scholar had studied carefully and utilized works written within the past 150 years by scholars from practically every country in Europe. An historian, he had studied carefully the most significant books of the most important historians—French, German, Yugoslav, Dutch, Danish, Swedish, Polish, Ukrainian, Italian, and Greek—the names of whom many American specialists and most young scholar-teachers could not even identify. This breadth of knowledge helps explain Seton-Watson's ability to understand developments within the Soviet Union and the wisdom of his judgments about Russian history and Soviet politics. Briefly, he was a learned scholar-teacher. I wonder how many learned scholars the United States possesses and whether any of those now in training will acquire the broad learning that was at the base of Seton-Watson's brilliant work.

The Imbalance Between Research and Instruction

Those who launched American expansion of Soviet studies after World War II were scholar-teachers, men who devoted their academic lives equally to teaching undergraduates and graduates and to research. They sought to train young men and women for the same kind of academic life—scholars "who would gladly teach."

This balance between research and teaching has been traditional in American universities, as in most universities outside the Soviet Union.

Careful attention to teaching undergraduates and the general public of informed men and women is critical in a democratic society, because public policy requires the free, knowledgeable support of the citizens. If their knowledge and insight are limited because only the specialists are informed, a democratic country's policies will inevitably remain unstable, no matter how sensible and shrewd they may be. For a number of reasons familiar to everyone acquainted with American university life, many scholar-teachers neglect undergraduates while research and publication attract an ever-growing concentration of their time and energy. As values have changed, as academic rewards have emphasized publication, as more and more funds become available for released time for writing, more and more of those trained have become only scholars. Universities assign teaching undergraduates to junior professors or to graduate assistants. They retain or attract eminent scholars by restricting their teaching to graduate seminars. The ideal appointment for a truly eminent scholar involves no teaching. Universities and their scholars use foundation funds not for library resources, scholarships, or graduate fellowships but to release productive scholars from teaching or to provide them with assistance so that they only rarely appear in a classroom. Jokes abound about a full professor's being absent full time. Graduate students meet the faculty members directing their work in airport lounges. Some outstanding senior scholars do not even read their graduate students' theses. Young scholars emulate their elders in a spiral that makes a mockery of higher education.

This neglect of teaching responsibilities is a travesty of education. In an era when scholar-teachers should pass on their learning and the excitement they acquire from their research to undergraduates and graduate students, we produce many half-baked one-sided products uninterested in and poorly equipped for this important function. It is therefore not surprising that few undergraduates in our major Soviet centers enter graduate work in the Soviet field; for many outstanding scholars in those centers do not instruct undergraduates and therefore close the opportunity to excite and attract "the best and the brightest."

In short, in the field of Soviet studies, the United States needs thousands of parish priests; it has instead produced many theologians. American undergraduates often lack the guidance and inspiration that dedicated scholar-teachers can provide. On the other hand, many scholars escape the simple but difficult questions and the relationship with the public that teaching provides. Americans have misused their resources, twisted their values, and betrayed the process of higher education.

Another phenomenon contributes to American neglect of teaching and even threatens the position of universities as research and instructional institutions. As recently as twenty or thirty years ago, young men and women joined university faculties because such institutions offered the opportunity to teach and to carry on research in a stimulating environment. Universities are no longer so attractive. Salaries have declined relatively; the amount of paperwork and committee activities has increased enormously; the role of students in university government has weakened faculty prerogatives and added a superfluous layer to all discussions; federal intervention to assure affirmative action and other programs has added complications; and the decline of student quality and interest in learning makes teaching less attractive. At the same time, research centers have sprung up, especially on the east and west coasts, offering scholars the opportunity to concentrate upon research and to work closely with other specialists on attractive narrowly defined subjects. These private and government institutions have drawn away from universities a significant number of the most able specialists on the Soviet Union and attract much of the time and energy of those who remain on campus. The continued decline of universities as attractive communities for research and instruction will spur this development, hastened by two other important changes. The first is the growing recognition that understanding the Soviet Union, its strengths and weaknesses, its internal politics and policies, and Soviet-American relations is such a complicated and multifaceted problem that team research seems the best response. Under ordinary circumstances, a university would constitute the ideal locus for such research, but the size of most universities, the strength of departmental barriers limiting cooperation, the dispersal of the different disciplines into scattered buildings, and the expense of some of the equipment needed will almost certainly lead more and more scholars away from the universities. Private or semiprivate research institutes such as the RAND Corporation, the Brookings Institute, the Hoover Institution, the Hudson Institute, and the so-called "think tanks" scattered around Washington and other major cities may therefore acquire the role in research on the Soviet Union that the great commercial laboratories and the government's national research institutes have acquired in many medical and physical sciences.

The information revolution and the development of remarkable ways of harnessing computers for research purposes provide universities a method of solving this problem. If American scholar-teachers and their institutions can secure the leadership and the necessary funds, they can utilize the new technology to regain for the universities the central role in research and instruction they are losing by uniting them through the computer network into a new community of learning.

Research

It is difficult to define the quality of American research. Fortunately, the United States does not have a newspaper entitled *The Truth*, and none of us is ever *certain* he has discovered and described accurately something in the social sciences or humanities. In short, I cannot comment on that aspect of our published research, except to recognize that some is of supremely high quality, that some is visibly incompetent, and that most is somewhere between the extremes.

My criticisms of much American research are of a different kind. First, more and more scholars produce narrowly defined publications of interest only to specialists and often in such an awkward and graceless style as to discourage even them. Most scholarly books are read only by scholars, most scholars read only highly specialized scholarly volumes, and the author's friends and relatives are often the only readers of many articles. In short, the time, energy, and resources devoted to research are essentially wasted. Thirty years ago Raymond Aron remarked that the gap between the knowledge American scholars possess and that of the public was enormous; American scholarship in its own way was excellent, but even the informed public was unaware of it. I believe that millions more Americans have read *The Russians*, by the journalist Hedrick Smith, than have read any of the American scholarly books on the Soviet Union produced in the last decade.

In short, one of the most serious shortcomings of the greatly expanded American programs is their slight impact upon the informed public. Most informed Americans obtain their information about the Soviet Union from the mass media, as shallow and faddish on this subject as it is on all others. Americans, even their leaders, seem to vacillate between two ridiculously extreme views of the Soviet system, some concluding that it is just like the American system and that the Soviet peoples resemble Americans in their values and beliefs, and others that the Soviet government is a monstrous conspiratorial group plotting constantly to conquer the world under a schedule their leaders have defined.

In addition, Soviet scholarship in the United States, and probably instruction in Soviet studies as well, has become increasingly politicized, to the point that the public discounts the research of some outstanding scholars because of suspicion that their political beliefs, whether conservative or liberal, affect their scholarly work. This is a special tragedy when one remembers the success the Robinsons, Moselys and Fainsods had in preventing politics from infecting and dividing the field as bitterly and destructively as it did Chinese studies in the 1950s. Robinson established the Russian Institute after the war to help train scholar-teachers dedicated to teaching, not to preaching. As a graduate student at Harvard and a post-doctoral Fellow at Columbia, under those who directed the great surge of Soviet studies, I can testify to the nature of the training these men provided. Although the issues facing the American people concerning the Soviet Union and its policies were just as critical and divisive thirty or forty years ago as they are now, I was not able to determine the political affiliations of these men. I have no knowledge of their political beliefs and actions in the 1950s and 1960s.

Many of the most eminent American scholars have abandoned that goal. Some who play active roles in government serve as open advisers to political candidates and have become politicized intellectuals, not scholars. They reflect what a French scholar sixty years ago defined as "*la trahison des clercs.*" They, their institutions, and those whom they train, are identified by their political leanings more than by the quality of their work. What a tragic change and loss!

This is especially true in political science and in those other aspects of Soviet studies most closely related to contemporary affairs, to public policy, and to increasingly common estimates of Soviet actions in the future. Many scholars advocate particular policies rather than seeking to provide the data necessary for the statesmen and the public to reach their own judgments. Often, specialists declare that Soviet policies will be those the specialists would adopt if they were the Soviet rulers. This flaw has been deepened by the invasion of the Soviet field by other politicized scholars who know no Russian, are totally uninformed about the Soviet Union (except for the shallow and uncertain information they acquire from the mass media), and utilize no Soviet materials available in translation. Soviet-American relations and the critical issue of arms control constitute the most damaging and scandalous illustrations. Men and women who are quite uninformed about the Soviet Union have been accepted as authorities—by both the informed public and confused citizens—on those central issues about which their knowledge is infinitesimal but their judgments remarkably confident.

Conclusion

Research and instruction concerning the Soviet Union in the United States have made great progress since the end of World War II, as American educational administrators and scholars took advantage of the freedoms Americans enjoy, the small but highly qualified base created before 1940, public interest and support, and the flow of men and women from the Soviet Union who contributed the knowledge and insight they had acquired from living and working in the Soviet system. The United States has a large number of well-staffed research and instructional centers sprinkled throughout the country, splendid libraries whose collections modern technology makes available to all, an active national organization, an abundance of professional journals and publishers, and a steady flow of publications of impressive quality on most aspects of Soviet history and life.

At the same time, the area of Soviet studies in the United States displays several major flaws. American education continues to concentrate upon the United States and Western Europe, so that research and instruction concerning the Soviet Union, and other parts of the world as well, are not an integral part of higher education but remain a kind of luxury on the periphery, dependent upon the federal government and private foundations for essential funding. The quality of training has declined sharply as Soviet studies have expanded. American specialists on the Soviet Union usually know no other foreign language but Russian, if that. Graduate training is generally restricted to just one discipline and to the twentieth century. Many outstanding scholars teach few if any undergraduates. Much research is so narrow and written with such limited grace and style that the expanded programs have had little effect upon students or upon that part of the public interested in acquiring knowledge and understanding of the Soviet Union. Finally, some of the most eminent members of the field have become directly engaged in politics at the highest and most visible levels, raising doubts concerning the objectivity of those in Soviet studies and depriving the country of the voice of trusted, non-political authority that the founders of this critical field set out to create.

No solution is in sight because neither the public nor educational leaders nor most specialists recognize the problem. Certainly the increased funding that most administrators and scholar-teachers seek will not repair the flaws; in fact, it would enlarge them. The United States still needs the revolution in higher education that seemed underway forty years ago; it must break away from its WASP framework and make research and instruction concerning all other parts of the world an essential part of the curriculum in all schools and colleges. Americans must require that all students acquire effective command of at least one other foreign language and that all scholar-teachers master several. Those especially interested in Soviet studies must therefore turn some of their energies from their traditional scholarly pursuits to active participation in this educational revolution. They must at the same time broaden and deepen the training they provide so that our scholar-teachers will possess the knowledge of the nature of the Soviet system and the knowledge of Russian history and culture necessary for understanding the different peoples who live in the Soviet Union. They must also abandon their efforts to directly affect American power and policy and return instead to their proper role—providing the basic knowledge and insight that their students and the informed public need so that their democratic government will obtain the popular understanding and support it requires for forming its policies toward the Soviet Union.

Notes on Contributors

Georg Brunner is Director of the Institute of East European Law and Professor of Law, University of Cologne, West Germany

R.V. Burks is Professor Emeritus of History, Wayne State University, Canton, Ohio

Robert F. Byrnes is Distinguished Professor of History, Indiana University, Bloomington, Indiana

Anatoly P. Fedoseyev is a former leading Soviet scientist, who in 1969 defected to England where, at the University of Cambridge, he continued his scientific work, and also wrote a number of books and articles on conditions of life and work in the USSR

Ferdinand J.M. Feldbrugge is Director of the Documentation Center on East European Law and is Professor of Law at the University of Leiden, Netherlands

Olimpiad S. Ioffe is Professor of Law, University of Connecticut, Hartford, Connecticut

Leszek Kolakowski is Professor of Philosophy at Oxford University and the University of Chicago, Chicago, Illinois

Ernst Kux is Professor of Politics, St. Gall Graduate School, Zurich, Switzerland

Eugene Kamenka is Professor of History of Ideas and Head of the History of Ideas Unit, Research School of Social Sciences, Institute of Advanced Studies, Australian National University, Canberra, Australia

Morton A. Kaplan is Professor of Political Science, University of Chicago, Chicago, Illinois

Vladislaw Krasnow is Associate Professor and Head of Russian Studies, The Monterey Institute of International Studies, Monterey, California

Richard Löwenthal is Professor of Political Science, Free University, West Berlin, West Germany

Terence P. McNeill is Lecturer in Politics, University of Hull, England

Alexander J. Matejko is Professor of Sociology, University of Alberta, Edmonton, Canada

Edward A. Shils is Professor of Sociology, University of Chicago, Chicago, Illinois

Alexander Shtromas is Reader in Politics and Contemporary History, University of Salford, England

Alice Erh-Soon Tay is Challis Professor of Jurisprudence and Head of the Department of Jurisprudence, Faculty of Law, University of Sydney, Australia

Michael Voslensky is Director of the Institute for Research into Contemporary USSR, Munich, West Germany

Peter J.D. Wiles is Professor of Economics, London School of Economics and Political Science, London, England

Index

NOTE: Letters in boldface following an entry indicate the author of the information: **GB** Georg Brunner; **RB** Richard Burks; **AF** Anatoly Fedoseyev; **FF** Ferdinand Feldbrugge; **OI** Olimpiad Ioffe; **EK** Eugene Kamenka; **MK** Morton Kaplan; **LK** Leszak Kolakowski; **VK** Vladislav Krasnov; **ML** Miriam London; **RL** Richard Lowenthal; **AM** Alexander Matejko; **TM** Terry McNeill; **AS** Alexander Shtromas; **AT** Alice Tay; **MV** Michael Voslensky; **PW** Peter Wiles